The Farlex Grammar Book
Volume III

Complete English Spelling and Pronunciation Rules

Simple Ways to Spell and Speak Correctly

Explore more books by Farlex at

farlex.com/books

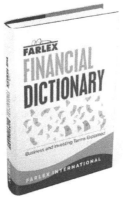
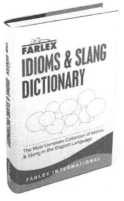

FARLEX INTERNATIONAL

FARLEX INTERNATIONAL LIMITED

a Farlex Group Company

• USA   • Ireland

farlex.com   farlex.ie

ISBN-10: 1978045824

ISBN-13: 978-1978045828

Table of contents

About the publisher

Farlex is the publishing team behind TheFreeDictionary.com, the award-winning reference destination with 1 billion+ annual visits.

The most comprehensive reference resource online, The Free Dictionary is a massive, easily searchable collection of dictionaries and encyclopedias from the most trusted publishers, including McGraw-Hill, Houghton Mifflin, HarperCollins, and many more.

Since its founding in 2003, TheFreeDictionary.com has grown to include a vast and diverse amount of reference content, including multiple thesaurus sources and specialty dictionaries covering fields such as science, medicine, law, finance, idioms and slang, acronyms, computing, and more, as well as dictionaries in 14 other languages. Farlex dictionary apps powered by The Free Dictionary have been downloaded tens of millions of times across multiple platforms, with top ratings after hundreds of thousands of user reviews.

With the three volumes of *The Farlex Grammar Book* (*Complete English Grammar Rules*, *Complete English Punctuation Rules*, and *Complete English Spelling and Pronunciation Rules*), Farlex brings its reputation for the most comprehensive, trusted, and easy-to-use reference products in the world to the most thorough English language guides available.

Complete English Spelling and Pronunciation Rules offers its readers unprecedented online integration. Every quiz in the book can be accessed for free at **TheGrammarBook.com**.

For more books from Farlex, visit **farlex.com/books**.

Preface

English is notorious for how difficult and unintuitive its spelling and pronunciation can be. Because it was derived from several other languages (such as Latin, Greek, French, and German) alongside the now unrecognizable Old English, it has been burdened with many oddities in how words are spelled and spoken aloud. It's no surprise, then, that the top two Google searches for "*How do you…*" are "*How do you **spell**…*" and "*How do you **say**…*"!

The purpose of this guide is to help you put an end to looking up individual words over and over again. Instead, we will provide a solid foundation of patterns, conventions, and rules that will help you recognize how certain words should be spelled and pronounced from the start. We'll touch on classic conventions like "I before E, except after C," but we'll also dive into the more thorough, structural rules of word formation. (We'll also explore the many, many exceptions and inconsistencies that accompany such conventions—the most problematic aspect for learners and native speakers alike.)

We'll start by thoroughly examining the letters of the alphabet, and all the speech sounds they can make. From there, we'll go over conventions for how words are spelled, followed by conventions for how they're pronounced. Every topic in the book can be read and understood individually, but throughout the book you will find cross-references to other sections and chapters to help make it clear how all the pieces relate to one another. If you're having trouble understanding something, try going back (or forward) to other related topics in the book.

Ultimately, mastering the intricacies of English spelling and pronunciation requires exposure and repetition—reading as much as possible and listening to how people speak, until recognizing the way words should look and sound becomes second nature. Let this book be your companion for every question you may have along the way.

Editor's Note

This book was written according to the standard spelling and pronunciation used in American English. While major differences between American and British English are usually addressed, some information in the book might not coincide with the styles, tendencies, or preferences of other English-speaking communities.

English Spelling and Pronunciation

Spelling refers to the way we structure words <u>visually</u> (using letters of the alphabet), while **pronunciation** refers to the way in which these words are formed <u>verbally</u> (using different speech sounds). Both spelling and pronunciation are notorious aspects of English, as there are many inconsistencies, irregularities, and seemingly illogical aspects to how each is formed. To help make sense of them, we've divided this guide into four major chapters: **The Alphabet, Spelling Conventions, Pronunciation Conventions**, and **Common Mistakes and Commonly Confused Words**.

The Alphabet

The first chapter will go into detail about the vowels and consonants that make up The Alphabet, describing the variety of sounds each letter can make. We'll also look at **digraphs, trigraphs**, and **tetragraphs** (sets of two, three, and four letters, respectively, that create single, unique speech sounds), as well as other letters, marks, and symbols that are not part of the regular alphabet but may still be encountered in English spelling.

Spelling Conventions

The second chapter will deal with the various conventions that can help us make sense of English spelling. Notice that we use the word *conventions*, not *rules*; while there are some concrete patterns in the way words are spelled, very few constitute real "rules," as most of them have many exceptions and irregularities.

The majority of these spelling conventions deal with affixes, which primarily comprise **prefixes** and **suffixes**. Prefixes are small, word-forming elements that attach to the beginning of words, while suffixes are word-forming elements that attach to the end of words. While prefixes are largely self-contained in their impact on spelling, there are a number of spelling conventions with suffixes that dictate the multiple aspects of words' spelling, such as changing Y to I before vowel suffixes, adding suffixes after silent E, and doubling consonants with vowel suffixes. We'll go in depth with each of these conventions, examining their various patterns and rules as well as all the various exceptions for each.

Closely related to suffixes is the notion of inflection in spelling, which refers to the ways in which a word's spelling may change to reflect its grammatical function in a sentence. Most instances of inflection are achieved by attaching a suffix (such as attaching "-s" or "-es" to form a plural), but some instances of inflection occur when the entire word changes (as with the inflection of personal pronouns, e.g., *I, me, my, mine*).

The remaining spelling conventions are much narrower in scope than suffixes and inflection. We'll discuss how to form contractions (words formed from two words joined together with an apostrophe), the three-letter rule (which states that words consisting of fewer than three letters will usually be grammatical function words), the "I Before E, Except After C" rule (which states that **I** will usually appear before **E** unless they both come after the letter **C**), and rules for capitalization (both for specific words in a sentence and the words in a title).

The final sections we'll cover in the Spelling Conventions chapter have to do with other languages and other dialects of English. First, we'll look at foreign loanwords and loan translations, which are words that are taken directly from other languages (either in translation or in the original language). After that, we'll compare the various differences in American English vs. British English spelling that tend to give writers trouble.

Pronunciation Conventions

The third chapter will cover various conventions for how words are pronounced. First, we'll look at tricky vowel sounds, specifically focusing on the difference between **monophthongs** (standard vowel sounds), **diphthongs** (two vowel sounds that glide together in a single syllable), and **triphthongs** (three vowel sounds that glide together in a single syllable).

After that, we'll look at tricky consonant sounds—specifically, how to form the /k/ sound, the /z/ sound, and the /ʒ/ sound (the **G** sound in *beige*), as well as the various ways of pronouncing the letter S.

Next, we'll go over the various silent letters. The most ubiquitous of these is **silent E**, which has a variety of different functions depending on the letters around it in a word, but **U** can also be silent, as can many different consonants.

The next convention we'll look at in this chapter is the way in which letters are grouped into **syllables**, as well as how syllables are divided and counted within a word. Closely related to that is **word stress**, which dictates which syllable within a word will receive the most vocal emphasis in speech. Finally, we'll look at **sentence stress**, which governs which words in a sentence receive more emphasis than others.

Common Mistakes and Commonly Confused Words

The final chapter in this guide deals with many different words that are either commonly misspelled or commonly confused with other words. Wherever possible, we'll try to provide useful mnemonic tricks to help remember the difference between them.

The Alphabet

Definition

The **alphabet** is the set of symbols known as **letters** that are used to form words. At its most basic, the English alphabet is composed of five vowels (letters representing speech sounds formed exclusively with an open airway) and 21 consonants (letters representing speech sounds formed with the tongue, teeth, and lips), for a total of 26 letters. Together, vowels and consonants form syllables in speech.

Every vowel and consonant has at least one speech sound associated with it, but most letters can have **several** sounds, with their pronunciation depending on where they appear in a word, what letter(s) appear around them, and, in some cases, the etymology (historical origin) of the word.

In this guide, we use the International Phonetic Alphabet (IPA) to represent the speech sounds made by each vowel, consonant, or combination of letters. These will always be offset by two slashes (for example, *apple* is pronounced /ˈæpəl/).

We'll briefly cover all of these here, but you can continue on to their individual sections to learn more about each.

Vowels

A **vowel** is a letter that represents a speech sound made with one's airway (the mouth and vocal chords) open and without touching one's tongue to the teeth, lips, or the roof of the mouth. Consonants, on the other hand, are formed by obstructing one's airway in some way so as to create a harder, more defined speech sound.

There are five letters that are considered to be true vowels: **A, E, I, O,** and **U.** The letter **Y** is often considered to be a "semi-vowel" because it functions sometimes as a vowel sound (as in *myth, any,* and *fly*) and sometimes as a soft consonant sound (as in *yard* and *bayou*).

Finally, it's worth mentioning that the letter **W,** which is typically considered a consonant, can also behave as a vowel, but this only occurs when it combines with another vowel in a digraph.

Vowel sounds are often divided into two categories: "short" vowels and "long" vowels.

Short Vowels

A short vowel sound is usually produced when a vowel is followed by one or more consonants in a syllable (except for single consonants followed by a **silent E**).

The Alphabet

Most vowel letters have a specific short-vowel sound—though **U** can create <u>two</u> types of short-vowel sounds, and the semi-vowel **Y** creates the same short vowel sound as the letter **I**.

Vowel Letter	IPA Symbol	Example Words
A a	/æ/	apple (/ˈæpəl/) map (/mæp/) track (/træk/) man (/mæn/)
E e	/ɛ/	set (/sɛt/) jet (/dʒɛ/) bend (/bɛnd/) met (/mɛt/)
I i	/ɪ/	tip (/tɪp/) strip (/strɪp/) imply (/ɪmˈplaɪ/) fin (/fɪn/)
O o	/ɑ/	top (/tɑp/) hot (/hɑt/) offer (/ˈɑfər/) pollen (/ˈpɑlən/)
U u	/ʌ/	cut (/kʌt/) hug (/hʌg/) mutt (/mʌt/) strut (/strʌt/)
U u	/ʊ/	put (/pʊt/) push (/pʊʃ/) full (/fʊl/) sugar (/ʃʊgər/)
Y y	/ɪ/	myth (/mɪθ/) system (/ˈsɪstəm/) rhythm (/ˈrɪðəm/) crypt (/krɪpt/)

Long Vowels

"Long" vowels are traditionally thought of as vowel sounds that approximate the pronunciation of the letter's name. For example, the long vowel sound of **I** is /aɪ/, which is the same way we say the letter **I** out loud. Let's look at the traditional long vowel sounds each letter makes, as well as a few example words for each:

Vowel Letter	IPA Symbol	Example Words
A a	/eɪ/	<u>a</u>te (/<u>eɪ</u>t/) pl<u>ai</u>n (/pl<u>eɪ</u>n/) alw<u>ay</u>s (/ˈɔlˌw<u>eɪ</u>z/)
E e	/i/	<u>ea</u>t (/<u>i</u>t/) f<u>ee</u>t (/f<u>i</u>t/) th<u>e</u>me (/θ<u>i</u>m/)
I i	/aɪ/	des<u>i</u>gn (/dɪˈz<u>aɪ</u>n/) s<u>i</u>ght (/s<u>aɪ</u>t/) t<u>i</u>le /t<u>aɪ</u>l/
O o	/oʊ/	t<u>o</u>ld (/t<u>oʊ</u>ld/) kn<u>ow</u> (/n<u>oʊ</u>/) r<u>o</u>pe (/r<u>oʊ</u>p/)
U u	/ju/	c<u>u</u>be (/k<u>ju</u>b/) imb<u>ue</u> (/ɪmbˈ<u>ju</u>/) h<u>u</u>ge (/h<u>ju</u>dʒ/)
Y y	(/aɪ/)	appl<u>y</u> (/ˈəpl<u>aɪ</u>/) rh<u>y</u>me (/r<u>aɪ</u>m/) h<u>y</u>pe (/h<u>aɪ</u>p/)
Y y	/i/	difficult<u>y</u> (/ˈdɪfɪˌkʌlt<u>i</u>/) friendl<u>y</u> (/ˈfrɛndl<u>i</u>/) happ<u>y</u> (/ˈhæp<u>i</u>/)

There are quite a few different conventions that dictate when a vowel will have a traditional long pronunciation; to learn more, go to the section on Vowels.

Other long vowel sounds

It's also worth mentioning that vowels can have other "long" sounds beyond those we've looked at above. These tend to occur in certain letter combinations—either vowel digraphs or combinations of vowels and consonants. For example:

Vowel Sound	Common Letters and Combinations	Example Words
/u/	• U • UE • UI • EW • O • OO • OU	• exclude (/ɪkˈsklud/) • true (/tru/) • bruise (/bruz/) • chew (/ʧu/) • prove (/pruv/) • tool (/tul/) • soup (/sup/)
/ɔ/	• O • OR • OUGH • A • AL • AU • AW	• across (/əˈkrɔs/) • orange (/ˈɔrənʤ/) • brought (/brɔt/) • water (/ˈwɔtər/) • false (/fɔls/) • cause (/kɔz/) • dawn (/dɔn/)
/ɜ/	• ER • IR • OR • UR • EAR	• perfect (/ˈpɜrˌfɪkt/) • stir (/stɜr/) • worse (/wɜrs/) • curve (/kɜrv/) • pearl (/pɜrl/)

Consonants

Consonants represent sounds that are made when part or all of the vocal tract is closed. Because they require a specific position of the lips, cheeks, tongue, etc., there is generally little to no difference in how consonants are pronounced between different speakers of English. (The pronunciation of vowels, on the other hand, can differ drastically depending on dialect).

There are 21 consonants letters: *B, C, D, F, G, H, J, K, L, M, N, P, Q, R, S, T, V, W, X, Y*, and *Z*. As we said previously, **Y** can sometimes function as a vowel (as in *myth* [/mɪθ/] or */dry/* [draɪ]), so it is often referred to as a **semi-vowel**. **W** can also function alongside vowels to form certain vowel sounds (as in *grow* [/groʊ/] or *draw* [/drɔ/]), but it can't function as a vowel on its own.

We'll very briefly go over the sounds each consonant makes, with examples for each. For more information about how the speech sounds are formed, spelling conventions regarding when they appear in a word, and more examples of each kind of sound, go to the section on Consonants.

Consonant	Speech Sound(s)
B b	**/b/:** • bag (/bæg/) • bubble (/ˈbʌbəl/) • slob (/slɑb/) **Silent B:** • doubt (/daʊt/) • debt (/dɛt/) • thumb (/θʌm/)
C c	**/k/ ("Hard" C):** • cap (/kæp/) • perfect (/ˈpɜrˌfɪkt/) • uncle (/ˈʌŋkəl/)

	/s/ ("Soft" C): • **central** (/ˈsɛntrəl/) • **exercise** (/ˈɛksərˌsaɪz/) • **icy** (/ˈaɪsi/) /ʃ/ (The "sh" sound): • **efficient** (/ɪˈfɪʃənt/) • **social** (/ˈsoʊʃəl/) • **ocean** (/ˈoʊʃən/) **Silent C:** • **ascend** (/əˈsɛnd/) • **muscle** (/ˈmʌsəl/) • **science** (/ˈsaɪəns/)
D d	/d/: • **deal** (/dil/) • **addle** (/ˈædəl/) • **bread** (/brɛd/) /t/: • **laughed** (/læft/) • **knocked** (/nɑkt/) • **helped** (/hɛlpt/) /dʒ/ (The "J" sound): • **education** (/ɛdʒuˈkeɪʃən/) • **graduate** (verb: /ˈgrædʒuˌeɪt/) • **individual** (/ɪndəˈvɪdʒuəl/) **Silent D:** • **handkerchief** (/ˈhæŋkərtʃɪf/) • **handsome** (/ˈhænsəm/) • **Wednesday** (/ˈwɛnzdeɪ/)
F f	/f/: • **feel** (/fil/) • **different** (/ˈdɪfrənt/) • **belief** (/bɪˈlif/) /v/: • **of** (/ɑv/)
G g	/g/ ("Hard" G): • **gap** (/gæp/) • **bag** (/bæg/) • **argue** (/ˈɑrgju/) /dʒ/ ("Soft" G): • **age** (/eɪdʒ/) • **logic** (/ˈlɑdʒɪk/) • **biology** (/baɪˈɑlədʒi/) /ʒ/ (The "other" soft G): • **garage** (/gəˈrɑʒ/) • **beige** (/beɪʒ/) • **genre** (/ˈʒɑnrə/) **Silent G:** • **gnaw** (/nɔ/) • **lasagna** (/ləˈzɑnjə/) • **deign** (/deɪn/)

H h	**/h/:** • house (/haʊs/) • hat (/hæt/) • hear (/hir/) **Silent H:** • hour (/aʊər/) • honor (/ˈɑnər/) • heir (/ɛr/)
J j	**/dʒ/:** • job (/dʒɑb/) • judge (/dʒʌdʒ/) • majority (/məˈdʒɔrəti/)
K k	**/k/:** • kick (/kɪk/) • donkey (/ˈdɔŋki/) • work (/wɜrk/) **Silent K:** • know (/noʊ/) • knife (/naɪf/) • knight (/naɪt/)
L l	**/l/:** • listen (/lɪsən/) • alter (/ɔltər/) • gel (/dʒɛl/) **Silent L:** • calf (/kæf/) • chalk (/tʃɔk/) • salmon (/ˈsæmən/)
M m	**/m/:** • make (/meɪk/) • almost (/ˈɔlˌmoʊst/) • team (/tim/) **Silent M:** • mnemonic (/nɪˈmɑnɪk/)
N n	**/n/:** • now (/naʊ/) • wander (/ˈwɑndər/) • fan (/fæn/) **/ŋ/ (The "ng" sound):** • distinct (/dɪˈstɪŋkt/) • synchronize (/ˈsɪŋkrəˌnaɪz/) • bank (/bæŋk/) **Silent N:** • autumn (/ˈɔtəm/) • column (/ˈkɑləm/) • hymn (/hɪm/)
P p	**/p/:** • part (/pɔrt/) • happy (/ˈhæpi/) • cheap (/tʃip/)

	Silent P: • pneuma (/ˈnumə/) • psalm (/sɑm/) • raspberry (/ˈræzˌbɛri/)
Q q **(almost always followed by U)**	**/kw/:** • quiet (/ˈkwaɪət/) • request (/rɪˈkwɛst/) • inquire (/ɪnˈkwaɪr/) **/k/:** • antique (/ænˈtik/) • conquer (/ˈkɑŋkər/) • mosquito (/məsˈkitoʊ/)
R r	**/r/:** • right (/raɪt/) • art (/ɑrt/) • endure (/ɪnˈdʊr/)
S s	**/s/:** • sand (/sænd/) • persuade (/pərˈsweɪd/) • this (/ðɪs/) **/z/:** • desert (/ˈdɛzɜrt/) • president (/ˈprɛzɪdənt/) • toys (/tɔɪz/) **/ʃ/ (The "sh" sound):** • controversial (/ˌkɑntrəˈvɜrʃəl/) • pressure (/ˈprɛʃər/) • sugar (/ˈʃʊgər/) **/ʒ/ (The "other" soft G sound):** • usual (/ˈjuʒuəl/) • measure (/ˈmɛʒər/) • illusion (/ɪˈluʒən/)
T t	**/t/:** • tap (/tæp/) • retire (/rɪˈtaɪr/) • react (/riˈækt/) **/ʃ/ (The "sh" sound):** • initial (/ɪˈnɪʃəl/) • patient (/ˈpeɪʃənt/) • action (/ˈækʃən/) **/tʃ/ (The "tch" sound):** • adventure (/ædˈvɛntʃər/) • situation (/ˌsɪtʃuˈeɪʃən) • question (/ˈkwɛstʃən/) **Silent T:** • castle (/ˈkæsəl/) • mortgage (/ˈmɔrgədʒ/) • ballet (/bæˈleɪ/)
V v	**/v/:** • vast (/væst/) • subversion (/səbˈvɜrʒən/) • give (/gɪv/)

	/f/: • have to (/hæ**f** tʊ/ in casual pronunciation)
W w	**/w/:** • **w**ay (/**w**eɪ/) • a**w**ake (/ə**ˈw**eɪk/) • bet**w**een (/bɪˈt**w**in/) **Silent W:** • **w**ho (/hu/) • **w**rap (/ræp/) • ans**w**er (/ˈænsər/)
X x	**/ks/:** • a**x**e (/æ**ks**/) • gala**x**y (/ˈgælə**ks**i/) • e**x**cellent (/ˈɛ**ks**ələnt/) **/gz/:** • e**x**ample (/ɪ**gˈz**æmpəl/) • e**x**ist (/ɪ**gˈz**ɪst/) • e**x**haust (/ɪ**gˈz**ɑst/) **/kʃ/:** • an**x**ious (/ˈæŋ**kʃ**əs/) • comple**x**ion (/kəmˈpɛ**kʃ**ən/) • obno**x**ious (/əbˈnɑ**kʃ**əs/) **/gʒ/:** • lu**x**ury (/ˈlʌ**gʒ**əri/) **/z/:** • **x**erography (/**z**ɪˈrɒgrəfi/) • **x**ylophone (/ˈ**z**aɪləˌfoʊn/) • an**x**iety (/æŋˈ**z**aɪəti/)
Y y	**/j/:** • **y**acht (/**j**ɑt/) • **y**oke (/**j**oʊk/) • law**y**er (/ˈlɔ**j**ər/)
Z z	**/z/:** • **z**eal (/**z**il/) • citi**z**en (/ˈsɪtə**z**ən/) • ja**zz** (/jæ**z**/) **/s/:** • blit**z** (/blɪt**s**/) • pret**z**el (/ˈprɛt**s**əl/) • *mozzarella* (ˌmɑt**s**əˈrɛlə) **/ʒ/:** • a**z**ure (/ˈæ**ʒ**ər/) • sei**z**ure (/ˈsi**ʒ**ər/)

Letter combinations that form single sounds

While most of the speech sounds we make are associated with specific letters, there are many that can also be formed by specific combinations of letters.

The most common form of such combinations is the **digraph**, which consists of two vowels or two consonants that create a single sound. Note that the examples below are only a small selection of the existing vowel and consonant digraphs; for more information, go to the sections on Vowels and Consonant Digraphs.

Vowel Digraphs	Pronunciation and Examples	Consonant Digraphs	Pronunciation and Examples
AI	/eɪ/: • fail (/feɪl/) • plain (/pleɪn/) • mail (/meɪl/)	CH	/ʧ/: • achieve (/əˈʧiv/) • beach (/biʧ/) • teacher (/ˈtiʧər/) /k/: • anchor (/ˈæŋkər/) • chemistry (/ˈkɛmɪstri/) • psychology (/saɪˈkɑləʤi/) /ʃ/: • brochure (/broʊˈʃʊr/) • chef (/ʃɛf/) • machine (/məˈʃin/)
AW	/ɔ/: • dawn (/dɔn/) • raw (/rɔ/) • thaw (/θɔ/)	DG	/ʤ/: • badge (/bæʤ/) • judge (/ʤʌʤ/) • fledgling (/ˈflɛʤlɪŋ/)
AY	/eɪ/: • pay (/peɪ/) • always (/ˈɔlˌweɪz/) • layer (/ˈleɪər/)	GH	/g/: • aghast (/əˈgæst/) • ghost (/goʊst/) • spaghetti (/spəˈgɛti/) /f/: • cough (/kɔf/) • enough (/ɪˈnʌf/) • rough (/rʌf/)
EA	/i/: • deal (/dil/) • bean (/bin/) • streak (/strik/) /ɜ/: • pearl (/pɜrl/) • search (/sɜrʧ/) • yearn (/jɜrn/) /ɛ/: • bread (/brɛd/) • dead (/dɛd/) • instead (/ɪnˈstɛd/)	NG	/ŋ/: • bang (/bæŋ/) • darling (/ˈdɑrlɪŋ/) • longing (/ˈlɔŋɪŋ/) /ŋk/: • angst (/ɑŋkst/) • length (/lɛŋkθ/) • strength (/strɛŋkθ/)
EE	/i/: • feel (/fil/) • street (/strit/) • meet (/mit/)	SH	/ʃ/: • shadow (/ˈʃæˌdoʊ/) • cushion (/ˈkʊʃən/) • publish (/ˈpʌblɪʃ/)
OA	/oʊ/: • coal (/koʊl/) • gloat (/gloʊt/) • oak (/oʊk/) /ɔ/: • broad (/brɔd/)	TH	/θ/: • thanks (/θæŋks/) • author (/ˈɔθər/) • teeth (/tiθ/) /ð/: • than (/ðæn/) • clothing (/ˈkloʊðɪŋ/) • smooth (/smuð/) /t/: • thyme (/taɪm/) • Theresa (/təˈrisə/) • Thomas (/ˈtɑməs/)

Although they are less common, there are also trigraphs (combinations of three letters) and even a few tetragraphs (combinations of four letters), which can be composed of vowels, consonants, or a combination of the two. Let's briefly look at each of these:

Trigraphs	Pronunciation and Examples	Tetragraphs	Pronunciation and Examples
TCH	/tʃ/: • batch (/bætʃ/) • ditch (/dɪtʃ/) • wretch (/rɛtʃ/)	OUGH	• /oʊ/: • although (/ɔlˈðoʊ/) • dough (/doʊ/) • thorough (/ˈθɝoʊ/) /u/: • through (/θru/) /ɔ/: • brought (/brɔt/) • fought (/fɔt/) • thought (/θɔt/) /aʊ/: • bough (/baʊ/) • drought (/draʊt/) • plough (/plaʊ/)
EAU	/oʊ/: • bureau (/ˈbjʊroʊ/) • château (/ʃæˈtoʊ/) • tableau (/tæˈbloʊ/) /ju/: • beauty (/ˈbjuti/) • beautiful (/ˈbjutɪfʊl/) /ɑ/: • bureaucracy (/bjʊrˈɑkrəsi/) /ə/: • bureaucrat (/ˈbjʊrəˌkræt/)	AIGH	/eɪ/: • straight
EOU/IOU	/ə/: • courageous (/kəˈreɪdʒəs/) • curvaceous (/kɝˈveɪʃəs/) • outrageous (/aʊtˈreɪdʒəs/) • gracious (/ˈgreɪʃəs/) • contagious (/kənˈteɪdʒəs/) • cautious (/ˈkɔʃəs/)	EIGH	/eɪ/: • eight (/eɪt/) • neighbor (/ˈneɪbər/) • weigh (/weɪ/) /aɪ/: • height (/haɪt/) • sleight (/slaɪt/)
IGH	/aɪ/: • bright (/braɪt/) • delight (/dɪˈlaɪt/) • highlight (/ˈhaɪˌlaɪt/)	AUGH	/ɔ/: • caught (/cɔt/) • fraught (/frɔt/) • taught (/tɔt/)

Other Letters, Marks, and Symbols

English contains many words that it adapted from different languages from around the world, especially Latin, Greek, French, and German. As the language evolved, though, certain typographical features from those languages were gradually changed or eliminated from modern English orthography, though some still appear in written English today.

The most common of these are **ligatures** (such as *æ* and *œ*, but also the symbol **&** and even the letter *W*) and **diacritics** (as in *résumé, voilà, crêpe, façade,* etc.), in addition to a few other outdated letters that overlapped with modern English until relatively recently. Continue on to the section Other Letters, Marks, and Symbols to learn more about all of these.

Quiz
(answers start on page 463)

1. All letters have at least ___ speech sound(s) associated with them.
a) 1
b) 2
c) 3
d) 4

2. How many **"true"** vowels are there?
a) 4
b) 5
c) 6
d) 7

3. Which of the following is considered a **semi-vowel**?
a) E
b) I
c) Y
d) R

4. A **digraph** is composed of how many letters?
a) 1
b) 2
c) 3
d) 4

Vowels

Definition

A **vowel** is a letter that represents a speech sound made with one's airway (the mouth and vocal chords) open and without touching one's tongue to the teeth, lips, or the roof of the mouth. Vowels are contrasted with **consonants**, which are formed by obstructing one's airway in some way so as to create a harder, more defined speech sound. Together, vowels and consonants form syllables in speech.

The Vowel Letters

There are five letters that are considered to be true vowels: **A, E, I, O,** and **U.** The letter **Y** is often considered to be a "semi-vowel" because it sometimes functions as a vowel sound (as in *myth, tryst, any,* or *fly*) and sometimes as a soft consonant sound (as in *yard, yet,* or *yonder*).

Finally, it's worth mentioning that the letter **W,** which is typically considered a consonant, can also behave as a vowel, but this only occurs when it combines with other vowels (known as vowel digraphs, which we'll look at a little further on).

Vowel Letters vs. Vowel Sounds

When we discuss vowels in this section, we will be taking the more traditional approach in describing the <u>letters</u> that create different vowel sounds. Modern linguistics takes a different approach, classifying each vowel <u>sound</u> as a unique value that is not specifically related to the particular letter(s) that creates it.

For example, in looking at two words, *apple* and *ate*, we will focus on the <u>vowel letter</u> **A,** which creates two different sounds depending on the spelling of the word—that is, **A** is the vowel in both words, but it behaves differently in each to create two distinct vowel sounds.

Linguistics, on the other hand, treats the **A** in *apple* (/ˈæpəl/) as a different vowel altogether from the **A** in *ate* (/eɪt/), regardless of the fact that they are both formed by the same vowel letter.

This guide will attempt to bridge the gap between the two. What we will refer to as a **vowel** is the letter that produces a variety of different sounds, whereas the unique pronunciation according to the letter's place and purpose in different spellings will be referred to as its **vowel sound**. When and where appropriate, we'll include the International Phonetic Alphabet (IPA) pronunciation for each different vowel sound.

Finally, it should be noted that, for the sake of clarity and conciseness, the pronunciations listed here and elsewhere in the guide are based on **General American English** pronunciations. There is often a wide variety of specific differences in dialect across the United States for different spelling patterns, and to differentiate pronunciations for each would result in a guide that is too cumbersome to be of any real, practical use.

Short vowels

Very broadly speaking, vowels are either **short** or **long** in their pronunciation, depending on how they are used in a word.

"Short" vowels are the most common vowel sounds in English. A short vowel sound is usually produced when a vowel is followed by one or more consonants in a syllable (except for single consonants followed by a **silent E**, which we'll look at later).

Most vowel letters have a specific short-vowel sound. Uniquely, **U** can create <u>two</u> types of short-vowel sounds; it's not possible to tell which pronunciation it will use just by looking at the spelling alone, so consult a dictionary if you're not sure. The semi-vowel **Y** can also create a short vowel sound, but it is the same as the letter **I**.

Let's look at some examples of each type of short vowel:

Vowel Letter	IPA Symbol	Example Words	IPA Pronunciation
A a	/æ/	apple map track man	/ˈæpəl/ /mæp/ /træk/ /mæn/
E e	/ɛ/	set jet bend met	/sɛt/ /dʒɛt/ /bɛnd/ /mɛt/
I i	/ɪ/	tip strip imply fin	/tɪp/ /strɪp/ /ɪmˈplaɪ/ /fɪn/
O o	/ɑ/	top hot offer pollen	/tɑp/ /hɑt/ /ˈɑfər/ /ˈpɑlən/
U u	/ʌ/	cut hug mutt strut	/kʌt/ /hʌg/ /mʌt/ /strʌt/
U u	/ʊ/	put push full sugar	/pʊt/ /pʊʃ/ /fʊl/ /ʃʊgər/
Y y	/ɪ/	myth system rhythm crypt	/mɪθ/ /ˈsɪstəm/ /ˈrɪðəm/ /krɪpt/

As we already noted, the letter **U** can create two distinct short-vowel sounds. However, the second short-vowel sound (/ʊ/) is actually somewhat uncommon with the vowel letter **U**; it occurs more often with the vowel digraphs "**OO**" and "**OU**," and occasionally with the letter **O** on its own. For example:

• f<u>oo</u>t (/fʊt/)
• w<u>oo</u>d (/wʊd/)
• s<u>oo</u>t (/sʊt/)
• sh<u>ou</u>ld (/ʃʊd/)
• c<u>ou</u>ld (/kʊd/)
• w<u>o</u>man (/ˈwʊmən/)
• w<u>o</u>lf (/wʊlf/)

Weak Vowels (The Schwa)

Sometimes a short vowel's sound changes in certain words to reflect the fact that it is not **stressed** (vocally emphasized) in the syllable. These are known as **weak** or **reduced vowels**, and they are represented by a **schwa** (/ə/) in pronunciation guides.

The schwa can occur with any of the vowel letters. The sound of the schwa can actually vary slightly, depending on the word, approximating a brief "uh," "ih," or "eh," but it's always considered the same vowel sound regardless. For example:

A a	E e	I i	O o	U u
<u>a</u>pply (/<u>ə</u>ˈplaɪ/)	pres<u>e</u>nt (/ˈprɛz<u>ə</u>nt/)	pup<u>i</u>l (/ˈpjup<u>ə</u>l/)	doct<u>o</u>r (/ˈdɑkt<u>ə</u>r/)	meas<u>u</u>re (/ˈmɛʒ<u>ə</u>r/)
stand<u>a</u>rd (/ˈstænd<u>ə</u>rd/)	lev<u>e</u>l (/ˈlɛv<u>ə</u>l/)	weev<u>i</u>l (/ˈwiv<u>ə</u>l/)	doll<u>o</u>p (/ˈdɑl<u>ə</u>p/)	circ<u>u</u>s (/ˈsɜrk<u>ə</u>s/)
postm<u>a</u>n (/ˈpoʊstm<u>ə</u>n/)	fath<u>e</u>r (/ˈfɑð<u>ə</u>r/)	cred<u>i</u>ble (/ˈkrɛd<u>ə</u>bəl/)	<u>o</u>ppose (/<u>ə</u>ˈpoʊz/)	s<u>u</u>pply (/s<u>ə</u>ˈplaɪ/)

Even the semi-vowel **Y** can occasionally form the schwa sound, as in:
• *s<u>y</u>ringe* (/s<u>ə</u>ˈrɪndʒ/)
• *c<u>y</u>lindrical* (/s<u>ə</u>ˈlɪndrɪkəl/)
• *vin<u>y</u>l* (/ˈvaɪn<u>ə</u>l/)

The schwa is also used in words that end in a consonant + "-le" to add an unstressed vowel sound to the final syllable of the word. For example:
• *a<u>ble</u>* (/ˈaɪ<u>bə</u>l/)
• *mono<u>cle</u>* (/ˈmɑnə<u>kə</u>l/)
• *ap<u>ple</u>* (/ˈæ<u>pə</u>l/)
• *un<u>cle</u>* (/ˈʌn<u>kə</u>l/)
• *fi<u>ddle</u>* (/ˈfɪ<u>də</u>l/)

Words with stressed or unstressed vowels

Many words have vowels that can be either stressed **or** unstressed, depending on how they are used in a sentence. For example, the word *convert* can be pronounced in two ways: with the stress on *con-* or on *-vert*. When the word is pronounced *convert*, the **O** takes on a normal, stressed short-vowel sound (/kɑnvɜrt/). In this form, the word is a **noun**, meaning "one who has been converted." When it is pronounced *convert*, the **O** becomes unstressed and instead takes the sound of the schwa (/kən'vɜrt). With this pronunciation, the word is used as a **verb**, meaning "to change something to another form or purpose."

Here are some other examples of words that can be either nouns or verbs, depending on their pronunciation:

Word	Noun	Verb
record	**record** (/ˈrɛkərd/) Meaning: "a unit of information preserved in some way for future access"	**record** (/rəˈkɔrd/) Meaning: "to preserve for future access"
permit	**permit** (/ˈpɜrˌmɪt/) Meaning: "an official certificate of permission; a license"	**permit** (/pərˈmɪt/) Meaning: "to allow to do something"
rebel	**rebel** (/ˈrɛbəl/) Meaning: "a person who revolts against a government or other authority"	**rebel** (/rɪˈbɛl/) Meaning: "to revolt or act in defiance of authority"

Notice that an unstressed syllable is **not** always represented by a schwa; sometimes it has the same vowel sound, just with less emphasis.

When learning a new word that has multiple pronunciations representing different grammatical functions, it's important to know how each version is pronounced so your meaning is understood correctly. Go to the section on **Word Stress** to learn more.

Long vowels

The traditional way of teaching **"long"** vowels is the mnemonic rule that they sound like the letter they represent. While this is not technically accurate from a linguistic point of view—the sounds are not elongated "versions" of short vowels—it is a useful term when trying to learn how to pronounce the different vowel sounds. (We can also form other long vowel sounds that do **not** sound like their vowel letter. We'll look at these and other types of vowel sounds further on.)

With the exception of long **E**, all of these long vowels are **diphthongs** (single syllables in which the vowel "glides" from one vowel sound to another. Also note that **Y** can create two long-vowel sounds: either that of a long **I** or a long **E**.

For example:

Vowel Letter	IPA Symbol	Example Word	IPA Pronunciation
A a	/eɪ/	<u>a</u>te	/<u>eɪ</u>t/
E e	/i/*	<u>e</u>at	/<u>i</u>t/
I i	/aɪ/	s<u>i</u>ght	/s<u>aɪ</u>t/
O o	/oʊ/	t<u>o</u>ld	/t<u>oʊ</u>ld/
U u	/ju/*	c<u>u</u>e	/kj<u>u</u>/
Y y	/aɪ/	appl<u>y</u>	/ˈəpl<u>aɪ</u>/
Y y	/i/	happ<u>y</u>	/ˈhæpi/

(*Note that the traditional transcription for long **E** is /iː/ while long **U** is transcribed /juː/. The triangular colon (ː) represents the elongation of the vowel sound. However, in most American dictionaries, this colon is omitted because the sounds represented by /i/ and /u/ do not change, so the elongation is inherent. This guide follows the convention of omitting the triangular colon so that IPA pronunciations match what would be found in an American dictionary.)

When vowels become long

There are a few general "rules" that we can follow that dictate when a vowel will be long in its pronunciation. While there are many exceptions to these rules, they are still helpful in identifying common trends in English spelling.

It should be noted that when the following rules apply to **Y**, it produces the long **I** sound. We'll look at instances in which it sounds like long **E** later on.

Silent E

The most common way to form a traditional long vowel is when it comes before a single consonant that is followed by a **silent E**. For example:

Vowel Letter	IPA Symbol	Example Words	IPA Pronunciation
A a	/eɪ/	gr<u>ape</u> w<u>ake</u> br<u>ave</u> m<u>ate</u>	/greɪp/ /weɪk/ /breɪv/ /meɪt/
E e	/i/	concr<u>ete</u> th<u>eme</u> conc<u>ede</u> sc<u>ene</u>	/ˈkɑnkrit/ /θim/ /kənˈsid/ /sin/
I i	/aɪ/	m<u>ice</u> str<u>ike</u> t<u>ile</u> f<u>ine</u>	/maɪs/ /straɪk/ /taɪl/ /faɪn/
O o	/oʊ/	h<u>ope</u> n<u>ote</u> b<u>one</u> d<u>ole</u>	/hoʊp/ /noʊt/ /boʊn/ /doʊl/
U u	/ju/*	f<u>use</u> h<u>uge</u> m<u>ule</u> m<u>ute</u>	/fjus/ /hjudʒ/ /mjul/ /mjut/
Y y	/aɪ/	st<u>yle</u> rh<u>yme</u> h<u>ype</u> megab<u>yte</u>	/staɪl/ /raɪm/ /haɪp/ /ˈmɛgəˌbaɪt/

(*There are many exceptions to this rule when it comes to **U**, in which the vowel sound created sounds like "oo" [/u/] rather than "you" [/ju/]. We'll look at some examples of this further on.)

It's important to note that if the consonant followed by a silent **E** is an **R**, the vowel sound often (though not always) changes slightly. Sometimes a schwa (/ə/) is added to the sound, as in *tire* (/ˈtaɪər/), but most of the time the vowel sound changes altogether, as in *bare* (/bɛr/). These are known as **r-colored vowels**, which we'll look at further on.

One-syllable words ending in one vowel

If a word has only one syllable and it ends in a vowel, the vowel is often (though not always) long. Note that this generally only occurs with the letters **E** and **Y** (and occasionally **O**). For instance:

E e (/i/)	Y y (/aɪ/)	O o (/oʊ/)
b<u>e</u>	wr<u>y</u>	n<u>o</u>
m<u>e</u>	tr<u>y</u>	pr<u>o</u>
w<u>e</u>	fl<u>y</u>	g<u>o</u>
h<u>e</u>	wh<u>y</u>	y<u>o</u>

We can also often (though not always) apply this rule to many single-syllable prefixes that end in **E, I,** and **O**, as in:
- **pr<u>e</u>**existing (/ˌpriːɡˈzɪstɪŋ/)
- **r<u>e</u>**direct (/ˌriːdəˈrɛkt/)
- **pr<u>o</u>**-America (/proʊ əˈmɛrəkə/)
- **c<u>o</u>**operation (/koʊ ɑpəˈreɪʃən/)
- **b<u>i</u>**annual (/baɪˈænuəl/)
- **tr<u>i</u>**mester (/traɪˈmɛstər/)

Long I in -*igh*

When a consonant is followed by "-igh," **I** usually has a long pronunciation (/aɪ/) and **GH** becomes silent, as in:
- sl**<u>igh</u>**t (/slaɪt/)
- br**<u>igh</u>**t (/braɪt/)
- th**<u>igh</u>** (/θaɪ/)
- h**<u>igh</u>** (/haɪ/)
- n**<u>igh</u>**t (/naɪt/)
- s**<u>igh</u>**t (/saɪt/)
- s**<u>igh</u>** (/saɪ/)

However, if an **E** comes before "-igh," the vowel sound becomes that of a long **A** (/eɪ/),* as in:
- w**<u>eigh</u>** (/weɪ/)
- sl**<u>eigh</u>** (/sleɪ/)
- n**<u>eigh</u>**bor (/ˈneɪbər/)
- fr**<u>eigh</u>**t (/freɪt/)
- **<u>eigh</u>**t (/eɪt/)

(*There are two notable exceptions to this sub-rule—*sl**eigh**t* (/slaɪt/) and *h**eigh**t* (/haɪt/)—which both have the long **I** (/aɪ/) vowel sound.)

Before "-ld" and "-nd"

The vowel **I** often becomes long when it comes before the consonant combination "-nd," while **O** is often long when it comes before the letters "-ld." For instance:

O + "-ld" (/oʊld/)	I + "-nd" (/aɪnd/)
c<u>old</u>	f<u>ind</u>
m<u>old</u>	gr<u>ind</u>
s<u>old</u>	bl<u>ind</u>
b<u>old</u>	b<u>ind</u>
beh<u>old</u>	beh<u>ind</u>
g<u>old</u>	k<u>ind</u>
f<u>old</u>	rem<u>ind</u>
t<u>old</u>	r<u>ind</u>

Vowel digraphs

Digraphs are single sounds created by the specific combination of two letters. When two vowels are used together within the same syllable, the first of the two is often (but not always) elongated while the second becomes silent. The most common vowel combinations that work this way are **AI, AY, EA, EE, OA, OE, OW** and **UE**. For example:

Vowel Combination	IPA Symbol	Example Word	Full IPA Pronunciation
AI	/eɪ/	fail plain stain mail	/feɪl/ /pleɪn/ /steɪn/ /meɪl/
AY	/eɪ/	pay always wayward layer	/peɪ/ /ˈɔlˌweɪz/ /ˈweɪwərd/ /ˈleɪər/
EA	/i/	deal bean streak beak	/dil/ /bin/ /strik/ /bik/
EE	/i/	feel street preen meet	/fil/ /strit/ /prin/ /mit/
OA	/oʊ/	coal gloat oak moan	/koʊl/ /gloʊt/ /oʊk/ /moʊn/
OE	/oʊ/	doe toe goes throes	/doʊ/ /toʊ/ /goʊz/ /θroʊz/
OW	/oʊ/	grow know own throws	/groʊ/ /noʊ/ /oʊn/ /θroʊz/
UE	/ju/	hue fuel cue imbue	/hju/ /fju(ə)l/ /kju/ /ɪmbˈju/

It's important to remember that there are many exceptions to this rule: diphthongs and other vowel sounds can be made from many of these (and other) vowel digraphs, which we'll look at further on.

Finally, note that if a vowel or vowel digraph is followed by an **R**, the vowel sound usually changes slightly, either becoming one of the short vowels we looked at earlier or a <u>different</u> long vowel sound (which we'll look at more closely below). In some dialects, a schwa (ə) is pronounced before the "r" as well. For example:
- f<u>air</u> (/fɛ<u>(ə)r</u>/)
- b<u>ear</u> (/bɛ<u>(ə)r</u>/)
- f<u>ear</u> (/fɪ<u>(ə)r</u>/)
- h<u>ear</u>d (/h<u>ɜr</u>d/)
- d<u>eer</u> (/dɪ<u>(ə)r</u>/)
- b<u>oar</u> (/b<u>ɔr</u>/)

The other long Y

As we noted above, **Y** can sound both like **I** (/aɪ/) and **E** (/i/) as a long vowel.

Long **Y** takes an **E** sound when it is used at the end of a word that is more than one syllable (except for the word *apply*). For example:
- friendl<u>y</u> (/ˈfrɛndl<u>i</u>/)
- happ<u>y</u> (/ˈhæp<u>i</u>/)
- happil<u>y</u> (/ˈhæpəl<u>i</u>/)
- difficult<u>y</u> (/ˈdɪfɪˌkʌlt<u>i</u>/)
- sill<u>y</u> (/ˈsɪl<u>i</u>/)
- tin<u>y</u> (/ˈtaɪn<u>i</u>/)
- luck<u>y</u> (/ˈlʌk<u>i</u>/)

It is less common for this kind of long **Y** to appear in the middle of a word, unless it is ending the first word of a compound, as in:
- *any*where (/ˈɛn<u>i</u>ˌwɛr/)
- *every*body (/ˈɛvr<u>i</u>ˌbɑdi/)
- *lady*bug (/ˈleɪd<u>i</u>ˌbʌg/)

Other long vowel sounds

In addition to the "traditional" long vowels, there are also other long vowel sounds that do not sound like the letter they are associated with.

We'll look each of these long sounds below, listing common vowel letters or digraphs that form the sound, along with example words and their full IPA pronunciations. Keep in mind that these don't include diphthongs or triphthongs, both of which we'll look at more closely in other sections.

Note on the symbols
Although all of the following vowel sounds are considered long, they generally do **not** have a triangular colon (꞉) shown after their IPA symbols in American dictionaries (just like the long **E** and **U** sounds that we looked at already). This is because each symbol is not used elsewhere as a short sound, and so it does not need to be distinguished by the colon. Because we are using General American pronunciation in this guide, we will remain consistent with how American dictionaries would most likely transcribe the sounds—just be aware that they might be shown with a ꞉ in British and international dictionaries.

/u/ (/uː/)

This long vowel occurs when a long U vowel sound does not have the consonant **Y** (/j/) intonation at the beginning of the sound; phonetically, it sounds like "oo." This pronunciation can occur in many of the same instances as the "traditional" long **U** (/ju/), so consult a dictionary or pronunciation guide if you're not sure which is correct.

Common Vowel Letter(s)	Example Words	Full IPA
U	rule exclude dune truth	/rul/ /ɪkˈsklud/ /dun/ /truθ/
UE	blue true glue flue	/blu/ /tru/ /glu/ /flu/
UI	bruise cruise suit juice	/bruz/ /kruz/ /sut/ /dʒus/
EW	chew strewn brewed knew	/ʧu/ /strun/ /brud/ /nu/
O	prove lose shoe tomb	/pruv/ /luz/ /ʃu/ /tum/ ("b" becomes silent)
O (as a final sound)	do to two who	/du/ /tu/ /tu/ /whu/
OO	loot tool choose moot	/lut/ /tul/ /ʧuz/ /mut/
OU	through acoustic wound (as in an injury) soup youth*	/θru/ /əˈkustɪk/ /wund/ /sup/ /juθ/*

(*Although words containing *you* produce the same sound as long **U** (/ju/), the **Y** sound (/j/) is actually coming from **Y** as a consonant, rather than the sound being considered a true single vowel.)

/ɔ/ (/ɔː/)

This vowel sound is like a cross between an **A** and an **O**. Phonetically, it sounds like "aw" or "au."

Common Vowel Letter(s)	Example Words	Full IPA
O	across cloth often song	/əˈkrɔs/ /klɔθ/ /ˈɔf(t)ən/ (sometimes the **T** is pronounced, other times not) /sɔŋ/
OR	Florida forest historical orange	/flɔrɪdə/ /fɔrəst/ /hɪˈstɔrɪkəl/ /ˈɔrəndʒ/
OUGH	thought fought brought sought	/θɔt/ /fɔt/ /brɔt/ /sɔt/
A	water war warrant quarter	/ˈwɔtər/ /wɔr/ /ˈwɔrənt/ /ˈkwɔrtər/
AL	already salt false walk	/ɔlˈrɛdi/ /sɔlt/ /fɔls/ /wɔk/ (**L** becomes silent)
AW	dawn raw thaw hawk	/dɔn/ /rɔ/ /θɔ/ /hɔk/
AU	author August cause taught	/ˈɔθər/ /ˈɔgəst/ /kɔz/ /tɔt/

/ɜ/ (/ɜː/)

This is a distinct sound that often occurs when **E, I, O,** or **U** is followed by an **R** but the vowel is stressed. It can also occur when **R** follows the digraph "**EA**." Phonetically, it sounds like "uhr."

A simple way of thinking about this vowel sound is that it acts as an elongated schwa (ə)—in fact, some dictionaries transcribe the sound as /əː/. Others simply write /ər/ (because it always occurs with an **R**), while others variously use the symbols /ɚ/ or /ɝ/ for these sounds (known as "r-colored" schwas). However, for the sake of conciseness and clarity, this guide will only use /ɜ/.

Common Letter Combinations	Example Words	Full IPA
ER	her	/hɜr/
	nerve	/nɜrv/
	perfect	/ˈpɜrˌfɪkt/
	were	/wɜr/
IR	bird	/bɜrd/
	stir	/stɜr/
	swirl	/swɜrl/
	fir	/fɜr/
OR	word	/wɜrd/
	work	/wɜrk/
	worse	/wɜrs/
	worthy	/wɜrði/
UR	nurse	/nɜrs/
	purple	/ˈpɜrpəl/
	curve	/kɜrv/
	fur	/fɜr/
EAR	Earth	/ɜrθ/
	pearl	/pɜrl/
	search	/sɜrtʃ/
	yearn	/yɜrn/
Other specific instances	journey	/ˈdʒɜrni/
	colonel	/ˈkɜrnəl/

Quiz

(answers start on page 463)

1. Which of the following letters is only **sometimes** considered a vowel?

a) A
b) I
c) E
d) Y
e) U
f) O

2. Which of the following words features a traditional **long** vowel?

a) set
b) pale
c) cot
d) pull
e) tip

3. The **schwa** is represented by which of the following vowel symbols?

a) ʊ
b) ɔ
c) ɜ
d) ə

4. A vowel is usually long when:

a) It comes before a single consonant followed by the letter "e"
b) It comes before a double consonant
c) It is used in an unstressed syllable
d) It comes before the consonant cluster "ck"

5. What is the correct IPA pronunciation for the word *press*?

a) prɪs

b) prəs

c) prɛs

d) prʊs

Consonants

Definition

In addition to vowels, the English alphabet is also made up of **consonants**. While vowels represent open-mouthed speech sounds, consonants represent sounds that are made when part or all of the vocal tract is closed. Because they require a specific position of the lips, cheeks, tongue, etc., there is generally little to no difference in how consonants are pronounced between different speakers of English. (The pronunciation of vowels, on the other hand, can differ drastically depending on dialect).

There are 21 consonants: *B, C, D, F, G, H, J, K, L, M, N, P, Q, R, S, T, V, W, X, Y,* and *Z*. Note that **Y** can <u>sometimes</u> function as a vowel (as in *myth* [/mɪθ/] or *dry* [/draɪ/]), so it is often referred to as a **semivowel**. **W** can also function <u>alongside</u> vowels to form certain vowel sounds (as in *grow* [/groʊ/] or *draw* [/drɔ/]), but it can't function as a vowel on its own.

Forming consonant sounds

Each consonant letter has at least one specific speech sound associated with it, but certain combinations of letters (known as digraphs) produce other specific sounds as well. For the most part, we'll be focusing on the sounds that consonants can make on their own, but we'll also look at certain instances in which a consonant's sound *changes* when it appears next to certain vowels or other consonants. For the unique speech sounds that specific consonant combinations create, see the section on Consonant Digraphs.

B b

The consonant **B** (pronounced "bee," IPA: /bi/) is formed by softly pressing the lips together before passing air through the mouth. The vocal cords are used to make a sound when this happens, so it is known as a **voiced** speech sound. This is the only sound associated with **B** in English, so the same character is used in IPA transcription: /b/.

For example:
- **boy** (/bɔɪ/)
- **break** (/breɪk/)
- **badly** (/ˈbædli/)
- **able** (/ˈeɪbəl/)
- **embarrass** (/ɪmˈbɛrəs/)
- **imbue** (/ɪmˈbju/)
- **dab** (/ˈdæb/)
- **verb** (/vɜrb/)
- **describe** (/dɪˈskraɪb/)

Silent B

The only exception to the pronunciation of **B** is the rare time that it is silent in a word. This usually occurs when **B** follows the letter **M**. Less commonly, silent **B** can occur when **B** <u>precedes</u> the letter **T**. For example:

MB	BT
climb (/klaɪm/)	
lamb (/læm/)	debt (/dɛt/)
thumb (/θʌm/)	doubt (/daʊt/)
numb (/nʌm/)	subtle (/'sʌtəl/)
bomb (/bɔm/)	
comb (/koʊm/)	

Be careful, though, because not every occurrence of **MB** or **BT** will produce a silent **B**. If in doubt, consult a good dictionary that provides pronunciation guides.

C c

The letter **C** (pronounced "cee," IPA: /si/) commonly produces <u>two</u> different sounds, depending on how it is used in a word. These are known as "**hard C**" and "**soft C**." Generally speaking, there are predictable patterns that determine whether **C** will be hard or soft, depending on the vowel that follows it. (Note that digraphs featuring the letter **C** have their own patterns of pronunciation.)

Hard C

Hard **C** has the same consonant sound as the letter **K**, transcribed in IPA as /k/. It is made by closing the vocal tract at the back of the throat before forcing air through.

The hard **C** sound generally occurs when **C** is followed by the vowels **A, O,** and **U**. For example:

CA	CO	CU
cap (/kæp/)	corner (/'kɔrnər/)	cushion (/'kʊʃən/)
cat (/kæt/)	cover (/'kʌvər/)	cute (/kjut/)
catch (/kætʃ/)	coat (/koʊt/)	curve (/kɜrv/)

The hard **C** sound also occurs when **C** appears before the consonants **T, R**, and **L**, as well as when **C** is the last letter of a word. For example:

CT	CR	CL	Final letter
act (/ækt/)	crawl (/krɔl/)	climb (/klaɪm/)	arc (/ark/)
perfect (/'pɜr ˌfɪkt/)	create (/kri'eɪt/)	clean (/klin/)	graphic (/'græfɪk/)
predict (/prɪd'ɪkt/)	accrue (/ə'kru/)	uncle (/'ʌŋkəl/)	cardiac (/'kɑrdi ˌæk/)

Soft C

Soft **C** has the same consonant sound as the letter **S**; both are transcribed in IPA as /s/. It is made by forcing air between the tongue and the roof of the mouth and out past the teeth. This is known as a **sibilant** speech sound, meaning it produces a *hissing* effect. The vocal cords are not engaged to produce a sound, so this is an **unvoiced** speech sound.

The soft **C** sound usually occurs when **C** is followed by the vowels **E, I,** and **Y,** as in:

CE	CI	CY
central (/ˈsɛntrəl/)	circle (/ˈsɜrkəl/)	juicy (/ˈdʒusi/)
celebrate (/ˈsɛləˌbreɪt/)	city (/ˈsɪti/)	icy (/ˈaɪsi/)
nice (/naɪs/)	exercise (/ˈɛksərˌsaɪz/)	cylinder (/ˈsɪlɪndər/)

Producing the /ʃ/ sound

Occasionally, **C** produces the sound most commonly made by the digraph **SH**, transcribed in IPA as /ʃ/. This sound is made by forming a narrow passageway with the sides of the tongue against the top teeth and then forcing air through partly open lips. Like the /s/ sound of soft **C**, it is **unvoiced**, meaning the vocal cords do not vibrate.

Generally speaking, **C** produces the /ʃ/ sound when it appears after a vowel and is followed by the letter **I** and another vowel. For example:
• efficient (/ɪˈfɪʃənt/)
• facial (/ˈfeɪʃəl/)
• precious (/ˈprɛʃəs/)
• social (/ˈsoʊʃəl/)

C also produces this sound in a handful of words in which it is followed by **EA**, as in:
• ocean (/ˈoʊʃən/)
• crustacean (/krəˈsteɪʃən/)

Silent C

C often becomes silent when it comes after the letter **S** and is followed by **E** or **I**. For example:
• ascend (/əˈsɛnd/)
• descend (/dɪˈsɛnd/)
• muscle (/ˈmʌsəl/; **LE** here produces a sound like **EL**)
• obscene (/ɑbˈsin/)
• scent (/sɛnt/)
• science (/ˈsaɪəns/)

We can also think of **C** as silent in the digraph **CK**, which is pronounced the same as **K** on its own: /k/. For instance:
• attack (/əˈtæk/)
• bucket (/ˈbʌkət/)
• locker (/ˈlɑkər/)
• stack (/stæk/)
• truck (/trʌk/)
• wicked (/ˈwɪkəd/)

D d

The consonant **D** (pronounced "dee," IPA: /di/) is usually pronounced by softly pressing the tongue to the roof of the mouth before forcing air through. The vocal cords are used to make a sound as well, making this a **voiced** speech sound. It is unique to the letter **D**, so the IPA transcription for the sound is simply /d/. For the most part, this sound does not change, regardless of where **D** appears in a word. However, there are three general exceptions to this rule.

Producing the /t/ sound

When the suffix "-ed" is used to form the simple past tense of a verb, **D** often takes on the speech sound of the letter **T** (/t/). This occurs when "-ed" follows an **unvoiced** consonant sound—that is, /f/, /k/, /p/, /s/, /ʃ/, /tʃ/, and /θ/. For example:

/f/	/k/	/p/	/s/	/ʃ/	/tʃ/	/θ/
briefed (/brift/) laughed (/læft/) puffed (/pʌft/)	baked (/beɪkt/) knocked (/nɑkt/) sacked (/sækt/) worked (/wɜrkt/)	dropped (/drɑpt/) helped (/hɛlpt/) jumped (/dʒʌmpt/) mapped (/mæpt/)	aced (/eɪst/) based (/beɪst/) diced (/daɪst/) passed (/pæst/)	blushed (/blʌʃt/) crashed (/kræʃt/) extinguished (/ɪkˈstɪŋgwɪʃt/) pushed (/pʊʃt/)	approached (/əˈproʊtʃt/) branched (/bræntʃt/) hunched (/hʌntʃt/) patched (/pætʃt/)	birthed (/bɜrθt/) frothed (/frɔθt/)

Note that verbs ending in /t/ (also an unvoiced consonant sound) are an exception to this rule, and **D** is pronounced /d/ as normal, as in:
• knotted (/ˈnɑtɪd/)
• potted (/ˈpɑtɪd/)
• heated (/ˈhitɪd/)
• plated (/ˈpleɪtɪd/)
• greeted (/ˈgritɪd/)

Producing the /dʒ/ sound

Very rarely, the letter **D** produces the same sound as the consonant **J**, transcribed in IPA as /dʒ/. This sound is made by first stopping airflow by pressing the tongue against the roof of the mouth and then forcing air through a narrow gap between the two. It is formed the same way as the **CH** sound (transcribed as /tʃ/), except that it is **voiced**, meaning the vocal chords are vibrated.

This happens in some words in which **D** is preceded by a vowel and followed by the letter **U**, as in:
• assiduous (/əˈsɪdʒuəs/)
• education (/ɛdʒuˈkeɪʃən/)
• graduate (verb: /ˈgrædʒuˌeɪt/)
• individual (/ɪndəˈvɪdʒuəl/)
• residual (/rɪˈzɪdʒuəl/)
(However, be aware that in some dialects this sound change is not seen, with **D** still pronounced as a standard /d/ sound.)

There is also one instance where a **D** followed by an **I** produces the /dʒ/ sound: *soldier* (/ˈsoʊldʒər/).

Additionally, **D** contributes to a /dʒ/ sound in the consonant combinations **DG** and **DJ**, which we'll look at in the section on Consonant Digraphs.

Silent D

When **D** appears in a large consonant cluster (especially when **D** comes after **N**), it is occasionally left unpronounced. For example:

• han**d**kerchief (/ˈhæŋkərtʃɪf/)
• han**d**some (/ˈhænsəm/)
• gran**d**father (/ˈgrænfaðər/)
• gran**d**mother (/ˈgræ[n]mʌðər/; **N** is also sometimes silent)
• gran**d**daughter (/ˈgrændɔtər/; first **D** is silent, but second **D** is pronounced)
• gran**d**son (/ˈgrænsʌn/)
• san**d**wich (/ˈsænwɪtʃ/)
• We**d**nesday (/ˈwɛnzdeɪ/)

(Note that for many of these words—with the exception *handkerchief* and *Wednesday*—the **D** may be pronounced in some dialects but left out in others.)

F f

The letter **F** (pronounced "ef," IPA: /ɛf/) is almost always pronounced as a **voiceless** or **unvoiced labiodental fricative**—that is, by pressing the front top teeth against the lower lip (the meaning of "labiodental") as air is expelled through the mouth without engaging the vocal cords. This is represented in IPA as /**f**/. For example:

• feel (/fil/)
• fair (/fɛr/)
• foot (/fʊt/)
• after (/ˈæftər/)
• different (/ˈdɪfrənt/)
• effect (/ɪˈfɛkt/)
• life (/laɪf/)
• belief (/bɪˈlif/)
• off (/ɔf/)

There is only one word in English in which **F** is pronounced differently: *of* (/ɑv/). Rather than taking the standard pronunciation, **F** is here pronounced like the letter **V** (IPA: /v/), which is called a **voiced labiodental fricative**. This means that instead of just pushing air between the teeth and lower lip, the vocal chords are vibrated at the same time.

G g

Like **C**, the letter **G** (pronounced "gee," IPA: /dʒi/) has two standard pronunciations: "**hard G**" and "**soft G**." Again, there are patterns that dictate whether **G** will be hard or soft in a word, though these are a bit less reliable than they were for hard and soft **C**. (And, again, there are separate rules for when **G** appears in consonant digraphs.)

Hard G

"Hard **G**" is a distinct sound not shared with any other consonant, transcribed in IPA as /**g**/. It is pronounced by closing the vocal tract at the back of the throat as air is pushed through and the vocal cords are vibrated (making this a **voiced** speech sound).

Like **C**, **G** makes a "hard" sound when it is followed by the vowels **A, O,** and **U**. For example:

GA	GO	GU
gap (/gæp/)	go (/gɔ/)	guest (/gɛst/)
gate (/geɪt/)	gossip (/ˈgasəp/)	gut (/gʌt/)
gall (/gɔll/)	gouge (/gaʊdʒ/)	argue (/ˈɑrgju/)

The hard **G** sound also occurs when **G** appears before the consonants **L, R**, and sometimes **H**,* as well as when **G** is the last letter of a word (and is not preceded by **N**). For example:

GL	GR	GH	Final letter
glove (/glʌv/)	grow (/groʊ/)	ghost (/goʊst/)	bag (/bæg/)
glean (/glin/)	agree (/əˈgri/)	ghastly (/ˈgæstli/)	dog (/dɔg/)
gargle (/ˈgɑrgəl/)	flagrant (/ˈfleɪgrənt/)	spaghetti (/spəˈgɛti/)	catalog (/ˈkætəlɔg/)

(*Note: The digraph **GH** can produce several different sounds, as well as being silent, depending on the vowel(s) or consonant(s) that precede it. The /g/ sound is uncommon in this combination, usually only occurring when a word <u>begins</u> with **GH**.)

Soft G

Soft **G** has the same consonant sound as the letter **J**: both are transcribed in IPA as /dʒ/. It is made by first stopping airflow by pressing the tongue against the roof of the mouth and then forcing the air between a narrow gap. It is a **voiced** consonant sound, meaning the vocal chords are vibrated.

Like soft **C**, the soft **G** sound typically occurs when **G** is followed by the vowels **E, I**, and **Y**, as in:

GE	GI	GY
germ (/dʒɜrm/)	fragile (/ˈfrædʒəl/)	gym (/dʒɪm/)
age (/eɪdʒ/)	giant (/ˈdʒaɪənt/)	biology (/baɪˈɑlədʒi/)
fringe (/frɪndʒ/)	logic (/ˈlɑdʒɪk/)	Egypt (/ˈidʒəpt/)

It's important to note, though, that there are many exceptions to these patterns, and it is quite common to see hard **G** pronunciations that occur with these combinations (particularly **GE** and **GI**). For example:
• get (/gɛt/ or /gɪt/)
• gear (/gɪr/)
• gecko (/ˈgɛkoʊ/)
• gift (/gɪft/)
• giggle (/ˈgɪgəl/)
• gill (/gɪl/)
• gynecology (/gaɪnəˈkɑlədʒi/)
Note as well that these patterns become even less reliable when **G** is used in different digraphs, especially **NG** and **GG**.

The other soft G

While /dʒ/ is the most common speech sound used for a soft **G**, there is a second, similar pronunciation that appears in some foreign loanwords ending in **GE** after a vowel. It is the same sound used for **SU** in certain words (such as *pleasure* or *usual*), and the IPA transcription is /ʒ/. The sound is formed in the same way as /dʒ/, except the tongue is not pressed against the roof of the mouth initially. (It is also the same formation as the digraph **SH** (/ʃ/) except that it is voiced, meaning a sound is made with the vocal cords.)

There is no reliable spelling pattern that dictates when a soft **G** will be pronounced /ʒ/ rather than /dʒ/, so we simply have to learn them individually. Here are a few examples:
• garage (/gəˈrɑʒ/)*
• beige (/beɪʒ/)
• massage (/məˈsɑʒ/)
• rouge (/ruʒ/)
• genre (/ˈʒɑnrə/)

(*It is also common to hear this word pronounced with the standard soft **G** at the end: /gəˈrɑdʒ/.)

Silent G

Occasionally, **G** becomes silent when it comes <u>before</u> the letter **N**. For example:

- **gn**aw (/nɔ/)
- **gn**at (/næt/)
- **gn**ash (/næʃ/)
- ali**gn** (/əˈlaɪn/)
- si**gn** (/saɪn/)
- arrai**gn** (/əˈreɪn/)
- dei**gn** (/deɪn/)
- fei**gn** (/feɪn/)
- impu**gn** (/ɪmˈpjun/)
- lasa**gn**a (/ləˈzɑnjə/)

H h

As a single letter, the consonant **H** (pronounced "aitch," IPA: /eɪtʃ/) has only one pronounced sound, transcribed in IPA as /h/. It is formed by slightly constricting the back of the throat as air is passed through; the vocal chords are not engaged, so it is an **unvoiced** speech sound.

Silent H

However, a single **H** is also occasionally silent. The spelling of the word on its own is usually not enough to dictate whether **H** is pronounced or silent, though, so we simply have to memorize such words. Here are a few examples of words where **H** is either pronounced or silent:

H is pronounced	H is silent
house (/haʊs/)	hour (/aʊər/)
hat (/hæt/)	honor (/ˈɑnər/)
hear (/hir/)	heir (/ɛr/)
herd (/hɜrd/)	herb* (/ɛrb/)

(*This pronunciation is most common in American English. In British English, the **H** is usually pronounced: /hɛrb/.)

The only times a single **H** is predictably silent are when it appears <u>between</u> two vowels or else ends a word <u>after</u> a vowel. For example:

- gra**h**am (/ˈgreɪəm/ or /græm/)
- anni**h**ilate (/əˈnaɪəˌleɪt/)
- ve**h**icle (/ˈviɪkəl/)**

- cheeta**h** (/ˈtʃitə/)
- tabboule**h** (/təˈbulɪ/)
- hurra**h** (/hʊˈrɑ/)

(**The **H** is silent in *vehicle* for the vast majority of English speakers, but in some dialects it may also be pronounced: /ˈvihɪkəl/.)

H in consonant digraphs

Finally, it's important to note that **H** appears in many letter combinations where it can either be silent or create a range of unique pronunciations, depending on the combination. Go to the section on Consonant Digraphs to learn more about how **H** behaves in such instances.

J j

The letter **J** (pronounced "jay," IPA: /ʤeɪ/) almost always has the same sound as soft **G**: /ʤ/. For instance:

- job (/ʤɑb/)
- judge (/ʤʌʤ/)
- jeer (/ʤɪr/)
- injury (/ɪnʤəri/)
- project (/prɑʤɛkt/)
- majority (/məˈʤɔrəti/)

Also like soft **G**, the letter **J** occasionally produces the /ʒ/ sound. This usually only happens in foreign loan words, as in:

- Taj Mahal (/tɑʒ məˈhɑl)
- Beijing (ˌbeɪʒˈɪŋ/)

However, this pronunciation is not consistently applied, and sometimes the normal /ʤ/ sound is used instead.

Very rarely, **J** also has the same sound as **Y** when used as a consonant. (Note that the IPA symbol for this sound looks like a lowercase **j**: /j/.) For example:

- fjord (/fjɔrd/)
- hallelujah (/hæləˈlujə/)

K k

The letter **K** (pronounced "kay," IPA: /keɪ/) has the same consonant sound as hard **C**: /k/. For example:

- kick (/kɪk/)
- kiss (/kɪs/)
- kangaroo (/ˌkæŋgəˈru/)
- koala (/koʊˈɑlə/)
- bake (/beɪk/)
- work (/wɜrk/)
- donkey (/ˈdɔŋki/)
- skin (/skɪn/)
- market (/ˈmɑrkət/)

Silent K

Like **G**, **K** sometimes becomes silent when it appears before the letter **N**, usually at the beginning of a word. For example:

- know (/noʊ/)
- knife (/naɪf/)
- knight (/naɪt/)
- knock (/nɑk/)
- knot (/nɑt/)
- knee (/ni/)
- knack (/næk/)
- knit (/nɪt/)
- knead (/nid/)

L l

The consonant sound for the letter **L** (pronounced "ell," IPA: /ɛl/) is formed by lightly pressing the tip of the tongue against the roof of the mouth while air passes through. At the same time, the vocal cords are engaged to create a sound, making this a **voiced** speech sound. In IPA, this sound is transcribed as /l/.

L is often (but not always) doubled if it appears after a vowel in the middle or at the end of a word. For example:

- listen (/lɪsən/)
- lips (/lɪps/)
- long (/lɔŋ/)
- last (/læst/)
- below (/bɪˈloʊ/)

- bellow (/ˈbɛloʊ/; notice how the pronunciation of **E** changes with two **L**s)
- alter (/ɔltər/)
- cold (/koʊld/)
- fell (/fɛl/)
- tell (/tɛl/)
- gel (/dʒɛl/; in this instance, the pronunciation is the same as words with two **L**s)

Silent L

L sometimes becomes silent when it appears before the consonants **F, V, K,** and **M** after the vowel **A**, as well as before **D** after the vowels **OU**. In some cases, this silent **L** elongates or otherwise modifies the vowel sound that comes before it, giving the slight impression of an /l/ sound without being distinctly pronounced. Here are a few common examples:

LF	LV	LK	LM	LD
calf (/kæf/) half (/hæf/)	calves (/kævs/) halves (/hævs/)	balk (/bɔk/) chalk (/tʃɔk/) talk (/tɔk/) walk (/wɔk/)	almond (/ˈamənd/) balm (/bɑm/) calm (/kɑm/) palm (/pɑm/) psalm (/sɑm/) salmon (/ˈsæmən/)	could (/kʊd/) should (/ʃʊd/) would (/wʊd/)

The strange pronunciation of *colonel*

There is one word in which **L** produces a completely different speech sound: *colonel*. Rather than an expected pronunciation of /kɔlənəl/ or /kɔloʊnəl/, the middle **L** is actually pronounced as an **R**, with the second **O** made silent: /kɜrnəl/. This strange pronunciation is the result of the word coming into spoken English from the French *coronel* (with a silent second **O**), which itself came from the Italian word *colonello*. As it entered the English language more regularly, writers kept the word's spelling closer to the original Italian, but the French pronunciation was so widely spoken that it has remained the preferred pronunciation to this day.

M m

The consonant sound for the letter **M** (pronounced "em," IPA: /ɛm/) is formed by pursing the lips together while the vocal cords are engaged; it is therefore a **voiced** speech sound. This sound is unique to the letter, so the IPA transcription uses the same character: **/m/**.

M produces the same sound regardless of where it appears in a word. For example:
- make (/meɪk/)
- merry (/mɛri/)
- mode (/moʊd/)
- woman (/ˈwʊmən/)
- almost (/ˈɔlˌmoʊst/)
- armor (/ˈɑrmər/)
- tram (/træm/)
- dam (/dæm/)
- team (/tim/)

Silent M

There is one word that features a **silent M**: *mnemonic*. Here, the **N** is pronounced but not the **M**: (/nɪˈmɑnɪk/). This pronunciation also is true for the adverbial form of the word, *mnemonically* (/nɪˈmɑnɪk[ə]li/).

N n

The consonant **N** (pronounced "en," IPA: /ɛn/) creates a similar sound to that of **M**. The airway is still blocked, but the tongue is pressed against the roof of the mouth just behind the teeth, while the lips are kept open. The vocal cords are again engaged to produce a sound, so it is a **voiced** speech sound. In IPA, this sound is transcribed as /**n**/.

N almost always produces the same sound, regardless of its position. For example:

• now (/naʊ/)
• near (/nɪr/)
• nag (/næg/)
• energy (/ˈɛnərdʒi/)
• wander (/ˈwɑndər/)
• enter (/ˈɛntər/)
• men (/mɛn/)
• fan (/fæn/)
• dawn (/dɔn/)

Producing the /ŋ/ sound

Occasionally, **N** forms the sound /ŋ/ (the sound formed by the digraph **NG**, as in *sing*) when it appears before the consonant sound /k/, most often represented by **C, CH, K,** or **Q**. For example:

NC	NCH	NK	NQ
distinct (/dɪˈstɪŋkt/)	anchor (/ˈæŋkər/)	ink (/ɪŋk/)	conquer (/ˈkɑŋkər/)
junction (/ˈdʒʌŋkʃən/)	bronchitis (/brɑŋˈkaɪtəs/)	bank (/bæŋk/)	relinquish (/rɪˈlɪŋkwɪʃ/)
puncture (/ˈpʌŋkʧər/)	synchronize (/ˈsɪŋkrəˌnaɪz/)	monkey (/ˈmʌŋki/)	tranquil (/ˈtræŋkwɪl/)

Silent N

N becomes silent when it appears after **M** at the <u>end</u> of a word. For example:

• autumn (/ˈɔtəm/)
• condemn (/kənˈdɛm/)
• column (/ˈkɑləm/)
• hymn (/hɪm/)
• solemn (/ˈsɑləm/)

P p

The consonant sound for the letter **P** (pronounced "pee," IPA: /pi/) is the **unvoiced** counterpart to the letter **B**. That is, they are both formed by pressing the lips together and then forcing air through the mouth, except the vocal cords do not make a sound when making the sound for the letter **P**. The IPA symbol for the sound is the same as the letter: /p/.

P nearly always makes the same sound, regardless of its position in a word (except in the digraph **PH**, which we'll look at separately). For example:

• part (/pɔrt/)
• play (/pleɪ/)
• president (/ˈprɛzəˌdɛnt/)
• apart (/əˈpɑrt/)
• deeply (/ˈdipli/)
• happy (/ˈhæpi/)
• atop (/əˈtɑp/)
• jump (/dʒʌmp/)
• cheap (/ʧip/)

Silent P

Occasionally, **P** can be silent when it is followed by the letters **N, S,** or **T,** usually in certain letter combinations that come from words of Greek origin or influence. For example:

PN	PS	PT
pneuma (/ˈnumə/)	psychology (/saɪˈkɑlədʒi/)	ptarmigan (/ˈtɑrmɪgən/)
pneumatic (/nuˈmætɪk/)	psalm (/sɑm/)	pterodactyl (/ˌtɛrəˈdæktɪl/)
pneumonia (/nuˈmoʊnjə/)	pseudo (/ˈsudoʊ/)	ptisan (/ˈtɪzæn)

Silent **P** occurs in a handful of other words, as well:

- cupboard (/ˈkʌbərd/)
- raspberry (/ˈræzˌbɛri/)
- corps (/kɔr/; both **P** and **S** are silent, unless the word is plural, in which case **S** is pronounced /z/)
- coup (/ku/)
- receipt (/rɪˈsit/)

Q q

The letter **Q** (pronounced "cue," IPA: /kju/) has the same speech sound as **K**: /k/. It is almost always followed by the letter **U,** and the two letters together most commonly form a /kw/ sound. This usually occurs when they appear at the beginning or in the middle of a word. For example:

- **qu**iet (/ˈkwaɪət/)
- **qu**ick (/kwɪk/)
- **qu**een (/kwin/)
- re**qu**est (/rɪˈkwɛst/)
- e**qu**ipment (/ɪˈkwɪpmənt/)
- in**qu**ire (/ɪnˈkwaɪr/)

QU does not always result in a /kw/ sound, though; sometimes it is simply a hard /k/, such as:

- anti**qu**e (/ænˈtik/)
- bou**qu**et (/buˈkeɪ/)
- con**qu**er (/ˈkɑŋkər/)
- li**qu**or (/ˈlɪkər/)
- mos**qu**ito (/məsˈkitoʊ/)

Finally, there *are* a handful of words in which **Q** is not followed by a **U,** but nearly all of them come from other languages, such as *Iraq, burqa,* or *qabab* (usually written in English as *kebab*).

R r

The consonant sound for the letter **R** (pronounced "ar," IPA: /ɑr/) is formed by narrowing the airway at the back of the throat as air is pushed through and the vocal cords are engaged (making it a **voiced** speech sound). The IPA transcription for the sound is the same character as the letter: /**r**/.

R always produces the same speech sound, which can appear anywhere in a word. For example:

- **r**ight (/raɪt/)
- **r**oll (/roʊl/)
- **r**ead (/rid/)
- a**r**t (/ɑrt/)
- po**r**k (/pɔrk/)
- ca**r**e (/kɛr/)
- ta**r** (/tɑr/)
- endu**r**e (/ɪnˈdʊr/)
- e**rr**o**r** (/ˈɛrər/)

It's important to mention that **R** often has the effect of altering the sound of a vowel that comes before it. To learn more about this, go to the section on Vowels.

S s

The consonant **S** (pronounced "ess," IPA: /ɛs/) has four different pronunciations, depending on the word it appears in. We'll briefly cover each sound here, but go to the section Pronouncing the Letter S to learn more.

Producing the /s/ sound

The primary sound associated with the letter **S** is the same as a soft **C**, transcribed in IPA as /s/. It is made by forcing air between the tongue and the roof of the mouth and out past the teeth. This is known as a **sibilant** speech sound, meaning it produces a *hissing* effect. The vocal cords are not engaged to produce a sound, so this is an **unvoiced** speech sound.

The /s/ sound can be made whether **S** is at the beginning, middle, or end of a word. For example:
• sand (/sænd/)
• see (/si/)
• soft (/sɑft/)
• assent (/əˈsɛnt/)
• basic (/ˈbeɪsɪk/)
• persuade (/pərˈsweɪd/)
• gas (/gæs/)
• this (/ðɪs/)
• tapes (/teɪps/)

However, when S appears in the middle or at the end of a word, it can also often make the sound /z/.

Producing the /z/ sound

S also often makes the same sound as the letter **Z**, transcribed in IPA as /z/. The sound is formed the same way as /s/, but it is **voiced**, meaning the vocal cords are engaged while making the sound.

S only produces the /z/ sound when it appears in the middle or at the end of certain words (it does not create this sound at the beginning of a word). For example:
• desert (/ˈdɛzɜrt/)
• easy (/ˈizi/)
• president (/ˈprɛzɪdənt/)
• has (/hæz/)
• goes (/goʊz/)
• toys (/tɔɪz/)

Producing the /ʃ/ sound

S most commonly produces the /ʃ/ sound in the digraph **SH**, but it can also occur when **S** appears on its own. The sound is made by forming a narrow passageway with the sides of the tongue against the top teeth and then forcing air through partly open lips. Like the /s/ sound, it is **unvoiced**, meaning the vocal cords do not vibrate.

Generally speaking, **S** produces the /ʃ/ sound when it appears after a consonant and is followed by the letter **I** and another vowel; it is also sometimes formed when **S** is followed by the letter **U**. For example:
• controversial (/ˌkɑntrəˈvɜrʃəl/)
• tension (/ˌkɑntrəˈvɜrʃəl/)
• obsession (/ˌkɑntrəˈvɜrʃəl/)

• issue (/ˈɪʃu/)
• pressure (/ˈprɛʃər/)
• sugar (/ˈʃʊgər/)
• sure (/ˈʃʊr/)

Producing the /ʒ/ sound

S also forms another sound when it is used in combination with certain vowels. It is the same sound used for **GE** in certain foreign loanwords (such as *beige* or *garage*), and the IPA transcription is /ʒ/. The sound is formed in the same way as /ʃ/ except that it is **voiced**, meaning a sound is made with the vocal cords while air is being pushed through the mouth.

The /ʒ/ sound is most often pronounced when **S** appears after a vowel and is followed by **UAL**, **URE**, or **ION**. For example:

SUAL	SURE	SION
usual (/ˈjuʒuəl/)	exposure (/ɪkˈspoʊʒər/)	collision (/kəˈlɪʒən/)
casual (/ˈkæʒəwəl/)	leisure (/ˈliʒər/)	division (/dɪˈvɪʒən/)
visual (/ˈvɪʒəwəl/)	measure (/ˈmɛʒər/)	illusion (/ɪˈluʒən/)

T t

The consonant sound for the letter **T** (pronounced "tee," IPA: /ti/) is produced by pressing the tip of the tongue against the roof of the mouth and then forcing air through. No sound is made with the vocal cords, making it an **unvoiced** speech sound. The IPA transcription for this sound is the same as the letter: /t/.

On its own, **T** can produce the speech sound /t/ anywhere in a word. For example:

• tap (/tæp/)
• toll (/toʊl/)
• trunk (/trʌŋk/)
• banter (/bæntər/)
• retire (/rɪˈtaɪr/)
• attribute (/ˈætrəˌbjut/)
• apt (/æpt/)
• react (/riˈækt/)
• sat (/sæt/)

Producing the /ʃ/ sound

The letter **T** can also form the /ʃ/ (**SH**) sound when it is followed by **IAL**, **IEN**, or (most commonly) **ION**. These combinations are usually preceded by a vowel, but they sometimes come after consonants too. For example:

TIAL	TIEN	TION
initial (/ɪˈnɪʃəl/) partial (/ˈpɑrʃəl/) spatial (/ˈspeɪʃəl/)	patient (/ˈpeɪʃənt/) patience (/ˈpeɪʃəns/)	education (/ˌɛdʒuˈkeɪʃən/) rational (/ˈræʃənəl/) mention (/ˈmɛnʃən/) action (/ˈækʃən/) function (/ˈfʌŋkʃən/)

Producing the /tʃ/ sound

While **T** usually produces the /ʃ/ sound when it is followed by a vowel, it can sometimes produce the /tʃ/ sound as well. This sound (most commonly associated with the digraphs **CH**) is made by first stopping airflow by pressing the tongue against the roof of the mouth and then forcing air through a narrow gap between the two. It is formed the same way as the **J** sound (transcribed as /dʒ/), except that it is **unvoiced**, meaning the vocal chords are not vibrated.

T most commonly produces the /ʧ/ sound when it is followed by **U**, but it can also occur when **TI** follows the letter **S**. For example:

TU	TI
adventure (/ædˈvɛnʧər/)	bastion (/ˈbæsʧən/)
century (/ˈsɛnʧəri/)	Christian (/ˈkrɪsʧən/)
eventually (/ɪˈvɛnʧəwəli/)	congestion (/kənˈdʒɛsʧən/)
fortune (/ˈfɔrʧən/)	digestion (/daɪˈdʒɛsʧən/)
future (/ˈfjuʧər/)	exhaustion (/ɪgˈzɑsʧən/)
picture (/ˈpɪkʧər/)	question (/ˈkwɛsʧən/)
nature (/ˈneɪʧər/)	suggestion (/səˈdʒɛsʧən/)
situation (/ˌsɪʧuˈeɪʃən)	

Pronouncing *equation* and *righteous*

Uniquely, the word *equation* is pronounced /ɪˈkweɪʒən/; it is the only instance in which **TI** produces a /ʒ/ sound rather than /ʃ/ or /ʧ/.

Another time **T** creates a unique pronunciation is in the word *righteous* (pronounced /ˈraɪʧəs/), which the only instance in which **TE** produces the /ʧ/ sound.

These pronunciations also carry over to words derived from them, as in *equational* (/ɪˈkweɪʒənəl/) or *righteousness* (/ˈraɪʧəsnəs/).

Silent T

Occasionally, the letter **T** becomes silent in a word. This occurs in some words when **T** comes after the letter **S** and is followed by a schwa (/ə/), as in:
- apostle (/əˈpɑsəl/)
- castle (/ˈkæsəl/)
- nestle (/ˈnɛsəl/)
- pestle (/ˈpɛsəl/)*
- thistle (/ˈθɪsəl/)
- whistle (/ˈwɪsəl/)
- wrestle (/ˈrɛsəl/)
- christen (/ˈkrɪsən/)
- fasten (/ˈfæsən/)
- glisten (/ˈglɪsən/)
- hasten (/ˈheɪsən/)
- listen (/ˈlɪsən/)
- moisten (/ˈmɔɪsən/)
- Christmas (/ˈkrɪsməs/)

In a few words, silent **T** also occurs with other consonant combinations. For example:
- mortgage (/ˈmɔrgəʤ/)
- often (/ˈɔfən/)*
- soften (/ˈsɔfən/)

Finally, certain loanwords that come from French maintain a silent **T** at the end of the word. For instance:
• ballet (/bæˈleɪ/)
• bouquet (/buˈkeɪ/)
• gourmet (/gʊərˈmeɪ/)
• valet (/væˈleɪ/)

(*Depending on regional dialect or personal preference, the **T** is sometimes pronounced in *pestle* [/ˈpɛstəl/] and *often* [/ˈɔftən/].)

V v

The letter **V** (pronounced "vee," IPA: /vi/) always* produces the same speech sound, transcribed in IPA as /v/. This sound is formed the same way as the letter **F**—by pressing the front top teeth against the lower lip as air is expelled through the mouth—except that the vocal cords are engaged, making it a **voiced** speech sound.

V forms this sound regardless of where it appears in a word. It can appear at the beginning or in the middle of a word; it is usually not the last letter of a word, almost always being followed by **E**. For example:
• vast (/væst/)
• very (/ˈvɛri/)
• voice (/vɔɪs/)
• advertise (/ˈædvərˌtaɪz/)
• invitation (/ˌɪnvɪˈteɪʃən/)
• subversion (/səbˈvɜrʒən/)
• have (/hæv/)
• give (/gɪv/)
• nerve (/nɜrv/)

*have to

In standard pronunciation, **V** always produces the /v/ speech sound. However, it is sometimes pronounced as an /f/ in the phrase *have to*, especially colloquially. So while the pronunciation /hæv tʊ/ would be considered standard, /hæf tʊ/ is also fairly common.

W w

As a distinct consonant, the letter **W** ("double U," pronounced "dubbel yuu," IPA: /ˈdʌbəlju/) creates a **voiced** speech sound, formed by constricting the entire mouth and pursing the lips into a narrow gap while the vocal cords are vibrated. It is transcribed in IPA as /w/.

This consonant sound may appear at the beginning or in the middle of a word, generally when **W** is followed by a vowel. For example:
• way (/weɪ/)
• wire (/waɪər/)
• work (/wɜrk/)
• awake (/əˈweɪk/)
• between (/bɪˈtwin/)
• otherwise (/ˈʌðərˌwaɪz/)

Silent W with consonants

In some consonant combinations, **W** is not pronounced at all. This occurs in some words beginning with **WH** when it is followed by **O**, as in:
• **who** (/hu/)
• **whole** (/hoʊl/)
• **whom** (/hum/)
• **whose** (/huz/)

W also becomes silent in most words that begin **WR**. For instance:
- wrap (/ræp/)
- wreck (/rɛk/)
- wrestle (/ˈrɛsəl/)
- wrist (/rɪst/)
- write (/raɪt/)
- wrong (/rɔŋ/)
- wrung (/rʌŋ/)

Finally, there are three words in which **W** is silent <u>after</u> another consonant:
- answer (/ˈænsər/)
- sword (/sɔrd/)
- two (/tu/)

Silent W after vowels

When **W** follows the vowels **A, E,** or **O** and either ends the word or is followed by a consonant, it is no longer distinctly pronounced. Instead, it usually serves to alter the vowel or else elongate the sound into a diphthong. For example:
- bow (/boʊ/ or /baʊ/)
- drawl (/drɔl/)
- fawn (/fɔn/)
- flew (/flu/)
- grow (/groʊ/)
- strewn (/strun/)

In some cases, **W** can become silent <u>between</u> two vowels as well, as in:
- coward (/ˈkaʊərd/)
- jewel (/ˈdʒuəl/)
- flower (/ˈflaʊər/)

To learn more about how vowels change their sounds in different letter arrangements, go to the sections on Vowels, Diphthongs, and Triphthongs.

X x

The letter **X** (pronounced "ex," IPA: /ɛks/) does not have a single, unique consonant sound associated with it; instead, it is usually formed from a combination of two other sounds. It almost always appears in the middle or at the end of a word (other than a few exceptions, which we'll look at later).

Pronounced as /ks/

Most commonly, **X** is pronounced as a combination of the **unvoiced** sounds /k/ and /s/. For example:
- axe (/æks/)
- expert (/ˈɛkspərt/)
- dexterity (/dɛksˈtɛrəti/)
- galaxy (/ˈɡæləksi/)
- excellent (/ˈɛksələnt/)
- box (/bɑks/)
- fix (/fɪks/)
- phoenix (/ˈfinɪks/)
- index (/ˈɪndɛks/)

Pronounced as /gz/

When **X** appears before a stressed vowel sound (and almost always after the letter **E**) it becomes **voiced** as the combination of the sounds /g/ and /z/. For instance:

- example (/ɪgˈzæmpəl/)
- exact (/ɪgˈzækt/)
- executive (/ɪgˈzɛkjətɪv/)
- exist (/ɪgˈzɪst/)
- exude (/ɪgˈzud/)
- exotic (/ɪgˈzɑtɪk/)
- exhaust (/ɪgˈzɑst/)
- exhibit (/ɪgˈzɪbɪt/)

(Note that the **H** is **silent** in the last two of these examples.)

Pronounced as /kʃ/ or /gʒ/

In a few rare instances, **X** is pronounced as /kʃ/ instead of /ks/, as in:

- anxious (/ˈæŋkʃəs/)
- complexion (/kəmˈpɛkʃən/)
- flexure (/ˈflɛkʃər/)
- sexual (/ˈsɛkʃuəl/)

Even less commonly, **X** is pronounced as /gʒ/ instead of /gz/:

- luxury (/ˈlʌgʒəri/)
- luxurious (/ləgʒˈəriəs/)

Pronounced as /z/

X predominantly appears in the middle or at the end of words. However, it does appear as the first letter of a few words, in which case it usually has the same sound as the letter **Z** (IPA: **/z/**). For example:

- xanthan (/ˈzænθən/)
- xenolith (/ˈzɛnəlɪθ/)
- xenophobia (/ˌzɛnəˈfoʊbiə/)
- xerography (/zɪˈrɒgrəfi/)
- xylophone (/ˈzaɪləˌfoʊn/)

Note that other than the rare words of which **X** is the first letter, **X** also has the /z/ pronunciation in one other word: *anxiety* (/æŋˈzaɪəti/).

Y y

The letter **Y** (pronounced "wye," IPA: /waɪ/) is often referred to as a "**semivowel**" because it can act as <u>either</u> a vowel or a consonant, depending on where it appears in a word.

When it functions as a consonant, the speech sound for **Y** is formed by first pressing the sides of the tongue up to the roof of the mouth to form a narrow passageway, as air is pushed through and the vocal cords are vibrated; then, mid-sound, this passageway is widened with the tongue to let more air through at a time. Because the vocal cords are engaged, it is a **voiced** speech sound. In IPA transcription, it is written as /j/. (Do not confuse this symbol with the consonant letter **J**; they produce very different sounds.)

As a consonant, **Y** almost always appears at the beginning of a word. For example:

- yacht (/jɑt/)
- yank (/jæŋk/)
- yard (/jɑrd/)
- yearn (/jɜrn/)
- yes (/jɛs/)
- yet (/jɛt/)
- yoga (/ˈjoʊgə/)
- yoke (/joʊk/)
- you (/ju/)
- yuck (/jʌk/)
- yummy (/ˈjʌmi/)

Much less commonly, **Y** can appear as a consonant in the middle of a word:
- canyon (/ˈkænjən/)
- lanyard (/ˈlænjərd/)
- lawyer (/ˈlɔjər/)
- pinyon (/ˈpɪnjən/)
- unyielding (/ənˈjildɪŋ/)
- vineyard (/ˈvɪnjərd/)

However, **Y** never appears at the end of a word as a consonant; it <u>always</u> functions as a vowel in that location. For more information on how **Y** behaves as a vowel, see the section on Vowels.

Z z

The letter **Z** (pronounced "zee," IPA: /zi/, in American English and "zed," IPA: /zɛd/, in British English) almost always produces the same consonant sound, transcribed in IPA as **/z/**. It is formed the same way as the sound /s/—by forcing air between the tongue and the roof of the mouth and out past the teeth—except that the vocal cords are vibrated to create sound, making /z/ a **voiced** speech sound.

Z most often appears in the middle of a word after a vowel. For example:
- amazing (/əˈmeɪzɪŋ/)
- Amazon (/ˈæməˌzɑn/)
- bizarre (/bəˈzɑr/)
- breeze (/briz/)
- brazen (/ˈbreɪzən/)
- citizen (/ˈsɪtəzən/)
- emblazon (/ɛmˈbleɪzən/)
- freezing (/frizɪŋ/)
- size (/saɪz/)

Z also usually maintains the /z/ pronunciation if it is doubled in the middle of a word, as in:
- blizzard (/ˈblɪzərd/)
- dazzle (/ˈdæzəl/)
- fuzzy (/ˈfʌzi/)
- muzzle (/ˈmʌzəl/)
- nozzle (/ˈnɑzəl/)
- tizzy (/ˈtɪzi/)

Z *can* appear at the beginning or end of a word, but it is much less common. It is usually (but not always) doubled if it ends the word. For instance:
- zig (/zɪg/)
- zag (/zæg/)
- zeal (/zil/)
- zucchini (/zuˈkini/)
- buzz (/bʌz/)
- fizz (/fɪz/)
- jazz (/jæz/)
- topaz (/ˈtoʊˌpæz/)

Z can also appear after the letter **T** at the end of some words, but its pronunciation changes (which we'll look at a little later).

"-ize" and "-ization"

Perhaps the most common use of **Z** is in the suffix "-ize" (which indicates a verb formed from a noun or adjective) and its derivative "-ization" (which indicates a noun formed from such a verb).* For example:

IZE	IZATION
realize (/ˈriə‚laɪz/)	realization (/ˌriələˈzeɪʃən/)
specialize (/ˈspɛʃə‚laɪz/)	specialization (/ˌspɛʃələˈzeɪʃən/)
visualize (/ˈvɪʒwə‚laɪz/)	visualization (/ˌvɪʒwələˈzeɪʃən/)

(*In British English, these suffixes are more commonly spelled "-ise" and "-isation.")

Producing the /s/ sound

In words in which **Z** appears after the letter **T**, it is pronounced /s/ rather than /z/. For example:
- blitz (/blɪts/)
- klutz (/klʌts/)
- glitzy (/glɪtsi/)
- pretzel (/ˈprɛtsəl/)
- quartz (/kwɔrts/)
- waltz (/wɔlts/)

Note that this /ts/ sound also occurs when **Z** is doubled in certain foreign loanwords, as in *pizza* (/ˈpitsə/), *mozzarella* (ˌmɑtsəˈrɛlə), and *mezzo* (/ˈmɛtsoʊ/).

Producing the /ʒ/ sound

Finally, there are two instances in which **Z** will be pronounced as /ʒ/ rather than /z/: *azure* (/ˈæʒər/) and *seizure* (/ˈsiʒər/).

Consonant Digraphs

Definition

A **consonant digraph** is a combination of two consonant letters that form a single **consonant speech sound** (technically known as a **consonant phoneme**). Sometimes the combination results in one letter becoming silent, but many times the pairing produces a unique sound that neither letter would form on its own.

The Digraphs

There is a huge range of digraphs in English. For the sake of conciseness, this section will only cover **consonant** digraphs that create unique sounds. Those that only result in one of the letters becoming silent are covered in the section on Consonants, while digraphs formed from a combination of two **vowels** are discussed in the sections on Vowels, Diphthongs, and Triphthongs

The digraphs we'll look at here are **CH, DG, DJ, GH, NG, PH, SH, SS, TH**, and **WH**.

CH

The digraph **CH** forms three distinct phonemes: /ʧ/, /k/, and /ʃ/. There are few reliable spelling patterns that indicate when **CH** will form one sound over another, so we simply have to memorize the different pronunciations. Below, we'll look at some common examples of each.

Producing the sound /ʧ/

The most common sound made by **CH** is /ʧ/, which is formed by first pressing the tip of the tongue against the roof of the mouth before forcing air through (to form the /t/ sound) and then quickly pressing the sides of the tongue against the top teeth and constricting the back of the throat (to form the /ʃ/ [SH] sound). This is why the symbol for /ʧ/ is a combination of /t/ and /ʃ/.

CH often comes after **T** when it makes this sound (forming a trigraph), but it can also do so on its own.

For example:
- achieve (/ə'ʧiv/)
- arch (/arʧ/)
- batch (/bæʧ/)
- beach (/biʧ/)
- charge (/ʧarʤ/)
- child (/ʧaɪld/)
- church (/ʧɜrʧ/)
- ditch (/dɪʧ/)
- purchase (/'pɜrʧəs/)
- reach (/riʧ/)
- teacher (/'tiʧər/)
- match (/mæʧ/)
- much (/mʌʧ/)
- which (/wɪʧ/)

Producing the sound /k/

Less often, **CH** produces the same sound as a **K** or hard **C**, transcribed in IPA as /k/. This sound almost always occurs when **CH** appears at the beginning or in the middle of a word. For example:

Beginning Position	Mid Position
	anchor (/'æŋkər/)
chemistry (/'kɛmɪstri/)	archive (/'ar͵kaɪv/)
choir (/'kwaɪər/)	psyche (/'saɪki/)
chord (/kɔrd/)	psychology (/saɪ'kalədʒi/)
chorus (/'kɔrəs/)	schedule (/'skɛʤʊl/)*
Christmas (/'krɪsməs/)	synchronize (/'sɪŋkrə͵naɪz/)
	technology (/tɛk'nalədʒi/)

Other than the word ache (/eɪk/), which ends in a silent E, there is only one standard word that ends in **CH** pronounced as /k/: *stomach* (/'stʌmək/). However, certain abbreviated forms of other words will sometimes end this way as well, such as *psych* (/saɪk/, short for *psychology*) or *tech* (/tɛk/, short for *technology*).

(*Note that in British English, *schedule* is often pronounced with a /ʃ/ sound rather than /k/: /'ʃɛdjuːl/.)

Producing the sound /ʃ/

Even less commonly, **CH** can be pronounced /ʃ/ (like the digraph **SH**), usually (but not always) when it appears between two vowels. For instance:

- brochure (/broʊˈʃʊr/)
- **chef** (/ʃɛf/)
- machine (/məˈʃin/)
- mustache (/ˈmʌˌstæʃ/)
- parachute (/ˈpɛrəˌʃut/)

DG and DJ

The digraphs **DG** and **DJ** both create the same consonant sound produced by the letter **J**, represented in IPA by the symbol /dʒ/. **DG** is often followed by the letter **E** (which is made silent), while **DJ** is almost always <u>preceded</u> by the letter **A**. Neither digraph can appear at the very beginning* or very end of a word; they must always follow and be followed by at least one other letter.

For example:

DG words	DJ words
abridged (/əˈbrɪdʒd/)	adjacent (/əˈdʒeɪsənt/)
badge (/bædʒ/)	adjective (/ˈædʒɪktɪv/)
judge (/dʒʌdʒ/)	adjourn (/əˈdʒɜrn/)
fledgling (/ˈflɛdʒlɪŋ/)	adjunct (/ˈæˌdʒʌŋkt/)
lodging (/ˈlɑdʒɪŋ/)	adjust (/əˈdʒʌst/)

(*A few foreign loanwords *do* begin with **DJ**, such as *djinni* [/dʒɪˈni/], an Islamic word for a supernatural spirit that influences the actions of people on Earth.)

judgment vs. *judgement*

The verb *judge* can be made into a noun by adding the suffix "-ment" onto the end. In American English, this ending <u>replaces</u> the **E** that normally follows **DG** forming the word *judgment* (/ˈdʒʌdʒmənt/). In American English, this is always considered the correct spelling.

In British English, however, it is equally common to see the word spelled as *judgement* (the pronunciation remains the same: /ˈdʒʌdʒmənt/), though *judgment* tends to be favored in legal and business writing.

Regardless, if the accuracy of your spelling needs to be precise, you should spell the word *judgment* as it is <u>always</u> correct, no matter where in the world you are.

GH

The digraph **GH** can form two sounds—/g/ and /f/—and can also be silent. **GH** only makes the hard /g/ sound when it is at the beginning of a syllable (and usually the beginning of a word). However, when **GH** follows vowels within the same syllable, it can either be silent or produce the /f/ sound—the spelling alone will not dictate which pronunciation it yields, making it a particularly difficult digraph to learn.

Producing the sound /g/

The hard /g/ sound is not very common for the digraph **GH**, but there are a few common words in which it appears:
- **aghast** (/əˈgæst/)
- **ghetto** (/ˈgɛtoʊ/)
- **gherkin** (/ˈgɜrkɪn/)
- **ghost** (/goʊst/)
- **ghoul** (/gul/)
- spaghetti (/spəˈgɛti/)

Producing the sound /f/

The /f/ phoneme is also not common for this digraph. When **GH** is pronounced this way, it almost always comes after the vowels **OU**. For example:

- cough (/kɔf/)
- enough (/ɪˈnʌf/)
- rough (/rʌf/)
- slough (/slʌf/)
- tough (/tʌf/)
- trough (/trɔf/)

GH can also produce the /f/ sound after the vowel digraph **AU**, but this only occurs in the word *laugh* (/læf/), as well as any derivative words like *laughter* or *laughing*.

(There *is* another word that follows this spelling pattern—*draught* (/dræft/—but this is chiefly a British English spelling of the word *draft*).

Silent GH

The most common pronunciation for **GH** is actually none at all. While the /g/ and /f/ pronunciations of the digraph are relatively uncommon, there are many words in which **GH** is silent.

Like the /f/ pronunciation, silent **GH** also appears after **OU** and **AU**, but it also follows the vowels **AI**, **EI**, and **I**. Be careful, though; even though several words may have the same vowels coming before silent **GH**, not all of them have the same pronunciation. For example:

OU + GH	AU + GH	AI + GH	EI + GH	I + GH
bought (/bɔt/)	caught (/kɔt/)		eight (/eɪt/)	bright (/braɪt/)
dough (/doʊ/)	daughter (/dɔtər/)		neighbor (/ˈneɪbər/)	high (/haɪ/)
fought (/fɔt/)	fraught (/frɔt/)	straight (/streɪt/)	height (/haɪt/)	night (/naɪt/)
ought (/ɔt/)	haughty (/ˈhɔti/)		sleight (/slaɪt/)	sight (/saɪt/)
through (/θru/)	naughty (/ˈnɔti/)		weigh (/weɪ/)	thigh (/θaɪ/)

In all of the above, **GH** is actually forming tetragraphs (and one trigraph) with the vowels to which it is attached; go to these sections to learn more about the sounds these can make.

hiccup vs. *hiccough*

Hiccup is the usual and traditional spelling of the word referring to an involuntary spasm of the diaphragm that results in a sharp inhalation of breath followed by a sudden closing of the glottis. The word is an onomatopoeia, mimicking the sound made when this happens.

Hiccough means the same thing, but its spelling is a more recent variation (supposedly because of an association being made between a *cough* and a *hiccup*).

Regardless of the spelling, though, the word is pronounced the same way: /ˈhɪkʌp/. This is the only instance in which **GH** is pronounced as /p/, rather than being silent or producing the sounds /g/ or /f/.

Producing two separate sounds

We must be careful when **G** and **H** appear next to each other but function in two separate syllables. This usually happens in compound words in which a word ending in **G** is attached to another word beginning in **H**. In this case, **GH** is no longer a digraph and each letter is pronounced individually. For example:

- doghouse (/ˈdɔɡˌhaʊs/)
- foghorn (/ˈfɔɡˌhɔrn/)
- leghorn (/ˈlɛɡˌhɔrn/)
- staghound (/ˈstæɡˌhaʊnd/)

Additionally, when a word ending in the digraph **NG** (which we'll look at next) forms a compound with a word beginning with **H**, it results in a separate pronunciation of the sounds /ŋ/ and /h/:

- clearinghouse (/ˈklɪrɪŋˌhaʊs/)

- longhand (/ˈlɔŋˌhænd/)
- longhouse (/ˈlɔŋˌhaʊs/)
- stronghold (/ˈstrɔŋˌhoʊld/)
- wrongheaded (/ˈrɔŋˌhɛdɪd/)

NG

The digraph **NG** almost always produces the same speech sound, represented in IPA by the symbol /ŋ/. This phoneme is formed by closing the back of the throat while keeping the mouth open and vibrating the vocal cords (making it a **voiced** speech sound).

NG can appear in the middle or at the end of a word, and it always comes after a vowel; it never appears at the beginning of a word. For example:
- bang (/bæŋ/)
- clang (/klæŋ/)
- dinghy (/ˈdɪŋi/)
- darling (/ˈdɑrlɪŋ/)
- fangs (/fæŋz/)
- hanged (/hæŋd/)
- longing (/ˈlɔŋɪŋ/)
- stringy (/ˈstrɪŋi/)
- winged (/wɪŋd/)

The most common occurrence of the digraph **NG** is in the suffix **ING**, which is used to form the gerund and present participle forms of verbs (as in the example *longing* above). Some other examples include:
- acting (/ˈæktɪŋ/)
- braving (/ˈbreɪvɪŋ/)
- dreaming (/ˈdrimɪŋ/)
- feeling (/ˈfilɪŋ/)
- hearing (/ˈhirɪŋ/)
- running (/ˈrʌnɪŋ/)
- seeing (/ˈsiɪŋ/)
- talking (/ˈtɔkɪŋ/)
- wearing (/ˈwɛrɪŋ/)

Producing the sound /ŋk/

In some dialects, **NG** will produce a /k/ sound after /ŋ/ when the digraph is followed by **ST** or **TH**:
- angst (/ɑŋkst/)
- length (/lɛŋkθ/)
- strength (/strɛŋkθ/)

This /ŋk/ sound only occurs in the three root words above, but it can also carry over to words derived from them, such as *lengthy* or *strengthen*.

Producing the sound /ŋg/

In some words, **N** and **G** appear next to each other but function separately across two separate syllables. This is not a true digraph (since two sounds are made from the two letters together), but, due to the proximity of the two letters, the sound /ŋ/ is still made. This results in the pronunciation /ŋg/. For example:
- anger (/ˈæŋgər/)
- finger (/ˈfɪŋgər/)
- hunger (/ˈhʌŋgər/)
- language (/ˈlæŋgwədʒ/)
- single (/ˈsɪŋgəl/)
- tangle (/ˈtæŋgəl/)

Producing the sounds /ŋg/ and /ndʒ/

Finally, it's worth noting that **NG** does not <u>always</u> result in the /ŋ/ phoneme. In some words in which **N** and **G** are split between two syllables, **N** carries its standard pronunciation (/n/) while **G** can create either a **hard G** (/g/) or (more commonly) **soft G** (/dʒ/) sound. For example:

Produces /ŋg/	Produces /ndʒ/
	angel (/ˈeɪndʒəl/)
congratulations (/kənˌgrætʃəˈleɪʃənz/)	change (/tʃeɪndʒ/)
congruence (/ˈkɒngruəns/)	danger (/ˈdeɪndʒər/)
engaged (/ɛnˈgeɪdʒd/)	dingy (/ˈdɪndʒi/)
engrave (/ɪnˈgreɪv/)	lounge (/laʊndʒ/)
ingrained (/ɪnˈgreɪnd/)	manger (/ˈmeɪndʒər/)
ungrateful (/ʌnˈgeɪtfəl/)	stingy (/ˈstɪndʒi/)
	strange (/streɪndʒ/)

PH

The digraph **PH** makes the same speech sound as that of the letter **F**, transcribed in IPA as **/f/**. This digraph can appear anywhere in a word. For example:

Beginning Position	Mid Position	End Position
phantom (/ˈfæntəm/)	alphabet (/ˈælfəˌbɛt/)	autograph (/ˈɔtəˌgræf/)
pheasant (/ˈfɛzənt/)	catastrophic (/ˌkætəˈstrɑfɪk/)	digraph (/ˈdaɪˌgræf/)
philosophy (/fəˈlɑsəfi/)	elephant (/ˈɛləfənt/)	nymph (/nɪmf/)
phoenix (/ˈfinɪks/)	emphasize (/ˈɛmfəˌsaɪz/)	morph (/mɔrf/)
photograph (/ˈfoʊtəˌgræf/)	lymphoma (/lɪmˈfoʊmə/)	paragraph (/ˈpærəˌgræf/)
physical (/ˈfɪzɪkəl/)	orphan (/ˈɔrfən/)	triumph (/ˈtraɪəmf/)

Producing two separate sounds

We must be careful when **P** and **H** appear next to each other but function in two separate syllables. This usually happens in compound words in which a word ending in **P** is attached to another word beginning in **H**. In this case, **PH** is no longer a digraph and each letter is pronounced individually. For example:

- loophole (/ˈlupˌhoʊl/)
- haphazard (/hæpˈhæzərd/)
- uphill (/ˈʌpˈhɪl/)
- uphold (/ʌpˈhoʊld/)
- upholstery (/ʌpˈhoʊlstəri/)

Note that the **H** in *upholstery* may also be silent: /əˈpoʊlstəri/. **H** is also silent in the word *shepherd* (/ˈʃɛpərd/), which is derived from the Old English word *sceaphierde—sceap* ("sheep") + *hierde* ("herder").

SH

The **SH** digraph always produces the same sound, represented in IPA by the symbol /ʃ/. This sound is formed by forming a narrow passageway with the sides of the tongue against the top teeth and then forcing air through partly open lips. It is **unvoiced**, meaning the vocal cords do not vibrate.

Like **PH**, the **SH** digraph can appear anywhere in a word.

Beginning Position	Mid Position	End Position
shadow (/ˈʃæˌdoʊ/)	ashen (/ˈæʃən/)	accomplish (/əˈkɑmplɪʃ/)
sheets (/ʃits/)	cushion (/ˈkʊʃən/)	blush (/blʌʃ/)
shining (/ˈʃaɪnɪŋ/)	dashboard (/ˈdæʃˌbɔrd/)	diminish (/dɪˈmɪnɪʃ/)
shoulder (/ˈʃoʊldər/)	fashion (/ˈfæʃən/)	lavish (/ˈlævɪʃ/)
shrewd (/ʃrud/)	pushover (/ˈpʊˌʃoʊvər/)	publish (/ˈpʌblɪʃ/)
shudder (/ˈʃʌdər/)	township (/ˈtaʊnʃɪp/)	wash (/wɑʃ/)

Producing two separate sounds

We must be careful when **S** and **H** appear next to each other but function in two separate syllables, usually when a prefix ending in **S** is attached to a word beginning in **H**. In this case, **SH** is no longer a digraph and each letter is pronounced individually, as in *mishap* (/ˈmɪsˌhæp/) or *disheartening* (/dɪsˈhɑrtənɪŋ/).

This rule also applies when a word beginning with a **silent H** is preceded by a suffix ending in **S**: the **S** is pronounced normally, while the **H** remains silent in the second syllable, as in *dishonest* (/dɪˈsɑnəst/) or *dishonor* (/dɪˈsɑnər/).

SS

The digraph **SS** appears in the middle or at the end of a word—it never appears at the beginning—and it can make three different speech sounds.

Producing the sound /s/

Most often, the digraph **SS** simply makes the same sound as a single **S**: /s/. For example:

- across (/əˈkrɔs/)
- assemble (/əˈsɛmbəl/)
- boss (/bɔs/)
- brass (/bræs/)
- blossom (/ˈblɑsəm/)
- dissuade (/dɪˈsweɪd/)
- express (/ɪkˈsprɛs/)
- message (/ˈmɛsɪdʒ/)
- success (/səkˈsɛs/)

Producing the sound /ʃ/

Sometimes when **SS** appears in the middle of a word, it creates the same sound as the digraph **SH**: /ʃ/. This pronunciation most often occurs when **SS** is followed by **ION**; less commonly, it can also occur when the digraph is followed by **URE** or **UE**. For example:

SS + ION	SS + URE	SS + UE
admission (/æd'mɪʃən/) compassion (/kəm'pæʃən/) expression (/ɪk'sprɛʃən/) transmission (/trænz'mɪʃən/) session (/'sɛʃən/)	assure (/ə'ʃʊr/) commissure (/('kɒm ə ˌʃɜr/) fissure (/'fɪʃər/) pressure (/'prɛʃər/)	issue (/'ɪʃu/) tissue (/'tɪʃu/)

Producing the sound /z/

In a few cases, **SS** produces the same sound as the letter **Z**, transcribed in IPA as /z/. This can only occur when **SS** appears between two vowels. For example:

- brassiere (/brə'zɪər/)
- dessert (/dɪ'zɜrt/)
- dissolve (/dɪ'zɑlv/)
- Missouri (/mə'zʊri/)
- possess (/pə'zɛs/; note that the second **SS** is pronounced /s/)
- scissors (/'sɪzərz/)

TH

The digraph **TH** most often produces one of two similar but distinct sounds: /θ/ and /ð/.

The sound /θ/ is made by lightly pressing the tip of the tongue against the bottom of the top two teeth as air is forced through the mouth. The vocal cords are not engaged, making this an **unvoiced** speech sound. The /ð/ phoneme is formed the exact same way, except the vocal cords **are** engaged, making it a **voiced** speech sound.

TH is usually pronounced /θ/ when it is followed by a consonant or appears at the very end of a word, while it is more likely to take the /ð/ pronunciation when it is followed by **E** or **I**, especially in the middle or at the end of a word. However, this is not always the case, and the spelling of the word alone won't always indicate whether **TH** produces /θ/ or /ð/. We therefore have to memorize the pronunciation of **TH** whenever we encounter it.

Words producing the sound /θ/

Beginning Position	Mid Position	End Position
thanks (/θæŋks/)	anthem (/'ænθəm/)	bath (/bæθ/)
theater (/'θiətər/)	author (/'ɔθər/)	depth (/dɛpθ/)
thing (/θɪŋ/)	cathedral (/kə'θidrəl/)	length (/lɛŋkθ/)
thorough (/'θɜroʊ/)	healthful (/'hɛlθfəl/)	mirth (/mɜrθ/)
thread (/θrɛd/)	mathematics (/ˌmæθə'mætɪks/)	teeth (/tiθ/)
through (/θru/)	nothing (/'nʌθɪŋ/)	warmth (/wɔrmθ/)
Thursday (/'θɜrz ˌdeɪ/)	prosthetic (/prɑ'sθɛtɪk/)	youth (/juθ/)

Words producing the sound /ð/

Beginning Position	Mid Position	End Position (usually followed by E)
than (/ðæn/)	bother (/ˈbaðər/)	breathe (/brið/)
the (/ði/)	clothing (/ˈkloʊðɪŋ/)	lathe (/leɪð/)
them (/ðɛm/)	either (/ˈaɪðər/ or /ˈiðər/)	loathe (/loʊð/)
this (/ðɪs/)	rhythm (/ˈrɪðəm/)	smooth (/smuð/)
though (/ðoʊ/)	together (/təˈgɛðər/)	soothe (/suð/)
thus (/ðʌs/)	whether (/ˈwɛðər/)	teethe (/tið/)
thy (/ðaɪ/)	wither (/ˈwɪðər/)	wreathe (/rið/)

Producing the sound /t/

In some words, **TH** produces the sound /t/, making the **H** silent. This most often occurs in proper nouns, such as:

- **Thames** (/tɛmz/)
- **Thailand** (/ˈtaɪˌlænd/)
- **Theresa** (/təˈrisə/)
- **Thomas** (/ˈtɑməs/)

There is also one common noun in English that features a **TH** pronounced as /t/: *thyme* (/taɪm/). It is pronounced the exact same way as *time*.

How to pronounce posthumous

The word *posthumous* is unique in that **TH** is not pronounced as /θ/, /ð/, or /t/. Instead, the digraph is pronounced /tʃ/ (the sound commonly made by **CH**), resulting in the pronunciation /ˈpɑstʃʊməs/ (or /ˈpɑstʃəməs/, with the first **U** reduced to a schwa).

Note that in British English, however, *posthumous* is pronounced as /ˈpɒstjʊməs/, with **TH** producing the sound /t/ (with a silent **H**) while **U** is elongated into the diphthong /jʊ/.

Producing two separate sounds

As with other digraphs, we must be careful when **T** and **H** appear next to each other but function in two separate syllables. This usually happens in compound words in which a word ending in **T** is attached to another word beginning in **H**. In this case, **TH** is no longer a digraph and each letter is pronounced individually. For example:

- **anthill** (/ˈæntˌhɪl/)
- **boathouse** (/ˈboʊtˈhaʊs/)
- **hothead** (/ˈhɑtˌhɛd/)
- **lighthouse** (/ˈlaɪtˌhaʊs/)
- **shorthand** (/ˈʃɔrtˌhænd/)

WH

In modern English, the digraph **WH** usually represents a /w/ sound, with **H** becoming silent. For instance:

- **what** (/wʌt/)
- **where** (/wɛr/)
- **when** (/wɛn/)
- **why** (/waɪ/)
- **which** (/wɪtʃ/)
- **wheel** (/wil/)
- **whisper** (/ˈwɪspər/)
- **white** (/waɪt/)

While not common in modern English, however, some dialects *do* pronounce the **H** very subtly, though it comes <u>before</u> the /w/ sound, producing the phoneme /hw/. Therefore, all of the words above might be pronounced in the following way:

- **what** (/hwʌt/)
- **where** (/hwɛr/)
- **when** (/hwɛn/)

- **why** (/hwaɪ/)
- **which** (/hwɪʧ/)
- **wheel** (/hwil/)
- **whisper** (/ˈhwɪspər/)
- **white** (/hwaɪt/)

Finally, in some consonant combinations, **W** is not pronounced at all. This occurs in some words beginning with **WH** when it is followed by **O**, as in:

- **who** (/hu/)
- **whole** (/hoʊl/)
- **whom** (/hum/)
- **whose** (/huz/)

Note that the pronunciations for these four words do not change across dialect.

Quiz
(answers start on page 463)

1. Which of the following is **not** something a digraph can do?

a) Form a unique speech sound different from either individual letter
b) Form a sound from one letter alone
c) Form two sounds from each of the letters
d) Become silent

2. Which of the following is the most **common** speech sound for the digraph **CH**?

a) /ʧ/
b) /k/
c) /ʃ/
d) Silent (not pronounced)

3. The digraphs **DG** and **DJ** both produce which of the following phonemes?

a) /dg/
b) /dʒ/
c) /ŋg/
d) /dj/

4. Which of the following is the most **common** speech sound for the digraph **GH**?

a) /g/
b) /f/
c) /ʃ/
d) Silent (not pronounced)

5. True or False: The spelling *judgment* is always considered correct.

a) True
b) False

6. Which of the following is **not** a speech sound that can be made by the digraph **SS**?

a) /s/
b) /ʃ/
c) /ʒ/
d) /z/

7. Which of the following is the **least** common pronunciation of the digraph **TH**?

a) /θ/
b) /ð/
c) /t/
d) /ʧ/

Trigraphs

Definition

A **trigraph** is a group of three letters that together form a single specific sound. Trigraphs may consist solely of consonants or vowels, or they may be a combination of both.

Consonant Trigraphs vs. Consonant Clusters

Before we look at different trigraphs, it's important to draw a distinction between trigraphs and **consonant clusters**.

Consonant trigraphs are often confused with **consonant clusters** (also called **consonant blends**), which are groups of two to three consonant letters that are pronounced individually in quick succession. For example, the word *script* contains two consonant clusters: *scr* and *pt*. Even though the sounds blend together quickly, the first cluster is not a trigraph and the second cluster is not a digraph, because each letter is pronounced individually: /**skrɪpt**/.

Another aspect that can cause confusion is that a consonant cluster may also consist of a single consonant combined with a consonant digraph (two letters forming a unique sound), as in *s**ch**ool* (/s**k**ul/) or ***th**row* (/**θ**roʊ/). The fact that two of the three letters create a single, specific sound that is then merged quickly with the sound of a third letter (plus the ubiquity of such combinations) makes it seem as though the three together form a single trigraph, but this is not the case.

Consonant Trigraphs

TCH

The most common and perhaps the only *true* consonant trigraph in English is **TCH**, which forms the sound /ʧ/.

It almost always appears at the end of base words, as in:
• batch (/bæʧ/)
• botch (/bɑʧ/)
• catch (/kæʧ/)
• clutch (/klʌʧ/)
• ditch (/dɪʧ/)
• etch (/ɛʧ/)
• itch (/ɪʧ/)
• hatch (/hæʧ/)
• match (/mæʧ/)
• notch (/nɑʧ/)
• patch (/pæʧ/)
• pitch (/pɪʧ/)
• stitch (/stɪʧ/)
• wretch (/rɛʧ/)

Except when we add suffixes to words like those above, there are only a few instances in which **TCH** appears mid-word, such as *butcher* (/ˈbʊʧər/), *ketchup* (/(ˈkɛʧəp/), and *tetchy* (/ˈtɛʧi/). There is also a slang word derived from Yiddish that both **begins** with the trigraph and contains it mid-word: *tchotchke* (/ˈʧɑʧkə/), meaning "a cheap knick-knack or trinket."

TCH vs. CH

The consonant digraph CH also commonly forms the /ʧ/ sound, and it can sometime be difficult to determine which spelling to use. However, there are a few simple conventions we can follow.

Use *CH* at the beginning of words

Other than the slang term *tchotchke*, words can only begin with the /ʧ/ sound when it is formed from the **CH** spelling, such as:

- **chair** (/ʧɛr/)
- **challenge** (/ʧæləndʒ/)
- **charge** (/ʧɑrdʒ/)
- **cheek** (/ʧik/)
- **cheese** (/ʧiz/)
- **cherish** (/ʧɛrɪʃ/)
- **chicken** (/ʧɪkən/)
- **child** (/ʧaɪld/)
- **chocolate** (/ʧɔk(ə)lɪt/)
- **choose** (/ʧuz/)
- **chunky** (/ʧʌŋki/)
- **church** (/ʧɜrʧ/)

Use *CH* after vowel digraphs

You may have noticed that none of the **TCH** words we looked at earlier featured a "traditional" long vowel sound (i.e., one that "says the name" of the vowel letter); they all had short vowel sounds before **TCH**.

When long vowel sounds precede the /ʧ/ sound in a word, they are always made by **vowel digraphs**, in which case /ʧ/ is always spelled **CH**. Additionally, digraphs that form other vowel sounds will also be followed by **CH** rather than **TCH**. For instance:

- av**ouch** (/əˈvaʊʧ/)
- b**each** (/biʧ/)
- b**eech** (/biʧ/)
- br**each** (/briʧ/)
- br**eeches** (/ˈbriɪʧɪz/)
- c**ouch** (/kaʊʧ/)
- deb**auch** (/dəˈbɔʧ/)
- **each** (/iʧ/)
- gr**ouch** (/graʊʧ/)
- imp**each** (/ɪmˈpiʧ/)
- l**eech** (/liʧ/)
- m**ooch** (/muʧ/)
- **ouch** (/aʊʧ/)
- p**each** (/piʧ/)
- p**ouch** (/paʊʧ/)
- p**ooch** (/puʧ/)
- r**each** (/riʧ/)
- scr**eech** (/skriʧ/)
- sp**eech** (/spiʧ/)
- t**each** (/tiʧ/)
- t**ouch** (/tʌʧ/)
- tr**eachery** (/ˈtrɛʧəri/)
- v**ouch** (/vaʊʧ/)

The only standard exception to this rule is the word *aitch* (/eɪʧ/), which is the word for the letter **H**.

Use *CH* after other consonants

When the /ʧ/ sound comes after the consonants **L, N,** or **R** at the end of a word, it is always spelled **CH**. For example:

L + CH	N + CH	R + CH
be**l**ch (/bɛl**ʧ**/) fi**l**ch (/fil**ʧ**/) gu**l**ch (/gʌl**ʧ**/) mu**l**ch (/mʌl**ʧ**/) sque**l**ch (/skwɛl**ʧ**/) zi**l**ch (/zɪl**ʧ**/)	be**n**ch (/bɛ**nʧ**/) bra**n**ch (/bræ**nʧ**/) dre**n**ch (/drɛ**nʧ**/) fli**n**ch (/flɪ**nʧ**/) hu**n**ch (/hʌ**nʧ**/) lau**n**ch (/lɔ**nʧ**/) lu**n**ch (/lʌ**nʧ**/) mu**n**ch (/mʌ**nʧ**/) wre**n**ch (/rɛ**nʧ**/)	a**r**ch (/ar**ʧ**/) chu**r**ch (/ʧɜ**rʧ**/) lu**r**ch (/lɜ**rʧ**/) ma**r**ch (/mar**ʧ**/) pa**r**ch (/par**ʧ**/) sco**r**ch (/skɔr**ʧ**/) to**r**ch (/tɔr**ʧ**/) sea**r**ch (/sɜr**ʧ**/)

Usually use *TCH* after single-letter short vowels

When the /ʧ/ sound is preceded by a single vowel letter making a **short vowel** sound, it is much more likely to be spelled **TCH**, as we saw from the examples earlier. However, there are several exceptions to this rule that will be spelled **CH** instead. Unfortunately, we just have to memorize these exceptions. Here are the most common:

• att**a**ch (/əˈtæ**ʧ**/)
• det**a**ch (/dɪˈtæ**ʧ**/)
• enr**i**ch (/ɪnˈrɪ**ʧ**/)
• m**u**ch (/mʌ**ʧ**/)
• ostr**i**ch (/ˈɔstrɪ**ʧ**/)
• r**i**ch (/rɪ**ʧ**/)
• sandw**i**ch (/ˈsændwɪ**ʧ**/)
• spin**a**ch (/ˈspɪnɪ**ʧ**/)
• s**u**ch (/sʌ**ʧ**/)
• wh**i**ch (/wɪ**ʧ**/)

SCH

In most English words, **SCH** represents a **consonant cluster** of the sounds /s/ and /k/, as in *school, scheme,* or *schedule,* rather than a true trigraph forming a single sound. (However, see the note about *schedule* further down.)

However, in certain foreign loan words from German and slang words derived from Yiddish, **SCH** is can be used to represent the sound /ʃ/ (like the **SH** in *show*). For example:

German loanwords	Meaning	Yiddish slang	Meaning
schadenfreude (/ˈʃadənˌfrɔɪdə/)	Happiness or pleasure derived from someone else's failure or misfortune.	schlemiel (/ʃləˈmil/)	A clumsy, awkward, or bungling person.
schnapps (/ʃnaps/)	Any strong dry liquor, or a sweet, flavored liqueur.	schlep (/ʃlɛp/)	*verb* To carry (something) or move with difficulty and in an awkward, clumsy manner. *noun* A tedious or arduous journey or task; a clumsy, awkward, or stupid person.
schnauzer (/ˈʃnaʊzər/)	A German breed of terrier.	schlock (/ʃlɑk/)	Something (especially goods or merchandise) that is cheap, trashy, or of inferior quality.
schnitzel (/ˈʃnɪtsəl/)	A thin slice of veal or other meat, usually fried.	schmooze (/ʃmuz/)	To chat or gossip casually with someone, especially for personal gain or self-promotion.
schuss (/ʃʊs/)	*noun* A high-speed downhill run on ski or snowboard. *verb* To perform such a run.	schmaltz (/ʃmalts/)	Excessive or exaggerated sentimentalism, especially in art, music, or writing.
schwa (/ʃwɑ/)	A weak or reduced unstressed vowel, represented by the symbol /ə/.	schmear (/ʃmɪər/)	1. A spreadable topping (such as cream cheese). 2. Several things or matters considered together. 3. An illicit monetary inducement; a bribe.
		schmuck (/ʃmʌk/)	An oafish, clumsy, or foolish person.
		schnoz (/ʃnɑz/)	A person's nose, especially one that is larger than usual.
		schtick (more commonly *shtick*)* (/ʃtɪk/)	A particular recognizable gimmick, routine, or characteristic.

(*Note that the Yiddish slang terms all have variant spellings beginning "*sh-*.")
Finally, it's worth noting that the word *schedule*, pronounced /ˈskɛdʒul/ in American English, is typically (though not always) pronounced /ˈʃɛdjul/ in British English.

Vowel trigraphs

Vowel trigraphs almost always form diphthongs, two vowel sounds that merge or "glide" together into a single compressed sound that acts as the nucleus of a syllable. Less commonly, vowel trigraphs can form triphthongs (three vowel sounds that glide together into one); in some rare instances, they can even reduce to a weak schwa sound /ə/.

EAU

This trigraph does not occur natively in English, but it does occur in several French loanwords and words adapted from French.

When it appears at the end of a word, **EAU** always creates the vowel sound /oʊ/ (the "long" **O** sound). This is most common in loanwords directly taken from French.

When **EAU** appears in the middle of a word, though, it can produce **three** vowel sounds: /ju/ (the "long" U sound), /ɑ/ (the vowel sound in the word *cot*), or the reduced weak vowel /ə/ (the schwa). Words in which **EAU** appears mid-word are *derived* from French, rather than direct loans.

Here are the examples most commonly appearing in English:

Pronounced /oʊ/	Pronounced /ju/	Pronounced /ɑ/	Pronounced /ə/
beau (/boʊ/) bureau (/ˈbjʊroʊ/) chateau (or château) (/ʃæˈtoʊ/) plateau (/plæˈtoʊ/) portmanteau (/ˈbjʊroʊ/) tableau (/tæˈbloʊ/)	beauty (originally from Anglo-French *beute*) (/ˈbjuti/) beautiful (/ˈbjutɪfʊl/) beauteous (/ˈbjutiəs/) beautician (/ˈbjutɪʃən/)	bureaucracy (from French *bureaucratie*) (/bjʊrˈɑkrəsi/) bureaucratize (/bjʊrˈɑkrətaɪz/)	bureaucrat (/ˈbjʊrəˌkræt/) bureaucratic (/ˌbjʊrəˈkrætɪk/)

Vowels + "-ous"

When the suffix "-ous" (used to form adjectives from nouns and verbs) attaches to a word, it can end up following the vowels **E**, **I**, or **U**. While **-UOUS** always creates two syllables with two vowel sounds (/ju.əs/), **-EOUS** and **-IOUS** can both result in a single reduced vowel sound (/əs/); we can think of **EOU** and **IOU** as vowel trigraphs in such situations.

EOU

EOU functions as a trigraph when "-eous" comes after the consonants **C** and **G**, or **T**. (After other consonants, it forms two syllables: /i.əs/.) In addition to making the single vowel sound /ə/, "-eous" also affects the pronunciation of the consonants: **C** is pronounced /ʃ/, while **G** is pronounced /dʒ/.

While this isn't a very common occurrence (especially **C** + **EOUS**), let's look at some examples in which it occurs:

C + EOUS	G + EOUS
Cretac**eous** (/krɪˈteɪʃəs/)	advanta**geous** (/ˌædvənˈteɪdʒəs/)
curvac**eous** (/kɜrˈveɪʃəs/)	coura**geous** (/kəˈreɪdʒəs/)
herbac**eous** (/ɜrˈbeɪʃəs/)	gor**geous** (/ˈgɔrdʒəs/)
rosac**eous** (/roʊˈzeɪʃəs/)	outra**geous** (/aʊtˈreɪdʒəs/)

There's also one unique instance in which **EOUS** results in a consonant forming the /tʃ/ sound: *right**eous*** (/ˈraɪtʃəs/). Every other instance of **T** + **EOUS** results in the pronunciation /ti.əs/, so we just have to memorize the exceptional way *righteous* is pronounced.

IOU

Like **EOU**, **IOU** acts as a trigraph when "-ious" comes after the consonants **C** and **G**; unlike **EOU**, it also functions this way after the consonant **T**. Once again, "-ious" also affects the pronunciation of the consonants it follows: **C** and **T** are both pronounced /ʃ/, while **G** is pronounced /dʒ/.

While the two endings behave in a similar way, it is much more common for words to end in "-ious" than "-eous." For example:

C + IOUS	G + IOUS	T + IOUS
atrocious (/əˈtroʊʃəs/)		ambitious (/æmˈbɪʃəs/)
capricious (/kəˈprɪʃəs/)	contagious (/kənˈteɪdʒəs/)	cautious (/ˈkɔʃəs/)
conscious (/ˈkɑnʃəs/)	egregious (/əˈgridʒəs/)	expeditious (/ˌɛkspəˈdɪʃəs/)
gracious (/ˈgreɪʃəs/)	litigious (/lɪˈtɪdʒəs/)	facetious (/fəˈsiʃəs/)
judicious (/dʒuˈdɪʃəs/)	prestigious (/prɛˈstɪdʒəs/)	infectious (/ɪnˈfɛkʃəs/)
luscious (/ˈlʌʃəs/)	prodigious (/prəˈdɪdʒəs/)	nutritious (/nuˈtrɪʃəs/)
precious (/ˈprɛʃəs/)	religious (/rɪˈlɪdʒəs/)	pretentious (/prɪˈtɛnʃəs/)
suspicious (/səˈspɪʃəs/)		repetitious (/ˌrɛpɪˈtɪʃəs/)
vicious (/vɪʃəs/)		superstitious (/ˌsupərˈstɪʃəs/)

Single-word vowel trigraphs

If we don't count words formed with the suffix "-ous," **EAU** is the only vowel trigraph that can be found in a variety of words. There are several others, though, that act as standalone words. Each of these ends in **E** and has either **W** or **Y** (which act as vowels in this capacity) as its central letter:

• **awe** (/ɔ/)
• **aye** (/aɪ/)
• **ewe** (/ju/)
• **eye** (/aɪ/)
• **owe** (/oʊ/)

Vowel-consonant trigraphs

There are two trigraphs that use a combination of vowel and consonant letters: **IGH** (which forms a vowel sound) and **DGE** (which forms a consonant sound).

IGH

The trigraph **IGH** always produces the same vowel sound: /aɪ/ (the "long I" sound). It usually occurs in the middle of a word, most commonly followed by the letter **T** (or when it is used in the first part of a compound word). It can also appear at the end of a word without a consonant following it, but this is much less common.

The Alphabet

Mid-position	Final position
affright (/əˈfraɪt/)	
alight (/əˈlaɪt/)	
aright (/əˈraɪt/)	
blight (/blaɪt/)	
bright (/braɪt/)	
delight (/dɪˈlaɪt/)	
fight (/faɪt/)	
flight (/flaɪt/)	
fright (/fraɪt/)	
highlight (/ˈhaɪˌlaɪt/)	high (/haɪ/)
highway (/ˈhaɪˌweɪ/)	nigh (/naɪ/)
light (/laɪt/)	sigh (/saɪ/)
lightning (/ˈlaɪtnɪŋ/)	thigh (/θaɪ/)
might (/maɪt/)	
night (/maɪt/)	
playwright (/ˈpleɪˌraɪt/)	
plight (/plaɪt/)	
right (/raɪt/)	
righteous (/raɪtʃəs/)	
sight (/saɪt/)	
slight (/slaɪt/)	
tight (/taɪt/)	
tonight (/təˈnaɪt/)	

Notice that we don't include any examples in which **IGH** appears after the vowels **A** (as in *straight*) or **E** (as in *neighbor*). In these cases, the four letters are working together to form a single sound, sequences known as **tetragraphs**; we'll look at these more closely in a separate section.

DGE

The letter combination **DGE** is typically considered a trigraph because the three letters always function together to form the same sound as the letter **J** (/ʤ/). For example:

- ba**dge** (/bæʤ/)
- blu**dge**on (/ˈblʌʤən/)
- bri**dge** (/brɪʤ/)
- bu**dge** (/bʌʤ/)
- bu**dge**t (/bʌʤɪt/)
- curmu**dge**on (/kərˈmʌʤən/)
- fi**dge**t (/fɪʤɪt/)
- fri**dge** (/frɪʤ/)
- fu**dge** (/fʌʤ/)
- do**dge** (/dɔʤ/)
- ga**dge**t (/gæʤɪt/)
- gru**dge** (/grʌʤ/)
- ju**dge** (/ʤʌʤ/)
- mi**dge** (/mɪʤ/)
- partri**dge** (/ˈpɑrtrɪʤ/)
- porri**dge** (/ˈpɔrɪʤ/)
- ri**dge** (/rɪʤ/)
- smi**dge**n (/ˈsmɪʤən/)
- wi**dge**t (/wɪʤɪt/)

Digraph or trigraph?

It's worth mentioning that we can also consider **DG** separately as a **consonant digraph**. (We include **DG** in the consonant digraphs section of this guide.) For instance, in words in which **DGE** is followed by N or T (as in *smidgen* and *budget*), the letter **E** makes its own vowel sound, which goes against the concept of a trigraph making a single indivisible speech sound.

Additionally, words that end in **DGE** will have **E** omitted when a vowel suffix is added such as "-ing" (*bri**dg**ing, ju**dg**ing*, etc.) or "-y" (*do**dg**y, e**dg**y*, etc.), but **DG** will still retain the /ʤ/ pronunciation. Silent E is still required to form this sound initially, but the digraph **DG** can stand on its own in a suffixed word and still create this sound.

Regardless, distinguishing between the digraph **DG** and the trigraph **DGE** is not especially important, so long as it is clear that the word is forming the /ʤ/ sound when **DG** is present.

Vowel-R trigraphs in British English

Finally, it's worth nothing that in British English (**Received Pronunciation**), the letter **R** is not normally pronounced as a consonant when it follows a vowel sound within the same syllable; instead, it can elongate the existing vowel sound, reduce it to a schwa (/ə/), or else alter it into a diphthong or triphthong. **R** can therefore combine with vowels to form trigraphs that we would normally not include in American English.

We won't spend too much time on them here, but let's look at a few examples of the combinations and sounds these trigraphs might make. (The IPA transcriptions for these examples will include the long vowel mark [ː] to reflect how they normally are written in Received Pronunciation.)

A Combinations	*E* Combinations	*I* Combinations	*O* Combinations	*U* Combinations	Silent *E* Combinations
air (/ɛə/) dinosaur (/ˈdaɪnəˌsɔː/) extraordinary (/ɪkˈstrɔːdənərɪ/)	amateur (/ˈæmətə/) deer (/dɪə/) ear (/ɪə/) Georgian (/ˈʤɔːʤjən/) heir (/ɛə/)	behaveiour (/bɪˈheɪvjə/) pier (/pɪə/)	choir (/kwaɪə/) door (/dɔː/) flour (/ˈflaʊə/) oar (/ɔː/)	curl (/kɜːl/) fur (/fɜː/) hurt (/hɜːt/) nurse (/nɜːs/)	care (/kɛə/) future (/ˈfjuːtʃə/) here (/hɪə/) lyre (/laɪə/) mire (/maɪə/) store (/stɔː/)

Quiz

(answers start on page 463)

1. How many letters make up a trigraph?

a) 1
b) 2
c) 3
d) 4

2. True or False: Consonant trigraphs are also known as consonant clusters.

a) True
b) False

3. Which of the following words contains a trigraph?

a) discharge
b) dispatch
c) discourteous
d) displaying

4. Which of the following words **does not** contain a trigraph?

a) instruct
b) schnauzer
c) itchy
d) smidge

5. When is the /ʧ/ sound spelled **CH** rather than **TCH**?

a) When a word begins with the /ʧ/ sound
b) When the /ʧ/ sound comes after a long vowel sound
c) When the /ʧ/ sound comes after the consonants **L, N,** or **R**
d) All of the above
e) None of the above

6. What sound is made by the trigraph **IGH**?

a) /eɪ/
b) /aɪ/
c) /i/
d) /ə/

Tetragraphs

Definition

A **tetragraph** is a sequence of four letters that together form a single sound. In native English words, these only occur when **GH** is used in conjunction with various vowel pairs to form specific vowel sounds: **AIGH, AUGH, EIGH,** and **OUGH.** For the first three of these, it could be argued that they are not really tetragraphs—that **GH** is simply silent following vowel **digraphs**—but we'll examine them here for the sake of completeness. First, let's look at the combination that *can* be called a true tetragraph.

OUGH

The sequence **OUGH** is quite common, but it is also one of the trickiest to learn because it can result in **six** different sounds. In two of these, **GH** makes the sound /f/, so it is functioning as a digraph paired with the vowel digraph **OU**, which can make either the /ɔ/ (as in *cot*) or /ʌ/ (as in *up*) sounds:

- cough (/kɔf/)
- enough (/ɪˈnʌf/)
- rough (/rʌf/)
- slough (/slʌf/)
- tough (/tʌf/)
- trough (/trɔf/)

When **OUGH** is functioning like a true tetragraph (forming a single vowel sound), it can be pronounced /oʊ/ (as in *go*), /u/ (as in *too*), /ɔ/ (as in *got*), or /aʊ/ (as in *cow*). The sounds created are unique to its spelling (that is, not all of them could not be formed from the digraph **OU** alone).

Let's look at some examples of each:

Pronounced /oʊ/	Pronounced /u/	Pronounced /ɔ/	Pronounced /aʊ/
although (/ɔlˈðoʊ/) borough* (/ˈbɜroʊ/) dough (/doʊ/) though (/ðoʊ/) thorough* (/ˈθɜroʊ/)	slough** (/slu/) through (/θru/)	bought (/bɔt/) brought (/brɔt/) fought (/fɔt/) ought (/ɔt/) thought (/θɔt/) wrought (/rɔt/)	bough (/baʊ/) doughty (/daʊti/) drought (/draʊt/) plough (usually spelled *plow*) (/plaʊ/) sough (/saʊ/ or /sʌf/)

(*In British English, *borough* and *thorough* are pronounced /ˈbʌrə/ and /ˈθʌrə/, respectively.)
(**Slough* takes this pronunciation when it means "a depression or hole filled with mud," "a swamp, marsh, or bog," or "a degraded or despairing condition." When *slough* means "an outer layer or covering" or "to discard an outer layer," it is pronounced /slʌf/.)

Other combinations

There are three other combinations of letters that could be considered tetragraphs in English. In these, the **GH** is usually simply silent—its presence doesn't dictate a pronunciation that is unique from the vowel digraph it follows. However, there are a couple of exceptions.

AIGH

This combination is pronounced /eɪ/ (the "long A" sound) and only appears in the word *straight* or words derived from it (*straightaway, straighten, straighter*, etc.).

EIGH

Like **AIGH**, this combination is also usually pronounced /eɪ/. For example:
• **eight** (/eɪt/)
• freight (/freɪt/)
• inveigh (/ɪnˈveɪ/)
• neigh (/neɪ/)
• neighbor (/ˈneɪbər/)
• sleigh (/sleɪ/)
• weigh (/weɪ/)

However, there are two words in which **EIGH** it is pronounced /aɪ/ (the "long I" sound): *height* (/haɪt/ and *sleight* (/slaɪt/). (This pronunciation also carries over to words derived from these two, such as *heighten* or *sleighted*.)

AUGH

There are two words in which **GH** produces the sound /f/ in this combination: *laugh* (/læf/) and *draught* (/dræft/ or /drɑft/), which is the British English spelling for *draft*.

Otherwise, **AUGH** will always produce the sound /ɔ/ and will always be followed by the letter **T**:
• **aught** (/ɔt/)
• **caught** (/cɔt/)
• **daughter** (/ˈdɔtər/)
• **distraught** (/dɪˈstrɔt/)
• **fraught** (/frɔt/)
• **naught** (/nɔt/)
• **onslaught** (/ˈɔnˌslɔt/)
• **slaughter** (/ˈslɔtər/)
• **taught** (/tɔt/)

Quiz

(answers start on page 463)

1. Which of the following is **not** a sound made by the tetragraph **OUGH**?

a) /oʊ/

b) /u/

c) /aɪ/

d) /aʊ/

e) /ɔ/

2. What is the pronunciation of the word *though*?

a) /ðɔ/

b) /ðoʊ/

c) /ðaʊ/

d) /ðu/

3. What is the pronunciation of the word *brought*?

a) /brɔt/

b) /broʊt/

c) /braʊt/

d) /brut/

4. In which of the following words is **OUGH** pronounced /u/?

a) thought

b) thorough

c) though

d) through

5. Which of the following tetragraphs is usually pronounced /eɪ/?

a) AIGH

b) EIGH

c) AUGH

d) A & B

e) B & C

f) None of the above

Other Letters, Marks, and Symbols

English contains many words that it adapted from different languages from around the world, especially Latin, Greek, French, and German. As the language evolved, certain typographical features from those languages were gradually changed or eliminated from modern English orthography, though some still appear in written English today.

The most common of these are **ligatures** and **diacritics**; we'll briefly go over both of these here, but you can continue on to their individual sections to learn more. There are also a few other outdated letters that overlapped with modern English until relatively recently, which we'll look at further on in this section.

Ligatures

A **ligature** is a combination of two or more letters joined into a single unit.

The most well-known of these originated in Latin as distinct letters within the language: **Æ/æ** (used in words like *encyclopædia, leukæmia,* and *pædiatric*) and **Œ/œ** (used in words like *diarrhœa, œsophagus,* and *manœuvre*). In modern English, these two letters were eventually divided into **AE** and **OE**, respectively, and eventually reduced to just **E** in American English.

There is another Latin ligature that *is* used in English today: **&**, a conjoined **E** and **T** known as an ampersand, which is used to mean "and" in informal or stylized writing. For example:
• "I work at Daniels **&** Jones Insurance Co."
• "My brother loves hip-hop, but I'm more of an R**&**B [rhythm and blues] fan myself."
• "Please send me a report on profit **&** loss for this quarter."

Finally, there is one last ligature that actually ended up becoming part of the modern English alphabet: **W**, two **U**s (originally two **V**s) joined into a single letter.

Diacritics

A **diacritic** (or **diacritical mark**) is a mark added to a letter, usually to indicate a specific pronunciation of that letter.

Of the various languages using the Latin alphabet, English is one of the few that generally does not use diacritical marks, other than in certain foreign loanwords (especially from French) whose diacritics have been retained.

The most common of these that appears in English is called an **acute accent**. For example:
• café
• exposé
• purée
• résumé
• touché

While this is the most common, other diacritics are sometimes used as well, such as the **grave accent** (*à la carte, vis-à-vis, voilà*), the **circumflex** (*crêpe, pâté, tête-à-tête*), the **cedilla** (*façade, garçon, soupçon*), the **tilde** (*jalapeño, piñata, señora*), and the **dieresis** (*doppelgänger, Noël, über*).

Other Outdated Letters

In addition to ligatures and diacritics, there are two other outdated letters that were used in English until relatively recently. These are the "**long S**" and the letter **thorn**, though the latter has only been used in very specific circumstances. Let's look at both.

Long S (ʃ)

The **long S** (ſ), also called a **medial S** or **descending S**, is a form of the lowercase S that was once used in certain locations in a word.

This older form of the lowercase S began in Roman cursive, originally looking more like a checkmark (✓) or the mathematical symbol for a square root (√). This was eventually straightened and elongated, forming the basis for the symbol used in the International Phonetic Alphabet for the sound made by **SH** (ʃ) and the mathematical symbol for integrals (∫). As printing presses became more common, the bottom portion of the symbol was cut off to accommodate typeface limitations, resulting in ſ (not to be confused with a lowercase **f** or **r**).

Traditionally, long S was used in the middle or at the beginning of a word (except when an initial S was capitalized). If a word had two Ss, only the first would be long. ſ was also normally not used in front of a lowercase **f**, due to their similar appearance. Here are some examples:
• best→beſt
• distress→diſtreſs
• son→ſon
• success→ſucceſs
• transfer→transfer ("short" S is used instead before an **F**)

In the late-18th century, ſ was only used in the middle of words when it appeared before another lowercase **s**, as in *Congreſs* or *aſſeſs*—words like *son* or *intense* would use the standard "short" S instead. Near the beginning of the 19th century, printing presses stopped using long S altogether; it was still used in handwriting until the late 19th century, at which point it disappeared completely.

Thorn (Þ, þ)

The **thorn** (Þ, lowercase þ) was a letter used in Old English to represent the sounds /ð/ and /θ/.

Over time, the shape of this character became indistinguishable from the letter **Y**, and, during the 14th century, the sounds /ð/ and /θ/ began to be represented by the consonant digraph **TH**. This led to the thorn eventually being discarded from English altogether.

However, there is a curious remnant of the letter thorn that still exists in modern English in the form of the pseudo-archaic phrase *ye olde*. This clichéd phrase is sometimes used in the names of shops, restaurants, and pubs to suggest something quaintly old-fashioned (as in "Ye Olde Sweet Shoppe"). However, it is not using the second-person plural pronoun *ye*, but in fact the definite article *the* spelled with a thorn (graphically converted to a Y, which Þ eventually came to resemble when it was still in use).

This has led to such names being mistakenly pronounced like the second person plural pronoun *ye* (/ji/), when in fact it should be pronounced the same as the definite article *the* (/ði/).

Other than this one specific instance, the letter Þ is completely extinct in modern English.

Quiz

(answers start on page 463)

1. Which of the following is a **ligature**?

a) Þ

b) ſ

c) æ

d) ç

2. What type of diacritical mark most commonly appears in foreign loanwords?

a) Acute accent (e.g., é)

b) Tilde (e.g., ñ)

c) Circumflex (e.g., â)

d) Dieresis (e.g., ö)

3. Traditionally, where could a **long S** appear in a word?

a) At the beginning of the word

b) In the middle of the word

c) At the end of the word

d) A & B

e) B & C

f) A & C

4. Which of the following words can be spelled with a variant of the letter **thorn** in certain contexts?

a) old

b) ye

c) we

d) that

Diacritics

Definition

A **diacritic** (or **diacritical mark**) is a mark added to a letter, usually to indicate a specific pronunciation of that letter.

Of the various languages using the Latin alphabet, English is one of the few that generally does not use diacritical marks. Those words that do contain them are typically foreign loanwords whose diacritics have been retained in English. The most common of these that appear in English are known as **accents** (either acute, as in *café*, or grave, as in *vis-à-vis*).

There are, however, a few diacritics that *are* used in native English words.

Diacritics in Native English Words

Tittle

The only diacritical mark that is used natively in English words is the **tittle** (also called a **superscript dot**). It is the small dot that appears above lowercase **i** and **j**.

Unlike the majority of other diacritic marks, the tittle does not indicate a specific way to pronounce the letters. (At least not in English; in other languages, such as Turkish, the tittle distinguishes two different vowel sounds that **I** can represent.) Instead, it originated as a means of distinguishing **i** and **j** from other letters in writing, as older lettering styles (especially Gothic writing) gave letters curves and widths that led them to blend into one another.

Because it does not influence pronunciation, instead being a part of the letter itself, the tittle is usually not considered among the diacritical marks one might encounter in English, but it's still worth knowing about.

Dieresis

The **dieresis** (**diaeresis** in British English; also called a **tréma** or an **umlaut**) is a pair of dots that appears over certain vowels to indicate a hiatus—that is, a pause between two adjacent vowel sounds, especially when they are the same letter. The dieresis indicates that the two vowels are pronounced separately, as opposed to forming a digraph or diphthong.

While there are a few words that are still commonly spelled with a dieresis, the majority have abandoned it altogether.

For example:
• Chloë (more commonly *Chloe*)
• coöperate (more commonly *cooperate* or, especially in British English, *co-operate*)
• deäctivate (more commonly *deactivate*)
• Eloïse (more commonly *Eloise*)
• naïve (originally from French, often simplified as *naive*)
• noöne (more commonly *no one*, sometimes *no-one*)
• preëmpt (more commonly *preempt* or, especially in British English, *pre-empt*)
• reëlect (more commonly *reelect* or, especially in British English, *re-elect*)
• reënter (more commonly *reenter* or, especially in British English, *re-enter*)
• Zoë (more commonly *Zoe*)
• zoölogy (more commonly *zoology*)

In a few words, the dieresis is used to indicate that an **E** at the end of a word is not silent, most famously the name *Brontë*.

Grave Accent

An **accent** is a short, diagonal mark written above a letter to indicate that it is pronounced a certain way. The **grave accent** slants from the left down to the right, as in *à, è, ì*, etc. (This is in contrast to the **acute accent**, which slopes the opposite way: *á, é, í*, etc.)

In English, the grave accent is almost only used in poetry or song lyrics (and even then, only rarely) to indicate additional syllables at the end of words that would otherwise be silent (especially past participles ending in "-ed"). This is generally done to maintain meter, the basic rhythmic structure created by stress on alternating syllables. For example:

Oh, on this blessèd day,
An old friend walkèd up to me,
He longèd for a world in which,
He would forever lovèd be.

While mostly reserved for poetry, the grave accent can be useful in other instances. For example, the past participle *learned* (pronounced /ˈlɜrnd/) can be used as an adjective to describe someone who has a profound amount of knowledge, in which case it is pronounced /ˈlɜrnɪd/. To distinguish this pronunciation, the word is sometimes written as *learnèd*, as in:
• "She is a renowned and learnèd professor."
• "This truly is a blessèd occasion!"

However, this is not common in everyday writing, and the grave accent is essentially unused in modern English. (When an accent is used, it is also not uncommon to use an acute accent instead, as it is more commonly encountered in foreign loanwords than the grave accent.)

Diacritics in Foreign Loanwords

By far, the majority of the diacritics we encounter in English are carried over from other languages in foreign loanwords (words that are used in English without translation). The most common of these are acute or grave accents used in French words, but other diacritics are sometimes used as well. However, because diacritics are not standard in English (and are not easily produced on most English keyboards), it is more common for English writers to simply omit them.

Because the pronunciation shifts indicated by these diacritical marks are specific to the languages in which they are used, we won't go over their functions or patterns here; instead, this section will simply list some common examples of the different diacritics one might encounter in English writing.

Acute Accent

The **acute accent** is the most commonly used diacritic in English. It almost always appears in loanwords taken from French, though there are a few terms from other languages that feature the acute accent as well.

For example:
• apéritif (French; usually *aperitif*)
• adiós (Spanish; usually *adios*)
• blasé (French; usually spelled with the accent)
• café (French; often simply *cafe*)
• cliché (French; usually spelled with the accent, but also commonly spelled without it)
• communiqué (French; usually spelled with the accent)
• coup d'état (French; usually spelled with the accent)
• canapé (French; usually spelled with the accent)
• divorcé(e) (French; *divorcé* refers to a man who has divorced, while *divorcée* is a woman who has divorced; *divorcee*, with no accent, is often used in English to refer to either a man or a woman)
• décor (French; often simply *decor*)
• éclair (French; often simply *eclair*)
• exposé (French; usually spelled with the accent to distinguish it from the verb *expose*)
• fiancé(e) (French; *fiancé* refers to a man engaged to be married, while *fiancée* refers to a woman; both terms are usually spelled with the accent in English)

- maté (Spanish; the accent mark is usually added in English to distinguish from the English word *mate*)
- matinée (French; often simply *matinee*)
- née (French; often simply *nee*)
- Pokémon (Japanese; the accent is often added in English to indicate the correct pronunciation of the word, but it is just as often left out)
- purée (French; often simply *puree*)
- résumé (French; often *resumé* or simply *resume*)
- saké (Japanese; the accent is sometimes added in English to indicate the correct pronunciation of the word, but it is more often left out)
- soirée (French; often simply *soiree*)
- touché (French; usually spelled with the accent)

Grave Accent

Other than the rare instances we looked at previously, the **grave accent** (a reverse of the acute accent above) only appears in English in loanwords taken from French.

For example:
- à la carte (French; often simply *a la carte*)
- chèvre (French; usually spelled with the accent)
- crèche (French; usually spelled with the accent)
- crème brûlée (French; can be spelled *crème brulée, creme brulée*, or simply *creme brulee*)
- déjà vu (French; often simply *deja vu*)
- discothèque (French; often simply *discotheque*)
- bric-à-brac (French; usually simply *bric-a-brac*)
- vis-à-vis (French; usually simply *vis-a-vis*)
- voilà (French; usually simply *voila*)

Circumflex

The **circumflex** is a combination of both the acute and grave accent, forming a single pointed mark that appears above vowels. It only appears in English in loanwords taken from French, above the letters **E** and **A**. For instance:
- château (French; often simply *chateau*)
- coup de grâce (French; often simply *coup de grace*)
- crème brûlée (French; can be spelled *crème brulée, creme brulée*, or simply *creme brulee*)
- crêpe (French; often simply *crepe*)
- mêlée (French; usually simply *melee*)
- papier-mâché (French; often simplified as *paper mache* or *maché*)
- pâté (French; often written with just the acute accent, *paté*)
- tête-à-tête (French; often simply *tete-a-tete*)

Cedilla

The cedilla is a tail-like mark that appears under certain consonants, usually the letter **C**. Only a few French loanwords that feature a cedilla are used in English, and those that do usually have the cedilla dropped by English writers due to its rarity and unfamiliarity. For example:
- façade (formally written with the cedilla, but often simplified as *facade*)
- garçon (formally written with the cedilla, but often simplified as *garcon*)
- soupçon (formally written with the cedilla, but often simplified as *soupcon*)

Tilde

The **tilde** is a wavy line that is placed over certain letters to indicate a nasal pronunciation. In English, it only appears in loanwords from Spanish, in which case it is only used over the letter **N**. For instance:
- El Niño (usually spelled with the tilde)

• español (not common in English, but usually spelled with the tilde when it is used)
• jalapeño (usually spelled with the tilde, but often simplified as *jalapeno*)
• La Niña (usually spelled with the tilde)
• mañana (not common in English, but usually spelled with the tilde when it is used)
• piñata (usually spelled with the tilde, but sometimes simplified as *pinata*)
• piñon (usually spelled with the tilde, but sometimes written as *pinyon* or *pinon*)
• quinceañera (not common in English, but usually spelled with the tilde when it is used)
• señor (usually spelled with the tilde, but sometimes simplified as *senor*)
• señora (usually spelled with the tilde, but sometimes simplified as *senora*)

Dieresis

Other than the rare (and now mostly obsolete) instances we looked at earlier, the **dieresis** is only used in a few words taken from another language. The dieresis is most associated with German words, though it does occur in French as well. (We included *naïve* in our previous section because it has become a standard word in English.) In German, it is known as an **umlaut**, and it indicates a shift in the way a vowel is produced, rather than a pause between two vowel sounds. For example:

• doppelgänger (formally written with the dieresis, but usually written without it)
• Fräulein (formally written with the dieresis, but usually written without it)
• Möbius (most often used in the phrase *Möbius strip* or *Möbius band*; usually spelled without the dieresis)
• Noël (French; often simplified as *Noel*)
• Schrödinger (most often used in the phrase *Schrödinger's cat*; commonly spelled without the dieresis)
• über (formally written with the dieresis, but now usually written without it)

Quiz

(answers start on page 463)

1. True or False: Diacritics are commonly used in English.

a) True
b) False

2. Which of the following diacritical marks is never used in native English words?

a) Grave accent (e.g., è)
b) Cedilla (e.g., ç)
c) Dieresis (e.g., ö)

3. What type of diacritical mark most commonly appears in foreign loanwords?

a) Acute accent (e.g., é)
b) Tilde (e.g., ñ)
c) Circumflex (e.g., â)
d) Dieresis (e.g., ö)

4. Foreign loanwords from which language most often have diacritics in English?

a) Spanish
b) German
c) Latin
d) French

Ligatures

Definition

In writing, a **ligature** is a combination of two or more letters joined into a single unit. There were many ligatures used in English at one time, formed to make typesetting easier (known as **typographical ligatures**), but these were all discarded as printing became easier and less expensive. However, there are two other ligatures that originated in Latin and were carried over into English as distinct letters: Æ (in lowercase, æ) and Œ (in lowercase, œ).

While these two letters were eventually divided in modern English (and eventually reduced to just **E/e** in American English), there is another Latin ligature that *is* used in English today: **&** (known as an ampersand).

Finally, there is one other ligature that arose as Latin evolved over time and is now a part of the modern English alphabet: **W**.

Æ/æ and Œ/œ

Not counting **W** (which is now considered a single letter) and **&** (which is a stylistic representation of a specific word, rather than just two conjoined letters), the two ligatures that survived in English until relatively recently are *Æ/æ* (a combination of **A** and **E**) and *Œ/œ* (a combination of **O** and **E**). Over time, they were divided back into separate letters, creating the vowel digraphs *AE* and *OE*.

In American English, however, most of the words featuring these divided ligatures dropped the **A** and **O**, leaving just the **E** behind. (In most cases, the pronunciation is the same in both American and British English, though in some words beginning with "e-/oe-," the pronunciation varies slightly.)

For example:

Spelling with ligature	British English	American English
Spelled "æ"	Spelled "ae"	Spelled "e"
anæmia	anaemia	anemia
anæsthesia	anaesthesia	anesthesia
bacteræmia	bacteraemia	bacteremia
cæsium	caesium	cesium
diæresis	diaeresis	dieresis
encyclopædia	encyclopaedia	encyclopedia
æon	aeon	eon
fæces	faeces	feces
frænum	fraenum	frenum
hæmoglobin	haemoglobin	hemoglobin
hæmophilia	haemophilia	hemophilia
hæmorrhage	haemorrhage	hemorrhage
hæmorrhoid	haemorrhoid	hemorrhoid
ischæmia	ischaemia	ischemia
leukæmia	leukaemia	leukemia
orthopædic	orthopaedic	orthopedic
pædiatric	paediatric	pediatric
palæography	palaeography	paleography
palæontology	palaeontology	paleontology
septicæmia	septicaemia	septicemia
synæsthesia	synaesthesia	synesthesia
toxæmia	toxaemia	toxemia
uræmia	uraemia	uremia

Spelled "œ"	Spelled "oe"	Spelled "e"
apnœa	apnoea	apnea
cœliac	coeliac	celiac
diarrhœa	diarrhoea	diarrhea
dyspnœa	dyspnoea	dyspnea
œdema	oedema	edema
œsophagus	oesophagus (/iːˈsɑfəgəs/)	esophagus (/ɪˈsɑfəgəs/)
œstrogen	oestrogen (/ˈiːstrədʒən/)	estrogen (/ˈɛstrədʒən/)
œstrus	oestrus (/ˈiːstrəs/)	estrus (/ˈɛstrəs/)
fœtus	foetus	fetus
gonorrhœa	gonorrhoea	gonorrhea
manœuvre	manoeuvre	maneuver
subpœna	subpoena	subpena

Words spelled "ae" and "oe" in both regions

Not many words retain the Latin-based digraphs in American English, but there are a few words that do:

Words with "ae"	Words with "oe"
aegis	amoeba
aesthetic	Oedipus
archaeology	Phoebe
paean	phoenix

Note that all the words featuring "ae" (and the word *amoeba*) have variant spellings with just "e" (*egis, esthetic, archeology, pean,* and *ameba*), but these are far less common.

Words with single letters in both regions

While American English much more commonly drops the additional vowels in the Latin digraphs "ae" and "oe," there are some words in both American and British English that only retain the **E**:
- chimera (derived from Latin *Chimaera*)
- demon (though *daemon* is sometimes used in stylized writing)
- ecology (originally *oecology*)
- economy (derived from Latin *oeconomia*)
- ecumenical (derived from Latin *oecumenicus*)
- enigma (derived from Latin *aenigma*)
- homeopathy (still spelled *homoeopathy* in British English, but less commonly)
- hyena (less commonly, *hyaena*)
- fetid (less commonly, *foetid*, derived from the incorrect Latin term *foetidus*)
- medieval (less commonly, *mediaeval*)
- primeval (much less commonly, *primaeval*)

Using "-ae" to form plurals

Nouns taken directly from Latin that end in "-a" are made plural using "-ae" in both American and British English. (Note, however, that the Latinate "-ae" ending has been replaced in modern English by the standard plural suffix "-s" in many common, everyday words.)

For example:
- alga→algae
- amoeba→amoebae
- antenna→antennae (more commonly *antennas*)
- aorta→aortae (more commonly *aortas*)
- cloaca→cloacae
- copula→copulae (more commonly *copulas*)
- cornea→corneae (more commonly *corneas*)
- ephemera→ephemerae

- formula→formul**ae** (more commonly *formulas*)
- hernia→herni**ae** (more commonly *hernias*)
- hyperbola→hyperbol**ae** (more commonly *hyperbolas*)
- placenta→placent**ae**
- pupa→pup**ae**
- retina→retin**ae** (more commonly *retinas*)
- scapula→scapul**ae**
- supernova→supernov**ae**
- vertebra→vertebr**ae**
- uvula→uvul**ae**

&

The symbol **&** (known as an **ampersand**) is used in writing to represent the word *and*. The symbol is actually a stylized ligature that combines the two letters of the Latin word *et* (also meaning "and") into a single symbol. (The term *ampersand* is actually a contraction of the phrase *and per se and*—a blend of English and Latin meaning "and (the symbol &) by itself means and.")

The ampersand is especially common in commercial names of companies and brands, and it is often featured in logos and graphic designs. Commonly recognized abbreviations that feature the word *and* often use ampersands as well. For example:
- "Daniels **&** Jones Insurance Co."
- "I just need some R**&**R [rest and relaxation]."
- "My brother loves hip-hop, but I'm more of an R**&**B [rhythm and blues] fan myself."
- "During the course of the audit, we will need P**&**L [profit and loss] reports for the last three fiscal years."

In more formal or academic writing, some style guides also recommend using an ampersand for parenthetical citations of sources written by two or more authors, as in:
- The authors assert that reliance on "antiquated methodology and outdated preconceptions" is still rampant in many government agencies (Smith, Burke, **&** Robertson, 2002).

However, other style guides recommend spelling out *and* completely, so check your school's or employer's preferred style guide to be sure which you should use. If in doubt, use *and* instead of **&**.

Finally, because the ampersand represents *et*, it was formerly used to write the abbreviated form of the Latin phrase *et cetera* (meaning "and so on"), appearing as *&c.*. For example:
- "Various contracts, receipts, invoices, **&c.**, were strewn about the office."

In modern English, though, this looks rather peculiar, and it is much more common to write the abbreviation as *etc.*

W

The letter **W** (pronounced "double U") is most commonly associated with the consonant sound /w/, as in *wise* (/waɪz/) or *weak* (/wik/), though it can also pair with certain vowels to create vowel digraphs and diphthongs.

In Classical Latin, the letter **V** was originally used to represent the /w/ sound at the beginning of a word, or the /u/ sound in the middle of a word. Therefore, the Latin noun *via* would have been pronounced /ˈwia/, while the Latin preposition *cum* would have been spelled *cvm* and pronounced /kum/.

Over time, the sound /w/ associated with the Latin **V** at the beginning of words shifted to that of a voiced bilabial fricative—essentially the /v/ sound we now associate with the letter **V** (as in *vest*, /vɛst/). In the Late Middle Ages, the shape of the letter **V** was rounded to a **U** when it appeared in the middle of a word; by the mid-16th century, **V** was used to represent the consonant sound /v/, while **U** was used to represent the vowel sound /u/.

Eventually, the vowel digraph **uu** (hence the name, "double-U") began to be used to represent the /w/ sound to distinguish it from the letter **V** and the newly formed **U**. This digraph was also written as **VV**, which was eventually combined into a ligature that resembled its current typographical shape, **W**.

Quiz

(answers start on page 463)

1. Which of the following ligatures is still used in modern English?

a) Æ

b) Œ

c) &

d) W

e) A & B

f) C & D

2. The letter W originated as which letter in Classical Latin?

a) X

b) U

c) Y

d) V

3. How is the ligature Æ/æ usually represented in modern American English?

a) AE/ae

b) A/a

c) E/e

4. What letters form the ligature **&**?

a) E and T

b) A and E

c) A and T

d) O and E

Spelling Conventions

Because modern English has been formed from and influenced by a variety of different languages—Latin, Greek, French, German, etc.—in addition to its evolution from Old and Middle English, the ways in which words are spelled and created can often seem inconsistent, illogical, and even contradictory.

Adding to the problem is that there is no single unified consensus governing English (unlike, for example, the *Académie française*, a council that acts as the official authority on the French language), so there are many discrepancies and differences in how words are spelled, pronounced, and even used grammatically in different parts of the world.

While there may be no single set of "rules" for English spelling, there are many different conventions and patterns we can use to help to make it easier to grasp. We'll briefly review these conventions below, but you can continue on to each individual section to learn more.

Affixes

An **affix** is an element that is added to a base word or root to create a new or inflected form. The most common affixes in English are **prefixes**, which attach to the beginning of a base or root word, and **suffixes**, which attach to the end. (There are a few other types of affixes that occur in English, but these are much less common; to learn more, go to the full section on Affixes.)

Prefixes

A **prefix** is a letter or group of letters that is added to the <u>beginning</u> of a root or base word to create a new word with a unique meaning. Let's briefly look at some common examples; continue on to the Prefixes section to learn more.

- **<u>a</u>typical** (**<u>not</u>** typical)
- **<u>bi</u>directional** (having **<u>two</u>** directions)
- **<u>co</u>operate** (operate **<u>together</u>**)
- **<u>de</u>fuse** (to **<u>remove</u>** a fuse)
- **<u>ex</u>**-boyfriend (**<u>former</u>** boyfriend)
- **<u>fore</u>arm** (**<u>front part of the</u>** arm)
- **<u>hyper</u>active** (**<u>overly</u>** active)
- **<u>im</u>mature** (**<u>not</u>** mature)
- **<u>mal</u>adjusted** (**<u>wrongly</u>** adjusted)
- **<u>non</u>functional** (**<u>not</u>** functional)
- **<u>out</u>number** (to be **<u>greater</u>** in number)
- **<u>post</u>production** (**<u>later</u>** in production)
- **<u>re</u>start** (start **<u>again</u>**)
- **<u>semi</u>serious** (**<u>half</u>** serious)
- **<u>trans</u>generational** (**<u>cross</u>** generational)
- **<u>ultra</u>violet** (**<u>beyond</u>** the violet end of the visible spectrum)

Suffixes

A **suffix** is a letter or group of letters added onto the <u>end</u> of a root or base word to change its meaning. There is a huge range of suffixes in English, which can be broadly categorized as either **inflectional** or **derivational**.

Inflectional Suffixes

Inflectional suffixes are used to modify the ***grammatical*** meaning of a word; they do not change a word from one part of speech to another, nor do they alter the fundamental meaning of the word.

Inflectional suffixes can be used with nouns, verbs, adjectives, and adverbs. For example:

Suffixes with Nouns (form plurals)	Suffixes with Verbs (form participles or third-person singular)	Suffixes with Adjectives or Adverbs (form comparatives or superlatives)
bank→bank**s** car→car**s** pizza→pizza**s** toy→toy**s** coach→coach**es** watch→watch**es** dish→dish**es** box→box**es** ox→ox**en** child→child**ren** brother→brethr**en**	hear→hear**s** run→run**s** think→think**s** approach→approach**es** catch→catch**es** do→do**es** burn→burn**ed** hope→hop**ed** open→open**ed** eat→eat**en** give→giv**en** got→gott**en** care→car**ing** hear→hear**ing** pass→pass**ing**	big→bigg**er** fast→fast**er** happy→happi**er** high→high**er** sad→sadd**er** slow→slow**er** big→bigg**est** fast→fast**est** happy→happi**est** high→high**est** sad→sadd**est** slow→slow**est**

Derivational Suffixes

Unlike inflectional suffixes, **derivational suffixes** create a new word based on the meaning of the word to which they attach. In many cases, the new word will belong to a completely different part of speech (or **word class**). These are sometimes referred to as **class-changing suffixes**.

While there are too many derivational suffixes to list here, let's go over some of the most common ones in day-to-day writing and speech. To learn more about the meanings they create, continue on to the section covering Suffixes.

Suffixes that form nouns	Suffixes that form verbs	Suffixes that form adjectives	Suffixes that form adverbs
block→block**age** propose→propos**al** arrogant→arrog**ance** free→free**dom** employ→employ**ee** exist→exist**ence** teach→teach**er** clarify→clarif**ication** criticize→critic**ism** equal→equal**ity** entertain→entertain**ment** dark→dark**ness** educate→educat**or** decide→deci**sion** translate→transla**tion**	fright→fright**en** pure→pur**ify** apology→apolog**ize** caffeine→caffein**ate**	adore→ador**able** logic→logic**al** gold→gold**en** beauty→beauti**ful** sense→sens**ible** comedy→comed**ic** history→histor**ical** child→child**ish** home→home**less** friend→friend**ly** glamor→glamor**ous** mess→mess**y**	easy→easi**ly** side→side**ways** like→like**wise** home→home**ward**

You may have noticed that some of the suffixes we looked at above have very similar appearances and uses—for example, -able vs. -ible, -ic vs. -ical, and -tion vs. -sion. This can cause some confusion for writers as to which suffix is appropriate for certain words. Continue on to the section Commonly Confused Suffixes to learn more about the subtle differences between these suffixes and when to use them.

Additionally, there are many instances in which adding a suffix to a word results in a change to the original word's spelling, which can prove difficult for writers to remember. For example, nouns that end in "-y" will end in "-ies" when becoming plural (as in *candy→candies*); the Silent E at the end of a word will usually be dropped when adding a suffix (as in *bake→baking*); and a single consonant at the end of a word will often be doubled when adding a suffix beginning with a vowel (as in *drag→dragged*). To learn more about the different instances in which suffixes change the spelling of base words, go to the section Spelling Conventions with Suffixes.

Inflection in Spelling

Closely related to suffixes is the notion of **inflection**—changes in a word's spelling that reflect changes in its grammatical function in a sentence. Inflection is divided into two broad categories: conjugation and declension.

Conjugation

Conjugation specifically refers to the inflection of verbs. In terms of spelling changes, it refers to changing a verb's structure to reflect past tense (as in *walk→walked*), continuous tense (as in *walk→walking*), or the third person singular (as in *walk→walks*).

Declension

Declension, on the other hand, is the inflection of nouns, pronouns, adjectives, and adverbs. We'll briefly cover how each part of speech is inflected here, but you can continue on to the full section on Inflection in Spelling to learn more.

Declension of nouns

The declension of nouns most often entails forming plurals by adding "-s" or "-es" (as in *cake→cakes* or *beach→beaches*). We go into greater detail about this in the section on Forming Plurals. A few nouns can also be declined to reflect gender (as in *actor→actress* or *bachelor→bachelorette*), but this is not very common.

Declension of pronouns

The declension of pronouns involves changes in how personal pronouns are spelled depending on their grammatical person (first person, second person, or third person), number (singular or plural), gender (masculine or feminine), and case (objective, subjective, or possessive). There are also specific forms for reflexive pronouns (those that are the object of their own action). For example, consider these variations of the first-person pronouns (which are all gender neutral):

• *I* (singular, subjective case)
• *me* (singular, objective case)
• *mine* (singular, possessive case)
• *myself* (singular, reflexive)
• *we* (plural, subjective case)
• *us* (plural, objective case)
• *ours* (plural, possessive case)
• *ourselves* (plural, reflexive)

Declension of adjectives and adverbs

Adjectives and adverbs are both inflected the same way to create two degrees of comparison between two or more people, things, actions, etc.

The first is known as the comparative degree, which, for adjectives, expresses a higher or lower degree of an attribute, or, for adverbs, indicates how an action is performed. In both cases, we form the comparative degree by attaching the suffix "-er" to the end of the word or by using the words *more* or *less* before it. (Note that adverbs that can take the "-er" suffix can also be used as adjectives.) For example:

	Adjectives	**Adverbs**
formed with "-er" (one-syllable adverbs, one-syllable adjectives, and two-syllable adjectives ending in "-y")	big→bigg**er** weak→weak**er** happy→happi**er** small→small**er**	hard→hard**er** quick→quick**er** fast→fast**er** late→lat**er**
formed with "more/less" (adverbs ending in "-ly"; adjectives with three or more syllables, or adjectives with two syllables not ending in "-y")	**more/less** careful **more/less** caring **more/less** intelligent **more/less** beautiful	**more/less** carefully **more/less** efficiently **more/less** happily **more/less** recently

The second degree of comparison is known as the **superlative degree**, which is used to describe characteristics that are the highest or lowest compared to someone or something else. We form the superlative degree in the same way as the comparative, but, instead of "-er," we use "-est," and, instead of *more/less*, we use ***most/least***. For example:

	Adjectives	Adverbs
formed with "-er" (one-syllable adverbs, one-syllable adjectives, and two-syllable adjectives ending in "-y")	big→bigg**est** weak→weak**est** happy→happi**est** small→small**est**	hard→hard**est** quick→quick**est** fast→fast**est** late→lat**est**
formed with "more/less" (adverbs ending in "-ly"; adjectives with three or more syllable, or adjectives with two syllables not ending in "-y")	**most/least** careful **most/least** caring **most/least** intelligent **most/least** beautiful	**most/least** carefully **most/least** efficiently **most/least** happily **most/least** recently

Forming Contractions

Another way that we alter the spelling of a word is when we create **contractions**. These are formed when words are shortened by omitting one or more letters, which are most often replaced with an apostrophe.

The most common type of contraction is when two words are joined together and one of them (usually the second) is shortened. It's important to remember that the apostrophe marks the **letters** that are left out of the contracted word; it does **not** mark the space that was between the words. For example:

✖ "This plan **does'nt** make any sense." (incorrect)

✖ "This plan **does'n't** make any sense." (incorrect)

✔ "This plan **doesn't** make any sense." (correct)

We'll go over some of the most common contractions here, but you can continue on to the full section on Forming Contractions to learn more.

Contracting *is, am,* and *are*

The most common type of two-word contraction occurs when the present simple tense forms of the verb *be* (*is, am, are*) are combined with the subject of a clause—usually a proper noun, personal pronoun, or question word (*who, what, where, when, why,* and *how*). For example:

Be conjugation	Contracted form	Example sentences
is	's	• "Jonathan**'s** coming over later." • "I think she**'s** pretty happy with the results." • "I can't believe it**'s** still raining outside!" • "How**'s** your project coming, Billy?"
am	'm	• "I**'m** going to the park later, if you want to come with me." • "You know the reason why I**'m** angry!"
are	're	• "You**'re** being so annoying!" • "I think we**'re** going to be late." • "Who**'re** you taking to the dance?"

Contracting other auxiliary verbs

In addition to the three forms of *be*, there are four other auxiliary verbs that can also be contracted as enclitics: *have* (and its conjugations *has* and *had*), *did, will,* and *would.* For example:

Auxiliary verb	Contracted form	Example sentences
have	've	• "I've been thinking about what you said." • "We think we've found a pretty elegant solution." • "Why've they been avoiding us?"
has	's	• "She's been rather quiet lately." • "Johnny's applied to be a police officer." • "It's been about a week since I last heard from them."
had	'd	• "We'd dreamed about living in Ireland for years before we finally moved here." • "I'd been feeling a little unwell, so I took Monday off from work." • "She'd never been prouder of herself before that moment."
did	'd	• "Who'd you ask to cover your shift on Monday?" • "What'd you think of the movie?" • "How'd you do on the test?"
will	'll	• "He'll call you in the morning." • "If you wash the dishes, I'll take out the trash." • "What'll they do with all that money?"
would	'd	• "He told you he'd call you in the morning." • "I'd like to go to the amusement park for my birthday." • "I thought she'd be here by now."

Contracting *not*

The adverb *not* is used to express negative actions, so, unlike the words we've looked at so far, it only contracts with verbs, not personal pronouns or question words. However, we can only do this with auxiliary verbs, not main verbs.

Another difference from the words we've looked at so far is that when we contract *not*, we don't omit all of the letters leading up to the final consonant; instead, we only omit **-o-** and replace it with an apostrophe. What's especially unusual about contractions of *not* is that sometimes the *first* word is altered as well. There's no specific pattern to help us gauge when (or how) these extra alterations will occur, so we have to memorize them:

• is + not = isn't
• are + not = aren't
• was + not = wasn't
• were + not = weren't

• have + not = haven't
• has + not = hasn't
• had + not = hadn't

• do + not = don't
• does + not = doesn't
• did + not = didn't

• can + not = cannot = can't
• could + not = couldn't

• will + not = won't
• would + not = wouldn't

- shall + not = sha**n't**
- should + not = should**n't**

- might + not = might**n't**
- must + not = must**n't**

Remember that this is just a cursory summary of contractions; there are many other informal contractions we can form, as well as several one-word and even three-word contractions. For more information on all of these, go to the section on Forming Contractions.

Inconsistent Spelling Rules

Because English spelling is often so haphazard, there are a few different sets of rules that have been popularized in an attempt to help standardize the way words are spelled. The problem is that there are many exceptions to each of them, which means that they are not the most reliable methods for determining a word's spelling. However, they are still useful to know, so we will briefly touch on them here; continue on to their full sections to learn more about each.

I Before E, Except After C

Perhaps the best known spelling convention in English is "I Before E, Except after C," meaning that **I** comes before **E** in most words, except when both letters immediately follow **C**. Due to the simplicity of the rule and its easily remembered rhyming mnemonic, it is often one of the first rules taught to those learning English spelling. The full rhyme typically goes like this:

"**I** before **E**,
Except after **C**,
Or when sounding like **A**
As in *neighbor* or *weigh*."

In addition to the "**A**" sound (/eɪ/) described in the rhyme, there are many exceptions and special cases that we have to consider when deciding whether **I** should come before **E**.

When the letters sound like *E* (/i/)

The "**I** before **E**" rule is most useful if we focus on instances when **E** and **I** are put together as vowel digraphs—that is, two vowels working together to form a single speech sound.

With this in mind, the basic rule "**I** before **E**, except after **C**" is fairly reliable when **IE** or **EI** function as digraphs that produce the sound /i/ (the way the letter **E** is said aloud as a word). For example:

I before E	Except after C
ach**ie**ve (/əˈtʃ**i**v/)	**ce**iling (/ˈs**i**lɪŋ/)
bel**ie**ve (/bɪˈl**i**v/)	con**ce**ive (/kənˈs**i**v/)
f**ie**ld (/f**i**ld/)	de**ce**it (/dɪˈs**i**t/)
gr**ie**f (/gr**i**f/)	per**ce**ive (/pərˈs**i**v/)
p**ie**ce (/p**i**s/)	re**ce**ipt (/rɪˈs**i**t/)
sh**ie**ld (/ʃ**i**ld/)	

E before I when sounding like *A* (/eɪ/)

The second half of the rhyme—"when sounding like *A*"—alludes to the fact that **E** often comes before **I** <u>without</u> **C** when **EI** is pronounced /eɪ/ (the way the letter **A** is said aloud as a word).

This is especially common when **EI** is followed by a silent GH, as in:
- fr**eigh**t (/fr**eɪ**t/)
- **eigh**t (/**eɪ**t/)
- inv**eigh** (/ɪnˈv**eɪ**/)
- n**eigh**bor (/ˈn**eɪ**bər/)
- sl**eigh** (/sl**eɪ**/)
- w**eigh**t (/w**eɪ**t/)

(Remember this when using these roots in other words, as in *eighteen* or *weightless*.)

And sometimes when sounding like *I* (/aɪ/)

Less commonly, the digraph **EI** produces the sound /aɪ/ (the way the letter **I** is said aloud as a word).

There are only a few common root words in which this is the case:
- f**ei**sty (/ˈf**aɪ**sti/)
- h**ei**ght (/h**aɪ**t/)
- h**ei**st (/h**aɪ**st/)
- sl**ei**ght (/sl**aɪ**t/)

Just be sure not to confuse the spelling for *slight* (an adjective meaning "small in size, degree, or amount") with *sleight* (a noun meaning "skill or dexterity" or "a clever trick or deception")—they both sound the same, but have sl**ight**ly different spellings.

Exceptions and other helpful tips

The main problem with the "I Before E" rule is that there are many different exceptions, as well as other special cases that dictate which letter will come first in a given word. There are too many to quickly summarize here, so continue on to the full section on I Before E, Except After C to learn more.

The Three-Letter Rule

A less popularly taught spelling rule is known as "The Three-Letter Rule," which states that "**content words**" (words that communicate meaningful information, such as nouns, (most) verbs, adjectives, and adverbs) will almost always be spelled with at least three letters. Words that are spelled with only one or two letters, on the other hand, will almost always be "**function words**"—words that perform grammatical functions to help construct a sentence, such as pronouns, prepositions, conjunctions, articles, or particles.

Determining spelling using the three-letter rule

The three-letter rule is a useful convention to follow when we're trying to determine the spelling of short, single-syllable words. Many one- and two-letter function words are **homophones** of short content words: they have different spellings, but their pronunciations are the same.

Spelling Conventions

Function Words	Content Words
aw (*interjection*)	*awe* (*noun*)
be (*auxiliary verb*)	*bee* (*noun*)
by (*preposition*)	*buy* (*verb*)
do (*auxiliary verb*)	*dew* (*noun*) *due* (*adjective*) *doe* (*noun*)
er (*interjection*)	*err* (*verb*) *ere* (*preposition/conjunction*)
hi (*informal interjection*)	*high* (*adjective/adverb*)
in (*preposition/particle*)	*inn* (*noun*)
I (*pronoun*)	*aye* (*noun*) *eye* (*noun*)
lo (*interjection*)	*low* (*adjective/adverb*)
of (*preposition*)	*off* (*adjective/adverb/preposition*)
or (*conjunction*)	*oar* (*noun*) *ore* (*noun*)
ow (*interjection*)	*owe* (*verb*)
to (*preposition/particle*)	*too* (*adverb*) *two* (*noun/determiner*) *toe* (*noun*) *tow* (*verb/noun*)
us (*pronoun*)	*use* (*verb/noun*)
we (*pronoun*)	*wee* (*adjective*)

Even where a short content word does not have a homophonic function word from which it needs to be distinguished, we still commonly find silent, seemingly extraneous letters in three-letter words that would have the same pronunciation with only two letters. For example:

ad<u>d</u>	pa<u>w</u>
bo<u>w</u>	pe<u>a</u>
cu<u>e</u>	pi<u>e</u>
di<u>e</u>	ra<u>w</u>
dy<u>e</u>	ro<u>e</u>
eb<u>b</u>	ro<u>w</u>
eg<u>g</u>	ru<u>e</u>
fo<u>e</u>	ry<u>e</u>
ho<u>e</u>	sa<u>w</u>
hu<u>e</u>	se<u>a</u>
il<u>l</u>	se<u>e</u>
jo<u>e</u>	so<u>w</u>
la<u>w</u>	su<u>e</u>
la<u>y</u>	te<u>a</u>
li<u>e</u>	te<u>e</u>
od<u>d</u>	ti<u>e</u>
	vi<u>e</u>

As with the "I Before E" rule, there are many exceptions to this convention. Go to the full section on The Three-Letter Rule to learn more.

Rules for Capitalization

Capitalization refers to certain letters being in the **upper case**. While there are some words that are always capitalized no matter where they appear in a sentence, most words are only capitalized if they appear at the beginning of a sentence.

There are also various conventions regarding the capitalization of words in the titles of creative or published works, but these can be difficult to learn because there is no single, generally accepted rule to follow.

Letters can also be capitalized in other specific circumstances, too. Let's briefly look at some of the capitalization conventions here; to learn more, go to the Rules for Capitalization.

Capitalizing the first word of a sentence

<u>T</u>he first word of a sentence is always capitalized.

<u>W</u>e also capitalize the first letter of a full sentence that is directly quoted within another sentence, as in:

• <u>J</u>ohn said, "<u>Y</u>ou'll never work in this city again!"
• <u>T</u>he other day, my daughter asked, "<u>W</u>hy do I have to go to school, but you don't?"

<u>N</u>ote that we do **not** capitalize the first word in the quotation if it is a word, phrase, or sentence fragment incorporated into the natural flow of the overall sentence; we also do not set it apart with commas. <u>F</u>or example:

• <u>M</u>y brother said he feels "<u>r</u>eally bad" about what happened.
• <u>B</u>ut I don't want to just "<u>s</u>ee how things go"!

Proper Nouns

Proper nouns are used to identify a <u>unique</u> person, place, or thing (as opposed to **common nouns**, which identify generic or nonspecific people or things).

The most common proper nouns are names of people, places, or events:

• "Go find <u>J</u>eff and tell him that dinner is ready."
• "I lived in <u>C</u>incinnati before I moved to <u>N</u>ew <u>Y</u>ork."
• "My parents still talk about how great <u>W</u>oodstock was in 1969."

The names of organizations, companies, agencies, etc., are all proper nouns as well, so the words that make up the name are all capitalized. However, unlike the names of people or places, these often contain **function words**, which are **not** capitalized. For example:

• "You'll have to raise your query with the <u>D</u>epartment <u>of</u> <u>F</u>oreign <u>A</u>ffairs <u>a</u>nd <u>T</u>rade."
• "I've been offered a teaching position at the <u>U</u>niversity <u>of</u> <u>P</u>ennsylvania."

Acronyms and Initialisms

Acronyms and **initialisms** are abbreviations of multiple words using just their initial letters (or fragments of each word); like the initials of a person's name, these letters are usually capitalized. Acronyms are distinguished by the fact that they are read aloud as a single word, while initialisms are spoken aloud as individual letters, rather than a single word. (Because the two are so similar in appearance and function, though, it is very common to simply refer to both as acronyms.)

For example:

Acronyms	Initialisms
NASA (acronym of "National Aeronautics and Space Administration")	**USA** (initialism of "United States of America")
AWOL (acronym of "Absent Without Leave")	**ATM** (initialism of "Automated Teller Machine")
SWAT (acronym of "Special Weapons and Tactics")	**UFO** (initialism of "Unidentified Flying Object")

However, there are some acronyms that have become so common in modern English that they are not capitalized at all. For example, the word *scuba* is actually an acronym of "self-contained underwater breathing apparatus," but it is now <u>only</u> written as a regular word. Similarly, *ASAP* (which stands for "as soon as possible" and can be pronounced as an acronym or an initialism) is commonly spelled with lowercase letters as *asap* due to how frequently it is used in everyday speech and writing.

There are also two initialisms that are <u>always</u> in lowercase: *i.e.* (short for the Latin *id est*, meaning "that is") and *e.g.* (short for the Latin *exempli gratia*, meaning "for example").

Capitalizing titles and headlines

While proper nouns, acronyms, and initialisms all have fairly standard conventions for capitalization, an area that gives writers difficulty is capitalizing headlines or the titles of written works. Different style guides prescribe different rules and recommendations, so there is little consensus on which words need to be capitalized in a title.

That said, it is generally agreed that you should capitalize the first and last word of the title, along with any **content words** (nouns, pronouns, verbs, adjectives, and adverbs). "Function words" (prepositions, articles, and conjunctions) are generally left in lowercase. This convention is sometimes known as **title case**, and some style guides recommend following it without exception, even for longer function words like *between* or *upon*.

For example:
• "<u>N</u>ew <u>R</u>egulations <u>f</u>or <u>S</u>chools <u>S</u>coring below <u>N</u>ational <u>A</u>verages"
• "<u>A</u>n <u>A</u>nalysis of the <u>D</u>ifferences between <u>F</u>ormatting <u>S</u>tyles"
• "<u>P</u>resident to <u>C</u>onsider <u>O</u>ptions after <u>R</u>esults of <u>FBI</u> <u>I</u>nvestigation"
• "<u>O</u>utrage over <u>P</u>rime <u>M</u>inister's <u>R</u>esponse to <u>C</u>orruption <u>C</u>harges"

Many styles guides consider longer function words (such as the conjunction *because* or the prepositions *between* or *above*) to add more meaning than short ones like *or* or *and*. Because of this, it is a common convention is to capitalize function words that have more than three letters in addition to "major" words like nouns and verbs. Here's how titles following this convention look:

• "<u>N</u>ew <u>R</u>egulations for <u>S</u>chools <u>S</u>coring <u>B</u>elow <u>N</u>ational <u>A</u>verages"
• "<u>A</u>n <u>A</u>nalysis <u>of</u> <u>t</u>he <u>D</u>ifferences <u>B</u>etween <u>F</u>ormatting <u>S</u>tyles"
• "<u>P</u>resident <u>t</u>o <u>C</u>onsider <u>O</u>ptions <u>A</u>fter <u>R</u>esults <u>of</u> <u>FBI</u> <u>I</u>nvestigation"
• "<u>O</u>utrage <u>O</u>ver <u>P</u>rime <u>M</u>inister's <u>R</u>esponse <u>t</u>o <u>C</u>orruption <u>C</u>harges"

However, there are a lot of other variations that different writers and styles guides choose to implement. Continue on to the full section on Rules for Capitalization to learn more.

Other Aspects of Spelling

In addition to the conventions we've looked at so far, there are other elements informing how words are spelled and used in English. One important aspect is how many words and phrases enter English from different languages around the world. These are broadly known as **borrowings**, and they are subdivided into two categories: **loanwords** and **loan translations**.

Another aspect that causes writers confusion is the discrepancy between the American style of English compared to the British style. We'll briefly look at both of these aspects here, but you can continue on to their full sections for more information about each.

Foreign Loanwords and Loan Translations

A **loanword** is a term taken from another language and used without translation; it has a specific meaning that (typically) does not otherwise exist in a single English word. Sometimes the word's spelling or pronunciation (or both) is slightly altered to accommodate English orthography, but, in most cases, it is preserved in its original language.

A **loan translation** (also known as a **calque**), on the other hand, is a word or phrase taken from another language but translated (either in part or in whole) to corresponding English words while still retaining the original meaning.

We'll look at some examples of both here, but you can continue on to the full section on Foreign Loanwords and Loan Translations to learn more.

Foreign Loanwords

Loanword	Language of origin	Notes on spelling, pronunciation, and meaning
aficionado	Spanish	Literally "fond of," in English it refers to an ardent fan, supporter, or devotee of some subject or activity.
café	French	In English, *café* (also spelled *cafe*, without the accent mark) only refers to a small restaurant in which one can buy food and drinks, usually coffee. In French, *café* (itself a loanword from Italian *caffè*) primarily refers to coffee itself, rather than an establishment that serves it.
chow mein	Chinese	Adapted from Chinese *ch'ao mein*, meaning "fried noodles." In English, it typically refers to a dish consisting of chopped vegetables and meat that is served with these noodles.
et cetera	Latin	Literally meaning "and (*et*) the rest (*cetera*)," it is used more figuratively in English to mean "and other unspecified things of the same type of class" or "and so forth."
faux pas	French	Literally "false step," used in English to mean "a breach in decorum, etiquette, or good manners."
haiku	Japanese	A type of poem that traditionally juxtaposes two disparate ideas or images in 17 *on* (Japanese sound units), separated in three phases of 5, 7, and 5. In English, *on* was translated to syllables, so haikus in English are typically written in three lines of 5, 7, and 5 syllables, respectively.
kindergarten	German	Literally "child garden," referring in both languages to a program or class for young children serving as an introduction to elementary school.
orangutan	Malay	Literally meaning "man of the woods," in English it refers to arboreal apes with shaggy, reddish-brown hair.
prima donna	Italian	Literally meaning "first lady," referring to the leading female singer in an opera company. It is more commonly used in English to refer to a self-centered, temperamental, petulant person.
smorgasbord	Swedish	Adapted from the Swedish term *smörgåsbord*, meaning "open-faced sandwich table." It refers specifically to a buffet-style meal consisting of a variety of different dishes. By extension in English, it is used figuratively to describe a wide variety of different options or elements, as in, "The festival features a **smorgasbord** of musical talents."
vigilante	Spanish	Literally meaning "watchman," it is used in English to refer to a person who pursues and punishes suspected criminals outside of the law.

Loan Translations (Calques)

While loanwords feature little or no change to the spelling (or phonetic spelling) of the original word, loan translations—typically idiomatic words or phrases—are translated literally into English (but retain the original meaning or one very similar). For example:

Loan translation	Language of origin	Notes on meaning
angel hair	Italian (*capelli d'angelo*)	Very thin, long pasta. In English, it is more commonly written as *angel hair pasta*.
brainwashing	Chinese (*xi nao*)	"Calculated, forcible indoctrination meant to replace a person's existing beliefs, convictions, or attitudes."
devil's advocate	Latin (*advocatus diaboli*)	This term originated in the Roman Catholic Church, referring to an official whose role was to deliberately argue against the canonization of potential saint, in order to expose any possible character flaws of the candidate or weaknesses of evidence in favor of canonization. In modern English, the term refers to anyone who argues against something either for the sake of argument alone, or to help clarify or determine the validity of the opposing cause (rather than due to personal opinions or convictions).
flea market	French (*marché aux puces*)	A type of informal bazaar consisting of vendors who rent space to sell or barter various goods or merchandise. The term is popularly thought to refer to a particular market in Paris known as the *marché aux puces*, so-called because most of the items being sold were of such age that they were likely to have gathered fleas over time.
lose face	Chinese (*tiu lien*)	The phrase means "humiliation" in Chinese, but in English it means "to do something resulting in the loss of status, reputation, or respect from others." The related term *save face* comes from this meaning in English, rather than as a loan translation from Chinese.
masterpiece	Dutch (*meesterstuk*)	Originally meaning "the work for which an artist or craftsman is granted the rank of master in a guild or academy," it is used in modern English to refer to any creation that is considered a person's greatest work or is of outstanding quality.
rest in peace	Latin (*requiescat in pace*)	Said of someone who has passed away, and commonly written on tombstones.
world-view	German (*Weltanschauung*)	An overall conception of life, the world, and humanity's place therein.

American English vs. British English Spelling

While English is fairly uniform in terms of structure and spelling across the various regions in which it is the native language, there are a few prominent differences that have arisen over the years. These differences are most notably codified between two major English-speaking regions, resulting in American English (AmE) and British English (BrE).

Most of these differences have to do with the endings of certain types of words, as in "-er" vs. "-re," "-or" vs. "-our," and "-ize" vs. "-ise." There are also differences involving whether a final consonant will remain single (AmE) or be doubled (BrE) after a vowel suffix, as well as whether words once featuring Latin ligatures will be spelled with a single vowel (AmE) or a vowel digraph (BrE). We'll briefly look at examples of each of these here, but for more in-depth information and exceptions, you can continue on to the full section on American English vs. British English Spelling.

"-er" vs. "-re"

Many words in British English are spelled with "-re" when that ending follows a consonant. This spelling is a reflection of the French spellings of the words from which they were derived. In American English, we usually find "-er" after a consonant at the end of a word, a practice started in the 19th century to more naturally reflect the word's pronunciation.

For example:

American English	British English
calib**er**	calib**re**
cent**er**	cent**re**
fib**er**	fib**re**
goit**er**	goit**re**
lit**er**	lit**re**
lust**er**	lust**re**
maneuv**er**	manoeuv**re**
meag**er**	meag**re**
met**er**	met**re**
och**er**	och**re**
reconnoit**er**	reconnoit**re**
sab**er**	sab**re**
scept**er**	scept**re**
sepulch**er**	sepulch**re**
somb**er**	somb**re**
spect**er**	spect**re**
theat**er**	theat**re**

"-ize" vs. "-ise"

In American English, the suffix "-ize" is used to form verbs, and it is ultimately derived from the Greek "-*izein*." This Greek suffix became "-iser" in Old French, and it is this form from which the British English "-ise" is derived.

This is a very standard convention, and almost all of the hundreds of words ending in "-ize" in American English will be spelled "-ise" in British English; here are just a few examples:

American English	British English
apolog**ize**	apolog**ise**
bapt**ize**	bapt**ise**
character**ize**	character**ise**
democrat**ize**	democrat**ise**
equal**ize**	equal**ise**
fictional**ize**	fictional**ise**
general**ize**	general**ise**
hypnot**ize**	hypnot**ise**
ideal**ize**	ideal**ise**
jeopard**ize**	jeopard**ise**
legal**ize**	legal**ise**
marginal**ize**	marginal**ise**
normal**ize**	normal**ise**
organ**ize**	organ**ise**
popular**ize**	popular**ise**
rational**ize**	rational**ise**
sensational**ize**	sensational**ise**
theor**ize**	theor**ise**
visual**ize**	visual**ise**
western**ize**	western**ise**

There are, however, verbs that only end in "-ise" regardless of region (such as *advertise, compromise,* or *televise*) as well a few that only end in "-ize" (such as *capsize, prize,* and *seize*).

Doubling L before vowel suffixes

In American English, we follow the rule that if the word has an emphasis on the final syllable before the vowel suffix, then the **L** is doubled. However, most words ending in a single **L** are stressed on the first syllable, so **L** remains singular. In

British English, a final **L** that follows a vowel is almost always doubled before "-ed," "-er," and "-ing" **regardless** of where the stress occurs in the word.

For example:

American English	British English
barrel→barreled, barreling	barrel→barrelled, barrelling
cancel→canceled, canceling	cancel→cancelled, cancelling
dial→dialed, dialing	dial→dialled, dialling
duel→dueled, dueling	duel→duelled, duelling
fuel→fueled, fueling	fuel→fuelled, fuelling
grovel→groveled, groveling	grovel→grovelled, grovelling
label→labeled, labeling	label→labelled, labelling
model→modeled, modeling	model→modelled, modelling
rival→rivaled, rivaling	rival→rivalled, rivalling
signal→signaled, signaling	signal→signalled, signalling
travel→traveled, traveling	travel→travelled, travelling

"e" vs. "ae" and "oe"

Many words (especially medical terms) that were derived from Latin roots originally made use of the **ligatures** æ and œ to represent specific diphthongs. Over time these specialized characters were divided back into separate letters, creating the vowel digraphs *ae* and *oe*.

In American English, however, most of the words featuring these divided ligatures dropped the **A** and **O**, respectively, leaving just the **E** behind.

American English	British English
Spelled "e"	**Spelled "ae"**
anesthesia	anaesthesia
bacteremia	bacteraemia
encyclopedia	encyclopaedia
eon	aeon
feces	faeces
hemophilia	haemophilia
hemorrhage	haemorrhage
ischemia	ischaemia
leukemia	leukaemia
orthopedic	orthopaedic
pediatric	paediatric
paleontology	palaeontology
septicemia	septicaemia
toxemia	toxaemia
Spelled "e"	**Spelled "oe"**
apnea	apnoea
celiac	coeliac
diarrhea	diarrhoea
dyspnea	dyspnoea
edema	oedema
esophagus	oesophagus
estrogen	oestrogen
fetus	foetus
gonorrhea	gonorrhoea
maneuver	manoeuvre
subpena	subpoena

There are also a variety of other less common spelling differences that only arise in a handful of words, as well as some specific word pairs that have slightly different spelling between American and British English. To learn more about all of these, go to the full section on American English vs. British English Spelling.

Quiz
(answers start on page 463)

1. To what part of a word does a **prefix** attach?

a) The beginning of a word
b) The middle of a word
c) The end of a word
d) Either the beginning or the end

2. Which of the following can be inflected to indicate **gender**?

a) Verbs
b) Pronouns
c) Adjectives
d) Adverbs

3. Which of the following forms of the verb *be* is **never** shortened in a contraction?

a) is
b) am
c) are
d) been

4. Which of the following is a **function word**?

a) add
b) an
c) aye
d) awe

5. When is the rule "**I** before **E**, except after **C**" most often true?

a) When the two vowels form the /eɪ/ sound
b) When the two vowels form the /i/ sound
c) When the two vowels form the /aɪ/ sound
d) When the two vowels form the /ɪ/ sound

6. Which of the following **must** be capitalized?

a) verbs
b) second-person pronouns
c) proper nouns
d) the last word of a sentence

7. Which term refers to foreign words that are used in English **without** being translated from the original language?

a) Foreign loanwords
b) Loan translations

8. What is the convention in **American English** regarding the Latin diphthongs "ae" and "oe"?

a) Always keep both letters
b) Usually keep both letters
c) Always drop the "a-" and the "o-"
d) Usually drop the "a-" and the "o-"

Affixes

Definition

An **affix** is an element that is added to a base word or root to create a new or inflected form. The most common affixes are **prefixes**, which attach to the beginning of a base or root word, and **suffixes**, which attach to the end. We'll briefly cover both of these here, but you can continue on to their individual sections to learn more.

There are also a number of other, less common affixes that are used in English, which we'll look at further on.

Prefixes

A **prefix** is a group of letters that is added to the <u>beginning</u> of a root or base word to change its meaning in a sentence. Prefixes are never **inflectional**—that is, they do not change the grammatical function of a word without changing its basic meaning. Instead, prefixes are only ever **derivational**, serving to create new words with unique meanings.

Prefixes generally do not affect the spelling of the root word to which they are attached, but we do sometimes have to alter the prefix *itself* depending on the spelling of the word it precedes. For example, the prefix **in-** can change to **ig-** (before *n-*), **il-** (before *l-*), **im-** (before *b-, m-,* or *p-*), or **ir-** (before **r-**).

In addition, many prefixes are only able (or only tend) to attach to certain parts of speech. For example, the prefix **un-** (meaning "not") generally only attaches to adjectives, as in **un**happy or **un**comfortable; when **un-** means "to do the opposite of," it only attaches to verbs, as in **un**cork or **un**lock. Attaching **un-** to a noun, on the other hand, is usually not done—for instance, **un**building or **un**sky are incorrect.

Let's briefly look at some common prefixes one might encounter:

Prefix	Meaning	Usually attaches to	Example words
anti- (Occasionally hyphenated; sometimes **ant-** before a vowel, especially *a-*)	1. Equal and opposite to. 2. Opposing; against; prejudicial to. 3. Counteracting; destroying; neutralizing. 4. Enemy of or rival to; false version of.	1. nouns, Greek roots 2. adjectives, nouns 3. adjectives, nouns 4. nouns	1. *antarctic, anticatalyst, anticlimax, antidote, antihero, antimatter, antipodes, antithesis, antonym* 2. *antagonist, antiapartheid, anticolonial, anticorruption, antidiscrimination, antiestablishment, antigovernment, antisocial, anti-war* 3. *anti-aircraft, antibacterial, anticonvulsive, antidepressant, antifungal, antifreeze, antihistamine, antipyretic, antitoxin, antiviral* 4. *antichrist, antipope*
auto- (occasionally reduced to **aut-** before vowels)	1. Self; one's own; of, regarding, or performed by the same person or thing. 2. Derived from *automatic* (sometimes hyphenated). 3. Derived from *automobile* (sometimes hyphenated).	1. nouns, adjectives, Latin and Greek roots 2. nouns, verbs 3. nouns	1. *autarchy, autism, autobiography, autoclave, autocracy, autograph, autoimmune, automatic, automobile, automotive, autonomy, autopsy* 2. *autofocus, autocorrect, autopilot, autosave, autosuggest, auto-tune* 3. *autobus, autocross, automaker, auto-mechanic*
bi- (Very rarely, becomes **bin-** before vowels)	1. Two. 2. Having or involving two. 3. Occurring at intervals of two; less formally, occurring twice within that interval.	1. nouns, Latin roots (and, less often, verbs) 2. adjectives 3. adjectives, adverbs	1. *biceps, bicycle, bifurcate, bipartisan, biped, bisect* 2. *bifocal, biconcave, biconvex, bilingual, binaural, binocular, bidirectional, bilateral, bipolar* 3. *biannual, bicentennial, bihourly, bimonthly, biweekly*

co- Occurs before roots beginning with vowels or the consonants *h-* and *gn-*; it is also used to form newer compound terms (which are often hyphenated). This prefix is the common reduced form of **com-**, the original Latin prefix, which occurs before roots beginning with *b-, m-,* or *p-*. It also takes three other forms, depending on the letter it precedes: • **col-** before roots beginning with *l-* • **cor-** before roots beginning with *r-* • **con-** before roots beginning with consonants other than *b-, h-, gn-, l-, m-, p-* or *r-*	1. From the original prefix: together; together with; joint; jointly; mutually. Also used as an intensifier. 2. In newer terms, **co-** can indicate: joint(ly), mutual(ly), or together (with); partnership or equality; a subordinate or assistant; to the same degree or extent; or (in mathematics) the complement of an angle.	1. Latin roots 2. adjectives, nouns, verbs	1. • (co-): *coagulate, coerce, coincide, cognate, cognizance* • (com-): *combat, combine, combust, commingle, commiserate, commit, compact, compare, complex* • (col-): *collaborate, collapse, colleague, collect, collide, collude* • (con-): *conceal, conceive, condemn, conduct, confer, confine, congress, congratulate, conjoin, connect, connive, conquer, conscience, constant, contact, contain, converge* • (cor-): *correct, correlate, correspond, corrode, corrupt* 2. *co-author, codependent, codominant, co-driver, coexist, coeducation, co-manage, cooperate, co-pilot, cosine, cotangent, co-worker*
de- (sometimes hyphenated when followed by a vowel)	1. To reverse; to do or cause to be the opposite. 2. To extract, remove, or eliminate from; to be without. 3. Out of; away from; off. 4. To reduce; to lower; to move down from. 5. Thoroughly or completely (used as an intensifier).	1. nouns, verbs, Latin roots 2. nouns, verbs, Latin roots 3. nouns, verbs, Latin roots 4. nouns, Latin roots 5. verbs	1. *decaffeinate, decelerate, decriminalize, decode, decommission, decompose, deconstruct, de-emphasize, desegregate, destabilize* 2. *debunk, decalcify, deglaze, de-ice, delouse, despair, dethrone* 3. *decamp, defect, deflect, deplane, detrain* 4. *declass, degrade, deject, demean, descend, detest* 5. *debrief, defraud, despoil*
dis- (becomes **dif-** when combining with Latin roots beginning *f-*)	1. Lacking; without; not. 2. To do or cause to be the opposite. 3. Apart; out of; away from; off. 4. To extract, cancel, remove, or release. 5. Indicating intensive force.	1. adjectives, nouns 2. verbs 3. verbs, Latin roots 4. nouns, verbs 5. verbs, Latin roots	1. *disability, disadvantage, disbelief, disease, dishonest, disservice, dissimilar, distemper, distrust, disuse* 2. *disagree, disassociate, disavow, disbelieve, disconnect, discredit, disgrace, disprove* 3. *differ, difficulty, diffraction, diffuse, discard, discord, discharge, disembark, dispense* 4. *disbar, disbud, disburse, disenfranchise, disenchant, disentangle* 5. *disannul, disembowel, disturb*
ex- (always hyphenated)	Former.	nouns	*ex-banker, ex-boyfriend, ex-girlfriend, ex-husband, ex-marine, ex-partner, ex-priest, ex-teacher, ex-wife*
fore-	1. Before; earlier; previous in time. 2. In front of; at or near the front; before or previous in position or location.	1. verbs 2. nouns	1. *forebear, forebode, forecast, foreclose, forego, forejudge, foresee, foreshadow, foretell, forewarn* 2. *forearm, forebrain, foredeck, forefather, forefinger, foreground, forehead, foreleg, foreman, foresail*
mis- (**Mis-** is in many ways identical to **mal-**, though **mis-** is much more likely to be paired with verbs.)	1. Bad; wrong; improper; imperfect; defective; abnormal. 2. Badly; wrongly; improperly; imperfectly; defectively; abnormally.	1. nouns 2. verbs	1. *misadventure, misbalance, misconception, misconduct, misconnection, misdiagnosis, misdirection, misdeed, misgivings, mishap, misinformation, misperception, mismatch, mistrust* 2. *misadjust, misbehave, miscalculate, miscarry, miscast, miscommunicate,*

Spelling Conventions

			misconstrue, misdial, misdiagnose, mishear, misinform, misinterpret, mislabel, mislead, mistake, mismanage, misrepresent, misspell
non- (**Non-** is often hyphenated according to the preference of the writer, but it is more commonly attached *without* a hyphen in American English.)	Indicating total negation, exclusion, failure, or deficiency.	adjectives, nouns	nonaggression, nonalcoholic, nonavailability, nonbeliever, nonchalant, noncombatant, non-cooperation, noncompliance, nondisclosure, noneducational, nonemergency, nonevent, nonexistent, nonfiction, nonfunctional, nonhazardous, nonhuman, noninfectious, nonlethal, nonpayment, nonprofit, nonsmoking, nonworker
out-	1. Surpassing; going beyond; excelling over others. 2. External to; outside; away from the center. 3. Indicating an emergence, protrusion, or issuing-forth. 4. Beyond what is normal, acceptable, or agreeable.	1. verbs 2. noun, verbs 3. nouns 4. adjectives, verbs	1. outargue, outclass, outdistance, outdo, outfox, outlast, outgrow, outgun, outmaneuver, outmatch, outnumber, outpace, outperform, outrank, outrun, outsmart, outshine 2. outback, outboard, outbound, outcast, outcross, outdate, outdoors, outfield, outfit, outgoing, outhouse, outlaw, outlier, outline, outpatient, outpost, outreach, outside, outsource 3. outburst, outcome, outcrop, outgrowth, outpouring 4. outlandish, outsized, outspoken, outstay
pre- (Often hyphenated before other vowels, especially *e-*, though this is less common in American English. Always hyphenated before proper nouns and non-letters)	1. Before; in front of. 2. Earlier than or beforehand in time. 3. Before, in advance, or instead of the normal occurrence.	1 & 2. adjectives, nouns, verbs, Latin roots 3. verbs	1. preamble, precede, precinct, predate, preeminent, preface, prefer, prefix, prefrontal, prelude, preposition, preside, pretext 2. precept, precipitation, precocious, pre-date, predict, pre-emption, prehistory, preindustrial, prejudice, premature, premonition, prenatal, preparation, preproduction, prescience, preserve, preschool, preshow, presume, preview 3. preadmit, preapprove, preassign, prebook, preclean, precondition, predestine, predetermine, preoccupy, preorder, prepay, pre-position
pro-	1. Supporting; promoting; in favor of. 2. Forward; forth; toward the point. 3. In place or on behalf of; acting or substituting for. 4. Beforehand; in advance; prior to. 5. In front; before.	1. nouns (usually hyphenated, but not always) 2, 3, 4 & 5. Greek and Latin roots (less commonly, adjectives, nouns, and verbs)	1. pro-American, pro-Britain, pro-Catholic, pro-choice, pro-life, pro-peace, pro-revolution, prowar 2. problem, proceed, proclaim, procreate, procrastination, profess, profound, program, progress, project, prolong, promote, propel, prosecute, protest, proverb 3. proconsul, procure, pronoun, proper, prorate, proportion 4. proactive, prognosis, prohibit, prophet, proscribe 5. proboscis, profane, pronominal, prologue, protect
re- (This prefix becomes **red-** before Latin roots beginning with vowels. It is hyphenated when paired with English roots if the resultant spelling would be the same as an existing word; it may also be	1. Once more; again (in the same manner, direction, etc.). 2. Once more; again (with the aim of improving, fixing, or substituting).	verbs, Latin roots	1. reaffirm, reappear, reboot, recognize, recopy, re-cover, recur, re-dress, redecorate, redeploy, redesign, rediscover, reelect, reenact, reenter, rehearse, rehire, relearn, rehydrate, relive, reload, reregister, re-sign, restart, retry, reunite 2. reapply, reapportion, rebrand,

hyphenated before English roots beginning with vowels, especially *e-*, but this is often up to the discretion of the writer and is not usually done in American English.)	3. Anew; restored to the original place, condition, etc. 4. Against; back or in reverse; opposite; in response to. 5. Used as an intensive with Latin root verbs.		*recalculate, rekindle, relabel, relocate, remarry, reschedule, reseal, rethink, retry* 3. *reacquire, readjust, realign, rebuild, recapture, receive, regain, rehabilitate, renew, replace, restore* 4. *react, rebel, rebuff, recant, recede, reciprocate, recite, recoil, redact, redeem, redress, refer, regress, reject, relate, remove, resign, respond, return* 5. *redolent, refine, regard, regret, relieve, remedy, repent*
semi-	1. Half. 2. Incompletely; partially; partly; somewhat, almost, or resembling. 3. Occurring twice within a certain period of time.	1 & 2. adjectives, nouns 3. adjectives	1. *semicircle, semicolon, semicylinder, semidiameter, semidome, semifinal, semioval, semiovate* 2. *semiarticulate, semiautomatic, semiconductor, semiconscious, semidarkness, semidetached, semidry, semiformal, semiliterate, semiofficial, semipermanent, semiprofessional, semiserious, semiretired, semitransparent, semivowel* 3. *semiannual, semimonthly, semiweekly*
trans- (usually becomes **tran-** before roots beginning with *s-*)	1. Across; beyond; through; on the other side. 2. Completely change or alter.	1. adjectives, verbs, Latin roots 2. nouns, verbs, Latin roots	1. *transaction, transatlantic, transcend, transfer, transfix, transfuse, transgenerational, transgress, transient, translucent, transmit, transnational, transpacific, transparent, transplant, transport* 2. *transcribe, transduce, transfigure, transform, transgender, translate, transliterate, transmute, transubstantiate*
un- (1) Hyphenated before proper nouns and adjectives.	1. Not. 2. Used to form certain negative adjectival phrases. 3. Opposite of or contrary to; lacking or absent.	1. adjectives (not counting nouns formed from prefixed adjectives) 2. past-participle adjectives + prepositions 3. nouns	1. *unable, unaccompanied, un-American, unbelievable, unbiased, un-British, uncertain, unclear, undue, unemployed, unending, unfamiliar, unforeseen, ungraceful, unguided, unhappy, unhealthy, uninformed, unjust, unkind, unknowing, unlawful, unlikely, unlucky, unmanned, unpersuaded, unprofessional, unrated, unreasonable, unscathed, unsolved, untried, untrustworthy, unwise, unwritten* 2. *unasked-for, uncalled-for, undreamed-of, un-get-at-able, unheard-of* 3. *unbelief, unconcern, uninterest, unmilitary, unrest, untruth*
un- (2)	1. To reverse, erase, or undo an action or effect. 2. To deprive of, extract, or remove. 3. To free, remove, or release from. 4. Used as an intensifier with existing verbs that have the same meaning.	1. verbs 2. nouns 3. nouns 4. verbs	1. *unbend, unbind, unbolt, unclog, uncoil, uncork, undo, undress, unfasten, unfold, unfurl, unhook, unload, unlock, unplug, unscrew, unscramble, unseal, unsheathe, unravel, unroll, untangle, unwind* 2. *unbalance, uncloak, unfrock, unhorse, unman, unmask, unseat, unveil* 3. *unburden, unbox, uncage, uncrate, unearth, unharness, unhitch, unleash, unwrap unyoke* 4. *unloose, unravel*

Suffixes

A **suffix** is a group of letters that is added onto the <u>end</u> of a base or root word to change its meaning. Unlike prefixes, which can only be **derivational** (forming a new word with a unique meaning), suffixes can be either derivational or **inflectional** (meaning that the grammatical function of the word is changed, but its basic meaning is not).

Inflectional Suffixes

Inflectional suffixes can be applied to nouns (to form plurals), adjectives and adverbs (to form comparatives and superlatives), and verbs (to indicate tense and grammatical person). In some cases, the same suffix may be used with different parts of speech to create different types of inflection. For example:

Suffix	Part of Speech Inflected	Grammatical Function	Example Words
"-s"	Verbs	Forms the third-person singular for most verbs.	hear→hears run→runs think→thinks write→writes
"-s"	Nouns	Changes most nouns from singular to plural.	bank→banks car→cars pizza→pizzas toy→toys wire→wires
"-es"	Verbs	Forms the third-person singular for verbs ending in a sibilant sound (/s/, /z/, /ʧ/, or /ʃ/) created by the endings "-ss," "-z," "-x," "-sh," "-ch," or "-tch," as well as verbs ending in a consonant + **O**.	approach→approaches catch→catches do→does go→goes hush→hushes pass→passes quiz→quizzes
"-es"	Nouns	Forms the plural for nouns ending in a sibilant sound (/s/, /z/, /ʧ/, or /ʃ/) as created by the endings "-ss," "-z," "-x," "-sh," "-ch," or "-tch."	coach→coaches watch→watches dish→dishes box→boxes bus→buses kiss→kisses waltz→waltzes
"-ed"	Verbs	Forms the past simple tense and past participle of most verbs.	ask→asked burn→burned dare→dared hope→hoped open→opened talk→talked walk→walked
"-en"	Verbs	Forms the past participle of some irregular verbs.	be→been drive→driven eat→eaten give→given got→gotten sink→sunken write→written
"-en"	Nouns	Changes certain irregular nouns from singular to plural.	ox→oxen child→children brother→brethren
"-ing"	Verbs	Forms the present participle of verbs (as well as the gerund form.)	build→building

				care→caring hear→hearing pass→passing read→reading see→seeing wear→wearing
"-er"	Adjectives and Adverbs	Forms the **comparative degree** for many adjectives and adverbs.		big→bigger fast→faster* happy→happier high→higher* sad→sadder slow→slower*
"-est"	Adjectives and Adverbs	Forms the **superlative degree** for many adjectives and adverbs.		big→biggest fast→fastest* happy→happiest high→highest* sad→saddest slow→slowest*

(*These words function either as adjectives or adverbs, depending on their use. Those without an asterisk only function as adjectives.)

Derivational Suffixes

While there is only a limited number of inflectional suffixes, there is a huge amount of **derivational suffixes**. These can create a word with a new meaning that belongs to the same part of speech, but, in many cases, derivational suffixes end up changing the part of speech of the word altogether.

We'll look at a lot more of these in the section on Suffixes, but let's look at some common ones here.

Suffixes that form nouns

Suffixes that form nouns most often attach to verbs, but some attach to adjectives or even other nouns. For example:

Suffix	Suffix meaning	Attaches to	Example words
"-al"	An action or process.	Verbs	approve→approval betray→betrayal bury→burial deny→denial dispose→disposal propose→proposal renew→renewal reverse→reversal
"-er"	A person or thing performing or capable of a particular action.	Verbs	bake→baker compose→composer defend→defender employ→employer interview→interviewer keep→keeper teach→teacher write→writer
"-hood"	1. A state, quality, or condition. 2. A group sharing a state, quality, or condition.	Nouns	adult→adulthood boy→boyhood brother→brotherhood child→childhood father→fatherhood girl→girlhood knight→knighthood man→manhood mother→motherhood

Spelling Conventions

			parent→parenthood sister→sisterhood woman→womanhood
"-ication"	A state, condition, action, process, or practice, or the result thereof.	Verbs ending in "-fy"	amplify→amplification clarify→clarification dignify→dignification falsify→falsifiication glorify→glorification identify→identification justify→justification modify→modification quantify→quantification simplify→simplification unify→unification
"-ism"	1. An action, process, or practice. 2. A state, condition, or quality. 3. A doctrine, theory, or set of guiding principles.	1. Verbs 2 & 3. Adjectives	active→activism antagonize→antagonism baptize→baptism criticize→criticism colloquial→colloquialism conservative→conservatism exorcize→exorciism feminine→feminism liberal→liberalism metabolize→metabolism modern→modernism pacific→pacifism
"-ment"	An action or process, or the result thereof.	Verbs	adjust→adjustment bereave→bereavement contain→containment disappoint→disappointment employ→employment fulfill→fulfillment judge→judgment move→movement place→placement resent→resentment treat→treatment
"-ness"	A state, condition, trait, or measurement thereof.	Adjectives	alert→alertness cold→coldness dark→darkness exact→exactness fierce→fierceness happy→happiness kind→kindness like→likeness selfish→selfishness useful→usefulness
"-tion"	A state, condition, action, process, or practice, or the result thereof.	Verbs	act→action affect→affection communicate→communication complete→completion direct→direction educate→education evolve→evolution inscribe→inscription interrupt→interruption misconceive→misconception resolve→resolution subscribe→subscription translate→translation

Suffixes that form verbs

Derivational suffixes that create verbs attach to nouns and adjectives:

Suffix	Suffix meaning	Attaches to	Example words
"-en"	1. To become or cause to become. 2. To come or cause to have.	1. Adjectives 2. Nouns	black→black**en** broad→broad**en** cheap→cheap**en** fright→fright**en** hard→hard**en** heart→heart**en** length→length**en** red→redd**en** sharp→sharp**en** sick→sick**en** strength→strength**en**
"-ify"	To make or cause to become.	Adjectives, nouns	ample→ampl**ify** beauty→beaut**ify** clear→clar**ify** diverse→divers**ify** dignity→dign**ify** glory→glor**ify** just→just**ify** pure→pur**ify** null→null**ify** simple→simpl**ify** type→typ**ify**
"-ize"	To become or cause to become; to do or make that to which the suffix is attached.	Adjectives, nouns	accessory→accessor**ize** apology→apolog**ize** capital→capital**ize** civil→civil**ize** economy→econom**ize** empathy→empath**ize** fertile→fertil**ize** industrial→industrial**ize** legal→legal**ize** human→human**ize** standard→standard**ize** theory→theor**ize** union→union**ize**

Suffixes that form adjectives

Derivational suffixes that create adjectives usually attach to nouns; much less often, they attach to verbs. For example:

Suffix	Suffix meaning	Attaches to	Example words
"-able"	Possible; capable of; suitable for.	Verbs	adore→adorable break→breakable debate→debatable do→doable excite→excitable live→livable manage→manageable read→readable stop→stoppable
"-al"	Having the characteristics of or relating to.	Nouns	artifice→artificial bride→bridal brute→brutal center→central emotion→emotional form→formal logic→logical music→musical politics→political space→spatial tide→tidal
"-ful"	1. Full of; characterized by. 2. Tending or able to.	1. Nouns 2. Verbs	beauty→beautiful care→careful delight→delightful forget→forgetful grace→graceful joy→joyful law→lawful mourn→mournful play→playful respect→respectful waste→wasteful
"-ic"	Having the characteristics of or relating to.	Nouns	acid→acidic base→basic comedy→comedic galaxy→galactic hero→heroic irony→ironic magnet→magnetic myth→mythic nostalgia→nostalgic poetry→poetic rhythm→rhythmic system→systemic
"-ish"	1. Typical of, similar to, or related to. 2. Of or associated with (a particular nationality, region, or language). 3. Inclined to or preoccupied with.	Nouns	book→bookish boy→boyish Britain→British child→childish clown→clownish Denmark→Danish

			fiend→fiend**ish** girl→girl**ish** nightmare→nightmar**ish** prude→prud**ish** self→self**ish** Spain→Span**ish** Sweden→Swed**ish**
"-less"	Lacking; deprived of; without.	Nouns	aim→aim**less** blame→blame**less** color→color**less** doubt→doubt**less** home→home**less** hope→hope**less** limit→limit**less** need→need**less** point→point**less** rest→rest**less** self→self**less** time→time**less** use→use**less**
"-ous"	Possessing; characterized by; full of.	Nouns	advantage→advantage**ous** caution→caut**ious** disaster→disastr**ous** fame→fam**ous** glamor→glamor**ous** joy→joy**ous** malice→malic**ious** nutrition→nutrit**ious** religion→religi**ous** pretense→pretent**ious** poison→poison**ous** suspicion→suspic**ious**
"-y"	1. Characterized by; consisting or having the quality of; filled with. 2. Tending or inclined to.	1. Nouns 2. Verbs	bulk→bulk**y** class→class**y** dream→dream**y** ease→eas**y** leak→leak**y** mess→mess**y** rain→rain**y** rope→rop**y** shine→shin**y** smell→smell**y** wimp→wimp**y**

Suffixes that form adverbs

By far the most common and well-known suffix that creates adverbs by attaching to adjectives is "**-ly.**" However, there are two others derivational suffixes that form adverbs: "**-ways/-wise**" and "**-ward.**" For example:

Suffix	Suffix meaning	Attaches to	Example words
"**-ly**"	1. In a certain or specified manner. 2. At that interval of time.	1. Adjectives 2. Nouns (units of time)	abrupt→abrupt**ly** calm→calm**ly** day→dai**ly** double→doub**ly** easy→easi**ly** extreme→extreme**ly** full→ful**ly** happy→happi**ly** lucky→lucki**ly** month→month**ly** probable→probab**ly** quiet→quiet**ly** right→right**ly** smart→smart**ly** true→tru**ly** whole→whol**ly** year→year**ly**
"**-ways/-wise**" ("-wise" is much more common, especially in American English, except with the root *side*, which almost always becomes *sideways*)	1. In a specified manner, direction, or position. 2. With reference or in regard to. (sometimes hyphenated)	Nouns, adjectives	clock→clock**wise** business→business**wise** edge→edge**wise** (occasionally: *edgeways*) health→health-**wise** length→length**wise** (occasionally: *lengthways*) like→like**wise** other→other**wise** side→side**ways** weather→weather-**wise**
"**-ward**"	In a specified direction or position.	Nouns, adjectives, adverbs	back→back**ward** down→down**ward** east→east**ward** fore→for**ward** front→front**ward** home→home**ward** north→north**ward** on→on**ward** south→south**ward** to→to**ward** west→west**ward**

Other Affixes

While prefixes and suffixes are by far the most common types of affixes in English, there are a few others that appear less often: interfixes, simulfixes, circumfixes, infixes, and suprafixes. Some of these are like prefixes and suffixes, in that they attach a new letter or letters to an existing base word or root to create a new term; others function by *changing* a letter within a word, or by changing the *pronunciation* of a word.

Interfixes

An interfix (also known as a **linking element**) is a single letter (usually a vowel, and especially **O**) that doesn't have specific meaning in itself, but instead acts as a connector between different words, roots, or word-forming elements.

For example:
- arachn**o**phobia (**O** replaces "-id" from *arachnid*)
- disc**o**graphy (**O** attaches to the word *disc*)
- ego**t**ism (**T** attaches to the word *ego*)
- embryo**n**ic (**N** attaches to the word *embryo*)
- film**o**graphy (**O** attaches to the word *film*)
- hallucin**o**gen (**O** replaces "-ation" from *hallucination*)
- herb**i**cide (**I** attaches to the word *herb*)
- ion**o**sphere (**O** attaches to the word *ion*)
- klept**o**mania (**O** replaces "-es" from the Greek root *kleptes*)
- lob**o**tomy (**O** replaces "-e" from *lobe*)
- pest**i**cide (**I** attaches to the word *pest*)
- speed**o**meter (**O** attaches to the word *speed*)
- trache**o**tomy (**O** replaces "-a" from *trachea*)

There are also a number of informal, colloquial, or humorous terms that writers sometimes coin by using an interfix with a noun and familiar ending to mimic the structure of standard words. For example:
- applause-**o**-meter (mimics words like *speedometer*)
- blog**o**sphere (mimics words like *atmosphere*)
- rodent**i**cide (mimics words like *pesticide*)
- germ**o**phobia/germ**a**phobia (mimics words like *arachnophobia*)
- smell-**o**-vision (mimics the word *television*)

Simulfixes

A **simulfix** is a letter or group of letters that changes within a word (rather than being added to it) to indicate a shift in grammatical meaning. The most common of these occur in nouns that have irregular plural forms or verbs with irregular conjugations. For example:

Irregular Nouns	Irregular Verbs
man→m**e**n	swim→sw**a**m→sw**u**m
woman→wom**e**n	sing→s**a**ng→s**u**ng
mouse→m**i**ce	see→s**aw**
goose→g**ee**se	run→r**a**n
louse→l**i**ce	grow→gr**ew**
tooth→t**ee**th	ride→r**o**de
foot→f**ee**t	sit→s**a**t
knife→kni**v**es	get→g**o**t
wolf→wol**v**es	give→g**a**ve
leaf→lea**v**es	drive→dr**o**ve
thief→thie**v**es	think→th**ought**

Circumfixes

Circumfixes are word elements that appear at both the end and beginning of a base word, usually forming transitive verbs. There are only a few words that could be said to feature circumfixes in English:
- **en**light**en**
- **en**liv**en**
- **em**bold**en**
- **e**vapor**ate**

Infixes

Infixes are words or word elements that appear within a base word, usually separated by hyphens. There are no "true" infixes in English; instead, they are all formed colloquially in speech and writing, typically for the sake of adding emphasis to a word.

Most commonly, infixes are used with words that have more than two syllables, and they usually consist of expletives (curse words) or minced oaths (euphemistic expressions meant to represent expletives without using the actual words).

For example:
• abso-**bloody**-lutely
• fan-**frickin'**-tastic
• un-**stinkin'**-believable

Suprafix

A **suprafix** (sometimes called a **superfix**) is unique among affixes in that it refers to a change in a word's *pronunciation* to indicate a difference in grammatical function and meaning, rather than a change in spelling. The name comes from the term *suprasegmental*, which refers to speech sounds like stress and pitch rather than those related to the pronunciation of letters.

Most often, suprafixes occur with words that can function as either a noun or a verb. For example:

Word	Noun	Verb
contest	**con**·test (/ˈkɑn.tɛst/)	con·**test** (/kənˈtɛst/)
desert	**des**·ert (/ˈdɛz.ərt/)	de·**sert** (/dɪˈzɜrt/)
increase	**in**·crease (/ˈɪn.kris/)	in·**crease** (/ɪnˈkris/)
object	**ob**·ject (/ˈɑb.dʒɛkt/)	ob·**ject** (/əbˈdʒɛkt/)
permit	**per**·mit (/ˈpɜr.mɪt/)	per·**mit** (/ˈpɜr.mɪt/)
present	**pres**·ent (/ˈprɛz.ənt/	pre·**sent** (/prɪˈzɛnt/)
project	**proj**·ect (/ˈprɑdʒ.ɛkt/)	pro·**ject** (/prəˈdʒɛkt/)
rebel	**reb**·el (/ˈrɛb.əl/)	re·**bel** (/rɪˈbɛl/)
record	**rec**·ord (/ˈrɛk.ərd/)	re·**cord** (/rəˈkɔrd/)
refuse	**ref**·use (/ˈrɛf.juz/)	re·**fuse** (/rɪˈfjuz/)
subject	**sub**·ject (/ˈsʌb.dʒɛkt/)	sub·**ject** (/səbˈdʒɛkt/)

Quiz
(answers start on page 463)

1. Which type of affix appears at the **beginning** of a word?

a) Prefix
b) Suffix
c) Interfix
d) Suprafix

2. Which type of affix appears in the **middle** of a word?

a) Prefix
b) Suffix
c) Interfix
d) Suprafix

3. Which type of affix can be **inflectional**?

a) Prefix
b) Suffix
c) Interfix
d) Suprafix

4. To which part of a word do *circumfixes* attach?

a) The beginning
b) The middle
c) The end
d) A & B
e) B & C
f) A & C

5. Which type of affix changes the **pronunciation** of a word, rather than the spelling?

a) Prefix
b) Suffix
c) Interfix
d) Suprafix

Prefixes

Definition

Prefixes are **morphemes** (specific groups of letters with particular semantic meaning) that are added onto the <u>beginning</u> of **roots** and **base words** to change their meaning. Prefixes are one of the two predominant kinds of affixes—the other kind is suffixes, which come at the <u>end</u> of a root word.

Unlike suffixes, which can be either inflectional (changing only the grammatical function of a word without changing its basic meaning) or derivational (creating a word with an entirely new meaning), prefixes can <u>only</u> be derivational; adding a prefix always changes the basic meaning of the word.

In this section, we'll look at some of the most commonly used prefixes, but first let's look at some conventions regarding how they're used.

Adding prefixes to words

Prefixes generally do not affect the spelling of the root word to which they are attached: they are simply placed immediately before the word without a space (although some, as we'll discuss later, may be attached with a hyphen).

However, while a root word's spelling does not change with a prefix, we do sometimes have to alter the prefix *itself* depending on the spelling of the word it precedes. For example, the prefix **a-** becomes **a<u>n</u>-** when coming before a vowel; the prefix **in-**, meanwhile, can change to **ig-** (before *n-*), **il-** (before *l-*), **im-** (before *b-, m-,* or *p-*), or **ir-** (before **r-**).

In addition, many prefixes are only able (or only tend) to attach to certain parts of speech. For example, the prefix **un-** (meaning "not") generally only attaches to adjectives, as in *unhappy* or *uncomfortable*; when **un-** means "to do the opposite of," it only attaches to verbs, as in *uncork* or *unlock*. Attaching **un-** to a root noun, on the other hand, is usually not done. For instance, *undesk* or *unsky* are incorrect. While technically correct words, *unhuman* and *unbelief* are not very common; we would more usually write *nonhuman* and *disbelief*.

Adding prefixes to foreign roots

Many prefixes will attach to both existing English base words as well as roots derived from foreign stems (parts of longer words used to form combinations), most often Latin or Greek.

When we look at examples of common prefixes further on, we'll distinguish when prefixes attach to existing English words (adjectives, nouns, or verbs), Latin and/or Greek roots, or both. Note that some guides may call prefixes that attach to foreign-language roots "combining forms" rather than prefixes, a distinction that we'll touch upon next.

Prefixes vs. Combining Forms

When defining different prefixes, a distinction is sometimes made between "true" prefixes and "**combining forms**" of words. The precise definition of one compared to the other is not often clear, and, depending on the source, the distinction between the two is often inconsistent or contradictory.

The simplest explanation tends to be that a prefix can only attach to a base word (an English word that can be used on its own without a prefix or suffix), while a combining form is an adaptation of a larger word (typically Greek or Latin) that only attaches to another combining form (meaning neither element cannot stand on its own as an independent word).

What complicates this distinction is the fact that a morpheme could be considered a prefix in one instance and a combining form in another. For example, *auto-*, meaning "of or by the same person or thing," functions like a "true" prefix in the word *autoimmune*, but it is usually considered a combining form, as in the word *autonomy*. Likewise, *ex-* as a prefix meaning "former" (as in *ex-boyfriend*) is sometimes contrasted with *ex-* as a combining form meaning "out" (as in *exclude*), yet the morpheme is more often considered a prefix in both cases by most dictionaries.

In reality, prefixes and combining forms behave the same way and essentially perform the same function in a word, so there's no real benefit in dividing them into two separate categories. Doing so simply adds an unnecessary complication, especially for those learning the fundamentals of the language. As such, the list of common prefixes we'll look at next makes no distinction between prefixes and combining forms—it's more important to understand the different meanings they can have so that we can see a pattern in the way words are formed and spelled.

Common prefixes

In the table below, we'll look at different prefixes that commonly appear in English, noting their various meanings, the parts of speech they most typically attach to, and several example words in which they appear.

It's important to note that this is by no means a complete list; there are far too many to include here. Rather, it is intended to give you an idea of how prefixes are used and how they may affect the meaning and spelling of words we use every day.

Prefix	Meaning	Usually attaches to	Example words
a- (1) (**an-** before a vowel)	Not; without.	adjectives, Greek roots (and, less commonly, nouns)	*agnostic, amoral, apathy, apolitical, asexual, asymmetry, atonal, atypical, anaerobic, anarchy, anecdote, anemia, anesthetic*
a- (2)	1. On; in; towards. 2. In a certain condition or state. 3. Of.	1. nouns 2. verbs 3. adjectives (and occasionally nouns)	1. *aback, aground, aside, away* 2. *abide, ablaze, afloat, ashamed, asleep, awake* 3. *afar, afresh, akin, anew*
ab- (Changes to **abs-** before *c-* or *t-*; sometimes reduces to **a-** before Latin roots beginning with *v-*.)	Away from; outside of; opposite to; off.	French and Latin roots (and, rarely, adjectives)	*abdicate, abduct, abhor, abject, abnormal, abscess, abscond, absolute, absorb, abstain, abstract, avert*
ad- This prefix has many forms, usually changing to match the consonant it precedes: • **a-** before roots beginning with *sc-* or *sp-* • **ac-** before roots beginning with *c-* or *q-* • **af-** before roots beginning with *f-* • **ag-** before roots beginning with *g-* • **al-** before roots beginning with *l-* • **an-** before roots beginning with *n-* • **ap-** before roots beginning with *p-* • **as-** before roots beginning with *s-* • **at-** before roots beginning with *t-*	To; toward; near to; in the direction or vicinity of.	Latin roots	• (ad-): *adapt, address, adequate, adrenal, advance, adventure* • (a-): *ascend, ascertain, aspire, aspect* • (ac-): *accept, accident, acquire, acquit* • (af-): *affair, affect, affirm, affix* • (ag-): *aggrandize, aggravate, aggression* • (al-): *allege, allot, allow, allure* • (an-): *annex, annihilate, annotate, announce* • (ap-): *appall, appeal, applaud, apply, approve* • (as-): *assail, assault, assemble, assert, assign* • (at-): *attain, attempt, attire, attribute, attract*
ante- (Occasionally becomes **anti-**)	1. Prior to; earlier than. 2. Before; in front of.	1. adjectives 2. nouns, Latin roots	1. *antediluvian, antenatal, antepenultimate* 2. *antecedent, anticipate, antechamber, antechoir, anteroom*
anti- (Occasionally hyphenated; sometimes **ant-** before a vowel, especially *a-*)	1. Equal and opposite to. 2. Opposing; against; prejudicial to. 3. Counteracting; destroying; neutralizing. 4. Enemy of or rival to; false version of.	1. nouns, Greek roots 2. adjectives, nouns 3. adjectives, nouns 4. nouns	1. *antarctic, anticatalyst, anticlimax, antidote, antihero, antimatter, antipodes, antithesis, antonym* 2. *antagonist, antiapartheid, anticolonial, anticorruption, antidiscrimination, antiestablishment, antigovernment, antisocial, anti-war* 3. *anti-aircraft, antibacterial,*

			*anti*convulsive, **anti**depressant, **anti**fungal, **anti**freeze, **anti**histamine, **anti**pyretic, **anti**toxin, **anti**viral 4. **anti**christ, **anti**pope
auto- (occasionally reduced to **aut-** before vowels)	1. Self; one's own; of, regarding, or performed by the same person or thing. 2. Derived from *automatic* (sometimes hyphenated). 3. Derived from *automobile* (sometimes hyphenated).	1. nouns, adjectives, Latin and Greek roots 2. nouns, verbs 3. nouns	1. *autarchy*, *autism*, *autobiography*, *autoclave*, *autocracy*, *autograph*, *autoimmune*, *automatic*, *automobile*, *automotive*, *autonomy*, *autopsy* 2. *autofocus*, *autocorrect*, *autopilot*, *autosave*, *autosuggest*, *auto-tune* 3. *autobus*, *autocross*, *automaker*, *auto-mechanic*
be-	1. To make, cause to be, or act as. 2. Adorned, covered, or provided with. 3. Thoroughly, excessively, completely; all over or all around. 4. At; about; against; for; on; over; regarding; to.	1. adjectives, nouns 2. adjectives (past participles ending in *-ed*) 3. verbs (acts as an intensive) 4. intransitive verbs (makes them transitive)	1. *becalm*, *bedim*, *befriend*, *beguile*, *belate*, *belittle*, *besiege*, *bewitch* 2. *bejewelled*, *beloved*, *bespectacled* 3. *bedevil*, *bedrivel*, *befog*, *behave*, *belong*, *bemuse*, *berate*, *bereave*, *beset*, *bespatter*, *besmirch* 4. *befall*, *befit*, *beget*, *begrudge*, *belabor*, *bemoan*, *bespeak*, *bewail*
bi- (Very rarely, becomes **bin-** before vowels)	1. Two. 2. Having or involving two. 3. Occurring at intervals of two; less formally, occurring twice within that interval.	1. nouns, Latin roots (and, less often, verbs) 2. adjectives 3. adjectives, adverbs	1. *biceps*, *bicycle*, *bifurcate*, *bipartisan*, *biped*, *bisect* 2. *bifocal*, *biconcave*, *biconvex*, *bilingual*, *binaural*, *binocular*, *bidirectional*, *bilateral*, *bipolar* 3. *biannual*, *bicentennial*, *bihourly*, *bimonthly*, *biweekly*
bio- (sometimes **bi-** before **o-**)	1. Indicating living organisms or organic life. 2. Indicating a person's life, career, or accomplishments.	1. adjectives, nouns, Greek or Latin roots 2. Used with the Greek root *graphia*	1. *bioavailability*, *biochemistry*, *biodegradable*, *biodiversity*, *bioelectric*, *bioengineer*, *biology*, *bioluminescence*, *bionics*, *biophysics*, *biopsy*, *biotic* 2. *biography*
co- Occurs before roots beginning with vowels or the consonants *h-* and *gn-*; it is also used to form newer compound terms (which are often hyphenated). This prefix is the common reduced form of **com-**, the original Latin prefix, which occurs before roots beginning *b-*, *m-*, or *p-*. It also takes three other forms, depending on the letter it precedes: • **col-** before roots beginning with *l-* • **cor-** before roots beginning with *r-* • **con-** before roots beginning with consonants other than *b-*, *h-*, *gn-*, *l-*, *m-*, *p-* or *r-*	1. From the original prefix: together; together with; joint; jointly; mutually. Also used as an intensifier. 2. In newer terms, co- can indicate: joint(ly), mutual(ly), or together (with); partnership or equality; a subordinate or assistant; to the same degree or extent; or (in mathematics) the complement of an angle.	1. Latin roots 2. adjectives, nouns, verbs	1. • (co-): *coagulate*, *coerce*, *coincide*, *cognate*, *cognizance* • (com-): *combat*, *combine*, *combust*, *commingle*, *commiserate*, *commit*, *compact*, *compare*, *complex* • (col-): *collaborate*, *collapse*, *colleague*, *collect*, *collide*, *collude* • (con-): *conceal*, *conceive*, *condemn*, *conduct*, *confer*, *confine*, *congress*, *congratulate*, *conjoin*, *connect*, *connive*, *conquer*, *conscience*, *constant*, *contact*, *contain*, *converge* • (cor-): *correct*, *correlate*, *correspond*, *corrode*, *corrupt* 2. *co-author*, *codependent*, *codominant*, *co-driver*, *coexist*, *coeducation*, *co-manage*, *cooperate*, *co-pilot*, *cosine*, *cotangent*, *co-worker*

contra- (becomes **contro-** in one instance before *v-*)	Opposite; against; in the opposite direction.	nouns, Latin roots	*contraband, contraception, contradiction, contradistinction, contraindication, contrast, contravene, controversy*
counter- (This is derived from the original Latin prefix **contra-**; it is often used in more modern word formations, though this is not always the case.)	1. Opposing; against; opposite. 2. Corresponding or complementary; offsetting. 3. In response to; thwarting or refuting.	adjectives, nouns, verbs (less commonly, Latin roots or words whose meaning is derived from Latin origins)	1. *counterclaim, counterclockwise, counterculture, counterfeit, counterintuitive, countermand, counterproductive, countervail* 2. *counteract, counterbalance, counterfoil, countermelody, counterpart, countersign, countervail, counterweight* 3. *counterattack, counterexample, counteroffer, counteroffensive, countermarch, countermeasure, counterpoint, counterproposal, counterstrike*
de- (sometimes hyphenated when followed by a vowel)	1. To reverse; to do or cause to be the opposite. 2. To extract, remove, or eliminate from; to be without. 3. Out of; away from; off. 4. To reduce; to lower; to move down from. 5. Thoroughly or completely (used as an intensifier).	1. nouns, verbs, Latin roots 2. nouns, verbs, Latin roots 3. nouns, verbs, Latin roots 4. nouns, Latin roots 5. verbs	1. *decaffeinate, decelerate, decriminalize, decode, decommission, decompose, deconstruct, de-emphasize, desegregate, destabilize* 2. *debunk, decalcify, deglaze, de-ice, delouse, despair, dethrone* 3. *decamp, defect, deflect, deplane, detrain* 4. *declass, degrade, deject, demean, descend, detest* 5. *debrief, defraud, despoil*
dia- (becomes **di-** before vowels)	Across; between; from point to point; through; throughout.	Latin and Greek roots	*diagnosis, diagonal, diagram, dialect, dialogue, diameter, diaper, diaphragm, diocese*
dis- (becomes **dif-** when combining with Latin roots beginning *f-*)	1. Lacking; without; not. 2. To do or cause to be the opposite. 3. Apart; out of; away from; off. 4. To extract, cancel, remove, or release. 5. Indicating intensive force.	1. adjectives, nouns 2. verbs 3. verbs, Latin roots 4. nouns, verbs 5. verbs, Latin roots	1. *disability, disadvantage, disbelief, disease, dishonest, disservice, dissimilar, distemper, distrust, disuse* 2. *disagree, disassociate, disavow, disbelieve, disconnect, discredit, disgrace, disprove* 3. *differ, difficulty, diffraction, diffuse, discard, discord, discharge, disembark, dispense* 4. *disbar, disbud, disburse, disenfranchise, disenchant, disentangle* 5. *disannul, disembowel, disturb*
en- (1) (becomes **em-** before words beginning with *b-* or *p-*, except in the word *enplane*)	1. To make or cause to be. 2. To go or put in, on, or near. 3. To cover, surround, or provide with. 4. Indicating intensive force.	1. adjectives, nouns 2. nouns 3. nouns 4. verbs	1. *enable, enamour, embitter, endear, engender, enrich, enslave, enthrone, entomb entrust* 2. *embattle, encircle, enplane, enthrone, entomb* 3. *encapsulate, enclose, engulf, enmesh, empower, enrobe* 4. *enkindle, enlighten, enliven, enrage, entangle*
en- (2) (becomes **em-** before words beginning with *b-* or *p-*)	In; inside; into; within.	Latin or Greek roots	*energy, endemic, emphasis, empathy, employ, enthusiasm*

ex- (1) (reduced to **e-** before *b-, d-, g-, j-, l-, m-, n-, r-* and *v-*, or becomes **ef-** before *f-*)	1. Away; from; outward; out of; upwards. 2. Completely; thoroughly.	Latin roots (occasionally attaches to existing nouns and verbs, but the meaning is derived from their Latin origin)	1. *ebullient, edify, **ef**fect, **ef**face, **ef**fort, **e**gress, **e**ject, **e**lation, **e**mancipate, **e**merge, **e**normous, **ex**alt, **ex**cel, **ex**change, **ex**clude, **ex**communicate, **ex**patriate, **ex**perience, **ex**tol, **e**vacuation, **e**valuate, **e**vaporation* 2. *exacerbation, exasperate, excruciate, exhilarate, exhortation, expect, exuberant*
ex- (2) (always hyphenated)	Former.	nouns	*ex-banker, ex-boyfriend, ex-girlfriend, ex-husband, ex-marine, ex-partner, ex-priest, ex-teacher, ex-wife*
fore-	1. Before; earlier; previous in time. 2. In front of; at or near the front; before or previous in position or location.	1. verbs 2. nouns	1. ***fore**bear, **fore**bode, **fore**cast, **fore**close, **fore**go, **fore**judge, **fore**see, **fore**shadow, **fore**tell, **fore**warn* 2. ***fore**arm, **fore**brain, **fore**deck, **fore**father, **fore**finger, **fore**ground, **fore**head, **fore**leg, **fore**man, **fore**sail*
hyper-	1. Above; beyond; higher; over. 2. Extreme; exceedingly; abnormally excessive.	nouns, adjectives, verbs, Greek and Latin Roots	1. ***hyper**charge, **hyper**extend, **hyper**immune, **hyper**sonic* 2. ***hyper**active, **hyper**alert, **hyper**acuity, **hyper**bole, **hyper**calcemia, **hyper**inflation, **hyper**sensitive, **hyper**tension, **hyper**thermia, **hyper**vigilance*
hypo- (occasionally reduced to **hyp-** before a vowel, especially *o-*)	1. Beneath; lower; underneath. 2. Abnormally deficient; less or lower than normal.	nouns and adjectives, but more commonly Greek and Latin Roots	1. ***hyp**abyssal, **hypo**dermic, **hypo**chondria, **hypo**crisy, **hypo**stasis, **hypo**tenuse, **hypo**thesis* 2. ***hyp**algesia, **hypo**allergenic, **hypo**glycemia, **hypo**mania, **hypo**tension, **hypo**thermia, **hyp**oxia*
in- This prefix also takes four other forms, depending on the letter it precedes: • **i-** before roots beginning with *gn-* • **il-** before roots beginning with *l-* • **im-** before roots beginning with *b-, m-,* or *p-* • **ir-** before roots beginning with *r-* Note that in meanings 2 & 3, **in-** functions as a less common variant of **en-** when forming verbs.	1. Not; non-; opposite of; without. 2. Into; in; on; upon. 3. To make or cause to be.	1. adjectives, Latin roots 2. adjectives, nouns, verbs, Latin roots 3. nouns	1. ***i**gnoble, **i**gnominious, **i**gnorant, **il**legal, **il**literate, **il**logical, **im**balanced, **im**becile, **im**material, **im**mature, **im**movable, **im**practical, **im**perfect, **im**possible, **in**nocent, **in**nocuous, **in**sane, **in**sincere, **in**tolerable, **ir**rational, **ir**reparable, **ir**reversible* 2. ***il**luminate, **il**lusion, **il**lustrate, **im**bue, **in**filtrate, **in**flux, **in**land, **in**nervate, **in**novate, **in**nuendo, **in**quire, **in**scribe, **in**sect, **in**tend, **ir**radiate, **ir**rigate* 3. ***in**flame, **im**peril, **im**prove*
mal-	1. Bad; wrong; improper; imperfect; defective; abnormal. 2. Badly; wrongly; improperly; imperfectly; defectively; abnormally.	1. nouns, Latin roots 2. adjectives, verbs, Latin roots (**Mal-** most commonly attaches to modern nouns and adjectives that are derived from verbs via suffixation; it's far less common for it to attach to non-suffixed verbs, though it does happen.)	1. ***mal**absorption, **mal**ady, **mal**adjustment, **mal**feasance, **mal**function, **mal**aise, **mal**efactor, **mal**ice, **mal**nutrition, **mal**practice* 2. ***mal**adjusted, **mal**adroit, **mal**administer, **mal**content, **mal**formed, **mal**function, **mal**ign, **mal**nourished, **mal**odorous*

mid-	At, near, or approximating the middle.	nouns	*mid*afternoon, *mid*air, *mid*brain, *mid*day, *mid*land, *mid*life, *mid*morning, *mid*night, *mid*point, *mid*range, *mid*size, *mid*summer, *mid*way
mis- (**Mis-** is in many ways identical to **mal-**, though **mis-** is much more likely to be paired with verbs.)	1. Bad; wrong; improper; imperfect; defective; abnormal. 2. Badly; wrongly; improperly; imperfectly; defectively; abnormally.	1. nouns 2. verbs	1. *mis*adventure, *mis*balance, *mis*conception, *mis*conduct, *mis*connection, *mis*diagnosis, *mis*direction, *mis*deed, *mis*givings, *mis*hap, *mis*information, *mis*perception, *mis*match, *mis*trust 2. *mis*adjust, *mis*behave, *mis*calculate, *mis*carry, *mis*cast, *mis*communicate, *mis*construe, *mis*dial, *mis*diagnose, *mis*hear, *mis*inform, *mis*interpret, *mis*label, *mis*lead, *mis*take, *mis*manage, *mis*represent, *mis*spell
non- (**Non-** is often hyphenated according to the preference of the writer, but it is more commonly attached *without* a hyphen in American English.)	Indicating total negation, exclusion, failure, or deficiency.	adjectives, nouns	*non*aggression, *non*alcoholic, *non*availability, *non*believer, *non*chalant, *non*combatant, *non*-cooperation, *non*compliance, *non*disclosure, *non*educational, *non*emergency, *non*event, *non*existent, *non*fiction, *non*functional, *non*hazardous, *non*human, *non*infectious, *non*lethal, *non*payment, *non*profit, *non*smoking, *non*worker
ob- This prefix can also take three other forms, depending on the letter it precedes: • **oc-** before roots beginning with *c-* • **of-** before roots beginning with *f-* • **op-** before roots beginning with *p-*	1. To; toward; across; away from; over. 2. Against; before; blocking; facing, concealing.	Latin roots	1. *ob*ey, *ob*fuscate, *ob*lige, *ob*scure, *ob*serve, *ob*tain, *oc*casion, *oc*cur, *of*fer, *op*portune 2. *ob*ject, *ob*lique, *ob*sess, *ob*struct, *ob*vious, *oc*cult, *oc*cupy, *of*fend, *op*ponent, *op*press
over-	1. Above; higher than; upon; across; outer. 2. Superior; higher-ranking. 3. Resulting in an inverted, reverse, or downwards movement or position. 4. Excessive or excessively; too much; above, beyond, or more than is normal or acceptable.	1. nouns, verbs 2. nouns 3. nouns, verbs 4. adjectives, nouns, verbs	1. *over*alls, *over*arch, *over*cast, *over*coat, *over*deck, *over*garment, *over*hand, *over*hang, *over*lap, *over*lay, *over*leaf, *over*pass, *over*see, *over*seas, *over*take, *over*view 2. *over*lord, *over*seer 3. *over*board, *over*throw, *over*rule, *over*turn, *over*whelm 4. *over*abundant, *over*achieve, *over*analyze, *over*bearing, *over*built, *over*charge, *over*compensate, *over*confident, *over*cook, *over*dose, *over*draw, *over*dress, *over*emphasize, *over*extend, *over*hear, *over*joyed, *over*laden, *over*look, *over*medicate, *over*pay, *over*qualified, *over*react, *over*regulate, *over*simplify, *over*stay, *over*think, *over*work
out-	1. Surpassing; going beyond; excelling over others. 2. External to; outside; away from the center.	1. verbs 2. noun, verbs 3. nouns 4. adjectives, verbs	1. *out*argue, *out*class, *out*distance, *out*do, *out*fox, *out*last, *out*grow, *out*gun, *out*maneuver, *out*match, *out*number, *out*pace, *out*perform, *out*rank, *out*run, *out*smart, *out*shine

	3. Indicating an emergence, protrusion, or issuing-forth. 4. Beyond what is normal, acceptable, or agreeable.		2. *outback*, *outboard*, *outbound*, *outcast*, *outcross*, *outdate*, *outdoors*, *outfield*, *outfit*, *outgoing*, *outhouse*, *outlaw*, *outlier*, *outline*, *outpatient*, *outpost*, *outreach*, *outside*, *outsource* 3. *outburst*, *outcome*, *outcrop*, *outgrowth*, *outpouring* 4. *outlandish*, *outsized*, *outspoken*, *outstay*
post- (Don't confuse this prefix with the word *post*—referring to the mail system—when it is used in compound words such as *postcard* or *postmark*.)	1. Behind; in back of. 2. Later than or afterwards in time.	adjectives, nouns, verbs, Latin roots	1. *postcranial*, *posterior*, *postfix*, *postorbital*, *postposition*, *postscript* 2. *postapocalyptic*, *postcolonial*, *postdoctoral*, *postelection*, *postgame*, *postgraduate*, *postindustrial*, *postmodernism*, *postproduction*, *postpone*, *postpositive*, *postmortem*, *postwar*
pre- (Often hyphenated before other vowels, especially *e*-, though this is less common in American English. Always hyphenated before proper nouns and non-letters)	1. Before; in front of. 2. Earlier than or beforehand in time. 3. Before, in advance, or instead of the normal occurrence.	1 & 2. adjectives, nouns, verbs, Latin roots 3. verbs	1. *preamble*, *precede*, *precinct*, *predate*, *preeminent*, *preface*, *prefer*, *prefix*, *prefrontal*, *prelude*, *preposition*, *preside*, *pretext* 2. *precept*, *precipitation*, *precocious*, *pre-date*, *predict*, *pre-emption*, *prehistory*, *preindustrial*, *prejudice*, *premature*, *premonition*, *prenatal*, *preparation*, *preproduction*, *prescience*, *preserve*, *preschool*, *preshow*, *presume*, *preview* 3. *preadmit*, *preapprove*, *preassign*, *prebook*, *preclean*, *precondition*, *predestine*, *predetermine*, *preoccupy*, *preorder*, *prepay*, *pre-position*
pro-	1. Supporting; promoting; in favor of. 2. Forward; forth; toward the point. 3. In place or on behalf of; acting or substituting for. 4. Beforehand; in advance; prior to. 5. In front; before.	1. nouns (usually hyphenated, but not always) 2, 3, 4 & 5. Greek and Latin roots (less commonly, adjective, nouns, and verbs)	1. *pro-American*, *pro-Britain*, *pro-Catholic*, *pro-choice*, *pro-life*, *pro-peace*, *pro-revolution*, *prowar* 2. *problem*, *proceed*, *proclaim*, *procreate*, *procrastination*, *profess*, *profound*, *program*, *progress*, *project*, *prolong*, *promote*, *propel*, *prosecute*, *protest*, *proverb* 3. *proconsul*, *procure*, *pronoun*, *proper*, *prorate*, *proportion* 4. *proactive*, *prognosis*, *prohibit*, *prophet*, *proscribe* 5. *proboscis*, *profane*, *pronominal*, *prologue*, *protect*
re- (This prefix becomes **red-** before Latin roots beginning with vowels. It is hyphenated when paired with English roots if the resultant spelling would be the same as an existing word; it may also be hyphenated before English roots beginning vowels, especially *e*-, but this is often up to the discretion of the writer and is not usually done in American English.)	1. Once more; again (in the same manner, direction, etc.). 2. Once more; again (with the aim of improving, fixing, or substituting). 3. Anew; restored to the original place, status, etc. 4. Against; back or in reverse; opposite; in response to. 5. Used as an intensive with Latin root verbs.	verbs, Latin roots	1. *reaffirm*, *reappear*, *reboot*, *recognize*, *recopy*, *re-cover*, *recur*, *re-dress*, *redecorate*, *redeploy*, *redesign*, *rediscover*, *reelect*, *reenact*, *reenter*, *rehearse*, *rehire*, *relearn*, *rehydrate*, *relive*, *reload*, *reregister*, *re-sign*, *restart*, *retry*, *reunite* 2. *reapply*, *reapportion*, *rebrand*, *recalculate*, *rekindle*, *relabel*, *relocate*, *remarry*, *reschedule*, *reseal*, *rethink*, *retry* 3. *reacquire*, *readjust*, *realign*,

			rebuild, *recapture*, *receive*, *regain*, *rehabilitate*, *renew*, *replace*, *restore* 4. *react*, *rebel*, *rebuff*, *recant*, *recede*, *reciprocate*, *recite*, *recoil*, *redact*, *redeem*, *redress*, *refer*, *regress*, *reject*, *relate*, *remove*, *resign*, *respond*, *return* 5. *redolent*, *refine*, *regard*, *regret*, *relieve*, *remedy*, *repent*
self- (Note that this prefix is almost always hyphenated.)	1. Of, with, in, regarding, or performed by the same person or thing. 2. Automatic; automatically.	1. nouns, adjectives 2. adjectives (usually past or present participles)	1. *self-analysis*, *self-confidence*, *self-control*, *self-deprecating*, *self-destruct*, *self-esteem*, *self-evident*, *self-fulfilling*, *self-image*, *self-importance*, *self-indulgent*, *self-interest*, *self-preservation*, *self-promotion*, *self-respect*, *self-righteous*, *selfsame*, *self-sufficient*, *self-worth* 2. *self-adhesive*, *self-driving*, *self-loading*, *self-propelled*, *self-pollinating*, *self-replicating*, *self-regulating*, *self-starting*
semi-	1. Half. 2. Incompletely; partially; partly; somewhat, almost, or resembling. 3. Occurring twice within a certain period of time.	1 & 2. adjectives, nouns 3. adjectives	1. *semicircle*, *semicolon*, *semicylinder*, *semidiameter*, *semidome*, *semifinal*, *semioval*, *semiovate* 2. *semiarticulate*, *semiautomatic*, *semiconductor*, *semiconscious*, *semidarkness*, *semidetached*, *semidry*, *semiformal*, *semiliterate*, *semiofficial*, *semipermanent*, *semiprofessional*, *semiserious*, *semiretired*, *semitransparent*, *semivowel* 3. *semiannual*, *semimonthly*, *semiweekly*
sub- When used with Latin roots, **sub-** sometimes takes different forms depending on the consonant it precedes: • **su-** before roots beginning with *s-* • **suc-** before roots beginning with *c-* • **sug-** before roots beginning with *g-* • **sup-** before roots beginning with *p-* • **sur-** before roots beginning with *r-* • occasionally **sus-** before some roots beginning with *c-, p-*, or *t-*	1. Under; below; beneath; outside or outlying. 2. At a secondary or lower position in a hierarchy. 3. Incompletely or imperfectly; partially; less than, almost, or nearly. 4. Forming a smaller part of a larger whole. 5. Up to; up from under or beneath.	1, 2, 3, & 4. adjectives, nouns, verbs, and Latin roots 5. Latin roots	1. *subaqueous*, *subcutaneous*, *subdermal*, *subject*, *submarine*, *submerge*, *submit*, *subscribe*, *subsoil*, *substrata*, *substitution*, *subterranean*, *subtle*, *subtitle*, *suburb*, *subway*, *subzero*, *suppose*, *surrogate*, *suspire* 2. *subagent*, *subaltern*, *subchief*, *subclerk*, *subcommittee*, *subcontractor*, *subeditor*, *sublet*, *subofficer*, *subordinate*, *subtreasury*, *subwriter* 3. *subarctic*, *subaquatic*, *subhuman*, *subnormal*, *subtropics* 4. *subarea*, *subcategory*, *subchapter*, *subcontinent*, *subcounty*, *subdepartment*, *subdivide*, *subfossil*, *subgenus*, *subplot*, *subregion*, *subsection*, *subspecies*, *subtype*, *subunit* 5. *sublime*, *subsist*, *substance*, *subtraction*, *succeed*, *suggest*, *support*, *surreptitious*, *susceptible*, *suspect*, *suspend*, *sustain*

Spelling Conventions

trans- (usually becomes **tran-** before roots beginning with *s-*)	1. Across; beyond; through; on the other side. 2. Completely change or alter.	1. adjectives, verbs, Latin roots 2. nouns, verbs, Latin roots	1. ***trans**action, **trans**atlantic, **trans**cend, **trans**fer, **trans**fix, **trans**fuse, **trans**generational, **trans**gress, **trans**ient, **trans**lucent, **trans**mit, **trans**national, **trans**pacific, **trans**parent, **trans**plant, **trans**port* 2. ***trans**cribe, **trans**duce, **trans**figure, **trans**form, **trans**gender, **trans**late, **trans**literate, **trans**mute, **tran**substantiate*
ultra-	1. Located beyond or on the far side of a certain point; exceeding the normal range or limit of a certain threshold. 2. Extremely; more than customary. 3. Radically; excessively; on the fringe of what is considered normal or acceptable.	adjectives, nouns	1. ***ultra**filter, **ultra**microscope, **ultra**sonic, **ultra**sound, **ultra**structure, **ultra**violet* 2. ***ultra**dense, **ultra**dry, **ultra**efficient, **ultra**fine, **ultra**high, **ultra**hot, **ultra**modern, **ultra**powerful, **ultra**vacuum* 3. ***ultra**conservative, **ultra**liberal, **ultra**nationalism, **ultra**orthodox, **ultra**violence*
un- (1) Hyphenated before proper nouns and adjectives. Note that some adjectives that are preceded by **un-** will have noun-form equivalents that take the prefix **in-** instead, as in *un**equal**/in**equality*** or *un**stable**/in**stability***.	1. Not. 2. Used to form certain negative adjectival phrases. 3. Opposite of or contrary to; lacking or absent.	1. adjectives (not counting nouns formed from prefixed adjectives) 2. past-participle adjectives + prepositions 3. nouns	1. ***un**able, **un**accompanied, **un**-American, **un**believable, **un**biased, **un**-British, **un**certain, **un**clear, **un**due, **un**employed, **un**ending, **un**familiar, **un**foreseen, **un**graceful, **un**guided, **un**happy, **un**healthy, **un**informed, **un**just, **un**kind, **un**knowing, **un**lawful, **un**likely, **un**lucky, **un**manned, **un**persuaded, **un**professional, **un**rated, **un**reasonable, **un**scathed, **un**solved, **un**tried, **un**trustworthy, **un**wise, **un**written* 2. ***un**asked-for, **un**called-for, **un**dreamed-of, **un**-get-at-able, **un**heard-of* 3. ***un**belief, **un**concern, **un**interest, **un**military, **un**rest, **un**truth*
un- (2) The first usage of **un-** forms adjectives or, less commonly, nouns, while this second usage forms verbs.	1. To reverse, erase, or undo an action or effect. 2. To deprive of, extract, or remove. 3. To free, remove, or release from. 4. Used as an intensifier with existing verbs that have the same meaning.	1. verbs 2. nouns 3. nouns 4. verbs	1. ***un**bend, **un**bind, **un**bolt, **un**clog, **un**coil, **un**cork, **un**do, **un**dress, **un**fasten, **un**fold, **un**furl, **un**hook, **un**load, **un**lock, **un**plug, **un**screw, **un**scramble, **un**seal, **un**sheathe, **un**ravel, **un**roll, **un**tangle, **un**wind* 2. ***un**balance, **un**cloak, **un**frock, **un**horse, **un**man, **un**mask, **un**seat, **un**veil* 3. ***un**burden, **un**box, **un**cage, **un**crate, **un**earth, **un**harness, **un**hitch, **un**leash, **un**wrap **un**yoke* 4. ***un**loose, **un**ravel*
under-	1. Located beneath or below; lower in position. 2. Inferior; lesser or lower in rank. 3. Less (in degree, amount, rate, etc.), usually than is considered appropriate or normal.	1. nouns, verbs 2. nouns 3. adjectives, nouns, verbs	1. ***under**arm, **under**belly, **under**clothes, **under**cover, **under**foot, **under**garment, **under**ground, **under**lay, **under**lie, **under**mine, **under**pass, **under**pin, **under**score, **under**sea, **under**tone, **under**tow, **under**water* 2. ***under**boss, **under**classmen,

			*under*graduate, *under*secretary, *under*sheriff, *under*study 3. *under*age, *under*appreciate, *under*developed, *under*employed, *under*estimate, *under*feed, *under*fund, *under*nourished, *under*pay, *under*rate, *under*report, *under*staff, *under*weight
up-	1. Up; upper; upwards; higher. 2. Greater; better; denoting increase.	1. nouns, verbs 2. nouns, verbs	1. *update*, *up*heave, *up*hold, *up*end, *up*land, *up*load, *up*on, *up*right, *up*roar, *up*root, *up*sell, *up*set, *up*stairs, *up*take, *up*wind 2. *up*grade, *up*lift, *up*rate, *up*scale, *up*start, *up*tick, *up*turn

Hyphenating prefixes

As you can see from the examples we've looked at, the vast majority of prefixes don't require a hyphen when they are attached to a root. However, it is sometimes the case that adding a prefix to a stem can result in a word that is difficult or confusing to read, or else results in a spelling that overlaps with an existing word. In these cases, we can use a hyphen between the prefix and the stem word to clarify the meaning of the new word.

Multiple vowels

Many writers choose to add a hyphen when the last letter of the prefix and the first letter of the root are both vowels (especially when they are the same letter) so as to avoid creating a word that is difficult or confusing to read. For example:
• *co-* + *operate* = *co-operate* (work/operate together)
• *de-* + *emphasize* = *de-emphasize* (lessen or reverse the emphasis on something)
• *re-* + *elect* = *re-elect* (elect again)

Note that this hyphen is almost always optional and up to the writer's discretion, and many double-vowel prefixed words are now commonly spelled <u>without</u> the hyphen (especially in American English). If in doubt, you can probably omit the hyphen, but use a good dictionary or check your school's or business's style guide to be sure.

Confusing spellings

Another instance when we might use a hyphen is when the resulting spelling would be confusing or awkward to read. For example:
• *co-* + *worker* = *co-worker* (compare with *coworker*, which could be confusing because it spells *cow* at the beginning)
• *de-* + *ice* = *de-ice* (compare with *deice*, which seems like it could be pronounced /deɪs/)

Again, using the prefix <u>without</u> a hyphen is often a correct way to spell the word as well, so the hyphen is purely up to the writer's discretion.

Creating words with a different meaning

When adding a prefix (especially *de-* and *re-*) creates a word that looks the same as (or similar to) an existing word with a different meaning, we should use a hyphen to avoid confusion. For example:
• *co-* + *op* = *co-op* (shortening of *cooperative*; compare with *coop*, which means "a small cage or enclosure")
• *de-* + *stress* = *de-stress* (meaning "to reduce stress"; without the hyphen, *destress* looks very similar to *distress*, which means "to cause strain, anxiety, or suffering")
• *re-* + *cover* = *re-cover* (meaning "to cover again"; compare with *recover*, meaning "to get back" or "to be restored to normal")
• *re-* + *dress* = *re-dress* (meaning "to dress again"; compare with *redress*, meaning "to rectify" or "to make amends to")

With proper nouns and adjectives

When a prefix is paired with a proper noun or a proper adjective, we use a hyphen so we don't have a capital letter appearing in the middle of a word. While hyphens have been almost always optional in our previous examples, we <u>always</u>

use a hyphen with proper words. For example:

• *pro + Canada = **pro**-Canada* (in favor of Canada; <u>not</u> *proCanada*)
• *pre + Industrial Revolution = **pre**-Industrial Revolution* (before the beginning of the Industrial Revolution; <u>not</u> *preIndustrial Revolution*)
• *un + American = **un**-American* (not in alignment with the ideals or principles of America)

Note that some style guides suggest using an en dash (–) instead of a hyphen when a prefix is used with a proper noun or adjective that is already a compound, as in the second example. Using this method, it would look like this:

• ***pre**–Industrial Revolution*

However, this is entirely a personal preference, unless the style guide used by your school or employer specifically prescribes its use.

With *self-* and *ex-*

In addition to proper nouns and adjectives, we almost always use a hyphen with the prefixes *self-* and *ex-* (when it means "former"), as in:

• *self- + conscious = **self-conscious*** (<u>not</u> *selfconscious*)
• *ex- + boyfriend = **ex-boyfriend*** (<u>not</u> *exboyfriend*)

Quiz
(answers start on page 463)

1. Prefixes attach to which part of a root or base word?

a) The beginning
b) The middle
c) The end

2. True or false: Attaching a prefix will usually alter the spelling of the base word.

a) True
b) False

3. Which of the following prefixes can mean "again"?

a) ad-
b) re-
c) de-
d) contra-
e) All of the above
f) None of the above

4. Which of the following prefixes can mean "not"?

a) dis-
b) in-
c) non-
d) un-
e) All of the above
f) None of the above

5. Which of the following prefixed words is **incorrect**?

a) unwavering
b) embattled
c) maldiagnose
d) preeminent

6. Which of the following prefixed words **must** have a hyphen?

a) disappoint
b) selfesteem
c) excommunicate
d) codependent
e) All of the above
f) None of the above

Suffixes

Definition

Suffixes are **morphemes** (specific groups of letters with particular semantic meaning) that are added onto the <u>end</u> of root words to change their meaning. Suffixes are one of the two predominant kinds of affixes—the other kind is prefixes, which come at the <u>beginning</u> of a root word.

There is a huge range of suffixes in English, which can be broadly categorized as either **inflectional** or **derivational**.

Inflectional and Derivational Suffixes

Suffixes are used to change the grammatical function of an existing word. Sometimes this change is minor, with the word retaining its basic meaning and word class (part of speech) but conforming to the grammatical rules required by the structure of the sentence; these are known as **inflectional suffixes**. More often, the addition of a suffix results in the formation of a word that is in a completely <u>different</u> class and shares a meaning similar to the original root word; these are called **derivational suffixes**.

Inflectional Suffixes

Inflection refers to the changing of a word's spelling according to the grammatical structure of a sentence. This is often accomplished by adding a specific suffix onto the end of a root word.

These inflectional suffixes are only used to modify the ***grammatical*** meaning of a word; they do not change a word from one part of speech to another, nor do they alter the fundamental meaning of the word. For example, the suffix "-s" is used with most nouns to indicate that they are plural (i.e., more than one), as in *boys* and *girls*. The basic meanings of the root words *boy* and *girl* do not change; they've simply been **inflected** to show that the speaker is talking about more than one.

Inflectional suffixes can be used with nouns, verbs, adjectives, and adverbs. The tables below show all of the inflectional suffixes used with these parts of speech, as well as examples of each.

Inflectional Suffixes of Nouns

Suffix	Grammatical Function	Example Words
"-s"	Changes most nouns from singular to plural.	bank→banks car→cars pizza→pizzas toy→toys wire→wires
"-es"	Forms the plural for nouns ending in a sibilant sound (/s/, /z/, /ʧ/, or /ʃ/) as created by the endings "-ss," "-z," "-x," "-sh," "-ch," or "-tch."	coach→coaches watch→watches dish→dishes box→boxes bus→buses kiss→two kisses waltz→waltzes
"-en"	Changes certain irregular nouns* from singular to plural.	ox→oxen child→children brother→brethren

(*There are many irregular plural forms of nouns that do not adhere to any specific spelling pattern. To learn more about these and other rules for making nouns plural, see the section on Forming Plurals.)

Inflectional Suffixes of Verbs

Suffix	Grammatical Function	Example Words
"-s"	Forms the third-person singular for most verbs.	hear→hears run→runs think→thinks write→writes
"-es"	Forms the third-person singular for verbs ending in a sibilant sound (/s/, /z/, /ʧ/, or /ʃ/) created by the endings "-ss," "-z," "-x," "-sh," "-ch," or "-tch," as well as verbs ending in a consonant + **O**.	approach→approaches catch→catches do→does go→goes hush→hushes pass→passes quiz→quizzes
"-ed"	Forms the past simple tense and past participle of most verbs.	ask→asked burn→burned dare→dared hope→hoped open→opened talk→talked walk→walked
"-en"	Forms the past participle of some irregular verbs.	be→been drive→driven eat→eaten give→given got→gotten sink→sunken write→written
"-ing"	Forms the present participle and gerund of verbs.	build→building care→caring hear→hearing pass→passing read→reading see→seeing wear→wearing

Inflectional Suffixes of Adjectives and Adverbs

Suffix	Grammatical Function	Example Words
"-er"	Forms the **comparative degree** for many adjectives and adverbs.	big→bigger fast→faster* happy→happier high→higher* sad→sadder slow→slower*
"-est"	Forms the **superlative degree** for many adjectives and adverbs.	big→biggest fast→fastest* happy→happiest high→highest* sad→saddest slow→slowest*

(*These words function either as adjectives or adverbs, depending on their use. Those without an asterisk only function as adjectives.)

Derivational Suffixes

Unlike inflectional suffixes, **derivational suffixes** create a new—though related—meaning in the word that's formed. In many cases, the word formed by the addition of a derivational suffix will belong to a completely different part of speech (or **word class**). Suffixes that cause a shift in word class are sometimes referred to as **class-changing suffixes**.

There are many, many derivational suffixes used in English—too many to list here. We'll just look at those most commonly encountered in day-to-day writing and speech.

It's important to note that many words in modern English feature suffixes used with Latin, Old English, or foreign-language roots. For the sake of simplicity, we'll mostly be focusing on examples of roots that can stand alone as words (with a few notable exceptions).

Suffixes that form nouns

Derivational suffixes that create nouns most often attach to verbs and (to a lesser degree) adjectives. However, several noun suffixes are also **class-maintaining**, meaning they form new nouns from other existing nouns. We'll look at some of these a little later.

Suffix	Suffix meaning	Attaches to	Example words
"-age"	An action, process, or its result; a thing or place used for such an action.	verbs (Often a class-maintaining suffix, as we'll see later.)	append→append**age** block→block**age** cover→cover**age** dote→dot**age** haul→haul**age** pack→pack**age** seep→seep**age** shrink→shrink**age** store→stor**age** use→us**age** wreck→wreck**age**
"-al"	An action or process.	verbs	approve→approv**al** betray→betray**al** bury→buri**al** deny→deni**al** dispose→dispos**al** propose→propos**al** renew→renew**al** reverse→revers**al**
"-ance"	An action, process, state, condition, or quality.	verbs most adjectives ending in "-ant"	appear→appear**ance** arrogant→arrog**ance** brilliant→brilli**ance** comply→compli**ance** deliver→deliver**ance** endure→endur**ance** fragrant→fragr**ance** ignorant→ignor**ance** perform→perform**ance** reluctant→reluct**ance** tolerate→toler**ance**
"-dom"	A state or condition.	adjectives (More often a class-maintaining suffix, as we'll see later.)	bored→bore**dom** free→free**dom** wise→wis**dom**
"-ee"	A person or thing receiving the effect of an action; less commonly, a person or thing	verbs	absent→absent**ee** address→address**ee** devote→devot**ee**

	controlling or performing a passive action.		employ→employ**ee** interview→interview**ee** nominate→nomin**ee** train→train**ee** trust→trust**ee**
"-ence"	An action, process, state, condition, or quality.	verbs most adjectives ending in "-ent"	absent→abs**ence** cohere→coher**ence** defer→defer**ence** evident→evid**ence** exist→exist**ence** intelligent→intellig**ence** lenient→leni**ence** occur→occurr**ence** patient→pati**ence** persist→persist**ence** revere→rever**ence** silent→sil**ence** transfer→transfer**ence**
"-er"	A person or thing performing or capable of a particular action.	verbs	bake→bak**er** compose→compos**er** cook→cook**er** defend→defend**er** employ→employ**er** interview→interview**er** keep→keep**er** teach→teach**er** write→writ**er**
"-ery"	The act, process, or practice of doing something, or a place for such.	verbs	bake→bak**ery** bribe→brib**ery** debauch→debauch**ery** distill→distill**ery** hatch→hatch**ery** mock→mock**ery** rob→robb**ery** trick→trick**ery**
"-ication"	A state, condition, action, process, or practice, or the result thereof.	verbs ending in "-fy"	amplify→amplif**ication** clarify→clarif**ication** dignify→dignif**ication** falsify→falsifi**ication** glorify→glorif**ication** identify→identif**ication** justify→justif**ication** modify→modif**ication** quantify→quantif**ication** simplify→simplif**ication** unify→unif**ication**
"-ism"	1. An action, process, or practice. 2. A state, condition, or quality. 3. A doctrine, theory, or set of guiding principles.	1. verbs 2 & 3. adjectives	active→activ**ism** antagonize→antagon**ism** baptize→bapt**ism** criticize→critic**ism** colloquial→colloquial**ism** exorcize→exorci**ism** feminine→femin**ism** liberal→liberal**ism** metabolize→metabol**ism**

Spelling Conventions

			modern→modern**ism** pacific→pacif**ism**
"-ist"	One who performs a particular action, process, or practice.	verbs (More often a class-maintaining suffix, as we'll see later.)	antagonize→antagon**ist** cycle→cycl**ist** exorcize→exorcic**ist** lobby→lobby**ist** theorize→theor**ist**
"-(i)ty" (The **i** is dropped if the preceding vowel sound is or becomes unstressed.)	A state, condition, trait, or quality.	adjectives	able→abili**ty** certain→certain**ty** cruel→cruel**ty** dual→duali**ty** equal→equali**ty** feminine→feminin**ity** frail→frail**ty** hilarious→hilari**ty** masculine→masculin**ity** mature→matur**ity** plural→plurali**ty** pure→puri**ty** secure→securi**ty**
"-ment"	An action or process, or the result thereof.	verbs	adjust→adjust**ment** bereave→bereave**ment** contain→contain**ment** disappoint→disappoint**ment** employ→employ**ment** fulfill→fulfill**ment** judge→judg**ment** move→move**ment** place→place**ment** resent→resent**ment** treat→treat**ment**
"-ness"	A state, condition, trait, or measurement thereof.	adjectives	alert→alert**ness** cold→cold**ness** dark→dark**ness** exact→exact**ness** fierce→fierce**ness** happy→happi**ness** kind→kind**ness** like→like**ness** selfish→selfish**ness** useful→useful**ness**
"-or"	A person or thing controlling or performing an action.	verbs	act→act**or** communicate→communicat**or** direct→direct**or** educate→educat**or** invest→invest**or** profess→profess**or** sail→sail**or** survive→surviv**or** translate→translat**or**
"-sion"	A state, condition, action, process, or practice, or the result thereof.	verbs	admit→admis**sion** allude→allu**sion** compel→compul**sion** convert→conver**sion** decide→deci**sion**

			divert→diver**sion** emit→emis**sion** extend→exten**sion** impress→impres**sion** invade→inva**sion** invert→inver**sion** obsess→obses**sion** propel→propul**sion** seclude→seclu**sion** suspend→suspen**sion** transmit→transmis**sion**
"-tion"	A state, condition, action, process, or practice, or the result thereof.	verbs	act→ac**tion** affect→affec**tion** communicate→communica**tion** complete→comple**tion** direct→direc**tion** educate→educa**tion** evolve→evolu**tion** inscribe→inscrip**tion** interrupt→interrup**tion** misconceive→misconcep**tion** resolve→resolu**tion** subscribe→subscrip**tion** translate→transla**tion**

Nouns formed from other nouns

As we mentioned already, many suffixes attach to existing nouns to create another noun with a new meaning. Because the words remain nouns, these suffixes are known as **class-maintaining suffixes**. (We looked at some of these already—they can be either class maintaining or class changing, depending on the root word that the suffix attaches to.)

Here are some of the most common:

Suffix	Suffix meaning	Example words
"-age"	1. A collection or group; a mass or amount. 2. A status, relationship, or connection. 3. A condition or state of being. 4. A place of residence. 4. A rate or measurement of.	acre→acre**age** bag→bagg**age** baron→baron**age** bond→bond**age** cube→cub**age** floor→floor**age** foot→foot**age** front→front**age** hermit→hermit**age** mile→mile**age** orphan→orphan**age** pasture→pastur**age** percent→percent**age** sewer→sewer**age** vicar→vicar**age** watt→watt**age**
"-(e)ry" (The **e** is usually dropped if the preceding vowel sound is or becomes unstressed.)	1. A group, collection, category, or class of things. 2. A state or condition of being. 3. The characteristic qualities, actions, or behavior. 4. A practice or occupation.	ancestor→ances**try** buffoon→buffoon**ery** circuit→circui**try** crock→crock**ery** dentist→dentis**try** image→imag**ery** peasant→peasan**try** pedant→pedan**try** prude→prud**ery**

Spelling Conventions

		scene→scenery snob→snobbery zealot→zealotry
"-ist"	1. One who produces, practices, plays, operates, or is otherwise connected to a specific thing or activity. 2. One who follows or adheres to a certain doctrine, theory, or set of guiding principles. 3. One who specializes in a specific field of study.	activism→activist anthropology→anthropologist art→artist bass→bassist biology→biologist Calvinism→Calvinist capitalism→capitalist feminism→feminist guitar→guitarist modernism→modernist novel→novelist pacifism→pacifist pharmacy→pharmacist piano→pianist psychiatry→psychiatrist racism→racist romanticism→romanticist science→scientist zoology→zoologist
"-dom"	1. A state, quality, or condition. 2. A specified domain or jurisdiction. 3. A particular rank or position.	duke→dukedom earl→earldom chief→chiefdom Christian→Christendom fan→fandom king→kingdom martyr→martyrdom prince→princedom star→stardom
"-hood"	1. A state, quality, or condition. 2. A group sharing a state, quality, or condition.	adult→adulthood boy→boyhood brother→brotherhood child→childhood father→fatherhood girl→girlhood knight→knighthood man→manhood mother→motherhood parent→parenthood sister→sisterhood woman→womanhood
"-ship"	1. A state, quality, or condition. 2. A particular rank, status, or position, or the time spent in such a position. 3. Skill, craft, or artistry employed in a particular profession or practice.	apprentice→apprenticeship champion→championship citizen→citizenship craftsman→craftsmanship dealer→dealership dean→deanship friend→friendship leader→leadership penman→penmanship professor→professorship scholar→scholarship sponsor→sponsorship workman→workmanship

"-(o)logy"

Another common suffix used to form nouns is the ending "-logy" (or **"-ology"** when following certain consonant sounds), which produces the meaning "a branch or field of knowledge, science, theory, or study."

This suffix usually does not attach to pre-existing English roots; instead, it more often connects to Greek or Latin roots. For example:

Root	Root Meaning	+ -(o)logy	New Meaning
astro-	star, celestial body, or outer space	astrology	Originally meaning "the science of the heavenly bodies," *astrology* now refers to the study of the positions and motions of planets, stars, and the moon in the belief that they influence human decisions and characteristics.
bio-	life	biology	The science of life and living animals.
cardio-	pertaining to the heart	cardiology	The scientific study of the structures, functions, and disorders of the heart.
geo-	earth (generally) or Earth (specifically)	geology	The scientific study of the origin and structures of the Earth.
ideo-	of or pertaining to ideas	ideology	A set of doctrines or beliefs that are held by an individual or shared by members of a social group.
neuro-	of or pertaining to a nerve or the nervous system	neurology	The scientific study of the structures, functions, and disorders of the nervous system.
psych-	mind, spirit, soul	psychology	The science and study of mental and behavioral processes.
theo-	God or gods	theology	The study of the divine and of religious truths.
zoo-*	animal, living being	zoology	The study of animals, including their physiology, development, and classification.

(*The root *zoo-* is a combining form derived from the Greek word *zoion*. The English word *zoo* is actually a shortening of the term *zoological garden*.)

Because the meaning of "-(o)logy" is so well established, it *is* sometimes attached to existing English words to create new terms that follow the pattern established by the Greek and Latin roots. For instance:

• anesthesia→anesthesi**ology**
• climate→climat**ology**
• criminal→crimin**ology**
• icon→icon**ology**
• music→music**ology**
• radiation→radi**ology**
• reflex→reflex**ology**

However, this combination is much less common than the use of Greek or Latin roots.

Suffixes that form verbs

Derivational suffixes that create verbs attach to nouns and adjectives.

Suffix	Suffix meaning	Attaches to	Example words
"-en"	1. To become or cause to become. 2. To come or cause to have.	1. adjectives 2. nouns	black→blacken broad→broaden cheap→cheapen fright→frighten hard→harden heart→hearten length→lengthen red→redden sharp→sharpen sick→sicken strength→strengthen
"-ify"	To make or cause to become.	adjectives, nouns	ample→amplify beauty→beautify clear→clarify diverse→diversify dignity→dignify glory→glorify just→justify pure→purify null→nullify simple→simplify type→typify
"-ize"	To become or cause to become; to do or make that to which the suffix is attached.	adjectives, nouns	accessory→accessorize apology→apologize capital→capitalize civil→civilize economy→economize empathy→empathize fertile→fertilize industrial→industrialize legal→legalize human→humanize standard→standardize theory→theorize union→unionize

"-ise" vs. "-ize"

In American English, the suffix "-ize" is used to change nouns and adjectives into verbs, as we have just seen, and it also appears in verbs that do not have standalone root words. British English, however, predominantly uses the synonymous suffix "-ise." For more information on this difference in spelling, go to the section on American English vs. British English.

"-ate"

There is also another common suffix that results in the creation of verbs: "**-ate**." However, while this ending does occasionally attach to pre-existing nouns or adjectives (meaning "to act on, cause to become or be modified, or furnish with"), it is much more likely to appear in verbs that come from the past participles of Latin verbs. Even many words that look like they come directly from nouns or adjectives are in fact derived from Latin. For example:

Formed from nouns and adjectives	Formed from Latin verbs
active→activ**ate** caffeine→caffein**ate** caliber→calibr**ate** hyphen→hyphen**ate** pollen→pollin**ate**	abbreviate→from Latin *abbreviatus* accentuate→from Latin *accentuatus* circulate→from Latin *circulatus* domesticate→from Latin *domesticatus* duplicate→from Latin *duplicatus* educate→from Latin *educatus* elongate→from Latin *elongatus* habituate→from Latin *habituatus* insulate→from Latin *insulatus* migrate→from Latin *migratus* notate→from Latin *notatus* separate→from Latin *separatus* translate→from Latin *translatus*

Suffixes that form adjectives

Derivational suffixes that create adjectives usually attach to nouns. Much less often, they attach to verbs.

Suffix	Suffix meaning	Attaches to	Example words
"**-able**"	Possible; capable of; suitable for.	verbs	adore→ador**able** break→break**able** debate→debat**able** do→do**able** excite→excit**able** live→liv**able** manage→manage**able** read→read**able** stop→stopp**able**
"**-al**"	Having the characteristics of or relating to.	nouns	artifice→artifici**al** bride→brid**al** brute→brut**al** center→centr**al** emotion→emotion**al** form→form**al** logic→logic**al** music→music**al** politics→politic**al** space→spati**al** tide→tid**al**
"**-en**"	Made of or resembling.	nouns	ash→ash**en** earth→earth**en** flax→flax**en** gold→gold**en** lead→lead**en** wax→wax**en** wood→wood**en**

Spelling Conventions

"-ful"	1. Full of; characterized by. 2. Tending or able to.	1. nouns 2. verbs	beauty→beauti**ful** care→care**ful** delight→delight**ful** forget→forget**ful** grace→grace**ful** joy→joy**ful** law→law**ful** mourn→mourn**ful** play→play**ful** respect→respect**ful** waste→waste**ful**
"-ible"	Possible; capable of; suitable for.	verbs	access→access**ible** collapse→collaps**ible** digest→digest**ible** divide→divis**ible** eat→ed**ible** flex→flex**ible** omit→omiss**ible** perceive→percept**ible** receive→recept**ible** sense→sens**ible** suggest→suggest**ible**
"-ic"	Having the characteristics of or relating to.	nouns	acid→acid**ic** base→bas**ic** comedy→comed**ic** galaxy→galact**ic** hero→hero**ic** irony→iron**ic** magnet→magnet**ic** myth→myth**ic** nostalgia→nostalg**ic** poetry→poet**ic** rhythm→rhythm**ic** system→system**ic**
"-ical"	Having the characteristics of or relating to.	nouns	acid→atom**ical** biology→biolog**ical** comedy→com**ical** history→histor**ical** myth→myth**ical** philosophy→philosoph**ical** type→typ**ical** whimsy→whims**ical**
"-ish"	1. Typical of, similar to, or related to. 2. Of or associated with (a particular nationality, region, or language). 3. Inclined to or preoccupied with.	nouns	book→book**ish** boy→boy**ish** Britain→Brit**ish** child→child**ish** clown→clown**ish** Denmark→Dan**ish** fiend→fiend**ish** girl→girl**ish** nightmare→nightmar**ish** prude→prud**ish** self→self**ish** Spain→Span**ish** Sweden→Swed**ish**

"-less"	Lacking; deprived of; without.	nouns	aim→aim**less** blame→blame**less** color→color**less** doubt→doubt**less** home→home**less** hope→hope**less** limit→limit**less** need→need**less** point→point**less** rest→rest**less** self→self**less** time→time**less** use→use**less**
"-ly"	1. Similar to or characteristic of. 2. Occurring at such intervals of time.	nouns	brother→brother**ly** coward→coward**ly** day→dai**ly** elder→elder**ly** friend→friend**ly** heaven→heaven**ly** hour→hour**ly** like→like**ly** love→love**ly** month→month**ly** miser→miser**ly** order→order**ly** scholar→scholar**ly** year→year**ly**
"-ous"	Possessing; characterized by; full of.	nouns	advantage→advantage**ous** caution→caut**ious** disaster→disastr**ous** fame→fam**ous** glamor→glamor**ous** joy→joy**ous** malice→malic**ious** nutrition→nutrit**ious** religion→relig**ious** pretense→pretent**ious** poison→poison**ous** suspicion→suspic**ious**
"-y"	1. Characterized by; consisting or having the quality of; filled with. 2. Tending or inclined to.	1. nouns 2. verbs	bulk→bulk**y** class→class**y** dream→dream**y** ease→eas**y** leak→leak**y** mess→mess**y** rain→rain**y** rope→rop**y** shine→shin**y** smell→smell**y** wimp→wimp**y**

Suffixes that form adverbs

By far the most common and well-known suffix that creates adverbs by attaching to adjectives is "**-ly.**" However, there are two others derivational suffixes that form adverbs: "**-ways/-wise**" and "**-ward.**"

Suffix	Suffix meaning	Attaches to	Example words
"**-ly**"	1. In a certain or specified manner. 2. At that interval of time.	1. adjectives 2. nouns (units of time)	abrupt→abrupt**ly** artistic→artistical**ly** calm→calm**ly** day→dai**ly** daring→daring**ly** double→doub**ly** easy→easi**ly** extreme→extreme**ly** full→ful**ly** happy→happi**ly** hour→hour**ly** lucky→lucki**ly** majestic→majestical**ly** month→month**ly** practical→practical**ly** probable→probab**ly** quiet→quiet**ly** right→right**ly** smart→smart**ly** true→tru**ly** whole→whol**ly** year→year**ly**
"**-ways/-wise**" ("**-wise**" is much more common, especially in American English, except with the root *side*, which almost always becomes *sideways*)	1. In a specified manner, direction, or position. 2. With reference or in regard to. (sometimes hyphenated)	nouns, adjectives	clock→clock**wise** business→business**wise** edge→edge**wise** (occasionally: *edgeways*) health→health-**wise** length→length**wise** (occasionally: *lengthways*) like→like**wise** other→other**wise** side→side**ways** weather→weather-**wise**
"**-ward**"	In a specified direction or position.	nouns, adjectives, adverbs	back→back**ward** down→down**ward** east→east**ward** fore→for**ward** front→front**ward** home→home**ward** north→north**ward** on→on**ward** south→south**ward** to→to**ward** west→west**ward**

Spelling changes

Finally, it's worth pointing out how the spelling of many words becomes slightly altered when a suffix is added. Even though these changes can at times seem haphazard, there are actually several guidelines we can follow to determine how a word's spelling might change if a suffix is added. Go to the section on Spelling Conventions with Suffixes to learn more.

Quiz
(answers start on page 463)

1. Suffixes are attached to which part of a root word?

a) The beginning
b) The middle
c) The end
d) All of the above

2. What kind of suffix only affects the **grammatical** function of a root word?

a) Derivational
b) Inflectional
c) Class-maintaining
d) Class-changing

3. Which of the following is the function of a **class-changing suffix**?

a) Changing the fundamental meaning of the root word
b) Changing the part of speech of the root word
c) Changing the grammatical function of the root word
d) A & B
e) B & C

4. What part of speech is formed by adding the suffix **"-ness"**?

a) Noun
b) Verb
c) Adjective
d) Adverb

5. What part of speech is formed by adding the suffix **"-ize"**?

a) Noun
b) Verb
c) Adjective
d) Adverb

6. What part of speech is formed by adding the suffix **"-wise"**?

a) Noun
b) Verb
c) Adjective
d) Adverb

7. Which of the following is **usually** a **class-maintaining** suffix?

a) "-or"
b) "-ate"
c) "-dom"
d) "-ous
e) A & D
f) B & C

Commonly Confused Suffixes

Because many suffixes overlap in their meaning, it can sometimes be confusing to determine which one is appropriate to use with a particular base word or root. To make things even more complicated, many suffixes also have alternate forms that are used in particular contexts or have evolved as the more accepted version.

In this section, we'll look at some of the most common pairs or sets of commonly confused suffixes. We'll give a very brief overview of each below, but for detailed spelling rules, conventions, and lists of examples for each, you can continue on to the individual sections.

"-er" vs. "-or" vs. "-ar"

The suffixes "-er," "-or," and "-ar" are all used to create nouns of agency (persons or things that perform an action) from verbs. Of the three, "-er" is by far the most common, while "-or" is much more common than "-ar." Because they perform the same function and are pronounced in the same way (/ər/), it can be difficult to decide which suffix is the correct one to use. Fortunately, of all the commonly confused suffixes, "-er," "-or," and "-ar" have the clearest spelling conventions indicating when each one is preferred.

"-tion" vs. "-sion"

The suffixes "-tion" and "-sion" are both used to create nouns from verbs (and, less commonly, adjectives and other nouns) to describe a state, condition, action, process, practice, or the result thereof. They are actually just permutations of the same suffix, "-ion," but there are specific conditions that will dictate which one we use, so it's worthwhile to consider them individually. For example, verbs ending in "-ize" will take the "-tion" ending when becoming nouns (e.g., *generalize* becomes *generalization*); verbs ending in "-mit," on the other hand, will take the "-sion" ending (e.g., *permit* becomes *permission*).

"-able" vs. "-ible"

The suffixes "-able" and "-ible" are both used to form adjectives meaning "possible, capable of, suitable for, or causing." Of the two, "-able" is much more common: it is what's known as a "living" or "productive" suffix, meaning that it is still being used to create new words. For example, *acceptable, honorable, palatable*, etc.
The variant "-ible," on the other hand, is only used in older words that have survived into modern English. Some common examples include *accessible, comprehensible*, and *sensible*.

"-ant" vs. "-ent"

The suffixes "-ant" and "-ent" are both used to form nouns of agency (persons or things who perform an action) and adjectives that describe a state or quality. They both derive from the conjugations of Latin and French verbs; in some cases, they seem to "attach" to existing base words (e.g., *accountant, persistent*), while other times they are adjacent to roots that could not exist on their own (*brilliant, resilient*).

"-ance/-ancy" vs. "-ence/-ency"

The suffixes "-ant" and "-ent" each have two related noun forms: "-ance/-ancy" and "-ence/-ency." These are all used to describe a state, quality, condition, or action typically associated with an adjective or noun of agency described by "-ant" or "-ent."

Many roots and base words can take all three endings (e.g., *expectant, expectance, expectancy*; *dependent, dependence, dependency*), but many others will only take *one* of the two possible noun endings (e.g., *pregnant* becomes *pregnancy*, but not *pregnance*; *different* becomes *difference*, but not *differency*).

Additionally, there are smaller subsets of words that will *only* be formed with "-ant," "-ance," "-ent," or "-ence," without having either of the other two endings. For example, the word *decongestant* is commonplace, but *decongestance* and *decongestancy* are not words; similarly, we can say *preference*, but not *preferent* or *preferency*.

138

"-ic" vs. "-ical"

The suffixes "-ic" and "-ical" both form adjectives meaning "of, resembling, characterized by, or relating to," and they can be notoriously difficult to distinguish. In many cases, words can be spelled either way, with one ending being simply more common than the other. Other times, the "-ic" and "-ical" versions will have similar but slightly *different* meanings, making each one more suitable in particular contexts.

Unfortunately, "-ic" and "-ical" form one of the least predictable pairs of suffixes, and, though there are a few spelling conventions we can rely on, more often than not we simply have to memorize which spelling is correct—or at least preferred.

American English vs. British English Suffixes

In addition to the existence of suffixes that are in themselves easy to confuse, there are several word endings that are spelled slightly differently in American English (AmE) as opposed to British English (BrE). For example, *color* (AmE) vs. *colour* (BrE); *center* (AmE) vs. *centre* (BrE); *defense* (AmE) vs. *defence* (BrE); or *realize* (AmE) vs. *realise* (BrE). For more information on these and other spelling conventions, head to the section that deals specifically with American English vs. British English.

Commonly Confused Suffixes: -able vs. -ible

The suffixes "-able" and "-ible" are both used to form adjectives meaning "possible, capable of, suitable for, or causing." Of the two, "-able" is much more common: it is what's known as a "living" or "productive" suffix, meaning that it is still being used to create new words. The variant "-ible," on the other hand, is only used in older words that have survived into modern English.

Because they are spelled so similarly and have the same pronunciation (/əbəl/), it can sometimes be hard to remember which is the correct one to use. Unfortunately, there are not very many conventions we can follow to know which suffix to use (and those that do exist are not always reliable). Instead, this section will focus on the different ways "-able" and "-ible" each attach to words, along with many examples for each.

Using "-able" with existing words

The suffix "-able" most commonly attaches to words (most often verbs) that could otherwise be complete without the suffix; in many cases, this occurs with no change to their spelling. Because "-able" is a productive suffix, there is a huge number of words it can be attached to. Let's just look at some common ones:

- accept→accept**able**
- adapt→adapt**able**
- adjust→adjust**able**
- avoid→avoid**able**
- bend→bend**able**
- break→break**able**
- build→build**able**
- buy→buy**able**
- catch→catch**able**
- chew→chew**able**
- consider→consider**able**
- depend→depend**able**
- distinguish→distinguish**able**
- do→do**able**
- elect→elect**able**
- employ→employ**able**
- enjoy→enjoy**able**

- expand→expand**able**
- fashion→fashion**able**
- favor→favor**able**
- fold→fold**able**
- govern→govern**able**
- grasp→grasp**able**
- guess→guess**able**
- honor→honor**able**
- know→know**able**
- lament→lament**able**
- laud→laud**able**
- laugh→laugh**able**
- limit→limit**able**
- market→market**able**
- mend→mend**able**
- mold→mold**able**
- obtain→obtain**able**
- order→order**able**
- pardon→pardon**able**
- pass→pass**able**
- pay→pay**able**
- predict→predict**able**
- prevent→prevent**able**
- punish→punish**able**
- question→question**able**
- reach→reach**able**
- reason→reason**able**
- remark→remark**able**
- shrink→shrink**able**
- speak→speak**able** (especially used in _unspeak**able**_)
- sustain→sustain**able**
- target→target**able**
- tax→tax**able**
- teach→teach**able**
- think→think**able** (especially used in _unthink**able**_)
- utter→utter**able**
- view→view**able**
- void→void**able**
- walk→walk**able**
- wear→wear**able**

Spelling changes with words that take "-able"

While many base words can take the "-able" suffix without changing their spelling, there are also many instances in which the spelling must be altered slightly in order for the suffix to be attached. The most common of these occur with words ending in silent E, but there are other instances in which a word's spelling will change in various ways.

Omitting silent E

The most common spelling change made to a word when "-able" is attached is for silent E to be omitted from the end of the word and replaced with the suffix (though this is not always the case). For example:

- abdicate→abdic**able**
- accrue→accru**able**
- allocate→allocat**able**
- argue→argu**able**
- assume→assum**able**
- automate→automat**able**
- breathe→breath**able**
- circulate→circulat**able**

- construe→constru**able**
- correlate→correlat**able**
- cultivate→cultivat**able**
- debate→debat**able**
- dilate→dilat**able**
- equate→equat**able**
- ignite→ignit**able**
- inflate→inflat**able**
- isolate→isolat**able**
- issue→issu**able**
- lapse→laps**able**
- locate→locat**able**
- palate→palat**able**
- relate→relat**able**
- rescue→rescu**able**
- translate→translat**able**
- value→valu**able**

Keeping silent E before "-able"

Note that there are many instances in which we do **not** omit a silent **E** when adding the vowel suffix "-able." This is especially true when it comes after **C** or **G** to make it clear that the consonants retain their "soft" pronunciations (/s/ and /ʒ/, respectively). For example:

	With "-able"	With other vowel suffixes
C + Silent E	dance→dan**ce**able efface→effa**ce**able notice→noti**ce**able replace→repla**ce**able trace→tra**ce**able	dan**c**ed, dan**c**er, dan**c**ing effa**c**ed, effa**c**ing noti**c**ed, noti**c**ing repla**c**ed, repla**c**ing tra**c**ed, tra**c**er, tra**c**ing
G + Silent E	age→a**ge**able bridge→brid**ge**able change→chan**ge**able discourage→discoura**ge**able manage→mana**ge**able	a**g**ed, a**g**ing* brid**g**ed, brid**g**ing chan**g**ed, chan**g**er, chan**g**ing discoura**g**ed, discoura**g**ing mana**g**ed, mana**g**er, mana**g**ing

(*In British English, the silent **E** is usually kept in the word *ageing*, whereas it is usually omitted in American English.)

While most common when coming after **C/G + E**, this convention of keeping **E** before "-able" does occur after other consonants as well. However, this is quite rare and, in many cases, is simply an alternative spelling (especially in American English, in which **E** is much more likely to be omitted).

Here are some examples in which you might see "-able" following a silent **E**:
- file→fil**e**able (but <u>not</u> *filable*)
- fine→fin**e**able (<u>more</u> commonly, *finable*)
- like→lik**e**able (<u>more</u> commonly, *likable*)
- live→liv**e**able (<u>more</u> commonly, *livable*)
- love→lov**e**able (<u>more</u> commonly, *lovable*)
- name→nam**e**able (<u>less</u> commonly, *namable*)
- shape→shap**e**able (<u>more</u> commonly, *shapable*)
- size→siz**e**able (<u>more</u> commonly, *sizable*)
- trade→trad**e**able (<u>more</u> commonly, *tradable*)

Doubling consonants before "-able"

When the last syllable of a verb contains a single short vowel followed by a single consonant, we usually have to double the consonant before "-able."
For example:
- bed→be**dd**able
- bid→bi**dd**able

- compel→compe**ll**able
- confer→confe**rr**able
- control→contro**ll**able
- cut→cu**tt**able
- defer→defe**rr**able
- deter→dete**rr**able
- dim→di**mm**able
- dip→di**pp**able
- drop→dro**pp**able
- expel→expe**ll**able
- fit→fi**tt**able
- flap→fla**pp**able
- forget→forge**tt**able
- hug→hu**gg**able
- hum→hu**mm**able
- map→ma**pp**able
- net→ne**tt**able
- program→proga**mm**able
- reset→rese**tt**able
- rip→ri**pp**able
- ship→shi**pp**able
- skip→ski**pp**able
- spot→spo**tt**able
- stop→sto**pp**able
- sum→su**mm**able
- swim→swi**mm**able
- transfer→transfe**rr**able
- transmit→transmi**tt**able
- win→wi**nn**able

Note that, in multi-syllable words, this is only the case if the final syllable is stressed in the base word. Otherwise, the final consonant is not doubled, as in *answerable, cancelable, limitable,* etc.

Replacing "-ate" with "-able"

We already saw that many verbs ending in "-ate" will take the suffix "-able" by omitting silent E. However, there are also quite a few words in which "-ate" is replaced altogether. Unfortunately, there is no spelling pattern we can use to indicate which "-ate" words will be changed this way; we just have to memorize them. Here are some of the most common:

- abominate→abomin**able**
- alienate→alien**able** (especially in the word *inalienable*)
- communicate→communic**able**
- delegate→deleg**able**
- demonstrate→demonstr**able**
- depreciate→depreci**able**
- differentiate→differenti**able**
- discriminate→discrimin**able**
- educate→educ**able**
- eradicate→eradic**able**
- estimate→estim**able**
- explicate→explic**able**
- extricate→extric**able**
- imitate→imit**able**
- litigate→litig**able**
- navigate→navig**able**
- negotiate→negoti**able**
- numerate→numer**able**
- operate→oper**able**
- penetrate→penetr**able**
- replicate→replic**able**

- satiate→sati**able**
- venerate→vener**able**

Changing Y to I before "-able"

When a suffix beginning with a vowel is attached to a word ending in a consonant + **Y**, we almost always change **Y** to the letter **I**. Because of this, verbs that end in "-y" <u>always</u> take the "-able" suffix, since we never have a word spelled "-iible." Let's look at some of the most common examples:

- certify→certif**i**able
- classify→classif**i**able
- deny→den**i**able
- envy→env**i**able
- falsify→falsif**i**able
- identify→identif**i**able
- justify→justif**i**able
- levy→lev**i**able
- notify→notif**i**able
- pity→pit**i**able
- ply→pl**i**able
- quantify→quantif**i**able
- rely→rel**i**able
- specify→specif**i**able
- unify→unif**i**able
- vary→var**i**able
- verify→verif**i**able

There are also two nouns ending in "-y" that can take "-able," but **Y** no longer changes to **I**—it is simply omitted:

- memory→memor**able**
- misery→miser**able**

Using "-able" and "-ible" with incomplete Latin roots

Because "-able" is so commonly used with existing base words, the most common tip to remembering the "-ible" variation is that it is usually used with Latin roots that cannot stand alone as words.

However, this is not a very reliable convention, because "-able" *also* attaches to many incomplete Latin roots (though "-ible" does so more commonly). There is only one rule we can use to know which ending is correct: if a root ends in a "soft" **C** (/s/) or **G** (/ʒ/), it will always be followed by "-ible," while a "hard" **C** (/k/) is always followed by "-able." (No Latin roots will end in a "hard" **G**, /g/.) Unfortunately, we just have to memorize the rest of these types of words:

Latin root + "-able"	Latin root + "-ible"
aff**able**	aud**ible**
ami**able**	comest**ible**
ami**c**able	compat**ible**
appli**c**able	corri**gible** (most commonly used in *incorrigible*)
culp**able**	cred**ible**
despi**c**able	ed**ible**
dur**able**	eli**gible**
flamm**able**	fall**ible***
fri**able**	feas**ible**
formid**able**	fran**gible**
herit**able**	gull**ible**
hospit**able**	horr**ible**
indomit**able**	indel**ible**
ineluct**able**	intelli**gible**
inevit**able**	invin**cible**
impe**cc**able	iras**cible**
inexor**able**	le**gible**
prob**able**	mis**cible**

malle**able**	neglig**ible**
verit**able**	ostens**ible**
vo<u>c</u>**able**	plaus**ible**
vulner**able**	poss**ible**
vi**able**	ris**ible**
	suscept**ible**
	tang**ible**
	terr**ible**
	vis**ible**

(*Note that the root *fall-* here is not the same as the verb *fall*.)

Using "-ible" with existing words

Though much less common than "-able," the "-ible" variant can also attach to existing base words with no change to its spelling. As with the Latin roots, there are generally no indications in the base word's spelling to indicate when "-ible" is correct, except for one: base words ending in "-uct" will (almost) always take "-ible" rather than "-able."

Let's look at some examples:
• access→access**ible**
• collect→collect**ible**
• combust→combust**ible**
• compact→compact**ible**
• compress→compress**ible**
• constr<u>uct</u>→constr<u>uct</u>**ible**
• contract→contract**ible**
• contempt→contempt**ible**
• controvert→controvert**ible** (especially in the word *incontrovertible*)
• convert→convert**ible**
• corrupt→corrupt**ible**
• ded<u>uct</u>→ded<u>uct</u>**ible**
• depress→depress**ible**
• destr<u>uct</u>→destr<u>uct</u>**ible**
• distract→distract**ible**
• erupt→erupt**ible**
• express→express**ible**
• flex→flex**ible**
• impress→impress**ible**
• ingest→ingest**ible**
• repress→repress**ible**
• resist→resist**ible**
• suggest→suggest**ible**
• suppress→suppress**ible**
• vend→vend**ible**

(Because "-able" is a productive suffix, meaning it is still being used to create new words, there may be instances in the future in which this rule is no longer true. For example, the term *instructable* has been gaining in popular usage in the last 30 years, but it is not found in the dictionary; *instructible*, meanwhile, *is* in the dictionary but has nearly become obsolete, which is why it isn't included above.)

"-ible" with silent E

Like "-able," the "-ible" ending can also replace silent E at the end of existing base words, as in:
• coerce→coerc**ible**
• collapse→collaps**ible**
• corrode→corrod**ible**
• deduce→deduc**ible**
• diffuse→diffus**ible**

- erode→erod**ible**
- evade→evad**ible**
- evince→evinc**ible**
- immerse→immers**ible**
- force→forc**ible**
- produce→produc**ible**
- reduce→reduc**ible**
- reverse→revers**ible**
- sense→sens**ible**
- submerge→submerg**ible**
- submerse→submers**ible**

However, as you can see by the size of the list, it is much less common for a silent **E** word to take "-ible" rather than "-able." If a word ends in a silent **E**, it will most likely take the "-able" suffix (and base words ending in "-ate" can <u>only</u> take "-able").

Other spelling changes with "-ible"

Sometimes an "-ible" word is related to an existing base word, but the spelling must change slightly to accommodate it. This also occurs with certain words when they attach to "-able" (e.g., when the suffix replaces "-ate" or "-y" becomes "-i-"), but "-ible" can result in much more drastic changes to the spelling of the base word.

The most consistent of these changes is for verbs ending in "-mit": with the exception of *limit* (which becomes *limitable*), all of these verbs take the "-ible" ending, with "-mit" changing to "-missible." Another common change occurs with verbs ending in "-nd," which changes to "-nsible" (however, *other* verbs ending in "-nd" can take "-able" instead, so we can't use this verb ending as a rule to determine the appropriate suffix). In addition to these, two other specific words have their endings change when attached to "-ible." Let's look at all the words that go through spelling changes with the "-ible" suffix:

"-mit" + "-ible"	"-nd" + "-ible"	Other endings + "-ible"
admit→admi**ss**ible omit→omi**ss**ible permit→permi**ss**ible remit→remi**ss**ible (slightly different meaning from *remittable*) transmit→transmi**ss**ible	apprehend→apprehe**ns**ible comprehend→comprehe**ns**ible defend→defe**ns**ible (slightly different meaning from *defendable*) respond→respo**ns**ible	divide→divi**s**ible perceive→perce**pt**ible (slightly different meaning from *perceivable*)

Words that can take <u>either</u> "-able" or "-ible"

In addition to the trends we've seen above, there are words ending in "-able" that can alternatively be spelled "-ible," and vice versa. In most cases, these are simply less common variants; other times, the meaning of the word is very similar but subtly different, depending on the ending used.

The table below shows all words that have acceptable variant spellings. For each pair, the most common spelling is in **bold**; if one is *much* more common than the alternative, it will be **<u>bold and underlined</u>**. Finally, if the two spellings have slightly different meanings, they'll be marked with an asterisk (*) and elaborated upon further on.

Ending in "-able"	Ending in "-ible"
<u>addable</u>	addible
ascendable	ascendible
<u>cognizable</u>	cognoscible
collectable	**collectible**
<u>condensable</u>	condensible
connectable	connectible
<u>correctable</u>	correctible
defendable*	**defensible***
discernable	**<u>discernible</u>**
discussable	discussible
distractable	**<u>distractible</u>**
dividable	**<u>divisible</u>**

eatable*	**edible***
erodable	**erodible**/erosible
evadable	evadible
excludable	excludible
expandable	expansible
extendable	extendible/**extensible**
ignitable	ignitible
lapsable	lapsible
passable	passible
perceivable*	**perceptible***
persuadable	persuasible
preventable	preventible
processable	processible
remittable*	remissible*
transfusable	transfusible
transmittable	**transmissible**/transmittible
vendable	**vendible**

*These pairs of words have slightly different meanings, which we'll look at next.

defendable vs. defensible

Defensible is the much more common adjective derived from the verb *defend*, but *defendable* is an acceptable variant. While they can be used nearly synonymously, there is actually a slight difference in their overall meanings. *Defensible* is generally used to describe something that is capable of being defended through logical (i.e., non-physical) means, such as an idea or a decision. While it can also relate to physical defense (such as in combat), the former meaning is much more common.

Defendable, on the other hand, is almost solely used to describe physical defense. Even in this use, though, it is a much less common variant of *defensible*.

eatable vs. edible

The words *eatable* and *edible* are nearly identical in meaning, but there is a subtle distinction in the way each is applied.

Edible is most commonly used to describe something that is fit to be eaten. For example, a piece of fruit is *edible*, but imitation plastic fruit is *inedible*.

The variant *eatable*, on the other hand, is typically used to refer only to the desirability of being eaten, rather than it being physically fit to be eaten. Something *edible* (capable of being eaten without causing harm) might be so repellent due to flavor, preparation, or texture as to be completely *uneatable*. However, even with this distinct meaning, *edible* is vastly more common than *eatable*. Additionally, *edible* can be used figuratively to achieve the same meaning, so unless you have a specific reason not to, you should always use *edible*.

perceivable vs. perceptible

Like *defendable* and *defensible*, *perceivable* and *perceptible* are separated by a cognitive, non-physical aspect in meaning. *Perceptible*, the more common of the two, means "capable of being perceived," whether by physical senses (such as touch, sight, or hearing) or cognitive senses (such as being able to notice when a person's behavior begins to change). *Perceivable*, on the other hand, is generally only used in reference to physical perceptions, not cognitive ones. As with *defensible* and *edible*, *perceptible* is much more common and has a broader meaning than its variant, making it the preferred spelling overall.

remittable vs. remissible

These two words are both derived from the verb *remit*, but are applied to different meanings the verb can have.

Remissible is the more traditional of the two adjectives, and it means "able to be pardoned or forgiven." *Remittable* takes the more modern meanings of *remit*, "capable of being transferred (such as a payment)" or "able to slacken, abate, or relax."

Remissible used to be the more common of the two, but in recent years it has been overtaken by *remittable*, likely due to the ubiquity of the productive "-able" suffix and the broader meaning of *remit* that it implies.

Quiz
(answers start on page 463)

1. Which of the following suffixes is used to create **new** words meaning "able to, suited for, or capable of"?

a) "-able"

b) "-ible"

2. For existing base words, which of the following endings will **only** take the "-able" suffix?

a) "-ide"

b) "-ect"

c) "-ate"

d) "-ss"

3. True or False: Only "-ible" can be used with incomplete Latin roots.

a) True

b) False

4. When verbs ending in "-mit" take the "-ible" suffix, what spelling change typically occurs?

a) "-mit" becomes "-mittible"

b) "-mit" becomes "-minsible"

c) "-mit" becomes "-misible"

d) "-mit" becomes "-missible"

5. Which is the correct way to spell *certify* with one of the suffixes we've looked at?

a) certifable

b) certifiable

c) certifible

d) certifiible

Commonly Confused Suffixes: -ant vs. -ent

The suffixes "-ant" and "-ent" are both used to form nouns of agency (persons or things who perform an action) and adjectives that describe a state or quality. They both derive from the conjugations of Latin and French verbs; in some cases, they seem to "attach" to existing base words (e.g., *accountant, persistent*), while other times they are adjacent to roots that could not exist on their own (*brilliant, resilient*).

The suffixes "-ant" and "-ent" are especially confusing because they are both common, have similar spellings, and are (usually) pronounced the exact same way (/ənt/). For words naturally ending in "-ant" or "-ent," there are no real clues to help us determine which ending is correct (beyond knowing the word's etymology); we just have to memorize them or check a dictionary to be sure. When "-ant" and "-ent" attach to existing base words, though, there are a few conventions we can follow to choose the correct one.

Finally, it's important to note that the conventions in this section are not intended to describe when a certain base or root word *can* take "-ant" or "-ent"; they are merely meant to help you decide which ending to use when you know that a word ends in one of the two.

Rules for words ending in "-ant"

Rule 1: Use "-ant" with verbs ending in "-ate"

Verbs that end in "-ate" can often be made into nouns of agency or, less commonly, adjectives by adding the suffix "-ant." Note that this suffix completely *replaces* "-ate". For example:

- accelerate→accelerant
- adulterate→adulterant
- anticipate→anticipant
- celebrate→celebrant
- communicate→communicant
- contaminate→contaminant
- desiccate→desiccant
- deviate→deviant
- dominate→dominant
- emigrate→emigrant
- exfoliate→exfoliant
- hesitate→hesitant
- immigrate→immigrant
- intoxicate→intoxicant
- irritate→irritant
- lubricate→lubricant
- migrate→migrant
- mutate→mutant
- officiate→officiant
- radiate→radiant
- stagnate→stagnant
- stimulate→stimulant
- tolerate→tolerant
- vacate→vacant

Rule 2: Use "-ant" with verbs ending in silent E

In addition to verbs ending in "-ate," the "-ant" ending will usually attach to verbs ending in other consonants + **silent E**. Unlike "-ate," though, "-ant" only replaces the silent **E** in these examples. For instance:

- aspire→aspirant
- confide→confidant*
- convulse→convulsant (used in the term *anticonvulsant*)
- determine→determinant
- dispute→disputant
- inhale→inhalant
- insure→insurant
- exhale→exhalant
- grieve→grievant
- observe→observant
- perspire→perspirant (used in the term *antiperspirant*)
- serve→servant

(*Not to be confused with *confident*; we'll talk about how to remember the difference a little further on.)

Note that there are a few exceptions to this rule. First, three verbs ending in "-ide" will take the "-ent" suffix instead:

- preside→president
- provide→provident
- reside→resident

Also, silent E can be used to dictate that final **C** and **G** take the "soft" pronunciation (/s/ and /dʒ/, respectively), as in *coalesce* or *emerge*. As we'll see further on, soft **C** and **G** are always followed by "-ent" rather than "-ant" (e.g., *coalescent* and *emergent*).

Rule 3: Use "-ant" with words ending in "-y"

Words ending in "-y" commonly take the related suffix "-ance," which exclusively forms nouns, but only a few will take "-ant" (usually to form adjectives). In nearly all of these, **Y** changes to **I**. For example:

- comply→compliant
- defy→defiant
- luxury→luxuriant

- rely→rel**i**ant
- var**y**→var**i**ant

Uniquely, the **Y** in the verb *occupy* does not change to **I**; it is simply omitted:

- occup**y**→occup**ant**

One exception to this rule is the verb *study*, which has the associated noun of agency *stud**ent***.

Rule 4: Use "-ant" if it comes after "-ct-" or "-lt-"

If a stem or base word ends in the consonant cluster "-ct-" or (less commonly) "-lt-," the ending will always be spelled "-ant." For example:

CT + "-ant"	LT + "-ant"
attra**ctant** disinfe**ctant** expe**ctant** hume**ctant** inje**ctant** o**ctant** prote**ctant** rea**ctant** relu**ctant** surfa**ctant**	consu**ltant** exu**ltant** resu**ltant**

Rule 5: Use "-ant" if it comes after "-or-"

If the last letters of the stem or root are "-or-," the word will always end in the suffix "-ant":

- col**orant**
- corrob**orant**
- deod**orant**
- expect**orant**
- ign**orant**
- od**orant**
- rob**orant**
- son**orant**

Rule 6: Use "-ant" if it follows a hard *C* or *G*

If a stem or base word ends in a "hard **C**" (the /k/ sound) or a "hard **G**" (the /g/ sound), the ending will always be spelled "-ant." For example:

Hard C + "-ant"	Hard G + "-ant"
appli**cant** communi**cant** desi**ccant** mendi**cant** signifi**cant** va**cant**	arro**gant** congre**gant** ele**gant** extrava**gant** fumi**gant** liti**gant** segre**gant**

(Many of these examples also fall under the "-ate" rule as well.)

This is also true when a hard **G** is followed by **N** or **R**:

GN + "-ant"	GR + "-ant"
benignant	
indignant	conflagrant
malignant	emigrant
poignant	flagrant
pregnant	fragrant
regnant	migrant
repugnant	vagrant
stagnant	

Rules for words ending in "-ent"

Rule 1: Use "-ent" if it follows a soft *C* or *G*

We saw already that words will take the "-ant" ending if it is preceded by a "hard **C**" (/k/) or a "hard **G**" (/g/). If the stem or base word ends in a "soft **C**" (/s/) or a "soft **G**" (/dʒ/), however, it will be followed by the "-ent" suffix or ending. For instance:

Soft C + "-ent"	Soft G + "-ent"
ascent	astringent
acquiescent	contingent
adjacent	convergent
complacent	diligent
decent	divergent
innocent	emergent
luminescent	indulgent
magnificent	intelligent
quiescent	negligent
reminiscent	stringent
reticent	tangent
translucent	urgent

There are a few exceptions to this, though:
• pageant (/ˈpædʒənt/)
• sergeant (/ˈsɑrdʒənt/)

Rule 2: Use "-ent" with verbs ending in "-er" or "-ere"

ER + -ent	ERE + -ent
defer→deferent	adhere→adherent
deter→deterrent	cohere→coherent
differ→different	inhere→inherent
refer→referent	revere→reverent

There is one exception to this, though it is uncommon in everyday speech or writing:
• alter→alterant

Rule 3: Use "-ent" if it follows "-id-"

If the root word ends in "-id-," it is much more likely that the suffix will be "-ent" rather than "-ant." For example:
• accident
• confident
• diffident

- diss**ident**
- ev**ident**
- inc**ident**
- occ**ident**
- str**ident**
- tr**ident**

As we said earlier, there are three verbs ending in "-ide" that are also associated with the "-ent" ending:

- preside→pres**ident**
- provide→prov**ident**
- reside→res**ident**

Finally, there are two exceptions in which "-id-" is followed by "-ant" instead: *confidant* (which we saw earlier) and *oxidant*. We can remember *confidant* (as opposed to *confident*) because it is pronounced with a secondary stress on *-dant* (/ˈkɑnfɪˌdɑnt/ or /ˈkɑnfɪˌdænt/), so the **A** sound is now distinctly audible. And we can remember the spelling of *oxidant* because it is something that causes *oxidation*.

Rule 4: Use "-ent" if it follows "-u-"

While there are a few words in which "-ant" follows "-u," it is much more likely for the ending to be "-ent." For instance:

- affl**uent**
- confl**uent**
- congr**uent**
- constit**uent**
- delinq**uent**
- eloq**uent**
- fl**uent**
- freq**uent**
- grandiloq**uent**
- mellifl**uent**
- seq**uent**
- subseq**uent**
- ung**uent**

As we said, though, there are a few words that **do** end in "-uant":

- contin**uant**
- evac**uant**
- fluct**uant**
- piq**uant**
- purs**uant**
- tr**uant**

Words that can take either "-ant" <u>or</u> "-ent"

To make matters even more complicated, there are a few words that can take <u>either</u> spelling. For some of these examples, one spelling is simply a less-common variant version of the other. However, in a few instances, the meaning of the word will determine which spelling is appropriate.

Variant spellings

In these examples, both spellings are considered correct, but one is much more common and is thus preferred over the other:

Preferred spelling	Variant spelling
ascend**ant**	ascend**ent**
propell**ant**	propell**ent**
repell**ent**	repell**ant**

Spelling determined by meaning

With these pairs of words, one particular spelling is more commonly associated with the word's meaning as a noun, while the other is associated with its meaning as an adjective.

Noun	Adjective
depend**ant** (especially in British English; more commonly *depend**ent*** in American English)	depend**ent** (<u>never</u> spelled *depend**ant*** as an adjective)
descend**ant** (<u>never</u> spelled *descend**ent*** as a noun)	descend**ent** (can be spelled *descend**ant*** as an adjective, but this is an uncommon variant)
pend**ant** (can be spelled *pend**ent*** as a noun, but this is an uncommon variant)	pend**ent** (can be spelled *pend**ant*** as an adjective, but this is an uncommon variant)

Remember, the word *independent* is an adjective, so, like the adjective *dependent*, it is <u>always</u> spelled with "-ent."

Words that we have to learn

While there are a few helpful conventions and spelling patterns we can follow to help us know whether a word takes the "-ant" or "-ent" ending, there are quite a few words we just have to memorize.

Words ending "-ant"	Words ending "-ent"
abund**ant**	absorb**ent**
accept**ant**	abstin**ent**
accord**ant**	adsorb**ent**
account**ant**	anteced**ent**
adam**ant**	appar**ent**
affi**ant**	belliger**ent**
allegi**ant**	benevol**ent**
ascend**ant**	compet**ent**
aspir**ant**	consist**ent**
assail**ant**	conveni**ent**
asson**ant**	correspond**ent**
attend**ant**	curr**ent**
blat**ant**	decad**ent**
brilli**ant**	defici**ent**
buoy**ant**	depend**ent**
claim**ant**	despond**ent**
clairvoy**ant**	effici**ent**
cogniz**ant**	emin**ent**
combat**ant**	equival**ent**
concord**ant**	excell**ent**
conson**ant**	excipi**ent**
cool**ant**	exist**ent**
coven**ant**	expedi**ent**
curr**ant**	ferv**ent**
defend**ant**	flatul**ent**
depress**ant**	flu**ent**
disson**ant**	fraudul**ent**
dorm**ant**	imman**ent**
eleph**ant**	immin**ent**
ench**ant**	inadvert**ent**
entr**ant**	inclem**ent**
err**ant**	incumb**ent**

exorbitant	independent
extant	insistent
exuberant	insolent
flagrant	insolvent
flamboyant	intelligent
flippant	intermittent
gallant	lenient
gallivant	malevolent
hydrant	negligent
important	obedient
incessant	omnipotent
infant	omniscient
informant	opponent
inhabitant	opulent
insouciant	patient
jubilant	penitent
merchant	permanent
militant	persistent
miscreant	pertinent
nonchalant	precedent
obeisant	prescient
peasant	prevalent
pedant	proficient
penchant	prominent
petulant	proponent
pleasant	prudent
pliant	recipient
pollutant	recurrent
rampant	redolent
redundant	remittent
relaxant	repellent
relevant	resilient
remnant	resplendent
repentant	respondent
restaurant	salient
retardant	sapient
sealant	sentient
sibilant	solvent
somnambulant	student
tenant	subservient
tremulant	sufficient
trenchant	transcendent
triumphant	transient
valiant	transparent
verdant	turbulent
vibrant	violent
vigilant	virulent

Quiz

(answers start on page 463)

1. How are both "-ant" and "-ent" **usually** pronounced?

a) /ænt/

b) /ənt/

c) /ɑnt/

d) /ɛnt/

2. Which of the following consonant clusters will be always followed by "**-ant**"?

a) CT

b) NT

c) ST

d) RT

3. Verbs with which of the following endings will take the "**-ent**" suffix?

a) -y

b) -ate

c) -ize

d) -ere

4. Which of the following verbs takes the "-ant" suffix to form a noun?

a) preside

b) provide

c) reside

d) confide

5. Which of the following words has an acceptable variant spelling of "-ent"?

a) colorant

b) elegant

c) ascendant

d) observant

6. Which of the following words **cannot** be spelled with "-ant" instead of "-ent"?

a) dependent

b) independent

c) pendent

d) descendent

Commonly Confused Suffixes: -ance and -ancy vs. -ence and -ency

The suffixes "-ant" and "-ent" each have two related noun forms: "-ance/-ancy" and "-ence/-ency." These are all used to describe a state, quality, condition, or action typically associated with an adjective or noun of agency described by "-ant" or "-ent."

However, there is not always a direct correlation between the "-nt," "-nce," and "-ncy" endings: not every word ending in "-ant" or "-ent" can become a noun ending in both "-ance/-ancy" or "-ence/-ency." Many roots and base words can indeed take all three endings (e.g., *expectant, expectance, expectancy*; *dependent, dependence, dependency*), but many others will only take *one* of the two possible noun endings (e.g., *pregnant* becomes *pregnancy*, but *not pregnance*; *different* becomes *difference*, but *not differency*). Additionally, there are smaller subsets of words that will *only* be formed with "-ant," "-ance," "-ent," or "-ence," without having either of the other two endings.

154

Note that the rules and conventions for when a word will take "-ance" vs. "-ence" or "-ancy" vs. "-ency" overlap almost entirely with choosing "-ant" vs "-ent," so this section will focus more on determining when particular "-ant" or "-ent" words have corresponding "-nce" or "-ncy" forms. There are no spelling patterns in such words to help us determine when or if "-ance/-ancy" or "-ence/-ency" can be used, so this section will only look at specific sets of example words. If you want to see more detailed rules for determining which ending is correct, go to the section Commonly Confused Suffixes: "-ant" vs. "-ent".

Words ending in "-ant"

Words that take both "-ance" and "-ancy"

The suffixes "-ance" and "-ancy" are simply variants of one another; as such, nouns with these two endings are almost always synonymous, with the only real difference being which one is more common. In the following table of examples, we've marked the most common form in **bold**—if it is overwhelmingly more common, it will be **<u>bold and underlined</u>**. (Note that we'll only make this distinction between "-ance" and "-ancy"—we won't be looking at how common "-ant" is compared to the others.)

-ant	-ance	-ancy
aberrant	aberrance	**aberrancy**
adamant	adamance	**adamancy**
ascendant	ascendance	**ascendancy**
attractant	attractance	**attractancy**
brilliant	**brilliance**	brilliancy
buoyant	buoyance	**buoyancy**
chatoyant	chatoyance	**chatoyancy**
compliant	**compliance**	compliancy
conversant	**conversance**	conversancy
deviant	**deviance**	deviancy
discordant	**discordance**	discordancy
elegant	**elegance**	elegancy
expectant	expectance	**expectancy**
extravagant	**<u>extravagance</u>**	extravagancy
exultant	**exultance**	exultancy
flagrant	flagrance	**flagrancy**
fragrant	fragrance	**fragrancy**
flamboyant	**flamboyance**	flamboyancy
hesitant	hesitance	**hesitancy**
instant	**<u>instance</u>**	instancy
irrelevant	**irrelevance**	irrelevancy
malignant	malignance	**malignancy**
militant	militance	**<u>militancy</u>**
petulant	**petulance**	petulancy
poignant	poignance	**poignancy**
precipitant	precipitance	**precipitancy**
preponderant	**<u>preponderance</u>**	preponderancy
protuberant	**<u>protuberance</u>**	protuberancy

radiant	**radiance**	radiancy
recalcitrant	**recalcitrance**	recalcitrancy
relevant	**relevance**	relevancy
reluctant	**reluctance**	reluctancy
repugnant	**repugnance**	repugnancy
significant	**significance**	significancy
undulant	**undulance**	undulancy
valiant	**valiance**	valiancy
vibrant	vibrance	**vibrancy**

Words that take either "-ance" _or_ "-ancy"

As we noted already, though, not every adjective or noun of agency ending in "-ant" will take both "-ance" or "-ancy" to become nouns of state or condition. In fact, more words ending in "-ant" will take only one of the forms, rather than both.

-ant	-ance	-ancy
abeyant	abeyance	
acceptant	acceptance	
abundant	abundance	
accordant	accordance	
accountant		accountancy
adjutant		adjutancy
affiant	affiance	
allegiant	allegiance	
ambulant	ambulance	
appurtenant	appurtenance	
arrogant	arrogance	
assistant	assistance	
attendant	attendance	
avoidant	avoidance	
benignant		benignancy
blatant		blatancy
brisant	brisance	
clairvoyant	clairvoyance	
cognizant	cognizance	
complaisant	complaisance	
concomitant	concomitance	
concordant	concordance	
consonant	consonance	
constant		constancy
consultant		consultancy
constant		constancy
continuant	continuance	

defiant	defiance	
dilatant		dilatancy
discrepant		discrepancy
distant	distance	
dominant	dominance	
dormant		dormancy
entrant	entrance	
errant	errancy	
exorbitant	exorbitance	
exuberant	exuberance	
flippant		flippancy
grievant	grievance	
ignorant	ignorance	
incessant		incessancy
infant		infancy
important	importance	
inobservant	inobservance	
insouciant	insouciance	
insurant	insurance	
intendant	intendance	
issuant	issuance	
iterant	iterance	
itinerant		itinerancy
jubilant	jubilance	
lieutenant		lieutenancy
luxuriant	luxuriance	
mendicant		mendicancy
mordant		mordancy
nurturant	nurturance	
obeisant	obeisance	
observant	observance	
occupant		occupancy
penetrant	penetrance	
piquant		piquancy
pleasant	pleasance	
pliant		pliancy
postulant		postulancy
pregnant		pregnancy
pursuant	pursuance	
puissant	puissance	
pursuant	pursuance	

radiant	radiance	
rampant		rampancy
reactant	reactance	
redundant		redundancy
reliant	reliance	
remonstrant	remonstrance	
repentant	repentance	
resemblant	resemblance	
resistant	resistance	
resonant	resonance	
sergeant		sergeancy
sibilant	sibilance	
sonant	sonance	
stagnant		stagnancy
suppliant	suppliance	
surveillant	surveillance	
sycophant		sycophancy
tenant		tenancy
tolerant	tolerance	
truant		truancy
vacant		vacancy
vagrant		vagrancy
variant	variance	
verdant		verdancy
vigilant	vigilance	

Words that don't take "-ance" or "-ancy"

While most "-ant" words will have associated forms ending in "-ance," "-ancy," or both, there is also a large number of terms that don't take **either** noun ending. There is nothing in the spelling of these words that makes it clear that they will not take either of the two endings, so we just have to memorize them:

abradant	examinant	participant
absonant	excitant	pedant
alterant	exhalant	penchant
accelerant	expectorant	permeant
administrant	extant	puissant
adulterant	fabricant	pollutant
claimant	flagellant	postulant
clamant	fluctuant	recreant
coagulant	fulgurant	reductant
colorant	fulminant	registrant
combatant	fumigant	relaxant
complainant	gallant	remnant
contestant	habitant	resultant
convulsant	humectant	retardant
coolant	hydrant	revenant

corroborant	immigrant	reverberant
culminant	incitant	ruminant
declarant	indicant	sealant
decongestant	indignant	servant
defendant	inebriant	simulant
deodorant	insulant	sonorant
depressant	irritant	stimulant
determinant	libellant	supplicant
discriminant	merchant	surfactant
discussant	migrant	toxicant
disinfectant	ministrant	tremulant
dispersant	mordant	triumphant
disputant	mutant	tyrant
emigrant	officiant	urticant
etchant	operant	vesicant
euphoriant	oxidant	visitant
evacuant	palpitant	

Words that only take "-ance"

While less common, there are also some nouns ending in "-ance" that *don't* have associated "-ant" forms. When this is the case, they do not have variant "-ancy" spellings either; they can only be formed from base words or roots using "-ance."

abidance	deliverance	performance
absorptance	disturbance	perseverance
acquaintance	emittance	pittance
acquittance	encumbrance	provenance
admittance	endurance	purveyance
affirmance	forbearance	quittance
alliance	forbiddance	reconnaissance
allowance	governance	remembrance
annoyance	guidance	remittance
appearance	hindrance	riddance
appliance	inductance	semblance
assurance	inheritance	severance
capacitance	luminance	substance
comeuppance	maintenance	sustenance
contrivance	malfeasance	temperance
conveyance	ordinance	utterance
countenance	parlance	vengeance
dalliance	penance	voidance

Words ending in "-ent"

The suffix "-ent" has the same function as "-ant," and it has the same behavior when forming nouns ending with "-ence" or "-ency": many "-ent" words will take both endings, many others will only take one or the other, while still others won't take either.

Words that take both "-ence" and "-ency"

As with "-ance/-ancy," nouns that end in "-ence" or "-ency" are almost always synonymous (though there *are* a few instances in which the "-ency" form has a slightly different meaning than "-ence"). Like in the previous table, the more common of the two is in **bold**, and if one is much more common than the other, it will be **bold and underlined**).

Spelling Conventions

-ent	-ence	-ency
adjacent	adjacence	**adjacency**
advertent	**advertence**	advertency
affluent	**affluence**	affluency
appetent	appetence	**appetency**
ascendent	ascendence	**ascendency**
belligerent	**belligerence**	belligerency
cadent	**cadence**	cadency
coherent	**coherence**	coherency
competent	**competence**	competency
complacent	complacence	**complacency**
concurrent	**concurrence**	concurrency
congruent	**congruence**	congruency
consistent	consistence	**consistency**
contingent	contingence	**contingency**
convenient	**convenience**	conveniency
convergent	**convergence**	convergency
correspondent	**correspondence**	correspondency
covalent	**covalence**	covalency
decadent	**decadence**	decadency
decumbent	decumbence	**decumbency**
dependent	**dependence**	dependency
despondent	despondence	**despondency**
detergent	detergence	**detergency**
divergent	**divergence**	divergency
ebullient	**ebullience**	ebulliency
effervescent	**effervescence**	effervescency
emergent	emergence (*the process or act of emerging*)	**emergency** (*a sudden, typically unexpected occurrence or situation requiring immediate action*)
eminent	**eminence**	eminency
esurient	**esurience**	esuriency
excellent	**excellence**	excellency (used exclusively as a title for high-ranking officials or Roman Catholic bishops and archbishops, rather than a complete synonym of *excellence*)
excrescent	**excrescence**	excrescency
exigent	exigence	**exigency**
expedient	expedience	**expediency**
flatulent	**flatulence**	flatulency
immanent	**immanence**	immanancy
imminent	**imminence**	imminency
impendent	**impendence**	impendency

impertinent	**impertinence**	impertinency
impotent	**impotence**	impotency
incipient	incipience	**incipiency**
inherent	**inherence**	inherency
insistent	**insistence**	insistency
insurgent	insurgence	**insurgency**
intermittent	intermittence	**intermittency**
lenient	lenience	**leniency**
lucent	lucence	**lucency**
nascent	**nascence**	nascency
omnipotent	**omnipotence**	omnipotency
opulent	**opulence**	opulency
permanent	**permanence**	permanency
persistent	**persistence**	persistency
pertinent	**pertinence**	pertinency
potent	potence	**potency**
precedent	**precedence**	precedency
prurient	**prurience**	pruriency
purulent	**purulence**	purulency
recipient	recipience	**recipiency**
refulgent	**refulgence**	refulgency
remittent	**remittence**	remittency
repellent	repellence	**repellency**
resident	**residence** (*a place in which one lives or resides, or the act thereof*)	residency (*more often meaning a particular stage in graduate medical training*)
resilient	**resilience**	resiliency
resplendent	**resplendence**	resplendency
respondent	**respondence**	respondency
reticent	**reticence**	reticency
salient	**salience**	saliency
somnolent	**somnolence**	somnolency
strident	stridence	**stridency**
subservient	**subservience**	subserviency
transcendent	**transcendence**	transcendency
transient	**transience**	transiency
translucent	translucence	**translucency**
transparent	transparence	**transparency**
truculent	**truculence**	truculency
valent	**valence**	valency
virulent	**virulence**	virulency

Words that take either "-ence" or "-ency"

While "-ant" words that can only take "-ance" or "-ancy" split this difference almost equally, "-ent" words are far more likely to only take the "-ence" ending.

-ent	-ence	-ency
abhorrent	abhorrence	
absent	absence	
absorbent	*	absorbency
abstinent	abstinence	
acquiescent	acquiescence	
adherent	adherence	
agent		agency
ambient	ambience	
ambivalent	ambivalence	
antecedent	antecedence	
arborescent	arborescence	
ardent		ardency
astringent		astringency
audient	audience	
beneficent	beneficence	
benevolent	benevolence	
candescent	candescence	
clement		clemency
coalescent	coalescence	
cogent		cogency
coincident	coincidence	
concrescent	concrescence	
concupiscent	concupiscence	
confident	confidence	
confluent	confluence	
consequent	consequence	
constituent		constituency
constringent		constringency
continent	continence	
convalescent	convalescence	
corpulent	corpulence	
current		currency
deferent	deference	
deficient		deficiency
dehiscent	dehiscence	
delinquent		delinquency
deliquescent	deliquescence	

deterrent	deterrence	
different	difference	
diffident	diffidence	
diligent	diligence	
dissident	dissidence	
efferent	efference	
efficient		efficiency
efflorescent	efflorescence	
effluent	effluence	
effulgent	effulgence	
eloquent	eloquence	
equipollent	equipollence	
evanescent	evanescence	
evident	evidence	
existent	existence	
feculent	feculence	
fervent		fervency
florescent	florescence	
fluent		fluency
fluorescent	fluorescence	
frequent		frequency
grandiloquent	grandiloquence	
immunocompetent	immunocompetence	
impudent	impudence	
incident	incidence	
incumbent		incumbency
indigent	indigence	
indulgent	indulgence	
innocent	innocence	
insolent	insolence	
intelligent	intelligence	
intransigent	intransigence	
iridescent	iridescence	
irreverent	irreverence	
jurisprudent	jurisprudence	
juvenescent	juvenescence	
lambent		lambency
latent		latency
luminescent	luminescence	
magnificent	magnificence	
magniloquent	magniloquence	

malevolent	malevolence	
munificent	munificence	
negligent	negligence	
omnificent	omnificence	
omnipresent	omnipresence	
omniscient	omniscience	
opalescent	opalescence	
patent		patency
patient	patience	
pearlescent	pearlescence	
pendent		pendency
penitent	penitence	
percipient	percipience	
pestilent	pestilence	
phosphorescent	phosphorescence	
preeminent	preeminence	
prepubescent	prepubescence	
prescient	prescience	
present	presence	
president		presidency
prevalent	prevalence	
prevenient	prevenience	
proficient		proficiency
prominent	prominence	
provident	providence	
prudent	prudence	
pubescent	pubescence	
pungent		pungency
putrescent	putrescence	
quiescent	quiescence	
recent		recency
recrudescent	recrudescence	
redolent	redolence	
referent	reference	
refluent	refluence	
regent		regency
remanent	remanence	
reminiscent	reminiscence	
renascent	renascence	
resurgent	resurgence	
reticent	reticence	

reverent	reverence	
rufescent	rufescence	
sapient	sapience	
senescent	senescence	
sequent	sequence	
silent	silence	
solvent		solvency
stringent		stringency
subjacent		subjacency
subsequent	subsequence	
subsistent	subsistence	
sufficient		sufficiency
tangent		tangency
tumescent	tumescence	
turbulent	turbulence	
urgent		urgency
vehement	vehemence	
violent	violence	

(*Note that *absorbance* also exists, but only in relation to physics—specifically denoting the measure of a substance's ability to absorb radiation. *Absorbent* and *absorbency* are the preferred spelling for all other meanings.)

Words that don't take "-ence" or "-ency"

As with "-ant," many adjectives and nouns of agency ending in "-ent" **cannot** be made into nouns ending in *either* "-ence" or "-ency."

abducent	crescent	gradient
abluent	decedent	ignescent
acescent	decrement	intent
acidulent	decrescent	intromittent
adducent	descendent	luculent
adsorbent	descent	malcontent
afferent	demulcent	mellifluent
ancient	detergent	mordent
aperient	diluent	nutrient
apparent	distent	opponent
ardent	docent	portent
ascent	eluent	procumbent
assent	emollient	proponent
assurgent	erumpent	rubefacient
candent	esculent	somnifacient
coefficient	excipient	student
component	extent	succedent
content	flocculent	torrent
cotangent	frutescent	unguent

Words that only end in "-ence"

Finally, there are also words that will only take the "-ence" ending. There are not that many of these words, but quite a few of them are very common in modern English.

- condescend**ence** (variant of *condescension*)
- condol**ence**
- confer**ence**
- consci**ence**
- circumfer**ence**
- divulg**ence**
- ess**ence**
- experi**ence**
- infer**ence**
- interfer**ence**
- merg**ence**
- prefer**ence**
- quintess**ence**
- sci**ence**
- subsid**ence**
- submerg**ence**
- transfer**ence**

Uniquely, the verb *tend* becomes *tendency*, not *tendent* or *tendence*. This is the only instance in which a word will take the "-ncy" ending, but not "-nt" or "-nce."

Commonly Confused Suffixes: -er, -or, and -ar

The suffixes "-er," "-or," and "-ar" are all used to create nouns of agency (indicating "a person or thing that performs an action") from verbs. Of the three, "-er" is by far the most common, while "-or" is much more common than "-ar." Because they perform the same function and are pronounced in the same way (/ər/), it can be difficult to decide which suffix is the correct one to use.

When a verb is changed into a noun of agency using a suffix, it will almost always be "-er." However, there are a few particular conventions we can follow to determine when we should use "-or" instead. (We use the "-ar" suffix much more rarely, so we will discuss it separately toward the end of the section.)

Rule 1: Use "-er" with verbs ending in a single consonant

When a verb ends in a single consonant, it will almost always take the suffix "-er." Note that if the consonant is preceded by a single vowel, the consonant will generally double before the suffix (though this is not always the case; go to the section Doubling Consonants with Vowel Suffixes to learn more).

For example:
- bat→bat**ter**
- barter→barte**rer**
- canvas→canvas**ser**
- cater→cate**rer**
- cheat→chea**ter**
- eat→ea**ter**
- embroider→embroide**rer**
- feel→fee**ler**
- fib→fib**ber**
- format→forma**tter**
- grab→grab**ber**
- loiter→loite**rer**
- loot→loo**ter**
- propel→prope**ller**
- rap→ra**pper**
- read→rea**der**

- scrub→scru**bber**
- sit→si**tter**
- shred→shre**dder**
- travel→trave**ler**
- yak→yak**ker**

There are several exceptions to this rule, though:

- conquer→conque**ror**
- council→counci**lor**
- counsel→counse**lor**
- offer→offe**ror**
- sail→sai**lor**

Rule 1.5: Use "-or" with multi-syllable verbs ending in "-it"

While single-syllable verbs that end in "-it" will usually take the suffix "-er" and have the final **T** doubled (as in *hitter, knitter, quitter, sitter*, etc.), verbs with two or more syllables ending in "-it" are much more likely to take the suffix "-or." For example:

- audit→audi**tor**
- credit→credi**tor**
- edit→edi**tor**
- exhibit→exhibi**tor**
- inherit→inheri**tor**
- inhibit→inhibi**tor**
- solicit→solici**tor**
- visit→visi**tor**

While this convention is fairly reliable, there are some exceptions:

- delimit→delimi**ter**
- profit→profi**ter**
- recruit→recrui**ter**

Also note that this convention does **not** apply when a silent E follows the final **T**.

Rule 2: Use "-er" with verbs ending in a silent E

Most verbs that end in a consonant + silent **E** will take the "-er" suffix (which replaces the final **E** of the root word). For instance:

- advertise→adverti**ser**
- bake→ba**ker**
- bathe→bat**her**
- change→chan**ger**
- code→co**der**
- divide→divi**der**
- frame→fra**mer**
- give→gi**ver**
- grate→gra**ter**
- hate→ha**ter**
- love→lo**ver**
- make→ma**ker**
- organize→organi**zer**
- page→pa**ger**
- ride→ri**der**
- slide→sli**der**
- time→ti**mer**
- write→wri**ter**

This is a reliable convention to follow, but there are some exceptions, most often when a word ends in "-ise":

- incise→inci**sor**
- previse→previ**sor**

- promise→promi**sor** (variant of *promiser*, used especially in legal writing)
- supervise→supervi**sor**
- survive→suvi**vor**

However, the most consistent exception is for verbs with more than one syllable that end in "-ate."

Rule 2.5: Use "-or" with multi-syllable verbs ending in "-ate"

When a word has more than one syllable and ends in "-ate," it will almost always take the "-or" suffix. Once again, the suffix <u>replaces</u> the silent **E** at the end. For example:

- accelerate→accelera**tor**
- administrate→administra**tor**
- animate→anima**tor**
- calculate→calcula**tor**
- coordinate→coordina**tor**
- educate→educa**tor**
- elevate→eleva**tor**
- generate→genera**tor**
- instigate→instiga**tor**
- liberate→libera**tor**
- motivate→motiva**tor**
- narrate→narra**tor**
- perpetrate→perpetra**tor**
- refrigerate→refrigera**tor**
- spectate→specta**tor**
- terminate→termina**tor**
- ventilate→ventila**tor**

Remember, single-syllable verbs ending in "-ate" will take the "-er" suffix, as in *gra**ter**, ha**ter**, ska**ter***, etc.

Rule 3: Use "-er" with verbs ending in consonant clusters

So far we've mostly looked at examples of verbs that end in a single consonant and a silent **E**, with a few different instances in which "-or" is (or might) be used instead of "-er."

However, when a verb ends in a consonant **cluster** (two or more consonants that quickly blend together in the same syllable), it is much more likely to take the "-er" suffix.

For example:

- adapt→adap**ter***
- bend→ben**der**
- boost→boos**ter**
- build→buil**der**
- busk→bus**ker**
- contend→conten**der**
- defend→defen**der**
- dust→dus**ter**
- forest→fores**ter**
- golf→gol**fer**
- grind→grin**der**
- help→hel**per**
- jump→jum**per**
- lend→len**der**
- mend→men**der**
- protest→protes**ter**
- respond→respon**der**
- shoplift→shoplif**ter**
- tempt→temp**ter**
- weld→wel**der**

However, there are a few common exceptions to this convention:

- invent→inventor
- invest→investor
- sculpt→sculptor
- torment→tormentor
- vend→vendor

(*Adapter can also be spelled *adaptor*, but this is a bit less common.)

Uniquely, we more commonly use "-or" when a word ends in the cluster **CT**.

Rule 3.5: Use "-or" with verbs ending in *CT*

While verbs ending in other consonant clusters will take the "-er" suffix, a verb that ends in **CT** will almost always be made into a noun with the suffix "-or," as in:

- abduct→abductor
- act→actor
- conduct→conductor
- contract→contractor
- correct→corrector
- direct→director
- eject→ejector
- instruct→instructor
- object→objector
- project→projector
- react→reactor
- reflect→reflector
- select→selector

Rule 4: Use "-er" with verbs ending in consonant digraphs

Like we do with verbs ending in consonant clusters (other than **CT**), we use the "-er" suffix with verbs ending in consonant digraphs, pairs of consonants that form a single unique consonant sound. This is also true of words ending in the consonant trigraph **TCH**.

For example:

- catch→catcher
- choreograph→choreographer
- cough→cougher
- etch→etcher
- laugh→laugher
- march→marcher
- publish→publisher
- sing→singer
- teach→teacher
- wash→washer
- watch→watcher

This is also true when a verb ends in a double consonant (except **SS**, as we'll see later). For example:

- bluff→bluffer
- buzz→buzzer
- call→caller
- distill→distiller
- mill→miller
- roll→roller
- spell→speller
- staff→staffer

Rule 4.5: There's no pattern for verbs ending in *SS*

While verbs ending in **FF, LL,** or **ZZ** will always take the suffix "-er," there is much less certainty for words ending in **SS**—there is no clear pattern, so we just have to memorize which suffix a particular word will take.

-er	-or
address→address**er**	assess→assess**or**
canvass→canvass**er**	compress→compress**or**
dress→dress**er**	confess→confess**or**
express→express**er**	depress→depress**or**
guess→guess**er**	possess→possess**or**
hiss→hiss**er**	process→process**or**
kiss→kiss**er**	profess→profess**or**
pass→pass**er**	suppress→suppress**or**
trespass→trespass**er**	transgress→transgress**or**

Using the suffix "-ar"

While "-er" is the most common suffix to form nouns of agency from verbs, the suffix "-or" performs the same function in certain instances. However, there is a third suffix that can be used to form these types of nouns, and it is pronounced the same way as the other two: "-ar."

Nouns of agency ending in "-ar"

Nouns of agency ending in the "-ar" suffix are much less common than "-er" or "-or," and there is no real convention to dictate when "-ar" is the appropriate ending.

There are only two nouns that can be directly derived from verbs using "-ar":

• beg→beg**ar**
• lie→li**ar**

There is a third verb that is connected to a noun of agency: *burgle→burgl**ar***. In this case, however, *burglar* is the original word (derived from Anglo-Latin) with the verb *burgle* derived from it, a process known as a "back-formation."

Finally, there are a few other nouns of agency that end in "-ar," but they are not derived from or directly connected to a verb, so "-ar" is not functioning as a suffix:

• burs**ar**
• registr**ar**
• schol**ar**
• vic**ar**

Other nouns ending in "-ar"

In addition to ending some nouns of agency, "-ar" appears at the ends of several other common nouns. However, it is not functioning as a suffix in these cases, as it does not change a different part of speech into a noun. For instance:

• alt**ar**
• avat**ar**
• calend**ar**
• chedd**ar**
• doll**ar**
• gramm**ar**
• guit**ar**
• hang**ar** (meaning "a large building or shelter, usually to house aircraft"; not related to the verb *hang*)
• mort**ar**
• nect**ar**
• pill**ar**
• rad**ar**
• vineg**ar**

Using "-ar" to form adjectives

While the suffix "-ar" is used to form a few nouns, it is much more commonly used to create adjectives, either on its own or as part of the larger suffix "-ular." (Both "-ar" and "-ular" are used to mean "like; resembling or relating to; of or belonging to.")

For example:
- angle→ang**ular**
- cell→cell**ular**
- circle→circ**ular**
- grain→gran**ular**
- line→line**ar**
- muscle→musc**ular**
- nucleus→nucle**ar**
- pole→pol**ar**
- populace→pop**ular**
- title→tit**ular**
- vehicle→vehic**ular**

Forming Comparative Adjectives and Comparative Adverbs

While many adjectives can be formed with the suffix "-ar," it's important to note that the suffix "-er" is the **only** ending that can be used to create **comparative adjectives** and **comparative adverbs**—adjectives and adverbs used to compare traits between two people or things. For example:

- bright→bright**er**
- dim→dimm**er**
- fast→fast**er**
- full→full**er**
- happy→happi**er**
- long→long**er**
- red→redd**er**
- slow→slow**er**
- tall→tall**er**
- witty→witti**er**

Forming other comparatives

Note that not all adjectives can become comparative by adding "-er." Only those that have one syllable or those with two syllables ending in "-y" can do so. For longer adjectives, we simply add the words *more* or *less* before them, as in:

- admirable→**more/less** admirable
- careful→**more/less** careful
- intelligent→**more/less** intelligent
- loyal→**more/less** loyal
- respectful→**more/less** respectful
- vivid→**more/less** vivid

Adverbs also have this restriction, though it is only single-syllable adverbs that can take the "-er" suffix; adverbs ending in "-y" are almost always formed by adding "-ly" to adjectives, and they take the words *more/less* to become comparative. For example:

- admirably→**more/less** admirably
- carefully→**more/less** carefully
- intelligently→**more/less** intelligently
- loyally→**more/less** loyally
- respectfully→**more/less** respectfully
- vividly→**more/less** vividly

Other adjectives are simply irregular, and have a specific comparative form that does not follow the convention above; here are some of the most common examples:

Adjectives	Adverbs
bad→**worse** fun→**more/less** fun far→**farther** (literal distance) or **further** (figurative distance) good→**better** little→**less** (when describing an amount)	badly→**worse** early→**earlier*** far→**farther** (literal distance) or **further** (figurative distance) little→**less** (when describing an amount) well→**better**

(*_Early_ is both an adjective and an adverb, and it has the same comparative form in both uses: _earlier_. This is irregular only as an adverb because it goes against the convention of adding _more/less_ to adverbs ending in "-ly.")

Quiz
(answers start on page 463)

1. Which of the following suffixes is **most** commonly used to form nouns from verbs?

a) -ar

b) -er

c) -or

2. Which of the following suffixes is **least** commonly used to form nouns from verbs?

a) -ar

b) -er

c) -or

3. In which of the following instances would we **most likely** use the suffix "**-or**"?

a) With verbs ending in a consonant digraph

b) With verbs ending in a single consonant

c) With verbs ending in a silent **E**

d) With verbs ending in **CT**

4. Which of the following verbs takes the "-er" suffix to become a noun of agency?

a) lie

b) narrate

c) work

d) inherit

5. Which part of speech is **most commonly** formed with the suffix "-ar"?

a) adjectives

b) adverbs

c) nouns

d) verbs

6. Which of the following suffixes is used to form **comparative** adjectives and adverbs?

a) -ar

b) -er

c) -or

d) A & B

e) B & C

f) All of the above

Commonly Confused Suffixes: -ic vs. -ical

The suffixes "-ic" and "-ical" both form adjectives meaning "of, resembling, characterized by, or relating to," and they are notoriously difficult to distinguish. In many cases, words can be spelled with either ending with no change in meaning, with one version simply more common than the other; in other instances, the "-ic" and "-ical" versions will have similar but slightly *different* meanings, making each one more suited in particular contexts.

However, there are also words that will only take "-ic" or "-ical," not both (or else have a variant spelling so uncommon as to be considered incorrect). While there are very few concrete "rules" dictating when this is the case, there *are* some general spelling conventions we can follow. We'll begin by looking at these different conventions, and then we'll compare words that can take both endings.

(For these spelling conventions, we'll only be looking at existing base words that become or are associated with adjectives ending in "-ic"; things become much less predictable when the suffixes attach to incomplete Greek or Latin roots.)

When to use "-ic"

The suffix "-ic" is by far the more common of the two ("-ical" is really just a variant of "-ic") and, as such, there are many more instances in which words will only end in "-ic."

Use "-ic" with nouns ending in "-d," "-de," or "-dy"

Existing nouns that end in "-d," "-de," or "-dy" will almost always take "-ic" ending when becoming adjectives. Note that with both "-de" and "-dy," though, the final vowel is replaced by "-ic," so each of these words will end in "-dic." Here are some of the most common examples:

• acid→acid**ic**
• comedy→comed**ic**
• episode→episod**ic**
• herald→herald**ic**
• melody→melod**ic**
• nomad→nomad**ic**
• parody→parod**ic**
• period→period**ic** (*Periodical* can also be used, but it more common as a noun referring to a publication issued at regular intervals)
• rhapsody→rhapsod**ic**

One outstanding exception is the noun *method*, which becomes *method**ical***. (*Methodic* is an accepted variant, but is very uncommon.)

Use "-ic" with nouns ending in "-ot" or "-ote"

There are not many nouns ending in "-ot" or "-ote" that become adjectives with "-ic," but this is still a reliable convention when distinguishing "-ic" vs. "-ical." As with "-de," we drop the silent E and replace it with "-ic." For instance:

• asymptote→asymptot**ic**
• anecdote→anecdot**ic***
• despot→despot**ic**
• idiot→idiot**ic**
• patriot→patriot**ic**
• Quixote→quixot**ic**
• zygote→zygot**ic**

(**Anecdotical* does exist, but is less common. However, a third adjective, *anecdotal*, is much more common than the "-ic" or "-ical" forms.)

Use "-ic" with nouns ending in "-et" or "-ete"

We can also use "-ic" with adjectives ending in "-et" or "-ete" following the same spelling pattern as "-ot" and "-ote."

• aesthete→aesthet**ic**
• athlete→athlet**ic**

- ballet→ballet**ic**
- diabetes→diabet**ic**
- diet→diet**ic** (note the unique spelling change)
- epithet→epithet**ic**
- magnet→magnet**ic**
- poet→poet**ic**
- prophet→prophet**ic**

The most common exception to this spelling convention is the noun *alphabet*, which most commonly becomes *alphabetical*. *Alphabetic* can also be used, but it is typically associated with a slightly different meaning. We'll look at this and other differentiated pairs further on.

Use "-ic" with nouns ending in "-esia" and "-esis"

In the examples we've looked at so far, the only spelling change we've encountered has been to drop silent E and replace it with "-ic" (with the exception of *dietetic*). With nouns ending in "-esia" and "-esis," though, we make more substantial changes: "-s-" is replaced with "-t-," and both "-ia" and "-is" become "-ic."

For example:
- anesthesia→anesthe**tic**
- diuresis→diure**tic**
- emesis→eme**tic**
- exegesis→exege**tic**
- genesis→gene**tic**
- kinesis→kine**tic**
- metathesis→metathe**tic**
- mimesis→mime**tic**
- paresis→pare**tic**
- prosthesis→prosthe**tic**
- synthesis→synthe**tic**

However, there are two prominent exceptions to this rule that take "-ical" instead:
- hypothesis→hypothe**tical**
- parenthesis→parenthe**tical**

Note that the other spelling changes we make remain the same—we just add "-al" to the very end.

Use "-ic" with nouns ending in "-os" and "-osis"

We change these nouns in a similar fashion to those ending in "-esia" and "-esis." For nouns ending in "-osis," we once again replace "-s-" with "-t-" and "-is" with "-ic;" for nouns ending in "-os," we simply replace "-s" with "-tic." For example:
- chaos→chao**tic**
- cirrhosis→cirrho**tic**
- fibrosis→fibro**tic**
- hypnosis→hypno**tic**
- melanosis→melano**tic**
- narcosis→narco**tic**
- necrosis→necro**tic**
- neurosis→neuro**tic**
- osmosis→osmo**tic**
- orthosis→ortho**tic**
- psychosis→psycho**tic**
- scoliosis→scolio**tic**
- symbiosis→symbio**tic**

Use "-ic" with nouns ending in "-pathy"

Another very reliable convention is that nouns ending in "-pathy" can only take the "-ic" suffix. We typically just replace "-y" with "-ic," forming "-pathic," but a few words will become becomes "-pathetic" instead.
- apathy→apa**thetic**

174

- empathy→empa**thic**/empath**etic***
- homeopathy→homeopa**thic**
- idiopathy→idiopa**thic**
- myopathy→myopa**thic**
- naturopathy→naturopa**thic**
- osteopathy→osteopa**thic**
- psychopathy→psychopa**thic**
- sociopath→sociopa**thic**
- sympathy→sympath**etic**
- telepathy→telepa**thic**

(*Empathic is an older term than *empathetic*, but the latter has become more common in everyday speech and writing, due in no small part to the structure and similar meaning of *sympathetic*. *Empathic* and *empathetic* are completely synonymous and equally acceptable, so choose whichever sounds better to your ear.)

Use "-ic" with nouns ending in "-ics" (usually)

The suffix "-ics" is actually a translation of the Greek suffix "-ika," which is the "neuter plural" form of "-ikos," from which "-ic" is derived. This neuter plural is used to form nouns from adjectives denoting particular activities or actions; professions, sciences, arts, or fields of study; or qualities or aspects. These "-ics" nouns are most often directly derived from adjectives ending in "-ic." For instance:

- academ**ics**→academ**ic**
- acoust**ics**→acoust**ic**
- acrobat**ics**→acrobat**ic**
- civ**ics**→civ**ic**
- econom**ics**→econom**ic***
- forens**ics**→forens**ic**
- genet**ics**→genet**ic**
- graph**ics**→graph**ic***
- gymnast**ics**→gymnast**ic**
- hydraul**ics**→hydraul**ic**
- kinet**ics**→kinet**ic**
- linguist**ics**→linguist**ic**
- pediatr**ics**→pediatr**ic**
- phon**ics**→phon**ic**
- thermodynam**ics**→thermodynam**ic**

However, despite the etymological link between "-ic" and "-ics," there are also a few "-ics" nouns that are only (or much more commonly) associated with "-ical" adjectives, such as:

- eth**ics**→eth**ical**
- hyster**ics**→hyster**ical**
- logist**ics**→logist**ical**
- mathemat**ics**→mathemat**ical**
- mechan**ics**→mechan**ical**
- opt**ics**→opt**ical**
- phys**ics**→phys**ical**
- polit**ics**→polit**ical**
- statist**ics**→statist**ical**
- theatr**ics**→theatr**ical**

(*These words also have common "-ical" variants, but they have slightly different meanings. We'll look at these and other such pairs of adjectives a little further on.)

When to use "-ical"

While "-ic" is much more common, there are a few cases in which "-ical" is used instead (or at least is greatly preferred).

Use "-ical" with nouns ending in "-ology"

One of the few spelling conventions that predictably indicates the use of "-ical" is when a noun ends in "-ology." While there are often "-ic" variants, "-ical" is almost always much more common.

Here are some of the most common examples:
• anthropology→anthropological
• archaeology→archaeological
• astrology→astrological
• biology→biological
• chronology→chronological
• ecology→ecological
• geology→geological
• iconology→iconological
• ideology→ideological
• meteorology→meteorological
• ontology→ontological
• pathology→pathological
• physiology→physiological
• psychology→psychological
• sociology→sociological
• theology→theological
• topology→topological
• zoology→zoological

There is a notable exception to this convention, though: the noun *apology* becomes *apologetic*, not *apological*.

Use "-ical" with nouns ending in "-ic"

One possible reason why the "-ical" variant has arisen in the evolution of English (and caused such confusion between the two suffixes) is to create adjectival forms of nouns that naturally end in "-ic." In such instances, we actually add a *different* suffix, "-al," to the end of the noun, which in turn creates the "-ical" ending. For example:
• cleric→clerical
• clinic→clinical
• critic→critical
• cynic→cynical
• empiric→empirical
• ethic→ethical
• fanatic→fanatical
• logic→logical
• medic→medical
• music→musical
• rhetoric→rhetorical
• skeptic→skeptical
• topic→topical

However, this convention is only really helpful when we know for certain that a noun ending in "-ic" does not also function as an adjective. Quite a few words ending in "-ic" can function as either nouns or adjectives (e.g., *academic, classic, magic*, etc.), and, while several of these have "-ical" variants, many others do not. To make matters more complicated, the "-ic" adjective sometimes has a slightly different meaning than the "-ical" equivalent, a problem that exists in quite a few "-ic/-ical" pairs.

Adjectives with different meanings when ending in "-ic" and "-ical"

All word pairs ending in "-ic" and "-ical" overlap in meaning, but some of them have differentiated over time, becoming more nuanced and specific in their modern usage. We'll look at some of the most common of these pairs, with brief explanations of how their meanings differ. (Note that we'll be looking at very abbreviated definitions, so the examples below may not cover every possible meaning of a given word.)

alphabetic vs. alphabetical

Alphabetic and *alphabetical* are synonymous, with two core meanings: 1) "arranged according to the order of the alphabet," and 2) "characterized by or relating to the alphabet." However, *alphabetical*, which is more common overall, is usually used in the context of the first meaning, as in:

• "The guidebook has the best places to visit listed in a series of **alphabetical** entries."

Alphabetic, on the other hand, is nowadays more typically used in relation to the second meaning, "characterized by or relating to the alphabet," as in:

• "English features an **alphabetic** writing system, whereas Chinese has a logographic writing system."

classic vs. classical

Classic is the more broadly applicable of this pair. It is generally used to describe something as being representative of the standard, traditional, or perfected norm; of the highest class or quality; or having lasting significance or worth. For instance:

• "The novel uses **classic** tropes established in film noir."
• "Their victory was largely due to a **classic** performance by their quarterback."
• "We've designed the rooms with a **classic** aesthetic that is both classy and comfortable."

Classic can also be used as a noun to describe an instance or example of these descriptions (as in, "The company's latest product is an instant **classic**."). When pluralized as *classics*, it can refer to the literature and/or languages of ancient Greece or Rome.

Classical can only be used as an adjective and is usually used more narrowly, referring to the art or culture of Ancient Greece or Rome, or the music produced in Europe in the 18th and 19th centuries. For example:

• "He is a professor of **classical** literature."
• "I only listen to the works of **classical** pianists."

comic vs. comical

As an adjective, *comic* is most commonly used to mean "of, characterized by, or having to do with comedy," as in:

• "The actress has incredible **comic** timing."
• "Some of the best **comic** writers in the business work on this show."

Comic can also simply mean "funny or humorous," but this definition is much more commonly associated with the term *comical* instead:

• "He had a knack for making **comical** facial expressions that delighted his audience."
• "Her unscripted comments were undeniably **comical**."

Unlike *comic*, *comical* can also have a negative connotation as well, indicating that something is ludicrous or pitiful in the way it provokes amusement. For example:

• "Their attempts to establish credibility were downright **comical**."
• "He had a look of almost **comical** dejection when I told him the job had already been filled."

economic vs. economical

Economic is used to describe that which is characterized by or relating to the *economy*, as in:

• "The president's proposed **economic** reform is being scrutinized by Congress."
• "It took several years for the country to recover from the **economic** downturn."

Economical, on the other hand, more often relates to being efficient, frugal, or prudent (with money or another resource):

• "With six children under one roof, our parents were forced to be **economical** early on."
• "The interior of the house was **economical** in its design, taking as much advantage of the limited space as possible."

electric vs. electrical (vs. electronic)

Electrical very broadly means "of, concerned with, operated by, or producing electricity." For example:

• "I need to take a safety course before I can operate any of the **electrical** equipment at work."
• "My sister is studying to be an **electrical** engineer."

Electric is used to talk about specific machines that are powered by electricity or musical instruments amplified by electronic devices:

• "I love my **electric** car, but it can't go very fast on the highway."
• "We always rely on our **electric** blankets during winter."
• "Of all things, my brother wants an **electric** harp for his birthday."

Finally, *electronic* refers to devices in which electrical currents are passed through and controlled by mechanical components such as transistors and circuitry. More recently, it has been used to identify information and data that can be sent, stored, or created using electronic equipment and systems. For example:

• "Many everyday items in modern houses have been turned into **electronic** gizmos, from the thermostat to the refrigerator to the toaster."
• "The advent of **electronic** mail ('e-mail') completely changed the way we do business now."

The term *electronics* is also commonly used as a collective noun indicating devices such as phones, computers, or video game systems that are powered by electronic components, as in, "The store specializes in **electronics** sold at discounted rates."

fantastic vs. fantastical

Fantastic once had the primary meaning of "existing in or having to do with fantasy or the imagination" or "strange and fanciful in appearance or conception."

However, in modern English, *fantastic* more commonly means "exceptionally good, wonderful, or desirable." For instance:

• "My sister received some **fantastic** news last night: she got the job!"
• "I thought the movie was really **fantastic**."

(Note that some sources still consider this usage to be informal, so *fantastic* may not be the best word to use in formal speech or writing.)

Fantastical retains the older sense of *fantastic*, as in "The story is full of many **fantastical** creatures and environments." It is a useful alternative when one wishes to describe something as "of or relating to fantasy" without causing confusion with the term *fantastic*.

graphic vs. graphical

Graphic and *graphical* are synonyms that both broadly mean "of, relating to, or represented by writing, pictures, or mathematical graphs," as in:

• "Please provide some **graphic/graphical** representations of the data for the board meeting, Jim."
• "It is the earliest language we know of that used **graphic/graphical** symbols to create a system of writing."

However, there are certain nouns that will usually take one form over the other. There are no clear rules governing these; they've just become established over time:

• "I'm studying **graphic** design in college."
• "All modern smartphones use a '**graphical** user interface,' meaning you interact with images to control what the phone does."
• "I'm currently working on a new **graphic** novel."
• "We're working on a new probabilistic **graphical** model for our work in machine learning."

It's also important to note that *graphic* has a common secondary meaning **not** shared by *graphical*: "vivid and explicit in representation," usually implying or referring to sexual or violent content. For example:

• "Please don't use such **graphic** language when the children are present."
• "These films are a bit too **graphic** for my taste."

Finally, we also use the collective noun *graphics* to refer to digital images created using computer software, as in:

• "The movie had spectacular **graphics**, but its story was a mess."

historic vs. historical

While *historic* and *historical* are technically full synonyms, they have fairly distinct meanings in modern English.

Historic primarily means "influential on, important to, or notable in the course of history." For example:

• "The **historic** accord between the two nations governed their relations for decades to come."
• "In 1903, the Wright brothers took a **historic** flight in the world's first airplane."

Historical, on the other hand, more generally means "of, relating to, based on, or concerned with past events," as in:

• "Many **historical** documents about the town's past residents were lost in the fire."
• "The film has tried to achieve an impressive degree of **historical** accuracy."
• "Her new **historical** novel is set in Russia in 1762."

lyric vs. lyrical

Lyrical means "expressing or characteristic of deep emotional significance or enthusiasm." For example:

• "His **lyrical** performance moved me so deeply that I felt compelled to weep and laugh at the same time."
• "Though the book is historical non-fiction, the author has such a beautiful command of the language that many

passages are downright **lyrical**."

Lyric, when it functions as an adjective, is usually related to a particular category of poetry, in which emotions and thoughts are expressed through airy, songlike words. For example:

• "As modernism and postmodernism have risen to prominence, **lyric** poets of the old style have become few and far between."

More often, though, *lyric* appears as the singular form of the noun *lyrics*, meaning "the words of a song." For example:

• "I had my favorite **lyric** from their song printed onto a poster."
• "Jess and Michael both seem to know the **lyrics** to every song on the radio.

magic vs. magical

The noun *magic* most commonly means "the process of using charms, rituals, spells, etc. to produce supernatural effects" or refers to such supernatural effects themselves. As an adjective, *magic* means "of, related to, or characterized by such supernatural elements or effects." For example:

• "With his **magic** wand, he conjured up a fierce otherworldly creature."
• "The world is populated with many **magic** spirits."

The adjective *magical* can also carry this same meaning, but it is less common than *magic*. Instead, it is more often used to refer to something as being "exceptionally enchanting, wonderful, or exciting," as in:

• "Samantha and I had a **magical** weekend together in Paris."
• "It has been **magical** seeing such a strong reaction to our film."

mythic vs. mythical

Mythical means "of or existing in a myth," and, by extension, "imaginary, fictitious, or fantastical." For example:

• "People still believe the **mythical** sasquatch exists, roaming the North American woodlands undetected."

(This is entirely synonymous with the word *mythological*, but *mythical* is more common.)

Mythic can also carry the above meaning, but it also has an exclusive definition of its own: "having the characteristics or nature of a myth." If something is *mythic*, rather than being fictitious or imaginary, it is elevated to the level of a legend in its scope or impact. Because it is more associated with real occurrences, it is also useful when describing something that has to do with the nature of mythology itself. For example:

• "My father's ability to attract friends and inspire confidence was almost **mythic**."
• "We can see in his novel the same **mythic** structures employed by Homer and Virgil."

optic vs. optical

The adjective *optic* is usually used to refer specifically to the eye or to the physical process of sight. Perhaps its most common usage in modern English is in the term "optic nerve" (the nerve that carries visual information from the eye to the brain).

Optical is much broader in its definition. While it can also relate to the eye or the sense of sight, it can also mean "of, producing, or related to visible light; designed or constructed to assist sight; having to do with the field of optics." For instance:

• optical zoom
• optical illusion
• optical fiber
• optical instruments
• optical defects
• optical astronomy

politic vs. political

The adjective *political* broadly means "of, involved, in, characterized by, or relating to politics," and it is by far the most common of the two terms. For example:

• "The company's **political** contributions have been heavily scrutinized in the wake of the scandal."
• "Her **political** career peaked in the late 2000s, but she first ran for office back in 1983."

Politic originally meant the same thing, but has now become archaic in that sense. Though uncommon in everyday speech or writing, it now means "pragmatic, shrewd, prudent, or judicious." For example:

• "His **politic** choice of investments did not surprise me, for my brother has never been one to gamble on uncertainty."

Adjectives ending in "-ic" and "-ical" with no difference in meaning

Although there are many adjectives with "-ic/-ical" variants of slightly different meaning, there are many more that are merely synonyms, with one form being more common than the other.

We'll look at some of these pairs below, with the more common spelling highlighted in **bold**. Be aware that this is not an exhaustive list, though; it is just meant to represent the pairs that are most likely to come up in everyday speech and writing.

"-ic"	"-ical"
analytic	**analytical**
anatomic	**anatomical**
biographic	**biographical**
botanic	**botanical**
categoric	**categorical**
cubic	cubical
cyclic	**cyclical**
diabolic	**diabolical**
egoistic	egoistical
egotistic	**egotistical**
geographic*	**geographical***
geometric	geometrical
ironic	ironical
mathematic	**mathematical**
metaphoric	**metaphorical**
metric	metrical
numeric	**numerical**
parasitic	parasitical
poetic	poetical
problematic	problematical
satiric	**satirical**
stoic	stoical
symbolic	symbolical

(*Geographic* and *geographical* are about equally common.)

Adjectives ending in "-ic" and "-ical" both become "-ically"

Finally, it's worth noting that when an adjective ending in "-ic" is made into an adverb by adding "-ly," we almost always change "-ic" to the "-ical" variant first. Since this applies to nearly every "-ic" adjective, let's just look at some common examples:
- artistic→artist**ically**
- basic→bas**ically**
- comic→com**ically**
- drastic→drast**ically**
- eccentric→eccentr**ically**
- fantastic→fantast**ically**
- gothic→goth**ically**
- hydraulic→hydraul**ically**
- idiotic→idiot**ically**
- jingoistic→jingoist**ically**
- kinetic→kinet**ically**
- laconic→lacon**ically**
- metallic→metall**ically**
- nostalgic→nostalg**ically**
- optimistic→optimist**ically**
- organic→organ**ically**
- prosthetic→prosthet**ically**
- realistic→realist**ically**

- scientific→scientif**ically**
- tragic→trag**ically**
- volcanic→volcan**ically**

However, there are two words ending in "-ic" that will simply use "-icly" as adverbs: ch**icly** and publ**icly**. (While *publically* is listed in some dictionaries as a variant spelling, it is extremely uncommon and will be regarded as incorrect by most readers.)

Quiz
(answers start on page 463)

1. True or False: "-ic" is more common than "-ical."

a) True
b) False

2. Which of the following nouns takes "-ical" to become an adjective, rather than "-ic"?

a) parody
b) homeopathy
c) geology
d) athlete

3. Which of the following nouns takes "-ic" to become an adjective, rather than "-ical"?

a) hypnosis
b) cynic
c) hypothesis
d) anthropology

4. True or False: Adjectives that can be spelled "-ic" or "-ical" always have the same meaning.

a) True
b) False

Commonly Confused Suffixes: -tion vs. -sion

The suffixes "-tion" and "-sion" are both used to create nouns from verbs (and, less commonly, adjectives and other nouns) to describe a state, condition, action, process, practice, or the result thereof. They are actually just permutations of the same suffix, "-ion," but there are specific conditions that will dictate which one we use, so it's worthwhile to consider them individually.

(There is also a third version, "-cion," but this only occurs in two specific instances: *coercion*, from the verb *coerce*, and *suspicion*, from the verb *suspect*.)

When to use "-tion"

The "-tion" ending is so ubiquitous because it is the more straightforward of the two to form. In most cases, "-ion" simply attaches to words ending in "-t" or "-te" (in which case it replaces the silent final E), so "-tion" is just the natural product of forming the noun. (Unlike "-sion," which more often alters the basic spelling of a word.)

With that in mind, there are some specific verb endings that *can* take the "-ion" suffix. In some cases, the resulting suffixed ending forms the basis for a spelling pattern that can be applied to *other* verbs.

Rule 1: Use "-tion" with verbs ending in "-ate"

A verb that ends in "-ate" will very often be able to become a noun using the "-ion" suffix. When this is the case, "-ion" replaces the silent E of the base word.

For example:
- abbreviate→abbrevia**tion**
- accommodate→accommoda**tion**
- celebrate→celebra**tion**
- communicate→communica**tion**
- cooperate→coopera**tion**
- dedicate→dedica**tion**
- depreciate→deprecia**tion**
- educate→educa**tion**
- exhilarate→exhilara**tion**
- fluctuate→fluctua**tion**
- formulate→formula**tion**
- generate→genera**tion**
- hallucinate→hallucina**tion**
- hesitate→hesita**tion**
- illuminate→illumina**tion**
- impersonate→impersona**tion**
- innovate→innova**tion**
- legislate→legisla**tion**
- liberate→libera**tion**
- manipulate→manipula**tion**
- migrate→migra**tion**
- negotiate→negotia**tion**
- notate→nota**tion**
- obliterate→oblitera**tion**
- operate→opera**tion**
- perpetuate→perpetua**tion**
- populate→popula**tion**
- radiate→radia**tion**
- rotate→rota**tion**

- separate→separa**tion**
- speculate→specula**tion**
- terminate→termina**tion**
- translate→transla**tion**

It's worth noting that, based on this pattern, "-ation" can function like a separate suffix of its own, attaching to other verbs not ending in "-ate." For instance:

- allege→alleg**ation**
- alter→alter**ation**
- cancel→cancell**ation**
- cause→caus**ation**
- compile→compil**ation**
- declare→declar**ation**
- exalt→exalt**ation**
- flirt→flirt**ation**
- float→flot**ation**
- inhale→inhal**ation**
- prepare→prepar**ation**
- strangle→strangul**ation**
- starve→starv**ation**

The use of "-ation" with verbs such as these is rather difficult to predict, because it occurs with so many different and varied endings; for the most part, we just have to memorize them. However, there are certain verb endings that *do* predictably take the "-ation" suffix at the end.

Rule 1.1 Use "-ation" with verbs ending in "-ize"

This is by far the most common verb ending to take the "-ation" suffix, which replaces the silent E at the end of the word. Though there are far too many words to include an exhaustive list here, let's look at some common examples:

- alphabetize→alphabetiz**ation**
- authorize→authoriz**ation**
- characterize→characteriz**ation**
- customize→customiz**ation**
- democratize→democratiz**ation**
- dramatize→dramatiz**ation**
- equalize→equaliz**ation**
- fictionalize→fictionaliz**ation**
- generalize→generaliz**ation**
- globalize→globaliz**ation**
- immunize→immuniz**ation**
- italicize→italiciz**ation**
- hospitalize→hospitaliz**ation**
- liberalize→liberaliz**ation**
- memorize→memoriz**ation**
- mobilize→mobiliz**ation**
- normalize→normaliz**ation**
- optimize→optimiz**ation**
- organize→organiz**ation**
- personalize→personaliz**ation**
- realize→realiz**ation**
- romanticize→romanticiz**ation**
- specialize→specializ**ation**
- stylize→styliz**ation**
- utilize→utiliz**ation**
- verbalize→verbaliz**ation**
- visualize→visualiz**ation**

Rule 1.2: Use "-ation" with verbs ending in "-ify"

The second most common verbs to take the "-ation" suffix are those ending in "-ify." However, instead of simply adding the suffix to the end of the word, we must make some changes to its overall spelling. First, **Y** changes **I**, then we add the letter **C** *and then* add "-ation." For example:

- amplify→amplif**ication**
- beautify→beautif**ication**
- certify→certif**ication**
- clarify→clarif**ication**
- classify→classif**ication**
- deify→deif**ication**
- edify→edif**ication**
- electrify→electrif**ication**
- falsify→falsif**ication**
- fortify→fortif**ication**
- gentrify→gentrif**ication**
- glorify→glorif**ication**
- humidify→humidif**ication**
- intensify→intensif**ication**
- justify→justif**ication**
- magnify→magnif**ication**
- mystify→mystif**ication**
- notify→notif**ication**
- objectify→objectif**ication**
- personify→personif**ication**
- ramify→ramif**ication**
- simplify→simplif**ication**
- specify→specif**ication**

Note that there are several verbs that end "-efy," and while this ending sounds the same as "-ify," such verbs take a different form when the "-tion" suffix is attached:

- lique**fy**→liquef**action**
- putre**fy**→putref**action**
- rare**fy**→raref**action**
- stupe**fy**→stupef**action**
- tume**fy**→tumef**action**

Rule 1.3: Use "-ation" with verbs ending in "-aim"

Not many verbs end in "-aim," but those that do can usually take the "-ation" suffix to become nouns (though only if the word has more than one syllable). Note that, when this happens, the letter **I** is omitted from "-aim." For example:

- acclaim→acclam**ation**
- declaim→declam**ation**
- disclaim→disclam**ation**
- exclaim→exclam**ation**
- proclaim→proclam**ation**
- reclaim→reclam**ation**

Rule 2: Use "-tion" with verbs ending in "-pt"

Verbs ending in "-pt" will simply take "-ion" to form nouns; they never use "-sion." For example:

- adopt→adop**tion**
- corrupt→corrup**tion**
- encrypt→encryp**tion**
- except→excep**tion**
- erupt→erup**tion**
- exempt→exemp**tion**
- intercept→intercep**tion**
- interrupt→interrup**tion**

(There are two exceptions to this: the verbs *adapt* and *tempt* take the "-ation" suffix rather than simply adding "-ion" to the end, becoming *adaptation* and *temptation*.)

In certain cases, though, a verb's ending will *change* to "-ption" to become a noun. Again, it is always "-tion" that is used with these verbs; we never have a word ending in "-psion."

Rule 2.1: Use "-ption" with verbs ending in "-scribe"

Verbs ending in the root "-scribe" will take the "-tion" suffix to become nouns. However, we omit the silent **E** and change **B** to **P**, as in:

• ascribe→ascri**ption**
• conscribe→conscri**ption**
• describe→descri**ption**
• inscribe→inscri**ption**
• prescribe→prescri**ption**
• proscribe→proscri**ption**
• subscribe→subscri**ption**
• transcribe→transcri**ption**

Rule 2.2: Use "-ption" with verbs ending in "-ceive"

Verbs ending in the root "-ceive" will also take the "-ption" ending. Like verbs ending in "-scribe," we have to make some changes to the overall spelling of the word when adding the suffix. In this instance, "-ive" is omitted and replaced by "-ption," as in:

• conceive→conce**ption**
• deceive→dece**ption**
• perceive→perce**ption**
• receive→rece**ption**

Rule 2.3: Use "-ption" with verbs ending in "-sume"

Finally, we also use "-ption" with verbs ending in "-sume." This time, though, we merely omit silent **E** and add "-ption" to the end:

• assume→assum**ption**
• consume→consum**ption**
• presume→presum**ption**
• resume→resum**ption**
• subsume→subsum**ption**

Rule 3: Use "-tion" with words ending in "-ct"

Like words ending in "-pt," most verbs and adjectives ending in "-ct" will simply take "-ion" to form nouns of quality or status. Other nouns simply end in "-ction" without being derived from a verb or adjective. Just remember that when the (/-ʃən/) sound follows a **C**, it will always be spelled "-ction."

Quite a few words will take this ending, so let's just look at some common examples:

• abstract→abstrac**tion**
• act→ac**tion**
• attract→attrac**tion**
• auc**tion**
• benefac**tion**
• connect→connec**tion**
• correct→correc**tion**
• deduct→deduc**tion***
• distinct→distinc**tion**
• distract→distrac**tion**
• elect→elec**tion**
• extinct→extinc**tion**
• frac**tion**
• func**tion**
• instruct→instruc**tion**

- intersect→intersec**tion**
- junc**tion**
- object→objec**tion**
- obstruct→obstruc**tion**
- perfect→perfec**tion**
- protect→protec**tion**
- react→reac**tion**
- reflect→reflec**tion**
- subtract→subtrac**tion**
- trac**tion**
- transact→transac**tion**

*The noun *deduction* is also associated with a different, unrelated verb: *deduce*. In fact, most verbs that end in "-duce" will take the "-tion" suffix in the same way, as in:

- deduce→deduc**tion**
- induce→induc**tion**
- introduce→introduc**tion**
- produce→produc**tion**
- reduce→reduc**tion**
- seduce→seduc**tion**
- transduce→transduc**tion**

Finally, this "-ction" spelling pattern is applied to another verb that is completely different from what we've seen so far: *suck*→suc**tion**.

Rule 4: Use "-tion" with verbs ending in "-ete"

If a verb (or, less commonly, an adjective) ends in "-ete," then it will take the "-ion" suffix by omitting the silent **E** at the end.

- complete→comple**tion**
- concrete→concre**tion**
- delete→dele**tion**
- deplete→deple**tion**
- excrete→excre**tion**
- replete→reple**tion**
- secrete→secre**tion**

Uniquely, the verb *compete* does not become *competion*, but *compe**tition***. (Also following this pattern, the verb *repeat* becomes *repe**tition***.)

---

discrete vs. discreet (vs. discretion)

The noun *discretion* is very similar in structure to the other words we looked at in Rule 4, and, based on that pattern, we would expect it to be derived from the adjective *discrete*, meaning "distinct, unconnected, or separate in function or form." *Discretion*, however, is actually the noun form of the adjective *discreet*, meaning "careful to avoid social awkwardness or discomfort, especially by not sharing delicate information." (The noun form of *discrete* is actually *discrete**ness***.)

Because *discrete* and *discreet* are both pronounced the same way (/dɪˈskrit/), and the noun *discretion* **looks** like it ought to be derived from *discrete*, it's easy to get these two terms confused. Here's a helpful mnemonic to help remember the appropriate meaning for the two different spellings:

- *Discrete* means "separate" or "distinct," so we must **separate** the last two **E**s with a **T**.

Rule 5: Use "-tion" with verbs ending in "-ute"

Like verbs ending "-ete," we can simply attach "-ion" to verbs ending in "-ute" by omitting the silent **E**, as in:

- attribute→attribu**tion**
- contribute→contribu**tion**
- dilute→dilu**tion**

- distribute→distribu**tion**
- execute→execu**tion**
- institute→institu**tion**
- pollute→pollu**tion**
- persecute→persecu**tion**
- substitute→substitu**tion**

Rule 5.1: Use "-ution" for verbs ending in "-olve"

Like "-ation" and "-ption," the "-ution" ending can also function as a separate suffix in certain circumstances. Here, it is applied to verbs ending in "-olve," taking the place of the letters **V** and **E**. For instance:

- absolve→absolu**tion**
- evolve→evolu**tion**
- involve→involu**tion**
- resolve→resolu**tion**
- revolve→revolu**tion**
- solve→solu**tion**

Rule 6: Use "-tion" with words ending in "-it" or "-ite"

- contrite→contri**tion**
- edit→edi**tion**
- erudite→erudi**tion**
- exhibit→exhibi**tion**
- expedite→expedi**tion**
- extradite→extradi**tion**
- fruit*→frui**tion**
- ignite→igni**tion**
- inhibit→inhibi**tion**
- intuit→intui**tion**
- prohibit→prohibi**tion**
- transit→transi**tion**

(*Meaning "to produce fruit"; the noun *fruition* is more usually used figuratively.)

Note, however, that verbs ending in "-mit" do **not** take the "-tion" ending, but rather "-mi**ssion**," which we'll look at a little bit further on.

Rule 6.1: Use "-ition" with verbs ending in "-ose"

The "-ition" ending is also commonly used with verbs ending in "-ose." With these words, it replaces the silent **E** at the end:

- appose→apposi**tion**
- compose→composi**tion**
- decompose→decomposi**tion**
- depose→deposi**tion**
- dispose→disposi**tion**
- juxtapose→juxtaposi**tion**
- impose→imposi**tion**
- oppose→opposi**tion**
- propose→proposi**tion**
- suppose→supposi**tion**
- transpose→transposi**tion**

When to use "-sion"

Rule 1: Use "-sion" when it is pronounced /-ʒən/

One of the distinguishing features of the "-sion" ending compared to "-tion" is the fact that it most often forms the /-ʒən/ sound, as heard in the word *vision* (/ˈvɪʒən/). This can easily be considered a rule unto itself, because "-tion" never makes the /-ʒən/ sound; it is always pronounced /-ʃən/, as in *portion* (/ˈpɔrʃən/).

That being said, there are still specific spelling patterns that dictate *when* (and, in some cases, *how*) a word can take the "-sion" ending, so it's important to look at the different spelling conventions associated with this suffix.

Rule 2: Use "-sion" with verbs ending in "-de"

One of the most reliable spelling indicators of when a verb will take "-sion" rather than "-tion" is when it ends in "-de." This is most commonly seen in words ending in "-ade" and (even more so) "-ude," but it also occurs in "-ide" and "-ode" words as well. Regardless of the vowel that precedes it, "-de" is always omitted and replaced by "-sion."

For example:

Verbs ending in "-ade"	Verbs ending in "-ide"	Verbs ending in "-ode"	Verbs ending in "-ude"
abrade→abrasion corrode→corrosion dissuade→dissuasion evade→evasion invade→invasion persuade→persuasion pervade→pervasion	collide→collision decide→decision elide→elision provide→provision	corrode→corrosion erode→erosion explode→explosion implode→implosion	allude→allusion collude→collusion conclude→conclusion delude→delusion elude→elusion exclude→exclusion extrude→extrusion include→inclusion intrude→intrusion obtrude→obtrusion occlude→occlusion preclude→preclusion protrude→protrusion seclude→seclusion

We also use the "-sion" suffix with verbs ending in "-cede," but the resultant nouns are both spelled and pronounced differently, so we'll look those examples separately further on.

Rule 3: Use "-sion" with verbs ending in "-ise" and "-use"

The "-sion" suffix is also used when a verb ends in "-ise" or, more commonly, "-use." However, unlike with words ending in "-de," this is because only silent E is omitted when it takes the suffix "-ion" rather than the word's spelling being *changed* to "-sion."

For example:

Verbs ending in "-ise"	Verbs ending in "-use"
incise→incision revise→revision supervise→supervision	confuse→confusion contuse→contusion diffuse→diffusion effuse→effusion infuse→infusion fuse→fusion suffuse→suffusion transfuse→transfusion

It's also worth noting that there are two adjectives ending in "-ise" that can take the "-sion" ending to become nouns: *concise→concision* and *precise→precision*. Likewise, two non-verbs ending in "-use" follow this pattern as well: the adjective *profuse* becomes *profusion*, and the noun *recluse* becomes *reclusion*.

Rule 4: Use "-sion" with verbs ending in "-pel"

Another instance in which we use the "-sion" ending instead of "-tion" is for verbs ending in "-pel." Again, the spelling of the word changes slightly to accommodate the suffix, this time changing from "-pel" to "-pul-," followed by "-sion."

- compel→comp**ulsion**
- expel→exp**ulsion**
- impel→imp**ulsion**
- propel→prop**ulsion**
- repel→rep**ulsion**

Though not ending in "-el," the verb *convulse* also has a noun that has this form: *conv**ulsion***. There are a few other words that follow this spelling pattern, too, but they are not derived from existing base verbs:

- av**ulsion**
- em**ulsion**
- ev**ulsion**
- rev**ulsion**

When "-sion" is pronounced /-ʃən/

The suffix "-sion" is most often pronounced /-ʒən/, but there are some instances in which it is pronounced /-ʃən/, the same as "-tion."

The most common spelling associated with this pronunciation is "-ssion," and there are a few conventions determining when this spelling will occur. (It can also be pronounced this way after the letter **N**, but we'll look at that separately further on.)

Rule 5: Use "-sion" with verbs ending in "-mit"

As we mentioned in Rule 6 above, the "-tion" suffix is used with words ending in "-it" **except** for verbs specifically ending in "-mit." For words with this ending, the "-ion" suffix changes the final **T** to **SS**.

For example:
- admit→admi**ssion**
- commit→commi**ssion**
- emit→emi**ssion**
- omit→omi**ssion**
- permit→permi**ssion**
- remit→remi**ssion**
- submit→submi**ssion**
- transmit→transmi**ssion**

Rule 6: Use "-sion" with verbs ending in "-cede"

Another verb ending that follows this pattern is "-cede." Similar to "-mit," we replace "-de" with "-ssion." Note as well that this suffix also changes the pronunciation of the vowel **E** from /i/ in "-cede" (/sid/) to /ɛ/ in "-cession" (/sɛʃən/).

For example:
- accede→acce**ssion**
- concede→conce**ssion**
- intercede→interce**ssion**
- precede→prece**ssion**
- recede→rece**ssion**
- secede→sece**ssion**

This pattern is also used for the very similarly spelled verbs *proceed* (*proce**ssion***) and *succeed* (*succe**ssion***).

Rule 7: Use "-sion" with verbs ending in "-ss"

Finally, many verbs that naturally end in a double **S** will simply take "-ion" on the end with no other change to the words' spelling. For example:

- aggress→aggre**ssion**

- compress→compre**ssion**
- concuss→concu**ssion**
- confess→confe**ssion**
- depress→depre**ssion**
- digress→digre**ssion**
- discuss→discu**ssion**
- egress→egre**ssion**
- express→expre**ssion**
- impress→impre**ssion**
- obsess→obse**ssion**
- oppress→oppre**ssion**
- percuss→percu**ssion**
- possess→posse**ssion**
- profess→profe**ssion**
- regress→regre**ssion**
- suppress→suppre**ssion**
- transgress→transgre**ssion**

"-tion" vs. "-sion" after *N* and *R*

Many spelling guides indicate that "-sion" very often occurs after the consonants **N** and **R**. While this is true, "-tion" **also** commonly occurs after these consonants, so we cannot use **N** or **R** on their own to decide whether a word's ending will be "-tion" or "-sion."

Thankfully, there are a few other spelling patterns that *can* help us determine the correct ending to use.

After *N*

Because "-ntion" and "-nsion" are both pronounced the same way (/-nʃən/), we must rely on the spelling of the verb to which the suffix attaches in order to decide which one is correct.

When to use "-tion"

When verbs end in "-tain," "-vene," or "-vent," we use the "-tion" suffix. (Note that "-tain" becomes "-tention," and "-vene" becomes "-vention.") For instance:

- abstain→absten**tion**
- circumvent→circumven**tion**
- contravene→contraven**tion**
- convene→conven**tion**
- detain→deten**tion**
- invent→inven**tion**
- prevent→preven**tion**
- retain→reten**tion**

Note that there is one verb ending in "-ent" that will take "-sion" rather than "-tion": *dissent→dissension* (though it has an accepted variant spelling of *dissention*).

When to use "-sion"

While we use "-tion" after verbs ending in "-ent," we use "-sion" after verbs ending in "-end," as in:

- apprehend→apprehe**nsion**
- ascend→asce**nsion**
- comprehend→comprehe**nsion**
- descend→desce**nsion** (more commonly *descent*)
- distend→diste**nsion**
- extend→exte**nsion**
- reprehend→reprehe**nsion**
- suspend→suspe**nsion**

However, there are two notable exceptions to the "-end" rule: the verb *intend* becomes the noun *intention*, and the verb *contend* becomes *contention*. (The noun *attention* is also etymologically related to the verb *attend*, but the two are not directly related in modern meaning. The noun of state, condition, action, process, or practice derived from *attend* is *attend**ance**.*)

There are also a few specific verbs with endings other than those we've seen that can take "-sion" after **N**:
• decline→decle**nsion**
• expand→expa**nsion**

Note that the noun *pretense* (or *pretence* in British English) and the adjective *tense* both take the "-sion" suffix as well: *pretension* and *tension*. The adjective *intense* can also become *intension* (which rhymes with *intention* but means "the state of being or the act of becoming intense"), but this is fairly uncommon compared to the synonym *intensity*.

After *R*

Focusing purely on pronunciation, a word will always take the "-sion" ending after **R** when it is pronounced /-rʒən/; "-rtion" is always pronounced /-rʃən/.
(Note, though, that "-rsion" can *also* be pronounced /-rʃən/ depending on the speaker's dialect [especially in British English], so it's still important consider the base word's spelling when deciding which suffix to use.)

When to use "-tion"

Generally speaking, we use "-tion" with verbs ending in "-rt," as in:
• assert→asse**rtion**
• contort→conto**rtion**
• desert→dese**rtion**
• distort→disto**rtion**
• exert→exe**rtion**
• extort→exto**rtion**
• insert→inse**rtion**

When to use "-sion"

However, there is a major exception to the "-rt" rule: we use "-sion" with words ending in "-vert," with the final **T** being replaced by the suffix. For example:
• convert→conve**rsion**
• divert→dive**rsion**
• extrovert→extrove**rsion**
• introvert→introve**rsion**
• invert→inve**rsion**
• revert→reve**rsion**
• subvert→subve**rsion**

We also use the "-sion" ending after **R** with three other types of verb endings, too: "-erse," "-ur," and "-erge." For instance:
• asperse→aspe**rsion**
• averse→ave**rsion**
• disperse→dispe**rsion**
• emerge→eme**rsion** (the synonym *emerg**ence*** is much more common)
• excur→excu**rsion** (though the verb *excur* is now obsolete)
• immerse→imme**rsion**
• incur→incu**rsion**
• recur→recu**rsion**
• submerge→subme**rsion** (the verb *submerse* is also related, though it may be a back-formation from *submersion*)

When to use "-cion" and "-cian"

As we mentioned at the beginning of the section, there is actually a third variation of this suffix in addition to "-tion" and "-sion": "-cion." It is used to form the nouns *coer**cion*** and *suspi**cion***.

A very similar suffix, "-cian" (also pronounced /-ʃən/), is used much more commonly than "-cion," but it has a different function and meaning than "-tion," "-sion," and "-cion." Rather than indicating a state, condition, action, process, or practice, "-ician" indicates a person who practices, performs, or specializes in a particular subject or activity. For example:

- arithmetic→arithmet**ician**
- beauty→beaut**ician**
- diet→diet**ician** (also spelled *dietitian*)
- electricity→electr**ician**
- magic→mag**ician**
- mathematics→mathemat**ician**
- music→mus**ician**
- optics→opt**ician**
- pediatrics→pediatr**ician**
- statistics→statist**ician**

Quiz
(answers start on page 463)

1. Which of the following is the most common permutation of the "-ion" suffix?

a) -cian
b) -cion
c) -sion
d) -tion

2. Which of the following words takes the suffix "-tion"?

a) expand
b) educate
c) invert
d) omit

3. Which of the following words takes the suffix "-sion"?

a) propel
b) justify
c) intend
d) suppose

4. True or False: The suffixes "-cian" and "-cion" have the same function and meaning.

a) True
b) False

5. True or False: The suffixes "-tion" and "-sion" can both be pronounced /-ʃən/.

a) True
b) False

Spelling Conventions with Suffixes

Forming new words with suffixes can often be tricky because, in many cases, the spelling of the original root word must be altered to accommodate the attachment of the suffix. However, even though such spelling changes can sometimes seem erratic, they usually follow specific conventions that help us determine how to form the new word.

Vowel Suffixes vs. Consonant Suffixes

Before we look at the spelling conventions for suffixes as a whole, it's important to distinguish between the two broad categories: **vowel suffixes** (those that begin with a vowel letter) and **consonant suffixes** (those that begin with a consonant letter). Let's look at a few of the most common examples of each:

Vowel Suffixes	Consonant Suffixes
-able	-dom
-ate	-ful
-ed	-less
-er	-ly
-est	-ment
-ible	-ness
-ic	-ry
-ion	-s
-ify	-ship
-ize	-sion
-ing	-tion
-ous	-ward
-y	-wise

The Primary Rules

These spelling rules are the most complex, resulting in spelling irregularities that often prove difficult for learners and native speakers alike. We'll give a brief overview of these rules below, but be aware that there are usually several exceptions and special cases within each rule. To learn more about these more complex primary rules, continue on to their individual sections.

Rule 1: Dropping silent E with vowel suffixes

When a silent E appears at the end of a word, its most common purpose is to change the pronunciation of vowels (as well as the consonants **C** or **G**) within the word.
When a vowel suffix is attached to a word with a silent **E**, it often (though not always) results in **E** being <u>omitted</u>.

For example:

Root Word	✔ Correctly Suffixed Words	✘ Incorrectly Suffixed Words
bake	baked, baker, baking	bakeed, bakeer, bakeing
communicate	communicated, communicating, communication	communicateed, communicateer, communicateing
dispose	disposable, disposal, disposing	disposeable, disposeal, disposeing
fame	famed, famous	fameed, fameous
fine	fined, finest, fining	fineed, fineing, finey
ice	iced, icing, icy	iceed, iceing, icey
store	storage, stored, storing	storeage, storeed, storeing
use	usage, used, user, using	useage, useed, useer, useing

Rule 2: Keeping silent E with consonant suffixes

Unlike vowel suffixes, when a **consonant suffix** is attached to a word ending in a silent **E**, we nearly always keep the **E** in the word.

For example:

Root Word	✔ Correctly Suffixed Words	✘ Incorrectly Suffixed Words
bare	barely, bareness, bares	barly, barness, bars
care	careful, careless, cares	carful, carless, cars
complete	completely, completeness, completes	completly, completness, complets
home	homeless, homely, homeward	homless, homly, homward
like	likely, likeness, likewise	likly, likness, likwise
peace	peaceful, peaceless	peacful, peacless
state	statehood, stateless, stately	stathood, statless, statly
wake	wakeful, wakeless, wakes	wakful, wakless, waks

Although these two rules regarding silent E are fairly reliable, there are quite a few exceptions to both. Check out the section on Adding Suffixes after Silent E to learn more.

Rule 3: Change Y to I before a suffix

When we add both vowel and consonant suffixes to words ending in **Y**, we usually change it to the letter **I**. For example:

With Vowel Suffixes	With Consonant Suffixes
apply→appliance, applied, applies	beauty→beautify, beautiful
colony→colonial, colonies, colonize	contrary→contrarily, contrariness, contrariwise
envy→enviable, envied, envious	eery→eerily, eeriness
happy→happier, happiest	happy→happily, happiness
luxury→luxuriant, luxuriate, luxurious	lively→likelihood, likeliness
marry→marriage, married, marries	merry→merrily, merriment, merriness
pity→pitiable, pities	pity→pitiful, pitiless
tidy→tidied, tidier, tidiest	trustworthy→trustworthily, trustworthiness
worry→worried, worrier, worries	weary→weariful, weariness, wearisome

Again, there are some exceptions to this rule. Most notably, we **don't** change **Y** to **I** before the vowel suffix "-ing" (e.g., *apply* becomes *app**ly**ing*). To learn more about this and other exceptions, go to the section Changing Y to I with Suffixes.

Rule 4: Doubling Consonants with Vowel Suffixes

When a single-syllable word ends in a vowel + a consonant, we almost always double the consonant when a vowel suffix is attached. If we don't, it could end up looking as though the root word had a silent **E** that's been omitted. For example:

Root Word	✔ Correctly Suffixed Words	✖ Incorrectly Suffixed Words
bar	barred, barring	bared, baring (looks like the root word is *bare*)
dot	dotted, dotting	doted, doting (looks like the root word is *dote*)
fat	fatten, fatter, fattest, fatty	faten, fater, fatest, faty (looks like the root word is *fate*)
hop	hopped, hopper, hopping, hoppy	hoped, hoper, hoping, hopy (looks like the root word is *hope*)
mad	madden, madder, maddest	maden, mader, madest (looks like the root word is *made*)
rob	robbed, robber, robbing	robed, rober, robing (looks like the root word is *robe*)
slim	slimmed, slimmer, slimming	slimed, slimer, sliming (looks like the root word is *slime*)

Rule 5: Doubling the consonant when the final syllable is emphasized

When a multi-syllable word is vocally stressed on the final syllable, we almost always double the final consonant before a vowel suffix; when the vocal stress is on a *different* syllable, we generally <u>don't</u> double the suffix. For example:

Emphasis on final syllable	Suffixed Words	Emphasis on other syllable	Suffixed Words
begin (/bɪˈgɪn/)	beginner, beginning	bicker (/ˈbɪkər/)	bickered, bickering
forget (/fərˈgɛt/)	forgettable, forgetting	forfeit (/ˈfɔrfɪt/)	forfeited, forfeiting, forfeiture
incur (/ɪnˈkɜr/)	incurrable, incurred, incurring	interpret (/ɪnˈtɜrprət/)	interpreted, interpreter, interpreting
omit (/oʊˈmɪt/)	omitted, omitting	open (/ˈoʊpən/)	opened, opener, opening
transmit (/trænzˈmɪt/)	transmittable, transmitted, transmitting	travel (/ˈtrævəl/)	traveled, traveler, traveling

Note that in British English, a final **L** is almost always doubled before vowel suffixes, even when the stress is on the first syllable of the word (e.g., *travel* becomes *trave**ll**ed* or *trave**ll**ing*). There are also a number of exceptions regarding the doubling of consonants before vowel suffixes in single- and multi-syllable words; to learn more, go to the section Doubling Consonants with Vowel Suffixes.

The Lesser Rules

There are a few other spelling conventions for suffixes that aren't as complex as the ones we've looked at so far. These "lesser" rules apply to a much narrower range of words and have few or no exceptions, so we'll examine them in their entirety here.

Rule 6: Adding K to verbs ending in C

Most verbs do not end in a **C** after a vowel; they usually have a **K** at the end to make the /k/ sound more definitive. A few do have a final **C**, though, so to avoid a spelling that might indicate a "soft C" sound (/s/), we add a **K** before suffixes beginning with **E, I,** or **Y.** For example:
• frolic→frol**icked**, frol**icker**, frol**icking**
• mimic→mimi**cked**, mimi**cker**, mimi**cking**
• panic→pani**cked**, pani**cking**, pani**cky**
• picnic→picni**cked**, picni**cker**, picni**cking**
• traffic→traffi**cked**, traffi**cker**, traffi**cking**

Note that we **don't** do this when we attach consonant suffixes or vowel suffixes that begin with **A:**
• frolic→frol**ics**, frol**icsome**
• mimic→mimi**cal**, mimi**cry**, mimi**cs**
• panic→pani**cs**
• picnic→picni**cs**
• traffic→traffi**cable**, traffi**cs**

Rule 7: "-ic" + "-ly" = "-ically"

Almost all adjectives that end in "-ic" have a variant spelling that ends in "-ical," and vice versa. The two forms are often synonymous, with one form simply being preferred over the other (though in some cases the two forms have similar but distinct meanings).

However, when adding the suffix "-ly" to words ending in "-ic" to form adverbs, we almost always change "-ic" to "ical" (even with words that **don't** have an "-ical" variant), thus yielding the ending **"-ically."**

For example:
• academic→academ**ically**
• acoustic→acoust**ically**
• basic→bas**ically**
• democratic→democrat**ically**
• drastic→drast**ically**
• enthusiastic→enthusiast**ically**
• genetic→genet**ically**
• historic→histor**ically**
• ironic→iron**ically**
• majestic→majest**ically**
• organic→organ**ically**
• poetic→poet**ically**
• realistic→realist**ically**
• specific→specif**ically**
• tragic→trag**ically**

Note that there are two words that do not conform to this rule:
• chic→chic**ly**
• public→publi**cly**

Luckily, these are the only exceptions we have to memorize; all other adjectives ending in "-ic" take the adverbial ending "-ically."

Rule 8: Change IE to Y before "-ing"

Very rarely, a verb will end in "-ie." When this happens, we have to change the vowel digraph to **Y** so that we can attach the present participle suffix "-ing." Note that this is the only suffix that results in an unusual spelling for these words; others will attach according to the patterns we've already looked at. For example:

• boogie→boog**ied**, boog**ies**, boog**ying**
• die→d**ied**, d**ies**, d**ying**
• lie→l**ied**, l**ies**, l**ying**
• tie→t**ied**, t**ies**, t**ying**
• vie→v**ied**, v**ies**, v**ying**

There are very few verbs that end in **IE**, so there are no exceptions to this rule.

Rule 9: Don't change verbs ending in a vowel

There aren't many verbs that end in a vowel other than **Y** or silent **E**. Many of those that are used in English often originated from another language or are abbreviated forms of longer, more technical terms that are now used as verbs. Regardless of origin, when a verb ends in a vowel other than **Y** or **E**, we don't make any changes to the root spelling when adding a vowel suffix. For example:

• cameo→cameo**ed**, cameo**ing**
• conga→conga**ed**, conga**ing**
• disco→disco**ed**, disco**ing**
• echo→echo**ed**, echo**ing**
• halo→halo**ed**, halo**ing**
• henna→henna**ed**, henna**ing**
• safari→safari**ed**, safari**ing**
• shanghai→shanghai**ed**, shanghai**ing**
• ski→ski**ed**, ski**ing**
• subpoena→subpoena**ed**, subpoena**ing**
• taxi→taxi**ed**, taxi**ing**
• veto→veto**ed**, veto**ing**

Quiz

(answers start on page 463)

1. Silent **E** is generally **not** omitted before which types of suffixes?

a) Vowel suffixes
b) Consonant suffixes
c) Both

2. In general, when do we double the final consonant in multi-syllable words?

a) When the final syllable is stressed
b) When the first syllable is stressed
c) When the emphasis shifts to the suffix itself
d) Always
e) Never

3. Which of the following is an **incorrectly** suffixed form of the word *apply*?

a) applied
b) applies
c) applying
d) applyable

4. Which of the following words has its spelling changed before the suffix "-ly"?

a) vague
b) basic
c) complete
d) slim

5. Which of the following words does **not** have its spelling changed before the suffix "-ing"?

a) panic
b) store
c) echo
d) tie

6. Which of the following suffixed words is spelled **incorrectly**?

a) enterring
b) preferring
c) opening
d) traveling

Changing Y to I with Suffixes

The letter **Y** is often referred to as a **semi-vowel** because it can behave as either a vowel or a consonant depending on its position and function in a word. When it appears at the end of a word, **Y** is always considered a vowel because it creates a vowel sound.

Changing Y to I before a suffix

However, a final **Y** isn't flexible in the way it is pronounced, and it doesn't function well with other letters when a suffix is attached. In most cases, we must change it to the letter **I**, which makes the word easier to read and pronounce. This is generally true for both vowel and consonant suffixes. For example:

With Vowel Suffixes	With Consonant Suffixes
apply→appliance, applied, applies	beauty→beautify, beautiful
colony→colonial, colonies, colonize	contrary→contrarily, contrariness, contrariwise
envy→enviable, envied, envious	eery→eerily, eeriness
happy→happier, happiest	happy→happily, happiness
luxury→luxuriant, luxuriate, luxurious	likely→likelihood, likeliness
marry→marriage, married, marries	merry→merrily, merriment, merriness
pity→pitiable, pities	pity→pitiful, pitiless
tidy→tidied, tidier, tidiest	trustworthy→trustworthily, trustworthiness
worry→worried, worrier, worries	weary→weariful, weariness, wearisome

Exception 1: Don't change Y to I before "-ing"

You may have noticed that none of the words above featured the ending "-ing." This is because we never change **Y** to **I** when it is followed by this suffix. To maintain the meaning of the word with "-ing," we need to keep the syllable that **Y** provides. We can't have a word ending in **IING** (unless the root word ends in **I**, as in *skiing* or *taxiing*), and if we simply replace **Y** with "-ing," the meaning of the word will change (or seem to change).

Let's look at the examples from above again, this time adding "-ing":

Root Word	✔ Correctly Suffixed Word	✖ Incorrectly Suffixed Words
apply	applying	appling, appliing
envy	envying	enving, enviing
marry	marrying	marring, marriing
pity	pitying	piting, pitiing
tidy	tidying	tiding, tidiing
worry	worrying	worring, worriing

Exception 2: *shy, sly, spry, wry*

For these single-syllable adjective words, it is preferred to keep the **Y** when a suffix is added to make them into adverbs, nouns, or comparative/superlative adjectives. While the words *can* be spelled with an **I**, this is usually seen as an acceptable (but less common) variant. Note, however, that with the suffix "-ness" (and in some cases "-ly"), **Y** is always kept. For example:

Root Word	✔ Preferred Suffix Spellings	✔ Variant Suffix Spellings	✘ Incorrect Suffix Spellings
shy	shyer, shyest, shyly, shyness	shier, shiest, shily (now rare)	shiness
sly	slyer, slyest, slyly, slyness	slier, sliest, slily	sliness
spry	spryer, spryest, spryly, spryness	sprier, spriest	spriness
wry	wryer, wryest, wryly, wryness	wrier, wriest	wrily, wriness

Sub-exception 1: *shy, shies, shied, shying*

Note that the word *shy* can also function as a verb, which means that it can take other inflectional suffixes to conjugate for tense, aspect, and grammatical person. Like all words ending in **Y**, the suffix "-ing" (which indicates the present participle form) attaches to *shy* with no other change in spelling: *shying*.

However, when it is put into the simple past tense or the **first-person singular**, **Y** <u>is</u> changed to **I**: *shied, shies*. Unlike with other vowel suffixes, this altered spelling is the only one that is correct; we can't keep **Y** with "-ed" or "-es."

Note that this pattern also applies to other regular single-syllable verbs ending in a consonant + **Y**:
• cry→ cries, cried, crying
• dry→ dries, dried, drying
• fry→ fries, fried, frying
• ply→ plies, plied, plying
• try→ tries, tried, trying

Sub-exception 2: *dryer vs. drier*

Like the other single-syllable words we just looked at, the word *dry* will in some cases keep its **Y** and other times have it replaced with **I**. However, there are specific instances for each, depending on the meaning of the root word.

For example, when *dry* is an adjective meaning "not wet," we replace **Y** with **I** to form the comparative adjective *drier* (we do the same thing to form the superlative adjective *driest*). However, when *dry* is a verb meaning "to make or become not wet," we <u>keep</u> **Y** to form the noun *dryer* ("a machine that makes things dry"). Both forms are considered acceptable for each meaning, but keeping the spellings distinct like this helps make your meaning clearer to the reader.

In addition, as we saw at the end of the previous sub-exception, there are certain ways we <u>must</u> spell the word *dry*, especially when it is being conjugated as a verb. Take a look at the table below to see all the various ways we add suffixes to *dry*:

Replace Y with I (preferred)	Don't replace Y with I (preferred)	Y is <u>always</u> replaced with I	Y is <u>never</u> replaced with I
drier (comparative adjective)	dryer (noun of agency)	dried (simple past tense)	drying (present participle)
driest (superlative adjective)	dryly (adverb)	dries (third-person singular)	dryness (noun of quality)

Exception 3: Don't change Y to I when it comes after a vowel

When **Y** comes after another vowel at the end of a word, we do not change it to an **I** regardless of the type of suffix that attaches to it.

For example:

Root Word	✔ Correctly Suffixed Words	✖ Incorrectly Suffixed Words
annoy	annoyance, annoyed, annoys	annoiance, annoied, annoies
buy	buyable, buyer, buys	buiable, buier, buies
convey	conveyance, conveyer, conveyor	conveiance, conveier, conveior
deploy	deployable, deployed, deployment	deploiable, deploied, deploiment
joy	joyful, joyless, joyous	joiful, joiless, joious
play	played, player, playful	plaied, plaier, plaiful
toy	toyed, toyish, toyless	toied, toiish, toiless

Irregular verbs ending in a vowel + Y

Be careful of the exception we just looked at, however: several verbs ending in a vowel (especially **A**) + **Y** have **irregular conjugations** for the past tense, meaning their past tense and past participle forms aren't formed by adding "-ed." Unfortunately, we just have to memorize which verbs are irregular and how they are conjugated. For example:

Root Word	✔ Irregular Form(s)	✖ Incorrect Form
buy	b*ought*	bu*yed*
lay	l*aid*	la*yed*
may	m*ight*	ma*yed*
pay* (to spend money)	p*aid*	pa*yed*
say	s*aid*	sa*yed*
slay (to kill)	sl*ew*, sl*ain*	sla*yed***

(*The most common meanings of the word *pay*—having to do with spending or yielding money or profits—form the irregular past tense *paid*. However, a less common nautical meaning of the verb—to cover with pitch or tar—<u>does</u> have a regular past-tense form: *payed*.)

(**Through colloquial usage, *slayed* is becoming an acceptable past tense/past participle form for *slay*, especially because another meaning of the word—"to amuse"—<u>does</u> take the regular form *slayed*.)

Quiz
(answers start on page 463)

1. In general, **Y** is changed to **I** before which types of suffixes?

a) Vowel suffixes
b) Consonant suffixes
c) Both
d) Neither

2. Which of the following suffixes **never** results in **Y** changing to **I**?

a) -ing
b) -ic
c) -ize
d) -ed

3. Which of the following suffixed words is spelled **incorrectly**?

a) pitiable
b) enviable
c) justifiable
d) enjoiable

4. Which of the following suffixed words is spelled **correctly**?

a) buyed
b) played
c) sayed
d) mayed

5. When we add the suffix "-ly," the **preferred** spelling is to **keep Y** for which of the following words?

a) weary
b) shy
c) happy
d) merry

Adding Suffixes after Silent E

When **E** appears at the end of a word, it is usually rendered silent. This silent E often determines the pronunciation of vowels, as well as the consonants **C** and **G**.

When a vowel suffix attaches to a word with a silent final **E**, it generally results in **E** being omitted or replaced. When it is followed by a consonant suffix, on the other hand, **E** usually remains in place within the word. However, there are quite a few exceptions to both of these conventions, as we'll see.

Dropping silent E with vowel suffixes

When a vowel suffix is attached to a word with a silent **E**, it often (though not always) results in **E** being omitted—the vowel of the suffix is able to take over the duties of **E** so that the pronunciation of the root word does not change. In the case of suffixes beginning with **E**, they simply replace the silent **E**.

For example:

Root Word	✔ Correctly Suffixed Words	✖ Incorrectly Suffixed Words
argue	argued, arguer, arguing	argueed, argueer, argueing
bake	baked, baker, baking	bakeed, bakeer, bakeing
communicate	communicated, communicating, communication	communicateed, communicateer, communicateing
dispose	disposable, disposal, disposing	disposeable, disposeal, disposeing
excite	excitable, excited, exciting	exciteable, exciteed, exciteing
fame	famed, famous	fameed, fameous
give	giver, giving	giveer, giveing
ice	iced, icing, icy	iceed, iceing, icey
manage	managed, manager, managing	manageed, manageer, manageing
tile	tiled, tiler, tiling	tileed, tileer, tileing
store	storage, stored, storing	storeage, storeed, storeing
use	usage, used, user, using	useage, useed, useer, useing

Although the convention of omitting silent **E** before a vowel suffix is the most common approach, there are notable exceptions to the silent E rule.

Exception 1: Keeping silent E before "-able"

There are many instances in which we do **not** omit a silent **E** when adding the vowel suffix "-able." This is especially true when it comes after **C** or **G** (to make it clear that the consonants retain their "soft" pronunciations). For example:

	With "-able"	With other vowel suffixes
C + Silent E	dance→dan**ce**able efface→effa**ce**able notice→noti**ce**able replace→repla**ce**able trace→tra**ce**able	danced, dancer, dancing effaced, effacing noticed, noticing replaced, replacing traced, tracer, tracing
G + Silent E	age→a**ge**able bridge→brid**ge**able change→chan**ge**able discourage→discoura**ge**able manage→mana**ge**able	aged, aging* bridged, bridging changed, changer, changing discouraged, discouraging managed, manager, managing

(*In British English, the silent **E** is usually kept in the word *ageing*, whereas it is usually omitted in American English.)

While most common when coming after **C/G + E**, this convention of keeping **E** before "-able" does occur after other consonants as well. However, this is quite rare and, in many cases, is simply an alternative spelling (especially in American English, in which **E** is much more likely to be omitted).

Here are some examples in which you might see "-able" following a silent **E**:
• file→fil**e**able (but <u>not</u> *filable*)
• fine→fin**e**able (<u>more</u> commonly, *finable*)
• like→lik**e**able (<u>more</u> commonly, *likable*)
• live→liv**e**able (<u>more</u> commonly, *livable*)
• love→lov**e**able (<u>more</u> commonly, *lovable*)
• name→nam**e**able (<u>less</u> commonly, *namable*)
• shape→shap**e**able (<u>more</u> commonly, *shapable*)
• size→siz**e**able (<u>more</u> commonly, *sizable*)
• trade→trad**e**able (<u>more</u> commonly, *tradable*)

Exception 2: Keeping silent E before "-ous"

The suffix "-ous" creates a few exceptions to the silent **E** rule, though these <u>only</u> occur in words in which silent **E** follows the consonant **G**. For example:
• advantage→advanta**ge***ous*
• courage→coura**ge***ous*
• outrage→outra**ge***ous*

(There are other words ending in "-eous," such as *courteous*, *gorgeous*, or *righteous*. However, in these words the **E** is not a remnant of the root + "-ous"; instead, such words' spellings are due to their evolution from other languages, such as Latin, French, or Old English.)

Exception 3: Words ending in "-ee," "-oe," and "-ye"

The silent **E** that appears in words with these three endings is functionally important, making their meanings and pronunciations clear to the reader. Because of this, silent **E** is **not** omitted when followed by the verb suffixes "-ing," "-able," or (in one instance) "-ist." For example:

Words ending in "-ee"	Words ending in "-oe"	Words ending in "-ye"
agree→agre**e**able, agre**e**ing decree→decre**e**ing foresee→foresee**e**able, foresee**e**ing free→fre**e**able, fre**e**ing guarantee→guarante**e**ing see→se**e**able, se**e**ing	canoe→cano**e**able, cano**e**ing, cano**e**ist hoe→ho**e**ing snowshoe→snowsho**e**ing	dye→dy**e**able, dy**e**ing eye→ey**e**able, ey**e**ing

However, when we add suffixes that **do** begin with **E** to these endings, we must drop the silent **E**—we never have a word with three **Es** in a row. Let's look at the same words again, this time adding **E** suffixes:

Words ending in "-ee"	Words ending in "-oe"	Words ending in "-ye"
agree→agreed decree→decreed, decreer foresee→foreseen, foreseer free→freed, freer, freest guarantee→guaranteed see→seen, seer	canoe→canoed hoe→hoed, hoer snowshoe→snowshoed, snowshoer	dye→dyed, dyer eye→eyed, eyer

Exception 4: The odd case of "-y"

When the vowel suffix "-y" is attached to a word ending in silent **E** to form an adjective, it *sometimes* replaces the **E**, but other times it does not. Like some of the examples we looked at with "-able," these are occasionally just variant (but acceptable) spellings of the same word. In some instances, only one form is correct.

Unfortunately, there is no predictable pattern to know when to omit or keep the silent **E** when adding the suffix "-y," so we just have to learn which is the correct (or more common) spelling. If you're not sure, check a good dictionary.

Let's look at some common examples:

E is usually omitted	E is usually kept	E is always omitted	E is always kept
flake→flaky (variant spelling: *flakey*) lace→lacy (variant spelling: *lacey*) rope→ropy (variant spelling: *ropey*)	home→homey (variant spelling: *homy*) price→pricey (variant spelling: *pricy*)	ice→icy (not *icey*) scare→scary (not *scarey*) spice→spicy (not *spicey*)	hoke→hokey (not: *hoky*) dice→dicey (not *dicy*)

Exception 5: Words ending in "-er"

This is more of an extension of the silent **E** rule than an exception to it, but it is a peculiar enough usage that it's worth highlighting.

In some words that end in "-er," **E** is also omitted when certain vowel suffixes are attached, even though **E** is neither silent nor at the end. This has to do with the origins of the words: originally, the ending was "-re," which can still be seen in the British English spellings, as in *calibre, centre, fibre, spectre,* or *theatre*. Even though they are spelled with "-er" in American English, we still treat them the same way with certain vowel suffixes, as in:

- caliber→calibrate
- center→central
- fiber→fibrous
- specter→spectral
- theater→theatrical

However, when we conjugate the verb *center* with "-ed" (*centered*) and "-ing" (*centering*), we do **not** omit **E** in American English.

Keeping silent E with consonant suffixes

When a word ending in a silent **E** is attached to a **consonant suffix**, we nearly always keep the **E** in the word. While other vowels are usually able to do the job of silent **E** in dictating the word's pronunciation and meaning, consonants cannot; therefore, we have to leave the **E** in place so the reader is not confused while reading.

For example:

Root Word	✔ Correctly Suffixed Words	✘ Incorrectly Suffixed Words
bar<u>e</u>	bar<u>e</u>ly, bar<u>e</u>ness, bar<u>e</u>s	bar**ly**, bar**ness**, bar**s**
car<u>e</u>	car<u>e</u>ful, car<u>e</u>less, car<u>e</u>s	car**ful**, car**less**, car**s**
complet<u>e</u>	complet<u>e</u>ly, complet<u>e</u>ness, complet<u>e</u>s	complet**ly**, complet**ness**, complet**s**
hom<u>e</u>	hom<u>e</u>less, hom<u>e</u>ly, hom<u>e</u>ward	hom**less**, hom**ly**, hom**ward**
lik<u>e</u>	lik<u>e</u>ly, lik<u>e</u>ness, lik<u>e</u>wise	lik**ly**, lik**ness**, lik**wise**
peac<u>e</u>	peac<u>e</u>ful, peac<u>e</u>less	peac**ful**, peac**less**
stat<u>e</u>	stat<u>e</u>hood, stat<u>e</u>less, stat<u>e</u>ly	stat**hood**, stat**less**, stat**ly**
wak<u>e</u>	wak<u>e</u>ful, wak<u>e</u>less, wak<u>e</u>s	wak**ful**, wak**less**, wak**s**

Although we usually keep silent **E** when we add a consonant suffix, there are a few specific exceptions to this rule. There are not as many exceptions as with the vowel suffixes, but it's still important to know when to omit silent E with consonant suffixes.

Exception 1: Consonant + LE + "-ly"

When **E** appears after a consonant + **L**, it is providing a vowel to complete the final syllable of the word. When we attach the suffix "-ly" to words that have this spelling pattern, it takes over this final syllable and replaces both **L** and **E**. For example:
- ab<u>le</u>→ab**ly**
- brist<u>le</u>→brist**ly**
- bub<u>ble</u>→bub**bly**
- dou<u>ble</u>→dou**bly**
- grist<u>le</u>→grist**ly**
- sensi<u>ble</u>→sensi**bly**
- subt<u>le</u>→subt**ly**
- this<u>tle</u>→this**tly**
- volu<u>ble</u>→volu**bly**

There are two exceptions within this exception, though. When we form adverbs from the adjectives *brittle* and *supple*, it is standard to <u>keep</u> the silent **E** because it still denotes a distinct syllable that is not replaced by "-ly":
- britt<u>le</u>→britt<u>le</u>**ly**
- sup<u>ple</u>→sup<u>ple</u>**ly**

(However, omitting E is also considered an acceptable variant, especially with *brittle*. Omitting **E** with *supple* yields *supply*, which already has another specific meaning, so it is considered more standard to keep the **E**.)

Exception 2: *truly* and *duly*

Most adjectives ending in "-ue" have a **Q** (or, in one case, a **G**) before the two vowels. The silent **E** makes it clear that the three letters together form a single-syllabled hard consonant sound (**QUE**=/k/; **GUE**=/g/), so we keep it when we add the consonant suffix "-ly" to form adverbs. For example:
- brus<u>que</u>→brus<u>que</u>**ly**
- grotes<u>que</u>→grotes<u>que</u>**ly**
- uni<u>que</u>→uni<u>que</u>**ly**
- va<u>gue</u>→va<u>gue</u>**ly**

In the words *true* and *due*, on the other hand, silent **E** does not determine the pronunciation of another letter—it's just there so the word does not end in a **U**, so when we add "-ly" to form an adverb, we drop the **E**:
- tru<u>e</u>→tru**ly**
- du<u>e</u>→du**ly**

However, there's also an exception to this exception: when the word *blue* is made into an adverb with "-ly," we <u>keep</u> the silent **E**, resulting in *blu<u>e</u>ly*. Luckily, this word is fairly uncommon in everyday speech and writing, but it's still good to know how it is spelled in comparison to *truly* and *duly*.

Exception 3: "-ment" with *argue, acknowledge,* and *judge*

The consonant suffix "-ment" typically behaves like any other when it follows silent **E**—that is, **E** is kept in the word. For instance:

• advertis**e**→advertis**ement**
• baffl**e**→baffl**ement**
• encourag**e**→encourag**ement**
• excit**e**→excit**ement**
• manag**e**→manag**ement**
• pav**e**→pav**ement**
• retir**e**→retir**ement**

However, when "-ment" follows the verbs *argue, acknowledge,* and *judge,* we <u>omit</u> the **E** instead of keeping it:

• argu**e**→argu**ment**
• acknowledg**e**→acknowledg**ment**
• judg**e**→judg**ment**

acknowledgment vs. *acknowledgement* and *judgment* vs. *judgement*

Be aware that both *acknowledgment* and *judgment* **can** be spelled with the silent **E**—in British English, this is actually the more common spelling. However, in American English, it is preferred (and often considered more correct) to omit the **E** for these two words.
Argument, on the other hand, can only be spelled the one way; *argu<u>e</u>ment* is <u>never</u> correct.

More information on silent E

All of the conventions we've looked at in this section have to do with the purpose and functionality of silent **E** in root words; knowing how it works will help you remember whether to keep or omit it before a suffix. If you're not clear on the different ways this silent vowel letter works, go to the section on Silent E to learn more.

Quiz

(answers start on page 463)

1. Silent **E** is generally *not* omitted before which type of suffixes?

a) Vowel suffixes

b) Consonant suffixes

c) Both

2. When silent **E** follows **C** or **G**, which vowel suffix does *not* result in it being omitted?

a) -ed

b) -ing

c) -able

d) -al

3. When does adding the suffix "-ly" result in silent **E** being *omitted*?

a) When the root word ends in a consonant + LE

b) When the root word ends "-ee," "-oe," or "-ye"

c) When **E** determines the pronunciation of **C, G**, or a vowel

d) A & C

e) All of the above

f) There is no predictable pattern

4. Which of the following suffixed words is spelled **correctly**?

a) raceing

b) dicy

c) judgment

d) homless

5. When do we *keep* silent **E** before the vowel suffix "-y"?

a) When the root word ends in a consonant + LE

b) When the root words are *true* and *due*

c) When **E** determines the pronunciation of **C, G**, or a vowel

d) There is no predictable spelling pattern

e) Always

f) Never

Doubling Consonants with Vowel Suffixes

Because most vowel suffixes are able to replace silent E by preserving the root word's pronunciation and meaning, we often have to double the final consonant of a root word when it precedes a vowel suffix to avoid confusion. This is especially true for single-syllable root words, but it occurs in certain words with two or more syllables as well.

Doubling the final consonant in single-syllable words

When a single-syllable word ends in a vowel + a consonant, we almost always double the consonant when a vowel suffix is attached; if we don't, we end up with the suffixed forms of root words that originally ended in silent E (or look as though they did). For example:

Root Word	✔ Correctly Suffixed Words	✖ Incorrectly Suffixed Words
bar	ba**rr**ed, ba**rr**ing	ba**r**ed, ba**r**ing (looks like the root word is *bare*)
dot	do**tt**ed, do**tt**ing	do**t**ed, do**t**ing (looks like the root word is *dote*)
fat	fa**tt**en, fa**tt**er, fa**tt**est, fa**tt**y	fa**t**en, fa**t**er, fa**t**est, fa**t**y (looks like the root word is *fate*)
hop	ho**pp**ed, ho**pp**er, ho**pp**ing, ho**pp**y	ho**p**ed, ho**p**er, ho**p**ing, ho**p**y (looks like the root word is *hope*)
jog	jo**gg**ed, jo**gg**er, jo**gg**ing	jo**g**ed, jo**g**er, jo**g**ing (looks like the root word is *joge*)
mad	ma**dd**en, ma**dd**er, ma**dd**est	ma**d**en, ma**d**er, ma**d**est (looks like the root word is *made*)
rob	ro**bb**ed, ro**bb**er, ro**bb**ing	ro**b**ed, ro**b**er, ro**b**ing (looks like the root word is *robe*)
slim	sli**mm**ed, sli**mm**er, sli**mm**ing	sli**m**ed, sli**m**er, sli**m**ing (looks like the root word is *slime*)
stop	sto**pp**able, sto**pp**ed, sto**pp**er, sto**pp**ing	sto**p**able, sto**p**ed, sto**p**er, sto**p**ing (looks like the root word is *stope*)
trek	tre**kk**ed, tre**kk**er, tre**kk**ing	tre**k**ed, tre**k**er, tre**k**ing (looks like the root word is *treke*)

This is a reliable rule to follow for single-syllable words that take vowel suffixes. Like most spelling rules, however, there are a number of specific exceptions.

Exception 1: Don't double a consonant that immediately follows another consonant

Keep in mind that the rule for single-syllable words only applies when the final consonant comes after a **vowel**: if two or more consonants occur together at the end of the word, we don't double the final one. For example:

• back→backed, backing
• clasp→clasped, clasping
• dark→darken, darkest
• herd→herder, herding
• long→longed, longing
• opt→opted, opting
• rest→rested, resting
• twitch→twitched, twitching

Exception 2: Don't double X or W

No words in English contain two **X**s in a row, and we only have two **W**s in a row when they occur in compound words (as in *glowworm*). This is because **X** forms two consonant sounds (/ks/), while a final **W** is technically functioning as a vowel, working with another vowel letter to create a vowel digraph. Thus, when a single-syllable word ends in one of these letters, we don't double it before a vowel suffix. For example:

Ending in X	Ending in W
ax→axed, axing	brew→brewed, brewing
coax→coaxed, coaxing	claw→clawed, clawing
fix→fixed, fixing	glow→glowed, glowing
tax→taxed, taxing	tow→towed, towing

Exception 3: Don't double a consonant after two vowels

Two vowels together in the same syllable form a vowel digraph, which makes a specific vowel sound. We don't need to double a consonant that immediately follows a vowel digraph because the pronunciation of the vowel sound won't be affected by the vowel suffixes. For example:

Root Word	✔ Correctly Suffixed Words	✖ Incorrectly Suffixed Words
bear	bearable, bearer, bearing	bearrable, bearrer, bearring
deem	deemed, deeming	deemmed, deemming
foul	fouled, fouler, foulest	foulled, fouller, foullest
heat	heatable, heater, heating	heattable, heatter, heatting
gain	gainable, gained, gaining	gainnable, gainned, gainning
oar	oared, oaring	oarred, oarring
shout	shouted, shouter, shouting	shoutted, shoutter, shoutting
wood	wooded, wooden, woody	woodded, woodder, wooddy

Sub-Exception: Words beginning with QU or SQU

The letter **U** always follows **Q** in native English words, and at the beginning of a word they create two consonant sounds: /kw/. We don't treat **U** like a separate vowel letter in this combination, so single-syllable words beginning with **QU** (or **SQU**) have their final consonants doubled before a vowel suffix. Fortunately, there are only a handful of common words in which this is the case:

Root Word	✔ Correctly Suffixed Words	✖ Incorrectly Suffixed Words
quip	quipped, quipping	quiped, quiping (looks like the root word is *quipe*)
quit	quitter, quitting	quiter, quiting (looks like the root word is *quite*)
quiz	quizzer, quizzing	quizer, quizing (looks like the root word is *quize*)
squat	squatted, squatting	squated, squating (looks like the root word is *squate*)

Note that most single-syllable words beginning with **QU** or **SQU** end in more than one consonant (as in *quick* or *squash*), have two internal vowels other than **U** (as in *squeak* or *squeal*), or else have a silent **E** after the final consonant (as in *quake* or *square*), which means there is no need to double the final consonant.

Doubling the consonant when the final syllable is emphasized

The rules for doubling final consonants are fairly straightforward for single-syllable words, but they become more complex when a word has two or more syllables. Luckily, there are conventions we can follow for these longer words as well, but they can be trickier to remember because they depend on the *pronunciation* of the word rather than its spelling alone.

When the final syllable of a multi-syllable word is vocally stressed, we almost always double the final consonant before a vowel suffix. In the examples below, the stressed syllables are shown in **bold**, with the IPA pronunciation included beneath each root word.

Emphasis on final syllable	Suffixed Words	Emphasis on other syllable	Suffixed Words
be**gin** (/bɪˈgɪn/)	begi**nn**er, begi**nn**ing	**bick**er (/ˈbɪkər/)	bickered, bickering
con**fer*** (/kənˈfɜr/)	confe**rr**able, confe**rr**ed, confe**rr**ing	con**sid**er (/kənˈsɪdər/)	considerable, considered, considering
for**get** (/fərˈgɛt/)	forge**tt**able, forge**tt**ing	**for**feit (/ˈfɔrfɪt/)	forfeited, forfeiting, forfeiture
in**cur** (/ɪnˈkɜr/)	incu**rr**able, incu**rr**ed, incu**rr**ing	in**ter**pret (/ɪnˈtɜrprət/)	interpreted, interpreter, interpreting
o**mit** (/oʊˈmɪt/)	omi**tt**ed, omi**tt**ing	**op**en (/ˈoʊpən/)	opened, opener, opening
pre**fer*** (/prɪˈfɜr/)	prefe**rr**ed, prefe**rr**ing	**prof**it (/ˈprɒfɪt/)	profitable, profited, profited
trans**mit** (/trænzˈmɪt/)	transmi**tt**able, transmi**tt**ed, transmi**tt**ing	**trav**el (/ˈtrævəl/)	traveled, traveler, traveling**

(*Not all vowel suffixes result in a doubled consonant for these words, as we'll see a little bit later.)
(**See **"American English vs. British English"** further on.)

Remember, all the other rules we've seen so far also apply: in addition to those in an emphasized syllable, we only double <u>single</u> consonants that come after a <u>single</u> vowel, are <u>not</u> followed by silent **E**, and are not **X** or **W**. In all other instances, the final consonant is **not** doubled. For example:

• careen→careened, careening
• decline→declined, declining
• entreat→entreated, entreating
• insist→insisted, insisting
• relax→relaxed, relaxing

But don't forget our sub-rule about **QU**—it also applies to words with more than one syllable, meaning we don't treat **U** as a vowel. For instance:

• acquit→acqui**tt**al, acqui**tt**ed
• equip→equi**pp**ed, equi**pp**ing

Exception 1: Doubled consonants in unstressed syllables

Note that there are several words that have primary emphasis on the first syllable but have doubled consonants when taking vowel suffixes. Most of these have a secondary stress on the last syllable, which might be part of the reason why their final consonants are doubled, but this is not always the case.

The situation is made more difficult by the fact that many of these words have variant or accepted alternative spellings in which the final consonant isn't doubled, and the preference for some of these variants often comes down to regional dialect. This leads to confusing spelling decisions such as *kidnaped vs. kidnapped* and *worshiped vs. worshipped*. Unfortunately, we just have to memorize these exceptions:

Emphasis on final syllable	Suffixed Words	Variant/Alternative Spellings
crystal (/ˈkrɪstəl/)	crystalline, crystallize	crystalize (*Crystalline* has only one spelling.)
input (/ˈɪnˌpʊt/)	inputted, inputting	*Input*, without a suffix, is often used instead of *inputted* for the past tense and past participle form.
kidnap (/ˈkɪdˌnæp/)	kidnapped, kidnapping	kidnaped, kidnaping (These variants are acceptable but less common in American English; in British English, only *kidnapped* and *kidnapping* are considered correct.)
program (/ˈproʊˌgræm/)	programmable, programmed, programmer, programming	programed, programing (Both variants are quite uncommon in modern English. Note that *programmable* and *programmer* are considered the only correct forms.)
worship (/ˈwɜrʃɪp/)	worshipped, worshipper, worshipping	worshiped, worshiper, worshiping (These variants are acceptable but less common in American English; in British English, only the double-consonant versions are considered correct.)

Exception 2: Words that change syllable stress

Finally, it's important to know that adding suffixes can sometimes **change** the pronunciation of the root word, resulting in stress being placed on a different syllable. When the syllabic stress moves to another part of the word as a result of a suffix, we must use the same spelling rules we've looked at already. This is especially common with verbs ending in "-fer." For example:

Root Word	Double consonant before suffix (No emphasis change)	Single consonant before suffix (Emphasis shifted)	Exceptions
confer (/kənˈfɜr/)	conferrable (/kənˈfɜrəbl/) conferred (/kənˈfɜrd/) conferring (/kənˈfɜr/)	conference (/ˈkɑnfrəns/)	
defer (/dɪˈfɜr/)	deferrable (/dɪˈfɜrəbəl/) deferred (/dɪˈfɜrd/) deferring (/dɪˈfɜrɪŋ/)	deference (/ˈdɛfərəns/)	
infer (/ɪnˈfɜr/)	inferred (/ɪnˈfɜrd/) inferring (/ɪnˈfɜrɪŋ/)	inference (/ˈɪnfərəns/)	inferable (/ɪnˈfɜrəbəl/) (*Inferrable* is an accepted but uncommon variant.)
prefer (/prɪˈfɜr/)	preferred (/prɪˈfɜrd/) preferring (/prɪˈfɜrɪŋ/)	preferable (/ˈprɛfərəbəl/) preference (/ˈprɛfərəns/)	*Preferable* is often pronounced *preferable* (/prɛˈfɜrəbəl/), but maintains the same spelling.
refer (/rɪˈfɜr/)	referral (/rɪˈfɜrəl/) referred (/rɪˈfɜrd/) referring (/rɪˈfɜrɪŋ/)	referee (/ˌrɛfəˈri/) reference (/ˈrɛfərəns/)	referable (/rɪˈfɜrəbəl/) (Many dictionaries list *referrable* as an alternate spelling when the word is pronounced /rɪˈfɜrəbəl/, while *referable* is shown with the pronunciation /ˈrɛfərəbəl/. However, the word is much more commonly spelled with one **R** and pronounced with a stress on the second syllable.)

Sub-Exception: Don't double consonants before "-ic"

Attaching the vowel suffix "-ic" usually results in the word's emphasis being placed on the syllable directly before it. According to the rules that we've seen so far, this should result in final consonants being doubled; however, this suffix is an exception to the rule, and single consonants are <u>never</u> doubled when they come before "-ic." For example:

• atom (/ˈætəm/) → atomic (/əˈtɑmɪk/)
• acrobat (/ˈækrəˌbæt/) → acrobatic (/ˌækrəˈbætɪk/)
• period (/ˈpɪriəd/) → periodic (/ˌpɪriˈɑdɪk/)
• symbol (/ˈsɪmbəl/) → symbolic (/sɪmˈbɑlɪk/)

Many other suffixes will change the pronunciation of a word without changing the root spelling. To learn more, see the section on Word Stress.

Doubling consonants in American English vs. British English

The rules regarding syllable stress and consonant doubling are all fairly consistent in American English, but there are some notable exceptions that occur in British English—specifically, words ending in **L**.

Doubling L before vowel suffixes (*traveled vs. travelled*)

Perhaps the most commonly confused spelling convention is whether or not to double the final **L** in two-syllable words before a vowel suffix. In American English, we follow the rule that we've already established: if the word has an emphasis on the final syllable before the vowel suffix, then the **L** is doubled. However, most words ending in a single **L** are stressed on the first syllable, so **L** remains singular. For example:

Emphasis on first syllable	Suffixed Words	Emphasis on last syllable	Suffixed Words
cance<u>l</u> (/ˈkænsəl/)	cance<u>l</u>ed, cance<u>l</u>ing	compe<u>l</u> (/kəmˈpɛl/)	compe<u>ll</u>ed, compe<u>ll</u>ing
equa<u>l</u> (/ˈikwəl/)	equa<u>l</u>ed, equa<u>l</u>ing	exce<u>l</u> (/ɪkˈsɛl/)	exce<u>ll</u>ed, exce<u>ll</u>ing (However, *exce<u>ll</u>ent*, with two Ls, is pronounced /ˈɛksələnt/.)
labe<u>l</u> (/ˈleɪbəl/)	labe<u>l</u>ed, labe<u>l</u>ing	lape<u>l</u> (/ləˈpɛl/)	lape<u>ll</u>ed
mode<u>l</u> (/ˈmɑdəl/)	mode<u>l</u>ed, mode<u>l</u>ing	prope<u>l</u> (/prəˈpɛl/)	prope<u>ll</u>ant, prope<u>ll</u>ed
trave<u>l</u> (/ˈtræəl/)	trave<u>l</u>ed, trave<u>l</u>ing	rebe<u>l</u> (/rɪˈbɛl/)	rebe<u>ll</u>ed, rebe<u>ll</u>ion

In British English, on the other hand, a final **L** that follows a vowel is almost always doubled before "-ed," "-er," and "-ing" **regardless** of where the stress occurs in the word.

For the sake of comparison, let's see the preferred American English spellings (with single **L**) of some common words alongside their preferred British English spellings (with doubled **L**):

American English	British English
barre<u>l</u>→barre<u>l</u>ed, barre<u>l</u>ing	barre<u>l</u>→barre<u>ll</u>ed, barre<u>ll</u>ing
cance<u>l</u>→cance<u>l</u>ed, cance<u>l</u>ing	cance<u>l</u>→cance<u>ll</u>ed, cance<u>ll</u>ing
dia<u>l</u>→dia<u>l</u>ed, dia<u>l</u>ing	dia<u>l</u>→dia<u>ll</u>ed, dia<u>ll</u>ing
due<u>l</u>→due<u>l</u>ed, due<u>l</u>ing	due<u>l</u>→due<u>ll</u>ed, due<u>ll</u>ing
fue<u>l</u>→fue<u>l</u>ed, fue<u>l</u>ing	fue<u>l</u>→fue<u>ll</u>ed, fue<u>ll</u>ing
grove<u>l</u>→grove<u>l</u>ed, grove<u>l</u>ing	grove<u>l</u>→grove<u>ll</u>ed, grove<u>ll</u>ing
labe<u>l</u>→labe<u>l</u>ed, labe<u>l</u>ing	labe<u>l</u>→labe<u>ll</u>ed, labe<u>ll</u>ing
mode<u>l</u>→mode<u>l</u>ed, mode<u>l</u>ing	mode<u>l</u>→mode<u>ll</u>ed, mode<u>ll</u>ing
riva<u>l</u>→riva<u>l</u>ed, riva<u>l</u>ing	riva<u>l</u>→riva<u>ll</u>ed, riva<u>ll</u>ing
signa<u>l</u>→signa<u>l</u>ed, signa<u>l</u>ing	signa<u>l</u>→signa<u>ll</u>ed, signa<u>ll</u>ing
trave<u>l</u>→trave<u>l</u>ed, trave<u>l</u>ing	trave<u>l</u>→trave<u>ll</u>ed, trave<u>ll</u>ing

If you're writing according to the styles of American English and you can't remember whether to double the final **L** or not, just check which syllable in the word is being stressed. If you're writing in British English, it's a good bet that the **L** should be doubled.

combating vs. *combatting*

The word *combat* has two different pronunciations with different syllabic stress: /ˈkɑmbæt/ (noun) and /kəmˈbæt/ (verb). When we add vowel suffixes to the word, the stress usually remains on the second syllable, but, unlike our previous examples, **T** remains <u>singular</u> in American English:

• comba<u>t</u>→comba<u>t</u>ed, comba<u>t</u>ing, comba<u>t</u>ive

Dictionaries often list *combatted* and *combatting* as acceptable variants in British English, but it is still most common in both styles for **T** to remain singular before the suffixes.

Note that *combative* is the <u>only</u> spelling considered correct in both American and British English.

focused vs. *focussed*

Another consonant ending that often confuses writers is the **S** in *focus*. Should it be *focused* or *focussed*? Again, there is a difference between American English and British English conventions.

In American English, the **S** is never doubled before a suffix, so its conjugations are *focused*, *focuses*, and *focusing*. The same rule applies to all forms of the word that have a vowel suffix, as in *focusable* and *focuser*.

This is the most common (and preferred) convention in British English as well, but it is not considered incorrect to spell the conjugations with a doubled **S**—*focussed*, *focusses*, *focussing*. (*Focusable* and *focuser* always take just one **S**). However, these double-**S** spellings are much less common and may be seen by some as incorrect, even within the UK.

No matter where in the world you are, it's best to keep the **S** in *focus* singular before a vowel suffix, because it's always the correct choice.

Quiz
(answers start on page 463)

1. In general, when do we double the final consonant in multi-syllable words?
a) When the first syllable is stressed
b) When the final syllable is stressed
c) When the emphasis shifts to the suffix itself
d) Always
e) Never

2. Which of these words would have a doubled consonant before a vowel suffix?
a) treat
b) open
c) tax
d) shop

3. Which of the following vowel suffixes **never** results in a doubled consonant?
a) al
b) ing
c) ic
d) able

4. In single-syllable words, we don't double the final consonant when it comes after two vowels **except**:
a) When the final consonant is **L** or **S**
b) When the word begins with **QU**
c) When it is followed by the suffix "-ous"
d) In British English

5. For words that have stress on the first syllable, which consonant is **usually** doubled in **British English**, but remains singular in **American English**?
a) C
b) L
c) S
d) R

Inflection in Spelling

Definition

Grammatical **inflection** (sometimes known as **accidence** or **flection** in more traditional grammars) is the way in which a word's spelling is changed in order to achieve a new, specific grammatical meaning.

Verbs are the most commonly inflected words, changing form to reflect grammatical tense and person. Collectively, this is known as **conjugation**.

The other parts of speech that can undergo inflection are nouns, pronouns, adjectives, and adverbs. Inflection of these parts of speech is known as **declension**.

Most inflection is done according to consistent spelling rules and patterns, but, as we'll see, there are also many words that are irregularly inflected.

Conjugation

When we discuss conjugating verbs, we usually refer to ways in which we change a verb's spelling to reflect tense or grammatical person.

For most verbs, this is achieved by adding various inflectional suffixes, which can be used to form the simple past tense/past participle, the present participle/gerund, and the third-person singular forms. For example:

Suffix	Grammatical Function	Example Words
"-s"	Forms the third-person singular for most verbs.	to end→it ends to hear→he hears to run→she runs to start→it starts to think→he thinks to write→she writes
"-es"	Forms the third-person singular for verbs ending in a sibilant sound (/s/, /z/, /ʃ/, or /ʧ/) created by the endings "-ss," "-zz," "-x," "-sh," "-ch," or "-tch," as well as verbs ending in a consonant + **O**.	to approach→he approaches to buzz→it buzzes to catch→she catches to go→he goes to hush→she hushes to pass→it passes
"-ed"	Forms the past participle of most verbs, used in the simple past tense, past perfect tense, and present perfect tense.	**Simple past tense:** • "I asked him for advice." • "We walked to the pier together." • "She signed up for a three-year contract." **Past perfect tense:** • "We had hoped for a better outcome." • "The movie had already ended when I turned on the TV." • "I had never watched a sunset before last night." **Present perfect tense:** • "I have lived in Italy for many years." • "He has never worked in this industry before." • "They have closed the restaurant for the weekend."

"-en"	Forms the past participle of some irregular verbs, used in the past perfect tense and present perfect tense (but **not** the simple past tense).	**Past perfect tense:** • "I had never be**en** to Spain before last summer." • "We had already eat**en** something by the time the meal was ready." • "She had already giv**en** her two weeks' notice when they offered her the promotion." **Present perfect tense:** • "I've ridd**en** on roller coasters before, but never one like this!" • "The film has gott**en** a lot of positive reviews." • "John's writt**en** a number of editorials on the topic in the past."
"-ing"	Forms the present participle of verbs, used in past, present, and future continuous tenses, as well as gerunds (which function as nouns).	**Continuous tenses:** • "I am build**ing** a treehouse for my kids." (present continuous tense) • "I was read**ing** about that in the paper this morning!" (past continuous tense) • "We'll be fly**ing** to Denver in the morning." (future continuous tense) **Gerunds:** • "I really love hik**ing**." • "Swimm**ing** is a great form of exercise." • "We're very fond of watch**ing** classic films."

It's important to note that there are also many so-called **irregular verbs**, which are conjugated in ways that do not follow the patterns we've just looked at. We'll cover these further on in this section.

Declension

The term **declension** refers to the inflection of the other parts of speech: nouns, pronouns, adjectives, and adverbs. For nouns, adjectives, and adverbs, we usually use inflectional suffixes, much like verbs. For *pronouns*, however, we usually change the word altogether, depending on the grammatical function of the word.

Declension of nouns

Generally, we only *decline* nouns to mark plurality—that is, whether there is more than one person, place, or thing being discussed. We usually do so by adding an "**-s**" to the end of the noun, as in *books, toys, tables*, etc. For nouns ending in "-s," "-x," "-z," or with consonant digraphs and trigraphs such as "-sh," "-ch," or "-tch", we add "**-es**" to make it plural, as in *buses, taxes, dishes, watches*, etc.

There are a few other spelling patterns that apply, which we'll look at in greater detail in the section Forming Plurals. There are also several **irregular** plurals, which we'll look at later in this section.

Indicating gender in nouns

We can also decline certain nouns to reflect grammatical **gender**. While this is very uncommon in English, when it does occur, nouns are almost always inflected with suffixes to become feminine, the most common of which is "**-ess**" (used primarily to identify a professional, noble, royal, or religious title of a woman). For example:

• steward**ess**
• wait**ress**
• act**ress**

- abb**ess**
- count**ess**
- duch**ess**
- princ**ess**

The other suffix most commonly associated with feminine nouns is "-ette," as in:

- suffrage**ette**
- bachelor**ette**
- brun**ette**

Other than the above examples, though, "-ette" is more commonly used to refer to non-gendered items that are small or diminutive, such as *cigarette, kitchenette, novelette, launderette, cassette*, and so on.

Uniquely, there is one word that is inherently feminine that can take the suffix "-er" to become masculine: *widow* (meaning a woman whose spouse has died) becomes masculine by adding "-er"—*widow**er*** (a man whose spouse has died).

There are other nouns that are inherently gendered in English (such as *king* and *queen*), but we won't go over them here because they do not follow specific spelling patterns or have their spellings changed to reflect their gender.

Declension of pronouns

For the most part, only personal pronouns are subject to inflection. We decline personal pronouns based on case (subjective or objective), gender (masculine or feminine), person (first person, second person, or third person), and number (singular or plural).

Case

Personal pronouns change form to reflect the subjective case, the objective case, and the possessive case.

When a personal pronoun is acting as the **subject** of a verb (that is, it is the person or thing <u>doing</u> the action), it is said to be in the subjective case. For instance:

- "**I** know that **she** said that." (Both pronouns are subjective, as both are agents of their respective actions.)
- "**He** told *her* to be quiet." (Here, only *he* is in the subjective case; *her*, the recipient or "object" of his action, is in the **objective** case.)

A personal pronoun is in the **objective case** when it is a *direct* or *indirect object* of a verb, or else if it is the **object of a preposition**. For example:

- "I can't believe he fired **you**." (*You* is the direct object of the verb *fired*.)
- "Please send **them** a thank you card." (*Them* is the indirect object of the verb *send*.)
- "You can't say that *to* **me**!" (*Me* is the object of the preposition *to*; together they form the prepositional phrase *to me*.)

Finally, the **possessive case** (also called the **genitive case**) inflects a personal pronoun to mark possession. These inflections can be divided into possessive pronouns and possessive determiners, which are similar but have distinct grammatical functions. **Possessive determiners** function grammatically like adjectives, modifying a noun or nouns. For example:

- "**My** dad's glasses went missing." (*My* is a possessive determiner that shows the relation of *dad* to the speaker.)
- "He said it was **his** computer." (*His* is a possessive determiner that modifies *computer*.)

Possessive pronouns, on the other hand, are personal pronouns in the possessive case that have the grammatical function of nouns. For example:

- "I can see **mine** through the window!"
- "Jenny seems pretty sure that the book is **hers**."

Gender

Personal pronouns are only inflected for gender when they are in the third person and singular—first-person and second-person pronouns (singular or plural) and third-person plural pronouns always remain gender neutral. Here are the gendered pronouns in English:

Third-person feminine singular: *she, her, hers, herself*
Third-person masculine singular: *he, him, his, himself*

The third-person singular can also be **neuter** (gender neutral). This is used when a personal pronoun represents a thing or an animal. Animals can sometimes take gendered personal pronouns if they are pets or domesticated animals; otherwise, they take the third-person neuter form:

Third-person neuter singular: *it, its, its own, itself*

Remember, when there are multiple people or things, we use the ungendered forms of *they*:

Third-person plural: *they, them, their, theirs, themselves*

Person

Grammatical person refers to the perspectives of the personal pronouns used to identify a person in speech and text—that is, it distinguishes between a speaker (first person), a person being spoken to (second person), and others beyond that (third person).

First-person pronouns tell what is directly happening to the speaker or narrator:

Singular: *I, me, my, mine, myself*

Plural: *we, us, our, ours, ourselves*

We use the **second-person pronouns** to indicate those who are being addressed directly by the speaker:

Singular/Plural: *you, you, your, yours, yourself (singular), yourselves (plural)*

Third-person pronouns are used to talk about someone or something that is not the speaker and is not being directly addressed:

Feminine singular: *she, her, hers, herself*

Masculine singular: *he, him, his, himself*

Neuter singular: *it, its, its own, itself*

However, when there are multiple people or things, we use the un-gendered forms of *they*:

Third-person plural: *they, them, their, theirs, themselves*

Number

Personal pronouns, unlike nouns, have various specific inflections depending on whether they are singular or plural. For the most part, only the **first-person** and **third-person** personal pronouns have plural forms; the only plural **second-person** pronoun is the reflexive pronoun *yourselves*.

There are no rules or guidelines for how we change the personal pronouns for number because doing so affects all the other forms; we simply have to memorize their various forms. The table below shows a breakdown of all the personal pronouns and their various inflections for number (as well as case, person, and gender).

Person	Number	Gender	Subjective Case	Objective Case	Possessive Determiner	Possessive Pronoun	Reflexive Pronoun
First Person	Singular	Masculine / Feminine	I	me	my	mine	myself
First Person	Plural	Masculine / Feminine	we	us	our	ours	ourselves
Second Person	Singular/Plural	Masculine / Feminine	you	you	your	yours	yourself (*yourselves* if plural)
Third Person	Singular	Feminine	she	her	her	hers	herself
Third Person	Singular	Masculine	he	him	his	his	himself
Third person	Singular	Neuter	it	it	its	its (own)	itself
Third person	Plural	Neuter (Gender Neutral)	they	them	their	theirs	themselves

Reflexive Pronouns and Intensive Pronouns

Reflexive and **intensive pronouns** are identical in appearance, formed by adding "-self" or "-selves" to the pronouns *my, our, your, her, him, it, them,* or *one*.

Reflexive pronouns are used when someone or something is both the subject and the object of the same verb. When this happens, the reflexive pronoun is used as the object of the verb to represent the person or thing; a reflexive pronoun can never be used as the subject of a verb.

For example:
- "I wish you could hear **yourselves** right now!"
- "She admitted to **herself** that she was wrong."
- "The vole hides **itself** beneath the ground for safety."
- "The players have really outdone **themselves** today!"
- "One should strive to better **oneself** every day."

Intensive pronouns look identical to reflexive pronouns, but they are used to add emphasis to a person's (or thing's) <u>role</u> in an action. For example:
- "I told them **myself** that the report would be finished on time."
- "You need to do the work **yourselves**, or you will never learn the material."
- "The president **herself** will be speaking at the ceremony."

Reflexive and intensive pronouns are not typically considered inflections of personal pronouns. However, because they are mostly formed <u>from</u> personal pronouns, we have grouped them together here with the other types of personal pronoun declension.

whom and *whomever*

Finally, two other pronouns that undergo declension are the relative pronouns *who* and *whoever*. These can be inflected as *whom* and *whomever*, which are in the objective case (that is, they function as the objects of verbs or pronouns). For example:
- "Mr. Dawson, **who<u>m</u>** I've had as a teacher for three years in a row, is writing a reference letter for my college application."
- "It is important that **who<u>m</u>ever** we choose is capable of running the branch without too much oversight."

However, this is becoming less common in everyday speech and writing, and *who* and *whoever* are increasingly being used in every situation.

Declension of adjectives

Adjectives are inflected when we want to form comparisons between two people or things (comparative adjectives), or to identify the person or thing with the highest degree of a characteristic among a group (superlative adjectives).

For instance:
- "Mike is **strong**." (adjective)
- "I am **stronger** than him." (comparative adjective)
- "Jeff is the **strongest** of all of us." (superlative adjective)

The progression of inflection for adjectives is known as the degrees of comparison. The spelling rules that dictate how each degree is formed depend on how the base form (known as the positive degree) of the adjective is spelled.

Adjective spelling	How to modify	Positive degree	Comparative degree	Superlative degree
One syllable, ending in a consonant preceded by one vowel.	Add "-er" for comparative degree or "-est" for superlative degree. Double final consonant.	big	big**ger**	big**gest**
One syllable, ending in a consonant preceded by two vowels or another consonant.	Add "-er" for comparative degree or "-est" for superlative degree. Do **not** double final consonant if preceded by one vowel.	strong	strong**er**	strong**est**
One syllable, ending in an "e"	Add "-r" for comparative degree or "-st" for superlative degree.	large	larg**er**	larg**est**
Two syllables, ending in a "y"	Replace "y" with "i" and add "-er" for comparative degree or "-est" for superlative degree.	happy	happ**ier**	happ**iest**
Three or more syllables, or two syllables **not** ending in "y"	Add the words *more* or *less* before the adjective to make them comparative, or *most/least* to make them superlative.	clever	**more/less** careful	**most/least** careful

Declension of adverbs

We can also inflect adverbs when we want to compare the degree to which two actions are performed (comparative adverbs), or to identify the highest degree of how an action is performed (superlative adverbs).

For example:
• "Susan runs **fast**." (adverb)
• "Janet runs **faster** than Susan." (comparative adverb)
• "Betty runs the **fastest**." (superlative adverb)

The progression of inflection for adverbs is known (like adjectives) as the degrees of comparison. Again, the spelling rules that dictate how each degree is formed depend on how the base form (known as the positive degree) of the adverb is spelled.

Adverb spelling	How to modify	Positive degree	Comparative degree	Superlative degree
One syllable, ending in a consonant	Add "-er" for comparative degree or "-est" for superlative degree.	fast	fast**er**	fast**est**
One syllable, ending in an "e"	Add "-r" for comparative degree or "-st" for superlative degree.	late	lat**er**	lat**est**
Adverbs ending in a "y"	Add the words *more* or *less* before the adverb to make it comparative, or *most/least* to make it superlative.	carefully	**more/less** carefully	**most/least** carefully

Irregular Inflection

While most words that can be inflected in English follow predictable and reliable patterns, there are a huge number of **irregular inflections** across the various parts of speech. The most notorious of these are irregular verbs, but there are also irregular plurals, irregular adjectives, and irregular adverbs. (Pronouns have such unique inflections that they could all be considered irregular in their own right.)

Irregular verbs

Verbs present the greatest challenge when it comes to learning about regular and irregular inflection. A huge variety of verbs are irregular, which means they have past simple tense and past participle forms that defy the normal conventions. That means that every irregular verb has three unique conjugations that must be memorized. In addition, the verb *be* is known as being **highly irregular**, because it has **six** irregular conjugations in addition to its base and present participle form—*eight* in all!

We'll briefly look at the rules for conjugating regular verbs and then look at some common irregular verbs below. (Note that all verbs, whether regular or irregular, conjugate the same way to form present participles, taking "-ing" at the end of the base form. Because of this, we won't include the present participle form in the breakdowns below.)

Conjugating regular verbs

The majority of verbs take the suffix "-ed" with their base form (the infinitive of the verb without *to*) to create **both** the past simple tense and past participle. There are some instances in which the verb's spelling must change slightly to accommodate this, but these rules are straightforward and consistent. Here are some common regular verb inflections:

Base Form	Past Simple Tense	Past Participle
play	played	played
bake	baked	baked
listen	listened	listened
approach	approached	approached
gather	gathered	gathered
climb	climbed	climbed
chop	chopped	chopped
copy	copied	copied
panic	panicked	panicked

Conjugating irregular verbs

Irregular verbs do not have spelling rules that we can follow to create the past simple tense and past participles. This means that the only way of knowing how to spell these forms is to memorize them for each irregular verb individually. Here are a few common examples:

Base Form	Past Simple Tense	Past Participle
see	saw	seen
grow	grew	grown
give	gave	given
think	thought	thought
throw	threw	thrown
drive	drove	driven
ride	rode	ridden
run	ran	run
swim	swam	swum
sit	sat	sat

Conjugating *be*

As we mentioned above, the verb *be* is unique among verbs for having a huge variety of conjugations. Not only does it have irregular inflections for the past simple tense and past participle, but it also has specific forms depending on **plurality** and **grammatical person** (first person, second person, and third person). The table below shows a breakdown of all the different ways we conjugate *be*.

Grammatical person	Base form	Present Tense Singular	Present Tense Plural	Present Participle	Past Tense Singular	Past Tense Plural	Past Participle
n/a	be			being			been
first person		I **am**	we **are**		I **was**	we **were**	
second person		you **are**	you **are**		you **were**	you **were**	
third person		he/she/it **is**	they **are**		he/she/it **was**	they **were**	

Irregular plurals

While the vast majority of nouns are made into plurals by adding "-s" or "-es," there are quite a few that have **irregular** plural forms that defy this convention. These are completely unique words that, for the most part, do not follow any rules or conventions for how they are spelled. Here are some of the most common irregular nouns:

Noun	Irregular plural form
person	**people/persons***
mouse	**mice**
goose	**geese**
child	**children**
foot	**feet**
man	**men**
woman	**women**

(*Persons is also a plural form of person, but in modern English it is usually reserved for more formal, bureaucratic, or legal language, as in, "Any such **persons** found to be guilty of shoplifting will be prosecuted.")

Adding "-ves" instead of "-(e)s"

With some nouns that end in "-f," "-fe," or "-lf," we replace the endings with "-ves" to make them plural. Here are some common examples:

Noun	Irregular plural form
life	li**ves**
wife	wi**ves**
loaf	loa**ves**
leaf	lea**ves**
knife	kni**ves**
thief	thie**ves**
calf	cal**ves**
half	hal**ves**
wolf	wol**ves**

Words from Latin or Greek

There are also nouns taken from Latin or Greek that maintain their original plural forms. While following the established patterns of their original language, these plurals are different from the standard plural forms in English. However, as we'll see, some of these words have begun shifting toward more conventional plural forms, which are now used in addition to their original spellings.

For example:

Noun	Irregular plural form
index	ind**ices** (*indexes* is now also acceptable)
appendix	append**ices** (*appendixes* is now also acceptable)
fungus	fung**i**
criterion	criteri**a**
nucleus	nucle**i**
syllabus	syllab**i**
focus	foc**i**
cactus	cact**i** (*cactuses* is now also acceptable)
thesis	thes**es**
crisis	cris**es**
phenomenon	phenomen**a**

Irregular adjectives

The vast majority of adjectives follow the convention of adding "-er" when forming the comparative degree and "-est" for the superlative degree. However, there are a few adjectives that are irregular and have unique forms that do not conform to any spelling conventions. Because of this, they must all be memorized:

Irregular adjective	Comparative degree	Superlative degree
fun	more/less fun	most/least fun
bad	worse	worst
well (healthy)	better	best
good	better	best
far	farther/further	farthest/furthest
little (amount)	less	least
many/much	more	most

Adverbs

Unlike adjectives, which can only be considered irregular when forming the comparative and superlative degrees, some adverbs can be irregular in their basic form (known as the positive degree), which then extends to their comparative and superlative degrees. We'll briefly look at how regular adverbs are formed, then contrast them with irregular adverbs and their subsequent degrees of comparison.

Regular adverbs

The majority of adverbs are formed from adjectives. The standard way of doing this is by adding "-ly" to the end of the adjective. Sometimes, the adjective's spelling needs to be altered slightly to accommodate this, but the rules of doing so are fairly straightforward. Here are some common examples:

Adjective	Regular adverb	Spelling rule
beautiful	**beautifully**	Adjective + "-ly"
enthusiastic	**enthusiastically**	If the adjective ends in "-ic," it will change to "-ically."
happy	**happily**	If the adjective ends in a "-y," it will change to "-ily."
terrible	**terribly**	If the adjective ends in "-le," the ending is dropped and is replaced with "-ly."
due	**duly**	If the adjective ends in "-ue," the "e" on the end is dropped and is replaced with "-ly."

Irregular adverbs

Although most adverbs follow the above rules when they are formed from adjectives, there are a number of irregular adverbs that go against the conventions. Much of the time, irregular adverbs have the same spelling as their adjectival counterparts, but there are no clues in the adjectives' spelling as to when this is the case; like all irregular inflections, they just have to be memorized. Below are some of the most common irregular adverbs.

Adjective	Irregular adverb	Sources of confusion
fast	**fast**	*Last* becomes *lastly*, but *fast* becomes *fast*.
hard	**hard**	*Hardly (ever)* is an adverb of frequency, meaning "almost never."
straight	**straight**	
lively	**lively**	*Lively* still exists as an adverb in phrases like *step lively*; however, it is more often used as an adjective in the prepositional phrase *in a lively manner*.
late (tardy)	**late**	*Lately* is a different adverb that means "recently."
daily	**daily**	Adverbs of frequency that relate to units of time have the same form as both adjectives and adverbs.
early	**early**	
friendly	**no adverb**	Can only be used in adverbial prepositional phrases like *in a friendly manner*.
timely	**no adverb**	Can only be used in adverbial prepositional phrases like *in a timely manner*.
good	**well**	*Well* is the adverbial form of *good*; it can also function as a predicative adjective meaning "healthy."

Irregular degrees of comparison

Just like adjectives, most comparative and superlative adverbs are formed by adding "-er" or *more/less* (comparative) or "-est" or *most/least* (superlative).

However, there are some adverbs that have irregular comparative and superlative forms. We can't rely on the irregular adverbs we looked at above, either, because many of those adverbs are ***regular*** in how they inflect to become comparative or superlative, while certain regular adverbs can have ***irregular*** inflections. (For instance, the irregular adverb *straight* inflects regularly as *straighter* and *straightest*, while the regular adverb *badly* inflects irregularly as *worse* and *worst*).

As always, we just have to commit these irregular inflections to memory:

Adverb (positive degree)	Comparative degree	Superlative degree
badly	worse	worst
early	earlier	earliest
far	farther/further	farthest/furthest
little	less	least
well	better	best

Learning irregular inflection

As we've seen, words that inflect in irregular ways are, unfortunately, unpredictable by nature. Because there are no patterns for how they are formed, it can be very difficult to learn them.

The best way to learn irregular words is to pay close attention when you are reading—if a word looks like it has an unusual spelling compared to other words that are used in the same way, then it is probably an irregular inflection. In these cases, look up the word in a good dictionary and make a note of how it is used, then try to remember it for next time.

Quiz
(answers start on page 463)

1. Which of the following parts of speech are most often inflected?

a) Nouns
b) Adjectives
c) Adverbs
d) Verbs

2. How are most nouns inflected to indicate **plurality**?

a) By adding the suffix "-es"
b) By adding the suffix "-est"
c) By adding the suffix "-er"
d) By adding the suffix "-s"
e) A & B
f) B & C
g) A & D

3. Which of the following can be inflected to indicate **gender**?

a) Verbs
b) Pronouns
c) Adjectives
d) Adverbs

4. Which of the following verbs undergoes **irregular** inflection?

a) be

b) work

c) talk

d) sip

5. Which of the following is **not** an inflection of the adjective *good*?

a) gooder

b) goodest

c) better

d) best

e) A & B

f) B & C

g) A & D

Forming Plurals

Definition

Plurals of nouns are used to indicate when there is more than one person, place, animal, or thing. There are a number of ways we can make a noun plural, either by adding a suffix, changing the spelling the word, or both.

Adding "-s"

The normal method for making nouns plural is to add an "-s" at the end of the noun.

For example:

• one boy – two boys

• one girl – two girls

• one pen – two pens

• one pencil – two pencils

• one prize – two prizes

• one price – two prices

Adding "-es"

In other instances, we use the suffix "-es" instead of "-s." This occurs if a noun ends in a sibilant sound (/s/, /z/, /ʧ/, or /ʃ/) created by the endings "-ss," "-z," "-x," "-sh," "-ch," or "-tch." We also use this suffix with some nouns ending in a consonant + **O**.

For example:

• one coach – two coaches

• one witch – two witches

• one dish – two dishes

• one box – two boxes

• one bus – two buses

• one kiss – two kisses

• one waltz – two waltzes

• one tomato – two tomatoes

Words ending in "-y"

When the noun ends in a "-y" and it is preceded by a consonant, we change "y" to "i" and add "-es."

For example:
- one country – two countr**ies**
- one city – two cit**ies**
- one gallery – two galler**ies**
- one baby – two bab**ies**
- one lady – two lad**ies**
- one reality – two realit**ies**
- one fly – two fl**ies**
- one butterfly – two butterfl**ies**

However, when a word ends in a "-y" preceded by a *vowel*, then we simply add an "-s" as usual:
- one toy – two toy**s**
- one play – two play**s**
- one key – two key**s**
- one guy – two guy**s**

Irregular plurals

There are some nouns that are irregular—they either use unconventional suffixes, have letters change internally, or else become entirely new words. They do not adhere to predictable spelling rules or conventions, so we have to memorize their unique spellings.

Here are the most common ones:
- one man – two **men**
- one woman – two **women**
- one person – two **people***
- one mouse – two **mice**
- one goose – two **geese**
- one child – two **children**
- one tooth – two **teeth**
- one foot – two **feet**
- one ox – two **oxen**

(**Persons* is also a plural form of *person*, but in modern English it is usually reserved for more formal, bureaucratic, or legal language, as in, "Any such **persons** found to be guilty of shoplifting will be prosecuted.")

Be aware that irregular plural nouns cannot be made plural *again*; that is, you cannot have *childrens*, or *feets*. However, *people* is an exception—it can be pluralized as *peoples* in some cases.

Adding "-ves" vs. "-s"

With some nouns that end in "-f," "-fe," or "-lf," we replace the endings with "-ves" to make them plural. Below is a list of some common examples:
- one life – two li**ves**
- one wife – two wi**ves**
- one loaf – two loa**ves**
- one leaf – two lea**ves**
- one knife – two kni**ves**
- one thief – two thie**ves**
- one calf – two cal**ves**
- one half – two hal**ves**
- one wolf – one wol**ves**

However, many other words that end in "-f," "-fe," or "-lf" are simply made plural by adding an "-s" on the end. Here are some common examples:
- one chief – two chief**s**
- one brief – two brief**s**
- one safe – two safe**s**
- one gulf – two gulf**s**

- one belief – two belief<u>s</u>
- one roof – two roof<u>s</u>

And yet some other words can receive <u>either</u> "-ves" **or** "-s," such as:

- one handkerchief – two handkerchiefs – two handkerchie**ves**
- one hoof – two hoofs – two hoo**ves**
- one scarf – two scarfs – two scar**ves**

Unfortunately, there is no steadfast rule for which words will receive a "-ves" ending, an "-s" ending, or both—they are irregular and have to be memorized.

Words ending in "-ff" or "-ffe"

Words ending in "-ff" or "-ffe," on the other hand, have straightforward plural forms and *are* considered regular—we simply add "-s" to the end, as in:

- one cliff – two cliff**s**
- one bailiff – two bailiff**s**
- one giraffe – two giraffe**s**
- one gaffe – two gaffe**s**

Words with the same plural and singular forms

We also have some nouns that remain the same whether singular or plural.

For example:

- one fish – two **fish***
- one sheep – two **sheep**
- one bison – two **bison**
- one aircraft – two **aircraft**

(*Note that *fish* can also be pluralized as *fishes*. However, it is more common for this "-es" form to be used in reference to more than one <u>kind</u> of fish, as opposed to multiple fish in general.)

Uncountable nouns

Although similar in nature to the above nouns, uncountable nouns refer to things that cannot be divided into individual units, and that therefore **cannot** be made plural at all.

For example:

- **rice**
- **butter**
- **milk**
- **advice**
- **news**

To quantify them, we need to use a unit of measure, such as *one pound of rice, a bottle of milk, a piece of advice,* etc. (There are some colloquial exceptions. For instance, it's not uncommon to ask for "two coffees" when ordering at a café, even though *coffee* is traditionally considered an uncountable noun.)

Words from Latin or Greek

There are also nouns taken from Latin or Greek that maintain their original forms in the plural. However, as we'll see, some of these words have begun shifting toward more conventional plural forms, in addition to their original spellings.

For example:

- index – ind**ices** (*indexes* is now also acceptable)
- appendix – append**ices** (*appendixes* is now also acceptable)
- fungus – fung**i**
- criterion – criter**ia**
- nucleus – nucle**i**
- syllabus – syllab**i**
- focus – foc**i**
- cactus – cact**i** (*cactuses* is now also acceptable)

- thesis – thes**es**
- crisis – cris**es**
- phenomenon – phenomen**a**

Quiz

(answers start on page 463)

1. What is the correct plural form of the noun *batch*?

a) batchs
b) batches
c) batchies
d) batch

2. For words ending in "-f" or "-fe," in what instances do we replace the endings with "-ves" to make them plural?

a) always
b) never
c) Only if the endings are preceded by a vowel
d) We have to memorize when to do so

3. When a word ends in a consonant + "y," how is the word made plural?

a) By replacing the "y" with "-ies"
b) By replacing the "y" with "-es"
c) By adding "-s" to the end of the word
d) No change necessary

4. How can an **uncountable noun** be made plural?

a) Its singular form is the same as its plural form
b) It cannot be made plural
c) By using its original Latin or Greek ending
d) We have to memorize how to do so

5. Which of the following sentences is **incorrect**?

a) "There are a number of missing persons following the disaster."
b) "Many men and women sacrificed their lives in the line of duty."
c) "There are many different childrens trying to find their parents."
d) "The roofs of several houses have collapsed in the last half hour."

Forming Contractions

Contractions are formed when words are shortened by omitting one or more letters, which are most often replaced with an apostrophe. Contractions most commonly occur when two words that commonly appear next to each other in a sentence are combined into a new, singular word. Less commonly (predominantly in informal speech and writing), we can also contract single words into shorter forms, or we can even combine more than two words into a single contraction.

Contracting two words

Two-word contractions are by far the most common, but we cannot simply contract any two adjacent words. Instead, there are certain patterns dictating when and how a pair of words will be combined. Most of the time, it is the second word in the group that is shortened, which is known as an **enclitic**. Much less commonly, the **first** word used in a contraction has one or more letters replaced by an apostrophe; the shortened form of this first word is known as a **proclitic**, which we'll look at separately further on.

Finally, it's important to remember that the apostrophe marks the **letters** that are left out of the contracted word; it does **not** mark the space that was between the words:

✖ "This plan **does'nt** make any sense." (incorrect)
✖ "This plan **does'n't** make any sense." (incorrect)
✔ "This plan **doesn't** make any sense." (correct)

Contracting forms of *be*

The verb *be* is what's known as a linking verb, which connects the subject of a sentence to an adjective that describes it or another noun that renames it, and it is also used as an auxiliary verb to form the **continuous tense** of other verbs. Because of how common and ubiquitous the verb is, it is very commonly contracted with the subject of its clause; it can also contract with the question words *who, what, where, when, why*, and *how*, though this is slightly less formal.

Note, however, that we only contract the present simple tense forms of the verb—*is, am*, and *are*. While we technically <u>can</u> contract the past simple tense forms (*was* and *were*), both have the same endings as the present-tense forms *is* and *are*, respectively. Because of this, it is generally assumed that contracted *be* verbs are always in the present tense.

Let's look at how *is, am*, and *are* are contracted, as well as some example sentences.

Be conjugation	Contracted form	Examples sentences
is (used for third-person singular subjects)	**'s** (apostrophe replaces the vowel **i-**; pronounced /-z/ except after **T**, in which case it is pronounced /-s/)	• "Jonathan**'s** coming over later." • "I think she**'s** pretty happy with the results." • "He**'s** a bit of a grouch, huh?" • "I can't believe it**'s** still raining outside!" • "How**'s** your project coming, Billy?" • "When**'s** the next train?"
am (used for first-person singular subjects—only contracts with the word *I*)	**'m** (apostrophe replaces the vowel **a-**)	• "I**'m** a pretty easy-going guy." • "I**'m** going to the park later, if you want to come with me." • "You know the reason why I**'m** angry!"

232

are (used for second-person singular subjects, and first-, second-, and third-person plural subjects)	**'re** (apostrophe replaces the vowel **a-**)	• "You**'re** being so annoying!" • "I think we**'re** going to be late." • "They**'re** just jealous of your success." • "Who**'re** you taking to the dance?" • "What**'re** we going to bring to the dinner party?"

It's also worth mentioning that we do not end a sentence with a contracted *is, am,* or *are*. For instance:

✔ "Do you know where dad **is**?"

✘ "Do you know where dad**'s**?"

✔ "I wonder where they **are**."

✘ "I wonder where they**'re**."

Finally, we can also contract *is* with the adverb *so*. However, this is very informal, and it is generally only used in responses comparing something to what another speaker has said, as in:

• Speaker A: "Sorry, we're running late!"
• Speaker B: "That's OK, **so's** Jeff."

• Speaker A: "Your outfit is really cute today!"
• Speaker B: "**So's** yours!"

it's vs. *its*

A common mistake is to use an apostrophe with the word *its* when we want to indicate possession, instead of when writing a contraction of *it is*.

We usually express possession in writing by adding **'s** to the end of a noun, as in *Mary's, John's, the council's, the dog's,* etc. (As a matter of fact, this possessive **'s** is actually a contraction as well, stemming from the Old English suffix "-es"; however, this "-es" ending fell out of use, and we generally think of the possessive **'s** as a distinct syntactic and grammatical construct, rather than a contraction.)

Curiously, the possessive form for the personal pronoun *it* does <u>not</u> have an apostrophe, just an S—*its*. However, the possessive form <u>was</u> originally spelled *it's*, <u>with</u> the apostrophe. This was dropped in the 1800s, most likely due to the established prevalence of the contraction *it is*.

In any case, we can only use **'s** with *it* when forming a contraction of *it is*. If we write *its*, we are indicating gender-neutral possession for an object, animal, group, etc.

Let's look at a couple examples just to see the difference more clearly:

✔ "I'm really glad **it's** starting to get warmer; I hate the wintertime!"

✘ "I'm really glad **its** starting to get warmer; I hate the wintertime!"

✔ "The corporation recently revised **its** hiring policy."

✘ "The corporation recently revised **it's** hiring policy."

they're, there, and *their*

Similar to the issue with *it's* vs. *its*, the contraction *they're* (*they are*) is very commonly confused with the words *their* and *there*. The main issue is that all three have the same pronunciation—/ðɛər/.

Again, we simply have to consider what we mean compared to what we're trying to write. If we are using the plural personal pronoun *they* and the verb *are*, then we have to use the contraction *they're*; if we are indicating direction or location, we use the adverb/pronoun *there*; and if we're saying that something belongs to a group of people, we use the possessive determiner *their*. Here's a handy way of remembering the three different spellings: *they're* comes from two words because it has an apostrophe in the middle, while *there* contains the word *here*, another adverb/pronoun of direction and location (and we use *their* if it is not functioning like one of these other two).

For example:
- "I think **they're** (*they are*) going to be here soon."
- "We parked the car over **there** (direction/location) on the hill."
- "I don't believe in giving students standardized tests, because **their** (possession) scores don't necessarily reflect **their** ability to learn."

Contracting other auxiliary verbs

In addition to the three forms of *be*, there are four other auxiliary verbs that can also be contracted as enclitics: *have* (and its conjugations *has* and *had*), *did, will*, and *would*.

When we contract these four auxiliaries, we use an apostrophe to replace all of the letters leading up to the last consonant sound. We generally only contract these verbs with personal pronouns (except for *has*, which can attach to people's names) or question words.

Auxiliary verb	Contracted form	Examples sentences
have (forms the present perfect tense with any subject except the third-person singular)	**'ve** (apostrophe replaces the letters **ha-**)	• "I**'ve** been thinking about what you said." • "We think we**'ve** found a pretty elegant solution." • "I know you**'ve** been working around the clock." • "Why**'ve** they been avoiding us?"
has (forms the present perfect tense, but only with third-person singular subjects)	**'s** (apostrophe replaces the letters **ha-**)	• "She**'s** been rather quiet lately." • "Johnny**'s** applied to be a police officer." • "It**'s** been about a week since I last heard from them." • "Do you know why he**'s** fallen behind in his studies?"
had (forms the past perfect tense for all pronouns; does not contract with question words to avoid confusion with *did*)	**'d** (apostrophe replaces the letters **ha-**)	• "We**'d** dreamed about living in Ireland for years before we finally moved here." • "I**'d** been feeling a little unwell, so I took Monday off from work." • "He**'d** already prepared a lecture for the class when he found out that it had been canceled." • "She**'d** never been prouder of herself before that moment."
did (forms questions and expresses negative actions about the past; can only contract with questions words, except for *when*)	**'d** (apostrophe replaces the letters **di-**)	• "Who**'d** you ask to cover your shift on Monday?" • "What**'d** you think of the movie?" • "Why**'d** we have to drive all the way out here?" • "How**'d** you do on the test?" • "Ah, my keys! Where**'d** you find them?"

will (used to form future tenses, to express willingness or ability, to make requests or offers, to complete conditional sentences, to express likelihood in the immediate present, or to issue commands)	**'ll** (apostrophe replaces the letters **wi-**)	• "He**'ll** call you in the morning." • "If you wash the dishes, I**'ll** take out the trash." • "What**'ll** they do with all that money?" • "Two tickets, two medium sodas, and one large popcorn—that**'ll** be $30, please."
would (past-tense version of *will*; does not contract with question words to avoid confusion with *did*)	**'d** (apostrophe replaces the letters **woul-**)	• "He told you he**'d** call you in the morning." • "I**'d** like to go to the amusement park for my birthday." • "I thought she**'d** have been here by now."

It's also worth noting that we do not contract *have, has,* or *had* when they are functioning as main verbs (meaning "to possess"). For instance:

✔ "I **have** class in the morning."
✘ "I**'ve** class in the morning."

✔ "We **had** lots of pets when we were growing up."
✘ "We**'d** lots of pets when we were growing up."

✔ "I think he **has** a problem with how the class is being conducted."
✘ "I think he**'s** a problem with how the class is being conducted."

(Note that some dialects, especially in **British English**, do contract *have* as a main verb with the subject of the sentence, but this is rather informal.)

should've, would've, could've vs. *should of, would of, could of*

Contracted enclitics create speech sounds that are often not simply shortened versions of the full word's pronunciation. Because modern speech relies so heavily on contractions, this can occasionally lead to confusion as to what the proper spelling should be.

By far the most common source of confusion is when *have* is contracted as *'ve* and attached to a word ending in a consonant, most commonly *should, would,* and *could*. This results in **'ve** being pronounced /əv/ (what's known as a syllabic consonant), which sounds the same as *of* when it is unstressed in speech. Because of this, it is a common mistake to think that *should've, would've,* and *could've* are instead spelled *should of, would of,* and *could of.*

It's important to be aware that *should of, would of,* and *could of* are not correct in English, whether informal, colloquial, or otherwise; they literally do not mean anything. Be careful to always spell the shortened forms as the contractions *should've, would've,* and *could've,* and, if you are spelling them out in their entirety, *should have, would have,* and *could have.* These are the only correct spellings.

Finally, note that this also applies to the contractions *might've* and *must've;* the **'ve** in these is also pronounced like *of,* but *might of* and *must of* are always incorrect.

Contracting *not* with auxiliary verbs

The adverb *not* is used to express negative actions, so, unlike the words we've looked at so far, it only contracts with verbs, not personal pronouns or question words. However, we can only do this with auxiliary verbs, not main verbs.

Another difference from the words we've looked at so far is that when we contract *not,* we don't omit all of the letters leading up to the final consonant; instead, we only omit **-o-** and replace it with an apostrophe. What's especially unusual about contractions of *not* is that sometimes the *first* word is altered as well. There's no specific pattern to help us gauge when (or how) these extra alterations will occur, so we have to memorize them:

Primary auxiliary verbs

- is + not = is**n't**
- are + not = are**n't**
- was + not = was**n't**
- were + not = were**n't**

- have + not = have**n't**
- has + not = has**n't**
- had + not = had**n't**

- do + not = do**n't**
- does + not = does**n't**
- did + not = did**n't**

While we do not usually contract *not* with *am*, there are some varieties of English (such as Irish and Scottish English) in which this contraction (*amn't*) is still used informally.

However, certain dialects of American English use a modified *version* of *amn't*—the highly informal **ain't**. We'll look at this more in depth a little further on, along with other informal contractions.

Modal auxiliary verbs

- can + not = cannot = ca**n't** (In addition to omitting **-o-**, we also omit the final **-n** from *can*.)
- could + not = could**n't**

- will + not = w**o**n't (The **-ill** from *will* is replaced with an **-o-** before taking the contracted **-n't**. This strange spelling convention is due to the evolution of the word *will* from Old English in the 16th and 17th centuries.)
- would + not = would**n't**

- shall + not = sha**n't** (In addition to omitting **-o-**, we also omit **-ll** from *shall*, though this contraction is considered old-fashioned in modern English.)
- should + not = should**n't**

- might + not = might**n't** (uncommon)
- must + not = must**n't**

Note that we do not contract *not* with the modal verb *may*.

let's

There are a few contractions that have become the standard form in modern English—that is, the uncontracted form is no longer used (or sounds rather old-fashioned).

One of these is the two-word contraction *let's*, which is a contraction of the words *let us*. This contracted form is only used when expressing a suggestion, as in, "**Let's** go to the beach." It sounds awkward and overly formal to say "**Let us** go to the beach."

However, because *let's* is solely associated with this meaning, there are other instances in which *let us* would be the only correct choice. This occurs when *let* means "to allow or give permission" or "to cause or make." For example:

✔ "I hope mom will **let us** go to the movies." (correct)
✘ "I hope mom will **let's** go to the movies." (incorrect)

✔ "Please **let us** know the results." (correct)
✘ "Please **let's** know the results." (incorrect)

let's vs. *lets*

Finally, we have to be careful not to confuse the contraction *let's* with **lets**, which is the conjugation of the verb for third-person singular subjects.

One thing to remember is that *let's* is only used in imperative sentences, the sentence structure used to issue commands or, in this case, suggestions. Imperative sentences do not have subjects (the person or thing performing the action of a verb); instead, they simply use the bare infinitive of a verb on its own, as it is being used to command or instruct another person.

Lets, on the other hand, can only be used in "normal" (non-imperative) sentences that *do* have subjects, because it is dependent on the grammatical class of the subject used in the clause.

For instance:

✔ "**Let's** go get something to eat!" (correct)

✘ "**Lets** go get something to eat!" (incorrect)

✔ "This new technology **lets** people talk to each other from across the globe." (correct)

✘ "This new technology **let's** people talk to each other from across the globe." (incorrect)

Proclitics

When we form contractions from two words, we almost always omit one or more letters from the second one, as we've seen in the preceding examples. There are a few instances, though, in which only the **first** word has one or more letters replaced by an apostrophe. The shortened form of the first word is known as a **proclitic**.

The most common contraction that uses a proclitic in everyday speech and writing is the very informal *y'all*, which is used primarily in Southern dialects of American English:

• *you* + *all* = **y'all**

While common in colloquial speech and writing, this contraction should not be used in formal, academic, or professional writing.

Another informal proclitic contraction is *c'mon*, a combination of the words *come* + *on*. When we say "come on" aloud, we tend to reduce the first vowel sound of *-o-* in *come* to an unstressed schwa (/ə/). Because this sound is so minute and almost irrelevant in the word pair, it is replaced with an apostrophe (the non-functional silent E is simply omitted). However, this contraction is much less common in written English, and, like *y'all*, should be avoided in formal writing.

'tis, 'twas, 'twere, 'twill, 'twould

The word *it* can also be contracted as a proclitic (especially when followed by auxiliary verbs beginning with **W**), with the vowel **I** being replaced by an apostrophe. These terms have fallen out of use in modern English, and they generally only appear in poetic or old-fashioned writing. For instance:

• **'tis** = *it* + *is*
• **'twas** = *it* + *was*
• **'twere** = *it* + *were*
• **'twill** = *it* + *will*
• **'twould** = *it* + *would*

Be careful, though: when using an apostrophe at the beginning of a word, remember not to use a single opening quotation mark (') instead of an apostrophe (') by mistake.

✔ **'Twas** a night we would not soon forget. (correct)

✘ **'Twas** a night we would not soon forget. (incorrect)

Informal two-word contractions

It is very common in spoken English to create vocal "shortcuts" to help make words easier to pronounce. One of the ways this is achieved is by blending together two normally distinct words into a single informal contraction. Some of these informal contractions have become so prevalent in speech that they have begun to be represented in writing, as well.
In addition to the proclitic contractions *y'all* and *c'mon* that we looked at earlier, there are many other pairs of words that are informally contracted into new single words.

ain't

As we said previously, we do not contract *am* and *not* as we do with the other conjugations of the verb *be*—*amn't* is not acceptable (except in colloquial uses in certain dialects, such as Irish English).

However, there is a very common, but very informal, variant of *amn't* that is used in rural dialects of American English: *ain't*. In fact, it is so informal that, in addition to representing *am* + *not*, *ain't* can also be used to represent *are not*, *is not*, *have not*, and *has not*. For example:

• "I **ain't** (*am not*) joking, kids—get down off that shed!"
• "Look, I know you **ain't** (*are not*) stupid. I'm just asking you to be careful."

• "From what I heard, he **ain't** (*is not*) cut out for this job."
• "We **ain't** (*have not*) been to the Grand Canyon before!"
• "All I can tell you is she **ain't** (*has not*) been doing her fair share of the work."

Despite its prevalence in American English, *ain't* is considered extremely informal. While you may be fine using it in conversational speech or writing, you should avoid it in any formal situations in which proper grammar, spelling, and pronunciation are required.

Other informal two-word contractions

Note that, for most of these, we do not use an apostrophe to represent the missing letters; instead, they often act like distinct singular words, often with unique spellings that represent the pronunciation more than the original two words. Additionally, some of these contractions are only used in specific contexts. Because of how colloquial and informal these are, there are many possible contractions that can be created, as well as many permutations of those that are known. We'll just look at some of the most common examples:

Words being contracted	Contraction	Spelling and pronunciation differences	Usage
don't + know	**dunno** (/dʌˈnoʊ/)	Because **T** appears directly between two /n/ sounds, it becomes slightly difficult to enunciate clearly and is often left out in speech. However, when this happens, the /oʊ/ sound of *don't* also becomes arduous, and so it is flattened into a short **U** sound (as in *cut*).	*Dunno* is generally only used with the personal pronoun *I*. While *dunno* can simply replace *don't know* in a sentence, it can also be used without *I* to form one-word answers. For example: • "I **dunno** what you're talking about." • Speaker A: "Where did Lisa go?" Speaker B: "**Dunno**."
give + me	**gimme** (/ˈgɪmi/)	The final **-ve** of *give* is not a very strong consonant sound, and it tends to be glided over or omitted altogether when adjacent to the **m-** of *me*. In writing, we double the middle consonant to avoid creating a word that looks like it rhymes with *time*.	We almost exclusively use this contraction when *give me* is an imperative (command), and, because of its informal nature, it creates a directness not found in the original word pair that can make it seem rather impolite. For example: • "**Gimme** a minute! I haven't even turned the computer on yet!" • "Hey, **gimme** a bite of your sandwich!"
going + to	**gonna** (/gʌˈnə/)	The word *to* is often unstressed in speech, so it becomes elided into the schwa sound (/ə/) represented by **-a**. When *to* comes after *going*, we often soften the /-ɪŋ/ sound from "-ing" into a flat /-n/ sound by dropping the "-i-" and "-g;" we then double the remaining **N** to avoid a word that looks like it rhymes with *persona*.	We can only use this contraction when *to* is functioning as a particle introducing an infinitive verb, as in, "I'm **gonna** go to the park," or, "Are you **gonna** be finished soon?" We **cannot** use *gonna* when *to* is functioning as a preposition. For example: ✔ "I'm *going to* go to the park later." ✔ "I'm **gonna** go to the park later." ✔ "I'm *going to* the park later." ✘ "I'm **gonna** the park later."
got + to	**gotta** (/ˈgɑtə/)	The word *got* is commonly used in the phrase *have got to* to add emphasis to the expression *have to* (meaning "must"). It's so common, in fact, that *got to* has evolved in spoken English into the contraction *gotta*, with *to* being essentially reduced down to just the schwa sound (/ə/)—though we keep the two **T**s to keep the contraction from looking like it rhymes with *quota*.	*Got* is so common in *have got to* that, in colloquial speech, *have* is often omitted altogether. Just note that, as informal as *gotta* already is, it is much more informal for it to be used without *have*. Finally, note that when *have* (or *has* for the third-person singular) is present alongside *gotta*, it is almost always contracted with the subject of the clause (as we saw earlier in this section). For example:

			• "I can't come over tonight. I('ve) **gotta** study for the test." • "Hey, we('ve) **gotta** get out of here!"
got + you (ya)	**gotcha** (/ˈgɑʧə/)	The word *you* is sometimes colloquially spelled *ya* to reflect the quick, offhand pronunciation it often takes in everyday speech; it is this form that attaches to *got* in this contraction. The slide from the /t/ sound of **T** to the /j/ sound represented by **Y** creates a sound similar to /ʧ/ (as in *chat*), hence the spelling change from **y-** to **-ch-**.	This contraction is actually a shortening of the longer phrase "I have got you," usually meaning "I understand you" (though it can also mean "I've got a hold on you"). In many cases it can stand alone without a subject, but in some instances it is still preceded by *I, we,* or *they* (and even *have*, sometimes). For example: • Speaker A: "I need you to be here at 8 AM sharp." Speaker B: "**Gotcha**." • Speaker A: "Did you understand the instructions?" Speaker B: "Yeah, yeah, I **gotcha**." • "Don't worry, miss, you can let go of the rope, we've **gotcha**."
kind + of	**kinda** (/ˈkaɪndə/)	The word *of* is so unstressed in this combination that it is completely replaced by an **-a** attached to *kind* to represent the schwa sound (/ə/) it has become.	This informal contraction can be used anywhere *kind of* is used. For example: • "I usually hate romantic comedies, but I **kinda** want to see this one." • Speaker A: "Did you enjoy your trip?" Speaker B: "**Kinda**. It rained the whole time."
let + me	**lemme** (/ˈlɛmi/)	The final **-t** of *let* tends to be softened and glided over in speech, and when it is adjacent to the **m-** of *me*, it can be omitted altogether. Once again, we double the middle consonant to avoid creating a "long vowel" sound, which would result in a word that looks like it rhymes with *theme*.	Similar to *give me/gimme*, *lemme* is a contraction of the imperative *let me*, so it may come across as impolite—though not in every circumstance. For example: • "Man, **lemme** tell you: that was the toughest job I've ever done." • "Hey, **lemme** see your phone for a minute."
sort + of	**sorta** (/ˈsɔrtə/)	The word *of* is so unstressed that it is completely replaced by an **-a** to represent the unstressed /ə/ sound, exactly the same as in the contraction *kinda*. In fact, *kinda* and *sorta* are synonymous.	This informal contraction can be used anywhere *sort of* is used. For example: • "I usually hate romantic comedies, but I **sorta** want to see this one." • Speaker A: "Did you enjoy your trip?" Speaker B: "**Sorta**. It rained the whole time."
want + to	**wanna** (/ˈwɑnə/)	The double /t/ sound that occurs in *want to* is a bit cumbersome in quick, casual speech, leading to this informal contraction in which they are elided completely. In addition, the function word *to* is so unstressed in this combination that it is completely replaced by an **-a** to represent the schwa sound (/ə/).	This contraction can simply be used in place of *want to* in its normal usage. However, it is also used to stand in for the phrase "Do you want to" in informal questions. For example: • "Hey, **wanna** go grab a bite to eat?" • "I don't **wanna** go home yet!" • "I think they **wanna** see how things turn out first."

Contracting single words

While contractions are most commonly combinations of two words, they can also consist of single words reduced to shorter forms by omitting letters. There are only a few formally accepted contractions formed from "everyday" words; these simply omit a consonant between two vowels so that the first and last syllables glide from one to the next:

- *madam* = **ma'am**
- *never-do-well* = **ne'er**-do-well
- *over* = **o'er** (generally only used in poetic writing)
- *ever* = **e'er** (generally only used in poetic writing)

Appellations

The most common single-word contractions are **appellations**, which are additional words added to a person's name. These may be used to indicate respect for a person (known as **honorifics**) or to indicate a person's profession, royalty, rank, etc. (known as **titles**). Many appellations are shortened (some always so) by removing letters from the middle or end of the word; however, unlike most contractions, we do this by placing a **period** at the <u>end</u> of the word* rather than using an apostrophe in place of the omitted letters. Also unlike normal contractions, we pronounce these as whole words in speech, not as abbreviations. For example:

- **Capt.** (short for *Captain*)
- **Cmdr.** (short for *Commander*)
- **Col.** (short for *Colonel*)
- **Cpl.** (short for *Corporal*)
- **Dr.** (short for *Doctor*)
- **Esq.** (short for *Esquire*)
- **Fr.** (short for *Father*, a priest in the Roman Catholic or Anglican churches)
- **Hon.** (short for *Honorable*)
- **Jr.** (short for *Junior*)
- **Lt.** (short for *Lieutenant*)
- **Mr.** (short for *Mister*)
- **Mrs.** (originally a shortened form of *Mistress*; now only the contraction is used)
- **Prof.** (short for *Professor*)
- **Rev.** (short for *Reverend*)
- **Sr.** (short for *Senior*)
- **St.** (short for *Saint*)
- **Sgt.** (short for *Sergeant*)

(*In American English, we always put a period after an abbreviated appellation. In British English, however, this period [called a **full stop** in BrE] is usually <u>not</u> included, especially if the first and last letter of the contraction are the same as the full word.)

It's worth noting that all of these are abbreviations, but there is not a complete consensus as to whether they may actually be considered contractions or not. Some sources state that only those with letters omitted from the middle count as contractions (since that is more common for contractions in general), while other sources don't include any of these when discussing contractions. However, since we are including informal contractions such as *'bout* or *o'* (which we'll look at next) that have letters removed from the beginning or end of the word, we've decided to take a more inclusive approach.

Informal one-word contractions

English speakers also tend to form many **informal** one-word contractions, most often by shortening the beginning or end of words; when represented in writing, the omitted letters are usually replaced with an apostrophe. (Just note that these are not considered acceptable in anything except conversational speech or writing.)

For example:

Original word	Contraction	Example sentences
about	**'bout**	"I don't know what you're talking **'bout**."
around	**'round**	"We'll be coming **'round** a little later."
of	**o'**	"Wow, that's a big bowl **o'** cereal!"
suppose	**s'pose**	"I **s'pose** that could work."
them	**'em**	"We told **'em** not to get involved!"

Words ending in "-ing" can also be informally contracted by omitting "-g," reflecting a change in the pronunciation of the ending from /-ɪŋ/ to /-ɪn/, which is slightly easier to say in quick, casual speech. There are too many possible examples to include here, so we'll just consider a few that we may commonly encounter in conversational speech or writing:

• **comin'** (*coming*)
• **feelin'** (*feeling*)
• **goin'** (*going*)
• **lookin'** (*looking*)
• **makin'** (*making*)
• **tryin'** (*trying*)

till vs. *until* vs. *'til*

One single-word contraction that is prevalent, especially in American English, is *'til*—a contraction of the preposition *until*.

However, this is actually an unnecessary contraction. The confusion is caused by the word *till*, which is synonymous to (but actually <u>pre-dates</u>) *until*. Because of the seemingly extraneous "l" in *till*, many people presume it to be a misspelling, so instead they shorten it to *til* and add an apostrophe where they think *un-* should be.

While it is not necessarily "incorrect" to use *'til* instead of *until* or *till*, be aware that it is a nonstandard spelling and is not preferred by dictionaries. If you are writing in an academic or professional context, it is safer to stick with *until* or, if need be, *till*.

Contracting three words

Least common of all contractions are those formed from three words. In fact, there are only two standard three-word contractions that aren't considered informal or colloquial:

Original words	Contraction	Example sentence
jack-*of-the*-lantern	jack-o'-lantern	"My favorite part of Halloween is carving the jack-**o'**-lantern with my dad."
of + *the* + clock	o'clock	"It's 4 **o'clock** in the morning! Please go back to bed."

All other three-word contractions are very informal and would not be considered acceptable in anything but conversational English. Additionally, some of these may be more common in certain dialects than others. In many of these, each of the three words retains one or more of their letters, so we use multiple apostrophes in the place of those that are missing:

Original word	Contraction	Example sentence
could + *not* + **have**	couldn't've	"Boy, that interview **couldn't've** have gone any worse."
he + **would** + **have**	he'd've	"I don't see how **he'd've** known about it already."
I + *would* + **have**	I'd've	"That's not how **I'd've** done it."
it + *was* + *not*	'twasn't	"I've been trying to get more exercise, so **'twasn't** a problem walking home."
it + *will* + *not*	'twon't	"The show should be starting soon; **'twon't** be much longer now."
it + *would* + *not*	'twouldn't	"I'd like to get a new TV, but **'twouldn't** bother me to just keep using our old one."
ought + *not* + **have**	oughtn't've	"You **oughtn't've** come back here, Jonathan."
she + **would** + **have**	she'd've	"I know **she'd've** preferred to stay home."
should + *not* + **have**	shouldn't've	"We **shouldn't've** gotten mixed up in all this."
they + **would** + **have**	they'd've	"**They'd've** gotten away with it if those kids hadn't come snooping around!"

we + *would* + *have*	**we'd've**	"I thought **we'd've** been finished by now!"
what + *are* + *you*	**whatcha**	"**Whatcha** thinking about?"
who + *would* + *have*	**who'd've**	"**Who'd've** thought it could be so simple?"
would + *not* + *have*	**wouldn't've**	"Apparently they used some fancy new special effects in the movie, but I **wouldn't've** noticed the difference."
you + *would* + *have*	**you'd've**	"**You'd've** been proud of her, Mary. She really outdid herself this time."

Using contractions in formal writing

On a final note, it is worth mentioning that contractions, no matter how accepted or standard, are sometimes seen as undesirable in more formal or professional writing. Contractions are a reflection of shortcuts we take in spoken English, and, as such, they can be considered by some to indicate casual writing. While there are a few exceptions (*o'clock* and *Mrs.*, for instance, are now the only acceptable forms), if you are writing something very formal (or want to create a more formal tone in your writing), it is best to avoid contractions wherever possible.

Quiz

(answers start on page 463)

1. Which of the following is the most common type of contraction?

a) One-word contractions
b) Two-word contractions
c) Three-word contractions
d) All three are equally common

2. Which of the following are **most commonly** shortened in two-word contractions?

a) auxiliary verbs
b) action verbs
c) pronouns
d) adjectives

3. Which of the following is **not** considered an informal or nonstandard contraction?

a) so's
b) let's
c) ain't
d) s'pose

4. What is a **proclitic**?

a) A contracted word that attaches to the end of a word
b) A contracted word that attaches in between two other words
c) A contracted word that does not attach to another word
d) A contracted word that attaches to the beginning of a word

5. Which of the following contractions is **never** used in its fully spelled-out form in modern English?

a) I'd've
b) couldn't've
c) o'clock
d) can't

Enclitics

Definition

Enclitics are reduced or contracted forms of words. They are attached to the word that precedes them by an apostrophe, and they are dependent on that word for their meaning.

Enclitics generally consist of just one consonant sound and cannot stand on their own. In English, they are usually the unstressed forms of functional words such as auxiliary verbs, determiners, participles, and pronouns. As such, they have grammatical rather than lexical meaning (compared with suffixes, which create new words through inflection).

Examples

The majority of enclitics in English are reflected in the common contractions we use in speech and writing. Here are a few of the most common.

be

When unstressed, the present tense forms of the auxiliary verb *be* (*am/is/are*) become enclitics when they are contracted and attached to the noun that precedes them. For example:
- "I**'m** going shopping." (*am*)
- "Your father**'s** on the phone." (*is*)
- "They**'re** waiting outside." (*are*)

not

Not is used after auxiliary verbs to make them negative. When this occurs, it usually attaches to the auxiliary verb as an enclitic. Uniquely, its enclitic form ("*-n't*") has the apostrophe occurring within *not* itself, rather than between the enclitic and the head word. For example:
- "I have**n't** been to town in a long time."
- "We ca**n't** go to town without a car."
- "She should**n't** wait for us."

have

Have is used to form the **perfect** and **past** tenses. Its enclitic form, "*-'ve*," attaches to the subject in clauses without an auxiliary verb, and to the auxiliary verb itself in clauses that include one. For example:
- "I**'ve** never been here before."
- "We would**'ve** called you if we knew you were in town."
- "He might**'ve** read that book already, but I'm not sure."

will

The enclitic form of *will* is "*-'ll*," and it attaches to the subject of the clause.
- "We**'ll** all go together."
- "It**'ll** all work out in the end."
- "They**'ll** be there before you know it."

would/had

The words *would* and *had* share an identical enclitic form, "*-d*." When we encounter it in speech or text, we have to pay attention to the context to know which one is being used. For example:
- "They**'d** already cooked dinner when I got home." (had)

- "I**'d** been there many times before." (had)
- "We**'d** love to go with you!" (would)
- "She**'d** always play in the garden when she was young." (would)

Possessive "-'s"

The possessive "-*'s*" was originally a contraction of the Old English suffix "-es"; however, this "-es" ending fell out of use, and we generally think of the possessive -*'s* as a distinct syntactic and grammatical construct, rather than a contraction. It is, however, an enclitic, since its meaning is dependent on the word that precedes it, and it is joined to it by an apostrophe. For example:

- "The dog**'s** tail is wagging."
- "Daniel**'s** wallet is on the table."
- "Jen**'s** books are in the car."

Quiz

(answers start on page 463)

1. Enclitics are reduced forms of words attached to the word _____ them.

a) after
b) before

2. In the following sentence, which word could be used as an enclitic?
"I have never been far away from home."

a) never
b) have
c) been
d) I

3. In the following sentence, which word could be used as an enclitic?
"We will always be thinking about you."

a) about
b) be
c) we
d) will

4. In the following sentence, what word does the enclitic **in bold** represent?
"I**'d** always wanted to travel, and now I can."

a) had
b) would
c) did

5. In the following sentence, what does the enclitic **in bold** represent?
"Jake**'s** car is in the driveway."

a) is
b) was
c) has
d) possession

The Three-Letter Rule

Definition

The "**three-letter rule**" is a spelling convention stating that "**content words**"—words that communicate meaningful information, such as nouns, (most) verbs, adjectives, and adverbs—will almost always be spelled with at least three letters. Words that are spelled with only one or two letters, on the other hand, will almost always be "**function words**"—words that perform grammatical functions to help construct a sentence, such as pronouns, prepositions, conjunctions, articles, or particles.

The rule is most helpful when we are trying to identify content words that are homophones with function words (that is, they are pronounced the same way but are spelled differently). First, though, let's look a bit more closely at the difference between content words and function words.

Content Words vs. Function Words

Content words

A **content word** (also known as a **lexical word**) is a word that communicates a distinct lexical meaning within a particular context—that is, it expresses the specific **content** of what we're talking about at a given time. Nouns (e.g., *dog, Betty, happiness, luggage*), most* verbs (e.g., *run, talk, decide, entice*), adjectives (e.g., *sad, outrageous, good, easy*), and adverbs (e.g., *slowly, beautifully, never*) all have meaning that is considered *lexically* important.

In addition, content words are considered an **open class** of words, meaning that new words can be added to their various parts of speech without difficulty. For example, the word *email* is now an accepted and commonplace term, with a distinct lexical meaning as both a noun and a verb, but it wouldn't have made sense to anybody 100 years ago.

Finally, content words will always have at least one syllable that is emphasized in a sentence, so if a content word only has a single syllable, it will always be stressed. (Single-syllable function words like *a* or *of*, on the other hand, are very often—though not always—unstressed in speech.)

(*Auxiliary verbs are specific types of verbs that are used in the grammatical construction of tense and aspect or to express **modality**—that is, asserting or denying possibility, likelihood, ability, permission, obligation, or future intention. These types of verbs are fixed in their structure and are used to convey a relationship between other "main" verbs, so they are considered function words, which we'll look at next.)

Function words

A **function word** (also known as a **structure word**) is a word that primarily serves to complete the syntax and grammatical nuance of a sentence. These include **pronouns** (e.g., *he, she, it, they*), **prepositions** (e.g., *to, in, on, under*), **conjunctions** (e.g., *and, but, if, or*), **articles** (e.g., *a, an, the*), other **determiners** (e.g., *this, each, those*), and interjections (e.g., *ah, grr, hello*).

In addition to these other parts of speech, function words also include a specific subset of verbs known as auxiliary verbs, which add structural and grammatical meaning to other main verbs. These include the three primary auxiliary verbs *be, do,* and *have*, as well as a number of others known as modal auxiliary verbs, such as *can, may, must, will*, etc. For example:

• "I **am** going home."
• "We **do** not agree with the outcome."
• "You **must** tell me what we **can** say during the interview."

Another distinct aspect of function words is that they are considered a **closed class** of words, which, unlike content words, means that we **don't** (or very rarely) add new words to these groups. For instance, we generally cannot create a new preposition to describe a relationship between a noun and the rest of the sentence, just as we have specific conjunctions that already exist to connect words, phrases, or clauses together. (Note that interjections are an exception to this, as they can evolve or be added to over time.)

Finally, single-syllable function words are commonly (but not always) unstressed in a sentence—since they are not providing lexical meaning integral to the sentence, we often "skip over" them vocally. For example, in the sentence, "Bobby wants **to** walk **to the** playground," the particle *to*, the preposition *to*, and the definite article *the* are all said without (or without much) stress. The content words (*Bobby*, *wants*, *walk*, and *playground*), on the other hand, each have at least one syllable that is emphasized.

Determining spelling using the three-letter rule

The three-letter rule is a useful convention to follow when we're trying to determine the spelling of short, single-syllable words. Many one- and two-letter function words are **homophones** of short content words: they have different spellings, but their pronunciations are the same. (We'll also look at a few instances in which the spelling of such words is similar in all but one letter, but their pronunciations are affected by the change in addition to their meaning.)

By remembering that content words will almost always be three or more letters long, we can choose the correct spelling for the word we mean.

For example:

Function Words	Content Words
aw (/ɔ/) *interjection* used to express pity, sympathy, tenderness, or disbelief (sometimes spelled *aww*)	*awe* (/ɔ/) *noun* huge or overwhelming respect, wonder, or admiration, sometimes mixed with dread or fear
be* (/bi/) *auxiliary verb* used to denote grammatical, tense, aspect, mood, or passive voice	*bee* (/bi/) *noun* a winged insect capable of stinging that collects nectar and pollen
by (/baɪ/) *preposition* close or next to; via or with the help of; through or due to the agency, action, or invention of	*buy* (/baɪ/) *verb* to purchase with money
do* (/du/) *auxiliary verb* used to ask questions or form negatives	*dew* (/du, dju/) *noun* droplets of water that condense onto cool surfaces from the air, especially at night *due* (/du, dju/) *adjective* payable on demand or owed as a debt; conventional, proper, or fitting *doe* (/doʊ/) *noun* a female deer, or the female of various other non-primate mammals
er (/ə, ər/) *interjection* expressing hesitation, doubt, or uncertainty	*err* (/ɛr/) *verb* to make an error; to do what is incorrect, improper, or unacceptable *ere* (/ɛr/) *preposition/conjunction* (old-fashioned) before; prior to
ew (/ɪəu/) *interjection* an exclamation of disgust (sometimes spelled *eww*)	*ewe* (/ju/) *noun* a female sheep
hi (/haɪ/) *informal interjection* used to express greeting	*high* (/haɪ/) *adjective and adverb* elevated or extended to a relatively great degree upward
in (/ɪn/) *preposition/particle* within the area of; into from the outside (among other meanings)	*inn* (/ɪn/) *noun* a lodging house, tavern, or restaurant

I (/aɪ/) first-person singular pronoun (subjective case)	***aye*** (/aɪ/) *noun* an affirmative vote or response ***eye*** (/aɪ/) *noun* the organ responsible for vision
lo (/loʊ/) *interjection* used to express surprise or attract attention, largely reserved in modern English for the phrase *lo and behold*	***low*** (/loʊ/) *adjective or adverb* near to or rising only slightly above the ground; not high or tall
of (/ʌv/) *preposition* originating, derived, or resulting from	***off*** (/ɔf/) *adjective* not connected, attached, on, or operational; *adverb* from or at a place, position, or certain distance (can be a preposition as well, used to indicate the removal, detachment, or distance of something)
or (/ɔr/; when unstressed, /ər/) *conjunction* used to indicate one or more choices or alternatives	***oar*** (/ɔr/) *noun* a long, thin paddle used to row or steer a boat ***ore*** (/ɔr/) *noun* a naturally occurring mineral, typically metal, mined for its value
ow (/aʊ/) *interjection* used to express pain	***owe*** (/oʊ/) *verb* to be indebted or to have a moral obligation to
to (/tu/) *preposition* towards or in the direction of; *particle* used to form infinitives, as in *to go, to run, to walk*, etc.	***too*** (/tu/) *adverb* also or in addition; immensely, extremely, or excessively ***two*** (/tu/) *noun* the name of the number 2, the sum of 1 + 1; also used as a determiner, as in "two sandwiches," "two books," etc. ***toe*** (/toʊ/) *noun* one of the five digits of the foot ***tow*** (/toʊ/) *verb* to pull or draw from behind; *noun* the act or an instance of *towing*
us (/ʌs/) first-person plural pronoun (objective case)	***use*** (v. /juz/; n. /jus/) *verb* to employ for a purpose or put into practice; *noun* the act or an instance of *using*
we (/wi/) first-person plural pronoun (subjective case)	***wee*** (/wi/) *adjective* exceptionally small; tiny

Even where a short content word does not have a homophonic function word from which it needs to be distinguished, we still commonly find silent, seemingly extraneous letters in three-letter words that would have the same pronunciation with only two letters. We often find this when the final consonant of the word is doubled; other times, silent E or other silent vowels are added at the end of the word to "reinforce" the main vowel's pronunciation. For example:

add	joe	rue
bow	law	rye
cue	lay	saw
die	lie	sea
dye	odd	see
ebb	paw	sow
egg	pea	sue
foe	pie	tea
hoe	raw	tee
hue	roe	tie
ill	row	vie

Be, do, and *have* as main verbs

It is worth noting that the auxiliary verbs *be, do* and *have* can also function as "main" verbs in certain situations, meaning they classify as content words depending on the context. For example:
• "Please **do** your homework."
• "I **am** hungry."
• "We don't **have** time for this."

Do and *be* are not the only content words that have fewer than three letters, though. We'll look at some other examples next.

Exceptions

While the three-letter rule is fairly reliable for determining the spelling of common words, there are a few content words that have fewer than three letters.

Two-letter content words

The most common content words that go against the three-letter rule have two letters—the only one-letter words in English are *a* (an article), *I* (a pronoun), and *O* (an archaic interjection).

However, it's important to note that several of these two-letter content words are actually abbreviations of other words, and are often considered informal or nonstandard; others are colloquial terms, or are specific to a certain field, practice, or study. The number of two-letter content words used in everyday speech and writing is actually quite small.

Here is a full list of examples:
• *ab* (an informal noun, short for *abdominal muscle*)
• *ad* (a noun, short for *advertisement*)
• *ag* (an informal adjective or noun, short for *agriculture/agricultural*, as in, "There are many **ag** students," or, "We are studying **ag**.")
• *am* (first-person singular conjugation of *be* when used as a main verb, as in, "I **am** angry.")
• *be* (when used as a main verb, as in, "Please **be** careful.")
• *bi* (an informal adjective, short for *bisexual*)
• *bo* (a long staff weapon used in Japanese martial arts; more formally written *bō*, transcribed from Japanese)
• *do* (when used as a main verb, as in, "I have work to **do**.")
• *ec* (an informal noun, short for *economics*, as in, "I am studying home ec this semester.")
• *ed* (informal noun, short for *education*, as in, "I am studying special **ed** this semester.")
• *el* (the name for the letter **L**)
• *em* (the name for the letter **M**; also used as an adjective meaning "the length of an **M**," as in the term *em dash*)
• *en* (the name for the letter **N**; also used as an adjective meaning "the length of an **N**," as in the term *en dash*)
• *ex* (a nominalization of the suffix "ex-," used to refer to a former husband, wife, partner, etc., as in, "I ran into my **ex** the other day"; also the name for the letter **X**)
• *go* (main verb, meaning "to move, travel, or depart")
• *id* (in psychoanalytic theory, the part of the psyche that represents unconscious and primitive impulses and desires)
• *is* (third-person singular conjugation of *be* when used as a main verb, as in "She **is** angry.")
• *lo* (stylized shortening of *low*, as in *lo-fi* or *lo calorie*)
• *ma* (colloquial term for *mother*)
• *no* (a negative adjective, as in "I have **no** luck," or adverb, as in "I did **no** better this time.")
• *oh* (an alternative name for the number zero, as in "My area code is three oh three" [303])
• *ox* (a large domesticated bovine used as a draft animal)
• *pa* (a colloquial term for *father*)
• *pi* (the 16th letter of the Greek alphabet, π; used in mathematics as a transcendental number, approximately 3.14159)
• *up* (when used as an adjective [rather than a preposition/particle], as in "Your time is **up**.")

Letters of the alphabet written as words

In addition to the examples we looked at above, individual letters of the alphabet can operate as nouns when we talk them in a sentence, as in, "There is no **i** in team."

However, the appropriate way of writing single letters can be a thorny issue. They can often look incorrect if they are simply written as a lowercase letter with no other punctuation or formatting, so a common solution is to surround a single letter in quotation marks, as in:

• "There is no **"i"** in team."

The biggest problem, though, is how to write plurals of single letters. If a single letter is lowercase, then simply adding "-s" to the end can create confusion with existing words, as in:

• "There are three **is** in *intrinsic*." (Could be confused with the verb *is*.)
• "The word *aardvark* actually begins with two **as**." (Could be confused with the conjunction/adverb *as*.)
• "Remember that *pursue* is spelled with two **us**, not one." (Could be confused with the pronoun *us*.)
• "*Savvy* is one of the few words that contain two **vs**." (Could be confused with *vs.*, an abbreviation of the word *versus*.)

In these cases, surrounding the letter in quotation marks will not help. For instance, writing "is" does nothing to clear up the confusion with the word *is*, and writing "i"s is both incorrect and visually unappealing.

To combat this potential confusion, it is common to use an apostrophe between the alphabetical letter and the pluralizing "-s" without quotation marks, as in:

• "Be sure to mind your **p's** and **q's** while you're with your grandparents."

However, this use of apostrophes is sometimes frowned upon by linguists who feel the apostrophe should be reserved for possession or contraction. As a result, it is common for writers to capitalize single letters so that they are distinct from the "-s." For example:

• "There are four **Es** in *excellence*."
• "Let me make sure that I've dotted my **Is** and crossed my **Ts**."
• "*Savvy* is one of only a few words that contain two **Vs**."

Some writers will still opt to use apostrophes to make their writing even clearer, even when a letter is capitalized:

• "There are four **E's** in *excellence*."
• "Let me make sure that I've dotted my **I's** and crossed my **T's**."
• "*Savvy* is one of the few words that contain two **V's**."

In the end, there is no single, standardized way of writing single letters of the alphabet in a sentence; unless the style guide of your school or employer specifies how to write them, choose the style that you feel looks the best and is the least ambiguous. Whichever method you decide to use, just be consistent throughout your writing.

Alphabetic adjectives

Finally, it's also worth mentioning that letters of the alphabet can be used as adjectives in certain situations to describe the shape of something. These generally occur in very specific instances. The letter is almost always capitalized, and the terms are often (but not always) conjoined by a hyphen. For example:

• **A**-frame
• **D**-ring
• **H**-beam
• **I**-beam
• **K**-turn (more commonly known as a *three-point turn*)
• **O**-ring
• **P**-trap
• **S**-bend
• **T** intersection
• **T**-shirt (also variously written as *t-shirt, tee-shirt,* and *tee shirt*)
• **U**-bend
• **U**-turn
• **Y** intersection
• **Y**-turn (more commonly known as a *three-point turn*)

Quiz

(answers start on page 463)

1. According to the three-letter rule, what type of word will most commonly be spelled with at least three letters?

a) Content words
b) Function words

2. Which of the following is **not** a common characteristic of **function words**?

a) They only provide structural and grammatical meaning
b) They are usually closed-class words
c) They can have new words added to them over time
d) They are commonly unstressed when they have only one syllable

3. Which of the following parts of speech are **not** considered **content words**?

a) Nouns
b) Adjectives
c) Adverbs
d) Conjunctions

4. Which of the following is a **function word**?

a) add
b) an
c) aye
d) awe

5. Which of the following parts of speech are only **sometimes** considered **function words**?

a) Prepositions
b) Interjections
c) Auxiliary verbs
d) Determiners

6. When do content words contain only **one** letter?

a) When the word is the letter of the alphabet itself
b) In informal or colloquial shortenings
c) In foreign loanwords
d) Never

I Before E, Except After C

Perhaps the best known spelling convention in English is "I Before E, Except After C," meaning that **I** comes before **E** in most words, except when both letters immediately follow **C**. Due to the simplicity of the rule and its easily remembered rhyming mnemonic, it is often one of the first rules taught to those learning English spelling.

However, even though the basic element of the rule is straightforward, it is actually quite a bit more complicated. In fact, the full rhyme typically goes like this:
"**I** before **E**,
Except after **C**,
Or when sounding like **A**
As in *neighbor* or *weigh*."
As we can see, we have to use a word's pronunciation to decide whether or not **I** does indeed come after **E**. And this is not just limited to the "**A**" sound (/eɪ/) described in the rhyme—there are many exceptions and special cases that we have to consider when deciding whether **I** should come before **E**.

We'll begin by looking at the foundations of the rule, and then examine the various instances in which it doesn't apply (or the rule changes slightly).

When the letters sound like *E* (/i/)

The "**I** before **E**" rule is most useful if we focus on instances when **E** and **I** are put together as vowel digraphs—that is, two vowels working together to form a single speech sound.

With this in mind, the basic rule "**I** before **E**, except after **C**" is fairly reliable when **IE** or **EI** function as digraphs that produce the sound /i/ (the way the letter **E** is said aloud as a word).

For example:

I before E	Except after C
ach**ie**ve (/əˈʧiv/)	**cei**ling (/ˈsilɪŋ/)
bel**ie**ve (/bɪˈliv/)	con**cei**t (/kənˈsit/)
ch**ie**f (/ʧif/)	con**cei**ve (/kənˈsiv/)
f**ie**ld (/fild/)	de**cei**t (/dɪˈsit/)
gr**ie**f (/grif/)	de**cei**ve (/dɪˈsiv/)
p**ie**ce (/pis/)	per**cei**ve (/pərˈsiv/)
rel**ie**ve (/rɪˈliv/)	re**cei**pt (/rɪˈsit/)
sh**ie**ld (/ʃild/)	trans**cei**ver (/trænˈsivər/)

E before I when sounding like *A* (/eɪ/)

The second half of the rhyme—"Or when sounding like *A*"—alludes to the fact that **E** often comes before **I** <u>without</u> **C** when **EI** is pronounced /eɪ/ (the way the letter **A** is said aloud as a word).

This is especially common when **EI** is followed by a silent GH, as in:
• fr<u>eigh</u>t (/freɪt/)
• <u>eigh</u>t (/eɪt/)
• inv<u>eigh</u> (/ɪnˈveɪ/)
• n<u>eigh</u>bor (/ˈneɪbər/)
• sl<u>eigh</u> (/sleɪ/)
• w<u>eigh</u>t (/weɪt/)
(Remember this when using these roots in other words, as in *eighteen* or *weightless*.)

In some words, **EI** also produces this pronunciation before a single silent G or simply on its own. For instance:
• d<u>eig</u>n (/deɪn/)
• b<u>eig</u>e (/beɪʒ/)
• f<u>eig</u>n (/feɪn/)
• r<u>eig</u>n (/reɪn/)
• r<u>ei</u>n (/reɪn/)
• surv<u>ei</u>llance (/sərˈveɪləns/)
• v<u>ei</u>l (/veɪl/)
• v<u>ei</u>n (/veɪn/)

And sometimes when sounding like *I* (/aɪ/)

Less commonly, the digraph **EI** produces the sound /aɪ/ (the way the letter **I** is said aloud as a word).

There are only a few common root words in which this is the case:
• f<u>ei</u>sty (/ˈfaɪsti/)
• h<u>ei</u>ght (/haɪt/)
• h<u>ei</u>st (/haɪst/)
• sl<u>eigh</u>t (/slaɪt/)

Just be sure not to confuse the spelling for *slight* (an adjective meaning "small in size, degree, or amount") with *sleight* (a noun meaning "skill or dexterity" or "a clever trick or deception")—they both sound the same, but have **slightly** different spellings.

Exceptions to the /i/ rule (and tips for remembering them)

Even when we narrow the "**I** before **E**" rule to digraphs that form the /i/ sound, there are still quite a few common exceptions in which **E** comes before **I** but <u>not</u> after **C**. We'll look at a few of the most common examples, as well as some helpful tips to remember their spelling. Be aware that this is <u>not</u> an exhaustive list, just a few of the most common occurrences. As always, if you're unsure of a word's spelling, check a trusted dictionary.

weird

A very common word that goes against the "**I** before **E** when it sounds like /i/" rule is the word *weird*. A good way to remember that **E** should come first is the mnemonic "<u>*we*</u> are <u>*weird*</u>."

seize

The word *seize* is one of the only words in which **EI** is followed by **Z**. When you're trying to remember whether **E** comes before **I**, follow this memory tip: because *seize* is a verb, it needs to end in "-ize" like many other verbs formed from this suffix, so **I** should come <u>after</u> **E** in their digraph.

caffeine

If you're having trouble remembering how to spell *caffeine*, it helps to think of it as a combination of *coffee* + the suffix "-ine," which is often used to form chemical names. Since we treat the ending like a suffix, **I** has to come after **E**.

If we remember the correct spelling of *caffeine*, we can use it to remember how to spell other chemical names as well, such as *protein* or *codeine*.

either and *neither*

Uniquely, the words *either* and *neither* have two common pronunciations, with **EI** producing the /i/ or the /aɪ/ sound (/ˈiðər/ or /ˈaɪðər/; /ˈniðər/ or /ˈnaɪðər/). Both pronunciations are considered correct, and there is no change in meaning between them.

Here's a useful tip for remembering the correct spelling for these two exceptions:
   "**E** comes before **I** in *either* and *neither*, because the letters sound **either** like **E** or like **I**."

leisure

Like *either* and *neither*, the word *leisure* has two different pronunciations. In this instance, though, the **EI** digraph can form the sound /i/ (/ˈliʒər/, the "long" **E** sound) or the /ɛ/ sound (/ˈlɛʒər/, the "short" **E** sound). The first pronunciation is more common in American English, while the second is more common in British English.

No matter how we pronounce the word, though, we can remember its spelling because the digraph always makes an **E** sound (either long or short), so **E** must come before **I**.

Other helpful tips

Although there are many exceptions to the general "**I** before **E**, except after **C**" rule, there are a number of other conventions that we can use together with it to remember the order of **I** and **E** in a given word.

I before E <u>after</u> C when making the "sh" sound (/ʃ/)

E will usually come before **I** after **C** when it makes the /s/ sound, as in *ceiling* or *receive*. However, when **C** makes the /ʃ/ ("sh") sound, it is often followed by **IE** (and usually **N**). For example:
• an**cie**nt (/ˈeɪʃənt/)
• cons**cie**nce (/ˈkɑnʃəns/)
• defi**cie**nt (/dɪˈfɪʃənt/)
• effi**cie**nt (/ɪˈfɪʃənt/)
• gla**cie**r (/ˈgleɪʃər/)
• omnis**cie**nt (/ɑmˈnɪʃənt/)

Spelling dictated by suffixes

Adding a suffix to a word will often alter its spelling, sometimes producing words that go against the "**I** before **E**, except after **C**" rule. Remember that the spelling of suffixes takes precedence over normal conventions.

Changing Y to I before a Suffix

When a word ends in the letter **Y**, we almost always change it to **I** when attaching a suffix to the end. Therefore, almost any word that originally ends in **Y** will have **I** before **E** when we add a suffix beginning with **E**, even if the two vowels come after **C**.
For example:

Y + "-ed"	Y + "-er"	Y + "-es"
appl**y**→appl**ied**	angr**y**→angr**ier**	agen**cy**→agen**cies**
bur**y**→bur**ied**	blurr**y**→blurr**ier**	beaut**y**→beaut**ies**
carr**y**→carr**ied**	boun**cy**→boun**cier**	curren**cy**→curren**cies**
def**y**→def**ied**	earl**y**→earl**ier**	empt**y**→empt**ies**
fan**cy**→fan**cied**	flee**cy**→flee**cier**	glor**y**→glor**ies**
hurr**y**→hurr**ied**	jui**cy**→jui**cier**	lega**cy**→lega**cies**
notif**y**→notif**ied**	lovel**y**→lovel**ier**	marr**y**→marr**ies**
pit**y**→pit**ied**	magnif**y**→magnif**ier**	poli**cy**→poli**cies**
repl**y**→repl**ied**	quantif**y**→quantif**ier**	repl**y**→repl**ies**
stud**y**→stud**ied**	spi**cy**→spi**cier**	vacan**cy**→vacan**cies**

E + "-ing"

When the letter **E** is the last letter of a word, it is often omitted when a suffix is attached because it is silent in the word. However, we still find instances when adding the suffix "-ing" to a word results in **EI**. For example:

• b**ei**ng
• cano**ei**ng
• dy**ei**ng
• fle**ei**ng
• se**ei**ng

When forming two syllables

When **E** and **I** are split across two syllables (rather than functioning as a single digraph), the sound of the first syllable will usually let us know which letter goes first. If you're trying to remember the spelling of a particular word, say it aloud, slowly and carefully enunciating each syllable. This is an especially useful tip when remembering how to spell *science*, since it goes against the "**I** before **E**, except after **C**" rule.

(In these examples, a syllable break will be indicated by an interpunct [·] in each word, and by a dot [.] in their IPA pronunciations.)

I before E	E before I
cli·ent (/ˈklaɪ.ənt/)	a·the·ist (/ˈeɪ.θi.əst/)
di·et (/ˈdaɪ.ət/)	al·be·it (/ɔlˈbi.ɪt/)
qui·et (/ˈkwaɪ.ət/)	be·ing (/ˈbi.ɪŋ/)
sci·ence (/ˈsaɪ.əns/)	de·i·ty (/ˈdi.ɪ.ti/)
so·ci·e·ty (/səˈsaɪ.ə.ti/)	spon·ta·ne·i·ty (/ˌspɑn.təˈneɪ.əti/)

Quiz
(answers start on page 463)

1. When is the rule "**I** before **E**, except after **C**" most often true?

a) When the two vowels form the /eɪ/ sound
b) When the two vowels form the /i/ sound
c) When the two vowels form the /aɪ/ sound
d) When the two vowels form the /ɪ/ sound

2. When can **I** come before **E** *after* **C**?

a) When a word ending in "-cy" takes a suffix beginning in "-e"
b) When **C** makes a /ʃ/ sound
c) When **I** and **E** are in two separate syllables
d) A & C
e) B & C
f) All of the above
g) None of the above

3. Which of the following words is spelled **incorrectly**?

a) field
b) wierd
c) ceiling
d) grief

4. Which of the following words is spelled **correctly**?

a) believe
b) viel
c) recieve
d) cheif

5. Which of the following rhymes with the word *slight*?

a) weight
b) height
c) freight
d) eight

Rules for Capitalization

The **capitalization** of a word (meaning its first letter is in the **upper case**) often depends upon its context and placement within a sentence. While there are some words that are always capitalized no matter where they appear in a sentence—such as "proper" nouns and adjectives, as well as the first-person pronoun *I*—most words are only capitalized if they appear at the beginning of a sentence.

Determining when to capitalize words in the titles of creative or published works (such as novels, films, essays, plays, paintings, news headlines, etc.) can be very difficult because there is no single, generally accepted rule to follow. However, there are *some* standard conventions, which we'll discuss a little further on.

Capitalizing the first word of a sentence

The first word of a sentence is always capitalized. This helps the reader clearly recognize that the sentence has begun, and we make it clear that the sentence has ended by using **terminal punctuation marks** (e.g., periods, exclamation points, or question marks).

We also capitalize the first letter of a sentence that is directly quoted within another sentence. This is known as direct speech. For example:

• John said, "You'll never work in this city again!"
• Mary told him, "We should spend some time apart," which took him by surprise.
• The other day, my daughter asked, "Why do I have to go to school, but you don't?"

Sometimes, a portion of a larger statement will be quoted as a complete sentence on its own; this is especially common in journalistic writing. To preserve capitalization conventions, we still usually capitalize the first letter of the quoted speech (if it functions as a complete independent sentence), but we surround the capital letter in brackets to make it clear that the change was made by the person using the quotation. For instance:

• The president went on to say, "[W]e must be willing to help those less fortunate than ourselves."

Note that we do **not** capitalize the first word in the quotation if it is a word, phrase, or sentence fragment incorporated into the natural flow of the overall sentence; we also do not set it apart with commas:

• My brother said he feels "really bad" about what happened.
• But I don't want to just "see how things go"!

Trademarks beginning with a lowercase letter

Sometimes, a trademark or brand name will begin with a lowercase letter immediately followed by an uppercase letter, as in *iPhone, eBay, eHarmony*, etc. If writers decide to begin a sentence with such a trademarked word, they may be confused about whether to capitalize the first letter since it is at the beginning of a sentence, or to leave the first letter in lowercase since it is specific to the brand name. Different style guides have different requirements, but most guides recommend rewording the sentence to avoid the issue altogether:

✔ "Sales for the iPhone continue to climb." (correct and recommended)

Proper Nouns

Proper nouns are used to identify a <u>unique</u> person, place, or thing (as opposed to **common nouns**, which identify generic or nonspecific people or things). A proper noun names someone or something that is one of a kind; this is signified by capitalizing the first letter of the word, no matter where it appears in a sentence.

The most common proper nouns are names of people, places, or events:
• "Go find <u>J</u>eff and tell him that dinner is ready."
• "I lived in <u>C</u>incinnati before I moved to <u>N</u>ew <u>Y</u>ork."
• "My parents still talk about how great <u>W</u>oodstock was in 1969."

Proper nouns are similarly used for items that have a commercial brand name. In this case, the object that's being referred to is not unique in itself, but the brand it belongs to is. For example:
• "Pass me the <u>F</u>risbee."
• "I'll have a <u>P</u>epsi, please."
• "My new <u>M</u>ac<u>B</u>ook is incredibly fast."

The names of organizations, companies, agencies, etc., are all proper nouns as well, so the words that make up the name are all capitalized. However, unlike the nouns of people or places, these often contain **function words** (those that have only grammatical importance, such as articles, conjunctions, and prepositions), which are **not** capitalized. For example:
• "You'll have to raise your query with the <u>D</u>epartment <u>of</u> <u>F</u>oreign <u>A</u>ffairs <u>and</u> <u>T</u>rade."
• "I've been offered a teaching position at the <u>U</u>niversity <u>of</u> <u>P</u>ennsylvania."
• "<u>B</u>ay <u>A</u>rea <u>R</u>apid <u>T</u>ransit workers continue their strike for a fifth consecutive day."

These are often made into **acronyms** and **initialisms**, which we'll discuss a bit later.

Appellations

Appellations are additional words added to a person's name. These may be used to indicate respect for a person (known as **honorifics**) or to indicate a person's profession, royalty, rank, etc. (known as **titles**). Some appellations are always abbreviated before a person's name, such as *Dr.* (short for *Doctor*), *Mr.* (short for *Mister*), and *Mrs.* (originally a shortened form of *Mistress*), and some may be used in place of a person's name altogether (such as *Your Honor*, *Your Highness*, or *Your Majesty*).

Appellations are considered a "part" of the person's name and are also capitalized in writing as a proper noun. For example:
• "<u>D</u>r. Spencer insists we perform a few more tests."
• "I intend to ask <u>P</u>rofessor Regan about her dissertation on foreign policy."
• "<u>P</u>rince William is adored by many."
• "Please see if <u>M</u>r. Parker and <u>M</u>rs. Wright will be joining us this evening."
• "I have no further questions, <u>Y</u>our <u>H</u>onor."

Normal words can also function as appellations <u>after</u> a person's name to describe his or her appearance, personality, or other personal characteristics; these are formally known as **epithets**. They are usually accompanied by function words (especially the article *the*), which are **not** capitalized. For example:
• Alexander the <u>G</u>reat
• Ivan the <u>T</u>errible
• Charles the <u>B</u>ald

Proper Adjectives

Proper adjectives are formed from proper nouns, and they are also capitalized. They are often made from the names of cities, countries, or regions to describe where something comes from or to identify a trait associated with that place, but they can also be formed from the names of people. For example:

Proper Noun	Proper Adjective	Example Sentence
Italy	Italian	I love <u>I</u>talian food.
China	Chinese	How much does this <u>C</u>hinese robe cost?
Christ	Christian	In Europe, you can visit many ancient <u>C</u>hristian churches.
Shakespeare	Shakespearean	He writes in an almost <u>S</u>hakespearean style.

Sometimes, a word that began as a proper adjective can lose its "proper" significance over time, especially when formed from the name of a fictional character. In these cases, the word is no longer capitalized. Take the following sentence:
• "He was making **quixotic** mistakes."

The word *quixotic* was originally a proper adjective derived from the name "Don Quixote," a fictional character who was prone to foolish, grandiose behavior. Through time, it has come to mean "foolish" in its own right, losing its association to the character. As such, it is no longer capitalized in modern English.

Another example is the word *gargantuan*. Once associated with the name of a giant in the 16th-century book *Gargantua*, it has come to mean "huge" in daily use. Since losing its link with the fictional monster, it is no longer capitalized:
• "The couple built a **gargantuan** house."

Other capitalization conventions

While proper nouns, proper adjectives, and the first word in a sentence are always capitalized, there are other conventions for capitalization that have less concrete rules.

Reverential capitalization

Traditionally, words for or relating to the Judeo-Christian God or to Jesus Christ are capitalized, a practice known as **reverential capitalization**. This is especially common in pronouns, though it can occur with other nouns associated with or used as a metaphor for God. For example:
"Our **F**ather, who art in heaven, hallowed be thy **N**ame."
"We must always model our actions on the **L**ord's will, trusting in **H**is plan and in the benevolence of the **A**lmighty."

However, this practice is one of style rather than grammatical correctness. It is becoming slightly less common in modern writing, especially in relation to pronouns, and many modern publications (even some editions of the Bible) tend not to capitalize pronouns associated with God or Jesus Christ (though nouns such as "the Lamb" or "the Almighty" still tend to be in uppercase).

Finally, note that when the word *god* is being used to describe or discuss a deity in general (i.e., not the specific God of Christian or Jewish faith), it does not need to be capitalized. Conversely, any name of a specific religious figure must be capitalized the same way as any other proper noun, as in *Zeus, Buddha, Allah, Krishna*, etc.

Acronyms and Initialisms

Acronyms and **initialisms** are abbreviations of multiple words using just their initial letters; like the initials of a person's name, these letters are usually capitalized. Acronyms are distinguished by the fact that they are read aloud as a single word, while initialisms are spoken aloud as individual letters rather than a single word. (However, because the two are so similar in appearance and function, it is very common to simply refer to both as acronyms.)

Acronyms

Because acronyms are said as distinct words, they are usually (but not always) written without periods. In some cases, the acronym has become so common that the letters aren't even capitalized anymore.

For example:
• "Scientists from **NASA** have confirmed the spacecraft's location on Mars." (acronym of "National Aeronautics and Space Administration")
• "The officer went **AWOL** following the attack." (acronym of "Absent Without Leave")
• "I need those documents finished **A.S.A.P.**" (acronym or initialism of "As Soon As Possible"; also often written as *ASAP, asap,* and *a.s.a.p.*)
• "His **scuba** equipment turned out to be faulty." (Scuba is actually an acronym of "self-contained underwater breathing apparatus," but it is now only written as a regular word.)

It's worth noting that in British English, it is becoming increasingly common to write acronyms of well-known organizations with only the first letter capitalized, as in *Nafta* (North American Free Trade Agreement) or *Unicef* (United Nations International Children's Emergency Fund), while initialisms, such as **UN** or **UK**, are still written in all capital letters.

Initialisms

Like acronyms, it is most common to write initialisms without periods. However, in American English, it is also common to include periods between the letters of some initialisms. This varies between style guides, and it is generally a matter of personal preference; whether you use periods in initialisms or not, be sure to be consistent.

Here are some examples of common initialisms (some with periods, some without):
• "I grew up in the **US**, but I've lived in London since my early 20s." (initialism of "United States")
• "It took a long time, but I've finally earned my **Ph.D.**" (initialism of "Philosophiae Doctor," Latin for "Doctor of Philosophy")
• "I need to go to an **ATM** to get some cash." (initialism of "Automated Teller Machine")
• "The witness claimed to have seen a **U.F.O.** fly over the field last night." (initialism of "Unidentified Flying Object")

Notice that the **h** in *Ph.D.* remains lowercase. This is because it is part of the same word as **P** (*Philosophiae*); it is spoken aloud as an individual letter to help make the initialism distinct. While this mix of uppercase and lowercase letters in an initialism is uncommon, there are other instances in which this occurs. Sometimes, as with *Ph.D.*, the lowercase letters come from the same word as an uppercase letter; other times, the lowercase letter represents a function word (a conjunction, preposition, or article). For example:
• **AmE** (**Am**erican English)
• **BrE** (**Br**itish English)
• **LotR** (*Lord **of** **t**he **R**ings*)
• **DoD** (Department **of** Defense)

Finally, there are two initialisms that are <u>always</u> in lowercase: *i.e.* (short for the Latin *id est*, meaning "that is") and *e.g.* (short for the Latin *exempli gratia*, meaning "for example"). The only instance in which these initialisms *might* be capitalized is if they are used at the beginning of a sentence, but doing so, while not grammatically incorrect, is generally considered aesthetically unappealing and should be avoided.

Abbreviations in conversational English

In conversational writing, especially with the advent of text messages and online messaging, many phrases have become shortened into informal abbreviations (usually initialisms, but occasionally said aloud as new words). They are usually written without periods and, due to their colloquial nature, they are often left in lowercase. While there are thousands of conversational abbreviations in use today, here are just a few of the most common:
• **LOL** (short for "Laugh Out Loud," said as an initialism or sometimes as a word [/lɑl/])
• **OMG** (short for "Oh My God." Interestingly, the first recorded use of this initialism was in a letter from Lord John Fisher to Winston Churchill in 1917.)
• **BTW** (short for "By The Way")
• **BRB** (short for "Be Right Back")
• **BFF** (short for "Best Friend Forever")
• **IDK** (short for "I Don't Know")
• **FWIW** (short for "For What It's Worth")
• **FYI** (short for "For Your Information")
• **IMHO** (short for "In My Humble/Honest Opinion")
• **P2P** (short for "Peer-To-Peer," with the word *To* represented by the number *2*, a homophone)
• **TLC** (short for "Tender Loving Care")
• **TL;DR** (short for "Too Long; Didn't Read")
• **TTYL** (short for "Talk To You Later")

Because these are all very informal, they should only be used in conversational writing.

Capitalizing titles and headlines

There is much less standardization regarding how to capitalize titles or article headlines; different style guides prescribe different rules and recommendations.

That said, it is generally agreed that you should capitalize the first and last word of the title, along with any words of semantic significance—that is, nouns, pronouns, verbs, adjectives, and adverbs—along with proper nouns, proper adjectives, acronyms, and initialisms. "Function words," those that primarily add grammatical meaning rather than anything substantial (prepositions, articles, and conjunctions), are generally left in lowercase. This convention is sometimes known as **title case**, and some style guides recommend following it without exception, even for longer function words like *between* or *upon*.

For example:
• "<u>N</u>ew <u>R</u>egulations for <u>S</u>chools <u>S</u>coring below <u>N</u>ational <u>A</u>verages"
• "<u>A</u>n <u>A</u>nalysis of the <u>D</u>ifferences between <u>F</u>ormatting <u>S</u>tyles"
• "<u>P</u>resident to <u>C</u>onsider <u>O</u>ptions after <u>R</u>esults of <u>FBI</u> <u>I</u>nvestigation"
• "<u>O</u>utrage over <u>P</u>rime <u>M</u>inister's <u>R</u>esponse to <u>C</u>orruption <u>C</u>harges"

Some words can pose problems because they can in some instances be prepositions and in other instances be adverbs. For example, in the phrasal verb *take off*, *off* is functioning adverbially to complete the meaning of the verb, so it would be capitalized in a title:

✔ "<u>H</u>ome <u>B</u>usinesses <u>T</u>aking <u>O</u>ff in <u>I</u>nternet <u>A</u>ge"
✖ "<u>H</u>ome <u>B</u>usinesses <u>T</u>aking off in <u>I</u>nternet <u>A</u>ge"

Another group of words that often gives writers problems is the various forms of the verb *to be*, which conjugates as *is, am, are, was, were, been*, and *being*. Because many of its forms are only two or three letters, writers are often inclined not to capitalize them; however, because *to be* is a verb, we should <u>always</u> capitalize it when using title case:

✔ "<u>D</u>etermining <u>W</u>ho <u>I</u>s <u>R</u>esponsible for the <u>O</u>utcome" (correct)
✖ "<u>D</u>etermining <u>W</u>ho is <u>R</u>esponsible for the <u>O</u>utcome" (incorrect)

Capitalizing words longer than three letters

Function words are usually not capitalized in title case, but longer function words (such as the conjunctions *because* or *should* or the prepositions *between* or *above*) are often considered to add more meaning than short ones like *or* or *and*. Because of this, it is a common convention is to capitalize function words that have more than three letters in addition to "major" words like nouns and verbs. Here's how titles following this convention look:

• "<u>N</u>ew <u>R</u>egulations for <u>S</u>chools <u>S</u>coring **<u>B</u>elow** <u>N</u>ational <u>A</u>verages"
• "<u>A</u>n <u>A</u>nalysis of the <u>D</u>ifferences **<u>B</u>etween** <u>F</u>ormatting <u>S</u>tyles"
• "<u>P</u>resident to <u>C</u>onsider <u>O</u>ptions <u>A</u>fter <u>R</u>esults of <u>FBI</u> <u>I</u>nvestigation"
• "<u>O</u>utrage <u>O</u>ver <u>P</u>rime <u>M</u>inister's <u>R</u>esponse to <u>C</u>orruption <u>C</u>harges"

Some style guides specify that only function words that are longer than <u>four</u> letters should be capitalized. Following this convention, the first three examples would remain the same, but the word *over* in the fourth example would remain lowercase. However, the "longer than three letters" rule is much more common.

Capitalizing hyphenated compounds

When a compound word features a hyphen, there are multiple ways to capitalize it in a title. Because compound words always serve as nouns or adjectives (or, rarely, verbs), we always capitalize the first part of the compound. What is less straightforward is whether to capitalize the word that comes after the hyphen. Some style guides recommend capitalizing both parts (so long as the second part is a "major" word), while others recommend only capitalizing the first part. For example:

✔ "<u>H</u>ow to <u>R</u>egulate *<u>S</u>elf-<u>D</u>riving* <u>C</u>ars in the <u>N</u>ear <u>F</u>uture"
✔ "*<u>E</u>ighteenth-century* <u>W</u>arship <u>D</u>iscovered off the <u>C</u>oast of <u>N</u>orway"

Certain style guides are very specific about how to capitalize hyphenated compounds, so if your school or employer uses a particular guide for its in-house style, be sure to follow its requirements. Otherwise, it is simply a matter of personal preference whether hyphenated compounds should be capitalized in full or in part; as always, just be consistent.

Compounds with articles, conjunctions, and prepositions

Some multiple-word compounds are formed with function words (typically the article *the*, the conjunction *and*, or the preposition *in*) between two other major words. While capitalizing the major words in the compound is optional and up to the writer's personal preference, the function words will <u>always</u> be in lowercase:

✔ "<u>A</u>re *<u>B</u>rick-and-<u>M</u>ortar* <u>S</u>tores <u>B</u>ecoming <u>O</u>bsolete?"
✔ "<u>P</u>rices of *<u>O</u>ver-the-counter* <u>M</u>edications <u>S</u>et to <u>R</u>ise"
✖ "<u>B</u>usiness <u>T</u>ycoon <u>A</u>ppoints *<u>D</u>aughter-<u>I</u>n-<u>L</u>aw* as <u>N</u>ew <u>CEO</u>"

The only exception to this rule is when writers choose to capitalize every word in the title.

Start case

To eliminate the possible confusion caused by short "substance" words (e.g., forms of *to be*), long function words (e.g., *because* or *beneath*), and hyphenated compounds, some publications choose to simply capitalize every word in a title, regardless of the "types" of words it may contain. This is sometimes known as "**start case**" or "**initial case**." For instance:

• "New Regulations For Schools Scoring Below National Averages"
• "An Analysis Of The Differences Between Formatting Styles"
• "President To Consider Options After Results Of FBI Investigation"
• "Outrage Over Prime Minister's Response To Corruption Charges"

This is especially common in journalism and online publications, but it is usually not recommended for academic or professional writing.

Sentence case

"Sentence case" refers to titles in which only the first word has a capital letter, the same way a sentence is capitalized. (Again, proper nouns, proper adjectives, acronyms, and initialisms remain capitalized.) As with start case, sentence case is useful because it eliminates any possible confusion over which words *should* be capitalized. Titles following this convention look like this:

• "New regulations for schools scoring below national averages"
• "An analysis of the differences between formatting styles"
• "President to consider options after results of FBI investigation"
• "Outrage over Prime Minister's response to corruption charges"

Sentence case is not typically recommended by academic or professional style guides, though this is not always true. Some magazine and news publications use the style for their headlines as well, as do many websites.

Capitalizing subtitles

When a piece of work has both a main title and a secondary subtitle (separated by a colon), we apply the same capitalization rules to both—that is, the same types of words will be in uppercase or lowercase depending on which style is being used. We also capitalize the first word after the colon, treating the subtitle as its own. For example:

• *The Secret Agent: A Simple Tale*
• *Terminator 2: Judgment Day*
• *Angela's Ashes: A Memoir*
• *Vanity Fair: A Novel without a Hero* (sometimes written as *Vanity Fair: A Novel Without a Hero* due to the preference of capitalizing words longer than three letters)

This convention is also true in academic essays, whose subtitles tend to be longer and more detailed, giving the reader a brief explanation of what the essay is about:

• *From the Television to the Supermarket: How the Rise of Modern Advertising Shaped Consumerism in America*
• *True Crimes: A Look at Criminal Cases That Inspired Five Classic Films*

Note that if the main title is written in sentence case, then we only capitalize the first word of the subtitle (after the colon):

• *In their shoes: Women of the 1940s who shaped public policy*

However, this style is generally only used when a title appears in a list of references in an essay's bibliography (individual style guides will have specific requirements for these works cited pages).

Alternate titles

Sometimes a subtitle acts as an alternate title; in this case, the two are often separated with a semicolon or a comma, followed by a lowercase *or* (though the specific style is left to the writer's or publisher's discretion). However, the alternate title is still capitalized the same way as the main title, with the first word after *or* being capitalized even if it is a short function word. For example:

• *Frankenstein; or, The Modern Prometheus*
• *Moby-Dick; or, The Whale*
• *Twelfth Night, or What You Will*
• *Dr. Strangelove or: How I Learned to Stop Worrying and Love the Bomb*

Capitalizing headings

Headings are titles that identify or introduce a specific section within a larger academic essay or business document. In general, headings will be capitalized in the same manner as the document's title, usually having the first and last word capitalized as well as any nouns, adjectives, adverbs, and verbs (and, depending on the style guide being followed, any prepositions or conjunctions longer than three letters).

Sometimes a written work will have multiple **subheadings** of sections that belong within a larger heading. It is common for subheadings to be written in sentence case, but most style guide have specific requirements for when this can be done (for instance, if the subheading is the third or more in a series of headings), if at all.

Deciding how to capitalize a title

Ultimately, unless your school or employer follows one specific style guide, it is a matter of preference to decide how the title is formatted. No matter which style you adopt, the most important thing is to be consistent throughout your body of writing.

Quiz

(answers start on page 463)

1. Which of the following **must** be capitalized?

a) verbs
b) second-person pronouns
c) proper nouns
d) the last word of a sentence

2. When is the first word of quoted speech **not** capitalized?

a) When it is a quoted fragment that is part of the natural flow of the sentence
b) When it is introduced by reporting verbs such as *said* or *told*
c) When it is set apart by one or two commas
d) When a quoted portion of text is used as a complete sentence

3. Which of the following abbreviations is **never** capitalized?

a) a.k.a.
b) lol
c) fyi
d) i.e.

4. Which of the following titles has capitalization that is considered grammatically correct?

a) Demanding equality: A look at twentieth-century law reforms
b) Supreme Court Overturns Ruling of Lower Court in Controversial Corporate Tax Case
c) Agreement between Farmers and Government Is Approved by State Senate
d) B & C
e) All of the above
f) None of the above

5. Which of the following titles has capitalization that is considered grammatically **incorrect**?

a) New State-run Insurance Program to Be Available by December
b) A Comparison of Thematic Conventions in Eighteenth- and Nineteenth-Century Literature
c) Company to Release a New Up-To-Date Software Fix
d) A & C
e) All of the above
f) None of the above

Foreign Loanwords and Loan Translations

Definition

English takes many of its words from different languages around the world. These words are broadly known as **borrowings**, and they are subdivided into two categories: loanwords and loan translations.

A **loanword** is a term taken from another language and used without translation; it has a specific meaning that (typically) does not otherwise exist in a single English word. Sometimes the word's spelling or pronunciation (or both) is slightly altered to accommodate English orthography, but, in most cases, it is preserved in its original language.

A **loan translation** (also known as a **calque**), on the other hand, is a word or phrase taken from another language but translated (either in part or in whole) to corresponding English words while still retaining the original meaning.

Foreign Loanwords

English is influenced by a variety of different languages, and, for that reason, it has a huge number of loanwords, many of which are so entrenched in the language that they are rarely even considered to be of foreign origin. In some cases, the meaning of the word when used in English is slightly different or more specific than in the language from which it is taken, but this is not always the case.

A huge amount of words now considered part of the standard English lexicon are technically loanwords from Latin, Greek, or French. Many of these borrowings occurred during the formative years of modern English, and have since been assimilated through changes in spelling and pronunciation into the words we use every day. There are far too many of these loanwords to go over individually. Instead, let's look at some examples that best demonstrate how loanwords are borrowed without (or with very little) change in their original spelling, pronunciation, or meaning:

Loanword	Language of origin	Notes on spelling, pronunciation, and meaning
aficionado	Spanish	Literally "fond of," in English it refers to an ardent fan, supporter, or devotee of some subject or activity.
amateur	French	In French, the term refers to someone who is a lover of some activity. In English, it is used to describe someone who engages in a study, sport, or other activity as a pastime rather than in a professional capacity.
angst	German	In German, *Angst* generally means "fear or anxiety"; in English, it is used to describe an acute feeling of nonspecific anxiety, anguish, or apprehension, usually without a discernible cause.
bacteria	Latin	Plural of the Latin *bacterium*, meaning "a small stick," used to describe the appearance of bacteria when first identified in the early 19th century.
ballet	French	From the French *ballette*, literally "small dance," referring to a theatrical, classical dance characterized by precise conventional steps and graceful movements.
café	French	In English, *café* (also spelled *cafe*, without the accent mark) only refers to a small restaurant in which one can buy food and drinks, usually coffee. In French, *café* (itself a loanword from Italian *caffé*) primarily refers to coffee itself, rather than an establishment that serves it.
chow mein	Chinese	Adapted from Chinese *ch'ao mein*, meaning "fried noodles." In English, it typically refers to a dish consisting of chopped vegetables and meat that is served with these noodles.

cookie	Dutch	Adapted from the Dutch *koekje*, literally meaning "small cake," to refer to small, dry, usually crisp cakes made from sweetened dough.
delicatessen	German	Adapted from German *Delikatessen*, literally meaning "fancy food; a delicacy." In English, it is used to refer to small shops or eateries, known especially for selling chilled, cooked meats. It is often shortened to *deli*, which is also used as an adjective to describe such meats.
et cetera	Latin	Literally meaning "and (*et*) the rest (*cetera*)," it is used more figuratively in English to mean "and other unspecified things of the same type of class" or "and so forth."
faux pas	French	Literally "false step," used in English to mean "a breach in decorum, etiquette, or good manners."
haiku	Japanese	A type of poem that traditionally juxtaposes two disparate ideas or images in 17 *on* (Japanese sound units), separated in three phases of 5, 7, and 5. In English, *on* was translated to "syllables," so haikus in English are typically written in three lines of 5, 7, and 5 syllables, respectively.
jungle	Hindi	An anglicization of the Hindi spelling *jangal*, meaning "a desert, wasteland, forest, or uncultivated area." In English, it refers to an area of dense tropical trees and vegetation.
kindergarten	German	Literally "child garden," referring in both languages to a program or class for young children serving as an introduction to elementary school.
macho	Spanish	Literally meaning "male animal" in Spanish, in English it is used to describe a tough, masculine, or virile person, especially a man.
modus operandi	Latin	Literally "mode of operating," it refers in English to a person's standard method or manner of working (used in law enforcement to describe a criminal's or suspect's behavior).
noodle	German	Adapted from the term *Nudel*, with the same meaning (a thin, ribbon-like piece of pasta).
oeuvre	French	Literally meaning "work," it is more commonly used in English to refer to the sum of work produced by a creative person (a writer, painter, composer, etc.) over the course of a lifetime.
orangutan	Malay	Literally meaning "man of the woods," in English it refers to arboreal apes with shaggy, reddish-brown hair.
pajamas	Hindi	The Hindi term *pajama* originated from Persian *payjama*, which perhaps influenced the standard British English spelling, *pyjamas*.
patio	Spanish	In Spanish, this term refers to an inner courtyard of a house that has no roof. While it shares this meaning in English, it more often refers to a typically paved outdoor space adjoined to a house used for dining and recreation.
piano	Italian	In both languages, *piano* primarily refers to the musical instrument with a manual keyboard that triggers hammers to strike metal wires that then produce the sound. It is short for the longer Italian word *pianoforte*.
prima donna	Italian	Literally meaning "first lady," referring to the leading female singer in an opera company. It is more commonly used in English to refer to a self-centered, temperamental, petulant person.
quid pro quo	Latin	Literally, "something for something." In English, it is used to mean "something done in exchange or compensation for something else."

smorgasbord	Swedish	Adapted from the Swedish term *smörgåsbord*, meaning "open-faced sandwich table." It refers specifically to a buffet-style meal consisting of a variety of different dishes. By extension in English, it is used figuratively to describe a wide variety of different options or elements, as in, "The festival features a **smorgasbord** of musical talents."
sombrero	Spanish	In both languages, this term refers to a broad-brimmed hat with a high crown.
tycoon	Japanese	Adapted from the Japanese term *taikun*, meaning "great lord, prince, or high commander," a title used by foreigners when referring to the Japanese shogunate. In English, it was anglicized as *tycoon*, and it now means a wealthy, powerful, and influential businessperson or magnate.
umami	Japanese	Literally "tasty things," this term refers to the savory taste sensation occurring in broths and meats.
vigilante	Spanish	Literally meaning "watchman," it is used in English to refer to a person who pursues and punishes suspected criminals outside of the law.

Loan Translations (Calques)

While loanwords are used with little or no change to the spelling (or phonetic spelling) of the original word, loan translations are instead an idiomatic word or phrase that is translated literally into English, but used with the same or similar meaning as the original.

There are far fewer loan translations in English than there are loanwords, but there are still too many to include in this section, so let's just look at a few common examples:

Loan translation	Language of origin	Original word or phrase	Notes on meaning
angel hair	Italian	*capelli d'angelo*, literally "hair of an angel"	Very thin, long pasta. In English, it is more commonly written as *angel hair pasta*.
brainwashing	Chinese	*xi nao*, literally meaning "wash brain"	"Calculated, forcible indoctrination meant to replace a person's existing beliefs, convictions, or attitudes."
commonplace	Latin	*locus communis*	Originally referring to a literary passage that is generally applicable, in modern English it simply refers to that which is ordinary, common, uninteresting, or unremarkable.
devil's advocate	Latin	*advocatus diaboli*	This term originated in the Roman Catholic Church, referring to an official whose role was to deliberately argue against the canonization of potential saint, in order to expose any possible character flaws of the candidate or weaknesses of evidence in favor of canonization. In modern English, the term refers to anyone who argues against something either for the sake of argument alone, or to help clarify or determine the validity of the opposing cause (rather than due to personal opinions or convictions).
flea market	French	*marché aux puces*, literally "market of the fleas"	A type of informal bazaar consisting of vendors who rent space to sell or barter various goods or merchandise. The term is popularly thought to refer to a particular market in Paris known as the *marché aux puces*, so-called because most of the items being sold were of such age that they were likely to have gathered fleas over time.

it goes without saying	French	*cela/ça va sans dire*	This expression has the same meaning in English as it does in French—that is, "it is or should be generally understood or accepted as self-evident."
let the buyer beware	Latin	*caveat emptor*	This axiom holds that the buyer is responsible for assessing the quality of goods or services before purchasing them. While this loan translation is a common cliché in English, the Latin term itself is also sometimes used as a loan phrase.
lose face	Chinese	*tiu lien*	The phrase means "humiliation" in Chinese, but in English it means "to do something resulting in the loss of status, reputation, or respect from others." The related term *save face* comes from this meaning in English, rather than as another loan translation from Chinese.
masterpiece	Dutch	*meesterstuk*	Originally meaning "the work for which an artist or craftsman is granted the rank of master in a guild or academy," it is used in modern English to refer to any creation that is considered a person's greatest work or is of outstanding quality.
moment of truth	Spanish	*el momento de verdad*	The original Spanish phrase was used in bullfighting to describe the moment at which the matador makes the final, fatal sword thrust into the bull. In English, it more generally refers to a critically decisive or important moment that will test a person's character or resolve, or determine the outcome of something.
New Wave	French	*Nouvelle Vague*	Originally a movement of French cinema in the 1960s, the phrase became popularized as a name for a certain style of music in the late 1970s and early '80s, similar to punk rock but characterized by more melodic music and, often, the use of synthesizers.
rainforest	German	*Regenwald*	A dense tropical forest in an area of high annual rainfall.
rest in peace	Latin	*requiescat in pace*, literally "may he or she begin to rest in peace"	Said of someone who has passed away, and commonly written on tombstones.
wisdom tooth	Latin	*dens sapientiae*	One of the four rearmost molar teeth, so named due to their appearance at the onset of adulthood, usually between age 17–25.
world-view	German	*Weltanschauung*, literally "world perception"	An overall conception of life, the world, and humanity's place therein.

Quiz

(answers start on page 463)

1. Which term refers to foreign words that are used in English without being translated from the original language?

a) Foreign loanwords
b) Loan translations

2. The term **calque** is another word for to:

a) Foreign loanwords
b) Loan translations

American English vs. British English Spelling

While English is fairly uniform in terms of structure and spelling across the various regions in which it is the native language, there are a few prominent differences that have arisen over the years. These differences are most notably codified between two major English-speaking regions, resulting in American English (AmE) and British English (BrE). (It's important to remember that there are many other variations [Canadian English, Australian English, etc.] that may incorporate elements of both or may be subtly different in their own right, but the biggest and most consistent spelling changes are most easily divided into American and British variants.)

Most of the differences between these two varieties of English have to do with the **endings** of certain types of words, but there are differences that appear in other parts of the word as well. We'll start with one of the most common: words ending in "-er" vs. "-re."

"-er" vs. "-re"

Many words in British English are spelled with "-re" when that ending follows a consonant. This spelling is a reflection of the French spellings of the words from which they were derived. In American English, we (almost) universally find "-er" after a consonant at the end of a word. This (along with many other uniquely American spelling patterns) was established by Noah Webster in the 19th century to more naturally reflect the word's pronunciation.

For example:

American English	British English
caliber	cali**bre**
center	cen**tre**
fiber	fi**bre**
goiter	goi**tre**
liter	li**tre**
luster	lus**tre**
maneuver	mano**euvre** (the other spelling difference ["e" vs. "oe"] will be discussed later)
meager	mea**gre**
meter	me**tre** (when describing a unit of length)
ocher	och**re**
reconnoiter	reconnoi**tre**
saber	sa**bre**
scepter	scep**tre**
sepulcher	sepul**chre**
somber	som**bre**
specter	spec**tre**
theater	thea**tre**

This difference in spelling is maintained when we add most suffixes—for instance, the American English spelling *center* becomes *centered* or *centering*, while the British English conjugations are *centred* and *centring*. However, this is not always true; there are some vowel suffixes that, when attached to words ending in either "-er" or "-re," cause **E** to be omitted in **both** spellings:

• caliber, calibre→cali**brate**
• center, centre→cen**tral**, cen**tric**, cen**trist**
• fiber, fibre→fib**roid**, fib**rous**
• luster, lustre→lust**rous**
• meter, metre→met**ric**
• sepulcher, sepulchre→sepulch**ral**
• specter, spectre→spect**ral**
• theater, theatre→theat**rical**

Words that always end in "-er"

While there are quite a few words that have different endings in American vs. British English, there are many more by far that share the same ending, most common of which is "-er." For example:

• ang**er**
• aug**er**
• dang**er**
• badg**er**
• blubb**er**
• blust**er**
• clust**er**
• disast**er**
• eag**er**
• fing**er**
• holst**er**
• mast**er**
• met**er** (when used to describe an instrument that takes measurements)
• moth**er**
• riv**er**
• semest**er**
• sist**er**
• timb**er** (referring to trees or wood; has a separate meaning from *timbre*, referring to sound tones)
• trimest**er**
• udd**er**
• wat**er**

As a suffix, "-er" is used to indicate a noun of agency, in which case its spelling is the same in both regions. There are far too many to include here, so we'll just look at a few common examples:

• adopt**er**
• batt**er**
• cater**er**
• defend**er**
• embroider**er**
• formatt**er**
• giv**er**
• golf**er**
• loiter**er**
• propell**er**
• read**er**
• respond**er**
• shredd**er**
• travel**er***
• writ**er**

(*Note that while *traveler* is spelled with "-er" in both AmE and BrE, there is another spelling difference between the regions: in AmE, we only spell the word with one **L**, while, in BrE, it is spelled with two **L**s. We'll discuss this convention separately further on.)

Words that always end in "-re"

While the "-er" ending is much more common in both American and British English, there are also many words ending in "-re" that are standard in both regions. Almost all of these end in **C** + "-re," which ensures that we pronounce a "hard **C**" (/k/), rather than the soft **C** (/s/) that almost always accompanies **CE**.

For example:

• ac**re**
• chanc**re**
• euch**re**
• luc**re**
• massac**re**

- mediocre
- ogre
- timbre (referring to sound and tone; has a separate meaning from *timber*, referring to trees or wood)

In other cases, the "-re" ending is carried over from foreign loanwords and reflects the pronunciation of the final syllable, as in:

- cadre (/ˈkædri/ or /ˈkɑdreɪ/)
- chèvre (/ˈʃɛvrə/)
- émigré (/ˈɛmɪˌgreɪ/)
- double entendre (/ˈdʌbəl ɑnˈtɑndrə/)
- genre (/ˈʒɑnrə/)
- macabre (/məˈkɑbrə/, /məˈkɑb/, or /məˈkɑbər/)
- oeuvre (French pronunciation: /œvrə/)

"-or" vs. "-our"

The suffix "-or" is a word-forming element used to create nouns of state, condition, or quality that was originally derived from the Latin "-orem." Old French adapted the Latin ending as "-our," and it is this ending that originally informed the spelling in English. While British English retained the "-our" spelling for many words derived from Latin, American English dropped the silent U in most (but not all) spellings around the beginning of the 19th century.

Let's look at a breakdown of words that end in "-or" in American English and in "-our" in British English:

American English	British English
arbor	arbour
ardor	ardour
armor	armour
behavior	behaviour
candor	candour
clamor	clamour
clangor	clangour
color	colour
demeanor	demeanour
dolor	dolour
enamor	enamour
endeavor	endeavour
favor	favour
fervor	fervour
flavor	flavour
harbor	harbour
honor	honour
humor	humour
labor	labour
neighbor	neighbour
odor	odour
parlor	parlour
rancor	rancour
rigor	rigour
rumor	rumour
savior	saviour
savor	savour
splendor	splendour
succor	succour
tumor	tumour
valor	valour
vapor	vapour
vigor	vigour

268

This spelling difference *usually* carries forward when we add suffixes to the end of the word, but there are some exceptions, which we'll look at after these examples:

American English	British English
arbor→arbored, arbors	arbour→arboured, arbours
ardor→ardors	ardour→ardours
armor→armored, armorer, armors, armory	armour→armoured, armourer, armours, armoury
behavior→behavioral, behaviors	behaviour→behavioural, behaviours
candor→candors	candour→candours
clamor→clamored, clamoring, clamors	clamour→clamoured, clamouring, clamours
clangor→clangored, clangoring, clangors	clangour→clangoured, clangouring, clangours
color→colored, colorful, coloring, colors	colour→coloured, colourful, colouring, colours
demeanor→demeanors	demeanour→demeanours
dolor→dolors	dolour→dolours
enamor→enamored, enamoring, enamors	enamour→enamoured, enamouring, enamours
endeavor→endeavored, endeavoring, endeavors	endeavour→endeavoured, endeavouring, endeavours
favor→favored, favorer, favoring, favors	favour→favoured, favourer, favouring, favours
fervor→fervors	fervour→fervours
flavor→flavored, flavoring, flavors, flavorsome	flavour→flavoured, flavouring, flavours, flavoursome
harbor→harbored, harboring, harbors	harbour→harboured, harbouring, harbours
honor→honorable, honored, honoring, honors	honour→honourable, honoured, honouring, honours
humor→humored, humoring, humors	humour→humoured, humouring, humours
labor→labored, laborer, laboring, labors	labour→laboured, labourer, labouring, labours
neighbor→neighbored, neighborhood, neighboring, neighbors	neighbour→neighboured, neighbourhood, neighbouring, neighbours
odor→odorful, odorless, odors	odour→odourful, odourless, odours
parlor→parlors	parlour→parlours
rancor→rancors	rancour→rancours
rigor→rigors	rigour→rigours
rumor→rumored, rumoring, rumors	rumour→rumoured, rumouring, rumours
savior→savior	saviour→saviour
savor→savored, savoring, savors, savory	savour→savoured, savouring, savours, savoury
splendor→splendors	splendour→splendours
succor→succored, succoring, succors	succour→succoured, succouring, succours
tumor→tumors	tumour→tumours
valor→valors	valour→valours
vapor→vapored, vaporer, vaporish, vaporless, vapory	vapour→vapoured, vapourer, vapourish, vapourless, vapoury

The British English spellings for *some* of these words lose their distinctive **U** when they attach to a few specific suffixes: "-ous," "-ate," "-ation," "-ant," "-ific," and "-ize/-ise." (Also note that we must use prefixes to form some of these terms.) For example:

Construction	Examples
Adjective + "-ous"	arborous clamorous dolorous humorous odorous laborious rancorous rigorous tumorous valorous vaporous vigorous
Adjective + "-ate"	elaborate evaporate invigorate
Adjective + "-ation"	coloration enamoration
Adjective + "-ant"	colorant deodorant
Adjective + "-ific"	colorific honorific
Adjective + "-ize/-ise"	arborize/ise colorize/ise deodorize/ise vaporize/ise

Words that always end in "-or"

Like the suffix "-er," "-or" is also used to indicate a noun of agency, in which case it is spelled without a **U** in both regions. There are hundreds of words that take this ending, so let's just look at a few common examples:

• act**or**
• auth**or**
• calculat**or**
• counsel**or***
• direct**or**
• educat**or**
• elevat**or**
• generat**or**
• govern**or**
• instruct**or**
• invent**or**
• jur**or**
• liberat**or**
• motivat**or**
• narrat**or**
• process**or**

- profess**or**
- react**or**
- refrigerat**or**
- sculpt**or**
- spectat**or**
- terminat**or**
- vend**or**

(*Like *traveler vs. traveller*, *counselor* is spelled *counsellor* in British English.)

There are also other "non-agency" nouns that have the "-or" ending in both American and British English, as well. For instance:

- ancest**or**
- alligat**or**
- corrid**or**
- dec**or**
- err**or**
- fact**or**
- mirr**or**
- horr**or**
- sect**or**
- strid**or**
- stup**or**
- terr**or**
- torp**or**
- trait**or**

Words that always end in "-our"

While the "-our" spelling is distinctive to British English in most cases, there are a few words that will be spelled with the silent **U** in both regions:

- am**our**
- cont**our**
- det**our**
- glam**our**
- param**our**
- vel**our**

Note that, like some of the British English terms we looked at earlier, the **U** in *amour* and *glamour* is dropped when the suffix "-ous" is attached, resulting in *amorous* and *glamorous*. Likewise, *glamorize* is much more common than *glamourize*.

"-ize" vs. "-ise"

The suffix "-ize" is used to form verbs, and it is ultimately derived from the Greek verb-forming element "-izein" (later "-izare" in Latin). This Greek suffix became "-iser" in Old French, and it is this form from which the English ending "-ise" was originally derived. The French-origin ending is what still prevails in British English, but American English changed the ending to "-ize" to better approximate the original Greek. (For this reason, some British language authorities recommend the "-ize" ending, despite the prevalence of "-ise" in British English.)

This is a very standard convention, and almost all of the hundreds of words ending in "-ize" in American English will be spelled "-ise" in British English; here are just a few examples:

American English	British English
apologize	apologise
authorize	authorise
baptize	baptise
brutalize	brutalise
capitalize	capitalise
characterize	characterise
democratize	democratise
destabilize	destabilise
economize	economise
equalize	equalise
fictionalize	fictionalise
fossilize	fossilise
generalize	generalise
globalize	globalise
humanize	humanise
hypnotize	hypnotise
idealize	idealise
incentivize	incentivise
jeopardize	jeopardise
legalize	legalise
localize	localise
marginalize	marginalise
merchandize	merchandise*
naturalize	naturalise
normalize	normalise
optimize	optimise
organize	organise
personalize	personalise
popularize	popularise
rationalize	rationalise
revolutionize	revolutionise
sensationalize	sensationalise
socialize	socialise
theorize	theorise
tranquilize	tranquilise
verbalize	verbalise
visualize	visualise
westernize	westernise

(*The noun form is also spelled "merchandise" in both AmE and BrE, but the ending is pronounced /-daɪs/.)

Verbs that always end in "-ise"

While the American English convention of using the "-ize" ending for verbs is very reliable, there are a number of words that can **only** be spelled with "-ise," regardless of the preference of the region:
• advertise
• advise
• arise
• chastise
• circumcise
• comprise
• compromise
• despise

- dev**ise**
- disgu**ise**
- exc**ise**
- exerc**ise**
- franch**ise**
- improv**ise**
- inc**ise**
- prom**ise** (though this is pronounced /ˈprɑmɪs/)
- r**aise**
- repr**ise**
- rev**ise**
- r**ise**
- superv**ise**
- surm**ise**
- surpr**ise**
- telev**ise**

Most of these are derived from existing French verbs, which is why the ending "-ise" only attaches to incomplete roots.

Verbs that always end in "-ize"

There are also a handful of verbs that always take the "-ize" ending, even in British English:

- caps**ize**
- pr**ize** (when meaning "to value highly" or "estimate the worth of"; when it means "to force or move, as with a lever," it is usually spelled *prise* in British English)
- se**ize**
- s**ize**

"-lyze" vs. "-lyse"

The endings "-lyze" and "-lyse" are both derived from another suffix, "-lysis" (as in *analysis, paralysis*, etc.). Likely due to their pronunciation, they follow the same pattern as "-ize" and "-ise," with the former being standard in American English, while the latter is standard in British English. Fortunately, there are not many words that end with this suffix (and several are only used in medical terminology), and the American–British distinction holds true for each:

American English	British English
ana**lyze**	ana**lyse**
auto**lyze**	auto**lyse**
cata**lyze**	cata**lyse**
dia**lyze**	dia**lyse**
electro**lyze**	electro**lyse**
hemo**lyze**	haemo**lyse** (note the other spelling difference, which we'll address later)
hydro**lyze**	hydro**lyse**
para**lyze**	para**lyse**
photo**lyze**	photo**lyse**
plasmo**lyze**	plasmo**lyse**
pyro**lyze**	pyro**lyse**

Doubling consonants in American English vs. British English

Because most vowel suffixes are able to replace silent E by preserving the root word's pronunciation and meaning, we often have to double the final consonant of a root word when it precedes a vowel suffix to avoid confusion. This convention largely depends on the number of syllables and on which part of the word is stressed vocally (see the section Doubling Consonants with Vowel Suffixes to learn more about these rules). While this convention is applied fairly consistently in American English, there are some notable exceptions that occur in British English—specifically, words ending in **L**.

Doubling L before vowel suffixes

Perhaps the most commonly confused spelling convention is whether or not to double the final **L** in two-syllable words before a vowel suffix. In American English, we follow the rule that if the word has an emphasis on the final syllable before the vowel suffix, then the **L** is doubled. However, most words ending in a single **L** are stressed on the first syllable, so **L** remains singular.

(In the following table of examples, text in **bold** represents syllable stress.)

Emphasis on first syllable	Suffixed Words	Emphasis on last syllable	Suffixed Words
cancel (/ˈkænsəl/)	**can**celed, **can**celing	com**pel** (/kəmˈpɛl/)	com**pel**led, com**pel**ling
equal (/ˈikwəl/)	**e**qualed, **e**qualing	ex**cel** (/ɪkˈsɛl/)	ex**cel**led, ex**cel**ling (However, *excellent*, with two Ls, is pronounced /ˈɛksələnt/.)
label (/ˈleɪbəl/)	**la**beled, **la**beling	la**pel** (/ləˈpɛl/)	la**pel**led
model (/ˈmɑdəl/)	**mo**deled, **mo**deling	pro**pel** (/prəˈpɛl/)	pro**pel**lant, pro**pel**led
travel (/ˈtræəl/)	**tra**veled, **tra**veling	re**bel** (/rɪˈbɛl/)	re**bel**led, re**bel**lion

In British English, on the other hand, a final **L** that follows a vowel is almost always doubled before "-ed," "-er," and "-ing" **regardless** of where the stress occurs in the word.

For the sake of comparison, let's see the preferred American English spellings (with single **L**) of some common words alongside their preferred British English spellings (with doubled **L**):

American English	British English
barrel→barreled, barreling	barrel→barrelled, barrelling
cancel→canceled, canceling	cancel→cancelled, cancelling
dial→dialed, dialing	dial→dialled, dialling
duel→dueled, dueling	duel→duelled, duelling
fuel→fueled, fueling	fuel→fuelled, fuelling
grovel→groveled, groveling	grovel→grovelled, grovelling
label→labeled, labeling	label→labelled, labelling
model→modeled, modeling	model→modelled, modelling
rival→rivaled, rivaling	rival→rivalled, rivalling
signal→signaled, signaling	signal→signalled, signalling
travel→traveled, traveling	travel→travelled, travelling

If you're writing according to the styles of American English and you can't remember whether to double the final **L** or not, just check which syllable in the word is being stressed. If you're writing in British English, it's a good bet that the **L** should be doubled.

Doubling *L* in American English only

There are a few verbs ending in a single **L** in British English that more commonly end in **two** Ls in American English in their base (uninflected) forms.

For example:

American English	British English
appall	appal
distill	distil
enroll	enrol
enthrall	enthral
fulfill	fulfil
instill	instil

When these verbs attach to suffixes beginning with consonants, such as "-ment" or "-s," these spelling differences remain: American English prefers *distills, enrollment,* and *installment,* for example, while British English prefers *distils, enrolment,* and *instalment.*

When they attach to suffixes beginning with vowels (such as "-ation," "-ed," or "-ing"), on the other hand, **L** is doubled in both regions—e.g., *appalled, distillery, enrolling, installation.*

skillful vs. skilful and willful vs. wilful

Skill and *will* are both spelled with two **L**s in all varieties of English. However, when they attach to the suffix "-ful," British English spelling tends to drop the second **L**, resulting in *skilful* and *wilful.* In American English, there is no change in the root words, resulting in *skillful* and *willful.*

Other consonant doubling differences

combating vs. combatting

The word *combat* has two different pronunciations with different syllabic stress: /ˈkɑmbæt/ (noun) and /kəmˈbæt/ (verb). When we add vowel suffixes to the word, the stress usually remains on the second syllable, but, unlike our previous examples, **T** remains singular in American English:

• comba**t**→comba**t**ed, comba**t**ing, comba**t**ive

Dictionaries often list *comba**tt**ed* and *comba**tt**ing* as acceptable variants in British English, but it is still most common in both styles for **T** to remain singular before the suffixes.

Note that *combative* is the only spelling considered correct in both American and British English.

focused vs. focussed

Another consonant ending that often confuses writers is the **S** in *focus.* Should it be *focused* or *focussed*? Again, there is a difference between American English and British English conventions.

In American English, the **S** is never doubled before a suffix, so its conjugations are *focused, focuses,* and *focusing.* The same rule applies to all forms of the word that have a vowel suffix, as in *focusable* and *focuser.*

This is the most common (and preferred) convention in British English as well, but it is not considered incorrect to spell the conjugations with a doubled **S**—*focussed, focusses, focussing.* (*Focusable* and *focuser* always take just one **S**). However, these double-**S** spellings are much less common and may be seen by some as incorrect, even within the UK.

No matter where in the world you are, it's best to keep the **S** in *focus* singular before a vowel suffix, because it's always correct.

"e" vs. "ae" and "oe"

Many words (especially medical terms) that were derived from Latin roots originally made use of **ligatures**, which are single characters formed from two letters to create specific diphthongs. In English, the two ligatures that survived were œ and æ, but over time these specialized characters were divided back into separate letters, creating the vowel digraphs *ae* and *oe.*

In American English, however, most of the words featuring these divided ligatures dropped the **A** and **O**, leaving just the **E** behind. (In most cases, the pronunciation is the same in both American and British English, though in some words beginning with "e-/oe-," the pronunciation varies slightly.)

American English	British English
Spelled "e"	Spelled "ae"
anemia	anaemia
anesthesia	anaesthesia
bacteremia	bacteraemia
cesium	caesium
dieresis	diaeresis
encyclopedia	encyclopaedia
eon	aeon
feces	faeces
frenum	fraenum
hemoglobin	haemoglobin
hemophilia	haemophilia
hemorrhage	haemorrhage
hemorrhoid	haemorrhoid
ischemia	ischaemia
leukemia	leukaemia
orthopedic	orthopaedic
pediatric	paediatric
paleography	palaeography
paleontology	palaeontology
septicemia	septicaemia
synesthesia	synaesthesia
toxemia	toxaemia
uremia	uraemia
Spelled "e"	Spelled "oe"
apnea	apnoea
celiac	coeliac
diarrhea	diarrhoea
dyspnea	dyspnoea
edema	oedema
esophagus (/ɪˈsɑfəgəs/)	oesophagus (/iːˈsɑfəgəs/)
estrogen (/ˈɛstrədʒən/)	oestrogen (/ˈiːstrədʒən/)
estrus (/ˈɛstrəs/)	oestrus (/ˈiːstrəs/)
fetus	foetus
gonorrhea	gonorrhoea
maneuver	manoeuvre
subpena	subpoena

Words spelled "ae" and "oe" in both regions

Not many words retain the Latin-based digraphs in American English, but there are a few words that share the spelling in both regions:

Words with "ae"	Words with "oe"
aegis	amoeba
aesthetic	Oedipus
archaeology	Phoebe
paean	phoenix

Note that all the words featuring "ae" and the word *amoeba* have variant spellings with just "e" (*egis, esthetic, archeology, pean,* and *ameba*), but these are far less common.

Words with single letters in both regions

While American English much more commonly drops the additional vowel in the Latin digraphs "ae" and "oe," there are some words in both American and British English that only retain the **E**:

• chimera (derived from Latin *Chimaera*)
• demon (though *daemon* is sometimes used in stylized writing)
• ecology (originally *oecology*)
• economy (derived from Latin *oeconomia*)
• ecumenical (derived from Latin *oecumenicus*)
• enigma (derived from Latin *aenigma*)
• homeopathy (still spelled *homoeopathy* in British English, but less commonly)
• hyena (less commonly, *hyaena*)
• fetid (less commonly, *foetid,* derived from the incorrect Latin term *foetidus*)
• medieval (less commonly, *mediaeval*)
• primeval (much less commonly, *primaeval*)

Using "-ae" to form plurals

Words taken directly from Latin that end in "-a" are made plural using "-ae" in both American and British English. (Note, however, that the Latinate "-ae" ending has been replaced in modern English by the standard plural suffix "-s" in many common, everday words.)

For example:
• alga→alg**ae**
• amoeba→amoeb**ae**
• antenna→antenn**ae** (more commonly *antennas*)
• aorta→aort**ae** (more commonly *aortas*)
• cloaca→cloac**ae**
• copula→copul**ae** (more commonly *copulas*)
• cornea→corne**ae** (more commonly *corneas*)
• ephemera→ephemer**ae**
• formula→formul**ae** (more commonly *formulas*)
• hernia→herni**ae** (more commonly *hernias*)
• hyperbola→hyperbol**ae** (more commonly *hyperbolas*)
• placenta→placent**ae**
• pupa→pup**ae**
• retina→retin**ae** (more commonly *retinas*)
• scapula→scapul**ae**
• supernova→supernov**ae**
• vertebra→vertebr**ae**
• uvula→uvul**ae**

Less common differences

While the conventions we've looked at thus far encompass a fairly broad range of terms, there are some other spelling differences between the two regions that only exist for a small selection of words.

"-ward" vs. "-wards"

Adverbs and prepositions formed using the suffix "-ward" can also be spelled "-wards," with no change in meaning. While both spellings occur in American and British English alike, the "-ward" versions are more common in the US, while the "-wards" versions are more common in the UK:

More common in American English	More common in British English
afterward	afterwards
backward	backwards
downward	downwards
eastward	eastwards
forward	forwards
frontward	frontwards
homeward	homewards
inward	inwards
leeward	leewards
northward	northwards
onward	onwards
outward	outwards
rearward	rearwards
seaward	seawards
skyward	skywards
toward	towards
upward	upwards
westward	westwards
windward	windwards

It's important to note that many of the words ending in "-ward" can also function as adjectives, but those ending in "-wards" **cannot**, regardless of region. For example:

✔ "I just saw a van like that driving **eastward**." (adverb)

✔ "I just saw a van like that driving **eastwards**." (adverb)

✔ "There is a strong **eastward** wind coming in off the sea." (adjective)

✘ "There is a strong **eastwards** wind coming in off the sea." (adjective—incorrect)

✔ "I bumped into someone while I was walking **backward**." (adverb)

✔ "I bumped into someone while I was walking **backwards**." (adverb)

✔ "Her parents have a real **backward** way of thinking." (adjective)

✘ "Her parents have a real **backwards** way of thinking." (adjective—incorrect)

If you're trying to determine whether it should be spelled "-ward" or "-wards," remember that the option without an **S** is always correct.

"-ense" vs. "-ence"

A handful of nouns ending in "-ense" in American English will be spelled "-ence" in British English:

American English	British English
defense	defence
license	licence
offense	offence
pretense	pretence

The term *license/licence* is a bit of a special case, though—in British English, it **is** spelled *license* when it is functioning as a verb, as in, "The state *licensed* us to sell merchandise on these premises."

Also note that while *defence* is spelled with a **C** in British English, the derived terms *defensible* and *defensive* are spelled with an **S**, the same as in American English.

These four terms are the only ones that have a difference in their endings between American and British English; any other words ending in "-ense" (as in *expense* or *sense*) or "-ence" (as in *experience* or *patience*) are spelled the same in both regions.

"-og" vs. "-ogue"

Another spelling difference that is often pointed out between the two regions is that American spellings favor the ending "-og," while British spellings favor "-ogue." However, like "-ense" vs. "-ence," there are only four word pairs in which this is true:

American English	British English
analog	analogue
catalog	catalogue
dialog	dialogue
homolog	homologue

(Note that all of these terms can be spelled "-ogue" in American English, but this is less common. Additionally, *analog* is also preferred in British English when referring specifically to computers.)

This convention is not reliable, though, as there are quite a few words that only (or predominantly) end in "-ogue" in American English as well as British English:

• apologue
• demagogue
• epilogue
• ideologue
• monologue
• pedagogue
• prologue
• rogue
• synagogue
• travelogue
• vogue

Miscellaneous spelling differences

In addition to spelling patterns that affect multiple words, there are also a number of unique pairs that have specific spelling differences between them. In some cases, the difference in spelling reflects a subtle difference in meaning, pronunciation, or both; other times, the spelling is the only difference.

aging vs. *ageing*

These two spellings are about equally common in British English, but, in American English, *aging* is the preferred spelling by a wide margin. There is no difference in pronunciation (/ ˈeɪʤɪŋ/).

airplane vs. *aeroplane*

The terms *airplane* and *aeroplane* are both commonly used in British English, but, in American English, only *airplane* is in common use. Because of the additional O, there is a slight difference in the two forms' pronunciation: *airplane* is pronounced /ˈɛrˌpleɪn/, while *aeroplane* is pronounced /ˈɛərəˌpleɪn/.

aluminum vs. *aluminium*

Aluminum is an amended form of the word *alumium*, coined by the English chemist Sir Humphry Davy in 1807. In American English, this form came to be the standard spelling, but British scientists changed the ending again to form *aluminium*, which parallels the spelling of other metallic elements (such as *lithium, potassium,* and *sodium*). As with *aeroplane*, the additional vowel changes the overall pronunciation of the word (this time even affecting which syllable is stressed): *aluminum* is pronounced /əˈlumənəm/, while *aluminium* is pronounced /ˌæljʊˈmɪnɪəm/.

annex vs. *annexe*

The word *annex* can function as a noun and a verb in both American and British English. When functioning as a verb, it is spelled the same in both regions; as a noun, British English spells it with a silent E at the end, reflecting its French origin.

artifact vs. *artefact*

Artefact is the older spelling of the word, and it is still the favored version in British English. The variant, *artifact*, became the standard spelling in American English in the early 1900s. There is no difference in pronunciation between the two (/ˈɑrtəˌfækt/).

behoove vs. *behove*

The verb *behoove* is derived from the noun *behoof*, an archaic term meaning "advantage, benefit, or use." In British English, the verb is spelled *behove*, possibly in relation to the German *behoven*. While both spellings were originally pronounced the same way (/bɪˈhuv/), rhyming with *move* or *groove*, the British English spelling is now usually pronounced the same way as *rove* or *stove* (/bɪˈhəʊv/).

check vs. *cheque*

These spellings refer only to written slips that authorize a bank to pay the amount specified from a particular account, with *check* being preferred in the US and *cheque* the standard in the UK. Both spellings have the same pronunciation, /tʃɛk/. (The term *checking account* would therefore be written *chequing account* in British English, although the term *current account* is preferred.)

In every other use of *check*, both as a noun or a verb, it is spelled the same way in both regions.

chili vs. *chilli*

In American English, *chili* is the most common spelling, though *chile* (short for the Mexican Spanish term *chile con carne*) is also a common variant. In British English, though, *chilli* (with two **L**s) is more common.

cozy vs. *cosy*

Cozy is the preferred spelling in the US, while *cosy* is preferred in the UK. There is no change in pronunciation.

curb vs. *kerb*

The variant spelling *kerb* is favored in British English for one specific meaning: "a concrete stone border along the edge of a street forming part of a gutter." For any other meanings of *curb*, either as a noun or a verb, the spelling is the same in both regions.

draft vs. *draught*

Despite their starkly different spellings, *draft* and *draught* are both pronounced in very similar ways: /dræft/ (American English) and /drɑːft/ (British English).

The American English spelling *draft* rose to prominence to better represent the pronunciation phonetically, and it is used for <u>all</u> meanings of the word.

In British English, the spelling *draught* is commonly used as a noun or modifier when referring to a current of air drawn into an enclosed space or into one's lungs, a portion of a drink or the act of drinking, beer or wine that is stored in and served from a cask, or the act of pulling a heavy load. For example:
• "Do you feel a **draught** coming from the window?"
• "I prefer **draught** beer."
• "We need to buy a new **draught** horse."
• "He poured out a healthy **draught** of the tonic."
(The term *draughts* is also the name of the game that's called *checkers* in the US.)

Draft, on the other hand, is preferred when discussing a rough outline or preliminary plan or sketch (functioning either as a noun or a verb) or a check/cheque issued by the bank guaranteed against its own funds. For example:
• "Could you please **draft** a report for our December earnings?"
• "I have a few changes I need to make to the first **draft** of my essay."
• "Do you know how long it takes for the bank to issue a bank **draft**?"

gray vs. grey

In American English, *gray* is the most common spelling, while, in British English (and most other English-speaking regions), *grey* is preferred. This carries over to inflections of verbs (*grayed/greyed, graying/greying*) and the formation of comparative and superlative adjectives (*grayer/greyer, grayest/greyest*). There is no difference in pronunciation.

licorice vs. liquorice

The American English spelling of this noun, *licorice*, comes from Old French *licorece*, which specified the plant and/or its root from which candy, medicines, and liqueurs were flavored. The British English spelling, *liquorice*, is perhaps influenced by the process of distilling the root into a liquid.

In American English, the word is most commonly pronounced /ˈlɪkərɪʃ/, while the British English pronunciation is more commonly /ˈlɪkərɪs/—note that it is only the final **C** that changes in pronunciation, rather than the part of the word that is spelled differently.

mold vs. mould

Both in reference to fungi and to the cast used to form the shape of something, American English exclusively favors *mold*, while British English exclusively favors *mould*. This carries over to inflections of verbs (*molded/moulded, molding/moulding*, etc.) and the formation of adjectives (*moldy/mouldy, moldier/mouldier*, etc.). There is no difference in pronunciation.

Unlike the "-or/-our" difference, this discrepancy in spelling does not occur with any other words ending in "-old/-ould."

mom(my) vs. mum(my)

Mommy and its shortened form *mom* are distinct to American English, whereas *mummy* (when referring to a mother) and the shortened *mum* are distinct to British English. The reason for this difference in spelling (and subsequent pronunciation) has to do with regional evolutions of the term *mama*—another word for *mother* that represents infant speech sounds.

omelet vs. omelette

The American English *omelet* is an adaptation of the French-origin word *omelette*. British English simply prefers the original spelling, which remains standard in the region.

pajamas vs. pyjamas

In American English, the word for sleepwear is spelled *pajamas*, while British English favors *pyjamas*. This spelling difference likely has to do with the Urdu and Persian terms from which the word is derived and the alphabetic representation of the initial vowel sound; however, both spellings of the English term are pronounced the same way (/pəˈdʒɑməz/).

plow vs. plough

In all meanings of the word, American English favors the simplified spelling *plow*, while British English prefers the spelling *plough* (possibly to reflect the original Old English *plog* or *ploh*).

practice vs. practise

In British English, *practice* and *practise* follow the same pattern as *advice* and *advise*—that is, *practice* is used as a noun, while *practise* functions as a verb. The difference is that *practice* and *practise* are both pronounced /ˈpræktɪs/, while *advice* is pronounced /ædˈvaɪs/ and *advise* is pronounced /ædˈvaɪz/.

In American English (perhaps to avoid confusion, since the difference in spelling doesn't result in any change in pronunciation), the spelling *practice* is used for both the noun and the verb.

program vs. programme

In American English, *program* is used for every meaning of the word.

In British English, *program* is only used in reference to computer programming. For any other senses of the word, the longer form *programme* is used.

story vs. *storey*

In American English, *story* is used for every meaning of the word.

In British English, a *story* refers to a narrative of some kind, whether true or fictitious. A *storey*, on the other hand, refers to the horizontal section of a building.

tire vs. *tyre*

In American English, *tire* is used for every meaning of the word.

In British English, though, the spelling *tyre* is used specifically in reference to a rubber wheel covering, while *tire* is used as a verb meaning "to lose or reduce energy, strength, patience, or tolerance."

vise vs. *vice*

In American English, *vise* is either a noun (referring to a heavy clamp that holds something in place) or a verb (referring to the action performed by a *vise*). A *vice*, on the other hand, refers to a practice, habit, or behavior that is considered evil or immoral. Both spellings are pronounced /vaɪs/.

In British English, there is no such distinction; *vice* is used for each of these meanings.

yogurt vs. *yoghurt*

In British English, both *yogurt* and *yoghurt* are used, though the latter is a bit more common. In American English, it is almost exclusively written as *yogurt*.

Quotation marks in American and British English

Finally, in addition to differences in how words are spelled, there are also differences between how the two regions use **quotation marks**.

There are two forms of quotation marks: **double quotation marks** (" ") and **single quotation marks** (' '). American English almost exclusively uses double quotation marks (except when a quotation appears within a quotation), while British English tends to favor single quotation marks (although it is not uncommon to see double quotation marks used in British English as well).

In American English, a period or comma used at the end of direct speech always appears <u>within</u> the quotation marks. In British English, however, if the quotation ends in a period or comma, it is usually placed <u>outside</u> the quotation mark.

For example:

American English	British English
The CEO said, "This is a great day for the company." "I want to be a doctor when I grow up," Susy told us yesterday.	The CEO said, 'This is a great day for the company'. 'I want to be a doctor when I grow up', Susy told us yesterday.

Note that if a quoted sentence ends in a question mark or exclamation point that <u>belongs</u> to the quotation, it will appear <u>within</u> the quotation marks. If the question mark or exclamation point belongs to the <u>overall</u> sentence (that is, it isn't actually part of the quotation), it will appear <u>outside</u> the quotation marks. This is the same in both American and British English. For example:
• Samantha asked, 'How long will it take to get there?'
• But I don't want to just "see how things go"!

Quiz
(answers start on page 463)

1. Which of the following words is spelled according to **British English** spelling patterns?

a) color
b) theatre
c) enrollment
d) leukemia

2. Which of the following spellings occurs in **both** American and British English?

a) centers
b) centring
c) centered
d) central

3. Which of the following spellings is **incorrect** in **both** American and British English?

a) advertize
b) centralise
c) realise
d) specialize

4. What is the convention in **American English** regarding the Latin diphthongs "ae" and "oe"?

a) Always keep both letters
b) Usually keep both letters
c) Always drop the "a-" and the "o-"
d) Usually drop the "a-" and the "o-"

5. Which type of quotation marks are preferred in **British English**?

a) Double quotation marks
b) Single quotation marks

6. In **American English**, when do periods (full stops) and commas appear **within** quotation marks?

a) Always
b) Only if they belong to the quoted sentence
c) Only if they belong to the non-quoted sentence
d) Never

Pronunciation Conventions

Like spelling, English pronunciation is especially tricky due its seeming lack of consistency and intuitive structure.

The basic elements of pronunciation all relate to the specific vowel and consonant letters, all of which are described in the section on The Alphabet. In this section, we'll look at some of the more difficult aspects of pronunciation, specifically focusing on tricky vowel sounds and tricky consonant sounds that are hard to guess simply by looking at the letters of a word. We'll also look at the various silent letters, paying particular attention to the various roles of Silent E.

After that, we will discuss the ways in which syllables are formed and divided within words, and then we'll conclude by looking at the stress we place on syllables within a word and on particular words within a sentence.

Tricky Vowel Sounds

Vowel sounds are an especially tricky part of English pronunciation because of how flexible and malleable they can be. One particular aspect of vowel sounds that can be confusing is when multiple vowel sounds blend together within a single syllable, because there are no clear divisions between the sounds like there are for consonants. We'll briefly look at the three different ranges of vowel sounds in this section; continue on to the full section on Tricky Vowel Sounds to learn more about each.

Monophthongs

The most basic vowel sound is known as a **monophthong**, which is a single vowel sound within a single syllable. Most of these are **short vowels**, though there are some **long vowel** monophthongs as well. For example:

Short Vowel Monophthongs	Long Vowel Monophthongs
apple (/ˈæpəl/) bend (/bɛnd/) tip (/tɪp/) pollen (/ˈpɑlən/) cup (/kʌp/) put (/pʊt/) myth (/mɪθ/)	concrete (/ˈkɑnkrit/) friendly (/ˈfrɛndli/) feet (/fit/) exclude (/ɪkˈsklud/) across (/əˈkrɔs/) curve (/kɜrv/)

Diphthongs

A **diphthong** (pronounced /ˈdɪfθɔŋ/) is a single-syllable vowel sound in which the beginning of the sound **glides** to another, slightly different vowel sound. For this reason, diphthongs are often referred to as **gliding vowels**.

There are eight diphthongs in American English, four of which are "traditional" **long vowels** (vowel sounds that are pronounced the same way as the names of the letters), and four of which are produced by certain vowel digraphs or in combination with the letter **R**.

For example:

Traditional Long Vowel Diphthongs	Other Long Vowel Diphthongs
t<u>a</u>pe (/t<u>eɪ</u>p/)	b<u>oy</u> (/b<u>ɔɪ</u>/)
n<u>i</u>ce (/n<u>aɪ</u>s/)	p<u>ou</u>t (/p<u>aʊ</u>t/)
r<u>o</u>pe (/r<u>oʊ</u>p/)	d<u>ee</u>r (/d<u>ɪər</u>/)
c<u>u</u>be (/k<u>ju</u>b/)	st<u>airs</u> (/st<u>ɛər</u>z/)

Triphthongs

Very rarely, a single syllable may contain <u>three</u> vowel sounds that quickly glide together; these sounds are known as **triphthongs**.

There are three triphthongs that are generally agreed upon in American English: /aʊə/ ("ah-oo-uh"), /aɪə/ ("ah-ih-uh"), and /jʊə/ ("ee-oo-uh"). The first occurs when the digraph **OU** is followed by an **R**, the second occurs with the letter combination **IRE**, and the third occurs when **UR** is followed by a **Y, I,** or **silent E**. For example:

- s<u>our</u> (/s<u>aʊər</u>/)
- f<u>ire</u> (/f<u>aɪər</u>/)
- f<u>ury</u> (/ˈf<u>jʊər</u>i/)

Tricky Consonant Sounds

Unlike vowels, many consonant letters will generally make the same consonant sound no matter where they appear in a word. However, some consonant sounds can be made by several different letters when they appear in certain parts of a word or in combination with other consonants. Many of these are covered in the section on consonant digraphs, but there are a few sounds that can be made by several different single letters as well. We'll very briefly look at these sounds here, but you can continue on to the full section on Tricky Consonant Sounds to learn more.

Forming the /k/ Sound

The consonant sound **/k/** can be produced by the consonants **C, K,** and **X,** as well as the consonant digraphs **CC** and **CK** and the combination **QU.** For example:

Letter(s)	Examples
C	<u>c</u>over (/ˈ<u>k</u>ʌvər/) de<u>c</u>ade (/ˈdɛ<u>k</u>eɪd/) basi<u>c</u> (/ˈbeɪsɪ<u>k</u>/)
K	<u>k</u>ennel (/ˈ<u>k</u>ɛnəl/) ris<u>k</u>y (/ˈrɪs<u>k</u>i/) oa<u>k</u> (/oʊ<u>k</u>/)

X (in the sound combinations /ks/ and /kʃ/)	bo**x** (/bɑ**ks**/) to**x**ic (/ˈtɑ**ks**ɪk/) an**x**ious (/ˈæŋ**kʃ**əs/)
CC	o**cc**asion (/əˈ**k**eɪʒən/) a**cc**omplish (/əˈ**k**ɑmplɪʃ/) a**cc**use (/əˈ**k**juz/)
CK	ba**ck** (/bæ**k**/) ro**ck** (/rɑ**k**/) ca**ck**le (/ˈkæ**k**əl/)
QU	e**qu**ipment (/ɪˈ**kw**ɪpmənt/) techni**qu**e (/tɛkˈni**k**/) con**qu**er (/ˈkɑŋ**k**ər/)

Forming the /z/ Sound

The consonant sound /z/ is most often associated with the consonant **Z**, because the correlation between the sound and that letter is very reliable, but it can also be formed from the letters **S** and **X**. For example:

Letter(s)	Examples
Z	bi**z**arre (/bəˈ**z**ɑr/) **z**ap (/**z**æp/) bu**zz** (/bʌ**z**/)
S	cou**s**in (/ˈkʌ**z**ən/) activi**s**m (/ˈæktɪˌvɪ**z**əm/) ha**s** (/hæ**z**/)
X	e**x**ample (/ɪgˈ**z**æmpəl/) e**x**haust (/ɪgˈ**z**ɑst/) **x**ylophone (/ˈ**z**aɪləˌfoʊn/)

Forming the /ʒ/ Sound

The sound /ʒ/ does not have a specific letter or digraph commonly associated with it. Instead, the /ʒ/ sound occurs when the consonants **S**, **G**, and **J** appear next to or between certain vowels. For example:

Letter(s)	Examples
S	deci**s**ion (/dɪˈsɪʒən/) compo**s**ure (/kəmˈpoʊʒər/) amne**s**ia (/æmˈniʒə/)
G	bei**ge** (/beɪʒ/) camoufla**ge** (/ˈkæməˌflɑʒ/) rou**ge** (/ruʒ/)
J	déjà vu (/ˈdeɪʒæ ˈvu/) Di**j**on (/ˌdiˈʒɑn/) Ta**j** Mahal (/tɑʒ məˈhɑl/)

Pronouncing the Letter S

The letter **S** can sometimes be problematic for pronunciation due to the wide range of speech sounds it can represent. Its most common sound is the unvoiced sibilant /s/, but it also makes the /z/ sound (formed the same way, but with the vocal cords engaged), the /ʃ/ sound (the sound associated with the digraph **SH**), and the /ʒ/ sound (made like the /ʃ/ sound, but with the vocal cords engaged).

We'll go over some examples of how S reliably forms each of these sounds, but go to the full section on Pronouncing the Letter S to find out more information.

When *S* is only pronounced /s/

At the beginning of a word

S is almost always pronounced /s/ if it appears at the beginning of a word, as in:
- **s**at (/**s**æt/)
- **s**ocial (/**s**oʊʃəl/)
- **s**yllable (/ˈ**s**ɪləbəl/)
- **s**kip (/**s**kɪp/)
- **s**mall (/**s**mɔl/)
- **s**tart (/**s**tɑrt/)

The only exceptions to this rule are the words *sugar* and *sure*, pronounced /ˈʃʊgər/ and /ʃʊər/, respectively.

As a suffix

S is also always pronounced /s/ when it functions as a suffix coming after an **unvoiced**, non-sibilant consonant sound—that is, after /k/, /f/, /p/, /t/, and /θ/ (the unvoiced **TH** sound). For example:
• book<u>s</u> (/bʊk<u>s</u>/)
• laugh<u>s</u> (/læf<u>s</u>/)
• keep<u>s</u> (/kip<u>s</u>/)
• let'<u>s</u> (/lɛt<u>s</u>/)
• streng<u>th</u><u>s</u> (/strɛŋkθ<u>s</u>/)

SS at the end of a word

Like words that *begin* with **S**, words that end in **SS** <u>always</u> make the /s/ sound. For example:
• aby<u>ss</u> (/əˈbɪ<u>s</u>/)
• cra<u>ss</u> (/kræ<u>s</u>/)
• dre<u>ss</u> (/drɛ<u>s</u>/)
• fu<u>ss</u> (/fʌ<u>s</u>/)
• hi<u>ss</u> (/hɪ<u>s</u>/)
• to<u>ss</u> (/tɑ<u>s</u>/)

Words ending in "-se"

When **S** is followed by a silent E, it will reliably create the /s/ sound when it follows four specific consonants: **L, N, P,** and **R**. For example:
• fal<u>se</u> (/fɔl<u>s</u>/)
• respon<u>se</u> (/rɪˈspɑn<u>s</u>/)
• eclip<u>se</u> (/ɪˈklɪp<u>s</u>/)
• traver<u>se</u> (/trəˈvɜr<u>s</u>/)

When S is only pronounced /z/

As a suffix

If the suffix "-s" comes after a **voiced** consonant sound (/b/, /d/, /g/, /l/, /m/, /n/, /ŋ/, /r/, /ð/, /v/) or a vowel sound, the **S** will be pronounced as /**z**/. When adding "-s" to a word that ends in a voiced or unvoiced **sibilant** speech sound (/s/, /z/, /ʃ/, /ʒ/, /tʃ/, /dʒ/), the suffix becomes "-es" and is pronounced /**ɪz**/. (The same pronunciation is used if an apostrophe-S is added to a word with a sibilant speech sound at the end.)

For example:
• barb<u>s</u> (/bɑrb<u>z</u>/)
• dread<u>s</u> (/drɛd<u>z</u>/)
• egg<u>s</u> (/ɛg<u>z</u>/)
• lull<u>s</u> (/lʌl<u>z</u>/)
• Malcolm'<u>s</u> (/ˈmælkəm<u>z</u>/)
• wive<u>s</u> (/waɪv<u>z</u>/)
• buse<u>s</u> (/bʌs<u>ɪz</u>/)
• comprise<u>s</u> (/kəmˈpraɪz<u>ɪz</u>/)
• Trish'<u>s</u> (/ˈtrɪʃ<u>ɪz</u>/)
• garage<u>s</u> (/gəˈrɑʒ<u>ɪz</u>/)
• pitche<u>s</u> (/ˈpɪtʃ<u>ɪz</u>/)
• smudge<u>s</u> (/ˈsmʌdʒ<u>ɪz</u>/)

In the suffixes "-ism" and "-ise"

One of the few instances in which **S** *is* reliably pronounced /z/ is when the letter combination **SM** appears at the end of a word (most often as a part of the suffix "-ism"). For example:

- activi**sm** (/ˈæktɪˌvɪ**zəm**/)
- cha**sm** (/ˈkæ**zəm**/)
- materiali**sm** (/məˈtɪriəˌlɪ**zəm**/)
- organi**sm** (/ˈɔrgəˌnɪ**zəm**/)
- sarca**sm** (/ˈsɑrˌkæ**zəm**/)

The suffix "-ise" (used to form verbs, especially in British English) is also very reliable in producing the /z/ sound. For example:

- adverti**se** (/ˈædvərˌtaɪ**z**/)
- advi**se** (/ˌædˈvaɪ**z**/)
- ari**se** (/əˈraɪ**z**/)
- compromi**se** (/ˈkɑmprəˌmaɪ**z**/)
- devi**se** (/dəˈvaɪ**z**/)
- exerci**se** (/ˈɛksərˌsaɪ**z**/)
- improvi**se** (/ˈɪmprəˌvaɪ**z**/)
- revi**se** (/rəˈvaɪ**z**/)
- surpri**se** (/sərˈpraɪ**z**/)
- televi**se** (/ˈtɛləˌvaɪ**z**/)

(One exception to this convention is *promise*, which is pronounced /ˈprɑmɪ**s**/.)

Forming the /ʃ/ and /ʒ/ sounds

In addition to /s/ and /z/, **S** can also form the /ʃ/ (as in *wash*) and /ʒ/ (as in *beige*) sounds when it appears in combination with certain suffixes. We saw earlier how it forms the /ʒ/ sound when this combination comes after a vowel; however, several of the same combinations will yield the /ʃ/ sound if they come after **L**, **N**, or another **S**. For example:

S + "-ion"	S + "-ure"	S + "-ual"
propul**s**ion (/prəˈpʌl**ʃ**ən/)	cen**s**ure (/ˈsɛn**ʃ**ər/)	consen**s**ual (/kənˈsɛn**ʃ**uəl/)
dimen**s**ion (/dɪˈmɛn**ʃ**ən/)	in**s**ure (/ɪnˈ**ʃ**ʊər/)	sen**s**ual (/ˈsɛn**ʃ**uəl/)
pa**ss**ion (/ˈpæ**ʃ**ən/)	pre**ss**ure (/ˈprɛ**ʃ**ər/)	

Silent Letters

Because English has evolved from several different sources (Latin, Greek, French, German, Old English, etc.), it has had to assimilate the various spelling and pronunciation quirks of its predecessors. This has resulted in many instances in which particular letters become silent. While it may seem like silent letters serve no purpose in a word, they can actually help distinguish two words that are otherwise homophonous, help indicate the meaning or origin of a word, or even help us determine the overall pronunciation of a word.

We'll briefly look at the various silent letters here, but continue on to the full section on Silent Letters to learn more.

Silent Vowels

While silent consonants tend to give people the most difficulty due to how unpredictable and illogical they seem, there are also a few truly silent vowels (as opposed to vowel digraphs, which work together to form specific sounds). By far the most common of these is the **silent E**, but the letter **U** can also be truly silent in some cases.

Silent E

Silent E has a wide range of functions in determining the pronunciation of a word. We'll have a brief look at some of the most common of these conventions, but go to the full section on Silent E for more examples and in-depth information.

Dictating a word's pronunciation and meaning

One of the most common purposes of silent **E** is to help the reader determine the pronunciation of a vowel sound that comes before the previous consonant. In many cases, silent **E** also helps indicate a difference in meaning between a similarly spelled word that doesn't have an **E** at the end. Here are some examples:

Word without Silent E	Meaning	Word with Silent E	Meaning
bad (/bæd/)	(*adj.*) Not good or undesirable.	bad<u>e</u> (/beɪd/)	(*verb*) The simple past tense of *bid*.
them (/ðɛm/)	(*pron.*) The objective case of the personal pronoun *they*.	them<u>e</u> (/θim/)	(*noun*) A topic, subject, or idea.
grip (/grɪp/)	(*verb*) To hold onto something.	grip<u>e</u> (/graɪp/)	(*verb*) To complain in a nagging or petulant manner.
hop (/hɑp/)	(*verb*) To jump or leap a short distance.	hop<u>e</u> (/hoʊp/)	(*verb*) To wish for or desire (something).
cub (/kʌb/)	(*noun*) A young bear, lion, wolf, or certain other animal.	cub<u>e</u> (/kjub/)	(*noun*) A solid shape comprising six equal square faces.

Forming Soft *C* and *G*

In addition to changing vowel sounds, silent **E** changes the pronunciation of both **C** and **G**, indicating when they take their soft pronunciations (/s/ and /dʒ/, respectively). This most commonly occurs when **CE** comes after the letter **I** and when **GE** comes after the letter **A**, but it can occur with other vowels as well. For example:

Soft C	Soft G
ic<u>e</u> (/aɪs/)	ag<u>e</u> (/eɪdʒ/)
advic<u>e</u> (/æd'vaɪs/)	cag<u>e</u> (/keɪdʒ/)
sacrific<u>e</u> (/'sækrɪˌfaɪs/)	stag<u>e</u> (/steɪdʒ/)
fac<u>e</u> (/feɪs/)	oblig<u>e</u> (/ə'blaɪdʒ/)

Silent U

The letter **Q** is almost always followed by **U** to help it form the /k/ sound. However, **QU** is only silent in the **QU** combination when it appears at the end of a word (in which case it will always be followed by silent **E**); if it comes before any vowel other than silent **E**, the **U** creates a /w/ sound, as in *require* (/rɪ'kwaɪr/) or *quality* (/'kwɑlɪtɪ/).
For example:

• antique (/æn'tik/)
• bisque (/bɪsk/)
• critique (/krɪ'tik/)
• grotesque (/groʊ'tɛsk/)
• physique (/fɪ'sik/)
• plaque (/plæk/)
• technique (/tɛk'nik/)
• unique (/ju'nik/)

This pattern also occurs when **U** follows **G** at the end of a word, usually resulting in a "hard" **G** sound, /g/. For example:
- colleague (/ˈkɑlig/)
- epilogue (/ˈɛpəˌlɔg/)
- fatigue (/fəˈtig/)
- intrigue (/ɪnˈtrig/)
- league (/lig/)
- plague (/pleɪg/)
- rogue (/roʊg/)
- vague (/veɪg/)

Unlike **QU**, **GU** can result in a silent **U** in various positions within a word when it precedes another vowel, as in:
- **gu**arantee (/ˌgærənˈti/)
- beleа**gu**er (/bɪˈligər/)
- **gu**ess (/gɛs/)
- dis**gu**ise (/dɪsˈgaɪz/)
- lan**gu**or (/ˈlæŋgər/)
- **gu**itar (/gɪˈtɑr/)

It's important to note, however, that this pattern is not a concrete rule, and **U** is often pronounced as /w/ or /ju/ in these same letter patterns in other words. If you're ever unsure, check the word's pronunciation in a good dictionary.

Silent Consonants

Because consonants generally make distinct speech sounds (unlike vowels, which can be malleable and inconsistent, depending on the word), it is much more striking when they are silent in a word, because it looks quite odd.

There are many different silent consonants, so rather than look at all the specific circumstances that indicate when they are silent, we'll just look at some common examples of each. Go to the full section on Silent Letters for more complete information.

Silent B

- bom**b** (/bɔm/)
- clim**b** (/klaɪm/)
- dum**b** (/dʌm/)
- lam**b** (/læm/)
- de**b**t (/dɛt/)
- dou**b**t (/daʊt/)
- su**b**tle (/ˈsʌtəl/)

Silent C

- acquies**c**e (/ˌækwiˈɛs/)
- as**c**end (/əˈsɛnd/)
- fluores**c**ent (/fluˈrɛsənt/)
- mus**c**le (/ˈmʌsəl/)
- s**c**ent (/sɛnt/)
- dis**c**ipline (/ˈdɪsəplɪn/)
- fas**c**inate (/ˈfæsɪˌneɪt/)
- s**c**ience (/ˈsaɪəns/)
- s**c**issors (/ˈsɪzərz/)

Silent D

- han**d**kerchief (/ˈhæŋkərʧɪf/)
- han**d**some (/ˈhænsəm/)
- gran**d**father (/ˈgrænfɑðər/)
- san**d**wich (/ˈsænwɪʧ/)
- We**d**nesday (/ˈwɛnzdeɪ/)

(Note that, other than *handkerchief*, the **D** may be pronounced in some dialects but left out in others.)

Silent G

- align (/əˈlaɪn/)
- benign (/bəˈnaɪn/)
- campaign (/kæmˈpeɪn/)
- design (/dəˈzaɪn/)
- foreign (/ˈfɔrɪn/)
- gnome (/noʊm/)
- malign (/məˈlaɪn/)
- resign (/rəˈzaɪn/)
- sovereign (/ˈsɑvrɪn/)

Silent H

- annihilate (/əˈnaɪəˌleɪt/)
- cheetah (/ˈtʃitə/)
- graham (/ˈgreɪəm/ or /græm/)
- heir (/ɛr/)
- honest (/ˈɑnɪst/)
- hour (/aʊər/)
- rhetoric (/ˈrɛtərɪk/)
- rhyme (/raɪm/)
- savannah (/səˈvænə/)
- vehicle (/ˈviɪkəl/)
- whale (/weɪl/)
- what (/wʌt/)

Silent K

- knead (/nid/)
- knee (/ni/)
- knife (/naɪf/)
- knight (/naɪt/)
- knit (/nɪt/)
- knock (/nɑk/)
- knot (/nɑt/)
- know (/noʊ/)

Silent L

- calf (/kæf/)
- calm (/kɑm/)
- chalk (/tʃɔk/)
- half (/hæf/)
- halve (/hæv/)
- salmon (/ˈsæmən/)
- salve (/sæv/)
- talk (/tɔk/)
- could (/kʊd/)
- should (/ʃʊd/)

Silent M

- mnemonic (/nɪˈmɑnɪk/)

Silent N

- autumn (/ˈɔtəm/)
- condemn (/kənˈdɛm/)
- column (/ˈkɑləm/)
- hymn (/hɪm/)
- solemn (/ˈsɑləm/)

Silent P

- cupboard (/ˈkʌbərd/)
- pneumatic (/nuˈmætɪk/)
- pneumonia (/nuˈmoʊnjə/)
- psalm (/sɑm/)
- pseudo (/ˈsudoʊ/)
- psychiatry (/saɪˈkaɪətrɪ/)
- raspberry (/ˈræzˌbɛri/)
- receipt (/rɪˈsit/)

Silent T

- ballet (/bæˈleɪ/)
- bristle (/ˈbrɪsəl/)
- castle (/ˈkæsəl/)
- christen (/ˈkrɪsən/)
- glisten (/ˈglɪsən/)
- hustle (/ˈhʌsəl/)
- listen (/ˈlɪsən/)
- nestle (/ˈnɛsəl/)
- whistle (/ˈwɪsəl/)
- wrestle (/ˈrɛsəl/)

Silent W

- answer (/ˈænsər/)
- sword (/sɔrd/)
- two (/tu/)
- wrap (/ræp/)
- wreath (/riθ/)
- wreck (/rɛk/)
- wrestle (/ˈrɛsəl/)
- wrist (/rɪst/)
- write (/raɪt/)
- who (/hu/)
- whole (/hoʊl/)
- wrong (/rɔŋ/)

Syllables

A **syllable** is a sequence of speech sounds (formed from vowels and consonants) organized into a single unit that acts as a building block of a spoken word.

Syllables can be structured several ways, but they always contain a **nucleus** (the core of the syllable), which is almost always formed from a vowel sound. Syllables may also contain consonant sounds that form an **onset** (a sound before the nucleus), a **coda** (a sound after the nucleus), or both, but they do not have to contain either.

We'll briefly look at the different types of syllable structures here, but go to the full section on Syllables to learn more about each, as well as for in-depth information about rules for dividing syllables.

In this particular section, syllables will be marked by an interpunct (·) for "normal" words, and by a period in IPA transcriptions. Note that the syllable breakdowns in this section are based on the way dictionaries list them; in many cases, the syllable breaks in normal written words may be slightly different than the words' IPA transcriptions. For example, the word *application* is divided in the dictionary as *ap·pli·ca·tion*, while its IPA transcription is /ˌæp.lɪˈkeɪ.ʃən/ (the two **P**s are divided by an interpunct in the written form, but the /p/ sound only occurs in the first syllable in the IPA form). This variation has to do with the technical aspects of how different types of syllables are categorized, rather than the phonetic aspects of the word. (We will use a slightly different method when looking at Word Stress, which we'll cover further on.)

Types of syllables

Although syllables all perform the same basic function, not all syllables are structured the same way. There are **six** types of syllables that are identified in English based on a word's spelling and the type of sound the syllable's nucleus creates. The two most basic categories are **open** and **closed syllables**, but we also distinguish **silent E syllables, vowel-combination syllables, vowel-R syllables**, and **syllabic consonants**.

Open syllables

An **open syllable** (also known as a **free syllable**) is one that has a single vowel letter for its nucleus and does not have a consonant sound after the vowel. An open syllable can be a vowel sound on its own, or else have one or more consonant sounds that precede the nucleus.

When an open syllable is stressed, it will have a "traditional" long vowel sound forming its nucleus—that is, a vowel sound that "says the name" of the vowel letter. When an open syllable is **unstressed**, it is often shortened into a **schwa** (/ə/) or the "short **I**" sound (/ɪ/).

For example:

Multiple syllables (vowel is stressed)	Multiple syllables (vowel is unstressed)
a·corn (/ˈeɪ.kɔrn/)	a·loft (/əˈlɔft/)
cu·bi·cal (/ˈkju.bɪ.kəl/)	be·neath (/bɪˈniθ/)
e·ven (/ˈi.vɪn/)	cu·**bi**·cal (/ˈkju.**bɪ**.kəl/)
gra·vy (/ˈgreɪ.vi/)	de·bate (/dɪˈbeɪt/)
hel·**lo** (/hɛˈloʊ/)	**de**·ter·mine (/dɪˈtɜr.mɪn/)
i·tem (/ˈaɪ.təm/)	e·vent (/ɪˈvɛnt/)
mu·tate (/ˈmju.teɪt/)	grav·**i**·tate (/ˈgræv.ɪˌteɪt/)
o·cean (/ˈoʊ.ʃən/)	med·**i**·tate (/ˈmɛd.ɪˌteɪt/)
se·cret (/ˈsi.krɪt/)	re·lease (/rɪˈlis/)
vol·**ca**·no (/vɑlˈkeɪ.noʊ/)	ze·**bra** (/(ˈzi.**brə**/)

Notice that syllables formed with vowel digraphs in the nucleus are classed together in a separate category.

Closed syllables

A **closed syllable** is one in which a single vowel is followed by a **coda**, which consists of one or more consonant sounds at the end of the syllable (not including the consonant **R**, which is a separate category). Closed syllables often have an **onset** as well, but this is not always the case.

Closed syllables most often have short vowels forming their nuclei, but they may also have other long vowel sounds that do not "say the name" of the vowel letter. As in open syllables, the nuclei of closed syllables may be reduced to weak vowel sounds if the syllable is unstressed.

Multiple syllables (stressed vowel)	Multiple syllables (unstressed vowel)
ac·ci·dent (/ˈæk.sɪ.dənt/)	ac·ci·dent (/ˈæk.sɪ.dənt/)
com·mon (/ˈkɑm.ən/)	ap·par·ent (/əˈpɛr.ənt/)
e·vent (/ɪˈvɛnt/)	black·en (/ˈblæk.ən/)
for·bid (/fərˈbɪd/)	com·mon (/ˈkɑm.ən/)
hap·pen (/ˈhæp.ən/)	con·trol (/kənˈtroʊl/)
lad·der (/ˈlæd.ər/)	ex·cept (/ɪkˈsɛpt/)
pel·i·can (/ˈpɛl.ɪ.kən/)	hap·pen (/ˈhæp.ən/)
riv·er (/ˈrɪv.ər/)	mas·sage (/məˈsɑʒ/)
suc·cess (/səkˈsɛs/)	suc·cess (/səkˈsɛs/)
tem·per (/ˈtɛmp.ər/)	tra·di·tion (/trəˈdɪ.ʃən/)

Silent E syllables

One of the most common and well-known functions of **silent E** is to indicate that a vowel has a "long" sound before a single consonant. Because the vowel sound of the nucleus becomes long, we distinguish syllables formed with a silent **E** from closed syllables, which always have short or weak vowels.

Silent **E** syllables are generally either the only or the final syllable of a word. For example:

One syllable	Multiple syllables
bik<u>e</u> (/baɪk/)	con·**cret<u>e</u>** (/ˈkɑn.**krit**/)
cak<u>e</u> (/keɪk/)	de·**mot<u>e</u>** (/dɪ**moʊt**/)
mut<u>e</u> (/mjut/)	e·**vad<u>e</u>** (/ɪ**veɪd**/)
rop<u>e</u> (/roʊp/)	in·**sid<u>e</u>** (/ɪn**saɪd**/)
them<u>e</u> (/θim/)	re·**buk<u>e</u>** (/rɪ**bjuk**/)

Vowel-combination syllables

Syllables that have vowel sounds formed from a combination of letters as their nuclei are known as **vowel-combination syllables** (sometimes referred to as **vowel team syllables**).

Many of the nuclei in these types of syllables are vowel digraphs (pairs of vowel letters that form a single sound), but they can also be formed from certain combinations of vowels and consonants.

For example:

Vowel Digraphs	Vowel-Consonant Combinations
au·thor (/ˈɔ.θər/)	
be·l**ie**ve (/bɪˈliv/)	c**au**ght (/kɔt/)
child·h**oo**d (/ˈʧaɪld ˌhʊd/)	dr**ough**t (/draʊt/)
en·d**ear**·ing (/ɛnˈdɪr.ɪŋ/)	h**eigh**t·en (/ˈhaɪt.ən/)
her·**oe**s (/ˈhɪr.oʊs/)	in·s**igh**t (/ˈɪnˌsaɪt/)
melt·d**ow**n (/ˈmɛlt ˌdaʊn/)	n**eigh**·bor (/ˈneɪ.bər/)
pur·s**ue** (/pərˈsu/)	p**al**m (/pɑm/)
un·b**ear**·a·ble (/ʌnˈbɛr.ə.bəl/)	thor·**ough** (/ˈθɜr.oʊ/)

Vowel-R syllables

Vowel-R Syllables (also known as "**R-controlled syllables**") are syllables in which the nucleus is made up of a single vowel letter followed by **R**. This has the effect of changing the pronunciation of the vowel, either subtly or dramatically, so we categorize these syllables separately.

For example:
- a·**far** (/əˈfɑr/)
- dis·em·**bark** (/ˌdɪs.ɛmˈbɑrk/)
- a·**lert** (/əˈlɜrt/)
- **per**·fect (/ˈpɜrˌfɪkt/)
- af·**firm** (/əˈfɜrm/)
- **sir**·loin (/ˈsɜr.lɔɪn/)
- re·**morse** (/rɪˈmɔrs/)
- w**or**·thy (/ˈwɜr.ði/)
- fl**ur**·ry (/ˈflɜr.i/)
- t**ur**·tle (/ˈtɜr.təl/)

Syllabic consonants

A **syllabic consonant** refers to a syllable that has a consonant as its nucleus, rather than a vowel. When these words are pronounced out loud, the consonant will have a short reduced-vowel sound (/ə/) before it.

In most cases, syllabic consonants occur when **L** comes after a consonant and is followed by a **semi**-silent E, which indicates that the schwa sound will occur before the syllable; less commonly, this can also occur with **R** rather than **L**. Finally, the letter **M** can also create syllabic consonants after **S** and **TH**.

For example:

Consonant + LE	Consonant + RE	S + M	TH + M
ap·**ple** (/ˈæp.əl/)		bap·**tism** (/ˈbæp.tɪz.əm/)	
bi·cy·**cle** (/ˈbaɪ.sɪk.əl/)		cat·a·**clysm** (/ˈkæt.əˌklɪz.əm/)	
cra·**dle** (/ˈkreɪd.əl/)	a·**cre** (/ˈeɪ.kər/)	en·thu·si·**asm** (/ɛnˈθu.ziˌæz.əm/)	
fid·**dle** (/ˈfɪd.əl/)	mas·sa·**cre** (/ˈmæs.ə.kər/)	her·o·**ism** (/ˈhɛroʊˌɪz.əm/)	al·go·**rithm** (/ˈæl.gəˌrɪð.əm/)
la·**dle** (/ˈleɪd.əl/)	me·di·o·**cre** (/ˌmi.di·oʊ.kər/)	mi·cro·**cosm** (/ˈmaɪ.krəˌkɑz.əm/)	log·a·**rithm** (/ˈlɑ.gəˌrɪ.ð.əm/)
mus·**cle** (/ˈmʌs.əl/)	o·**gre** (/ˈoʊ.gər/)	par·ox·**ysm** (/pərˈɑkˌsɪz.əm/)	**rhythm** (/ˈrɪð.əm/)
star·**tle** (/ˈstɑrt.əl/)		sar·**casm** (/ˈsɑrˌkæz.əm/)	
ti·**tle** (/ˈtaɪt.əl/)		tour·**ism** (/ˈtʊəˌrɪz.əm/)	

Stress

Stress (sometimes known as **accent**) refers to the emphasis placed on syllables and words in speech. Stress on individual syllables is called **word stress**, while stress on words within a sentence is known as **sentence stress**.

Word stress can sometimes be determined by a word's function (noun, verb, etc.), as well as by certain structural cues such as suffixes. However, these conventions are often unreliable, and there are typically many exceptions that contradict them. Sentence stress, meanwhile, is primarily determined by the type of words the sentence comprises.

We'll briefly look each type of stress here, but you can continue on to their individual sections to learn more.

Word Stress

When we talk about word stress, we are describing the primary emphasis put on one specific syllable within a word—a word cannot have more than one syllable with primary emphasis. Because nearly all syllables must contain at least a vowel sound, we only apply stress to vowels, not consonant sounds.

While word stress can be very hard to predict for individual words, there are a few conventions that are commonly used. Just be aware that there are usually many exceptions to each of these conventions. (Go to the full article on Word Stress to learn more about these exceptions.)

Finally, note that the way we divide syllables will be slightly different in this section compared to the chapter on Syllables. In that section, we provide syllable breakdowns based on how they would be found in the dictionary. Because this part of the guide is more concerned with the phonetic placement of word stress, the examples we use will try to match the written form as closely as possible to the spoken form (the IPA transcriptions). For example, in this section we would divide the syllables of *application* as *app·li·ca·tion* to match the IPA transcription /ˌæp.lɪˈkeɪ.ʃən/ (with the /p/ sound of **PP** only occurring in the first syllable), while the way it would be divided in the dictionary is *ap·pli·ca·tion*. Just keep in mind that the syllable divisions in this section may not match up with how you might see them in the dictionary.

Determining stress based on word type

One common pronunciation convention many guides provide is that nouns and adjectives with two or more syllables will have stress placed on the first syllable, while verbs and prepositions tend to have their stress on the second syllable. For example:

Nouns	Adjectives	Verbs	Prepositions
app·le (/ˈæp.əl/)	beau·ti·ful (/ˈbyu.tə.fəl/)	a·pply (/əˈplaɪ/)	a·mong (/əˈmʌŋ/)
bott·le (/ˈbɑt.əl/)	clev·er (/ˈklɛv.ər/)	be·come (/bɪˈkʌm/)	a·round (/əˈraʊnd/)
cherr·y (/ˈtʃɛr.i/)	diff·i·cult (/ˈdɪf.ɪˌkʌlt/)	com·pare (/kəmˈpɛr/)	be·side (/bɪˈsaɪd/)
dia·mond (/ˈdaɪ.mənd/)	fa·vor·ite (/ˈfeɪ.vər.ɪt/)	di·scuss (/dɪˈskʌs/)	be·tween (/bɪˈtwin/)
el·e·phant (/ˈɛl.ə.fənt/)	happ·y (/ˈhæp.i/)	ex·plain (/ɪkˈspleɪn/)	de·spite (/dɪˈspaɪt/)
fam·i·ly (/ˈfæm.ə.li/)	litt·le (/ˈlɪt.əl/)	ful·fill (/fʊlˈfɪl/)	ex·cept (/ɪkˈsɛpt/)
knowl·edge (/ˈnɑl.ɪdʒ/)	mas·cu·line (/ˈmæs.kju.lɪn/)	la·ment (/ləˈmɛnt/)	in·side (/ˌɪnˈsaɪd/)
mu·sic (/ˈmju.zɪk/)	nar·row (/ˈnær.oʊ/)	ne·glect (/nɪˈglɛkt/)	out·side (/ˌaʊtˈsaɪd/)
pa·per (/ˈpeɪ.pər/)	or·ange (/ˈɔr.ɪndʒ/)	pre·vent (/prɪˈvɛnt/)	un·til (/ʌnˈtɪl/)
sam·ple (/ˈsæm.pəl/)	pleas·ant (/ˈplɛz.ənt/)	re·ply (/rɪˈplaɪ/)	u·pon (/əˈpɑn/)
ta·ble (/ˈteɪ.bəl/)	qui·et (/ˈkwaɪ.ət/)	suc·ceed (/səkˈsid/)	with·in (/wɪðˈɪn/)
win·dow (/ˈwɪn.doʊ/)	sim·ple (/ˈsɪm.pəl/)	tra·verse (/trəˈvɜrs/)	with·out (/wɪðˈaʊt/)

Initial-stress-derived nouns

When a word can operate as either a noun or a verb, we often differentiate the meanings by shifting the stress from the second syllable to the first (or **initial**) syllable—in other words, these nouns are **derived** from verbs according to their **initial stress**. For example:

Word	Noun	Verb
contest	con·test (/ˈkɑn.tɛst/)	con·test (/kənˈtɛst/)
desert	des·ert (/ˈdɛz.ərt/)	de·sert (/dɪˈzɜrt/)
increase	in·crease (/ˈɪn.kris/)	in·crease (/ɪnˈkris/)
object	ob·ject (/ˈɑb.dʒɛkt/)	ob·ject (/əbˈdʒɛkt/)
permit	per·mit (/ˈpɜr.mɪt/)	per·mit (/pərˈmɪt/)
record	rec·ord (/ˈrɛk.ərd/)	re·cord (/rəˈkɔrd/)
subject	sub·ject (/ˈsʌb.dʒɛkt/)	sub·ject (/səbˈdʒɛkt/)

Word stress dictated by suffixes

While the stress in many words is very difficult to predict, certain suffixes and other word endings will reliably dictate where stress should be applied within the word, either on the suffix itself, one syllable before the suffix, or two syllables before the suffix. Other suffixes, however, don't impact word stress at all. For example:

Stress is placed on the suffix	Stress is placed one syllable before the suffix	Stress is placed two syllables before the suffix	No change to stress
ab·sen·tee (/ˌæb.sənˈti/) en·gi·neer (/ˌɛn.dʒɪˈnɪər/) Jap·a·nese (/ˌdʒæp.əˈniz/) car·di·ol·o·gy (/ˌkɑr.di.ˈal.ə.dʒi/) der·ma·to·sis (/ˌdɜr.məˈtoʊ.sɪs/)	ad·van·ta·geous (/ˌæd.vənˈteɪ.dʒəs/) my·ster·i·ous (/mɪˈstɪr.i.əs/) bac·ter·i·a (/bæk.ˈtɪər.i.ə/) ed·i·tor·i·al (/ˌɛd.ɪ ˈtɔr.i.əl/) i·con·ic (/aɪˈkan.ɪk/) e·lec·tri·fy (/ɪˈlɛk.trəˌfaɪ/) rec·i·proc·i·ty (/ˌrɛs.əˈpras.ɪ.ti/) ex·haus·tion (/ɪgˈzɔs.tʃən/)	co·llab·o·rate (/kəˈlæb.əˌreɪt/) de·moc·ra·cy (/dɪˈmak.rə.si/) bib·li·og·ra·phy (/ˌbɪb.liˈag.rə.fi/) phi·los·o·phy (/fɪˈlas.ə.fi/)	or·phan·age (/ˈɔr.fə.nɪdʒ/) car·too·nish (/ˌkɑrˈtu.nɪʃ/) par·ent·hood (/ˈpɛr.əntˌhʊd/) re·gard·less (/rɪˈgard.lɪs/) to·geth·er·ness (/təˈgɛð.ər.nɪs/) per·i·lous (/ˈpɛr.ə.ləs/)

Sentence Stress

Sentence stress (also called **prosodic stress**) differs from the internal word stress placed on individual syllables, referring instead to the varying emphasis placed on certain words within a sentence.

In the most basic pattern, **content words** (nouns, verbs, adjectives, and adverbs) will always be stressed, while **function words** (pronouns, prepositions, conjunctions, articles, determiners, and auxiliary verbs) will often be unstressed. The back-and-forth between these stressed and unstressed words creates the rhythm of a sentence. For example:
- "*I* have *a* **favor** *to* **ask**."
- "**Jonathan** *will be* **late** *because his* **car broke down**."
- "*I'm* **going** *to the* **store** **later**."
- "*We do* **not agree** *with the* **outcome**."
- "**Please** *don't* **tell** *me* **how** *the* **movie ends**."

Emphatic stress

English speakers often place additional emphasis on a specific word or words to provide clarity, emphasis, or contrast; doing so provides the listener with more information than the words can provide on their own. For example:
- "I didn't think that George was upset." (No emphatic stress.)
- "*I* didn't think that George was upset." (Someone else might have thought George was upset.)
- "I didn't *think* that George was upset." (It was only a guess that George wasn't upset; alternatively, the statement may be a claim that one absolutely *knew* that George was upset, and was not merely guessing.)
- "I didn't think that George *was* upset." (At the time, it seemed like George wasn't upset at all.)
- "I didn't think that George was *upset*." (It seemed like George was displaying a different emotion.)

Quiz
(answers start on page 463)

1. Which of the following traditional long vowels is **not** considered a diphthong?

a) "Long A"
b) "Long E"
c) "Long I"
d) "Long O"
e) "Long U"

2. Which of the following is another term for a diphthong?

a) Combined vowel
b) Blended vowel
c) Vowel digraph
d) Gliding vowel

3. When does the letter **C** *not* form the /k/ sound?

a) Before the vowels **A, O,** and **U**
b) Before the vowels **E, I,** and **Y**
c) When it is followed by the consonants **L, R,** and **T**
d) When it is the last letter of a word with two or more syllables

4. Which of the following sounds is **not** made by the letter **S**?

a) /s/
b) /z/
c) /θ/
d) /ʃ/
e) /ʒ/

5. Which of the following is the most common silent letter?

a) B
b) E
c) U
d) H

6. What **must** a syllable contain?

a) An onset
b) A nucleus
c) A coda
d) A & B
e) B & C
f) All of the above

7. What type of speech sound receives stress in a word?

a) Consonant sounds
b) Vowel sounds
c) A & B

8. Which type of word is typically stressed in a sentence?

a) Content words
b) Function words
c) A & B

Tricky Vowel Sounds (Monophthongs, Diphthongs, and Triphthongs)

Vowel sounds are an especially tricky part of English pronunciation because of how flexible and malleable they can be. While consonant sounds are fairly uniform throughout various dialects, vowel sounds can have slight variations in pronunciation from one region to another.

Another aspect of vowel sounds that can be confusing is when multiple vowel sounds blend together within a single syllable. Because there are no clear divisions between the sounds like there are for consonants, these blended vowel sounds can be difficult to pronounce correctly. In this section, we'll look at the three ranges of vowel sounds: **monophthongs** (single vowel sounds within a syllable), **diphthongs** (two vowels sounds combined within a syllable), and **triphthongs** (three vowels sounds combined within a syllable).

Monophthongs

The most basic vowel sound is known as a **monophthong** (pronounced /ˈmɑnəfˌθɑŋ/). As the prefix "mono-" suggests, a monophthong is a single sound (to which the root "-phthong" refers) within a single syllable. Most of these are **short vowels**, though there are some **long vowel** monophthongs as well.

Short vowel monophthongs

Most of the monophthongs in English are commonly known as "**short vowels**," which are usually produced when a vowel is followed by one or more consonants in a syllable.

Most vowel letters have a specific short-vowel sound, though **U** can create <u>two</u> types of short-vowel sounds. The semi-vowel **Y** can also create a short vowel sound, but it is the same as the letter **I**.

Let's look at some examples of each type of short vowel:

Vowel Letter	IPA Symbol	Example Words
A a	/æ/	<u>a</u>pple (/ˈæpəl/) m<u>a</u>p (/mæp/) tr<u>a</u>ck (/træk/) m<u>a</u>n (/mæn/)
E e	/ɛ/	s<u>e</u>t (/sɛt/) j<u>e</u>t (/dʒɛ/) b<u>e</u>nd (/bɛnd/) m<u>e</u>t (/mɛt/)
I i	/ɪ/	t<u>i</u>p (/tɪp/) str<u>i</u>p (/strɪp/) <u>i</u>mply (/ɪmˈplaɪ/) f<u>i</u>n (/fɪn/)

301

O o	/ɑ/	t<u>o</u>p (/t<u>ɑ</u>p/) h<u>o</u>t (/h<u>ɑ</u>t/) <u>o</u>ffer (/ˈ<u>ɑ</u>fər/) p<u>o</u>llen (/ˈp<u>ɑ</u>lən/)
U u	/ʌ/	c<u>u</u>t (/k<u>ʌ</u>t/) h<u>u</u>g (/h<u>ʌ</u>g/) m<u>u</u>tt (/m<u>ʌ</u>t/) str<u>u</u>t (/str<u>ʌ</u>t/)
U u	/ʊ/	p<u>u</u>t (/p<u>ʊ</u>t/) p<u>u</u>sh (/p<u>ʊ</u>ʃ/) f<u>u</u>ll (/f<u>ʊ</u>l/) s<u>u</u>gar (/ˈʃ<u>ʊ</u>gər/)
Y y	/ɪ/	m<u>y</u>th (/m<u>ɪ</u>θ/) s<u>y</u>stem (/ˈs<u>ɪ</u>stəm/) rh<u>y</u>thm (/ˈr<u>ɪ</u>ðəm/) cr<u>y</u>pt (/kr<u>ɪ</u>pt/)

Long vowel monophthongs

Most of the traditional "**long vowels**" (vowel sounds that approximate the name of their corresponding vowel letters) are diphthongs, so we'll look at those further on. One traditional long vowel that *is* a monophthong, though, is "**long E**," represented in IPA by /i/. This sound is usually produced by the letter **E**, but it can also be formed by the letter **Y**, as well as a number of **vowel digraphs**. For example:

- m<u>e</u> (/<u>i</u>t/)
- concr<u>e</u>te (/ˈkɑnkr<u>i</u>t/)
- happ<u>y</u> (/ˈhæp<u>i</u>/)
- friendl<u>y</u> (/ˈfrɛndl<u>i</u>/)
- f<u>ee</u>l (/f<u>i</u>l/)
- <u>ea</u>t (/<u>i</u>t/)
- categor<u>ie</u>s (/ˈkætɪˌgɔr<u>i</u>z/)

There are also a few other long vowels besides those that sound like the names of vowel letters. Most of these occur in various vowel digraphs, though some can be produced by single letters, while others occur when a vowel is combined with the consonant **R**.

/u/

- exclude (/ɪkˈsklud/)
- prove (/pruv/)
- true (/tru/)
- cruise (/kruz/)
- chew (/ʧu/)
- loot (/lut/)
- through (/θru/)

/ɔ/

- water (/ˈwɔtər/)
- across (/əˈkrɔs/)
- thought (/θɔt/)
- dawn (/dɔn/)
- author (/ˈɔθər/)

/ɜ/

- nerve (/nɜrv/)
- stir (/stɜr/)
- work (/wɜrk/)
- curve (/kɜrv/)
- search (/sɜrʧ/)
- journey (/ˈʤɜrni/)

Diphthongs

A **diphthong** (pronounced /ˈdɪfθɔŋ/) is a single-syllable vowel sound in which the beginning of the sound **glides** to another, slightly different vowel sound. For this reason, diphthongs are often referred to as **gliding vowels**.

There are eight vowel sounds in American English that are generally agreed upon as being diphthongs. Four of these are the "traditional" **long vowels** (vowel sounds that are pronounced the same way as the names of the letters), but there are also a few others that occur with certain vowel digraphs or in combination with the letter **R**.

We'll briefly go over the different diphthongs here, but you can continue on to the full section on Diphthongs to learn more.

Traditional long vowels

With the exception of long **E** (/i/), all of the traditional long vowel sounds are diphthongs. These most predictably occur when the vowel letter is followed by a single consonant and a silent "e":

Vowel Letter	Vowel Sound (IPA Symbol)	How to pronounce it	Example word
A	/eɪ/	eh-ee	tape (/teɪp/)
I	/aɪ/	ah-ee	ice (/aɪs/)
O	/oʊ/	oh-oo	rope (/roʊp/)
U	/ju/	ee-oo	cube (/kjub/)

Other diphthongs

/ɔɪ/

This diphthong is pronounced "au-ee," and it occurs in in the vowel digraphs **OY** and **OI**. For example:

- b<u>oy</u> (/bɔɪ/)
- ann<u>oy</u> (/əˈnɔɪ/)
- r<u>oy</u>al (/ˈrɔɪəl/)
- empl<u>oy</u>ed (/ɪmˈplɔɪd/)

- c<u>oi</u>n (/kɔɪn/)
- f<u>oi</u>l (/fɔɪl/)
- ch<u>oi</u>ce (/tʃɔɪs/)
- n<u>oi</u>se (/nɔɪz/)

/aʊ/

This diphthong is pronounced "ah-oo," and it occurs with the digraphs **OU** and **OW**. For example:

- f<u>ou</u>nd (/faʊnd/)
- p<u>ou</u>t (/paʊt/)
- st<u>ou</u>t (/staʊt/)
- m<u>ou</u>th (/maʊθ/)

- t<u>ow</u>n (/taʊn/)
- cr<u>ow</u>d (/kraʊd/)
- ch<u>ow</u>der (/ˈtʃaʊdər/)
- sh<u>ow</u>er (/ˈʃaʊər/)

/ɪə/

Depending on dialect, the schwa (/ə/) that forms the second part of this diphthong is often not pronounced. When this diphthong is articulated fully, it is pronounced "ih-uh," and it usually occurs with the digraphs **EE**, **EA**, and **IE** when they are followed by an **R**. For example:

- d<u>eer</u> (/dɪər/)
- sh<u>eer</u> (/ʃɪər/)
- st<u>eer</u> (/stɪər/)

- d<u>ear</u> (/dɪər/)
- h<u>ear</u> (/hɪər/)
- app<u>ear</u> (/əpˈɪər/)

- p<u>ier</u> (/pɪər/)
- f<u>ier</u>ce (/fɪərs/)
- front<u>ier</u> (/frənˈtɪər/)

/ɛə/

Like /ɪə/, the schwa of /ɛə/ is often left out. When it is articulated fully, /ɛə/ is pronounced "eh-uh," and it usually occurs with the letter combinations **ARE**, **AIR**, and occasionally **EAR**. For example:

- fl<u>are</u> (/flɛər/)
- c<u>are</u> (/kɛər/)
- st<u>are</u> (/stɛər/)

- st<u>airs</u> (/stɛərz/)
- d<u>airy</u> (/dɛəri/)
- rep<u>air</u> (/rəˈpɛər/)

- w<u>ear</u> (/wɛər/)
- b<u>ear</u> (/bɛər/)
- p<u>ear</u> (/pɛər/)

Triphthongs

Very rarely, a single syllable may contain <u>three</u> vowel sounds that quickly glide together; this compound vowel sound is known as a **triphthong** (pronounced /ˈtrɪf θɔŋ/).

There are three triphthongs that are generally agreed upon in American English: /aʊə/ ("ah-oo-uh"), /aɪə/ ("ah-ih-uh"), and /jʊə/ ("ee-oo-uh"). We'll briefly look at each here, but you can find out more about them in the full section on Triphthongs.

/aʊə/

This triphthong is pronounced "ah-oo-uh," and it occurs when the digraph **OU** is followed by an **R**. For example:

• <u>our</u> (/a<u>ʊə</u>r/)
• h<u>our</u> (/<u>aʊə</u>r/; **H** is silent)
• fl<u>our</u> (/fl<u>aʊə</u>r/)
• s<u>our</u> (/s<u>aʊə</u>r/)

/aɪə/

This triphthong is pronounced "ah-ih-uh," and it occurs with the letter combination **IRE**. For example:

• f<u>ire</u> (/f<u>aɪə</u>r/)
• d<u>ire</u> (/d<u>aɪə</u>r/)
• insp<u>ire</u> (/ɪnˈsp<u>aɪə</u>r/)
• <u>Ire</u>land (/ˈ<u>aɪə</u>rlənd/)

/jʊə/

This triphthong is pronounced "ee-oo-uh," and it sometimes occurs when the combination **UR** comes after a hard consonant and is followed by an **E, Y,** or **I**. For example:

• c<u>ure</u> (/k<u>jʊə</u>r/)
• p<u>ure</u> (/p<u>jʊə</u>r/)
• f<u>ur</u>y (/ˈf<u>jʊə</u>ri/)
• c<u>ur</u>ious (/ˈk<u>jʊə</u>r.iəs/)

Quiz

(answers start on page 463)

1. A **triphthong** comprises how many vowel sounds?

a) 1
b) 2
c) 3
d) 4

2. Which of the following traditional long vowels is **not** considered a diphthong?

a) "Long A"
b) "Long E"
c) "Long I"
d) "Long O"
e) "Long U"

3. Which of the following is another term for a diphthong?

a) Combined vowel
b) Blended vowel
c) Vowel digraph
d) Gliding vowel

4. Which of the following words contains a **monophthong**?

a) indeed
b) employ
c) dear
d) kind

Diphthongs

Definition

A **diphthong** is a single-syllable vowel sound in which the beginning of the sound is different from the end sound—that is, the sound **glides** from one vowel sound to another. For this reason, diphthongs are often referred to as **gliding vowels**. A "pure" vowel sound that doesn't glide is known as a **monophthong**. It's also possible (though less common) to have a single syllable that glides between <u>three</u> vowel sounds; this is known as a triphthong, which we'll look at in another section.

There are eight vowel sounds in American English that are generally agreed upon as being diphthongs. We already encountered four of these when we looked at "traditional" **long vowels** (vowel sounds that are pronounced the same way as the names of the letters), but there are also a few others that occur. Let's start by reviewing the diphthongs that make up the traditional long vowels, and then we'll move on to the rest.

Traditional long vowels

With the exception of long **E** (/i/), all of the traditional long vowel sounds are diphthongs. These most predictably occur when the vowel letter is followed by a single consonant and a silent "e":

Vowel Letter	Vowel Sound (IPA Symbol)	How to pronounce it	Example word
A	/eɪ/	eh-ee	t<u>a</u>pe (/t<u>eɪ</u>p/)
I	/aɪ/	ah-ee	<u>i</u>ce (/<u>aɪ</u>s/)
O	/oʊ/	oh-oo	r<u>o</u>pe (/r<u>oʊ</u>p/)
U	/ju/*	ee-oo	c<u>u</u>be (/k<u>ju</u>b/)

(*Note that the traditional transcription for long **U** is /juː/. The triangular colon [ː] represents the elongation of the vowel sound. However, in most American dictionaries, this colon is omitted because the elongation of /ju/ is implied. This guide follows the convention of omitting the triangular colon so that the IPA pronunciations match what would be found in an American dictionary.)

The silent "e" rule is not the only instance when these long-vowel diphthongs occur. For more information on when a vowel creates the traditional long sound, go to the section overview on Vowels.

Other diphthongs

In addition to the four diphthongs listed above, there are two other diphthongs that regularly occur in American English pronunciation. There are also two others that are sometimes articulated (but aren't always included in IPA transcriptions).

Below, we'll look at each diphthong individually, listing common vowel digraphs that form the sound, along with example words and their full IPA pronunciations.

/ɔɪ/

This diphthong is pronounced "au-ee"—it begins with the /ɔ/ sound (as in *d<u>aw</u>n* or *d<u>oor</u>*) and glides to the /ɪ/ sound (as in *p<u>i</u>t*). It generally only occurs with the vowel combinations "**OY**" and "**OI**."

Common Digraphs	Example Words	Full IPA
OY	boy annoy royal employed	/bɔɪ/ /əˈnɔɪ/ /ˈrɔɪəl/ /ɪmˈplɔɪd/
OI	coin foil choice noise	/kɔɪn/ /fɔɪl/ /tʃɔɪs/ /nɔɪz/

/aʊ/

This diphthong is pronounced "ah-oo"—the vowel glides from the /æ/ sound (as in b*a*t) to the /ʊ/ sound (as in p*u*ll). It generally occurs with the digraphs "OU" and "OW."

Common Digraphs	Example Words	Full IPA
OU	found pout drought mouth	/faʊnd/ /paʊt/ /draʊt/ (GH becomes silent) /maʊθ/
OW	town crowd chowder shower	/taʊn/ /kraʊd/ /ˈtʃaʊdər/ /ˈʃaʊər/

Be careful, though, because many words that have "OU" or "OW" spellings will make the **long O** (/oʊ/) vowel sound, as in:

• though (/ðoʊ/; **GH** is silent)
• boulder (/boʊldər/)
• soul (/soʊl/)
• lower (/loʊər/)
• own (/oʊn/)
• growth (/groʊθ/)

Finally, some words that are spelled with "**OW**" can be pronounced <u>either</u> way, which alters the meaning of the word altogether. Let's look at some common examples:

Word	Pronounced /oʊ/	Pronounced /aʊ/
bow	1. (noun) A weapon that shoots arrows. 2. (noun) A knot composed of two or more loops.	1. (verb) To incline or bend forward. 2. (verb) To yield or submit.
row	1. (noun) A number of people or things arranged in a line. 2. (verb) To propel forward using the leverage of an oar or a similar instrument.	1. (noun) A noisy quarrel or argument. 2. (verb) To engage or participate in such a quarrel.
sow	(verb) To plant or scatter seed(s).	(noun) An adult female swine.

"R-Colored" Diphthongs

There are two other diphthongs that sometimes occur in American English: /ɪə/ and /ɛə/. These can be found in certain instances where a vowel sound is followed by an "r." However, it is very common in General American pronunciations to omit the schwa sound before the "r" in /ɪər/ and /ɛər/, and the standard transcription in (most) American dictionaries is often simply /ɪr/ or /ɛr/, respectively. While the IPA transcriptions used in this guide generally favor the trends of American dictionaries (and do not include the schwas as a result), we'll have a quick look below at when they might occur.

/ɪə/

When this diphthong is articulated, it is pronounced "ih-uh," quickly gliding from the short **I** sound /ɪ/ (as in *tip*) to an unstressed schwa (/ə/). It usually occurs with the digraphs "**EE**," "**EA**," and "**IE**" when they are followed by an "R."

Letter Combinations	Example Words	Full IPA	IPA in American Dictionaries
EER	b<u>eer</u>	/bɪər/	/bɪr/
	d<u>eer</u>	/dɪər/	/dɪr/
	sh<u>eer</u>	/ʃɪər/	/ʃɪr/
	st<u>eer</u>	/stɪər/	/stɪr/
EAR	d<u>ear</u>	/dɪər/	/dɪr/
	h<u>ear</u>	/hɪər/	/hɪr/
	sh<u>ear</u>	/ʃɪər/	/ʃɪr/
	app<u>ear</u>	/əpˈɪər/	/əpˈɪr/
IER*	p<u>ier</u>	/pɪər/	/pɪr/
	f<u>ier</u>ce	/fɪərs/	/fɪrs/
	front<u>ier</u>	/frənˈtɪər/	/frənˈtɪr/
	bandol<u>ier</u>	/ˌbændəˈlɪər/	/ˌbændəˈlɪr/

(*Note that "-ier" is often used to create the comparative form of adjectives that end in "y," as in *happier, fussier, busier*, etc. In this case, "-ier" is pronounced "ee-er," and its IPA notation is /iər/. This is **not** a diphthong, however, because it is stressed as two separate syllables.)

/ɛə/

When this diphthong is articulated, it is pronounced "eh-uh," quickly gliding from the short "**E**" sound /ɛ/ (as in *set*) to an unstressed schwa (/ə/). (In some dialects, the "**E**" sound sometimes raises up slightly to sound more like "ei"; for this reason, some dictionaries transcribe the diphthong as **/eə/** instead.)

This diphthong usually occurs with the letter combinations "**ARE**" and "**AIR**," but be careful: it also sometimes occurs with "**EAR**," which is often pronounced **/ɪər/**. All of the root "**EAR**" words that have the /ɛər/ pronunciation are listed below.

Letter Combinations	Example Words	Full IPA	IPA in American Dictionaries
ARE*	fl<u>are</u>	/flɛər/	/flɛr/
	c<u>are</u>	/kɛər/	/kɛr/
	st<u>are</u>	/stɛər/	/stɛr/
	ensn<u>are</u>	/ɪnˈsnɛər/	/ɪnˈsnɛr/
AIR	fl<u>air</u>	/flɛər/	/flɛr/
	st<u>air</u>s	/stɛərz/	/stɛrz/
	d<u>air</u>y	/dɛəri/	/dɛri/
	rep<u>air</u>	/rəˈpɛər/	/rəˈpɛr/

EAR	w**ear**	/w**ɛər**/	/w**ɛr**/
	b**ear**	/b**ɛər**/	/b**ɛr**/
	p**ear**	/p**ɛər**/	/p**ɛr**/
	sw**ear**	/sw**ɛər**/	/sw**ɛr**/
	t**ear** (meaning "to rip")	/t**ɛər**/	/t**ɛr**/

*The most notable exception to this rule is the short word *are*, which is pronounced "ahr" (/ɑr/).

It's also important to note that verbs ending in **ARE** keep this pronunciation even when they are made into a gerund or present participle, in which case the final "e" is replaced with "-ing." For example:

• d**aring** (/dɛ(ə)rɪŋ/)
• sh**aring** (/ʃɛ(ə)rɪŋ/)
• c**aring** (/kɛ(ə)rɪŋ/)
• st**aring** (/stɛ(ə)rɪŋ/)

Quiz
(answers start on page 463)

1. Which of the following words does **not** have a diphthong?

a) tape
b) meter
c) tile
d) tone
e) compute

2. How is the diphthong /ɔɪ/ pronounced?

a) ah-oo
b) eh-ee
c) oh-oo
d) au-ee

3. Which of the following letter combinations is **sometimes** represented by the diphthong /ɪə/?

a) EA
b) AI
c) OW
d) ARE
e) A & B
f) B & C

4. Which of the following letter combinations can **either** be represented by the diphthong /oʊ/ **or** /aʊ/?

a) OE
b) OU
c) OW
d) OA
e) A & B
f) B & C

5. What is the name for a vowel sound that does **not** glide from one sound to another?

a) zerophthong
b) monophthong
c) diphthong
d) triphthong

Triphthongs

Definition

Very rarely, the nucleus of a single syllable may contain <u>three</u> vowel sounds that quickly glide together; these sounds are known as **triphthongs**.

There are three triphthongs that are generally agreed upon in American English: /aʊə/ ("ah-oo-uh"), /aɪə/ ("ah-ih-uh"), and /jʊə/ ("ee-oo-uh"). These always come before an R sound in a word.

There is some disagreement among linguists as to whether the first two are truly triphthongs, or if they are simply two syllables that are merged closely together (/aʊ.ə/ and /aɪ.ə/). As we look at examples of each of the possible triphthongs below, we'll consider them as both single and double syllables. (For the purposes of this section, a syllable break will be indicated by a dot [.].)

/aʊə/ ("ah-oo-uh")

This vowel sound occurs when the digraph "**OU**" is followed by an "**R**."

Example Words	Triphthong (Single syllable)	No triphthong (Two syllables)
<u>**our**</u>	/a<u>ʊə</u>r/	/ˈa<u>ʊ.ə</u>r/
h<u>our</u>	/a<u>ʊə</u>r/ (H is silent)	/ˈa<u>ʊ.ə</u>r/
fl<u>our</u>	/fla<u>ʊə</u>r/	/ˈfla<u>ʊ.ə</u>r/
s<u>our</u>	/sa<u>ʊə</u>r/	/ˈsa<u>ʊ.ə</u>r/

/aɪə/ ("ah-ih-uh")

This triphthong is pronounced with the letter combination "**IRE**."

Example Words	Triphthong (One syllable)	No triphthong (Two syllables)
f<u>ire</u>	/fa<u>ɪə</u>r/	/ˈfa<u>ɪ.ə</u>r/
d<u>ire</u>	/da<u>ɪə</u>r/	/ˈda<u>ɪ.ə</u>r/
insp<u>ire</u>	/ɪnˈspa<u>ɪə</u>r/	/ɪnˈspa<u>ɪ.ə</u>r/
<u>Ire</u>land	/ˈa<u>ɪə</u>r.lənd/	/ˈa<u>ɪ.ə</u>r.lənd/

In addition to "IRE" words, there are a few other specific instances where this pronunciation may occur:
• pyre (/pa<u>ɪə</u>r/)
• choir (/kwa<u>ɪə</u>r/)

/jʊə/ ("ee-oo-uh")

This triphthong sometimes occurs when the digraph "**UR**" comes after a hard consonant and is followed by an **E, Y**, or **I**. Rather than breaking up the sound into two syllables like the previous two triphthongs, this one is often rounded to leave out the schwa altogether.

Example Words	Triphthong (schwa included)	No triphthong (schwa omitted)
c<u>ure</u>	/kj<u>ʊə</u>r/	/kj<u>ʊ</u>r/
p<u>ure</u>	/pj<u>ʊə</u>r/	/pj<u>ʊ</u>r/
f<u>ur</u>y	/ˈfj<u>ʊə</u>r.i/	/ˈfj<u>ʊ</u>r.i/
c<u>ur</u>ious	/ˈkj<u>ʊə</u>r.iəs/	/ˈkj<u>ʊ</u>r.iəs/

Quiz

(answers start on page 463)

1. How many vowel sounds occur in a single syllable in a triphthong?

a) 1
b) 2
c) 3
d) 4

2. What letter always appears when forming triphthongs?

a) E
b) R
c) Y
d) I

3. Which triphthong can be pronounced in the letter combination "**IRE**"?

a) /aʊə/
b) /aɪə/
c) /jʊə/

4. Which triphthong can be pronounced in the letter combination "**OUR**"?

a) /aʊə/
b) /aɪə/
c) /jʊə/

Tricky Consonant Sounds

Many consonants have a one-to-one relationship with the sounds they make—that is, a certain consonant letter will generally make the same consonant sound no matter where it appears in a word. However, some consonant sounds can be made by several different letters when they appear in certain parts of a word or in combination with other consonants. Many of these are covered in the section on consonant digraphs, but there are a few sounds that can be made by several different single letters as well, which is what we'll focus on in this section. We'll also take a close look at the letter **S**, as it can produce a wide range of speech sounds.

Forming the /k/ Sound

The consonant sound /k/ can be produced by the consonants **C, K** and **X**, as well as the consonant digraphs **CC** and **CK** and the combination **QU**.

Formed from the letter *C*

C most often produces the hard /k/ sound when it come before the vowels **A, O,** and **U**; when it is followed by the consonants **L, R,** and **T**; or when it is the last letter of a word with two or more syllables. For example:

- decade (/ˈdɛkeɪd/)
- cover (/ˈkʌvər/)
- focus (/ˈfoʊkəs/)
- declare (/dɪˈklɛr/)
- create (/kriˈeɪt/)
- act (/ækt/)
- basic (/ˈbeɪsɪk/)

Formed from the letter *K*

As a single letter, **K** is most often used to form the /k/ sound when it is followed by the vowels **E, I,** or **Y,** or at the end of one-syllable words when preceded by another consonant or a vowel digraph. For example:
- **kennel** (/ˈkɛnəl/)
- **kick** (/kɪk/)
- **ask** (/æsk/)
- **oak** (/oʊk/)
- **risky** (/ˈrɪski/)

Formed from the letter *X*

While the letter **X** *does* commonly create the /k/ sound, it does so in combination with the sibilant speech sounds /s/ and /ʃ/, which are pronounced much more distinctly than /k/.

X forms the /ks/ sound when it appears at the end of a word, after a consonant, or between two vowels (if the first one is stressed in the word). For example:
- **box** (/bɑks/)
- **expert** (/ˈɛkspərt/)
- **fix** (/fɪks/)
- **galaxy** (/ˈgæləksi/)
- **phoenix** (/ˈfinɪks/)
- **toxic** (/ˈtɑksɪk/)

The much less common /kʃ/ sound occurs when **X** is followed by the suffixes "-ious," "-ion," and "-ual." For instance:
- **anxious** (/ˈæŋkʃəs/)
- **noxious** (/ˈnɑkʃəs/)
- **obnoxious** (/əbˈnɑkʃəs/)

- **complexion** (/kəmˈpɛkʃən/)

- **sexual** (/ˈsɛkʃuəl/)

Formed from the digraph *CC*

We can also form the /k/ sound with the **digraph CC** following most of the same rules for "hard **C**" that we've seen already—that is, **CC** will produce the /k/ sound when it is followed by **A, O, U, L** or **R.** (No words are spelled **CCT.**)
- **occasion** (/əˈkeɪʒən/)
- **accomplish** (/əˈkɑmplɪʃ/)
- **accuse** (/əˈkjuz/)
- **acclaim** (/əˈkleɪm/)
- **accrue** (/əˈkru/)

CC also creates the /ks/ sound when it is followed by **E, I,** or, in one case, **Y:**
- **accident** (/ˈæksɪdənt/)
- **accent** (/ˈæksɛnt/)
- **coccyx** (/ˈkɑksɪks/)

Formed from the digraph *CK*

While **K** is used on its own to form the /k/ sound at the ends of words when it comes after vowel digraphs or other consonants, the consonant digraph **CK** is used when the /k/ sound is at the end of single-syllable words following a short vowel sound.

For example:
- **back** (/bæk/)

- check (/tʃɛk/)
- stick (/stɪk/)
- rock (/rɑk/)
- puck (/pʌk/)

In multi-syllable words, it more often appears in the middle when it is followed by **ET, LE**, or, less commonly, **O**.

For example:
- bracket (/ˈbrækɪt/)
- cackle (/ˈkækəl/)
- beckon (/ˈbɛkən/)

Formed from the letter *Q*

Other than in certain foreign loanwords, the consonant **Q** is always followed by the letter **U**, and the two letters together usually form the sound /kw/. If the sound /kw/ occurs within a single syllable, and the word is not a compound, it will almost always be spelled **QU**. For example:
- equipment (/ɪˈkwɪpmənt/)
- inquire (/ɪnˈkwaɪər/)
- quiet (/ˈkwaɪət/)
- quick (/kwɪk/)
- request (/rɪˈkwɛst/)
- squeeze (/skwiz/)

Less commonly, **QU** simply forms a hard /k/ sound. This can occur when **QU** is followed by a silent E at the end of a word, or when it is followed by a vowel + **R** or **T** in the middle of a word. For example:
- antique (/ænˈtik/)
- boutique (/buˈtik/)
- critique (/krɪˈtik/)
- grotesque (/groʊˈtɛsk/)
- technique (/tɛkˈnik/)
- unique (/juˈnik/)

- bouquet (/buˈkeɪ/; **T** is silent)
- conquer (/ˈkɑŋkər/)
- etiquette (/ˈɛtɪkɪt/)
- lacquer (/ˈlækər/)
- mosquito (/məsˈkitoʊ/)
- tourniquet (/ˈtɜrnɪkɪt/)

Forming the /z/ Sound

The consonant sound /z/ is most often associated with the consonant letter **Z**, because the correlation between the sound and that letter is very reliable. However, there are a few other letters (and combinations of letters) that can also result in the /z/ sound.

Formed from the letter *Z*

Z most often appears in the middle of a word after a vowel, but it can also appear at the beginning or (less commonly) end of a word. For example:
- bizarre (/bəˈzɑr/)
- brazen (/ˈbreɪzən/)
- citizen (/ˈsɪtəzən/)
- zig (/zɪg/)
- zag (/zæg/)
- topaz (/ˈtoʊˌpæz/)

Z also usually maintains the /z/ pronunciation if it is doubled in the middle or at the end of a word, as in:
- blizzard (/ˈblɪzərd/)
- dazzle (/ˈdæzəl/)
- fuzzy (/ˈfʌzi/)
- buzz (/bʌz/)
- fizz (/fɪz/)
- jazz (/jæz/)

Formed from the letter *S*

S only produces the /z/ sound when it appears in the middle or at the end of certain words. Unfortunately, there are no reliable spelling cues to indicate when **S** is pronounced /z/ rather than /s/ in this position, so we just have to memorize such words or check a dictionary. For example:
- acquisition (/ˌækwəˈzɪʃən/)
- cousin (/ˈkʌzən/)
- liaison (/liˈeɪzən/)
- president (/ˈprɛzɪdənt/)
- visit (/ˈvɪzɪt/)

One of the few instances in which **S** *is* reliably pronounced /z/ is when the letter combination **SM** appears at the end of a word (most often as a part of the suffix "-ism"). For example:
- activism (/ˈæktɪˌvɪzəm/)
- chasm (/ˈkæzəm/)
- materialism (/məˈtɪriəˌlɪzəm/)
- organism (/ˈɔrgəˌnɪzəm/)
- sarcasm (/ˈsɑrˌkæzəm/)

At the end of a word, **S** will be pronounced /z/ if it follows any vowel sound or any consonant sound <u>other than</u> /f/, /k/, /p/, /t/, and /θ/.
- has (/hæz/)
- was (/wʌz/)
- his (/hɪz/)
- she's (/ʃiz/)
- qualms (/kwɑmz/)
- runs (/rʌnz/)
- serves (/sɜrvz/)
- ages (/ˈeɪdʒɪz/)
- halves (/hævz/)

There are also a handful of words in which the consonant digraph **SS** forms the /z/ sound (as opposed to its usual /s/ sound) when it appears between two vowels:
- brassiere (/brəˈzɪər/)
- dessert (/dɪˈzɜrt/)
- dissolve (/dɪˈzɑlv/)
- Missouri (/məˈzʊri/)
- possess (/pəˈzɛs/; note that the second SS is pronounced /s/)
- scissors (/ˈsɪzərz/)

Formed with the letter *X*

The letter **X** almost always forms a blend of consonant sounds. Most of the time, it is the blend /ks/, as in *tax* (/tæks/). However, when it appears immediately before a stressed vowel sound (and almost always *after* the letter **E**) at the beginning of a word, it becomes **voiced** as the combination /gz/. For instance:
- example (/ɪgˈzæmpəl/)
- exaggerate (/ɪgˈzædʒəˌreɪt/)

- exist (/ɪgˈzɪst/)
- exhaust (/ɪgˈzɑst/)
- exhibit (/ɪgˈzɪbɪt/)

(Note that the **H** is **silent** in the last two of these examples.)

There are also a few words in which **X** *only* forms the /z/ sound, though most of these are not common in everyday speech and writing. For example:

- xanthan (/ˈzænθən/)
- xenolith (/ˈzɛnəlɪθ/)
- xerography (/zɪˈrɑgrəfi/)
- xylophone (/ˈzaɪləˌfoʊn/)

Forming the /ʒ/ Sound

Unlike most consonant sounds, the sound /ʒ/ does not have a specific letter or digraph commonly associated with it. Instead, the /ʒ/ sound occurs when various consonants appear next to or between certain vowels.

Formed with the letter S

The most common consonant that forms the /ʒ/ sound is **S** when it is followed by a specific suffix and (usually) preceded by a vowel. For example:

Vowel + S + "-ion"	Vowel + S + "-ure"	Vowel + S + "-ia"	Vowel + S + "-ual"
invasion (/ɪnˈveɪʒən/)	closure (/ˈkloʊʒər/)	ambrosia (/æmˈbroʊʒə/)	casual (/ˈkæʒuəl/)
cohesion (/koʊˈhiʒən/)	composure (/kəmˈpoʊʒər/)	amnesia (/æmˈniʒə/)	usual (/ˈjuʒuəl/)
decision (/dɪˈsɪʒən/)	exposure (/ɪkˈspoʊʒər/)	dysplasia (/dɪsˈpleɪʒə/)	visual (/ˈvɪʒuəl/)
explosion (/ɪkˈsploʊʒən/)	leisure (/ˈliʒər/)	fantasia (/fænˈteɪʒə/)	
inclusion (/ɪnˈkluʒən/)	measure (/ˈmɛʒər/)		

Formed from the letter *G*

The letter **G** takes a "soft" pronunciation when it appears after a vowel and immediately before an **E, I,** or **Y**. While /dʒ/ is the most common speech sound used for a soft **G**, the /ʒ/ sound is formed in some French loanwords ending in **GE**. For example:

- beige (/beɪʒ/)
- camouflage (/ˈkæməˌflɑʒ/)
- garage (/gəˈrɑʒ/)
- massage (/məˈsɑʒ/)
- rouge (/ruʒ/)

Formed from the letter *J*

Like soft **G**, the letter **J** occasionally produces the /ʒ/ sound instead of the normal /dʒ/ sound, though this only happens in foreign loanwords. For example:

- Beijing (/ˌbeɪʒˈɪŋ/)
- bijou (/ˈbiʒu/)
- déjà vu (/ˈdeɪʒæ ˈvu/)
- Dijon (/ˌdiˈʒɑn/)

• force majeure (/ˈfɔrs mæˈʒɜr/)
• Taj Mahal (/tɑʒ məˈhɑl/)

Pronouncing the Letter S

The letter **S** can sometimes be problematic for pronunciation due to the wide range of speech sounds it can represent. Its most common sound is the unvoiced sibilant /s/, made by forcing air between the tongue and roof of the mouth and out past the teeth without engaging the vocal cords. As we saw previously, **S** also commonly represents this sound's voiced counterpart, /z/, formed the same way but with the vocal cords engaged.

Which pronunciation the letter forms is much easier to determine when it appears at the beginning or end of a word.

At the beginning of a word

S is almost always pronounced /s/ if it appears at the beginning of a word, as in:
• sat (/sæt/)
• social (/ˈsoʊʃəl/)
• syllable (/ˈsɪləbəl/)
• skip (/skɪp/)
• small (/smɔl/)
• start (/stɑrt/)

The only exceptions to this rule are the words *sugar* and *sure*, both of which begin with the /ʃ/ sound (the sound associated with the consonant digraph **SH**).

At the end of a word

Suffixes, contractions, and possessives

When the suffixes "-s," "-es," or "-'s" are added to a word to form a plural, the grammatical third person, a contraction, or a possessive, then we can determine how it will be pronounced by looking at the speech sound immediately before it.

S is always pronounced /s/ when coming after an **unvoiced**, non-sibilant consonant sound—that is, after /k/, /f/, /p/, /t/, and /θ/ (the unvoiced **TH** sound). For example:
• books (/bʊks/)
• laughs (/læfs/)
• keeps (/kips/)
• let's (/lɛts/)
• strengths (/strɛŋkθs/)

If **S** comes after a **voiced** consonant sound (/b/, /d/, /g/, /l/, /m/, /n/, /ŋ/, /r/, /ð/, /v/) or a vowel sound, the **S** will be pronounced as /z/. When adding "-s" to a word that ends in a voiced or unvoiced **sibilant** speech sound (/s/, /z/, /ʃ/, /ʒ/, /ʧ/, /ʤ/), the suffix becomes "-es" and is pronounced /ɪz/. (The same pronunciation is used if an apostrophe-S is added to a word with a sibilant speech sound at the end.)

For example:
• barbs (/bɑrbz/)
• dreads (/drɛdz/)
• eggs (/ɛgz/)
• lulls (/lʌlz/)
• Malcolm's (/ˈmælkəmz/)
• wives (/waɪvz/)
• buses (/bʌsɪz/)
• comprises (/kəmˈpraɪzɪz/)
• Trish's (/ˈtrɪʃɪz/)

- garage**s** (/gəˈrɑʒɪ**z**/)
- pitche**s** (/ˈpɪtʃɪ**z**/)
- smudge**s** (/ˈsmʌdʒɪ**z**/)

Words ending in a single *S*

When a word ends naturally in a single **S** (that is, it is not a suffix), it usually tends to be the unvoiced /s/ pronunciation. However, there are a few words that are pronounced /z/ instead, with no indication from the spelling alone. For example:

Pronounced /s/	Pronounced /z/
atla**s** (/ˈætlə**s**/) bu**s** (/bʌ**s**/) circu**s** (/ˈsɜrkə**s**/) diagnos**is** (/ˌdaɪəgˈnoʊsə**s**/) ga**s** (/gæ**s**/) plu**s** (/plʌ**s**/) thi**s** (/ðɪ**s**/) ye**s** (/jɛ**s**/)	a**s** (/æ**z**/) ha**s** (/hæ**z**/) hi**s** (/hɪ**z**/) **is** (/ɪ**z**/) wa**s** (/wʌ**z**/)

Words ending in *SS*

Like words that *begin* with S, words that end in **SS** <u>always</u> make the /s/ sound. For example:

- aby**ss** (/əˈbɪ**s**/)
- cra**ss** (/kræ**s**/)
- dre**ss** (/drɛ**s**/)
- fu**ss** (/fʌ**s**/)
- hi**ss** (/hɪ**s**/)
- to**ss** (/tɑ**s**/)

Words ending in "-se"

When **S** is followed by a silent E, it will reliably create the /s/ sound when it follows four specific consonants: **L, N, P,** and **R**. For example:

- fal**se** (/fɔl**s**/)
- respon**se** (/rɪˈspɑn**s**/)
- eclip**se** (/ɪˈklɪp**s**/)
- traver**se** (/trəˈvɜr**s**/)

When "-se" comes after a vowel sound, it is much trickier to predict. Unfortunately, the only time we can be sure of S's pronunciation is when a word has the same spelling but has <u>two</u> pronunciations, one for a noun (or adjective) and one for a verb. When this is the case, the noun form will be pronounced with a final /s/, while the verb form will be pronounced with a final /z/. Otherwise, there is no clear pattern to when "-se" will be pronounced /s/ or /z/.

For example:

Pronounced /s/	Pronounced /z/
abu**se** (noun: /əˈbjus/)	abu**se** (verb: /əˈbjuz/)
cea**se** (/sis/)	appea**se** (/əˈpiz/)
clo**se** (adj.: /kloʊs/)	chee**se** (/ʧiz/)
conci**se** (/kənˈsaɪs/)	choo**se** (/ʧuz/)
diagno**se** (/ˌdaɪəgˈnoʊs/)	clo**se** (verb: /kloʊz/)
excu**se** (noun: /ɪˈkskjus/)	demi**se** (/dɪˈmaɪz/)
goo**se** (/gus/)	excu**se** (verb: /ɪˈkskjuz/)
hou**se** (noun: /haʊs/)	hou**se** (verb: /haʊz/)
loo**se** (/lus/)	plea**se** (/pliz/)
lou**se** (/laʊs/)	refu**se** (verb: /rɪˈfjuz/)
mou**se** (/maʊs/)	tho**se** (/ðoʊz/)
refu**se** (noun: /ˈrɛˌfjus/)	u**se** (verb: /juz/)
u**se** (noun: /jus/)	wi**se** (/waɪz/)

In the middle of a word

The conventions and patterns for how to pronounce **S** in the middle of a word are too varied and extensive to summarize here, but you can continue on to the section Pronouncing the Letter S to learn more.

Forming the /ʃ/ (and /ʒ/) sounds

In addition to /s/ and /z/, **S** can also form the /ʃ/ (as in *wash*) and /ʒ/ (as in *beige*) sounds when it appears in combination with certain suffixes. We saw earlier how it forms the /ʒ/ sound when this combination comes after a vowel; however, several of the same combinations will yield the /ʃ/ sound if they come after **L**, **N**, or another **S**. For example:

S + "-ion"	S + "-ure"	S + "-ual"
propul**sion** (/prəˈpʌlʃən/) dimen**sion** (/dɪˈmɛnʃən/) pa**ssion** (/ˈpæʃən/)	cen**sure** (/ˈsɛnʃər/) in**sure** (/ɪnˈʃʊər/) pre**ssure** (/ˈprɛʃər/)	consen**sual** (/kənˈsɛnʃuəl/) sen**sual** (/ˈsɛnʃuəl/)

Quiz

(answers start on page 463)

1. When does the letter **C** *not* form the /k/ sound?

a) Before the vowels **A, O,** and **U**
b) Before the vowels **E, I,** and **Y**
c) When it is followed by the consonants **L, R,** and **T**
d) When it is the last letter of a word with two or more syllables

2. The combination **QU** most often forms which of the following speech sounds?

a) /kw/
b) /ku/
c) /kju/
d) /ki/

3. In which of the following word endings is **S** always pronounced /z/?

a) "-ise"
b) "-ism"
c) "-ase"
d) "-ss"

4. Which of the following sounds is **not** made by the letter **S**?

a) /s/
b) /z/
c) /θ/
d) /ʃ/
e) /ʒ/

5. In which of the following words does **X** produce the /z/ sound?

a) exception
b) exert
c) exercise
d) exhale

6. Which of the following consonant digraphs is associated with the /ʒ/ speech sound?

a) SH
b) CH
c) GH
d) None

Forming the /k/ Sound

The consonant sound /k/ can be tricky because it can be formed from a number of different consonant letters—**C, CC, K, CK**, and **QU** can all be used to form this sound, depending where they occur in a word.

Forming the /k/ sound with *C*

The letter **C** can form either a "hard" sound (/k/) or a "soft" sound (/s/). **C** most often produces the hard /k/ sound when it come before the vowels **A, O,** and **U**; when it is followed by the consonants **L, R,** and **T**; or when it is the last letter of a word with two or more syllables. For example:

CA	CO	CU	CL	CR	CT	Final letter
advocate (/ˈædvəˌkeɪt/)	acoustic (/əˈkustɪk/)	articulate (/ɑrˈtɪkjələt/)	barnacle (/ˈbɑrnəkəl/)	across (/əˈkrɔs/)	act (/ækt/)	academic (/ˌækəˈdɛmɪk/)
call (/kɔl/)	corner (/ˈkɔrnər/)	cushion (/ˈkuʃən/)	climb (/klaɪm/)	democracy (/dɪˈmakrəsi/)	constructive (/kənˈstrʌktɪv/)	basic (/ˈbeɪsɪk/)
cap (/kæp/)	cover (/ˈkʌvər/)	cute (/kjut/)	clean (/klin/)	crawl (/krɔl/)	election (/ɪˈlɛkʃən/)	frolic (/ˈfralɪkk/)
catch (/kætʃ/)	coat (/koʊt/)	curve (/kɜrv/)	declare (/dɪˈklɛr/)	create (/kriˈeɪt/)	galactic (/gəˈlæktɪk/)	graphic (/ˈgræfɪk/)
decade (/ˈdɛkeɪd/)	economy (/ɪˈkanəmi/)	focus (/ˈfoʊkəs/)	incline (/ɪnˈklaɪn/)	lucrative (/ˈlukrətɪv/)	nocturnal (/nakˈtɜrnəl/)	havoc (/ˈhævək/)
pecan (/pɪˈkan/)	helicopter (/ˈhɛlɪˌkaptər/)	peculiar (/pɪˈkjuljər/)	nuclear (/ˈnukliər/)	microscope (/ˈmaɪkrəˌskoʊp/)	predict (/prɪˈdɪkt/)	maniac (/ˈmeɪniˌæk/)
scale (/skeɪl/)	scold (/skoʊld/)	sculpture (/ˈskʌlptʃər/)	uncle (/ˈʌŋkəl/)	sacrifice (/ˈsækrəˌfaɪs/)	selective (/səˈlɛktɪv/)	traffic (/ˈtræfɪk/)

Forming the /s/ sound

"Soft **C**" (/s/), on the other hand, is made when **C** is followed by the vowels **E, I,** and **Y,** as in:

CE	CI	CY
aced (/ˈeɪsd/)	advancing (/ədˈvænsɪŋ/)	bicycle (/ˈbaɪsɪkəl/)
central (/ˈsɛntrəl/)	circle (/ˈsɜrkəl/)	cylinder (/ˈsɪlɪndər/)
celebrate (/ˈsɛləˌbreɪt/)	city (/ˈsɪti/)	icy (/ˈaɪsi/)
nice (/naɪs/)	decide (/ˌdɪˈsaɪd/)	juicy (/ˈdʒusi/)
recent (/ˈrisənt/)	exercise (/ˈɛksərˌsaɪz/)	privacy (/ˈpraɪvəsi/)

Because of the way **C** becomes "soft" when followed by **E, I,** and **Y,** we usually form the /k/ sound with either **K** or **CK** before these vowels, as we'll see a bit later.

Forming the /k/ sound with *CC*

We can also form the /k/ sound in many words with the **digraph CC**, following most of the same rules for "hard **C**" that we've seen already—that is, **CC** will produce the /k/ sound when it is followed by **A, O, U, L** or **R**. (No words contain the cluster **CCT**—other than initialisms—and no words begin or end with **CC**.)

For example:

CCA	CCO	CCU	CCL	CCR
buccaneer (/ˌbʌkəˈnɪr/)	accommodate (/əˈkɑməˌdeɪt/)	accurate (/ˈækjərɪt/)		
desiccate (/ˈdɛsɪkeɪt/)	accomplish (/əˈkɑmplɪʃ/)	accuse (/əˈkjuz/)	acclaim (/əˈkleɪm/)	
impeccable (/ɪmˈpɛkəbəl/)	account (/əˈkaʊnt/)	hiccup (/ˈhɪkʌp/)	acclimate (/ˈækləˌmeɪt/)	accredit (/əˈkrɛdɪt/)
occasion (/əˈkeɪʒən/)	broccoli (/ˈbrɑkəli/)	occupy (/ˈɑkjəˌpaɪ/)	ecclesiastic (/ɪˌkliziˈæstɪk/)	accrue (/əˈkru/)
staccato (/stəˈkɑˌtoʊ/)	raccoon (/ræˈkun/)	occur (/əˈkɜr/)	occlude (/əˈklud/)	
	tobacco (/təˈbæˌkoʊ/)	succumb (/səˈkʌm/)		

Creating the /ks/ sound

If **CC** is followed by **E** or **I**, the first **C** still forms the /k/ sound, but the second **C** behaves like a single **C** and forms the /s/ sound. For example:
• accident (/ˈæksɪdənt/)
• accelerate (/ækˈsɛləˌreɪt/)
• accent (/ˈæksɛnt/)
• accept (/əkˈsɛpt/)
• access (/ˈækˌsɛs/)
• eccentric (/ɪkˈsɛntrɪk/)
• occident (/ˈɑksɪˌdɛnt/)
• succeed (/səkˈsid/)
• succinct (/səkˈsɪŋkt/)
• vaccine (/vækˈsin/)

Exceptions

The most common exceptions to this rule come from Italian loan words in which **CC** produces the /ʧ/ ("ch") sound when followed by **I** or **E**, as in:
• bocce (/ˈbɑʧi/)
• cacciatore (/kæʧəˈtɔri/)
• cappuccino (/ˌkæˌpuˈʧinoʊ/)
• fettuccine (/ˌfɛtəˈʧini/)
• focaccia (/foʊˈkɑʧə/)

Other exceptions come from abbreviations of words that are used in a new (often informal) way. In these, **CC** maintains a hard /k/ sound, despite being followed by E or I. For instance:

Word	IPA Pronunciation	Word Meaning & Origin
recce	/ˈrɛki/	Slang military abbreviation of *reconnaissance*, used as a noun or a verb.
soccer	/ˈsɑkər/	Now the established North American term for *association football*, originally formed from the abbreviation of the word *association* (*assoc.*) + the suffix "-er."
specced	/ˈspɛkt/	Past participle of *spec*, an informal abbreviation of *specification* used as a verb.
speccing	/ˈspɛkɪŋ/	Present participle of *spec*, an informal abbreviation of *specification* used as a verb.

One last exception is the word *flaccid*. The original pronunciation of the word follows the standard convention we've already seen, with **CC** producing the /ks/ sound: /ˈflæksɪd/. However, it is now much more commonly pronounced /ˈflæsɪd/, with **CC** producing a single soft /s/ sound.

Forming the /k/ sound with *K*

As a single letter, **K** is most often used to form the /k/ sound when it is followed by the vowels **E** or **I** (since a **C** before these letters would result in the /s/ sound), or at the end of one-syllable words when preceded by another consonant (we'll look at the digraph **CK** separately) or a vowel digraph. For example:

KE	KI	Final letter
bake (/beɪk/)	akimbo (/əˈkɪmˌboʊ/)	ask (/æsk/)
canker (/ˈkæŋkər/)	bikini (/bɪˈkini/)	book (/bʊk/)
keep (/kip/)	kick (/kɪk/)	creek (/krik/)
kennel (/ˈkɛnəl/)	kid (/kɪd/)	oak (/oʊk/)
key (/ki/)	kiss (/kɪs/)	park (/pɑrk/)
market (/ˈmɑrkɪt/)	kitchen (/ˈkɪtʃən/)	risk (/rɪsk/)
smoke (/smoʊk/)	skill (/skɪl/)	shriek (/ʃrik/)
skeleton (/ˈskɛlɪtən/)	skip (/skɪp/)	work (/wɜrk/)

K also appears before the vowel **Y**, as in the word *sky*, but this more often occurs when the suffix "-y" is attached to nouns already ending in **K** to form adjectives, as in:
• bulky (/ˈbʌlki/)
• cheeky (/ˈtʃiki/)
• cranky (/ˈkræŋki/)
• funky (/ˈfʌŋki/)
• husky (/ˈhʌski/)
• inky (/ˈɪŋki/)
• leaky (/ˈliki/)
• murky (/ˈmɜrki/)
• risky (/ˈrɪski/)

skeptic vs. *sceptic*

In American English, the word *skeptic* (/ˈskɛptɪk/) follows the spelling patterns we've just seen, with **K** being used when followed by **E**. However, the original spelling of the word is *sceptic* (with the same pronunciation), which is the preferred spelling in British English. Because **SC** usually produces the /s/ sound before **E** and **I** (as in *scepter* or *science*), skeptic has become the preferred spelling in American English.

This difference in spelling carries over to its derivative forms as well:

• skeptic→skeptical, skepticism
• sceptic→sceptical, scepticism

Forming the /k/ sound with *CK*

While **K** is used on its own to form the /k/ sound at the ends of words when it comes after vowel digraphs or other consonants, the consonant digraph **CK** is used when the /k/ sound is at the end of single-syllable words following a short vowel sound. For example:

ACK (/æk/)	ECK (/ɛk/)	ICK (/ɪk/)	OCK (/ɑk/)	UCK (/ʌk/)
back	beck	brick	block	buck
black	check	click	clock	chuck
crack	deck	kick	dock	duck
hack	fleck	lick	flock	luck
lack	neck	pick	knock	pluck
pack	peck	quick	lock	muck
snack	speck	stick	rock	stuck
track	wreck	trick	shock	truck

CK in multi-syllable words

As we've seen already, **C** is often the last letter of words with two or more syllables that end in a /k/ sound, usually coming after a short **I** sound (/ɪ/), as in *graphic* or *panic*.

The digraph **CK** most typically appears at the end of words with one syllable, but there are some common exceptions, such as *attack* or *hammock*. In multi-syllable words, it more often appears in the middle when it is followed by **ET, LE**, or, less commonly, **O**. For example:

CK+ET	CK+LE	CK+O
bracket (/ˈbrækɪt/)	buckle (/ˈbʌkəl/)	
bucket (/ˈbʌkɪt/)	cackle (/ˈkækəl/)	
cricket (/ˈkrɪkɪt/)	chuckle (/ˈʧʌkəl/)	beckon (/ˈbɛkən/)
jacket (/ˈʤækɪt/)	heckle (/ˈhɛkəl/)	gecko (/ˈgɛkoʊ/)
picket (/ˈpɪkɪt/)	knuckle (/ˈnʌkəl/)	hickory (/ˈhɪkəri/)
racket (/ˈrækɪt/)	pickle (/ˈpɪkəl/)	reckon (/ˈrɛkən/)
rocket (/ˈrɑkɪt/)	shackle (/ˈʃækəl/)	
ticket (/ˈtɪkɪt/)	tickle (/ˈtɪkəl/)	

(Note that this list does not include compound words or those formed by attaching suffixes to the end of single-syllable words.)

Adding *K* to verbs ending in *C*

Most verbs do not end in a **C** after a vowel; they usually have a **K** at the end to make the /k/ sound more definitive. A few do have a final **C**, though, so to avoid a spelling that might indicate a "soft C" sound (/s/), we add a **K** before suffixes beginning with **E**, **I**, or **Y**. For example:

• frolic→frolicked, frolicker, frolicking
• mimic→mimicked, mimicker, mimicking
• panic→panicked, panicking, panicky
• picnic→picnicked, picnicker, picnicking
• traffic→trafficked, trafficker, trafficking

Note that we **don't** do this when we attach consonant suffixes or vowel suffixes that begin with **A**:

• frolic→frolics, frolicsome
• mimic→mimical, mimicry, mimics
• panic→panics
• picnic→picnics
• traffic→trafficable, traffics

Don't add *K* when attaching the suffix "-ize"

When we <u>make</u> verbs from other parts of speech that end in C by attaching the suffix "-ize," we **don't** add a **K**. Instead, **C** remains on its own, but its pronunciation changes from the /k/ sound to the /s/ sound. For example:

• critic (/ˈkrɪtɪk/)→criticize (/ˈkrɪtɪˌsaɪz/)
• italic (/ɪˈtælɪk/)→italicize (/ɪˈtælɪˌsaɪz/)
• politic (/ˈpɑləˌtɪk/)→politicize (/pəˈlɪtɪˌsaɪz/)
• public (/ˈpʌblɪk/)→publicize (/ˈpʌblɪˌsaɪz/)
• mythic (/ˈmɪθɪk/)→mythicize (/ˈmɪθəˌsaɪz/)
• romantic (/roʊˈmæntɪk/)→romanticize (/roʊˈmæntəˌsaɪz/)

Forming the /k/ sound with *QU*

Other than in certain foreign loanwords, the consonant **Q** is always followed by the letter **U**, and the two letters together usually form the sound /kw/. If the sound /kw/ occurs within a single syllable, and the word is not a compound, it will almost always be spelled **QU**. For example:

• e**qu**ipment (/ɪˈkwɪpmənt/)
• elo**qu**ence (/ˈɛləkwəns/)
• in**qu**ire (/ɪnˈkwaɪər/)
• **qu**een (/kwin/)
• **qu**iet (/ˈkwaɪət/)
• **qu**ick (/kwɪk/)
• re**qu**est (/rɪˈkwɛst/)
• re**qu**ire (/rɪˈkwɛst/)
• s**qu**are (/skwɛər/)
• s**qu**eeze (/skwiz/)

QU does not always result in a /kw/ sound, though; sometimes it is simply a hard /k/. This most often occurs when **QU** is followed by a silent E at the end of a word, as in:

• anti**que** (/ænˈtik/)
• baro**que** (/bəˈroʊk/)
• bouti**que** (/buˈtik/)
• criti**que** (/krɪˈtik/)
• grotes**que** (/groʊˈtɛsk/)
• opa**que** (/oʊˈpeɪk/)
• pictures**que** (/ˈpɪktʃərəsk/)
• physi**que** (/fɪˈzik/)
• techni**que** (/tɛkˈnik/)
• uni**que** (/juˈnik/)

Less commonly, **QU** forms the /k/ sound in the middle of a word when followed by a vowel + **R** or **T**. For instance:

- briquette (/brɪˈkɛt/)
- bouquet (/buˈkeɪ/; **T** is silent)
- conquer (/ˈkɑŋkər/)
- etiquette (/ˈɛtɪkɪt/)
- lacquer (/ˈlækər/)
- liquor (/ˈlɪkər/)
- masquerade (/ˌmæskəˈreɪd/)
- mosquito (/məsˈkitoʊ/)
- tourniquet (/ˈtɜrnɪkɪt/)

Quiz
(answers start on page 463)

1. When is the letter **C** generally *not* able to form the /k/ sound?

a) When it is followed by a consonant
b) When it is followed by the vowels **A, O**, or **U**
c) When it is followed by the vowels **E, I**, or **Y**
d) None of the above

2. In which of the following words is **CC** pronounced /ks/?

a) accumulate
b) accentuate
c) accommodate
d) acclimate

3. Which ending correctly completes the following word?
"guideboo_"

a) c
b) cc
c) k
d) ck

4. When do we add **K** to words ending in **C**?

a) When attaching the suffix "-ed"
b) When attaching the suffix "-ing"
c) When attaching the suffix "-ize"
d) When attaching the suffix "-al"
e) A & B
f) B & C
g) All of the above

5. Which of the following words makes the sound /kw/?

a) disqualify
b) rescuing
c) brusque
d) accuse

6. When does **CK** typically appear at the end of a word? (Choose the answer that is most correct.)

a) In single-syllable words
b) In multi-syllable words
c) When preceded by a vowel digraph
d) When preceded by a short vowel sound
e) A & B
f) B & C
g) A & D

Forming the /z/ Sound

The consonant sound **/z/** is most often associated with the consonant letter **Z**, because the correlation between the sound and that letter is very reliable. However, there are a few other letters (and combinations of letters) that can also result in the /z/ sound. First, let's go over the letter **Z**, and then we'll look at other letters that can form this sound.

Forming the /z/ sound with *Z*

The letter **Z** (pronounced "zee," IPA: /zi/, in American English and "zed," IPA: /zɛd/, in British English) almost always produces the same consonant sound, transcribed in IPA as /z/. It is formed the same way as the sound /s/—by forcing air between the tongue and the roof of the mouth and out past the teeth—except that the vocal cords are vibrated to create sound, making /z/ a **voiced** speech sound.

In the middle of a word

Z most often appears in the middle of a word after a vowel. For example:
- amazing (/əˈmeɪzɪŋ/)
- Amazon (/ˈæməˌzɑn/)
- bizarre (/bəˈzɑr/)
- breeze (/briz/)
- brazen (/ˈbreɪzən/)
- citizen (/ˈsɪtəzən/)
- emblazon (/ɛmˈbleɪzən/)
- freezing (/frizɪŋ/)
- size (/saɪz/)

Z also usually maintains the /z/ pronunciation if it is doubled in the middle of a word, as in:
- blizzard (/ˈblɪzərd/)
- dazzle (/ˈdæzəl/)
- fuzzy (/ˈfʌzi/)
- muzzle (/ˈmʌzəl/)
- nozzle (/ˈnɑzəl/)
- tizzy (/ˈtɪzi/)

When *ZZ* is pronounced /ts/

In a few Italian loan words, **ZZ** has the same pronunciation as the consonant cluster **TZ**, /ts/ (as in *pretzel, quartz, waltz,* etc.). For example:
- mezzo (/ˈmɛtsoʊ/)
- mozzarella (/ˌmɑtsəˈrɛlə/)
- paparazzi (/ˌpɑpəˈrɑtsi/)
- pizza (/ˈpitsə/)

Z in other positions

Z *can* appear at the beginning or end of a word, but this is much less common. If it does end the word, it is usually (but not always) doubled. For instance:
- zig (/zɪg/)
- zag (/zæg/)
- zeal (/zil/)
- zucchini (/zuˈkini/)
- buzz (/bʌz/)
- fizz (/fɪz/)
- jazz (/jæz/)
- topaz (/ˈtoʊˌpæz/)

Z can also appear after the letter **T** at the end of some words, but its pronunciation changes (which we'll look at a little later).

"-ize" and "-ization"

Perhaps the most common use of **Z** is in the suffix "-ize" (which indicates a verb formed from a noun or adjective) and its derivative "-ization" (which indicates a noun formed from such a verb).* For example:

IZE	IZATION
reali**ze** (/ˈriəˌlaɪz/)	reali**z**ation (/ˌriələˈzeɪʃən/)
speciali**ze** (/ˈspɛʃəˌlaɪz/)	speciali**z**ation (/ˌspɛʃələˈzeɪʃən/)
visuali**ze** (/ˈvɪʒwəˌlaɪz/)	visuali**z**ation (/ˌvɪʒwələˈzeɪʃən/)

In British English, these suffixes are more commonly spelled "-ise" and "-isation," with the same pronunciation. There are a few words that are spelled this way in American English, though, which we'll look at further on.

Forming the /z/ sound with *S*

S only produces the /z/ sound when it appears in the middle or at the end of certain words. We'll briefly go over examples of these here, but there is more detail in the section on Pronouncing the Letter S.

In the middle of words

When **S** appears in the middle of a word, it can sometimes produce the /z/ sound if it comes between two vowels. For example:
- acqui**s**ition (/ˌækwəˈzɪʃən/)
- bu**s**y (/ˈbɪzi/)
- cou**s**in (/ˈkʌzən/)
- de**s**ert (*n.* /ˈdɛzərt/)
- ea**s**y (/ˈizi/)
- inci**s**or (/ɪnˈsaɪzər/)
- liai**s**on (/liˈeɪzən/)
- mu**s**ic (/ˈmjuzɪk/)
- poi**s**on (/ˈpɔɪzən/)
- pre**s**ent (*adj.* /ˈprɛzənt/)
- pre**s**ident (/ˈprɛzɪdənt/)
- pri**s**on (/ˈprɪzən/)
- rea**s**on (/ˈrizən/)
- vi**s**it (/ˈvɪzɪt/)

Unfortunately, this is not a reliable convention, and it can be pronounced /s/ in many other words.

At the end of words

Forming plurals, possessives, and the third-person singular

We use the suffix "-s" to create plurals of nouns and to inflect verbs for third-person singular subjects, and we use "-'s" to indicate possession for most nouns. When either of these endings comes after the consonant sounds /f/, /k/, /p/, /t/, and /θ/, they will produce the /s/ sound; after any other consonant or vowel sounds, "-s" or "-'s" (or "-es") is pronounced /-z/.

Pronunciation Conventions

For example:

Pronounced /s/	Pronounced /z/
	ages (/ˈeɪdʒɪz/)
	bathes (/beɪðz/)
antics (/ˈæntɪks/)	buzzes (/ˈbʌzɪz/)
bishop's (/ˈbɪʃəps/)	coach's (/koʊtʃɪz/)
creates (/kriˈeɪts/)	duties (/dutiz/)
Derrick's (/ˈdɛrɪks/)	frogs (/frɑgz/)
engulfs (/ɛnˈgʌlfs/)	Georgina's (/ˌdʒɔrˈdʒinəz/)
gets (/gɛts/)	holds (/hoʊtldz/)
kicks (/kɪks/)	judges (/ˈdʒʌdʒɪz/)
laughs (/læfs/)	marshes (/mɑrʃɪz/)
monoliths (/ˈmɑnəlɪθs/)	numerals (/ˈnumərəlz/)
Pat's (/pæts/)	Peter's (/pitərz/)
traps (/træps/)	qualms (/kwɑmz/)
unearths (/ʌnˈɜrθs/)	runs (/rʌnz/)
	serves (/sɜrvz/)
	watches (/wɑtʃɪz/)

Note that some nouns ending in "-f" or "-fe" change their spelling to "-ves" when becoming plural, and the pronunciation of the **S** changes accordingly:
- half (/hæf/)→hal**ves** (/hæ**vz**/)
- knife (/naɪf/)→kni**ves** (/naɪ**vz**/)
- life (/laɪf/)→li**ves** (/laɪ**vz**/)
- loaf (/loʊf/)→loa**ves** (/loʊ**vz**/)
- shelf (/ʃɛlf/)→shel**ves** (/ʃɛl**vz**/)
- thief (/θif/)→thie**ves** (/θi**vz**/)

The pluralization of several nouns ending in "-th" produces a similar effect. While the spelling doesn't change at all, the pronunciation changes from /θ/ to /ðz/. For example:
- booth (/buθ/)→boo**ths** (/bu**ðz**/)
- mouth (/maʊθ/)→mou**ths** (/maʊ**ðz**/)
- oath (/oʊθ/)→oa**ths** (/oʊ**ðz**/)
- path (/pæθ/)→pa**ths** (/pæ**ðz**/)
- truth (/truθ/)→tru**ths** (/tru**ðz**/)
- wreath (/riθ/)→wrea**ths** (/ri**ðz**/)

Words ending "-sm"

One instance in which **S** is <u>always</u> pronounced /z/ is when the letter combination **SM** appears at the end of a word (most often as a part of the suffix "-ism"), in which case a reduced vowel sound (the schwa, /ə/) is pronounced between **S** and **M**. For example:

• activi<u>sm</u> (/ˈæktɪˌvɪ<u>z</u>əm/)
• bapti<u>sm</u> (/ˈbæptɪ<u>z</u>əm/)
• cha<u>sm</u> (/ˈkæ<u>z</u>əm/)
• humani<u>sm</u> (/ˈhjuməˌnɪ<u>z</u>əm/)
• materiali<u>sm</u> (/məˈtɪriəˌlɪ<u>z</u>əm/)
• nationali<u>sm</u> (/ˈnæʃənəˌlɪ<u>z</u>əm/)
• organi<u>sm</u> (/ˈɔrgəˌnɪ<u>z</u>əm/)
• phanta<u>sm</u> (/ˌfænˈtæ<u>z</u>əm/)
• sarca<u>sm</u> (/ˈsɑrˌkæ<u>z</u>əm/)
• spirituali<u>sm</u> (/ˈspɪrɪʧəwəlɪ<u>z</u>əm/)

Vowel + *-se*

If a word ends in "-se" preceded by a vowel, the **S** will often form the /z/ sound. For example:

• appea<u>se</u> (/əˈpi<u>z</u>/)
• brow<u>se</u> (/braʊ<u>z</u>/)
• brui<u>se</u> (/bru<u>z</u>/)
• cau<u>se</u> (/kɔ<u>z</u>/)
• chee<u>se</u> (/ʧi<u>z</u>/)
• choo<u>se</u> (/ʧu<u>z</u>/)
• the<u>se</u> (/ði<u>z</u>/)
• espou<u>se</u> (/ɪˈspaʊ<u>z</u>/)
• pha<u>se</u> (/feɪ<u>z</u>/)
• prai<u>se</u> (/preɪ<u>z</u>/)
• ro<u>se</u> (/roʊ<u>z</u>/)
• wi<u>se</u> (/waɪ<u>z</u>/)

Unfortunately, this is not a very reliable convention. In fact, several pairs of words have the exact same vowel + "-se" spelling, but have different pronunciations. For instance:

Pronounced /s/	Pronounced /z/
case (/keɪs/)	phra<u>se</u> (/freɪ<u>z</u>/)
dose (/doʊs/)	no<u>se</u> (/noʊ<u>z</u>/)
geese (/gis/)	chee<u>se</u> (/ʧi<u>z</u>/)
moose (/mus/)	choo<u>se</u> (/ʧu<u>z</u>/)
mouse (/maʊs/)	carou<u>se</u> (/kəˈraʊ<u>z</u>/)
grease (/gris/)	ea<u>se</u> (/i<u>z</u>/)
obese (/oʊˈbis/)	Chine<u>se</u> (/ʧaɪˈni<u>z</u>/)
premise (/ˈprɛmɪs/)	demi<u>se</u> (/dɪˈmaɪ<u>z</u>/)

There are also a few pairs of words that have the same spelling, but whose pronunciation changes depending on meaning. For example:

Pronounced /s/	Pronounced /z/
abuse (noun) (/əˈbjus/)	abu<u>se</u> (verb) (/əˈbju<u>z</u>/)
close (adjective) (/kloʊs/)	clo<u>se</u> (verb) (/kloʊ<u>z</u>/)
diffuse (adjective) (/dɪˈfjus/)	diffu<u>se</u> (verb) (/dɪˈfju<u>z</u>/)
excuse (noun) (/ɪkˈskjus/)	excu<u>se</u> (verb) (/ɪkˈskju<u>z</u>/)
house (noun) (/haʊs/)	hou<u>se</u> (verb) (/haʊ<u>z</u>/)
use (noun) (/jus/)	u<u>se</u> (verb) (/ju<u>z</u>/)

One specific ending that <u>will</u> reliably produce the /z/ sound is the suffix "-ise" when it is used to form verbs. In American English, these are much more commonly represented by "-ize" instead, but there are a few words that must be spelled "-ise." This is because, rather than attaching to an existing base word to form a verb, this ending is part of the word's etymological origin. For example:
- adverti<u>se</u> (/ˈædvərˌta<u>ɪz</u>/)
- advi<u>se</u> (/ædˈva<u>ɪz</u>/)
- chasti<u>se</u> (/tʃæsˈta<u>ɪz</u>/)
- compromi<u>se</u> (/ˈkɑmprəˌma<u>ɪz</u>/)
- despi<u>se</u> (/dɪˈspa<u>ɪz</u>/)
- devi<u>se</u> (/dɪˈva<u>ɪz</u>/)
- disgui<u>se</u> (/dɪsˈga<u>ɪz</u>/)
- exci<u>se</u> (/ɪkˈsa<u>ɪz</u>/)
- exerci<u>se</u> (/ˈɛksərˌsa<u>ɪz</u>/)
- improvi<u>se</u> (/ˈɪmprəˌva<u>ɪz</u>/)
- inci<u>se</u> (/ɪnˈsa<u>ɪz</u>/)
- revi<u>se</u> (/rɪˈva<u>ɪz</u>/)
- supervi<u>se</u> (/ˈsupərˌva<u>ɪz</u>/)
- surmi<u>se</u> (/sərˈma<u>ɪz</u>/)
- surpri<u>se</u> (/sərˈpra<u>ɪz</u>/)
- televi<u>se</u> (/ˈtɛləˌva<u>ɪz</u>/)

One exception to this is the verb *promise*, which is pronounced /ˈprɑmɪs/.

Forming the /z/ sound with *SS*

While the consonant digraph **SS** most often forms the /s/ sound, it can occasionally form the /z/ sound in certain words in which it appears between two vowels. There are only a few words in which this is the case:
- bra<u>ss</u>iere (/brəˈ<u>z</u>ɪər/)
- de<u>ss</u>ert (/dɪˈ<u>z</u>ɜrt/)
- di<u>ss</u>olve (/dɪˈ<u>z</u>ɑlv/)
- Mi<u>ss</u>ouri (/məˈ<u>z</u>ʊri/)
- po<u>ss</u>ess (/pəˈ<u>z</u>ɛs/; note that the second <u>ss</u> is pronounced /s/)
- sci<u>ss</u>ors (/ˈsɪ<u>z</u>ərz/)

For all other words, **SS** between vowels will make the /s/ sound (as in *assess*, /əˈsɛs/) or the /ʃ/ sound (as in *session*, /ˈsɛʃən/).

Forming the /z/ sound with *X*

The letter **X** most often forms a blend of two unvoiced consonant sounds: /k/ and /s/. However, when it appears immediately before a stressed vowel sound (and almost always after the letter **E**) at the beginning of a word, it becomes **voiced** as the combination of the sounds /g/ and /z/. For instance:

- Ale**x**ander (/ˌælɪgˈzændər/)
- e**x**ample (/ɪgˈzæmpəl/)
- e**x**act (/ɪgˈzækt/)
- e**x**aggerate (/ɪgˈzædʒ əˌreɪt)
- e**x**ecutive (/ɪgˈzɛkjətɪv/)
- e**x**ist (/ɪgˈzɪst/)
- e**x**ude (/ɪgˈzud/)
- e**x**otic (/ɪgˈzɑtɪk/)
- e**x**haust (/ɪgˈzɑst/)
- e**x**hibit (/ɪgˈzɪbɪt/)

(Note that the **H** is **silent** in the last two of these examples.)

There is also another word in which **x** has this pronunciation but does <u>not</u> come after an **E**: *au**x**iliary* (/ɔgˈzɪləri/).

Finally, there are also a few words in which **x** *only* forms the /z/ sound, though most of these are not common in everyday speech and writing. For example:

- **x**anthan (/ˈzænθən/)
- **x**enolith (/ˈzɛnəlɪθ/)
- **x**erography (/zɪˈrɑgrəfi/)
- **x**ylophone (/ˈzaɪləˌfoʊn/)

Quiz

(answers start on page 463)

1. In which of the following words is **ZZ** *not* pronounced /z/?

a) fuzzy
b) blizzard
c) pizza
d) fizzle

2. When is **S** pronounced /z/ when it is used to form plurals, possessives, and the third-person singular?

a) After all consonant sounds
b) After the consonant sound /t/
c) After the consonant sound /f/
d) After the consonant sound /m/

3. In which of the following word endings is **S** always pronounced /z/?

a) -ise
b) -ism
c) -ase
d) -ss

4. In which of the following words does **X** produce the /z/ sound?

a) exception
b) exert
c) exercise
d) exhale

Forming the /ʒ/ (ZH) Sound

The consonant sound /ʒ/ can be especially tricky because, unlike most consonant sounds, it does not have a specific letter or digraph commonly associated with it. It is sometimes transcribed as **ZH**, but there are no native English words that feature this digraph; instead, the /ʒ/ sound occurs when various consonants appear next to or between certain vowels.

Formed with the letter S

The consonant that most commonly forms the /ʒ/ sound is **S** when it is followed by specific suffixes. Other than a certain set of exceptions in which it comes after an **R**, **S** is always preceded by a vowel when it forms the /ʒ/ sound. Let's look at examples of the various suffixes that combine with **S** to form this pronunciation.

Vowel + "-s-" + "-ion"

The most common suffix to form the /ʒ/ sound with **S** is "-ion," which is used to create nouns indicating an action or process, or the result thereof. Note that this combination only produces this sound when it follows a vowel or the letter **R** (as we'll see further on); if it comes after any other consonant, it produces the /ʃ/ sound (i.e., the sound of the digraph **SH**).

For example:

A + "-sion"	E + "-sion"	I + "-sion"	O + "-sion"	U + "-sion"
abrasion (/əˈbreɪʒən/) evasion (/əˈveɪʒən/) invasion (/ɪnˈveɪʒən/) occasion (/əˈkeɪʒən/) persuasion (/pərˈsweɪʒən/) pervasion (/pərˈveɪʒən/)	adhesion (/ædˈhiʒən/) cohesion (/koʊˈhiʒən/) lesion (/ˈliʒən/)	collision (/kəˈlɪʒən/) decision (/dɪˈsɪʒən/) division (/dɪˈvɪʒən/) incision (/ɪnˈsɪʒən/) precision (/priˈsɪʒən/) provision (/prəˈvɪʒən/) vision (/ˈvɪʒən/)	corrosion (/kəˈroʊʒən/) erosion (/ɪˈroʊʒən/) explosion (/ɪkˈsploʊʒən/) implosion (/ɪmˈploʊʒən/)	allusion (/əˈluʒən/) collusion (/kəˈluʒən/) conclusion (/kənˈkluʒən/) delusion (/dɪˈluʒən/) exclusion (/ɪksˈkluʒən/) illusion (/ɪˈluʒən/) inclusion (/ɪnˈkluʒən/) intrusion (/ɪnˈtruʒən/) protrusion (/proʊˈtruʒən/) seclusion (/sɪˈkluʒən/)

R + "-sion"

The only consonant that **S** can follow while forming the /ʒ/ sound is **R**, and it only occurs with the suffix "-ion." For example:
- aversion (/əˈvɜrʒən/)
- conversion (/kənˈvɜrʒən/)
- diversion (/dɪˈvɜrʒən/)
- excursion (/ɪkˈskɜrʒən/)
- incursion (/ɪnˈkɜrʒən/)
- immersion (/ɪˈmɜrʒən/)
- submersion (/səbˈmɜrʒən/)
- subversion (/səbˈvɜrʒən/)

Note that these pronunciations are often specific to American English; in British English (or even different dialects within American English), this combination can form the /ʃ/ (**SH**) sound instead.

Vowel + S + "-ure"

The suffix "-ure" is used to form nouns describing a condition, process, act, or function. **S** only forms the /ʒ/ sound with this suffix when it is preceded by the letter **O**, the digraph **EA** (pronounced /ɛ/), or (in one instance) the digraph **EI** (pronounced either /i/ or /ɛ/).

For example:
- closure (/ˈkloʊʒər/)

- compo<u>s</u>ure (/kəmˈpoʊʒər/)
- disclo<u>s</u>ure /dɪsˈkloʊʒər/
- expo<u>s</u>ure (/ɪkˈspoʊʒər/)
- enclo<u>s</u>ure (/ɪnˈkloʊʒər/)
- lei<u>s</u>ure (/ˈliʒər/ or /ˈlɛʒər/)
- mea<u>s</u>ure (/ˈmɛʒər/)
- plea<u>s</u>ure (/ˈplɛʒər/)
- trea<u>s</u>ure (/ˈtrɛʒər/)

Forming the /ʒ/ sound with the letter Z

There are two other words ending in "-ure" that create the /ʒ/ sound, but they are spelled with a **Z** rather than an **S**: *seizure* (/ˈsiʒər/) and *azure* (/ˈæʒər/). These are the only two instances in which **Z** can form the /ʒ/ sound.

Vowel + S + "-ia"

The suffix "-ia" is most often used to indicate the names of diseases and pathological conditions, territories or countries, or certain conditions or qualities. For example:

- ambro<u>s</u>ia (/æmˈbroʊʒə/)
- amne<u>s</u>ia (/æmˈniʒə/)
- A<u>s</u>ia (/ˈeɪʒə/)
- dyspla<u>s</u>ia (/dɪsˈpleɪʒə/)
- fanta<u>s</u>ia (/fænˈteɪʒə/)
- kinesthe<u>s</u>ia (/ˌkɪnəsˈθiʒə/)
- magne<u>s</u>ia (/mægˈniʒə/)
- synesthe<u>s</u>ia (/ˌsɪnəsˈθiʒə/)

Vowel + "-sual"

This ending is not really a suffix, but rather appears in adaptations of Latin root words. At its most basic, it only appears in three adjectives, but these words can be expanded, using other suffixes, to form nouns, verbs, and adverbs.

For example:

- ca<u>s</u>ual (/ˈkæʒuəl/); also forms *casually* (adv.), *casualty* (n.), and *casualness* (n.)
- u<u>s</u>ual (/ˈjuʒuəl/); also forms *usually* (adv.) and *usualness* (n.)
- vi<u>s</u>ual (/ˈvɪʒuəl/); also forms *visually* (adv.), *visuality* (n.), and *visualness* (n.)

Formed from the letter G

After the letter **S**, the consonant that most commonly forms the /ʒ/ sound is "**soft G.**"

The letter **G** can be considered "soft" when it appears after a vowel and immediately before an **E, I**, or **Y**. While /dʒ/ (the sound of the letter **J**) is the most common speech sound used for a soft **G** (as in *age, logic,* or *biology*), the /ʒ/ sound is formed in some French loanwords ending in **GE** (especially after the letter **A**). For this reason, it can be thought of as the "French soft G."

There is no reliable spelling pattern that dictates when a soft **G** will be pronounced /ʒ/ rather than /dʒ/, so we simply have to memorize these pronunciations:

- arbitra<u>ge</u> (/ˈɑrbɪˌtrɑʒ/)
- bei<u>ge</u> (/beɪʒ/)
- barra<u>ge</u> (/bəˈrɑʒ/)
- camoufla<u>ge</u> (/ˈkæməˌflɑʒ/)
- colla<u>ge</u> (/kəˈlɑʒ/)
- corsa<u>ge</u> (/kɔrˈsɑʒ/)
- dressa<u>ge</u> (/drəˈsɑʒ/)
- entoura<u>ge</u> (/ˌɑntʊˈrɑʒ/)
- gara<u>ge</u> (/gəˈrɑʒ/)*
- massa<u>ge</u> (/məˈsɑʒ/)
- monta<u>ge</u> (/mɑnˈtɑʒ/)

• mir<u>age</u> (/mɪˈrɑʒ/)
• ro<u>uge</u> (/ruʒ/)
• sabot<u>age</u> (ˈsæbəˌtɑʒ/)

(*It is also common to hear this word pronounced with the standard soft **G** at the end: /gəˈrɑdʒ/.)

There are also a few words in which **G** takes the /ʒ/ sound but does not appear at the end of the word:

• <u>g</u>enre (/ˈʒɑnrə/)
• lin<u>g</u>erie (/ˌlɑnʒəˈreɪ/)
• re<u>g</u>ime (/rəˈʒim/)

Formed from other letters

J

Like soft **G**, the letter **J** occasionally produces the /ʒ/ sound instead of the normal /dʒ/ sound, though this only happens in foreign loanwords. For example:

• Bei<u>j</u>ing (/ˌbeɪʒˈɪŋ/)
• bi<u>j</u>ou (/ˈbiʒu/)
• dé<u>j</u>à vu (/ˈdeɪʒæ ˈvu/
• Di<u>j</u>on (ˌdiˈʒɑn/)
• force ma<u>j</u>eure (/ˈfɔrs mæˈʒɜr/)
• Ta<u>j</u> Mahal (/tɑʒ məˈhɑl)

T and X

There is only one word in which **T** produces the /ʒ/ sound: *equation* (/ɪˈkweɪʒən/).
Likewise, there is one word in which **X** forms the /ʒ/ sound (in the combination /gʒ/): lu**x**ury (/ˈlʌg**ʒ**əri/).

Quiz
<small>(answers start on page 463)</small>

1. Which letter most commonly produces the /ʒ/ sound?

a) G
b) J
c) S
d) T

2. Which of the following words produces the /ʒ/ sound?

a) tension
b) discussion
c) expulsion
d) diversion

3. Which of the following words is usually pronounced with the /ʒ/ sound?

a) generic
b) germ
c) genre
d) gelatine

4. True or False: The letter **J** only forms the /ʒ/ sound in foreign loanwords.

a) True
b) False

Pronouncing the Letter S

The letter **S** can present some difficulties for pronunciation because of the variety of sounds it can make. Most often, it produces two distinct consonant sounds: /s/ and /z/. In some specific instances, **S** can also form the sounds /ʃ/ (as in *sure*) or /ʒ/ (as in *usual*). We'll briefly touch on these pronunciations as well, but first we'll focus on the /s/ vs. /z/ sounds.

Forming the /s/ and /z/ sounds

Determining which of these two possible pronunciations to use is very tricky because many words that have very similar spellings can have **S** pronounced as either /s/ or /z/, with very little indication as to which is correct. For instance, the noun *goose* is pronounced /gus/, while the verb *choose* is pronounced /ʧuz/; from the spelling alone, we can't tell why one is pronounced /s/ while the other is pronounced /z/.

While in many instances we simply have to memorize pronunciation oddities like these, there *are* some conventions that we can follow to help us determine which sound to make. This largely depends on where **S** appears in the word—at the beginning, the end, or in the middle.

At the beginning of a word

The pronunciation of **S** is the easiest to remember when it is the first letter of a word: it is almost always pronounced /s/, regardless of whether it is followed by a vowel or another consonant; it is <u>never</u> pronounced /z/. For example:

S + Vowel	S + Consonant
sap (/sæp/)	scare (/skɛr/)
set (/sɛt/)	skip (/skɪp/)
sip (/sɪp/)	slouch (/slaʊʧ/)
social (/ˈsoʊʃəl/)	small (/smɔl/)
subject (/ˈsʌbʤɪkt/)	snail (/sneɪl/)
syllable (/ˈsɪləbəl/)	spell (/spɛl/)
	square (/skwɛr/)
	start (/stɑrt/)
	swift (/swɪft/)

However, when **S** is followed by **H**, the two letters form a digraph that produces the sound /ʃ/, as in:
• share (/ʃɛr/)
• sheep (/ʃip/)
• ship (/ʃɪp/)
• shout (/ʃaʊt/)
• shriek (/ʃrik/)
• shuffle (/ˈʃʌfəl/)
• shy (/ʃaɪ/)

There are also two specific exceptions in which **S** creates the /ʃ/ sound on its own when it is followed by the vowel **U**: *sugar* (/ˈʃʊgər/) and *sure* (/ʃʊr/).

Finally, it should be noted that there are quite a few consonant letters that never or almost never follow **S** at the beginning of words: **B, D, F, G, J, R, V, X,** and **Z**. The only exceptions are a few foreign loanwords—such as *svelte* (/svɛlt/) from French (meaning "gracefully slender" or "sophisticated").

At the end of a word

The letter **S** can serve several different functions at the end of words, each of which can influence its pronunciation. Here, we'll look at when the inflectional suffixes "-s" and "-es" are used to form **plural nouns** and **third-person singular** verbs, when "-s" follows an apostrophe to form a **possessive** or a **contraction**, and when S appears naturally at the end of a word.

Forming plurals and the third-person singular

Nouns are usually made plural by adding "-s" or "-es" onto the end, without changing the spelling of the base noun itself. In the same way, we add "-s" or "-es" onto verbs to indicate actions done by a singular person or thing being described in the third person. Fortunately, the rules for pronunciation of both plural and third-person "-(e)s" are relatively straightforward. (Many words can function as both nouns and verbs, depending on context, so our examples will include both since the pronunciation rule applies to each in the same way.)

When "-s" forms the /s/ sound

S is always pronounced /s/ when it comes after an **unvoiced**, non-sibilant consonant sound—that is, after /k/, /f/, /p/, /t/, and /θ/ (the sound usually associated with **TH**). We always add a single "-s" after these sounds, never "-es."

For example:

/k/ + "-s"	/f/+ "-s"	/p/+ "-s"	/t/+ "-s"	/θ/+ "-s"
attacks (/əˈtæks/)	autographs (/ˈɔtəˌgræfs/)	blimps (/blɪmps/)	advocates (noun: /ˈædvəkɪts/; verb: /ˈædvəˌkeɪts/)	baths (/bæθs/)
bakes (/beɪks(/	beliefs (/brˈlifs/)	claps (/klæps/)	boots (/buts/)	births (/bɜrθs/)
cooks (/kʊks/)	chiefs (/ʧifs/)	drops (/drɑps/)	creates (/kriˈeɪts/)	cloths (/klɔθs/)
clinics (/ˈklɪnɪks/)	giraffes (/dʒəˈræfs/)	flips (/flɪps/)	deposits (/dɪˈpɑzɪts/)	deaths (/dɛθs/)
flicks (/flɪks/)	handcuffs (/ˈhændˌkʌfs/)	gasps (/gæsps/)	eats (/its/)	growths (/groʊθs/)
makes (/meɪks/)	laughs (/læfs/)	keeps (/kips/)	investigates (/ɪnˈvɛstɪˌgeɪts/)	lengths (/lɛŋkθs/)
picnics (/ˈpɪkˌnɪks/)	oafs (/oʊfs/)	naps (/næps/)	meets (/mits/)	myths (/mɪθs/)
rebukes (/rɪˈbjuks/)	photographs (/ˈfoʊtəˌgræfs/)	stamps (/stæmps/)	starts (/stɑrts/)	strengths (/strɛŋkθs/)
tasks (/tæsks/)	spoofs (/spufs/)	troops (/trups/)	trusts (/trʌsts/)	tenths (/tɛnθs/)
weeks (/wiks/)	troughs (/trɔfs/)	warps (/wɔrps/)	weights (/weɪts/)	unearths (/ʌnˈɜrθs/)

When "-(e)s" forms the /z/ sound

Whenever the inflectional suffix "-s" is added to a word ending in a **voiced** consonant sound (/b/, /d/, /g/, /l/, /m/, /n/, /ŋ/, /r/, /ð/, /v/) or a vowel sound, the S will be pronounced as /z/. When adding "-s" to a word that ends in a voiced or unvoiced **sibilant** speech sound (/s/, /z/, /ʃ/, /ʒ/, /ʧ/, /ʤ/), we need to create an extra syllable to add clarity between the two sounds, so the suffix becomes "-es" and is pronounced /ɪz/. We also add "-es" to words ending in a consonant + **Y** (which is then changed to an **I**) and *sometimes* the letter **O**, but this does not create an additional syllable.

Let's look at some examples:

Voiced, non-sibilant consonant + "-s"	Vowel + "-s"	Sibilant sound + "-es"	Consonant + Y + "-es"	O + "-es"
barbs (/barbz/) dreads (/drɛdz/) eggs (/ɛgz/) lulls (/lʌlz/) norms (/nɔrmz/) planes (/pleɪnz/) rings (/rɪŋz/) stars (/starz/) teethes (/tiðz/) waves (/weɪvz/)	aromas (/əˈroʊməz/) frees (/friz/) skis (/skiz/) tornados* (/tɔrˈneɪdoʊz/) values (/ˈvæljuz/) volleys (/ˈvaliz/)	buses (/bʌsɪz/) comprises (/kəmˈpraɪzɪz/) rashes (/ˈræʃɪz/) garages (/gəˈraʒɪz/) pitches (/ˈpɪtʃɪz/) smudges (/ˈsmʌdʒɪz/)	ability→abilities (/əˈbɪlətiz/) baby→babies (/ˈbaɪbiz/) embody→embodies (/ɛmˈbadiz/) mercy→mercies (/ˈmɜrsiz/) tragedy→tragedies (/ˈtrædʒədiz/) worry→worries (/ˈwɜriz/)	does (/dʌz/) goes (/goʊz/) heroes (/ˈhɪroʊz/) potatoes (/pəˈteɪtoʊz/) tomatoes (/təˈmeɪtoʊz/) vetoes (/ˈvitoʊz/)

(*Many words may be spelled either "-os" or "-oes," sometimes with one spelling preferred over the other, or else being equally common. While this won't affect the pronunciation of the word, be sure to check the dictionary if you're unsure of the preferred or proper spelling.)

Many nouns ending in **F** or **FE** will have their spelling changed to **VE** when "-s" is added to make them plural. This isn't always the case (as we saw from some of the examples earlier), but it happens quite often. When it does, the normal pronunciation rules apply and the added **S** is pronounced /z/. For example:

Singular	Plural
calf (/kæf/)	calves (/kævz/)
half (/hæf/)	halves (/hævz/)
knife (/naɪf/)	knives (/naɪvz/)
leaf (/lif/)	leaves (/livz/)
life (/laɪf/)	lives (/laɪvz/)
loaf (/loʊf/)	loaves (/loʊvz/)
sheaf (/ʃif/)	sheaves (/ʃivz/)
thief (/θif/)	thieves (/θivz/)
wife (/waɪf/)	wives (/waɪvz/)
wolf (/wʊlf/)	wolves (/wʊlvz/)

These are considered **irregular plurals**, and we simply have to memorize them. Go to the section on Forming Plurals to learn more.

Finally, it's worth mentioning that the pluralization of several nouns ending in "-th" produces a similar effect. While the spelling doesn't change at all, the pronunciation changes from /θ/ to /ðz/. For example:

• booth (/buθ/)→boo<u>ths</u> (/bu<u>ðz</u>/)
• mouth (/maʊθ/)→mou<u>ths</u> (/maʊ<u>ðz</u>/)
• oath (/oʊθ/)→oa<u>ths</u> (/oʊ<u>ðz</u>/)
• path (/pæθ/)→pa<u>ths</u> (/pæ<u>ðz</u>/)
• truth (/truθ/)→tru<u>ths</u> (/tru<u>ðz</u>/)
• wreath (/riθ/)→wrea<u>ths</u> (/ri<u>ðz</u>/)

Apostrophe + "-s"

When we indicate possession of a noun or form a contraction with the word *is*, we most commonly use an **apostrophe (')** + "-s."

While the rules regarding how to form possessives and contractions by using an apostrophe + "-s" are unique, the rules for how that **S** is <u>pronounced</u> are the same as what we've already seen for plurals and third-person singular verbs: **S** is pronounced /s/ when it follows unvoiced, non-sibilant consonants, and it is pronounced /z/ (or /ɪz/) when it follows voiced consonants, sibilants, and vowels. This rule also applies when apostrophe-S is used with proper nouns—that is, capitalized names of people, brands, companies, or places.

Let's look at some examples of both possessives and contractions using apostrophe-S (for the sake of simplicity, we'll only look at proper nouns for the possessives and pronouns for the contractions—with one exception):

	Possessives	Contractions
After unvoiced, non-sibilant consonants (pronounced /s̲/)	Bart'<u>s</u> (/bɑrt<u>s</u>/) Elizabeth'<u>s</u> (/ɪ'lɪzəbɪθ<u>s</u>/) its (/ɪt<u>s</u>/) Jeff'<u>s</u> (/dʒɛf<u>s</u>/) Mike'<u>s</u> (/maɪk<u>s</u>/) Philip'<u>s</u> (/'fɪlɪp<u>s</u>/)	it'<u>s</u> (/ɪt<u>s</u>/) let'<u>s</u> (/lɛt<u>s</u>/) that'<u>s</u> (/ðæt<u>s</u>/) what'<u>s</u> (/wʌt<u>s</u>/)
After voiced, non-sibilant consonants (pronounced /z̲/)	Aisling'<u>s</u> (/'æʃlɪŋ<u>z</u>/) Bob'<u>s</u> (/bɑb<u>z</u>/) Craig'<u>s</u> (/kreɪg<u>z</u>/) Dan'<u>s</u> (/dæn<u>z</u>/) Gustav'<u>s</u> (/'gʊstɑv<u>z</u>/) Isabel'<u>s</u> (/'ɪzə,bɛl<u>z</u>/) Malcolm'<u>s</u> (/'mælkəm<u>z</u>/) Rosalind'<u>s</u> (/'rɑzəlɪnd<u>z</u>/) Taylor'<u>s</u> (/'teɪlər<u>z</u>/)	there'<u>s</u> (/ðɛr<u>z</u>/) when'<u>s</u> (/wɛn<u>z</u>/) where'<u>s</u> (/wɛr<u>z</u>/)

After sibilant consonants (pronounced /ɪz/)	Coleridge's (/ˈkoʊlrɪdʒɪz/) Lynch's (/ˈlɪntʃɪz/) Joyce's (/ˈdʒɔɪsɪz/) Sanchez's (/ˈsæntʃɛzɪz/) Trish's (/ˈtrɪʃɪz/)	this's (/ˈðɪsɪz/)
After vowel sounds (pronounced /z/)	Amy's (/ˈeɪmiz/) Daphne's (/ˈdæfniz/) Joshua's (/ˈdʒɑʃuəz/) Keanu's (/kiˈɑnuz/) Omari's (/oʊˈmɑriz/) Leo's (/ˈlioʊz/) Matthew's (/ˈmæθjuz/)	he's (/hiz/) how's (/haʊz/) she's (/ʃiz/) who's (/huz/) why's (/waɪz/)

Words ending in S or SE

While there are some consistent, reliable rules regarding the pronunciation of **S** when it is *attached* to a word, it's a bit more complicated (and inconsistent) for words that naturally end in **S** (or **S** + silent E). However, there are still some conventions we can follow that are *usually* reliable.

Double S after short vowels

Because we use the suffix "-s" to inflect nouns and verbs, we don't usually have base words that end in a single **S** after a vowel or vowels. If the vowel makes a short sound, we typically <u>double</u> the **S** so it isn't confused for a plural noun or a third-person singular verb.

Like words that *begin* with **S**, words that end in **SS** <u>always</u> make the /s/ sound. Note that this is not always the case when **SS** appears mid-word (which we'll look at later), but it is always true at the end of words. For example:

Short vowel + SS	IPA Pronunciation
abyss	/əˈbɪs/
across	/əˈkrɑs/
boss	/bɑs/
crass	/kræs/
dress	/drɛs/
fuss	/fʌs/
hiss	/hɪs/
impress	/ɪmˈprɛs/
mattress	/ˈmætrɪs/
possess	/pəˈzɛs/
success	/səkˈsɛs/
toss	/tɑs/
underpass	/ˈʌndərˌpæs/

This is a fairly reliable convention. If a word ends in a short vowel sound followed by /s/ (and it isn't plural or in third-person singular), there's a good chance that it will be spelled **SS**—and if you know the word ends in **SS**, then you can be sure it is pronounced /s/.

However, there are some exceptions. There are some words that end in a short vowel sound followed by /s/ but are only spelled with a single **S**. In particular, words with a short **U** sound (/ʌ/) at the end are often followed by a single **S**. Much less commonly, there are a few words that have a long vowel sound followed by **SS**. For example:

Short vowel + S	Long vowel + SS
atla**s** (/ˈætləs/)	
bu**s** (/bʌs/)	
canva**s** (/ˈkænvəs/)	ba**ss** (referring to music) (/beɪs/)
circu**s** (/ˈsɜrkəs/)	edelwei**ss** (/ˈeɪdəlˌvaɪs/)
diagnosi**s** (/ˌdaɪəɡˈnoʊsəs/)	engro**ss** (/ɪnˈɡroʊs/)
ga**s** (/ɡæs/)	gnei**ss** (/naɪs/)
plu**s** (/plʌs/)	gro**ss** (/ɡroʊs/)
thi**s** (/ðɪs/)	spei**ss** (/spaɪs/)
viru**s** (/ˈvaɪrəs/)	
ye**s** (/jɛs/)	

Finally, it's worth noting that any adjective formed with the suffix "-ous" will be pronounced /s/ at the end, as in *ambitous* (/æmˈbɪʃəs/), *enormous* (/ɪˈnɔrməs/), *hilarious* (/hɪˈlɛriəs/), etc.

S + Silent E after long vowels

While we typically double **S** when it appears after a short vowel sound at the end of a word, when it comes after a long vowel sound, **S** is usually followed by a silent E.

Unfortunately, there's generally no clear way to predict if **S** will have an /s/ or /z/ pronunciation in these words. The only time we can be sure of its pronunciation is when a word has the same spelling but has <u>two</u> pronunciations, one for a verb and one for a noun (or, in one case, an adjective). When this is the case, the noun form will be pronounced with a final /s/, while the verb form will be pronounced with a final /z/. (Note that this only applies to words that can be both nouns and verbs, and <u>only</u> when one of the sounds changed between them is the final **S**.)

There are many examples that we could list—too many to include here. Instead, we'll just look a selection of some common words:

Pronounced /s/	Pronounced /z/
abu**se** (noun: /əˈbjus/)	abu**se** (verb: /əˈbjuz/)
ba**se** (/beɪs/)	accu**se** (/əˈkjuz/)
ca**se** (/keɪs/)	brow**se** (/braʊz/)
cea**se** (/sis/)	chee**se** (/tʃiz/)
clo**se**	choo**se**

(adj.: /kloʊs/)	(/ʧuz/)
concise (/kənˈsaɪs/)	close (verb: /kloʊz/)
decrease (noun: /ˈdiˌkris/) verb: /dɪˈkris/)	demise (/dɪˈmaɪz/)
diagnose (/ˌdaɪəgˈnoʊs/)	excuse (verb: /ɪˈkskjuz/)
dose (noun and verb: /doʊs/)	hose (/hoʊz/)
excuse (noun: /ɪˈkskjus/)	house (verb: /haʊz/)
increase (noun: /ˈɪnˌkris/) verb: /ɪnˈkris/)	nose (/noʊz/)
goose (/gus/)	please (/pliz/)
house (noun: /haʊs/)	refuse (verb: /rɪˈfjuz/)
loose (/lus/)	these (/ðiz/)
louse (/laʊs/)	those (/ðoʊz/)
mouse (/maʊs/)	use (verb: /juz/)
refuse (noun: /ˈrɛˌfjus/)	whose (/huz/)
use (noun: /jus/)	wise (/waɪz/)

S + Silent E after L, N, P, and R

S can also create the last sound of a word when it follows four specific consonants: **L, N, P,** and **R**. Again, we must add a silent **E** after this **S** to avoid such words being confused with plurals or third-person singular verbs. Unlike when **SE** follows vowels, **S** is almost always pronounced /s/ in these words, even for words that function as both nouns and verbs.

For example:

L + SE	N + SE	P + SE	R + SE
	condense (/kənˈdɛns/)		
avulse (/əˈvʌls/)	dispense (/dɪˈspɛns/)	apocalypse (/əˈpakəˌlɪps/)	adverse (/ædˈvɜrs/)
convulse (/kənˈvʌls/)	intense (/ɪnˈtɛns/)	collapse (/kəˈlæps/)	coarse (/kɔrs/)
else (/ɛls/)	license (/ˈlaɪsəns/)	eclipse (/ɪˈklɪps/)	endorse (/ɛnˈdɔrs/)
false (/fɔls/)	offense (/əˈfɛns/)	glimpse (/glɪmps/)	nurse (/nɜrs/)
impulse (/ˈɪmpʌls/)	response (/rɪˈspans/)	lapse (/læps/)	traverse (/trəˈvɜrs/)
pulse (/pʌls/)	suspense (/səˈspɛns/)	synapse (/ˈsɪnæps/)	worse (/wɜrs/)
	tense (/tɛns/)		

(One notable exception to this convention is the word *cleanse*, which is pronounced /klɛnz/.)

In the middle of a word

The pronunciation of **S** in the middle of a word largely follows the patterns we've already seen when it appears at the beginning or end, taking the /s/ or /z/ pronunciation depending on whether it appears next to vowels or certain consonants. When it appears in the middle of a word, there are also two other sounds it can create: /ʃ/ or /ʒ/.

Next to consonants

Mid-word, **S** most commonly comes between two vowels, but when it comes before or after a consonant, it most often appears <u>before</u> unvoiced consonant sounds (/f/, /k/, /l/, /p/, /t/) or the sibilant sound /tʃ/, or else <u>after</u> the voiced consonants /n/ or /r/. Next to these consonant sounds, **S** almost always forms the sound /s/.

For example:

S + /f/	S + /k/	S + /l/	S + /p/	S + /t/	S + /tʃ/	/n/ + S	/r/ + S
asphalt (/ˈæsˌfɔlt/) blasphemy (/ˈblæsfəmi/) disfigure (/dɪsˈfɪgjər/) hemisphere (/ˈhɛmɪˌsfɪr/) misfortune (/mɪsˈfɔrtʃən/) satisfy (/ˈsætɪˌsfaɪ/)	ask (/æsk/) discuss (/dɪˈskʌs/) confiscate (/ˈkɑnfɪˌskeɪt/) couscous (/ˈkuskus/) kiosk (/ˈkiˌɑsk/) muscular (/ˈmʌskjələr/) musket (/ˈmʌskət/) pesky (/ˈpeski/) vascular (/ˈvæskjələr/)	aslant (/əˈslænt/) asleep (/əˈslip/) dislike (/dɪsˈlaɪk/) disloyal (/dɪsˈlɔɪəl/) legislate (/ˈlɛdʒɪˌsleɪt/) mislabel (/mɪsˈleɪbəl/)	aspect (/ˈæsˌpɛkt/) crisp (/krɪsp/) dispel (/dɪˈspɛl/) inspect (/ɪnˈspɛkt/) gospel (/ˈgɑspəl/) hospital (/ˈhɑˌspɪtəl/) respond (/rɪˈspɑnd/) suspense (/səˈspɛns/) wasp (/wɑsp/)	abstract (/ˈæbstrækt/) best (/bɛst/) custard (/ˈkʌstərd/) establish (/ɪˈstæblɪʃ/) instant (/ˈɪnstənt/) master (/ˈmæstər/) prostrate (/ˈprɑstreɪt/) sustain (/səˈsteɪn/) understand (/ˌʌndərˈstænd/)	congestion (/kənˈdʒɛstʃən/) discharge (/ˈdɪsˌtʃɑrdʒ/) eschew (/ɛsˈtʃu/) exhaustion (/ɪgˈzɑstʃən/) mischief (/ˈmɪstʃəf/) posture (/ˈpɑstʃər/) question (/ˈkwɛstʃən/) suggestion (/səˈdʒɛstʃən/)	answer (/ˈænsər/) compensate (/ˈkɑmpənˌseɪt/) consider (/kənˈsɪdər/) handsome* (/ˈhænsəm/) inside (/ɪnˈsaɪd/) monsoon (/mɑnˈsun/) ransom (/ˈrænsəm/) sponsor (/ˈspɑnsər/)	arsenal (/ˈɑrsənəl/) corsage (/kɔrˈsɑʒ/) dorsal (/ˈdɔrsəl/) intersect (/ˌɪntərˈsɛkt/) fearsome (/ˈfɪrsəm/) forsake (/fɔrˈseɪk/) person (/ˈpɜrsən/) somersault (/ˈsʌmərˌsɔlt/) versus (/ˈvɜrsəs/)

(*The **D** is silent in *handsome*, so **S** still follows the /n/ sound and is still pronounced /s/.)

While this is a pretty reliable convention, there are some exceptions in which **S** is pronounced /z/ when it appears next to these consonants, such as:
• berserk (/bərˈzɜrk/*)
• gosling (/ˈgɑzlɪŋ/)
• grisly (/ˈgrɪzli/)
• jersey (/ˈdʒɜrzi/)
• measly (/ˈmizli/)
• muesli (/ˈmjuzli/*)
• muslin (/ˈmʌzlɪn/)
• tousle (/ˈtaʊzəl/*)
• transaction (/trænˈzækʃən/*)

(*S can also be pronounced as /s/ in these words, depending on local pronunciation.)

Next to B, D, and M

Except when it is at the end of a prefix attached to an existing base word or part of a compound word (in which case the individual words' pronunciations take precedence), **S** does not often appear before or after voiced consonant sounds other than /b/, /d/, and /m/. However, while **S** can form the /z/ sound next to these consonants (especially /m/), it commonly produces the /s/ sound as well; unfortunately, we just have to know which way it is pronounced for individual words. For example:

	Forms the /z/ sound	Forms the /s/ sound
/b/ + S	absolve (/æbˈzɑlv/) absorb (/əbˈzɔrb/) observe (/əbˈzɜrv/)	absent (/ˈæbsənt/) absurd (/əbˈsɜrd/) obsequious (/əbˈsikwiəs/) obsess (/əbˈsɛs/) obsidian (/əbˈsɪdiən/) obsolete (/ˌɑbsəˈlit/) subside (/səbˈsaɪd/)
S + /b/	husband (/ˈhʌzbənd/) lesbian (/ˈlɛzbiən/) raspberry* (/ˈræzˌbɛri/)	asbestos (/æsˈbɛstəs/) disband (/dɪsˈbænd/) disburse (/dɪsˈbɜrs/) smorgasbord (/ˈsmɔrgəsˌbɔrd/)
/d/ + S	adsorb (/ædˈzɔrb/) sudsy (/ˈsʌdzi/) woodsy (/ˈwʊdzi/)	bedside (/ˈbɛdˌsaɪd/) gladsome (/ˈglædsəm/) grandson** (/ˈgrændˌsʌn/) midsummer (/ˈmɪdˌsʌmər/)
S + /d/	eavesdrop (/ˈivzˌdrɑp/) Thursday (/ˈθɜrzˌdeɪ/) Tuesday (/ˈtuzˌdeɪ/) Wednesday*** (/ˈwɛnzˌdeɪ/) wisdom (/ˈwɪzdəm/)	disdain (/dɪsˈdeɪn/) jurisdiction (/ˌdʒʊrɪsˈdɪkʃən/) misdemeanour (/ˌmɪsdəˈminər/)
/m/ + S	clumsy (/ˈklʌmzi/) crimson (/ˈkrɪmzən/) damsel (/ˈdæmzəl/) damson (/ˈdæmzən/) flimsy (/ˈflɪmzi/) whimsy (/ˈwɪmzi/)	himself (/hɪmˈsɛlf/) homestead (/ˈhoʊmˌstɛd/) namesake (/ˈneɪmˌseɪk/)

S + /m/	abysmal (/ə'bɪzməl/)	
	charisma (/kə'rɪzmə/)	
	cosmetic (/kɑz'mɛtɪk/)	besmirch (/bɪ'smɜrtʃ/)
	cosmos (/'kɑzmoʊs/)	dismantle (/dɪ'smæntəl/)
	jasmine (/'dʒæzmɪn/)	dismay (/dɪ'smeɪ/)
	mesmerize (/'mɛzmə,raɪz/)	dismiss (/dɪ'smɪs/)
	miasma (/maɪ'æzmə/)	talisman (/'tælɪsmən/)
	plasma (/'plæzmə/)	
	transmit (/trænz'mɪt/)	

(*The **P** in *raspberry* is silent.
The **D in *grandson* can also be silent.
***The initial **D** in *Wednesday* is silent.)

One instance in which **S** is <u>always</u> pronounced /z/ is when the letter combination **SM** appears at the end of a word (most often as a part of the suffix "-ism"), in which case a reduced vowel sound (the schwa, /ə/) is pronounced between **S** and **M**. For example:

• activism (/'æktɪ,vɪzəm/)
• baptism (/'bæptɪzəm/)
• chasm (/'kæzəm/)
• humanism (/'hjumə,nɪzəm/)
• materialism (/mə'tɪriə,lɪzəm/)
• nationalism (/'næʃənə,lɪzəm/)
• organism (/'ɔrgə,nɪzəm/)
• phantasm (/,fæn'tæzəm/)
• sarcasm (/'sɑr,kæzəm/)
• spiritualism (/'spɪrɪtʃəwəlɪzəm/)

Between vowels

When **S** appears between two vowel sounds in the middle of a word, it tends to create the /z/ sound, but it is by no means uncommon for it to be pronounced /s/, too. Unfortunately, there's no clear way to be sure of whether **S** will take an /s/ or /z/ pronunciation in this position—we simply have to memorize individual words.

Here are some examples:

Pronounced /z/	Pronounced /s/
advisor (/æd'vaɪzər/)	awesome (/'ɑsəm/)
busy (/'bɪzi/)	beside (/bɪ'saɪd/)
cousin (/'kʌzən/)	carousel (/'kɛrə,sɛl/)
daisy (/'deɪzi/)	desolate (adjective: /'dɛsələt/ verb: /'dɛsə,leɪt/)
desert (adjective/noun: /'dɛzɜrt/ verb: /dɪ'zɜrt/)	disembark (/dɪsɛm'bɑrk/)

disaster (/dɪˈzæstər/)	fantasy (/ˈfæntəsi/)
disease (/dɪˈziz/)	gasoline (/ˈgæsəˌlin/)
easy (/ˈizi/)	jettison (/ˈdʒetɪsən/)
limousine (/ˈlɪməˌzin/)	nuisance (/ˈnusəns/)
lousy (/ˈlaʊzi/)	research (/ˈrisərtʃ/)
museum (/mjuˈziəm/)	
music (/mjuˈzɪk/)	
plausible (/ˈplɔzəbəl/)	
present (adjective/noun: /ˈprɛzənt/ verb: /priˈzɛnt/)	
prison (/ˈprɪzən/)	
thousand (/ˈθaʊzənd/)	
visible (/ˈvɪzəbəl/)	

Forming the /ʃ/ and /ʒ/ sounds

These two sounds are created when **S** is followed by certain letter combinations at the end of a word. In each case, the same combination can produce *either* the /ʃ/ or /ʒ/ sound, depending on the letter that <u>precedes</u> **S**.

S + "-ion"

When **S** is followed by the suffix "-ion," it creates the /ʃ/ sound if **S** comes after **L**, **N**, or another **S** (with some exceptions);* if **S** comes after a vowel sound, it will make the /ʒ/ sound. When **S** comes after **R**, it is usually pronounced /ʒ/ (especially in American English), but it can also be pronounced /ʃ/. For example:

	S + "-ion"	IPA Pronunciation
After L (Pronounced /ʃ/)	compulsion	/kəmˈpʌlʃən/
	emulsion	/ɪˈmʌlʃən/
	expulsion	/ɪkˈspʌlʃən/
	propulsion	/prəˈpʌlʃən/
	revulsion	/rɪˈvʌlʃən/
After N (Pronounced /ʃ/)	apprehension	/ˌæprɪˈhɛnʃən/
	dimension	/dɪˈmɛnʃən/
	expansion	/ɪkˈspænʃən/
	pension	/ˈpɛnʃən/
	tension	/ˈtɛnʃən/
After S (Pronounced /ʃ/)	admission	/ædˈmɪʃən/
	discussion	/dɪˈskʌʃən/
	emission	/ɪˈmɪʃən/
	passion	/ˈpæʃən/
	suppression	/səˈprɛʃən/

After R **(Pronounced /ʒ/ *or* /ʃ/)**	conversion diversion excursion immersion submersion	/kənˈvɜrʒən/ (or /kənˈvɜrʃən/) /dɪˈvɜrʒən/ (or /dɪˈvɜrʃən/) /ɪkˈskɜrʒən/ (or /ɪkˈskɜrʃən/) /ɪˈmɜrʒən/ (or /ɪˈmɜrʃən/) /səbˈmɜrʒən/ (or /səbˈmɜrʃən/)
After Vowels **(Pronounced /ʒ/)**	explosion illusion invasion lesion precision	/ɪkˈsploʊʒən/ /ɪˈluʒən/ /ɪnˈveɪʒən/ /ˈliʒən/ /priˈsɪʒən/

(*There are two words ending in **SSION** that can take either the /ʃən/ or the /ʒən/ pronunciation: *fission* [meaning "the splitting or breaking of one thing into two parts"] and *scission* [meaning "the act of dividing, cutting, or severing"]. The word *rescission* [which means "the act of rescinding"], on the other hand, is only pronounced /rɪˈsɪʒən/.)

S + "-ure"

S behaves in a similar way before the ending "-ure" as it does before "-ion": when it comes after **N** and **S**, it produces the /ʃ/ sound; after vowel sounds, it produces the /ʒ/ sound. Unlike **S** + "-ion," it does not come after **L** or **R**. And, of course, the word *sure* on its own can be pronounced /ʃʊər/ or /ʃɜr/.

For example:

	S + "-ure"	**IPA Pronunciation**
After N **(Pronounced /ʃ/)**	censure ensure insure licensure	/ˈsɛnʃər/ /ɛnˈʃʊər/ /ɪnˈʃʊər/ /ˈlaɪsənʃər/
After S **(Pronounced /ʃ/)**	assure fissure pressure	/əˈʃʊər/ /ˈfɪʃər/ /ˈprɛʃər/
After Vowels **(Pronounced /ʒ/*)**	closure exposure leisure measure	/ˈkloʊʒər/ /ɪkˈspoʊʒər/ /ˈliʒər/ or /ˈlɛʒər/ /ˈmɛʒər/

(*One exception to this convention is the word *erasure*, which is pronounced /ɪˈreɪʃər/.)

S + "-ual"

Less commonly, **S** will be followed by the ending "-ual." After the letter **N**, **S** is pronounced /ʃ/, while it is pronounced /ʒ/ after vowels:

	S + "-ual"	**IPA Pronunciation**
After N **(Pronounced /ʃ/)**	consensual sensual	/kənˈsɛnʃuəl/ /ˈsɛnʃuəl/
After Vowels **(Pronounced /ʒ/*)**	casual usual visual	/ˈkæʒuəl/ /ˈjuʒuəl/ /ˈvɪʒuəl/

Silent S

Finally, there are a few words in which **S** is not pronounced at all. Some of these are foreign loanwords; others are the result of spelling adjustments made to English words throughout the years. Regardless of their origin, there are no indicators in these words that tells us the **S** will be silent; they are all just special exceptions that we must memorize.

• ai<u>s</u>le (/aɪl/)
• apropo<u>s</u> (/ˌæprəˈpoʊ/)
• chamoi<u>s</u> (/ˈʃæmwɑ/ or /ˈʃæmi/)
• debri<u>s</u> (/dəˈbri/)
• bourgeoi<u>s</u> (/bʊərˈʒwɑ/)
• i<u>s</u>land (/ˈaɪlənd/)
• i<u>s</u>le (/aɪl/)
• patoi<u>s</u> (/ˈpætwɑ/)
• vi<u>s</u>count (/ˈvaɪˌkaʊnt/)

Quiz

(answers start on page 463)

1. Which of the following sounds is **not** made by the letter **S**?

a) /s/
b) /z/
c) /θ/
d) /ʃ/
e) /ʒ/

2. In which of the following words is **S** pronounced /ʃ/?

a) peruse
b) instinct
c) museum
d) mansion

3. In which position does the letter **S** *never* make the /z/ sound?

a) At the beginning of a word
b) In the middle of a word
c) At the end of a word
d) All of the above
e) None of the above

4. In which of the following contractions is **S** pronounced /ɪz/?

a) that's
b) there's
c) this's
d) how's

5. At the **end** of a word, what type of speech sound must **S** follow to produce the /z/ sound?

a) Voiced consonant sounds
b) Sibilant speech sounds
c) Vowel sounds
d) All of the above
e) None of the above

6. In which of the following words is **S** pronounced /z/?

a) dose (verb)
b) use (verb)
c) dose (noun)
d) use (noun)

Silent Letters

One of the trickiest aspects of English spelling and pronunciation is the presence of many different **silent letters**. Because English has evolved from several different sources (Latin, Greek, French, German, Old English, etc.), it has had to assimilate the various spelling and pronunciation quirks of all of its predecessors. This has resulted in many instances in which particular letters become silent. While it may seem like such silent letters serve no purpose in a word, this is not strictly true: silent letters can help distinguish two words that are otherwise homophonous, help indicate the meaning or origin of a word, or even help us determine the overall pronunciation of a word.

Silent letters vs. digraphs (and trigraphs and tetragraphs)

Most silent letters are actually part of different combinations that make specific unique speech sounds. These combinations are known as digraphs (two letters), trigraphs (three letters), and, much less commonly, tetragraphs (four letters). These can be made up of vowels, consonants, or a combination of both.

Because the "silent" letters in these combinations are actually serving a distinct phonemic purpose, we won't be looking at examples of them here—you can find more information in the sections on vowel digraphs, consonant digraphs, trigraphs, and tetragraphs.

Silent vowels

When we talk about silent letters, we are **usually** talking about silent consonants, as these are much less logical and much harder to predict than silent vowels (most of which are simply part of a vowel digraph, which we won't cover here). However, there is one silent vowel that has a huge impact on the spelling, pronunciation, and meaning of words and other letters.

Silent E

By far the best known and most versatile silent letter is **silent E** (sometimes known as "**magic E**"). We cover this particular silent letter more in depth in a separate section, but we'll give a brief overview of its most common functions here.

Dictating words' pronunciation and meaning

One of the most common purposes of silent **E** is to help the reader determine the pronunciation of a vowel sound that comes before the previous consonant. In many cases, silent **E** also helps indicate a difference in meaning between a similarly spelled word that doesn't have an **E** at the end. Here are some examples:

Word without Silent E	Meaning	Word with Silent E	Meaning
bad (/bæd/)	(*adj.*) Not good or undesirable.	bade (/beɪd/)	(*verb*) The simple past tense of *bid*.
them (/ðɛm/)	(*pron.*) The objective case of the personal pronoun *they*.	theme (/θim/)	(*noun*) A topic, subject, or idea.
grip (/grɪp/)	(*verb*) To hold onto something.	gripe (/graɪp/)	(*verb*) To complain in a nagging or petulant manner.
hop (/hɑp/)	(*verb*) To jump or leap a short distance.	hope (/hoʊp/)	(*verb*) To wish for or desire (something).
cub (/kʌb/)	(*noun*) A young bear, lion, wolf, or certain other animal.	cube (/kjub/)	(*noun*) A solid shape comprising six equal square faces.

Dictating pronunciation but not meaning

Silent **E** also has the same effect on pronunciation in words for which there is no **E**-less alternative:

A a	E e	I i	O o	U u	Y y
bale (/beɪl/)	concrete (/'kɑnkrit/)	bike (/baɪk/)	rope (/roʊp/)	fuse (/fjus/)	thyme (/taɪm/)
cake (/keɪk/)	impede (/ɪm'pid/)	tile (/taɪl/)	broke (/broʊk/)	mule (/mjul/)	hype (/haɪp/)
rave (/reɪv/)	scene (/sin/)	strike (/straɪk/)	trope (/troʊp/)	rebuke (/rɪ'bjuk/)	tyke (/taɪk/)

Changing C and G

The consonants **C** and **G** both have a "hard" and "soft" pronunciation. "**Hard C**" is pronounced the same as the letter **K** (/k/), while "**soft C**" has the same sound as the letter **S** (/s/). "**Hard G**" has a unique consonant sound (/g/), while "**soft G**" is pronounced like the letter **J** (/dʒ/).

In addition to changing vowel sounds, silent **E** changes the pronunciation of both **C** and **G**, indicating when they take their soft pronunciations (/s/ and /dʒ/, respectively). This most commonly occurs when **CE** comes after the letter **I** and when **GE** comes after the letter **A**, but it can occur with other vowels as well. For example:

Soft C	Soft G
ice (/aɪs/)	age (/eɪdʒ/)
advice (/æd'vaɪs/)	cage (/keɪdʒ/)
sacrifice (/'sækrɪˌfaɪs/)	stage (/steɪdʒ/)
face (/feɪs/)	oblige (/ə'blaɪdʒ/)

Changing TH

Silent **E** also has a bearing on the pronunciation of the consonant digraph **TH**. In most words that end in **TH**, it is pronounced as /θ/, an **unvoiced** consonant sound (meaning the vocal cords aren't vibrated to create noise). When a final **TH** is followed by **E**, however, it almost takes the **voiced** consonant sound /ð/.

Often, adding a silent **E** after **TH** also has the effect of changing the meaning of a word, usually from a noun to a verb. For example:

Word without Silent E	Meaning	Word with Silent E	Meaning
bath (/bæθ/)	(*noun*) The act of washing the body in water.	bathe (/beɪð/)	(*verb*) To immerse in water for the purposes of washing; to take a bath.
breath (/brɛθ/)	(*noun*) An instance of inhaling air into the lungs.	breathe (/brið/)	(*verb*) To inhale air into the lungs.
cloth (/klɔθ/)	(*noun*) Material made from woven or knitted fibers.	clothe (/kloʊð/)	(*verb*) To put on or provide clothing.
teeth (/tiθ/)	(*noun*) Plural of *tooth*.	teethe (/tið/)	(*verb*) Of babies, to grow teeth for the first time.
wreath (/riθ/)	(*noun*) A ring of entwined flowers, leaves, or other foliage.	wreathe (/rið/)	(*verb*) To form into or take the shape of a wreath.

There are a few other functions beyond dictating vowel and consonant pronunciation, so, if you'd like to learn more, see the section on Silent E.

Silent U

While **E** is the most commonly recognised silent vowel letter, due to its variety of uses and the spelling rules associated with it, there is another silent vowel with a much less elaborate purpose: **U**.

U is used in conjunction with **Q** to help it form the /k/ sound. However, when **QU** comes before any vowel other than silent E, the **U** creates a /w/ sound (as in *require* or *quadruple*). **U** is usually only silent in the **QU** combination when it appears at the end of a word (with just a few exceptions, such as the word mos**qui**to [/məˈskitoʊ/]), in which case it always will be followed by silent **E** (with the rare exception of a few foreign loan words).

For example:
• anti**que** (/ænˈtik/)
• baro**que** (/bəˈroʊk/)
• bis**que** (/bɪsk/)
• criti**que** (/krɪˈtik/)
• grotes**que** (/groʊˈtɛsk/)
• mysti**que** (/mɪˈstik/)
• physi**que** (/fɪˈsik/)
• pla**que** (/plæk/)
• statues**que** (/ˌstætʃuˈɛsk/)
• techni**que** (/tɛkˈnik/)
• tor**que** (/toʊrk/)
• uni**que** (/juˈnik/)

This pattern also occurs when **U** follows **G** at the end of words—in fact, it happens much more often. Most of the time, it results in a "hard" G sound, /g/, but there are a few instances in which silent **U** follows the digraph **NG**, /ŋ/:
• analo**gue** (/ˈænəlˌɔg/)
• bro**gue** (/broʊg/)
• catalo**gue** (/ˈkætəlˌɔg/)
• collea**gue** (/ˈkɑlig/)
• dialo**gue** (/ˈdaɪəˌlɔg/)
• epilo**gue** (/ˈɛpəˌlɔg/)
• fati**gue** (/fəˈtig/)
• haran**gue** (/həˈræŋ/)
• intri**gue** (/ɪnˈtrig/)
• lea**gue** (/lig/)
• pla**gue** (/pleɪg/)
• ro**gue** (/roʊg/)
• ton**gue** (/tʌŋ/)
• va**gue** (/veɪg/)
• vo**gue** (/voʊg/)

(Note that *analogue, catalogue, dialogue,* and *homologue* are all commonly spelled without **UE** in American English—*analog, catalog, dialog,* and *homolog*.)

Unlike **QU**, though, **GU** can result in a silent **U** in various positions within a word, rather than just at the end. In fact, **U** is often silent if it follows **G** and precedes another vowel, especially **E** and **I**:

GUA	GUE	GUI	GUO	GUY
guarantee (/ˌgær ənˈti/) guard (/gɑrd/)	baguette (/bæˈgɛt/) beleaguer (/bɪˈligər/) daguerreotype (/dəˈgɛərəˌtaɪp/) guerrilla (/gəˈrɪlə/) guess (/gɛs/) guest (/gɛst/)	beguile (/bəˈgaɪl/) disguise (/dɪsˈgaɪz/) guide (/gaɪd/) guild (/gɪld/) guile (/gaɪl/) guilt (/gɪlt/) guinea (/ˈgɪni/) guitar (/gɪˈtɑr/)	languor (/ˈlæŋgər/)	guy (/gaɪ/) guyot (/giˈoʊ/)

However, this pattern is not a concrete rule, and **U** is often pronounced as /w/ or /ju/ in these same letter patterns in other words—for instance, *guava* (/ˈgwɑvə/), *segue* (/ˈsɛgweɪ/), *linguist* (/ˈlɪŋgwɪst/), *ambiguous* (/æmˈbɪgjʊəs/), etc. Fortunately, **U** is more likely to be silent in these sequences than not, but it is important to be aware that this spelling convention is not always consistent.

Finally, **U** can be silent in a few words after other consonants, though these are much less common than **Q** or **G**. For example:
- bisc**u**it (/ˈbɪskɪt/)
- b**u**ild (/bɪld/)
- b**u**oyant (/ˈbɔɪənt/)
- b**u**y (/baɪ/)
- circ**u**it (/ˈsɜrkɪt/)
- fr**u**it (/fr**u**t/)
- fl**u**oride (/ˈflɔraɪd/)
- purs**u**it (/pərˈs**u**t/)
- recr**u**it (/rəˈkr**u**t/)
- s**u**it (/s**u**t/)

Silent consonants

Because consonants generally make distinct speech sounds (unlike vowels, which can be malleable and inconsistent, depending on the word), it is much more striking when they are silent in a word, because it looks quite odd to the eye.

We'll first look at instances in which individual letters are silent, due to a word's etymological origin or evolution of pronunciation; further on, we'll talk about when consonants become silent due to **doubling**.

Silent B

Silent B is usually the result of how a given word evolved from blends of Latin, Old English, and/or French. Sometimes, as in the word *doubt*, the silent **B** was added to the word to help it *resemble* Latin or draw a clearer connection to a related Latin term (in this case, *dubitare*, from which *dubious* is derived). In other cases, such as *limb* or *thumb*, the silent **B** doesn't have a clear etymological explanation at all—it's just an oddity we have to remember.

Most often, **B** is silent when it follows the letter **M**. Less commonly, silent **B** can occur when **B** <u>precedes</u> the letter **T**. For example:

MB	BT
bom<u>b</u> (/bɔm/)	
catacom<u>b</u> (/ˈkæt ə ˌkoʊm/)	
clim<u>b</u> (/klaɪm/)	
crum<u>b</u> (/krʌm/)	de<u>b</u>t (/dɛt/)
dum<u>b</u> (/dʌm/)	dou<u>b</u>t (/daʊt/)
lam<u>b</u> (/læm/)	su<u>b</u>tle (/ˈsʌtəl/)
num<u>b</u> (/nʌm/)	
plum<u>b</u>er (/plʌmər/)	
thum<u>b</u> (/θʌm/)	
wom<u>b</u> (/wum/)	

Silent C

C often becomes silent when it comes after the letter **S** and is followed by **E** or **I**. Like silent **B**, these **C**s come from the Latin origins of the words, in which **SC** was pronounced /sk/. Over time, the pronunciation dropped the hard /k/ sound made by **C**, but the spelling remained the same. For example:

S + C + E	S + C + I
abs<u>c</u>ess (/ˈæbsɛs/)	abs<u>c</u>ise (/æbˈsaɪz/)
acquies<u>c</u>e (/ˌækwiˈɛs/)	dis<u>c</u>ipline (/ˈdɪsəplɪn/)
adoles<u>c</u>ent (/ˌædəlˈɛsənt/)	fas<u>c</u>inate (/ˈfæsɪˌneɪt/)
as<u>c</u>end (/əˈsɛnd/)	iras<u>c</u>ible (/ɪˈræsəbəl/)
condes<u>c</u>end (/ˌkɑndəˈsɛnd/)	las<u>c</u>ivious (/ləˈsɪviəs/)
cres<u>c</u>ent (/ˈkrɛsənt/)	res<u>c</u>ind (/rɪˈsɪnd/)
des<u>c</u>end (/dɪˈsɛnd/)	resus<u>c</u>itate (/rɪˈsʌsɪˌteɪt/)
evis<u>c</u>erate (/ɪˈvɪsəˌreɪt/)	s<u>c</u>iatica (/saɪˈætɪkə/)
fluores<u>c</u>ent (/fluˈrɛsənt/)	s<u>c</u>ience (/ˈsaɪəns/)
incandes<u>c</u>ent (/ˌɪnkənˈdɛsənt/)	s<u>c</u>imitar (/ˈsɪmɪtar/)

miscellaneous (/ˌmɪsəˈleɪnɪəs/)	scintillate (/ˈsɪntɪlˌeɪt/)
muscle (/ˈmʌsəl/; **LE** here produces a sound like **EL**)	scion (/ˈsaɪən/)
nascent (/ˈneɪsənt/)	scissors (/ˈsɪzərz/)
obscene (/ɑbˈsin/)	viscid (/ˈvɪsɪd/)
oscillate (/ˈɑsɪˌleɪt/)	
scent (/sɛnt/)	

We can also think of **C** as silent in the consonant clusters **CK** and **CQ**, since **K** and **Q** are both pronounced /k/ with or without **C**. Here are a few examples of each:

CK	CQ
attack (/əˈtæk/)	acquaint (/əˈkweɪnt/)
bucket (/ˈbʌkət/)	acquiesce (/ˌækwiˈɛs/)
locker (/ˈlɑkər/)	acquire (/əˈkwaɪər/)
stack (/stæk/)	acquit (/əˈkwɪt/)
truck (/trʌk/)	lacquer (/ˈlækɛr/)
wicked (/ˈwɪkəd/)	racquet (/ˈrækɪt/)

Finally, **C** is *sometimes* silent in the words *arctic* (/ˈɑrktɪk/, /ˈɑrtɪk/) and *antarctic* (/æntˈɑrktɪk/, /æntˈɑrtɪk/), but this depends on regional dialect as well as personal preference.

Silent D

There are almost no words in which **D** is truly silent. Instead, when **D** appears in a large consonant cluster (especially when it appears after **N**), it is occasionally left unpronounced. For example:
- handkerchief (/ˈhæŋkərtʃɪf/)
- handsome (/ˈhænsəm/)
- grandfather (/ˈgrænfɑðər/)
- grandmother (/ˈgræ[n]mʌðər/; **N** is also sometimes silent)
- granddaughter (/ˈgrændɔtər/; first **D** is silent, but second **D** is pronounced)
- grandson (/ˈgrænsʌn/)
- sandwich (/ˈsænwɪtʃ/)

(Note that, for most of these words, the **D** may be pronounced in some dialects but left out in others.)

The only word in which **D** is silent due to the evolution of a word's spelling is the notorious *Wednesday* (/ˈwɛnzdeɪ/). It is derived from Old English *wodnesdæg*, which originally did pronounce the **D**.

Silent G

When **G** comes after **N**, they form a specific digraph that creates the phoneme /ŋ/, as in *sing* (/sɪŋ/) or *strong* (/strɔŋ/).

When **G** comes <u>before</u> the letter **N**, the two letters are typically pronounced separately. However, **G** occasionally becomes silent in certain words that were derived from French, Italian, or Old English. For example:
- align (/əˈlaɪn/)
- arraign (/əˈreɪn/)
- assign (/əˈsaɪn/)
- benign (/bəˈnaɪn/)
- bologna (/bəˈloʊni/)
- campaign (/kæmˈpeɪn/)

- champagne (/ʃæmˈpeɪn/)
- consign (/kənˈsaɪn/)
- deign (/deɪn/)
- design (/dəˈzaɪn/)
- feign (/feɪn/)
- foreign (/ˈfɔrɪn/)
- gnarl (/nærl/)
- gnash (/næʃ/)
- gnat (/næt/)
- gnaw (/nɔ/)
- gnome (/noʊm/)
- impugn (/ɪmˈpjun/)
- lasagna (/ləˈzɑnjə/)
- malign (/məˈlaɪn/)
- poignant (/ˈpɔɪnjənt/)
- reign (/reɪn/)
- resign (/rəˈzaɪn/)
- sign (/saɪn/)
- sovereign (/ˈsɑvrɪn/)
- vignette (/vɪˈnjɛt/)

Note, however, that in several of the verbs ending in "-gn," **G** will cease being silent when the suffixes "-ant," "-atory," or "-ation" are attached to the end of the word. For instance:

- assign→assignation (/ˌæsɪgˈneɪʃən/)
- benign→benignant (/bɪˈnɪgnənt/); benignity (/bɪˈnɪgnɪti/)
- consign→consignation (/ˌkɑnsɪgˈneɪʃən/)
- design→designation (/ˌdɛzɪgˈneɪʃən/)
- malign→malignant (/məˈlɪgnənt/); malignity (/məˈlɪgnɪti/)
- resign→resignation (/ˌrɛzɪgˈneɪʃən/)
- sign→signatory (/ˈsɪgnəˌtɔri/)

If you're trying to remember if a word features a silent **G**, say it with one of these suffixes attached and see if a /g/ sound arises.

Silent H

H is also occasionally silent at the beginnings of certain words. The spelling of the word on its own is usually not enough to dictate whether **H** is pronounced or silent, though, so we simply have to memorize such words. For the sake of comparison, let's look at some examples of words where **H** is either pronounced or silent:

H is pronounced	H is silent
hear (/hir/)	heir (/ɛr/)
herd (/hɜrd/)	herb* (/ɛrb/)
homophone (/ˈhoʊməfoʊn/)	homage (/ˈɑmɪdʒ/)
honey (/ˈhʌni/)	honest (/ˈɑnɪst/)
honk (/hɑŋk/)	honor (/ˈɑnər/)
house (/haʊs/)	hour (/aʊər/)

(*This pronunciation is most common in American English. In British English, the **H** is usually pronounced: /hɛrb/.)

Silent **H** can also appear mid word or at the end of a word, but only when it appears <u>between</u> two vowels (though not all words follow this convention) or else when a word ends with a vowel followed by **H**. For example:

Mid position	End position
anni<u>h</u>ilate (/əˈnaɪəˌleɪt/) graham (/ˈgreɪəm/ or /græm/) ni<u>h</u>ilism (/ˈnaɪəˌlɪzəm/) ve<u>h</u>ement (/ˈviəmənt/) ve<u>h</u>icle (/ˈviɪkəl/)*	cheeta<u>h</u> (/ˈʧitə/) hallelujah<u>h</u> (/ˌhæləˈluyə/) hurra<u>h</u> (/hʊˈrɑ/) Pharaoh<u>h</u> (/ˈfɛəroʊ/) savanna<u>h</u> (/səˈvænə/) tabboule<u>h</u> (/təˈbulɪ/)

(*The **H** is silent in *vehicle* for the vast majority of English speakers, but in some dialects it may also be pronounced: /ˈvihɪkəl/.)

While it is certainly not uncommon for **H** to be silent on its own, it is much more commonly silent when it occurs after other consonants.

Silent H in CH

The most common sound made by the digraph **CH** is /ʧ/, as in *achieve* (/əˈʧiv/) or *reach* (/riʧ/). Less commonly, the **H** essentially becomes silent, and the digraph produces the same sound as a **K** or hard **C**, transcribed in IPA as /k/. This sound almost always occurs when **CH** appears at the beginning or in the middle of a word. For example:

Beginning Position	Mid Position
chemistry (/ˈkɛmɪstri/) **ch**oir (/ˈkwaɪər/) **ch**ord (/kɔrd/) **ch**orus (/ˈkɔrəs/) **Ch**ristmas (/ˈkrɪsməs/)	an**ch**or (/ˈæŋkər/) ar**ch**ive (/ˈɑrˌkaɪv/) psy**ch**e (/ˈsaɪki/) psy**ch**ology (/saɪˈkɑlədʒi/) s**ch**edule (/ˈskɛdʒʊl/)* syn**ch**ronize (/ˈsɪŋkrəˌnaɪz/) te**ch**nology (/tɛkˈnɑlədʒi/)

There are only a few standard words that end in **CH** pronounced as /k/, such as *stomach* (/ˈstʌmək/) and *triptych* (/ˈtrɪptɪk/). However, certain abbreviated forms of other words will sometimes end this way as well, such as *psy**ch*** (/saɪk/, short for *psychology*) or *te**ch*** (/tɛk/, short for *technology*).

(*Note that in British English, *s**ch**edule* is often pronounced /ʃ/ rather than /sk/: /ˈʃɛdjuːl/.)

Silent H in GH

The digraph **GH** can form the sound /f/ (as in *cough*) or—much more commonly—be completely silent (as in *bought*). (Go to the section on consonant digraphs and tetragraphs to learn more about these spellings and pronunciations.)

Less commonly, the **H** in the digraph becomes silent, so it simply makes the sound of "hard" **G** (/g/):
• afghan (/ˈæfgæn/)
• aghast (/əˈgæst/)
• ghastly (/ˈgæstli/)
• gherkin (/ˈgɜrkɪn/)
• ghetto (/ˈgɛtoʊ/)
• ghost (/goʊst/)
• ghoul (/gul/)
• spaghetti (/spəˈgɛti/)
• yoghurt (/ˈyoʊgərt/; more commonly spelled *yogurt* in American English)

Silent H in RH

The commonest occurrences of silent **H** are in the pair **RH** (pronounced /r/). Most of the time, this combination appears at the beginning of a word. Many of these are specialized terms that come from mathematics, botany, anatomy, or medicine, so we'll just look at those that are more likely to appear in everyday speech or writing:
• rhapsody (/ˈræpsədi/)
• rhetoric (/ˈrɛtərɪk/)
• rheumatic (/rʊˈmætɪk/)
• rheumatoid (/ˈruməˌtɔɪd/)
• rhinoceros (/raɪˈnɑsərəs/)
• rhinoplasty (/ˈraɪnoʊˌplæsti/)
• rhinovirus (/ˌraɪnoʊˈvaɪrəs/)
• rhodium (/ˈroʊdiəm/)
• rhombus (/ˈrɑmbəs/)
• rhomboid (/ˈrɑmbɔɪd/)
• rhubarb (/ˈrubɑrb/)
• rhyme (/raɪm/)
• rhythm (/ˈrɪðəm/)

RH can also appear in the middle of words, mostly medical terminology. In each of these, **RH** is preceded by another **R**, and the whole cluster (**RRH**) is pronounced /r/:
• arrhythmia (/əˈrɪðmiə/)
• catarrh (/kəˈtɑr/)
• cirrhosis (/sɪˈroʊsɪs/)
• diarrhea (/ˌdaɪəˈriə/)
• hemorrhage (/ˈhɛmərɪdʒ/)
• hemorrhoid (/ˈhɛməˌrɔɪd/)
• myrrh (/mɜr/)
• pyorrhea (/ˌpaɪəˈriə/)
• seborrhea (/ˌsɛbəˈriə/)

Silent H in WH

Modern English words beginning with **WH** are almost all derived from Old English, in which they were originally spelled **HW**. Over time, the position of the letters reversed, and the digraph came to represent the /w/ sound, with **H** becoming silent. This spelling pattern seems to have influenced other words with initial /w/ sounds that were from languages other than Old English, too (such as *whip*).

For instance:

whack (/wæk/)	whiff (/wɪf/)
whale (/weɪl/)	while (/waɪl/)
wham (/wæm/)	whimper (/ˈwɪmpər/)
wharf (/wɔrf/)	whim (/wɪm/)
what (/wʌt/)	whine (/waɪn/)
wheat (/wit/)	whip (/wɪp/)
wheedle (/ˈwidəl/)	whirl (/wɪrl/)
wheel (/wil/)	whisper (/ˈwɪspər/)
wheeze (/wiz/)	whistle (/ˈwɪsəl/)
when (/wɛn/)	whit (/wɪt/)
where (/wɛr/)	white (/waɪt/)
whether (/ˈwɛðər/)	whittle (/ˈwɪtəl/)
whey (/weɪ/)	whopping (/ˈwɑpɪŋ/)
which (/wɪtʃ/)	whoosh (/wuʃ/)
	why (/waɪ/)

While not common in modern English, some dialects *do* still pronounce the **H** very subtly—though it comes <u>before</u> the /w/ sound, producing the phoneme **/hw/** as a reflection of the Old English origin. Here are just few examples of these terms with the alternative pronunciation:

• whack (/**h**wæk/)
• what (/**h**wʌt/)
• where (/**h**wɛr/)
• when (/**h**wɛn/)
• why (/**h**waɪ/)
• which (/**h**wɪtʃ/)
• wheel (/**h**wil/)
• whisper (/ˈ**h**wɪspər/)
• white (/**h**waɪt/)

Finally, it's important to remember that a few words beginning "who-" are pronounced /hu-/ or /hoʊ-/ rather than /wu-/ or /woʊ-/. Luckily, there are very few of these. For example:

• who (/**h**u/)
• whole (/**h**oʊl/)
• whom (/**h**um/)
• whose (/**h**uz/)

Silent H in XH

One last pair of consonants in which **H** *usually* becomes silent is **XH**. This combination also results in the pronunciation of **X** changing from /ks/ to /gz/ (a pattern that often occurs when **X** appears between two vowels). For example:

• ex<u>h</u>aust (/ɪgˈzɔst/)
• ex<u>h</u>ibit (/ɪgˈzɪbɪt/)
• ex<u>h</u>ilarate (/ɪgˈzɪləˌreɪt/)
• ex<u>h</u>ort (/ɪgˈzɔrt/)
• ex<u>h</u>ume (/ɪgˈzum/)

Note that there is one exception: *ex<u>h</u>ale* (/ɛksˈheɪl/). This pronunciation also carries over to any terms derived from *exhale*, such as *exhalant* or *exhalation*.

Silent K

K becomes silent if it appears before the letter **N** at the beginning of a word. This **KN** spelling is a relic of Middle English—itself derived from Germanic origins. While the original pronunciation reflected the two letters more closely, it became simplified in modern English to the /n/ sound. For example:

• <u>k</u>nack (/næk/)
• <u>k</u>napsack (/ˈnæpˌsæk/)
• <u>k</u>nave (/neɪv/)
• <u>k</u>nead (/nid/)
• <u>k</u>nee (/ni/)
• <u>k</u>neel (/nil/)
• <u>k</u>nell (/nɛl/)
• <u>k</u>nickers (/nɪkərz/)
• <u>k</u>nife (/naɪf/)
• <u>k</u>night (/naɪt/)
• <u>k</u>nit (/nɪt/)
• <u>k</u>nock (/nɑk/)
• <u>k</u>not (/nɑt/)
• <u>k</u>now (/noʊ/)
• <u>k</u>nuckle (/ˈnʌkəl)

Silent L

L sometimes becomes silent when it appears after the letter **A** and before the consonants **F, V, K,** and **M,** as well as before **D** after the vowels **OU.** Almost all of these instances of silent **L** occur when the combination appears at the end of the word; **ALF, ALV,** etc., appearing at the beginning or middle of a word will usually feature a non-silent **L.**

In some cases, this silent **L** elongates or otherwise modifies the vowel sound that comes before it, giving the slight impression of an /l/ sound without being distinctly pronounced. Here are a few common examples:

ALF	ALV	ALK	ALM	OULD
			a<u>l</u>mond (/ˈɑmənd/)	
		ba<u>l</u>k (/bɔk/)	ba<u>l</u>m (/bɑm/)	
beha<u>l</u>f (/bəˈhæf/)	ca<u>l</u>ve (/kæv/)	cha<u>l</u>k (/ʧɔk/)	ca<u>l</u>m (/kɑm/)	cou<u>l</u>d (/kʊd/)
ca<u>l</u>f (/kæf/)	ha<u>l</u>ve (/hæv/)	sta<u>l</u>k (/stɔk/)	pa<u>l</u>m (/pɑm/)	shou<u>l</u>d (/ʃʊd/)
ha<u>l</u>f (/hæf/)	sa<u>l</u>ve (/sæv/)	ta<u>l</u>k (/tɔk/)	psa<u>l</u>m (/sɑm/)	wou<u>l</u>d (/wʊd/)
		wa<u>l</u>k (/wɔk/)	sa<u>l</u>mon (/ˈsæmən/)	

(An exception to the **ALV** pattern above is the word *valve*— /vælv/.)

Similar to the **ALK** pattern above, the word cau**l**k is pronounced (/kɔk/). In fact, because of this similarity, it has a variant spelling of *calk* (likewise, *balk* has a variant spelling of *baulk*).

Finally, silent **L** also appears before **K** in two other words: *folk* and *yolk*, both of which originate in Old English. In these words, the appearance of **L** lets us know that **O** will have a "long" pronunciation as seen in words like *poke* or *stoke*: *folk* is pronounced /foʊk/ and *yolk* is pronounced /joʊk/.

Silent M

There is one word that features a **silent M**: **m**nemonic. Here, the **N** is pronounced but not the **M**: (/nɪˈmɑnɪk/). This pronunciation also is true for the adverbial form of the word, **mn**emonically (/nɪˈmɑnɪk[ə]li/).

Silent N

N becomes silent when it appears after **M** at the <u>end</u> of a word. For example:

• autum**n** (/ˈɔtəm/)
• condem**n** (/kənˈdɛm/)
• colum**n** (/ˈkɑləm/)
• hym**n** (/hɪm/)
• solem**n** (/ˈsɑləm/)

Note that **N** <u>is</u> pronounced in these words when they take certain vowel suffixes, such as "-al," "-ation," and "-ist":

• autumn→autum**n**al (/ɔˈtʌmnəl/)
• condemn→condem**n**ation (/ˌkɑndɛmˈneɪʃən/)
• column→colum**n**ist (/ˈkɑləmnɪst/)
• hymn→hym**n**al (/ˈhɪmn/), hym**n**ist (/ˈhɪmnɪst/)
• solemn→solem**n**ify (/səˈlɛmnɪfaɪ/), solem**n**ity (/səˈlɛmnɪti/)

Silent P

Occasionally, **P** can be silent when it is followed by the letters **N**, **S**, or **T**, usually in certain letter combinations that come from words of Greek origin or influence. For example:

PN	PS	PT
	psalm (/sam/)	asym**p**tote (/ˈæsɪmˌtoʊt/)
pneuma (/ˈnumə/)	**p**saltery (/ˈsɔltəri)	**p**tarmigan (/ˈtɑrmɪgən/)
pneumatic (/nuˈmætɪk/)	**p**seudo (/ˈsudoʊ/)	**p**terodactyl (/ˌtɛrəˈdæktɪl/)
pneumonia (/nuˈmoʊnjə/)	**p**soriasis (/səˈraɪəsɪs/)	**p**teropod (/ˈtɛrəˌpɑd/)
	psyche* (/ˈsaɪki/)	**p**tisan (/ˈtɪzæn/)

(*It's important to note that *psyche* is used as a prefix, "psych-" [derived from Greek "*psykhe-*"], which is used to create many other terms, such as *psychiatry, psychic, psychology, psychopath, psychotherapy*, etc. In each of these, **P** remains silent.)

Aside from words derived from Greek roots, silent **P** occurs in a handful of other words:

• cu**p**board (/ˈkʌbərd/)
• ras**p**berry (/ˈræzˌbɛri/)
• cor**p**s (/kɔr/; both **P** and **S** are silent, unless the word is plural, in which case **S** is pronounced /z/)
• cou**p** (/ku/)
• recei**p**t (/rɪˈsit/)

In the first two terms, **P** is made silent through a process called **elision**—the /p/ sound was initially present (as they were originally compound words of *cup + board* and *raspis + berry*), but because it is difficult to individually pronounce /p/ and /b/ next to each other in the same word, /p/ has been naturally omitted. The other three words come from French (which determines the pronunciation) via Latin (which determines the spelling).

Finally, there are some words in which **P** *tends* to become silent in everyday speech when it appears in the consonant cluster **MPT**. (Just be aware that this omission of the /p/ sound may be considered poor or improper diction by some.) For example:

- assum**p**tion (/əˈsʌmʃən/; more properly, /əˈsʌmpʃən/)
- contem**p**t (/kənˈtɛmt/; more properly, /kənˈtɛmpt/)
- em**p**ty (/ˈɛmti/; more properly, /ˈɛmpti/)
- exem**p**t (/ɪɡˈzɛmt/; more properly, /ɪɡˈzɛmpt/)
- prom**p**t (/prɑmt/; more properly, /prɑmpt/)
- tem**p**t (/tɛmt/; more properly, /tɛmpt/)
- redem**p**tion (/rɪˈdɛmʃən/; more properly, /rɪˈdɛmpʃən/)

Silent T

The letter **T** sometimes follows the pattern of **P** in *cupboard* and *raspberry* in that it becomes silent due to the complexity of the consonant sounds around it. This occurs in some words when **T** comes after the letter **S** and is followed by a reduced vowel sound, known as a schwa (/ə/), most commonly with the ending **LE**, and, less commonly, **EN**:

ST + LE	ST + EN
apos**t**le (/əˈpɑsəl/)	
bris**t**le (/ˈbrɪsəl/)	
bus**t**le (/ˈbʌsəl/)	
cas**t**le (/ˈkæsəl/)	chas**t**en (/ˈtʃeɪsən/)
epis**t**le (/ɪˈpɪsəl/)	chris**t**en (/ˈkrɪsən/)
gris**t**le (/ˈgrɪsəl/)	fas**t**en (/ˈfæsən/)
hus**t**le (/ˈhʌsəl/)	glis**t**en (/ˈglɪsən/)
jos**t**le (/ˈdʒɑsəl/)	has**t**en (/ˈheɪsən/)
nes**t**le (/ˈnɛsəl/)	lis**t**en (/ˈlɪsən/)
pes**t**le (/ˈpɛsəl/)*	mois**t**en (/ˈmɔɪsən/)
rus**t**le (/ˈrʌsəl/)	
this**t**le (/ˈθɪsəl/)	
whis**t**le (/ˈwɪsəl/)	
wres**t**le (/ˈrɛsəl/)	

This same pattern is why **T** is silent in the words *soften* (/ˈsɔfən/), *often* (/ˈɔfən/),* and *Christmas* /ˈkrɪsməs/.

(*Depending on regional dialect or personal preference, the **T** is sometimes pronounced in *pestle* [/ˈpɛstəl/] and *often* [/ˈɔftən/].)

Silent T in French loanwords

Certain loanwords that come from French maintain a silent **T** at the end of the word. For instance:

- balle**t** (/bæˈleɪ/)
- bouque**t** (/buˈkeɪ/)
- gourme**t** (/gʊərˈmeɪ/)
- vale**t** (/væˈleɪ/)

Other instances of silent T

T is also silent in the word *mortgage* (/ˈmɔrgədʒ/), which comes from the French term *morgage*, derived from Old French *mort gaige*, based on the Latin *mortus*. The English spelling reintroduced the **T** to be closer to Latin, but the pronunciation remained the same as the French.

Another odd instance of silent **T** is the word *boatswain*, pronounced /ˈboʊsən/ (note that **W** also becomes silent). This strange pronunciation is the result of a similar process that led to the silent **T** in *Christmas* or *soften*. Quite simply, the cluster of consonants is rather arduous to pronounce individually, so, over time, the trickier **T** and **W** sounds were elided (skipped over vocally).

In fact, because the pronunciation is so drastically different from its spelling, *boatswain* has a variant spelling of *bosun* to better reflect the modern pronunciation.

Luckily, this is a nautical term that isn't likely to appear in everyday speech or writing, but it's still worth knowing the correct pronunciation of the word.

Silent W

W, like **Y**, is considered a **semi-vowel**, which means that it can behave either like a vowel or a consonant depending on its position and function in a word. For example, it is functioning like a vowel when it pairs with other vowels to form vowel digraphs, as in *low* (/loʊ/), *draw* (/drɔ/), *stew* (/stu/), etc.; when **W** is used to articulate a distinct speech sound, as in *work* (/wɜrk/), it is functioning as a consonant.

However, **W** can also appear alongside several other consonants, and, in these combinations, **W** is not pronounced at all. This is due to the Old English origin of the words; **W** was pronounced initially, but as the pronunciation of the language evolved, it was eventually elided from speech.

Silent W in WR

By far the most common occurrence of silent **W** is when it comes before the consonant **R**. Notwithstanding compound words and those formed using prefixes, **WR** always appears at the beginning of words. For instance:

- w**r**ack (/ræk/)
- w**r**angle (/ˈræŋgəl/)
- w**r**ap (/ræp/)
- w**r**ath (/ræθ/)
- w**r**eak (/rik/)
- w**r**eath (/riθ/)
- w**r**eck (/rɛk/)
- w**r**estle (/ˈrɛsəl/)
- w**r**ist (/rɪst/)
- w**r**ite (/raɪt/)
- w**r**ong (/rɔŋ/)
- w**r**ung (/rʌŋ/)

Silent W in WH

This occurs in some words beginning with **WH** when it is followed by **O**, as in:

- **w**ho (/hu/)
- **w**hole (/hoʊl/)
- **w**hom (/hum/)
- **w**hose (/huz/)

Other Silent Ws

Finally, there are a few words in which **W** is silent <u>after</u> another consonant:
- ans**w**er (/ˈænsər/)
- boats**w**ain* (/ˈboʊsən/; note that **T** is also silent in this word)
- coxs**w**ain* (/ˈkɒksən/)
- gun**w**ale* (/ˈɡʌnəl/)
- s**w**ord (/sɔrd/)
- t**w**o (/tu/)

(*The rather odd pronunciation of these three terms stems from their nautical origin, as seafarers evolved the pronunciation to suit their own preferences.)

Silent TH

Finally, it's worth mentioning that the digraph **TH** (which makes the sounds /θ/, as in *bath*, or /ð/, as in *them*) is always silent in two words:
- as**th**ma (/ˈæzmə/)
- is**th**mus (/ˈɪsməs/)

Like **P** in *empty*, **TH** is sometimes made silent in everyday speech through casual elision—that is, the "proper" pronunciation includes the speech sound, but it is common in everyday speech to omit it (or glide over it quickly enough that it is indistinct). For **TH**, this occasionally happens when it is adjacent to **S** (like the two previous examples). For instance:
- clo**th**es (/kloʊz/; more properly, /kloʊð̠z/)
- de**pth**s (/dɛps/; more properly, /dɛpθs/)
- mon**th**s (/mʌns/; more properly, /mʌnθs/)

Silent doubled consonants

While there are many single consonants that are silent among others in a word, there are far more that are silent because there are two in a row when only one is needed to establish the correct consonant sound.

Doubling consonants at the ends of words

Many words have a doubled consonant at the end to help determine their meaning and pronunciation. In some cases, this doubled consonant distinguishes the word from another word with the same pronunciation. Other times, it simply indicates that the preceding vowel has a "short" sound.

(Certain vowels can be doubled in a similar way at the end of a word, but, because they comprise vowel digraphs with varying pronunciations, we have not included them here.)

The most common consonants to be doubled in this way are **F**, **L**, and (by far the most common) **S**; however, other consonants can appear doubled at the end of words as well. There are far too many examples to list here, but let's look at a few:

acros<u>s</u> asses<u>s</u>* ad<u>d</u> (extra **D** distinguishes it from the noun *ad*, short for *advertisement*) bas<u>s</u> blu<u>ff</u> bo<u>ss</u> bu<u>tt</u> (short for *buttocks*, but the extra **T** also helps distinguish it from the conjunction *but*) bu<u>zz</u> che<u>ss</u>	i<u>ll</u> in<u>n</u> (extra **N** distinguishes it from the preposition *in*) kne<u>ll</u> le<u>ss</u> ma<u>ss</u> me<u>ss</u> mi<u>ss</u> (extra **S** distinguishes it from the prefix "mis-") mi<u>tt</u>

di**ll** du**ll** eb**b** eg**g** er**r** (extra **R** distinguishes it from the interjection *er*) exces**s** fi**ll** fu**ll** fu**zz** gi**ll** gras**s** gues**s**	od**d** of**f** (extra **F** distinguishes it from the preposition *of*) pi**ll** que**ll** qui**ll** se**ll** stu**ff** stro**ll** tos**s** wat**t** wi**ll** ye**ll**

(*The first doubled **S** in *assess* is due to the word's Latin origin, *assessare*, which stems from a combination of the inflected prefix *ad-* and the root word *sedere*.)

Doubling consonants with Latin prefixes

Many words are derived from a combination of Latin roots and prefixes, and the final letter of certain Latin prefixes changes to match the first letter (or sound) of the root to which the prefix attaches. Note that many of these changes do not result in a silent consonant (for example, *in-* becomes *im-* in *imbue*). So, for the sake of conciseness, we'll only look at those prefixes whose changes create doubled silent letters; for more detailed information about the variations of certain Latin prefixes, go to the section on Prefixes.

Latin prefix	Meaning	Spelling change	Examples
ad-	To; toward; near to; in the direction or vicinity of.	**ac-** before roots beginning *q-* **af-** before roots beginning with *f-* **ag-** before roots beginning with *g-* **al-** before roots beginning with *l-* **an-** before roots beginning with *n-* **ap-** before roots beginning with *p-* **as-** before roots beginning with *s-* **at-** before roots beginning with *t-* (*Ad-* can also change to *ac-* before *c-*, but this changes the consonants' sounds (*-cc-* is pronounced /-ks-/), whereas **C** is truly silent in *acq-*.)	(ac-): *a**cq**uaint, a**cq**uiesce, a**cq**uire, a**cq**uit* (af-): *a**ff**air, a**ff**ect, a**ff**irm, a**ff**ix* (ag-): *a**gg**randize, a**gg**ravate, a**gg**re**ss*** (al-): *a**ll**ege, a**ll**ot, a**ll**ow, a**ll**ure* (an-): *a**nn**ex, a**nn**ihilate, a**nn**otate, a**nn**ounce* (ap-): *a**pp**all, a**pp**eal, a**pp**laud, a**pp**ly, a**pp**rove* (as-): *a**ss**ail, a**ss**ault, a**ss**emble, a**ss**ert, a**ss**ign* (at-): *a**tt**ain, a**tt**empt, a**tt**ire, a**tt**ribute, a**tt**ract*
com-	Together; together with; joint; jointly; mutually. Also used as an intensifier.	**com-** before roots beginning with *m-* **col-** before roots beginning with *l-* **cor-** before roots beginning with *r-* **con-** before roots beginning with *n-*	(com-): *co**mm**and, co**mm**ingle, co**mm**iserate, co**mm**it* (col-): *co**ll**aborate, co**ll**apse, co**ll**eague, co**ll**ect, co**ll**ide, co**ll**ude* (con-): *co**nn**ect, co**nn**ive, co**nn**otation* (cor-): *co**rr**ect, co**rr**elate, co**rr**espond, co**rr**ode, co**rr**upt*

ex-	Away; from; outward; out of; upwards.	Becomes **ef-** before *f-*	*efface, effect, effeminate, effort*
in-	1. Not; non-; opposite of; without. 2. Into; in; on; upon.	**il-** before roots beginning with *l-* **im-** before roots beginning with *m-* **ir-** before roots beginning with *r-*	(il-): *illegal, illiterate, illogical, illuminate, illusion, illustrate* (im-): *immaculate, immaterial, immature, immediate, immigrate, immobile* (in-): *innocent, innocuous, innervate, innovate, innuendo* (ir-): *irradiate, irrational, irreparable, irreversible, irrigate*
ob-	1. To; toward; across; away from; over. 2. Against; before; blocking; facing, concealing.	**oc-** before roots beginning with *c-* **of-** before roots beginning with *f-* **op-** before roots beginning with *p-*	(oc-): *occasion, occult, occupy, occur* (of-): *offer, offend* (op-): *opponent, oppress, opportune*
sub-	1. Under; below; beneath; outside or outlying. 2. At a secondary or lower position in a hierarchy. 3. Incompletely or imperfectly; partially; less than, almost, or nearly. 4. Forming a smaller part of a larger whole. 5. Up to; up from under or beneath.	**sup-** before roots beginning with *p-* **sur-** before roots beginning with *r-* (*Sub-* can also change to *suc-* before *c-* and *sug-* before *g-*, but this changes the consonants' sounds [*-cc-* is pronounced /-ks-/, and *-gg-* is pronounced /-dʒ-/], rather than one letter becoming silent.)	(sup-): *supplicate, suppose, support, suppress, supply* (sur-): *surreptitious, surrogate*

Doubling Consonants with Vowel Suffixes

Because most vowel suffixes are able to replace silent E by preserving the root word's pronunciation and meaning, we often have to double the final consonant of a root word when it precedes a vowel suffix to avoid confusion. This is especially true for single-syllable root words, but it occurs in certain words with two or more syllables as well. (We cover this more in depth in a separate section, so we'll just give a brief overview here.)

Doubling the final consonant in single-syllable words

When a single-syllable word ends in a vowel + a consonant, we almost always double the consonant when a vowel suffix is attached; if we don't, we end up with the suffixed forms of root words that originally ended in silent **E** (or look as though they did).

For example:

Root Word	✔ Correctly Suffixed Words	✖ Incorrectly Suffixed Words
bar	ba**rr**ed, ba**rr**ing	ba**r**ed, ba**r**ing (looks like the root word is *bare*)
dot	do**tt**ed, do**tt**ing	do**t**ed, do**t**ing (looks like the root word is *dote*)
hop	ho**pp**ed, ho**pp**er, ho**pp**ing, ho**pp**y	ho**p**ed, ho**p**er, ho**p**ing, ho**p**y (looks like the root word is *hope*)
jog	jo**gg**ed, jo**gg**er, jo**gg**ing	jo**g**ed, jo**g**er, jo**g**ing (looks like the root word is *joge*)
mad	ma**dd**en, ma**dd**er, ma**dd**est	ma**d**en, ma**d**er, ma**d**est (looks like the root word is *made*)
stop	sto**pp**able, sto**pp**ed, sto**pp**er, sto**pp**ing	sto**p**able, sto**p**ed, sto**p**er, sto**p**ing (looks like the root word is *stope*)

We only follow this pattern when a word has a single syllable, a single short vowel, and ends with a single consonant—we don't double consonants for words that end in consonant clusters or digraphs (e.g., *dark→darken*) or those that have vowel digraphs in the middle (e.g., *steam→steamed*). We also never double the consonant **X**, as it technically forms two distinct consonant sounds joined as one, /ks/.

Doubling the consonant when the final syllable is emphasized

When a word has two or more syllables, we almost always double the final consonant before a vowel suffix when the final syllable is vocally stressed. In the examples below, the stressed syllables are shown in **bold**, with the IPA pronunciation included beneath each root word.

Emphasis on final syllable	Suffixed Words	Emphasis on other syllable	Suffixed Words
be**gin** (/bɪˈgɪn/)	begi**nn**er, begi**nn**ing	**bick**er (/ˈbɪkər/)/)	bicke**r**ed, bicke**r**ing
for**get** (/fərˈgɛt/)	forge**tt**able, forge**tt**ing	**for**feit (/ˈfɔrfɪt/)	forfei**t**ed, forfei**t**ing, forfei**t**ure
in**cur** (/ɪnˈkɜr/)	incu**rr**able, incu**rr**ed, incu**rr**ing	in**ter**pret (/ɪnˈtɜrprət/)	interpre**t**ed, interpre**t**er, interpre**t**ing
o**mit** (/oʊˈmɪt/)	omi**tt**ed, omi**tt**ing	**o**pen (/ˈoʊpən/)	ope**n**ed, ope**n**er, ope**n**ing
trans**mit** (/trænzˈmɪt/)	transmi**tt**able, transmi**tt**ed, transmi**tt**ing	**trav**el (/ˈtrævəl/)	trave**l**ed, trave**l**er, trave**l**ing*

(*In American English, **L** is not doubled at the end of words in which the vocal stress is on the first syllable. In British English, though, it is much more common to double the final **L** regardless of which syllable is stressed, though this doesn't happen to any other letters. Go to the section on American vs. British English Spelling to learn more about such differences.)

Quiz

(answers start on page 463)

1. Which of the following is the most common silent **vowel**?

a) A

b) E

c) U

d) Y

2. The letter **U** is most commonly silent when it appears after which consonant (other than **Q**)?

a) B

b) C

c) G

d) L

3. When attached to the word *resign*, which of the following suffixes would make **G** no longer silent?

a) -ation

b) -ed

c) -er

d) -ing

4. Which consonants can be silent when they appear **after** the letter **M**?

a) B & G

b) B & H

c) B & N

d) H & N

5. When are the final consonants doubled in single-syllable words?

a) When they come after vowel digraphs

b) When they are part of a consonant cluster

c) When they are part of a consonant digraph

d) When they come after a single short vowel.

6. Which of the following words does **not** contain a silent letter in its **standard** pronunciation?

a) clothes

b) mortgage

c) Wednesday

d) honest

Silent E

Definition

The term **silent E** (sometimes called **magic E**) refers to the use of an unpronounced E after another letter (usually a consonant) at the end of a word. As its name suggests, silent E is not pronounced as a separate vowel sound; instead, its most common function is to dictate the pronunciation of the vowel (and occasionally the consonant) that comes before it. However, as we'll see later, there are many exceptions to this rule, as well as a number of other technical functions that silent E can perform.

Dictating both pronunciation and meaning

As we looked at in the section on vowels, silent E affects the way another vowel in the word is pronounced, changing the speech sound into what is commonly referred to as a "long vowel"—one that is pronounced like the name of the letter. Let's take a look at some similarly spelled words in which the addition of a silent E changes the pronunciation as well as the meaning. For example:

Word without Silent E	Meaning	Word with Silent E	Meaning
bad (/bæd/)	(*adj.*) Not good or undesirable.	bade (/beɪd/)	(*verb*) The simple past tense of *bid*.
them (/ðɛm/)	(*pron.*) The objective case of the personal pronoun *they*.	theme (/θim/)	(*noun*) A topic, subject, or idea.
grip (/grɪp/)	(*verb*) To hold onto something.	gripe (/graɪp/)	(*verb*) To complain in a nagging or petulant manner.
hop (/hɑp/)	(*verb*) To jump or leap a short distance.	hope (/hoʊp/)	(*verb*) To wish for or desire (something).
cub (/kʌb/)	(*noun*) A young bear, lion, wolf, or certain other animal.	cube (/kjub/)	(*noun*) A solid shape comprising six equal square faces.

Silent E also has this effect on the sound of **Y** when **Y** functions as a vowel (the "long" and "short" vowel sounds for **Y** are the same as **I**: /aɪ/ and /ɪ/, respectively). There are no standard pairs of words that have the same spelling except for silent **E**, but we can look at an example of two words with *similar* spelling to see the differences in pronunciation: *myth* (/mɪθ/) and *scythe* (/saɪð/). Notice how silent **E** also affects the pronunciation of **TH**; we'll look at this more closely further on.

Dictating pronunciation but not meaning

It's important to remember that silent **E** also has this effect in words that couldn't be spelled without it—that is, the word without the silent **E** would have no meaning. Therefore, only the pronunciation is dictated by silent **E**, not the meaning of the word compared to another.

For example:

A a	E e	I i	O o	U u	Y y
bale (/beɪl/)	concrete (/ˈkɑnkrit/)	bike (/baɪk/)	rope (/roʊp/)	fuse (/fjus/)	thyme (/taɪm/)
cake (/keɪk/)	impede (/ɪmˈpid/)	tile (/taɪl/)	broke (/broʊk/)	mule (/mjul/)	hype (/haɪp/)
rave (/reɪv/)	scene (/sin/)	strike (/straɪk/)	trope (/troʊp/)	rebuke (/rɪˈbjuk/)	tyke (/taɪk/)

Exceptions to the rule

While the silent **E** rule regarding vowel pronunciation is fairly consistent, there are many instances in which the preceding vowel does **not** become long. This is typically the result of spelling having changed over time, or of an **E** becoming silent after having once been pronounced. Some common examples include:

• are (/ɑr/)*
• above (/əˈbʌv/)
• come (/kʌm/)
• done (/dʌn/)
• have (/hæv/)
• give (/gɪv/)
• glove (/glʌv/)
• gone (/gɔn/)*
• love (/lʌv/)
• some (/sʌm/)
• none (/nʌn/)

(*Note that these vowel sounds are considered a *kind* of long vowel, but are not what is traditionally taught as one—that is, they do not sound like their vowel letters' names.)

Certain endings

This exception to the rule that silent **E** produces long vowels before single consonants is also often seen in many (though not all) multi-syllable words ending with "-ive," "-ine," and "-age." Much less commonly, it also happens with words ending in "-ate." (Note that, in the case of "-age" and "-ate," the short vowel sound for **A** changes from /æ/ to /ɪ/.)

For example:

IVE	INE	AGE	ATE
active (/ˈæktɪv/)	doctrine (/ˈdɑktrɪn/)	advantage (/ædˈvæntɪdʒ/)	accurate (/ˈækjərɪt/)
captive (/ˈkæptɪv/)	examine (/ɪgˈzæmɪn/)	bandage (/ˈbændɪdʒ/)	celibate (/ˈsɛlɪbɪt/)
defensive (/dɪˈfɛnsɪv/)	feminine (/ˈfɛmənɪn/)	courage (/ˈkɜrɪdʒ/)	corporate (/ˈkɔrpərɪt/)
effective (/ɪˈfɛktɪv/)	imagine (/ɪˈmædʒɪn/)	image (/ˈɪmɪdʒ/)	estimate* (/ˈɛstəmɪt/)
offensive (/əˈfɛnsɪv/)	medicine (/ˈmɛdəsɪn/)	outage (/ˈaʊtɪdʒ/)	frigate (/ˈfrɪgɪt/)

Many words ending in "-ine" also have a <u>different</u> long-vowel sound for the letter **I** (/i/, traditionally taught as the "long **E**" sound). This is especially true for the names of chemical compounds, but it occurs in other instances as well. For example:

• gasoline (/ˈgæsəˌlin/)
• glycine (/ˈglaɪˌsin/)
• latrine (/ləˈtrin/)
• limousine (/ˈlɪməˌzin/)
• marine (/məˈrin/)
• nicotine (/ˈnɪkəˌtin/)

- ravine (/rəˈvin/)
- saline (/seɪˈlin/)

(*As a noun, *estimate* is pronounced /ˈɛstəmɪt/. However, this word can also function as a verb, in which case it is pronounced /ˈɛstəmeɪt/, with silent **E** producing a "long **A**" as it usually does. There are other words like this that have two pronunciations dictated by **E**, which we'll look at next.)

Words with two pronunciations

Many words that have the exact same spelling will have two different meanings with two separate pronunciations. The standard rule that silent **E** will make the preceding vowel "long" applies to one of these pronunciations, but not the other (though **E** is silent in both); this difference in pronunciation lets us know which meaning we're using. For example:

Short vowel sound before final consonant	Meaning	Long vowel sound before final consonant	Meaning
advocate (/ˈædvəkɪt/)	(*noun*) Someone who represents or stands up for a certain cause.	advocate (/ˈædvəˌkeɪt/)	(*verb*) To speak for, represent, or support (something) publicly.
dove (/dʌv/)	(*noun*) A type of bird.	dove (/daɪv/)	(*verb*) Simple past tense of *dive*.
live (/lɪv/)	(*verb*) To exist or be alive.	live (/laɪv/)	(*adj.*) Having or showing the characteristics of life.
minute (/mɪˈnɪt/)	(*noun*) A unit of 60 seconds.	minute (/maɪˈnjut/)	(*adj.*) Very small, unimportant, or petty.
separate (/ˈsɛpəˌrɪt/)	(*adj.*) Detached; distinct; independent.	separate (/ˈsɛpəˌreɪt/)	(*verb*) To divide or keep apart.

Changing consonant sounds

In addition to changing the sound of preceding vowels, silent **E** can also have an impact on the pronunciation of certain consonant sounds, specifically those produced by **C**, **D**, and the digraph **TH**.

Changing C and G

The consonants **C** and **G** both have a "hard" and "soft" pronunciation. "**Hard C**" is pronounced the same as the letter **K** (/k/), while "**soft C**" has the same sound as the letter **S** (/s/). "**Hard G**" has a unique consonant sound (/g/), while "**soft G**" is pronounced like the letter **J** (/dʒ/).

When they come before a silent **E**, both **C** and **G** take their soft pronunciations. This most commonly occurs when **CE** comes after the letter **I** and when **GE** comes after the letter **A**, but it can occur with other vowels as well. For example:

Soft C	Soft G
ice (/aɪs/)	age (/eɪdʒ/)
advice (/ædˈvaɪs/)	cage (/keɪdʒ/)
sacrifice (/ˈsækrɪˌfaɪs/)	stage (/steɪdʒ/)
face (/feɪs/)	oblige (/əˈblaɪdʒ/)
fleece (/flis/)	college (/ˈkɑlɪdʒ/)
truce (/trus/)	refuge (/ˈrɛfjudʒ/)

This effect is also true when **CE** and **GE** come after **N** at the end of a word, as in:
- advance (/ədˈvæns/)
- essence (/ˈɛsəns/)
- glance (/glæns/)

- arrange (/əˈreɪndʒ/)
- cringe (/krɪndʒ/)
- orange (/ˈɔrəndʒ/)

Changing TH

Silent **E** also has a bearing on the pronunciation of the consonant digraph **TH**. In most words that end in **TH**, it is pronounced as /θ/, an **unvoiced** consonant sound (meaning the vocal cords aren't vibrated to create noise). When a final **TH** is followed by **E**, however, it almost takes the **voiced** consonant sound /ð/.

Often, adding a silent **E** after **TH** also has the effect of changing the meaning of a word, usually from a noun to a verb. For example:

Word without Silent E	Meaning	Word with Silent E	Meaning
bath (/bæθ/)	(*noun*) The act of washing the body in water.	bathe (/beɪð/)	(*verb*) To immerse in water for the purposes of washing; to take a bath.
breath (/brɛθ/)	(*noun*) An instance of inhaling air into the lungs.	breathe (/brið/)	(*verb*) To inhale air into the lungs.
cloth (/klɔθ/)	(*noun*) Material made from woven or knitted fibers.	clothe (/kloʊð/)	(*verb*) To put on or provide clothing.
teeth (/tiθ/)	(*noun*) Plural of *tooth*.	teethe (/tið/)	(*verb*) Of babies, to grow teeth for the first time.
wreath (/riθ/)	(*noun*) A ring of entwined flowers, leaves, or other foliage.	wreathe (/rið/)	(*verb*) To form into or take the shape of a wreath.

Ending some words in a vowel + **THE** will result in the /ð/ sound but will not change the meaning from a noun to a verb. For example:
- lathe (/leɪð/)
- scythe (/saɪð/)
- swathe (/sweɪð/)
- tithe (/taɪð/)

Other functions of Silent E

In addition to dictating pronunciation, meaning, or both, silent **E** also has a number of particular orthographic functions at the end of many words.

Providing a final syllable with a vowel

Each syllable in a word must contain a vowel sound. Many words are spelled with a final syllable consisting of a consonant + **L**, so an **E** is added to make sure the syllable is complete. While this **E** is often referred to as silent, in fact it *does* provide a very subtle, unstressed vowel sound—known as a **schwa** (/ə/)—*before* the consonant sound /l/.

This "semi-silent" **E** can also affect the pronunciation of the vowel sound that precedes the consonant + **LE**. Generally (there are exceptions), the rule is this: If a single vowel comes before a single consonant + **LE**, the vowel sound is "long"; if a single vowel comes before two consonants + **LE**, the vowel sound is "short"; and if a vowel **digraph** comes before a consonant + **LE**, the vowel sound is dictated by the digraph itself.

For example:

Single vowel + Consonant + LE	Single vowel + Two Consonants + LE	Vowel Digraph + Consonant + LE
able* (/ˈeɪbəl/)	assemble (/əˈsɛmbəl/)	beagle (/ˈbigəl/)
bugle (/ˈbjugəl/)	bundle (/ˈbʌnbəl/)	couple (/ˈkʌpəl/)
cable (/ˈkeɪbəl/)	cattle (/ˈkætəl/)	beetle (/ˈbitəl/)
cradle (/ˈkreɪdəl/)	curdle (/ˈkɜrdəl/)	feeble (/ˈfibəl/)
idle (/ˈaɪdəl/)	example (/ɪgˈzæmpəl/)	double (/ˈdʌbəl/)
ladle (/ˈleɪdəl/)	little (/ˈlɪtəl/)	inveigle (/ɪnˈveɪgəl/)
maple (/ˈmeɪpəl/)	paddle (/ˈpædəl/)	needle (/ˈnidəl/)
noble (/ˈnoʊbəl/)	marble (/ˈmɑrbəl/)	people (/ˈpipəl/)
soluble (/ˈsɑljubəl/)	middle (/ˈmɪdəl/)	steeple (/ˈstipəl/)
title (/ˈtaɪtəl/)	single (/ˈsɪŋgəl/)	trouble (/ˈtrʌbəl/)

(*The word *able* also acts as a suffix in many words, meaning "capable of, tending to, or suitable for." In this capacity, the vowel **A** is reduced to an unstressed schwa, as in *capable* [/ˈkeɪpəbəl/] or *suitable* [/ˈsutəbəl/].)

Note, though, that there *are* a few words in which **no** vowel letter is present in the final syllable. These occur when **M** is the last letter of the word after **S** or, less commonly, **TH**; we do not add silent **E** in these words. For example:
- enthusia**sm** (/ɛnˈθu.ziˌæz.əm/)
- tour**ism** (/ˈtʊəˌrɪz.əm/)
- rhy**thm** (/ˈrɪð.əm/)

While there is no vowel *letter* in the final syllable of these words, notice that there is still a vowel *sound*—an unstressed schwa (/ə/), just like we had in words ending in consonant + **LE**. (Go to the section on Syllables for more information about the different ways they are formed and identified.)

After final U and V

The vast majority of English words do not end in a **U** or a **V**. In a similar way to how **E** is added after words ending in a consonant + **L**, it is also added after words ending in **U** or **V** to help normalize their appearance. However, **unlike** when it appears after a consonant + **L**, this **E** is truly silent; it does not add a schwa or any other vowel sound to the word.

Finally, for words that end in a single vowel + **VE**, silent **E** may or may not affect the previous vowel's pronunciation (like many of the exceptions we looked at earlier). Unfortunately, the spelling of the word won't indicate when this is or is not the case, so we just have to memorize the pronunciation of such words.

For example:

U + E	V+ E
clue (/klu/)	above (/əˈbʌv/)
dialogue (/ˈdaɪəˌlɔg/)	brave (/breɪv/)
ensue (/ɪnˈsu/)	crave (/creɪv/)
fatigue (/fəˈtig/)	eve (/iv/)
opaque (/oʊˈpeɪk/)	have (/hæv/)
revenue (/ˈrɛvəˌnu/)	love (/lʌv/)
unique (/juˈnik/)	prove (/pruv/)
value (/ˈvælju/)	wove (/woʊv/)

Notice that the words ending in **GUE** or **QUE** don't have an additional syllable at the end, so **G** and **Q** are pronounced /g/ and /k/ while **U** and **E** both become silent. However, in some words, this letter combination <u>does</u> produce an extra syllable, in which case either **U** or **E** is pronounced. For instance:

• argue (/ˈɑrgju/)
• dengue (/ˈdɛngeɪ/)
• communiqué* (/kəmˌjunəˈkeɪ/)
• risqué* (/ˌrɪˈskeɪ/)
• segue (/ˈsɛgweɪ/)

(*_Communiqué_ and _risqué_ are loan words from French. Because of this, the final **E** is traditionally written with an accent mark. However, because these words have become common in English, this accent mark is often left off.)

Keeping a singular noun from ending in S

Another functional purpose of silent **E** is to keep a singular noun from ending in a single **S**. This ensures that the word is not mistaken for a plural noun or a third person singular verb.

For example:
• base (/beɪs/)
• course (/kɔrs/)
• cheese (/tʃis/)
• goose (/gus/)
• lease (/lis/)
• moose (/mus/)
• promise (/ˈprɑməs/)
• purse (/pɜrs/)
• spouse (/spaʊs/)
• verse (/vɜrs/)

Non-silent E

Finally, it's worth mentioning that while a single **E** following a consonant at the end of a word is <u>usually</u> silent (or else produces a reduced schwa), it does occasionally produce a true speech sound of its own. For example:
• ante (/ˈænti/)
• apostrophe (/əˈpɑstrəfi/)
• coyote (/kaɪˈoʊti/)
• hyperbole (/haɪˈpɜrbəˌli/)
• recipe (/ˈrɛsəpi/)

- sesam<u>e</u> (/ˈsɛsəm<u>i</u>/)
- simil<u>e</u> (/ˈsɪməl<u>i</u>/)
- syncop<u>e</u> (/ˈsɪnkəˌp<u>i</u>/)

E is also pronounced when it occurs at the end of words with a single consonant sound, as in:

- b<u>e</u> (/b<u>i</u>/)
- h<u>e</u> (/h<u>i</u>/)
- m<u>e</u> (/m<u>i</u>/)
- sh<u>e</u> (/ʃ<u>i</u>/)
- th<u>e</u> (/ðə/ or /ð<u>i</u>/)
- w<u>e</u> (/w<u>i</u>/)

Quiz
(answers start on page 463)

1. Which of the following is **not** a function of silent **E**?

a) Dictating a vowel's pronunciation
b) Adding a vowel to a final syllable
c) Indicating that a noun is plural rather than singular
d) Dictating a consonant's pronunciation

2. A vowel that precedes a consonant + silent **E** is most commonly pronounced in which way?

a) The same way as the name of the letter
b) As a "short" vowel
c) It becomes silent
d) Silent **E** has no effect

3. How does silent **E** affect the pronunciation of **C** and **G**?

a) It produces their "hard" pronunciation
b) It produces their "soft" pronunciation
c) It produces the /ð/ phoneme
d) It has no effect

4. In which of the following words is the vowel's pronunciation **not** made long by the silent **E**?

a) complete
b) provoke
c) determine
d) arcade

5. What speech sound does **E** produce when it appears at the end of a word after a consonant + **L**?

a) /ɛ/
b) /ə/
c) /i/
d) No sound

Syllables

Definition

A **syllable** is a sequence of speech sounds (formed from vowels and consonants) organized into a single unit. Syllables act as the building blocks of a spoken word, determining the pace and rhythm of how the word is pronounced.

Structure of a syllable

The three structural elements of a syllable are the **nucleus**, the **onset**, and the **coda**.

Syllables can be structured several ways, but they <u>always</u> contain a nucleus, which is (usually) formed from a vowel sound. The nucleus is the core of the syllable, indicating its individual "beat" within a word; the number of syllables in a word will be determined by the number of vowel sounds forming their nuclei.

Syllables may also contain consonant sounds that form an onset (a sound <u>before</u> the nucleus), a coda (a sound <u>after</u> the nucleus), or both, but they do not have to contain either.

For example, the word *open* (/ˈoʊpən/) contains two syllables: "o-" and "-pen." The first syllable <u>only</u> contains a nucleus (the vowel sound /oʊ/); because it does not end with a consonant sound, it is what's known as an **open syllable**. The second syllable, on the other hand, contains an onset (the consonant sound /p/), a nucleus (the reduced vowel sound /ə/), and a coda (the consonant sound /n/); it is what's known as a **closed syllable**.

We'll look at the different types of syllables further on, but first let's look at how we can represent syllables in writing.

Indicating syllables in writing

Because syllables are related solely to speech, we do not use symbols to represent them in everyday writing. However, there are certain ways that syllables *can* be demonstrated in written English, such as in dictionaries or other reference works.

Words with one syllable do not have any visual representation for them—there's no need, since the word itself *is* the syllable. If a word has more than one syllable, though, subsequent syllables are often identified by a mark known as an interpunct (·), also called a **midpoint, middle dot**, or **centered dot**. For example, the word *application* would appear as *ap·pli·ca·tion*. This is the symbol used in many dictionaries to delineate mid-word syllables; however, because the interpunct is such a specialized symbol, other sources commonly use hyphens (*ap-pli-ca-tion*) or slashes (*ap/pli/ca/tion*). In this guide, we will use **interpuncts** whenever a word's syllables need to be visualized.

When the pronunciation of a word is transcribed using the **International Phonetic Alphabet** (IPA), syllables usually are not represented at all except for the primary stress (ˈ) and, in some cases, secondary stress (ˌ). For example, the word *application* is transcribed in IPA as /ˌæplɪˈkeɪʃən/. Saying the word aloud, we can hear that the greatest vocal stress in the word is placed on the syllable /keɪ/, so it is marked with the symbol ˈ. The first syllable /æp/ has less stress, but it is still more forcefully pronounced than the rest of the syllables, so it is marked with the ˌ symbol. (Compare the pronunciation of *application* with that of the base word *apply*: /əˈplaɪ/. The first syllable is now **unstressed** and reduced to a schwa, so it is no longer marked with the ˌ symbol.)

However, unstressed syllables *can* be represented in IPA when they occur mid-word, either by periods (/ˌæp.lɪˈkeɪ.ʃən/) or spaces (/ˌæp lɪ ˈkeɪ ʃən/). While this guide usually does not mark unstressed syllables in IPA transcriptions, we will indicate them in this section with **periods**.

Written syllables vs. spoken syllables

You may have noticed in the example above that the syllables of *application* and *apply* are divided slightly differently in the written "dictionary" form compared to the phonetic "spoken" form (the IPA transcription). Specifically, the written form divides the double consonant **PP** between the first and second syllable (*ap·pli·ca·tion*), but as a digraph **PP** only makes a single consonant sound (/p/), so in the spoken form it only appears in the first syllable since it has a secondary stress (/ˌæp.lɪˈkeɪ.ʃən/). In *ap·ply*, on the other hand, the first syllable is **unstressed** and only consists of the reduced vowel sound /ə/, so the /p/ sound is now connected to the *second* syllable in the spoken form: /əˈplaɪ/. In fact, doubled consonants are almost always divided between syllables in the written form of a word, even though the sound they make can only belong to one syllable. Which syllable the consonant sound belongs to is determined by the type of vowel sound made by the nucleus, which is in turn dictated by what **type** of syllable it is.

We also sometimes see differences like this in words ending with the vowel suffixes "-ing" or "-ize." Many written forms treat such suffixes as individual syllables separate from the preceding consonant sound, while in speech the final syllable often *includes* the consonant. For example:

	Written syllables	**Spoken syllables**
"-ing" words	a·larm·ing ask·ing bak·ing eat·ing learn·ing think·ing	/əˈlɑr.mɪŋ/ /ˈæs.kɪŋ/ /ˈbeɪ.kɪŋ/ /ˈi.tɪŋ/ /ˈlɜr.nɪŋ/ /ˈθɪŋ.kɪŋ/
"-ize" words	at·om·ize cus·tom·ize in·ter·nal·ize mois·tur·ize re·al·ize ver·bal·ize	/ˈæt.əˌmaɪz/ /ˈkʌs.təˌmaɪz/ /ɪnˈtɜr.nəˌlaɪz/ /ˈmɔɪs.tʃəˌraɪz/ /ˈrɪəˌlaɪz/ /ˈvɜr.bəˌlaɪz/

Note that this is not **always** true for words ending in these suffixes, but it is common enough that it's worth pointing out.

There are other less predictable instances in which a written syllable division does not match the way it is spoken. Such deviations as these are fairly common in English because there is rarely a one-to-one correspondence between letters and sounds. Instead, we identify syllables divisions based on several *types* of syllables that commonly occur and the spelling and pronunciation conventions that they indicate.

Types of syllables

Although syllables all perform the same basic function—marking the verbal "beats" of a spoken word—not all syllables are structured the same way. In fact, there are **six** types of syllables that are identified in English based on a word's spelling and the type of sound the syllable's nucleus creates. The two most basic categories are **open** and **closed syllables**, but we also distinguish **silent E syllables, vowel-combination syllables, vowel-R syllables**, and **syllabic consonants**. By dividing syllables into these six categories, we can identify a number of patterns that help us use a word's spelling to determine its pronunciation, and vice versa.

Open syllables

An **open syllable** (also known as a **free syllable**) is one that has a single vowel letter for its nucleus and does not contain a **coda**—that is, it does not have a consonant sound after the vowel. An open syllable can be a vowel sound on its own, or else have an onset (one or more consonant sounds) that precedes the nucleus.

When an open syllable is stressed (i.e., it has the most vocal emphasis in the word), it will have a "traditional" long vowel sound forming its nucleus—that is, a vowel sound that "says the name" of the vowel letter. When an open syllable is **unstressed**, it is often shortened into a weak vowel—typically a **schwa** (/ə/) or the "short **I**" sound (/ɪ/). (For words with only a single open syllable, this vowel reduction only occurs in the articles *a* and *the*.)

For example:

One-syllable words	One-syllable words (when vowel is unstressed)	Multiple syllables (vowel is stressed)	Multiple syllables (vowel is unstressed)
a (/eɪ/)		a·corn (/ˈeɪ.kɔrn/)	a·loft (/əˈlɔft/)
by (/baɪ/)		cu·bi·cal (/ˈkju.bɪ.kəl/)	be·neath (/bɪˈniθ/)
go (/goʊ/)		e·ven (/ˈi.vɪn/)	cu·bi·cal (/ˈkju.bɪ.kəl/)
he (/hi/)	a (/ə/)	gra·vy (/ˈɡreɪ.vi/)	de·bate (/dɪˈbeɪt/)
I (/aɪ/)	the (/ðə/)	hel·lo (/hɛˈloʊ/)	de·ter·mine (/dɪˈtɜr.mɪn/)
me (/mi/)	(Note: When *the* is unstressed, it only takes the reduced pronunciation /ðə/ before words beginning with a consonant. When an unstressed *the* occurs before a **vowel**, it is normally still pronounced /ði/.)	i·tem (/ˈaɪ.təm/)	e·vent (/ɪˈvɛnt/)
so (/soʊ/)		mu·tate (/ˈmju.teɪt/)	grav·i·tate (/ˈɡræv.ɪˌteɪt/)
she (/ʃi/)		o·cean (/ˈoʊ.ʃən/)	med·i·tate (/ˈmɛd.ɪˌteɪt/)
the (/ði/)		se·cret (/ˈsi.krɪt/)	re·lease (/rɪˈlis/)
why (/waɪ/)		vol·ca·no (/vɑlˈkeɪ.noʊ/)	ze·bra (/ˈzi.brə/)

You may have noticed that none of the syllables we highlighted here feature vowel digraphs (two vowel letters forming a single vowel sound). This is because syllables with vowel digraphs (as well as other vowel-sound combinations) are typically classed together under a separate category, which we will look at further on.

Finally note that an open syllable cannot be followed by a <u>doubled</u> consonant; it can only be followed by a <u>single</u> consonant or a **consonant cluster** that acts as the onset of the next syllable. This is because a doubled consonant appearing mid-word will always be divided between syllables, with the first consonant forming the **coda** of a closed syllable and the second consonant forming the **onset** of the next syllable.

Closed syllables

In contrast to an open syllable, a **closed syllable** is one in which a single vowel is followed by a **coda**, which consists of one or more consonant sounds at the end of the syllable (except the consonant **R**—vowels followed by **R** form a specific syllable category, which we'll look at separately).

Closed syllables often have an **onset** as well (forming what's known as the CVC or consonant-vowel-consonant pattern). This is not always the case, though, especially when a closed syllable is at the beginning of a word.

Closed syllables most often have short vowels forming their nuclei, but they may also have other long vowel sounds that do not "say the name" of the vowel letter. Like those of open syllables, the vowels of closed syllables may be reduced to weak vowel sounds if the closed syllable is unstressed.

For example:

One-syllable words	One-syllable words (when vowel is unstressed)	Multiple syllables (stressed vowel)	Multiple syllables (unstressed vowel)
as (/æz/)		ac·ci·dent (/ˈæk.sɪ.dənt/)	ac·ci·dent (/ˈæk.sɪ.dənt/)
at (/æt/)		com·mon (/ˈkɑm.ən/)	ap·par·ent (/əˈpɛr.ənt/)
bed (/bɛd/)	an (/ən/)	e·vent (/ɪˈvɛnt/)	black·en (/ˈblæk.ən/)
cot (/kɑt/)	as (/əz/)	for·bid (/fərˈbɪd/)	com·mon (/ˈkɑm.ən/)
duck (/dʌk/)	at (/ət/)	hap·pen (/ˈhæp.ən/)	con·trol (/kənˈtroʊl/)
have* (/hæv/)	have* (/(h)əv/)	lad·der (/ˈlæd.ər/)	ex·cept (/ɪkˈsɛpt/)
myth (/mɪθ/)	of (/əv/)	pel·i·can (/ˈpɛl.ɪ.kən/)	hap·pen (/ˈhæp.ən/)
of (/ʌv/)		riv·er (/ˈrɪv.ər/)	mas·sage (/məˈsɑʒ/)
strut (/strʌt/)		suc·cess (/səkˈsɛs/)	suc·cess (/səkˈsɛs/)
task (/tæsk/)		tem·per (/ˈtɛmp.ər/)	tra·di·tion (/trəˈdɪ.ʃən/)

*Notice that the word *have* behaves like a normal closed syllable, with **A** taking the short vowel sound /æ/, even though it has a silent E at the end. A number of other words are pronounced with short vowels despite having silent **E** endings, such as *give* (/gɪv/), *gone* (/gɔn/), or *love* (/lʌv/), but most of the time a silent **E** indicates that the vowel sound in the syllable's nucleus is long, which goes against the normal pronunciation pattern for closed syllables. These are often identified separately as **Silent E Syllables**.

Exceptions

Although it is less common, a closed syllable *can* have a traditional long vowel as its nucleus. It is usually the letter **O** that takes this long pronunciation. For example:

• b**o**th (/boʊθ/)
• con·tr**o**l (/kənˈtroʊl/)
• gr**o**ss (/groʊs/)
• j**o**lt (/dʒoʊlt/)
• pa·tr**o**l (/pəˈtroʊl/)
• p**o**st (/poʊst/)
• r**o**ll (/roʊl/)
• t**o**ll (/toʊl/)

This is almost always the case when **O** is followed by "-ld." For instance:

• b**o**ld (/boʊld/)
• c**o**ld (/koʊld/)
• f**o**ld (/foʊld/)
• g**o**ld (/goʊld/)
• h**o**ld (/hoʊld/)
• m**o**ld (/moʊld/)
• **o**ld (/oʊld/)
• s**o**ld (/soʊld/)
• t**o**ld (/toʊld/)

The letter **I** can also have a long pronunciation in a closed syllable, typically when followed by "-nd," as in:

• be·h**i**nd (/bɪˈhaɪnd/)

- b<u>i</u>nd (/b<u>aɪ</u>nd/)
- bl<u>i</u>nd (/bl<u>aɪ</u>nd/)
- f<u>i</u>nd (/f<u>aɪ</u>nd/)
- gr<u>i</u>nd (/gr<u>aɪ</u>nd/)
- k<u>i</u>nd (/k<u>aɪ</u>nd/)
- m<u>i</u>nd (/m<u>aɪ</u>nd/)
- r<u>i</u>nd (/r<u>aɪ</u>nd/)
- w<u>i</u>nd (/w<u>aɪ</u>nd/, meaning "to twist or turn")

Silent E syllables

One of the most common and well-known functions of **silent E** is to indicate that a vowel has a "long" sound before a single consonant. Because the vowel sound of the nucleus becomes long, we distinguish syllables formed with a silent **E** from closed syllables, which always have short or weak vowels.

Silent **E** syllables are generally either the only or the final syllable of the word. For example:

One syllable	Multiple syllables
bik<u>e</u> (/baɪk/)	con·**cret<u>e</u>** (/ˈkɑn.**krit**/)
cak<u>e</u> (/keɪk/)	de·**mot<u>e</u>** (/dɪ**ˈmoʊt**/)
mut<u>e</u> (/mjut/)	e·**vad<u>e</u>** (/ɪ**ˈveɪd**/)
rop<u>e</u> (/roʊp/)	in·**sid<u>e</u>** (/ɪn**ˈsaɪd**/)
them<u>e</u> (/θim/)	re·**buk<u>e</u>** (/rɪ**ˈbjuk**/)

Exceptions to the Silent E rule

It's important to note that there are many exceptions to this rule; there are many words in which silent **E** appears at the end of syllables that have short-vowel nuclei, meaning there is little difference between them and normal closed syllables. Here are just a few examples:

- ac·**tiv<u>e</u>** (/ˈæk.**tɪv**/)
- ex·am·**in<u>e</u>** (/ɪgˈzæm.**ɪn**/)
- hav<u>e</u> (/hæv/)
- som<u>e</u> (/sʌm/)

For more information on the different exceptions, go to the section on Silent E.

Vowel-combination syllables

Just as we do with syllables in which silent **E** indicates a long-vowel sound for the nucleus, we separate syllables that have vowel sounds formed from a combination of letters as their nuclei. These kinds of syllables are known as **vowel-combination syllables** (sometimes referred to as **vowel team syllables**).

Many of the nuclei in these types of syllables are vowel digraphs, specific pairs of vowel letters that form single vowel sounds or diphthongs; however, the nucleus of a vowel-combination syllable can also be formed from certain combinations of vowels and consonants.

Many of these combinations, especially vowel digraphs, form a certain vowel sound in one instance, but a completely different sound in another. If you're not sure how a certain combination is supposed to be pronounced, check the pronunciation guide in a good dictionary.

There are too many vowel-sound combinations to list in this section; we'll give a brief overview here, but go to the Vowels section to learn more.

Vowel Digraphs	Vowel-Consonant Combinations
au·thor (/ˈɔ.θər/)	
be·**lieve** (/bɪˈliv/)	b**al**m (/bɑm/)
chew·a·ble* (/ˈtʃu.ə.bəl/)	c**au**ght (/kɔt/)
child·**hood** (/ˈtʃaɪld͵hʊd/)	dr**ough**t (/draʊt/)
cr**ui**se (/kruz/)	f**ough**t (/fɔt/)
en·**dear**·ing (/ɛnˈdɪr.ɪŋ/)	**height**·en (/ˈhaɪt.ən/)
her·**oes** (/ˈhɪr.oʊs/)	in·**sight** (/ˈɪn͵saɪt/)
melt·**down*** (/ˈmɛlt͵daʊn/)	**neigh**·bor (/ˈneɪ.bər/)
pur·**sue** (/pərˈsu/)	p**al**m (/pɑm/)
pain·ful (/ˈpeɪn.fəl/)	sh**ou**ld (/ʃʊd/)
s**ui**t (/sut/)	thr**ough** (/θru/)
un·**bear**·a·ble (/ʌnˈbɛr.ə.bəl/)	w**ou**ld (/wʊd/)
un·**beat**·a·ble (/͵ʌnˈbit.ə.bəl/)	

(*W, like Y, is often considered to function as a vowel rather than a consonant when used in digraphs like these.)

Vowel-R syllables

Also known as "**R-controlled syllables,**" these are syllables in which the nucleus is made up of a single vowel letter followed by **R**. This has the effect of changing the pronunciation of the vowel, either subtly or dramatically, so we categorize these syllables separately.

Vowel + R	Example Words	Full IPA
AR	a·**far** car dis·em·**bark** **par**·ti·cle **war**·lock	/əˈfɑr/ /kɑr/ /͵dɪs.ɛmˈbɑrk/ /ˈpɑr.tɪ.kəl/ /ˈwɔr.lɑk/
ER	a·**lert** her nerve **per**·fect su·**perb**	/əˈlɜrt/ /hɜr/ /nɜrv/ /ˈpɜr͵fɪkt/ /sʊˈpɜrb/
IR	af·**firm** bird mirth **sir**·loin swirl·ing	/əˈfɜrm/ /bɜrd/ /mɜrθ/ /ˈsɜr.lɔɪn/ /ˈswɜrl.ɪŋ/

379

OR	c<u>or</u>d	/c<u>ɔ</u>rd/
	re·**m<u>or</u>se**	/rɪ'm<u>ɔ</u>rs/
	st<u>or</u>k	/st<u>ɔ</u>rk/
	w<u>or</u>k	/w<u>ɜ</u>rk/
	w<u>or</u>·thy	/'**w<u>ɜ</u>r**.ði/
UR	c<u>ur</u>v·y	/'**k<u>ɜr</u>v**.i/
	fl<u>ur</u>·ry	/'**fl<u>ɜr</u>**.i/
	n<u>ur</u>se	/n<u>ɜr</u>s/
	p<u>ur</u>·ple	/'**p<u>ɜr</u>**.pəl/
	t<u>ur</u>·tle	/'**t<u>ɜr</u>**.təl/

Notice that **ER, IR,** and **UR** all (generally) result in the same vowel sound, /ɜ/. **OR** can also form this vowel sound, but it more often makes the vowel sound /ɔ/, while **AR** almost always makes the vowel sound /ɑ/.

Syllabic consonants

A **syllabic consonant** refers to a syllable that has a consonant as its nucleus, rather than a vowel. When these words are pronounced out loud, the consonant will have a short reduced-vowel sound (/ə/) before it.

In most cases, syllabic consonants occur when **L** comes after a consonant and is followed by a **semi-**silent E, which indicates that the schwa sound will occur before the syllable; less commonly, this can also occur with **R** rather than **L** (a pattern that is much more common in British English). Finally, the letter **M** can also create syllabic consonants *without* a silent E, most often when it follows the letter **S** (especially in the suffix "-ism") but occasionally after the digraph **TH** as well.

For example:

Consonant + LE	Consonant + RE	S + M	Suffix "-ism"	TH + M
ap·**ple** (/'æp.əl/)			ac·tiv·**ism** (/'æk.tə͵vɪz.əm/)	
bi·cy·**cle** (/'baɪ.sɪk.əl/)			bap·**tism** (/'bæp.tɪz.əm/)	
cra·**dle** (/'kreɪd.əl/)		an·eu·**rysm** (/'æn.jə͵rɪz.əm/)	cap·i·tal·**ism** (/'kæp.ɪ.tə͵lɪz.əm/)	
crum·**ple** (/'krʌmp.əl/)	a·**cre** (/'eɪ.kər/)	**chasm** (/'kæz.əm/)	es·cap·**ism** (/ɪ'skeɪ͵pɪz.əm/)	
fid·**dle** (/'fɪd.əl/)	lu·**cre** (/'lu.kər/)	cat·a·**clysm** (/'kæt.ə͵klɪz.əm/)	fem·i·n·**ism** (/'fɛmɪ͵nɪz.əm/)	al·go·**rithm** (/'æl.gə͵rɪð.əm/)
hus·**tle** (/'hʌs.əl/)	mas·sa·**cre** (/'mæs.ə.kər/)	en·thu·si·**asm** (/ɛn'θu.zi͵æz.əm/)	her·o·**ism** (/'hɛroʊ͵ɪz.əm/)	log·a·**rithm** (/'la.gə͵rɪ.ð.əm/)
la·**dle** (/'leɪd.əl/)	me·di·o·**cre** (/͵mi.di'oʊ.kər/)	mi·cro·**cosm** (/'maɪ.krə͵kɑz.əm/)	lib·er·al·**ism** (/'lɪbərə͵lɪz.əm/)	**rhythm** (/'rɪð.əm/)
mus·**cle** (/'mʌs.əl/)	o·**gre** (/'oʊ.gər/)	par·ox·**ysm** (/pər'ak͵sɪz.əm/)	man·ner·**ism** (/'mæn.ə͵rɪz.əm/)	
net·**tle** (/'nɛt.əl/)	wise·a·**cre** (/'waɪz͵eɪ.kər/)	phan·**tasm** (/'fæn͵tæz.əm/)	pac·i·**fism** (/'pæs.ɪ͵fɪz.əm/)	
star·**tle** (/'stɑrt.əl/)		sar·**casm** (/'sɑr͵kæz.əm/)	skep·ti·**cism** (/'skɛp.tɪ͵sɪz.əm/)	
ti·**tle** (/'taɪt.əl/)			tour·**ism** (/'tʊə͵rɪz.əm/)	
ve·hi·**cle** (/'vi.ɪ.kəl/)				

Other syllabic consonants

Some linguistics resources also identify the letters **L, M, N,** and **R** as being syllabic consonants when they follow reduced vowels, generally at the end of the word. In speech these reduced vowels are all but eliminated, with the speaker naturally gliding from one consonant sound to the next with no (or very little) vowel sound in between.

While dictionary transcriptions will transcribe these reduced vowels as a schwa (/ə/), as we have done in this guide, some sources will simply eliminate the vowel from the IPA transcription. Academic or scholarly sources that follow the IPA more strictly might, in addition to omitting /ə/, indicate a syllabic consonant by adding a small vertical mark (ˌ) beneath the normal consonant character (except for **R**, which is either transcribed as /ɹ/ or merged with /ə/ to form the symbol /ɚ/.

For example:

Examples	Standard IPA (with /ə/)	Academic IPA (without /ə/)
but·ter	/ˈbʌt.ər/	/ˈbɑt.l̩/ /ˈbʌt.ɹ/ or /ˈbʌt.ɚ/
but·ton	/ˈbʌt.ən/	/ˈbʌt.n̩/
cot·ton	/ˈkɑt.ən/	/ˈkɑt.n̩/
hos·tel	/ˈhɑs.təl/	/ˈhɑs.tl̩/
les·son	/ˈlɛs.ən/	/ˈlɛs.n̩/
let·ter	/ˈlɛt.ər/	/ˈlɛt.ɹ/ or /ˈlɛt.ɚ/
pis·tol	/ˈpɪs.təl/	/ˈpɪst.l̩/

Rules for dividing syllables

Now that we've looked at the different types of syllables into which a word may be divided, we can began examining *how* we divide a word into those syllables.

In this section, we will be relying on the written form to establish these conventions and rules. However, it's important to reiterate what we touched upon earlier: The exact divisions of syllable breaks can be slightly different in speech compared to the rather formulaic patterns of written words. Pronunciation differs drastically depending on where you are from, so particular details like syllabic stress or where a syllable actually begins in a word are often going to be different as well. (Even the IPA transcriptions that we'll feature here might not be the same as how a word is spoken in a certain region.)

That said, using these rules for syllable division in conjunction with identifying the types of syllables we looked at above *can* make a word's pronunciation easier to understand. Conversely, when you know how to divide a written word into pronounceable syllables, you can use the same methods to help determine the spelling of a *spoken* word based on its pronunciation alone.

1. Identify the number of syllables

The first, and most basic, step is to count how many syllables a word actually contains.

Because a syllable <u>must</u> contain a nucleus and a nucleus is almost always made up of a vowel sound, the easiest way to identify the number of syllables in a word is to identify the number of unique vowel sounds it contains. In many cases, this is as simple as counting the vowel letters in a word. For example, the word *letter* has two vowel letters (two **E**'s), and two syllables, *let·ter*; *word* has just one vowel letter (**O**), and only one syllable.

However, as we saw from the different types of syllables, nuclei may contain more than one vowel letter forming a single vowel sound (vowel digraphs), silent consonants that work in conjunction with vowels (vowel-consonant combinations), a silent **E** that occurs after the syllable's coda, or even just a syllabic consonant. Therefore, when trying to determine the number of syllables in a word, we must count all the vowel **sounds** in the word, not the individual letters.

As an example, let's determine the number of syllables in the word **unpronounceable**. We can see that it has *seven* vowel letters. The first two, **U** and **O**, are straightforward and act as the nuclei of two separate syllables. However, the next two vowels, **O** and **U**, act as a **digraph** that forms the diphthong /aʊ/, a single sound that "glides" from one vowel sound to another. Although two vowels comprise the diphthong, they function as the nucleus of **one** syllable. The next two vowels, **E** and **A**, look like they *could* form the digraph **EA**, but they actually function separately: **E** is silent, indicating that **C** takes the "soft" pronunciation /s/, while **A** begins the suffix "-able," so we only count **A** as a nucleus. Finally, the final **E** of the word is part of the "Consonant + **LE**" pattern that we looked at earlier, indicating that **L** functions as a syllabic consonant, with a very subtle reduced vowel sound occurring between it and the consonant **B**. After analysing the different vowels in the word, we can determine that *unpronounceable* has <u>five</u> distinct vowel sounds, and thus <u>five</u> syllables.

2. Words with one consonant between vowels

When a word has a single consonant letter that appears between two vowels, we have to use the *sound* of the first vowel to help us determine where the syllable break occurs. In general, if the preceding vowel is **stressed** and makes a **short** sound, then it is the nucleus of a **closed syllable** and the syllable break comes <u>after</u> the consonant (the syllable's coda). If, on the other hand, the preceding vowel is **unstressed**, or it is stressed and makes a traditionally **long** sound, then the syllable is **open** and the syllable break comes immediately <u>before</u> the consonant. For example:

Stressed syllable, short vowel sound	Stressed syllable, long vowel sound	Unstressed syllable, weak vowel sound
bod·y (/ˈbɑdi/)	**a**·li·en (/ˈeɪ.li.ən/)	**a**·part (/eˈpɑrt/)
cab·in (/ˈkæb.ɪn/)	**i**·tem (/ˈaɪ.təm/)	**a**·lert (/eˈlɜrt/)
del·i·cate (/ˈdɛl.ɪ.kɪt/)	**o**·pen (/ˈoʊ.pən/)	**be**·moan (/bɪˈmoʊn/)
frig·id (/ˈfrɪdʒ.ɪd/)	**pa**·tience (/ˈpeɪ.ʃəns/)	**de**·plore (/dɪˈplɔr/)
pan·ic (/ˈpæn.ɪk/)	**re**·cent (/ˈri.sənt/)	**re**·ceive (/rɪˈsiv/)
tal·is·man (/ˈtæl.ɪs.mən/)	**tu**·nic (/ˈtu.nɪk/)	**se**·lect (/sɪˈlɛkt/)

3. Words with multiple consonants

When two consonants appear next to each other in the middle of a multi-syllable word, it is most common that they will be divided <u>between</u> the syllables of the word. For instance:

• an·cient
• ban·ter
• cir·cle
• en·dure
• im·per·ti·nent
• man·ners
• ob·ject
• ras·cal

However, not all groups of consonants behave the same way, and so won't always split up between syllables. There are different trends we should be aware of, depending on the types of consonants that appear mid-word.

Divide syllables between double consonants

When a multi-syllable word has two of the **same** consonant appearing next to each other mid-word, we almost always divide the syllables <u>between</u> them. We do this because a doubled consonant is typically preceded by a **short** vowel sound, so the first consonant of the pair will form the coda of the short vowel's syllable. For example:

• ap·par·ent
• bag·gage
• cor·rect
• din·ner
• ec·cen·tric
• fid·dle
• grub·by
• hol·ler
• in·ner

- jag·ged
- mam·mal
- plan·ner
- suf·fice
- top·pings
- war·ran·ty

Note that this is usually **not** done when a word that naturally ends in a doubled consonant has a **vowel suffix** attached to it, such as *add·ing* or *sell·er*. This is because we usually must divide suffixes <u>separately</u> as syllables when they do not affect the spelling of a word, a convention that we'll look at more closely further on.

Dividing syllables between consonant clusters

While dividing the syllables around doubled consonants is fairly straightforward, it is a bit trickier to know when to divide **consonant clusters** between syllables. **Consonant clusters** (also called **consonant blends, consonant sequences**, or **consonant compounds**) are groups of two or three individual consonants that are pronounced in quick succession—they each make a distinct sound but "blend" together when spoken aloud. These are typically formed when **L, R,** or **S** appear with other consonant sounds. (It's important to note that consonant clusters are <u>not</u> the same as consonant digraphs, which form a <u>single</u> consonant sound. We <u>cannot</u> divide **consonant digraphs** across two syllables.)

Just as when a single consonant appears between two vowels, we first must look at the *type* of vowel sound that comes before a consonant cluster to determine where the syllable break will occur. If the cluster is preceded by a **short** vowel sound, the first consonant will usually form the **coda** of the previous syllable; if the vowel sound is traditionally **long** (i.e., it "says the name" of the vowel), then <u>both</u> consonants will form the **onset** of the <u>subsequent</u> syllable.

For example, compare the words *acrobat* and *apron*. Both start with **A**, are followed by consonant clusters (**CR** and **PR**), and have stress on the first syllable. However, the **A** in *acrobat* is pronounced /æ/—a short vowel—so we divide the syllable <u>between</u> the consonant cluster: *ac·ro·bat* (/ˈæk.rəˌbæt/). Conversely, the **A** in *apron* makes the long vowel sound /eɪ/, so the entire consonant cluster comes <u>after</u> the syllable break: *a·pron* (/ˈeɪ.prən/).

In addition, if the preceding syllable is unstressed and has a weak vowel sound (/ə/ or /ɪ/) as its nucleus, we *usually* (though not always) mark the syllable break <u>before</u> the consonant cluster.

Here are some more examples to help highlight the differences:

Short vowel nucleus (Divided between consonant cluster)	Long vowel nucleus (Divided before consonant cluster)	Weak vowel nucleus (Divided before consonant cluster)
ap·ri·cot* (/ˈæp.rɪˌkɑt/) fas·ter (/ˈfæs.tər/) jas·mine (/ˈdʒæz.mɪn/) in·teg·ri·ty (/ɪnˈtɛg.rɪ.ti/) mus·cu·lar (/ˈmʌs.kjʊ.lər/) ob·long (/ˈɑbˌlɔŋ/) prog·ress (noun: /ˈprɑgˌrɛs/) rep·li·cate (adj., noun: /ˈrɛp.lɪ.kɪt/ verb: /ˈrɛp.lɪˌkeɪt/)	a·ble (/ˈeɪ.bəl/) a·pri·cot* (/ˈeɪ.prɪˌkɑt/ du·pli·cate (adj., noun: /ˈdu.plɪ.kɪt/ verb: /ˈdu.plɪˌkeɪt/) fra·grant (/ˈfreɪ.grənt/) la·dle (/ˈleɪ.dəl/) mi·crobe (/ˈmaɪ.kroʊb/) o·gre (/ˈoʊ.gər/) sa·cred (/ˈseɪ.krɪd/) ti·gress (/ˈtaɪ.grɪs/) ti·tle (/ˈtaɪ.təl/)	a·gree (/əˈgri/) a·slant (/əˈslænt/) be·tween (/bɪˈtwin/) de·flate (/dɪˈfleɪt/) di·gress (/dɪˈgrɛs/ or /daɪˈgrɛs/) ma·tric·u·late (/məˈtrɪk.jəˌleɪt/) pro·gress (verb: /prəˈgrɛs/) re·spect (/rɪˈspɛkt/)

(**Apricot* can be pronounced either of these two ways, depending on the dialect, and the division of syllables changes accordingly.)

Note that when a single consonant follows a vowel and is adjacent to a cluster or digraph that precedes another vowel sound, the syllable break will occur after the <u>single</u> consonant. For example:

• an·chor
• en·thrall
• es·chew
• in·struct
• mar·shal
• nos·tril
• ob·struct
• pan·try
• pas·try

4. Dividing before syllabic consonants

When a word ends with the syllabic consonants "-le" or "-re", we mark the syllable division before the consonant that precedes them. For example:

• an·kle (/ˈæŋ.kəl/)
• bend·a·ble (/ˈbɛnd.ə.bəl/)
• fid·dle (/ˈfɪd.əl/)
• hus·tle* (/ˈhʌs.əl/)
• princ·i·ple (/ˈprɪn.sə.pəl/)
• star·tle (/ˈstɑr.təl/)
• this·tle* (/ˈθɪs.əl/)

• a·cre (/ˈeɪ.kər/)
• mas·sa·cre (/ˈmæs.ə.kər/)
• me·di·o·cre (/ˌmi.diˈoʊ.kər/)
• o·gre (/ˈoʊ.gər/)

(*Even though **ST** forms the /s/ sound, with **T** becoming silent, we still put the syllable break between the letters so that the first syllable remains closed and follows the pattern for a short vowel pronunciation.)

Exception 1: CK + LE

When "-le" comes after the consonant digraph **CK**, the syllable break occurs immediately before the letter **L** rather than the consonant adjacent to "-le." For instance:

• buck·le (/ˈbʌk.əl/)
• crack·le (/ˈkræk.əl/)
• knuck·le (/ˈnʌk.əl/)
• pick·le (/ˈpɪk.əl/)
• trick·le (/ˈtrɪk.əl/)

Exception 2: Syllabic M

Note that we <u>don't</u> indicate a syllable break before **M** when it functions as a syllabic consonant, even though it is *pronounced* as a separate syllable with a weak vowel sound for its nucleus:

• ac·tiv·ism (/ˈæk.tə.ˌvɪz.əm/)
• her·o·ism (/ˈhɛr.oʊ.ˌɪz.əm/)
• rhythm (/ˈrɪð.əm/)
• schism (/ˈskɪz.əm/)

5. Separate prefixes, suffixes, and compound words

When a word forms a compound by attaching to a prefix, suffix, and/or another word, there will *usually* be a syllable break where the different elements join together. Separating affixes and compound elements from a word can help us see the function of all the letters, so we can better understand how the word should be pronounced.

For instance, let's look again at the word *unpronounceable*. Immediately we can see that it contains the prefix "un-" and the suffix "-able," leaving the base word *pronounce*. This base word also contains a prefix, "**pro-**," which attaches to the root *nounce* (derived from Latin *nuntiare*, meaning "to announce"). Having counted the number of syllables in **Step 1**, we know there are five total, and, by using **Step 3**, we know that "-able" will have a syllable break dividing "a-" and "-ble."

The rest of the word, then, will be divided where the affixes are conjoined:
un·pro·nounce·a·ble (/ʌn.prəˈnaʊns.əb.əl/)

Let's look at some other examples:

Prefix + Base Word	Base Word + Suffix	Base Word + Base Word
an·ti·air·craft (/ˌæn.tiˈɛrˌkræft/)	be·**ing** (/ˈbi.ɪŋ/)	air·craft (/ˈɛrˌkræft/)
be·witch (/bɪˈwɪtʃ/)	cook·**er** (/ˈkʊk.ər/)	book·worm (/ˈbʊkˌwɜrm/)
co·ed·it (/koʊˈɛd.ɪt) /)	dan·ger·**ous** (/ˈdeɪn.dʒər.əs/) /)	class·room (/ˈklæsˌrum/)
de·brief (/diˈbrif/)	friend·**ly** (/ˈfrɛnd.li/)	draw·back (/ˈdrɔˌbæk/)
mis·com·mu·ni·cate (/mɪs.kəmˈjunɪˌkeɪt/)	i·de·al·**ize** (/aɪˈdi.əˌlaɪz/)	fire·fly (/ˈfaɪərˌflaɪ/)
pre·school (/ˈpriˌskul/)	man·age·**ment** (/ˈmæn.ɪdʒ.mənt/)	note·book (/ˈnoʊtˌbʊk/)
re·a·lign (/ˌri.əˈlaɪn/)	pa·tri·ot·**ic** (/ˌpeɪ.triˈɑt.ɪk/)	pas·ser·by (/ˈpæs.ərˈbaɪ/)
un·lock (/ʌnˈlɑk/)	strange·**ness** (/ˈstreɪndʒ.nɪs/)	turn·ta·ble (/ˈtɜrnˌteɪ.bəl/)

Suffixes and syllable divisions

It's important to note that we can't depend on this convention with all suffixes, as they can sometimes result in changes to a word's spelling, pronunciation, or both. For example, when the suffix "-ion" is added to the word *hesitate* (/ˈhɛ.zɪˌteɪt/), it changes the final /t/ sound to /ʃ/ (/ˌhɛzɪˈteɪʃən). Because the combination **TION** specifically creates this sound, the letters can't be divided across syllables.

Another common spelling convention occurs when a vowel suffix (especially "-ing") is added to a word that ends in a vowel + a single consonant. To avoid forming a word that looks like it had a silent E that was replaced by the suffix, we double the final consonant (for example, *hopping* comes from the word *hop*, compared to *hoping*, from the word *hope*). Because we now have a double consonant next to the syllable break with a short vowel preceding it, we have to divide the consonants between the two syllables: *hop·ping*. Because the spelling change is the direct result of adding the suffix, we can't simply mark the syllable break where the suffix begins—we must look at the new spelling in relation to our existing conventions. (As we saw earlier, if a word *naturally* ends in a double consonant, then we <u>do</u> mark the syllable division before the suffix because it hasn't changed the base word's spelling, as in *add·ing*, *class·es*, *fill·er*, *putt·ed*, etc.)

To learn more about the way words change when a suffix is added, go to the section Spelling Conventions with Suffixes.

Words with multiple pronunciations

There are many words in English that can have different pronunciations depending on how they are used in a sentence, and this can in turn affect where their syllable breaks occur. For example, the word *record* can be pronounced in two ways: with the stress on *rec-* or on *-cord*. When the word is pronounced *record* (/ˈrɛk.ərd/), the first syllable is stressed and becomes **closed**, so the syllable break occurs <u>after</u> the consonant **C**. In this form, the word is a **noun**, meaning "a unit of information preserved in some way for future access." However, when it is pronounced *record* (/rɪˈkɔrd/), the first syllable becomes unstressed and open, which means that the syllable break occurs <u>before</u> the consonant. With this pronunciation, the word is used as a **verb**, meaning "to preserve for future access."

Pronunciation Conventions

Here are some other examples of words that have multiple pronunciations with different syllable divisions:

Word	Noun	Verb
desert	**des**·ert (/ˈdɛz.ərt/) Meaning: "a place where few things can grow or live, especially due to an absence of water"	de·**sert** (/dɪˈzɜrt/) Meaning: "to abandon, forsake, or run away from"
present	**pres**·ent (/ˈprɛz.ənt/) Meaning: "the time occurring at this instant" or "a gift"	pre·**sent** (/prɪˈzɛnt/) Meaning: "to give, introduce, offer, or furnish"
project	**proj**·ect (/ˈprɑdʒ.ɛkt/) Meaning: "a particular plan, task, assignment, or undertaking"	pro·**ject** (/prəˈdʒɛkt/) Meaning: "to estimate, plan, or calculate" or "to throw or thrust forward"
rebel	**reb**·el (/ˈrɛb.əl/) Meaning: "a person who revolts against a government or other authority"	re·**bel** (/rɪˈbɛl/) Meaning: "to revolt or act in defiance of authority"
refuse	**ref**·use (/ˈrɛf.juz/) Meaning: "something discarded or thrown away as trash"	re·**fuse** (/rɪˈfjuz/) Meaning: "to decline or express unwillingness to do something"

Quiz

(answers start on page 463)

1. What **must** a syllable contain?

a) An onset
b) A nucleus
c) A coda
d) A & B
e) B & C
f) All of the above

2. Which of the following must a **closed syllable** contain?

a) An onset
b) A nucleus
c) A coda
d) A & B
e) B & C
f) All of the above

3. True or False: Syllable divisions in the written form of a word always match the way it is spoken aloud.

a) True
b) False

4. When are double consonants **not** divided between syllables?

a) When a final consonant is doubled before a vowel suffix
b) When a double consonant appears between two vowel sounds
c) When a word ending in a double consonant has a vowel suffix attached
d) Always
e) Never

5. Which of the following is the correct syllable division for the word *impractical*?

a) im·prac·ti·cal
b) imp·ract·i·cal
c) impr·ac·ti·cal
d) im·prac·tic·al

6. Which of the following words contains a **vowel-combination syllable**?

a) being
b) cereal
c) bacteria
d) engineer

7. How many syllables are in the word *reevaluated*?

a) 5
b) 7
c) 6
d) 4

Word Stress

Definition

Word stress, also called **lexical stress**, is the emphasis a speaker places on a specific syllable in a multi-syllable word.

Word stress is especially hard for non-native speakers to master. While there are a few conventions and general rules governing which syllable is stressed in a word based on its spelling alone, these conventions are often unreliable.

Before we look at these conventions and their exceptions, let's discuss how we can indicate syllables and word stress in writing.

Indicating syllables in writing

In this section, we'll be using different symbols to indicate syllable division in words. For the normal spelling of words, we'll be using a symbol known as an interpunct (·) (also called a **midpoint, middle dot**, or **centered dot**). For example, the word *application* would appear as *app·li·ca·tion*.

When the pronunciation of a word is transcribed using the **International Phonetic Alphabet** (IPA), there are three different symbols we use. For syllables that receive the **primary stress**, we use a short vertical line above and just before the syllable being emphasized ('); for secondary stress, we use the same vertical line, but it appears <u>below</u> and before the syllable (ˌ); and, while this guide usually does not mark unstressed syllables in IPA transcriptions, we will indicate them in this section with periods. Using *application* as an example again, its pronunciation would be transcribed in IPA as /ˌæp.lɪˈkeɪ.ʃən/.

Written syllables vs. spoken syllables

The syllable breakdowns in the written "dictionary" form of words are often divided slightly differently compared to the phonetic "spoken" form used in IPA transcriptions.

Specifically, the written form divides syllables according to established syllable "types," based on spelling patterns such as double consonants, short vowels contained within two consonants, and vowel digraphs. The spoken form, on the other hand, divides syllables according to the phonetic pronunciation of the word, and the difference between these two can sometime lead to syllable breakdowns that don't look like they correspond to one another. For example, the word *learning* is divided in the dictionary as *learn·ing*, but it is divided as /ˈlɜr.nɪŋ/ in IPA transcription—the placement of the first **N** is not the same.

Because this part of the guide is more concerned with the phonetic placement of word stress rather than the technical breakdown of syllables (as found in dictionary entries), the examples we use will try to match the written form as closely as possible to the spoken form. Looking at the *learning* example again, we would divide the syllables as *lear·ning* to match its IPA transcription. Just be aware that these will often be slightly different to what one may find in a dictionary. For more technical information on how syllables are formed and divided within words, check out the chapter on Syllables.

Primary vs. Secondary Stress

Every word has one syllable that receives a **primary stress**—that is, it is vocally emphasized more than any other syllable. Some longer words also have a **secondary stress**, which is more emphatic than the unstressed syllables but not as strong as the primary stress. (Some words can even have more than one secondary stress.)

Let's look at some examples, with the primary stress in **bold** and the secondary stress in *italics*:
- *ab*·sen·**tee** (/ˌæb.sənˈti/)
- **cem**·e·*ter*·y (/ˈsɛm.ɪˌtɛr.i/)
- *dis*·be·**lief** (/ˌdɪs.bɪˈlif/)
- *in*·for·**ma**·tion (/ˌɪn.fərˈmeɪ.ʃən/)
- **labo**·ra·*tor*·y (/ˈlæb.rəˌtɔr.i/; the initial **O** is usually silent)
- **mil**·i·*tar*·y (/ˈmɪl.ɪˌtɛr.i/)
- **or**·din·*ar*·y (/ˈɔr.dənˌɛr.i/)
- **sec**·re·*tar*·y (/ˈsɛk.rɪˌtɛr.i/)
- **tem**·po·*rar*·y (/ˈtɛm.pəˌrɛr.i/)
- *un*·a·**pol**·o·*get*·ic (/ˌʌn.əˌpal.əˈdʒɛt.ɪk/)

Unfortunately, secondary stress is extremely unpredictable. **Primary stress**, on the other hand, can often be predicted according to a few different conventions.

Determining word stress

There are only two consistent, reliable rules about word stress in English:
   1. Only the vowel sound within a syllable is stressed; stress is not applied to consonant sounds.

   2. Any given word, even one with many syllables, will only have one syllable that receives the primary stress in speech. Some longer words also receive a **secondary stress**, which we'll look at more closely further on. (By definition, single-syllable words only ever have a single stress, though certain **function words** can be unstressed altogether, which we'll discuss later.)

However, determining *which* syllable is emphasized in a given word is not always straightforward, as a word's spelling is usually not enough on its own to let us know the appropriate stress. There are a few general conventions that can help make this easier to determine, but there are many exceptions and anomalies for each.

Determining stress based on word type

One common pronunciation convention many guides provide is that nouns and adjectives with two or more syllables will have stress placed on the first syllable, while verbs and prepositions tend to have their stress on the second syllable. While there are many examples that support this convention, it is also very problematic because there are many exceptions that contradict it.

Let's look at some examples that support or contradict this convention.

Nouns and adjectives will have stress on the first syllable

Nouns	Adjectives
app·le (/ˈæp.əl/)	clev·er (/ˈklɛv.ər/)
bott·le (/ˈbɑt.əl/)	comm·on (/ˈkɑm.ən/)
busi·ness (/ˈbɪz.nɪs/; the I is silent)	diff·i·cult (/ˈdɪf.ɪˌkʌlt/)
cherr·y (/ˈʧɛr.i/)	fa·vor·ite (/ˈfeɪ.vər.ɪt/)
cli·mate (/ˈklaɪ.mɪt/)	fem·i·nine (/ˈfɛm.ə.nɪn/)
crit·ic (/ˈkrɪt.ɪk/)	funn·y (/ˈfʌn.i/)
dia·mond (/ˈdaɪ.mənd/)	happ·y (/ˈhæp.i/)
el·e·phant (/ˈɛl.ə.fənt/)	hon·est (/ˈɑn.ɪst/)
en·ve·lope (/ˈɛnvəˌloʊp/)	litt·le (/ˈlɪt.əl/)
fam·i·ly (/ˈfæm.ə.li/)	mas·cu·line (/ˈmæs.kju.lɪn/)
In·ter·net (/ˈɪn.tərˌnɛt/)	narr·ow (/ˈnær.oʊ/)
knowl·edge (/ˈnɑl.ɪʤ/)	or·ange (/ˈɔr.ɪnʤ/)
mu·sic (/ˈmju.zɪk/)	pleas·ant (/ˈplɛz.ənt/)
pa·per (/ˈpeɪ.pər/)	pre·tty (/ˈprɪ.ti/)
sam·ple (/ˈsæm.pəl/)	pur·ple (/ˈpɜr.pəl/)
satch·el (/ˈsæʧ.əl/)	qui·et (/ˈkwaɪ.ət/)
ta·ble (/ˈteɪ.bəl/)	sim·ple (/ˈsɪm.pəl/)
tel·e·phone (/ˈtɛl.əˌfoʊn/)	sub·tle (/ˈsʌt.əl/)
ton·ic (/ˈtɑn.ɪk/)	trick·y (/ˈtrɪk.i/)
win·dow (/ˈwɪn.doʊ/)	ug·ly (/ˈʌg.li/)

As we said already, though, there are many exceptions to this convention for both nouns and adjectives. Let's look at some examples:

Nouns	Adjectives
ba·na·na (/bə.ˈnæ.na/)	a·live (/ə.ˈlaɪv/)
ca·nal (/kə.ˈnæl/)	a·noth·er (/ə.ˈnʌð.ər/)

com·**put**·er (/kəm.ˈpju.tər/)	com·**plete** (/kəm.ˈplit/)
de·**fence** (/dɪ.ˈfɛns/)	dis·**tinct** (/dɪsˈtinkt/)
des·**sert** (/dɪ.ˈzɜrt/)	e·**nough** (/ɪ.ˈnʌf/)
di·**sease** (/dɪ.ˈziz/)	ex·**pen**·sive (/ɪk.ˈspɛn.sɪv/)
ex·**tent** (/ɪk.ˈstɛnt/)	ex·**tinct** (/ɪk.ˈtiŋkt/)
ho·**tel** (/hoʊ.ˈtɛl/)	i·**ni**·tial (/ɪ.ˈnɪ.ʃəl/)
ma·**chine** (/mə.ˈʃin/)	in·**tense** (/ɪn.ˈtɛns/)
pi·**a**·no (/pi.ˈæ.noʊ/)	po·**lite** (/pə.ˈlaɪt/)
po·**ta**·to (/pə.ˈteɪˌtoʊ/)	re·**pet**·i·tive (/rɪ.ˈpɛt.ɪ.tɪv/)
re·**ceipt** (/rɪ.ˈsit/)	un·**think**·a·ble (/ʌnˈθɪŋk.ə.bəl/)
re·**venge** (/rɪ.ˈvɛndʒ/)	
suc·**cess** (/sɪk.ˈsɛs/)	

Verbs and prepositions will have stress on the second syllable

Verbs	Prepositions
a·**pply** (/əˈplaɪ/)	a·**bout** (/əˈbaʊt/)
be·**come** (/bɪˈkʌm/)	a·**cross** (/əˈkrɔs/)
com·**pare** (/kəmˈpɛr/)	a·**long** (/əˈlɔŋ/)
di·**scuss** (/dɪˈskʌs/)	a·**mong** (/əˈmʌŋ/)
ex·**plain** (/ɪkˈspleɪn/)	a·**round** (/əˈraʊnd/)
ful·**fil** (/fʊlˈfɪl/)	be·**hind** (/bɪˈhaɪnd/)
in·**crease** (/ɪnˈkris/)	be·**low** (/bɪˈloʊ/)
ha·**rass** (/həˈræs/)	be·**side** (/bɪˈsaɪd/)
la·**ment** (/ləˈmɛnt/)	be·**tween** (/bɪˈtwin/)
ne·**glect** (/nɪˈglɛkt/)	de·**spite** (/dɪˈspaɪt/)
pre·**vent** (/prɪˈvɛnt/)	ex·**cept** (/ɪkˈsɛpt/)

qua·**dru**·ple (/kwɑˈdru.pəl/)	in·**side** (/ˌɪnˈsaɪd/)
re·**ply** (/rɪˈplaɪ/)	out·**side** (/ˌaʊtˈsaɪd/)
suc·**ceed** (/səkˈsid/)	un·**til** (/ʌnˈtɪl/)
tra·**verse** (/trəˈvɜrs/)	u·**pon** (/əˈpɑn/)
un·**furl** (/ʌnˈfɜrl/)	with·**in** (/wɪðˈɪn/)
with·**hold** (/wɪθˈhoʊld/)	with·**out** (/wɪðˈaʊt/)

As with nouns and adjectives, there are a huge number of exceptions that have primary stress placed on the first or third syllable. In fact, almost every verb beginning with **G, H, J, K, L**, and **M** has its primary stress placed on the <u>first</u> syllable, rather than the second.

Let's look at a few examples:

Verbs	Prepositions
ar·gue (/ˈɑr.gju/)	
beck·on (/ˈbɛk.ən/)	
can·cel (/ˈkæn.səl/)	
dom·i·nate (/ˈdɑm.əˌneɪt/)	
en·ter·**tain** (/ˌɛn.tərˈteɪn/)	
fas·ten (/ˈfæs.ən/)	**af**·ter (/ˈæf.tər/)
gam·ble (/ˈgæm.bəl/)	**dur**·ing (/ˈdʊr.ɪŋ/)
hin·der (/ˈhɪn.dər/)	**in**·to (/ˈɪn.tu/)
i·so·late (/ˈaɪ.səˌleɪt/)	**on**·to (/ˈɑn.tu/)
jin·gle (/ˈdʒɪŋ.gəl/)	**un**·der (/ˈʌn.dər/)
kin·dle (/ˈkɪn.dəl/)	
leng·then (/ˈlɛŋk.θən/)	
man·age (/ˈmæn.ɪdʒ/)	
nour·ish (/ˈnɜr.ɪʃ/)	
or·ga·nize (/ˈɔr.gəˌnaɪz/)	
per·ish (/ˈpɛr.ɪʃ/)	

qua·ver (/ˈkweɪ.vər/) **ram**·ble (/ˈræm.bəl/) **sa**·vor (/ˈseɪ.vər/) **threat**·en (/ˈθrɛt.ən/) un·der·**stand** (/ˌʌn.dərˈstænd/) **van**·ish (/ˈvæn.ɪʃ/) **wan**·der (/ˈwɑn.dər/) **yo**·del (/ˈjoʊd.əl/)	

Initial-stress-derived nouns

As we saw previously, we commonly place stress on the first syllable of a noun. When a word can operate as either a noun **or** a verb, we often differentiate the meanings by shifting the stress from the second syllable to the first (or **initial**) syllable—in other words, these nouns are **derived** from verbs according to their **initial stress**.

Let's look at a few examples of such words that change in pronunciation when functioning as nouns or verbs:

Word	Noun	Verb
contest	**con**·test (/ˈkɑn.tɛst/) Meaning: "a game, competition, or struggle for victory, superiority, a prize, etc."	con·**test** (/kənˈtɛst/) Meaning: "to dispute, contend with, call into question, or fight against"
desert	**des**·ert (/ˈdɛz.ərt/) Meaning: "a place where few things can grow or live, especially due to an absence of water"	de·**sert** (/dɪˈzɜrt/) Meaning: "to abandon, forsake, or run away from"
increase	**in**·crease (/ˈɪn.kris/) Meaning: "the act or process of growing larger or becoming greater"	in·**crease** (/ɪnˈkris/) Meaning: "to grow larger or become greater (in size, amount, strength, etc.)"
object	**ob**·ject (/ˈɑb.dʒɛkt/) Meaning: "any material thing that is visible or tangible"	ob·**ject** (/əbˈdʒɛkt/) Meaning: "to present an argument in opposition (to something)"
permit	**per**·mit (/ˈpɜr.mɪt/) Meaning: "an authoritative or official certificate of permission; license"	per·**mit** (/pərˈmɪt/) Meaning: "to allow to do something"
present	**pres**·ent (/ˈprɛz.ənt/) Meaning: "the time occurring at this instant" or "a gift"	pre·**sent** (/prɪˈzɛnt/) Meaning: "to give, introduce, offer, or furnish"

project	**proj**·ect (/ˈprɑdʒ.ɛkt/) Meaning: "a particular plan, task, assignment, or undertaking"	pro·**ject** (/prəˈdʒɛkt/) Meaning: "to estimate, plan, or calculate" or "to throw or thrust forward"
rebel	**reb**·el (/ˈrɛb.əl/) Meaning: "a person who revolts against a government or other authority"	re·**bel** (/rɪˈbɛl/) Meaning: "to revolt or act in defiance of authority"
record	**rec**·ord (/ˈrɛk.ərd/) Meaning: "information or knowledge preserved in writing or the like" or "something on which sound or images have been recorded for subsequent reproduction"	re·**cord** (/rəˈkɔrd/) Meaning: "to set down in writing or the like"
refuse	**ref**·use (/ˈrɛf.juz/) Meaning: "something discarded or thrown away as trash"	re·**fuse** (/rɪˈfjuz/) Meaning: "to decline or express unwillingness to do something"
subject	**sub**·ject (/ˈsʌb.dʒɛkt/) Meaning: "that which is the focus of a thought, discussion, lesson, investigation, etc."	sub·**ject** (/səbˈdʒɛkt/) Meaning: "to bring under control, domination, authority"

Although this pattern is very common in English, it is by no means a rule; there are just as many words that function as both nouns and verbs but that have <u>no</u> difference in pronunciation. For instance:

Word	Noun	Verb
amount	a·**mount** (/əˈmaʊnt/)	a·**mount** (/əˈmaʊnt/)
answer	**an**·swer (/ˈæn.sər/)	**an**·swer (/ˈæn.sər/)
attack	a·**ttack** (/əˈtæk/)	a·**ttack** (/əˈtæk/)
challenge	**chall**·enge (/ˈtʃæl.ɪndʒ/)	**chall**·enge (/ˈtʃæl.ɪndʒ/)
contact	**con**·tact (/ˈkɑn.tækt/)	**con**·tact (/ˈkɑn.tækt/)
control	con·**trol** (/kənˈtroʊl/)	con·**trol** (/kənˈtroʊl/)
forecast	**fore**·cast (/ˈfɔrˌkæst/)	**fore**·cast (/ˈfɔrˌkæst/)
monitor	**mon**·i·tor (/ˈmɑn.ɪ.tər/)	**mon**·i·tor (/ˈmɑn.ɪ.tər/)
pepper	**pep**·per (/ˈpɛp.ər/)	**pep**·per (/ˈpɛp.ər/)

report	re·**port** (/rɪˈpɔrt/)	re·**port** (/rɪˈpɔrt/)
respect	re·**spect** (/rɪˈspɛkt/)	re·**spect** (/rɪˈspɛkt/)
support	su·**pport** (/səˈpɔrt/)	su·**pport** (/səˈpɔrt/)
witness	**wit**·ness (/ˈwɪt.nɪs/)	**wit**·ness (/ˈwɪt.nɪs/)
worry	**worr**·y (/ˈwɜr.i/)	**worr**·y (/ˈwɜr.i/)

Word stress in compound words

Compound words are single words formed from two separate words, often from different parts of speech. These typically include compound nouns, compound adjectives, and compound verbs.

Compound nouns and compound verbs typically create pronunciation patterns that help us determine which of their syllables will have the primary stress. Compound adjectives, on the other hand, are most often pronounced as two separate words, with each receiving its own primary stress, so we won't be looking at them here.

We'll also briefly look at reflexive pronouns. Although these aren't technically compounds, they have a similarly predictable stress pattern.

Compound nouns

A compound noun is a noun consisting of two or more words working together as a single unit to name a person, place, or thing. Compound nouns are usually made up of two nouns or an adjective and a noun, but other combinations are also possible, as well.

In single-word compound nouns, whether they are conjoined by a hyphen or are simply one word, stress is almost always placed on the first syllable. For example:
- **back**·pack (/ˈbækˌpæk/)
- **bath**·room (/ˈbæθˌrum/)
- **draw**·back (/ˈdrɔˌbæk/)
- **check**-in (/ˈtʃɛkˌɪn/)
- **foot**·ball (/ˈfʊtˌbɔl/)
- **hand**·bag (/ˈhændˌbæg/)
- **green**·house (/ˈgrinˌhaʊs/)
- **hair**·cut (/ˈhɛrˌkʌt/)
- **log**·in (/ˈsʌn.ɪnˌlɔ/)
- **mo**·tor·cy·cle (/ˈmoʊ.tərˌsaɪ kəl/)
- **on**·look·er (/ˈɑnˌlʊkər/)
- **pas**·ser·by (/ˈpæs.ərˌbaɪ/)
- **son**-in-law (/ˈsʌn.ɪnˌlɔ/)
- **ta**·ble·cloth (/ˈteɪ.bəlˌklɔθ/)
- **wall**·pa·per (/ˈwɔlˌpeɪ.pər/)
- **web**·site (/ˈwɛbˌsaɪt/)

One notable exception to this convention is the word *af·ter·noon*, which has its primary stress on the third syllable: /ˌæf.tərˈnun/.

Single-word compound verbs

The term "compound verb" can refer to a few different things: phrasal verbs, which consist of a verb paired with a specific preposition or particle to create a new, unique meaning; prepositional verbs, in which a preposition connects a noun to a verb; combinations with auxiliary verbs, which form tense and aspect; and single-word compounds, in which a verb is combined with a noun, preposition, or another verb to create a new word. For the first three types of compound verbs, each word is stressed individually, but single-word compounds have a unique pronunciation pattern that we can predict.

For most single-word compound verbs, stress will be on the first syllable. However, if the first element of the compound is a two-syllable preposition, stress will be placed on the second element. For example:

- **air**·con·dit·ion (/ˈeɪr.kən͵dɪʃ.ən/)
- **ba**·by·sit (/ˈbeɪ.bi͵sɪt/)
- **cop**·y·ed·it (/ˈkɑ.pi͵ɛd.ɪt/)
- **day**·dream (/ˈdeɪ͵drim/)
- **down**·load (/ˈdaʊn͵loʊd/)
- **ice**-skate (/ˈaɪs͵skeɪt/)
- **jay**·walk (/ˈdʒeɪ͵wɔk/)
- **kick**-start (/ˈkɪk͵stɑrt/)
- o·ver·**heat** (/͵oʊ.vərˈhit/)
- **proof**·read (/ˈpruf͵rid/)
- **stir**-fry (/ˈstɜr͵fraɪ/)
- **test**-drive (/ˈtɛst͵draɪv/)
- un·der·**cook** (/͵ʌndərˈkʊk/)
- **wa**·ter·proof (/ˈwɔ.tər͵pruf/)

Reflexive Pronouns

Reflexive pronouns are not technically compounds ("-self" and "-selves" are suffixes that attach to a base pronoun), but they look and behave similarly. In these words, *-self/-selves* receives the primary stress.

- my·**self** (/maɪˈsɛlf/)
- her·**self** (/hərˈsɛlf/)
- him·**self** (/hɪmˈsɛlf/)
- it·**self** (/ɪtˈsɛlf/)
- one·**self** (/wʌnˈsɛlf/)
- your·**self** (/jərˈsɛlf/)
- your·**selves** (/jərˈsɛlvz/)
- them·**selves** (/ðəmˈsɛlvz/)

Word stress dictated by suffixes

While the stress in many words is very difficult to predict, certain suffixes and other word endings will reliably dictate where stress should be applied within the word. This can be especially useful for determining the pronunciation of longer words. (There are still some exceptions, but much fewer than for the other conventions we've seen.)

For the suffixes we'll look at, primary stress is either placed on the suffix itself, one syllable before the suffix, or two syllables before the suffix. Finally, we'll look at some suffixes that don't affect a word's pronunciation at all.

Stress is placed on the suffix itself

"-ee," "-eer," and "-ese"

These three suffixes all sound similar, but they have different functions: "-ee" indicates someone who benefits from or is the recipient of the action of a verb; "-eer" indicates someone who is concerned with or engaged in a certain action; and "-ese" is attached to place names to describe languages, characteristics of certain nationalities, or (when attached to non-place names) traits or styles of particular fields or professions.

For example:

-ee	-eer	-ese
ab·sen·**tee** (/ˌæbsən**ˈti**/)		Chi·**nese** (/tʃaɪ**ˈniz**/)
a·tten·**dee** (/əˌtɛn**ˈdi**/)	auc·tio·**neer** (/ˌɔk.ʃə**ˈnɪər**/)	Jap·a·**nese** (/ˌdʒæp.ə**ˈniz**/)
de·tai·**nee** (/dɪˌteɪ**ˈni**/)	com·man·**deer** (/ˌkɑ.mən**ˈdɪər**/)	jour·na·**lese** (/ˌdʒɜr.nə**ˈliz**/)
in·ter·view·**ee** (/ɪnˌtər.vyu**ˈi**/)	dom·i·**neer** (/ˌdɑm.ɪ**ˈnɪər**/)	Leb·a·**nese** (/ˌlɛb.ə**ˈniz**/)
li·cen·**see** (/ˌlaɪ.sən**ˈsi**/)	en·gi·**neer** (/ˌɛn.dʒɪ**ˈnɪər**/)	le·ga·**lese** (/ˌli.gə**ˈliz**/)
mort·ga·**gee** (/ˌmɔr.gə**ˈdʒi**/)	moun·tai·**neer** (/ˌmaʊn.tɪ**ˈnɪər**/)	Mal·**tese** (/ˌmɔl**ˈtiz**/)
pa·ro·**lee** (/pəˌroʊ**ˈli**/)	prof·i·**teer** (/ˌprɑf.ɪ**ˈtɪər**/)	Por·tu·**guese** (/ˌpɔr.tʃə**ˈgiz**/)
ref·e·**ree** (/ˌrɛf.ə**ˈri**/)	pupp·e·**teer** (/ˌpʌp.ɪ**ˈtɪər**/)	Si·a·**mese** (/ˌsaɪ.ə**ˈmiz**/)
ref·u·**gee** (/ˌrɛf.jʊ**ˈdʒi**/)	rack·e·**teer** (/ˌræk.ɪ**ˈtɪər**/)	Tai·wa·**nese** (/ˌtaɪ.wɑ**ˈniz**/)
trai·**nee** (/treɪ**ˈni**/)	vol·un·**teer** (/ˌvɑl.ɪn**ˈtɪər**/)	Vi·et·na·**mese** (/viˌɛt.nɑ**ˈmiz**/)
warr·an·**tee** (/ˌwɔr.ən**ˈti**/)		

(The word *employee* usually follows this same pattern, but it is one of a few words that has its primary stress on different syllables depending on dialect and personal preference.)

Some other words that feature the "-ee" ending also follow the same pattern, even though they are not formed from another base word. For instance:
- chim·pan·**zee** (/ˌtʃɪm.pæn**ˈzi**/)
- guar·an·**tee** (/ˌgær.ən**ˈti**/)
- jam·bo·**ree** (/ˌdʒæm.bə**ˈri**/)
- ru·**pee** (/ru.**ˈpi**/)

Be careful, though, because other words don't follow the pattern. For example:
- **ap**·o·gee (/**ˈæp**.əˌdʒi/)
- **co**·ffee (/**ˈkɔ**.fi/)
- co·**mmit**·tee (/kə**ˈmɪt**.i/)
- **kedg**·e·ree (/**ˈkɛdʒ**.əˌri/)
- **te**·pee (/**ˈti**.pi/)

"-ology"

This suffix is used to denote fields of scientific study or discourse; sets of ideas, beliefs, or principles; or bodies of texts or writings. Primary stress is placed on the syllable in which "-ol-" appears. For example:
- a·**strol**·o·gy (/ə**ˈstrɑl**.əˌdʒi/)
- bi·**ol**·o·gy (/baɪ**ˈɑl**.əˌdʒi/)
- car·di·**ol**·o·gy (/ˌkɑr.di**ˈɑl**.əˌdʒi/)
- e·**col**·o·gy (/ɪ**ˈkɑl**.əˌdʒi/)
- ge·**ol**·o·gy (/dʒi**ˈɑl**.əˌdʒi/)
- i·de·**ol**·o·gy (/ˌaɪ.di**ˈɑl**.əˌdʒi/)
- lex·i·**col**·o·gy (/ˌlɛk.sɪ**ˈkɑl**.əˌdʒi/)
- meth·o·**dol**·o·gy (/ˌmɛθ.ə**ˈdɑl**.əˌdʒi/)
- neu·**rol**·o·gy (/nʊ**ˈrɑl**.əˌdʒi/)

- psy·**chol**·o·gy (/saɪˈkɑl.ə.dʒi/)
- ra·di·**ol**·o·gy (/reɪ.diˈɑl.ə.dʒi/)
- so·ci·**ol**·o·gy (/ˌsoʊ.siˈɑl.ə.dʒi/)
- tech·**nol**·o·gy (/tɛkˈnɑl.ə.dʒi/)
- u·**rol**·o·gy (/jʊˈrɑl.ə.dʒi/)
- zo·**ol**·o·gy (/zuˈɑl.ə.dʒi/)

"-osis"

This suffix is used to form the names of diseases, conditions, and other medical processes. Stress is placed on the syllable in which "-o-" appears

- ac·i·**do**·sis (/ˌæs.ɪˈdoʊ.sɪs/)
- cir·**rho**·sis (/sɪˈroʊ.sɪs/)
- di·ag·**no**·sis (/ˌdaɪ.əgˈnoʊ.sɪs/)
- en·do·me·tri·**o**·sis (/ˌɛn.doʊˌmi.triˈoʊ.sɪs/)
- fib·**ro**·sis (/faɪˈbroʊ.sɪs/)
- hyp·**no**·sis (/hɪpˈnoʊ.sɪs/)
- mi·**to**·sis (/maɪˈtoʊ.sɪs/)
- ne·**cro**·sis (/nəˈkroʊ.sɪs/)
- os·te·o·po·**ro**·sis (/ˌɑs.ti.oʊ.pəˈroʊ.sɪs/)
- prog·**no**·sis (/prɑgˈnoʊ.sɪs/)
- sym·bi·**o**·sis (/ˌsɪm.biˈoʊ.sɪs/)
- tu·ber·cu·**lo**·sis (/tʊˌbɜr.kjəˈloʊ.sɪs/)

Stress is placed on syllable immediately before the suffix

"-eous" and -"ious"

These two suffixes are both used to form adjectives meaning "having, characterized by, or full of," most often attaching to base nouns.

In many cases, the **E** and **I** are pronounced individually, but for many other words they are silent, instead serving to mark a change in pronunciation for the previous consonant. For example:

-eous	-ious
ad·van·**ta**·geous (/ˌæd vənˈteɪ.dʒəs/)	am·**phib**·i·ous (/æmˈfɪb.i.əs/)
boun·te·ous (/ˈbaʊn.ti.əs/)	bo·**da**·cious (/boʊˈdeɪ.ʃəs/)
cou·**ra**·geous (/kəˈreɪ.dʒəs/)	con·**ta**·gious (/kənˈteɪ.dʒəs/)
dis·**cour**·te·ous (/dɪsˈkɜr.ti.əs/)	**du**·bi·ous (/ˈdu.bi.əs/)
ex·**tra**·ne·ous (/ɪkˈstreɪ.ni.əs/)	ex·pe·**diti**·ous (/ˌɛk spɪˈdɪʃ.əs/)
gas·e·ous (/ˈgæs.i.əs/)	fa·**ce**·tious (/fəˈsi.ʃəs/)
hid·e·ous (/ˈhɪd.i.əs/)	gre·**gar**·i·ous (/grɪˈgɛər.i.əs/)
ig·ne·ous (/ˈɪg.ni.əs/)	hi·**lar**·i·ous (/hɪˈlɛr.i.əs/)
misc·e·**lla**·ne·ous (/ˌmɪs.əˈleɪ.ni.əs/)	im·**per**·vi·ous (/ɪmˈpɜr.vi.əs/)
nau·seous (/ˈnɔ.ʃəs/)	ju·**dici**·ous (/dʒuˈdɪʃ.əs/)

out·**ra**·geous (/aʊt'**reɪ**.dʒəs/)	la·**bor**·i·ous (/lə'**bɔr**.i.əs/)
pit·e·ous (/'**pɪt**.i.əs/)	my·**ster**·i·ous (/mɪ'**stɪr**.i əs/)
righ·teous (/'**raɪ**.tʃəs/)	ne·**far**·i·ous (/nɪ'**fɛr**.i.əs/)
si·mul·**ta**·ne·ous (/ˌsaɪ.məl'**teɪ**.ni.əs/)	**ob**·vi·ous (/'**ɑb**.vi.əs/)
vi·tre·ous (/'**vɪ**.tri.əs/)	pro·**digi**·ous (/prə'**dɪdʒ**.əs/)
	re·**bell**·ious (/rɪ'**bɛl**.jəs/)
	su·per·**sti**·tious (/ˌsu.pər'**stɪ**.ʃəs/)
	te·**na**·cious (/te'**neɪ**.ʃəs/)
	up·**roar**·i·ous (/ʌp'**rɔr**.i.əs/)
	vi·**car**·i·ous (/vaɪ'**kɛr**.i.əs/)

"-ia"

This suffix is used to create nouns, either denoting a disease or a condition or quality.

In most words, the **I** is pronounced individually. In other words, it becomes silent and indicates a change in the pronunciation of the previous consonant. (In a handful of words, **I** blends with a previous vowel sound that is stressed before the final **A**.)

For example:
- ac·a·**de**·mi·a (/ˌæk.ə'**di**.mi.ə/)
- bac·**ter**·i·a (/bæk.'**tɪər**.i.ə/)
- cat·a·**to**·ni·a (/ˌkæt.ə'**toʊ**.ni.ə/)
- de·**men**·tia (/dɪ'**mɛn**.ʃə/)
- en·cy·clo·**pe**·di·a (/ɛnˌsaɪ.klə'**pi**.di.ə/)
- fan·**ta**·sia (/fæn'**teɪ**.ʒə/)
- hy·po·**ther**·mi·a (ˌhaɪ.pə'**θɜr**.mi.ə/)
- in·**som**·ni·a (/ɪn'**sɑm**.ni.ə/)
- leu·**ke**·mi·a (/lu'**ki**.mi.ə/)
- mem·or·a·**bil**·i·a (/ˌmɛm.ər.ə'**bɪl**.i.ə/)
- no·**stal**·gia (/nɑ'**stæl**.dʒə/)
- par·a·**noi**·a (/ˌpær.ə'**nɔɪ**.ə/)
- re·**ga**·li·a (/rɪ'**geɪ**.li.ə/)
- su·**bur**·bi·a (/sə'**bɜr**.bi.ə/)
- **tri**·vi·a (/'**trɪ**.vi.ə/)
- u·**to**·pi·a (/ju'**toʊ**.pi.ə/)
- xen·o·**pho**·bi·a (/ˌzɛn.ə'**foʊ**.bi.ə/)

"-ial"

The suffix "-ial" is used to form adjectives from nouns, meaning "of, characterized by, connected with, or relating to." Like "-ia," **I** is either pronounced individually or else becomes silent and changes the pronunciation of the previous consonant. For example:
- ad·**ver**·bi·al (/æd'**vɜr**.bi.əl/)
- bac·**ter**·i·al (/bæk'**tɪr**.i.əl/)
- con·fi·**den**·tial (/ˌkɑn.fɪ'**dɛn**.ʃəl/)
- def·e·**ren**·tial (/ˌdɛf.ə'**rɛn**.ʃəl/)
- ed·i·**tor**·i·al (/ˌɛd.ɪ'**tɔr**.i.əl/)

- fa·**mil**·i·al (/fəˈmɪl.jəl/)
- **gla**·cial (/ˈgleɪ.ʃəl/)
- in·flu·**en**·tial (/ˌɪn.fluˈɛn.ʃəl/)
- ju·**di**·cial (/dʒuˈdɪʃ.əl/)
- me·**mor**·i·al (/məˈmɔr.i.əl/)
- o·**ffici**·al (/əˈfɪʃ.əl/)
- pro·**ver**·bi·al (/prəˈvɜr.bi.əl/)
- ref·e·**ren**·tial (/ˌrɛf.əˈrɛn.ʃəl/)
- su·per·**fi**·cial (/ˌsu.pərˈfɪʃ.əl/)
- terr·i·**tor**·i·al (/ˌtɛr.ɪˈtɔr.i.əl/)
- ve·**stig**·i·al (/vɛˈstɪdʒ.i.əl/)

"-ic" and "-ical"

These two suffixes form adjectives from the nouns to which they attach. For both, the primary stress is placed on the syllable immediately before "-ic-." For example:

-ic	-ical
a·**tom**·ic (/əˈtɑm.ɪk)	an·a·**tom**·i·cal (/ˌæn.əˈtɑm.ɪ.kəl)
bur·eau·**crat**·ic (/ˌbjʊər.əˈkræt.ɪk)	bi·o·**log**·i·cal (/ˌbaɪ.əˈlɑdʒ.ɪ.kəl/)
cha·**ot**·ic (/keɪˈɑt.ɪk/)	chron·o·**log**·i·cal (/ˌkrɑn.əˈlɑdʒ.ɪ.kəl/)
dem·o·**crat**·ic (/ˌdɛm.əˈkræt.ɪk/)	di·a·**bol**·i·cal (/ˌdaɪ.əˈbɑl.ɪ.kəl/)
en·er·**get**·ic (/ˌɛn.ərˈdʒɛt.ɪk/)	e·**lec**·tri·cal (/ɪˈlɛk.trɪ.kəl/)
for·mu·**la**·ic (/ˌfɔr.mjəˈleɪ.ɪk/)	**far**·ci·cal (/ˈfɑr.sɪ.kəl/)
ge·**net**·ic (/dʒəˈnɛt.ɪk/)	ge·o·**graph**·i·cal (/dʒi.əˈgræf.ɪ.kəl/)
hyp·**not**·ic (/hɪpˈnɑt.ɪk/)	his·**tor**·i·cal (/hɪˈstɔr.ɪ.kəl/)
i·**con**·ic (/aɪˈkɑn.ɪk/)	in·e·**ffec**·tu·al (/ˌɪn.ɪˈfɛk.tʃu.əl/)
ki·**net**·ic (/kəˈnɛt.ɪk/)	lack·a·**dai**·si·cal (/ˌlæk.əˈdeɪ.zɪ.kəl/)
la·**con**·ic (/leɪˈkɑn.ɪk/)	**mu**·si·cal (/ˈmju.zɪ.kəl/)
mag·**net**·ic (/mægˈnɛt.ɪk/)	**nau**·ti·cal (/ˈnɔ.tɪ.kəl/)
no·**stal**·gic (/nəˈstæl.dʒɪk)	**op**·ti·cal (/ˈɑp.tɪ.kəl/)
opp·or·tu·**nis**·tic (/ˌɑp.ər.tuˈnɪs.tɪk/)	par·a·**dox**·i·cal (/pær.əˈdɑks.ɪ.kəl/)
pe·ri·**od**·ic (/ˌpɪər.iˈɑd.ɪk/)	psy·cho·an·a·**lyt**·i·cal (/ˌsaɪ.koʊ.æn.əˈlɪt.ɪ.kəl/)
re·a·**lis**·tic (/ˌri.əˈlɪs.tɪk/)	rhe·**tor**·i·cal (/rɪˈtɔr.ɪ.kəl/)
sym·pa·**thet**·ic (/ˌsɪm.pəˈθɛt.ɪk/)	sy·**mmet**·ri·cal (/sɪˈmɛt.rɪ.kəl/)
ti·**tan**·ic (taɪˈtæn.ɪk/)	ty·**ran**·ni·cal (/tɪˈræn.ɪ.kəl/)

ul·tra·**son**·ic (/ˌʌl.trəˈsɑn.ɪk/)	um·**bil**·i·cal (/ʌmˈbɪl.ɪ.kəl/)
vol·**can**·ic (/vɑlˈkæn.ɪk/)	**ver**·ti·cal (/ˈvɜr.tɪ.kəl/)
	whim·si·cal (/ˈwɪm.zɪ.kəl/)
	zo·o·**log**·i·cal (ˌzoʊ.əˈlɑdʒ.ɪ.kəl/)

While this pattern of pronunciation is very reliable, there are a few words (mostly nouns) ending in "-ic" that go against it:
• a·**rith**·me·tic* (/əˈrɪθ.mə.tɪk/)
• **her**·e·tic (/ˈhɛr.ɪ.tɪk/)
• **lu**·na·tic (/ˈlu.nə.tɪk/)
• **pol**·i·tics (/ˈpɑl.ɪ.tɪks/)
• **rhet**·o·ric (/ˈrɛt.ə.rɪk/)

(*This pronunciation is used when *arithmetic* is a noun. As an adjective, it is pronounced *a·rith·**me**·tic* [/ˌæ.rɪθˈmɛ.tɪk/].)

"-ify"

This suffix is used to form verbs, most often from existing nouns or adjectives. While the primary stress is placed immediately before "-i-," the second syllable of the suffix, "-fy," also receives a **secondary stress**. For instance:
• a·**cid**·i·fy (/əˈsɪd.əˌfaɪ/)
• be·**at**·i·fy (/biˈæt.əˌfaɪ/)
• **class**·i·fy (/ˈklæs.əˌfaɪ/)
• **dig**·ni·fy (/ˈdɪg.nəˌfaɪ/)
• e·**lec**·tri·fy (/ɪˈlɛk.trəˌfaɪ/)
• **fal**·si·fy (/ˈfɔlsəˌfaɪ/)
• **horr**·i·fy (/ˈhɔr.əˌfaɪ/)
• i·**den**·ti·fy (/aɪˈdɛn.təˌfaɪ/)
• **mag**·ni·fy (/ˈmægnəˌfaɪ/)
• **no**·ti·fy (/ˈnoʊ.təˌfaɪ/)
• ob·**jec**·ti·fy (/əbˈdʒɛk.təˌfaɪ/)
• per·**son**·i·fy (/pərˈsɑn.əˌfaɪ/)
• **rat**·i·fy (/ˈræt.əˌfaɪ/)
• so·**lid**·i·fy (/səˈlɪd.əˌfaɪ/)
• **tes**·ti·fy (/ˈtɛs.təˌfaɪ/)
• **ver**·i·fy (/ˈvɛr.əˌfaɪ/)

"-ity"

This suffix is the opposite of "-ic(al)"—that is, it is used to create nouns from adjectives. The I is pronounced in an individual syllable, with the word's primary stress occurring immediately before it. For instance:
• a·**bil**·i·ty (/əˈbɪl.ɪ.ti/)
• ba·**nal**·i·ty (/bəˈnæl.ɪ.ti/)
• ce·**leb**·ri·ty (/səˈlɛb.rɪ.ti/)
• dis·**par**·i·ty (/dɪˈspær.ɪ.ti/)
• e·**qual**·i·ty (/əˈkwɑl.ɪ.ti/)
• func·tion·**al**·i·ty (/ˌfʌŋk.ʃənˈæl.ɪ.tɪ/)
• gen·e·**ros**·i·ty (/ˌdʒɛn.əˈrɑs.ɪ.ti/)
• hu·**mid**·i·ty (/hjuˈmɪd.ɪ.ti/)
• i·**niq**·ui·ty (/ɪˈnɪk.wɪ.ti/)
• jo·vi·**al**·i·ty (/dʒoʊ.vi.ˈæl.ɪ.ti/)
• le·**gal**·i·ty (/liˈgæl.ɪ.ti/)
• ma·**jor**·i·ty (/məˈdʒoʊr.ɪ.ti/)
• nor·**mal**·i·ty (/noʊrˈmæl.ɪ.ti/)
• ob·**scur**·i·ty (/əbˈskʊər.ɪ.ti/)
• prac·ti·**cal**·i·ty (/præk.tɪˈkæl.ɪ.ti/)

- **qual**·i·ty (/ˈkwɑl.ɪ.ti/)
- rec·i·**proc**·i·ty (/ˌrɛs.əˈprɑs.ɪ.ti/)
- **scar**·ci·ty (/ˈskɛr.sɪ.ti/)
- tech·ni·**cal**·i·ty (/ˌtɛk.nɪˈkæl.ɪ.ti/)
- u·na·**nim**·i·ty (/ˌju.nəˈnɪm.ɪ.ti/)
- ve·**loc**·i·ty (/vəˈlɑs.ɪ.ti/)

"-tion" and "-sion"

These two syllables are used to create nouns, especially from verbs to describe an instance of that action. Depending on the word, the /ʃ/ or /tʃ/ sounds made by "-tion" and the /ʃ/ or /ʒ/ sounds made by "-sion" will be part of the stressed syllable or the final unstressed syllable. For example:

-tion	-sion
au·**diti**·on (/ɔˈdɪʃ.ən/)	a·**bra**·sion (/əˈbreɪ.ʒən/)
bi·**sec**·tion (/baɪˈsɛk.ʃən/)	a·**ver**·sion (/əˈvɜr.ʒən/)
can·ce·**lla**·tion (/ˌkæn.sɪˈleɪ.ʃən/)	co·**llisi**·on (/kəˈlɪʒ.ən/)
di·**screti**·on (/dɪˈskrɛʃ.ən/)	com·**pul**·sion (/kəmˈpʌl.ʃən/)
ex·**haus**·tion (/ɪgˈzɔs.tʃən/)	di·**ffu**·sion (/dɪˈfju.ʒən/)
flo·**ta**·tion (/floʊˈteɪ.ʃən/)	di·**men**·sion (/dɪˈmɛn.ʃən/)
grad·u·a·tion (/ˌgrædʒ.uˈeɪ.ʃən/)	e·**ro**·sion (/ɪˈroʊ.ʒən/)
hos·pi·tal·i·**za**·tion (/ˌhɑs.pɪ.təl.ɪˈzeɪʃ.ən/)	**fu**·sion (/ˈfju.ʒən/)
ig·**ni**·tion (/ɪgˈnɪʃ.ən/)	i·**llu**·sion (/ɪˈlu.ʒən/)
jur·is·**dic**·tion (/ˌdʒʊər.ɪsˈdɪk.ʃən/)	in·**va**·sion (/ɪnˈveɪ.ʒən/)
lo·co·**mo**·tion (/ˌloʊ.kəˈmoʊ.ʃən/)	**man**·sion (/ˈmæn.ʃən/)
mod·i·fi·**ca**·tion (/ˌmɑd.ə.fɪˈkeɪ.ʃən/)	ob·**sessi**·on (/əbˈsɛʃ.ən/)
nom·i·**na**·tion (/ˌnɑm.əˈneɪ.ʃən/)	o·**cca**·sion (/əˈkeɪ.ʒən/)
ob·**struc**·tion (/əbˈstrʌk.ʃən/)	per·**cussi**·on (/pərˈkʌʃ.ən/)
pros·e·**cu**·tion (/ˌprɑs.ɪˈkyu.ʃən/)	pro·**pul**·sion (/prəˈpʌl.ʃən/)
re·a·li·**za**·tion (/ˌri.ə.ləˈzeɪ.ʃən/)	re·**missi**·on (/rɪˈmɪʃ.ən/)
se·**cre**·tion (/sɪˈkri.ʃən/)	sub·**ver**·sion (/səbˈvɜr.ʒən/)
tra·**diti**·on (/trəˈdɪʃ.ən/)	su·**spen**·sion (/səˈspɛn.ʃən/)
u·ni·fi·**ca**·tion (/ˌju.nə.fɪˈkeɪ.ʃən/)	trans·**fu**·sion (/trænsˈfju.ʒən/)
vi·**bra**·tion (/vaɪˈbreɪ.ʃən/)	**ver**·sion (/ˈvɜr.ʒən/)

The word *television* is an exception to this rule, and in most dialects it has the primary stress placed on the first syllable: /ˈtɛl.ə.ˌvɪʒ.ən/.

Stress applied two syllables before the suffix

"-ate"

This suffix is most often used to create verbs, but it can also form adjectives and nouns. In words with three or more syllables, the primary stress is placed two syllables before the suffix. For example:

- ac·**cen**·tu·ate (/æk ˈsɛn.tʃu ˌeɪt/))
- bar·**bit**·ur·ate (/bɑr ˈbɪtʃ.ər.ɪt/)
- co·**llab**·o·rate (/kə ˈlæb.ə ˌreɪt/)
- diff·e·**ren**·ti·ate (/ ˌdɪf.ə ˈrɛn.ʃi ˌeɪt/)
- e·**nu**.me·rate (/ɪ ˈnu.mə ˌreɪt/)
- fa·**cil**·i·tate (/fə ˈsɪl.ɪ ˌteɪt/)
- ge·**stic**·u·late (/dʒɛ ˈstɪk.jə ˌleɪt/)
- hu·**mil**·i·ate (/hju ˈmɪl.i ˌeɪt/)
- in·**ad**·e·quate (/ɪn ˈæd.ɪ.kwɪt/)
- le·**git**·i·mate (/lɪ ˈdʒɪt.ə ˌmɪt/)
- ma·**tric**·u·late (/mə ˈtrɪk.jə ˌleɪt/)
- ne·**cess**·i·tate (/nə ˈsɛs.ɪ ˌteɪt/)
- o·**blit**·e·rate (/ə ˈblɪt.ə ˌreɪt/)
- par·**tic**·i·pate (/pɑr ˈtɪs.ɪ.ɪt/)
- re·**frig**·er·ate (/rɪ ˈfrɪdʒ.ə ˌreɪt/)
- **stip**·u·late (/ˈstɪp.jə ˌleɪt/)
- tri·**an**·gu·late (/traɪ ˈæŋ.gjə.leɪt/)
- un·**for**·tu·nate (/ʌn ˈfɔr.tʃə.nɪt/)
- **ver**·te·brate (/ˈvɜr.tə.brɪt/)

"-cy"

This suffix attaches to adjectives or nouns to form nouns referring to "state, condition, or quality," or "rank or office." For example:

- a·**dja**·cen·cy (/ə ˈdʒeɪ.sən.si/)
- **a**·gen·cy (/ˈeɪ.dʒən.si/)
- **bank**·rupt·cy (/ˈbæŋk.rʌpt.si/)
- com·**pla**·cen·cy (/kəm ˈpleɪ.sən.si/)
- de·**moc**·ra·cy (/dɪ ˈmɑk.rə.si/)
- ex·**pec**·tan·cy (/ɪk ˈspɛk.tən.si/)
- flam·**boy**·an·cy (/flæm ˈbɔɪ.ən.si/)
- **fre**·quen·cy (/ˈfri.kwən.si/)
- in·**sur**·gen·cy (/ɪn ˈsɜr.dʒən.si/)
- **in**·fan·cy (/ ˈɪnfən.si/)
- lieu·**ten**·an·cy (/lu ˈtɛn.ən.si/)
- ma·**lig**·nan·cy (/mə ˈlɪg.nən.si/)
- pro·**fici**·en·cy (/prə ˈfɪʃ.ən.si/)
- re·**dun**·dan·cy (/rɪ ˈdʌn.dən.si/)
- su·**prem**·a·cy (/sə ˈprɛm.ə.si/)
- trans·**par**·en·cy (/træns ˈpɛər.ən.si/)
- **va**·can·cy (/ˈveɪ.kən.si/)

Unlike some of the other suffixes we've looked at so far, this one has a number of exceptions. For these, the primary stress is placed <u>three</u> syllables before the suffix:

- **ac**·cur·a·cy (/ˈæk.jər.ə.si/)
- **can**·di·da·cy (/ˈkæn.dɪ.də.si/)
- **com**·pe·ten·cy (/ˈkɑm.pɪ.tən.si/)
- **del**·i·ca·cy (/ˈdɛl.ɪ.kə.si/)
- ex·**trav**·a·gan·cy (/ɪk ˈstræv.ə.gən.si/)
- im·**me**·di·a·cy (/ɪ ˈmi.di.ə.si/)

- **in**·ti·ma·cy (/ˈɪn.tɪ.mə.sɪ/)
- **lit**·er·a·cy (/ˈlɪt.ər.ə.sɪ/)
- le·**git**·i·ma·cy (/lɪˈdʒɪt.ə.mə.si/)
- **occ**·u·pan·cy (/ˈɑk.jə.pən.si/)
- **pres**·i·den·cy (/ˈprɛz.ɪ.dən.si/)
- **rel**·e·van·cy (/ˈrɛl.ɪ.vən.si/)
- **surr**·o·ga·cy (/ˈsɜr.ə.gə.si/)

Unfortunately, there are no patterns in these words to let us know that their primary stress will be in a different place; we just have to memorize them.

"-phy"

This ending is actually a part of other suffixes, most often "-graphy," but also "-trophy" and "-sophy." The primary stress in the word will appear immediately before the "-gra-," "-tro-," and "-so-" parts of the words. For example:

- **a**·tro·phy (/ˈæ.trə.fi/)
- bib·li·**og**·ra·phy (/ˌbɪb.liˈɑg.rə.fi/)
- cal·**lig**·ra·phy (/kəˈlɪg.rə.fi/)
- dis·**cog**·ra·phy (/dɪsˈkɑg.rə.fi/)
- eth·**nog**·ra·phy (/ɛθˈnɑg.rə.fi/)
- fil·**mog**·ra·phy (/fɪlˈmɑg.rə.fi/)
- ge·**og**·ra·phy (/dʒiˈɑg.rə.fi/)
- i·co·**nog**·ra·phy (/ˌaɪ.kəˈnɑg.rə.fi/)
- or·**thog**·ra·phy (/ɔrˈθɑg.rə.fi/)
- phi·**los**·o·phy (/fɪˈlɑs.ə.fi/)
- pho·**tog**·ra·phy (/fəˈtɑg.rə.fi/)
- ra·di·**og**·ra·phy (/ˌreɪ.dɪˈɑg.rə.fi/)
- so·**nog**·ra·phy (/səˈnɑg.rə.fi/)
- the·**os**·o·phy (/θiˈɑs.ə.fi/)
- ty·**pog**·ra·phy (/taɪˈpɑg.rə.fi/)

Suffixes that don't affect word stress

While many suffixes dictate which syllable is stressed in a word, there are others that usually do not affect the stress of the base word at all. Let's look at some examples of these (just note that this isn't an exhaustive list):

"-age"	"-ish"*	"-hood"	"-less"	"-ness"	"-ous"
an·chor·age brok·er·age cov·er·age e·**quip**·age her·mit·age lev·er·age or·phan·age me·ter·age pa·tron·age sew·er·age vic·ar·age	am·a·teur·ish ba·by·ish car·toon·ish dev·il·ish fe·ver·ish hea·then·ish og·re·ish pur·pl·ish tick·l·ish va·ga·**bond**·ish yell·ow·ish	a·**dult**·hood **broth**·er·hood **fath**·er·hood **like**·li·hood **moth**·er·hood **neigh**·bor·hood **par**·ent·hood **sis**·ter·hood **vic**·tim·hood **wo**·man·hood	ar·mor·less bo·di·less col·or·less di·**rec**·tion·less e·**mo**·tion·less **feath**·er·less hu·mor·less **lim**·it·less **mean**·ing·less o·dor·less pen·ni·less re·**gard**·less **struc**·ture·less **tick**·et·less vi·**bra**·tion·less **win**·dow·less	ad·**ven**·tur·ous·ness **bash**·ful·ness com·**pet**·i·tive·ness de·**ceit**·ful·ness e·**ffec**·tive·ness fa·**ce**·tious·ness glo·ri·ous·ness **hid**·e·ous·ness il·**lust**·ri·ous·ness **jag**·ged·ness **king**·li·ness li·**ti**·gious·ness **mean**·ing·ful·ness **nerv**·ous·ness o·**blique**·ness per·**sua**·sive·ness **quea**·si·ness re·**morse**·less·ness sub·**ver**·sive·ness to·**geth**·er·ness u·**biq**·ui·tous·ness **venge**·ful·ness **war**·i·ness **youth**·ful·ness **zeal**·ous·ness	an·**al**·o·gous **blas**·phe·mous **can**·cer·ous **dan**·ger·ous **fi**·brous **glam**·or·ous **li**·bel·ous **mu**·ti·nous o·dor·ous **per**·il·ous **ran**·cor·ous **scan**·dal·ous **treach**·er·ous **val**·or·ous

Inflectional suffixes (suffixes that form plurals, change verb tense, create comparative ajectives and adverbs, etc.) do not affect word stress either. Let's look at a few examples:
- a·**maze**→a·**maz**·ing (creates the present participle / gerund)
- **blank**·et→**blank**·et·ed (creates the past tense)
- **com**·pro·mise→**com**·pro·mis·es (creates the third-person singular form)
- **drows**·y→**drows**·i·er (creates the comparative form)
- **hap**·py→**hap**·pi·est (creates the superlative form)
- re·**sponse**→re·**spons**·es (creates the plural form)

*"-ish" at the end of verbs

The examples of the suffix "-ish" that we looked at previously were all adjectives formed from various parts of speech (usually nouns). However, "-ish" can also appear naturally at the end of verbs—that is, it doesn't attach to existing base words, but is rather the result of the word's evolution in English. For these verbs, primary stress always occurs on the syllable immediately before "-ish." For example:
- a·**ston**·ish (/əˈstɑn.ɪʃ/)
- **bran**·dish (/ˈbræn.dɪʃ/)
- **cher**·ish (/ˈtʃɛr.ɪʃ/)
- de·**mol**·ish (/dɪˈmɑl.ɪʃ/)
- ex·**tin**·guish (/ɪkˈstɪŋ.gwɪʃ/)
- **fur**·nish (/ˈfɜr.nɪʃ/)
- **gar**·nish (/ˈgɑr.nɪʃ/)
- im·**pove**·rish (/ɪmˈpɑv.rɪʃ/; the **E** is silent)
- **lan**·guish (/ˈlæŋ.gwɪʃ/)
- **nour**·ish (/ˈnɜr.ɪʃ/)
- **pub**·lish (/ˈpʌb.lɪʃ/)
- re·**plen**·ish (/rɪˈplɛn.ɪʃ/)
- **tar**·nish (/ˈtɑr.nɪʃ/)

Unstressed Words (Function Words)

We discussed earlier how words have at least one primary stress centered around a vowel sound; however, this is not always the case. This is because English consists of two types of words: **content words** and **function words**.

Content words (also known as **lexical words**) communicate a distinct lexical meaning within a particular context—that is, they express the specific **content** of what we're talking about at a given time. These include nouns, adjective, adverbs, and most verbs. Content words will always have at least one syllable that is emphasized in a sentence, so if a content word only has a single syllable, it will always be stressed.

Function words (also known as **structure words**) primarily serve to complete the syntax and grammatical nuance of a sentence. These include pronouns, prepositions, conjunctions, articles, determiners, and auxiliary verbs. In contrast to content words, single-syllable function words are commonly (but not always) unstressed in a sentence—since they are not providing lexical meaning integral to the sentence, we often "skip over" them vocally. Take the following sentence:
- "Bobby wants **to** walk **to the** playground."

The particle *to*, the preposition *to*, and the definitive article *the* are all said without (or without much) stress. The content words (*Bobby, wants, walk*, and *playground*), on the other hand, each have at least one syllable that is emphasized.

Let's look at some single-syllable function words that can either be stressed or unstressed in a given sentence:

Function Word	Stressed	Unstressed
a	/eɪ/	/ə/
an	/æn/	/ən/
am	/æm/	/əm/
are	/ɑr/	/ər/
be	/bi/	/bɪ/

can	/kæn/	/kən/
could	/kʊd/	/kəd/
do	/du/	/dʊ/ or /də/
have	/hæv/	/həv/
of	/ʌv/ or /ɑv/	/əv/ or /ə/
or	/ɔr/	/ər/
should	/ʃʊd/	/ʃəd/
the	/ði/	/ðə/ or /ðɪ/
to	/tu/	/tə/
was	/wɑz/	/wəz/
were	/wɜr/	/wər/
would	/wʊd/	/wəd/

Words with multiple pronunciations

It is not uncommon for English words to have more than one pronunciation even when there is no change in meaning, especially between different regional dialects. This difference usually occurs in the pronunciation of certain vowel or consonant sounds, but it can also affect which syllable in the word receives the primary stress.

For example:

Word	Pronunciation 1	Pronunciation 2
address (noun)	a·**ddress** /əˈdrɛs/	**add**·ress /ˈæd.rɛs/
adult	a·**dult** /əˈdʌlt/	**ad**·ult /ˈæd.ʌlt/
advertisement	ad·ver·**tise**·ment /ˌæd.vərˈtaɪz.mənt/ (AmE)	ad·**ver**·tise·ment /ædˈvɜr.tɪz.mənt/ (BrE)
applicable	**app**·li·ca·ble /ˈæp.lɪ.kə.bəl/	a·**ppli**·ca·ble /əˈplɪ.kə.bəl/
café	ca·**fé** /kæˈfeɪ/ (AmE)	**ca**·fé /ˈkæ.feɪ/ (BrE)
Caribbean	Car·i·**bbe**·an /ˌkær.əˈbi.ən/	Ca·**ribb**·e·an /kəˈrɪb.i.ən/
chauffeur	**chau**·ffeur /ˈʃoʊ.fər/	chau·**ffeur** /ʃoʊˈfɜr/
composite	com·**pos**·ite /kəmˈpɑz.ɪt/ (AmE)	**com**·pos·ite /ˈkɑm.pəz.ɪt/ (BrE)
controversy	**con**·tro·ver·sy /ˈkɑn.trəˌvɜr.si/	con·**trov**·er·sy /kənˈtrɑv.er.si/ (BrE)

employee	em·**ploy**·ee /ɛmˈplɔɪ.i/	em·ploy·**ee** /ɛm.plɔɪˈi/
fiancé(e)	fi·an·**cé(e)** /ˌfi.ɑnˈseɪ/	fi·an·cé(e) /fiˈɑn.seɪ/
garage	ga·**rage** /gəˈrɑʒ/ (*AmE*)	**gar**·age /ˈgær.ɑʒ/ (*BrE*)
kilometer	ki·**lom**·e·ter /kɪˈlɑm.ɪ.tər/	**kil**·o·me·ter /ˈkɪl.əˌmi.tər/
lingerie	lin·ge·**rie** /ˌlɑn.ʒəˈreɪ/ (*AmE*)	**lin**·ge·rie /ˈlæn.ʒə.ri/ (*BrE*)
preferable	**pref**·er·a·ble /ˈprɛf.ər.ə.bəl/	pre·**fer**·a·ble /prɪˈfɜr.ər.ə.bəl/
transference	trans·**fer**·ence /trænsˈfɜr.əns/	**trans**·fer·ence /ˈtræns.fər.əns/

Unfortunately, there's no way to predict when a word will have different stress patterns, as they are often the result of variations in regional dialects, rather than the origin of the words themselves. If you hear someone pronounce a word with an intonation you haven't heard before, check a reliable dictionary to see what is the most common pronunciation.

Quiz
(answers start on page 463)

1. What type of speech sound receives stress in a word?

a) Consonant sounds
b) Vowel sounds
c) A & B

2. How many syllables in a word can have **primary stress**?

a) 1
b) 2
c) 3
d) 4

3. Which of the following words can be **completely** unstressed?

a) run
b) book
c) off
d) of

4. Where does primary stress usually occur in words ending with the suffix "-ic"?

a) On the suffix itself
b) One syllable before the suffix
c) Two syllables before the suffix
d) Three syllables before the suffix

5. Where does primary stress usually occur in words ending with the suffix "-ate"?

a) On the suffix itself
b) One syllable before the suffix
c) Two syllables before the suffix
d) Three syllables before the suffix

6. When a word functions as both a noun and a verb, in what way are they often distinguished in speech?
a) The noun is stressed on the first syllable, while the verb is stressed on the second
b) The noun is stressed on the second syllable, while the verb is stressed on the first

7. Which of the following suffixes does **not** determine word stress?
a) "-ology"
b) "-phy"
c) "-tion"
d) "-hood"

Sentence Stress

Definition

Sentence stress (also called **prosodic stress**) refers to the emphasis placed on certain words within a sentence. This varying emphasis gives English a cadence, resulting in a natural songlike quality when spoken fluently.

Sentence stress is generally determined by whether a word is considered a "**content word**" or a "**function word**," and the vocal space between stressed words creates the **rhythm** of a sentence.

Content Words vs. Function Words

In the most basic pattern, **content words** will always be stressed, while **function words** will often be unstressed. Let's briefly discuss the difference between the two.

Content words

A **content word** (also known as a **lexical word**) is a word that communicates a distinct lexical meaning within a particular context—that is, it expresses the specific **content** of what we're talking about at a given time. Nouns (e.g., *dog, Betty, happiness, luggage*), most* verbs (e.g., *run, talk, decide, entice*), adjectives (e.g., *sad, outrageous, good, easy*), and adverbs (e.g., *slowly, beautifully, never*) all have meaning that is considered *lexically* important.

Content words will always have at least one syllable that is emphasized in a sentence, so if a content word only has a single syllable, it will always be stressed.

(*Auxiliary verbs are specific types of verbs that are used in the grammatical construction of tense and aspect or to express **modality**—that is, asserting or denying possibility, likelihood, ability, permission, obligation, or future intention. These types of verbs are fixed in their structure and are used to convey a relationship between other "main" verbs, so they are considered function words, which we'll look at next.)

Function words

A **function word** (also known as a **structure word**) is a word that primarily serves to complete the syntax and grammatical nuance of a sentence. These include **pronouns** (e.g., *he, she, it, they*), **prepositions** (e.g., *to, in, on, under*), **conjunctions** (e.g., *and, but, if, or*), **articles** (e.g., *a, an, the*), other **determiners** (e.g., *this, each, those*), and interjections (e.g., *ah, grr, hello*).

In addition to these parts of speech, function words also include a specific subset of verbs known as auxiliary verbs, which add structural and grammatical meaning to other main verbs. These include the three primary auxiliary verbs *be, do,* and *have,* as well as a number of others known as modal auxiliary verbs, such as *can, may, must, will,* and others.

Finally, function words, especially those with only one syllable, are commonly (but not always) unstressed in a sentence—since they are not providing lexical meaning integral to the sentence, we often "skip over" them vocally. For example, in the sentence, "Bobby wants *to* walk *to the* playground," the particle *to,* the preposition *to,* and the definite article *the* are all said without (or without much) stress. The content words (*Bobby, wants, walk,* and *playground*), on the other hand, each receive more emphasis to help them stand out and underline their importance to the meaning of the sentence.

Sentence Stress vs. Word Stress

While function words are often unstressed in a sentence, those that have more than one syllable still have internal word stress on one of their syllables. For example, the word *because* has two syllables (*be·cause*), with stress placed on the second syllable (/bɪˈkɔz/). However, in a sentence with a normal stress pattern, *because* will have less overall emphasis than the content words around it, which helps maintain the cadence and flow of the sentence in everyday speech.

Likewise, multi-syllable content words will have even more emphasis placed on the syllable that receives the primary stress. It is this syllable that is most articulated within a sentence, with the rest of the word being unstressed like the function words.

Examples of normal sentence stress

Let's look at some examples, with function words in *italics* and the primary stress of content words in **bold**:
- "*I* **have** *a* **fa**vor *to* **ask**."
- "**Jon**athan *will be** **late** *because his* **car broke down**."
- "*I'm* **go**ing *to the* **store la**ter."
- "*We do* **not agree** *with the* **out**come."
- "**Please** *don't* **tell** *me* **how** *the* **movie ends**."

(*Note that *be* is technically a content word here—it is the main verb in the phrase *will be late*—but it remains unstressed like a function word. Because they are often used as auxiliary verbs to form verb tense, conjugations of *be* are almost always unstressed in sentences irrespective of their technical grammatical function.)

Rhythm

English is what's known as a **stress-timed language**, which means that we leave approximately the same amount of time between stressed syllables in a sentence to create a natural cadence. These are sometimes referred to as the "beats" of a sentence.

This rhythm is easier to hear in sentences in which content words and function words alternate regularly, as in:
- "*I* **have** *a* **fa**vor *to* **ask**."

Things become more complicated when a sentence has multiple content or function words in a row.

Generally speaking, when multiple function words appear together, we vocally condense them into a single beat, meaning that they are spoken slightly faster than content words on either side.

When multiple single-syllable content words appear together, the reverse effect occurs: a greater pause is given between each word to create natural beats while still maintaining the proper amount of emphasis. (Content words with more than one syllable are usually not affected, since at least one part of the word is unstressed.)

Let's look at one of our previous examples to see this more clearly:
- "**Jon**athan *will be* **late** *because his* **car broke down**."

After the first syllable of the content word *Jonathan* is stressed, the words *will be* and the last two syllables of *Jonathan* are all unstressed and spoken together quickly to form a beat before the next content word, *late*. The next two words, *because his*, are also unstressed and spoken quickly to form the next beat. The next three words, *car broke down*, are all content words, and they are each stressed separately. Because of this, we add a slight pause between them to help the rhythm of the sentence sound natural.

This rhythmic pattern between stressed and unstressed words occurs when a sentence is spoken "neutrally"—that is, without any additional emphasis added by the speaker. However, we can add extra stress to any word in a sentence in order to achieve a particular meaning. This is known as emphatic stress.

Emphatic Stress

The convention regarding the stress and rhythm of content words and function words is consistent in **normal** (sometimes called "neutral") sentence stress. However, English speakers often place additional emphasis on a specific word or words to provide clarity, emphasis, or contrast; doing so lets the listener know more information than the words can provide on their own. Consider the following "neutral" sentence, with no stress highlighted at all:
• "Peter told John that a deal like this wasn't allowed."

Now let's look at the same sentence with emphatic stress applied to different words, and we'll see how its implied meaning changes accordingly:
• "*Peter* told John that a deal like this wasn't allowed." (Clarifies that *Peter*, as opposed to someone else, told John not to make the deal.)
• "Peter *told* John that a deal like this wasn't allowed." (Emphasizes the fact that John had been told not to make the deal but did so anyway.)
• "Peter told *John* that a deal like this wasn't allowed." (Clarifies that *John* was told not to make the deal, not someone else.)
• "Peter told John that a deal like this *wasn't* allowed." (Emphasizes that Peter said the deal was not allowed, indicating that John thought or said the opposite.)

Representing emphatic stress in writing

In writing, we normally use the *italic*, underline, or **bold** typesets to represent this emphasis visually. *Italics* is more common in printed text, while underlining is more common in handwritten text.

Another quick way to indicate emphatic stress in writing is to put the emphasized word or words in capital letters, as in:
• "Peter TOLD John that a deal like this wasn't allowed."

This is much less formal, however, and is only appropriate in conversational writing.

Quiz
(answers start on page 463)

1. Which type of word is typically stressed in a sentence?

a) Content words
b) Function words

2. Which of the following words would usually **not** be stressed in a sentence?

a) believe
b) person
c) happy
d) neither

3. What type of verb is usually unstressed in a sentence?

a) Action verbs
b) Phrasal verbs
c) Auxiliary verbs
d) Conditional verbs

4. How do we maintain rhythm when multiple content words appear in a row?

a) Say the words quickly, with minimal stress on each
b) Say the words with equal stress and a slight pause between each
c) Say the words quickly, with extra emphasis on each

Common Mistakes and Commonly Confused Words

English has a large number of **homophones**—words that have the same pronunciation but different meanings. In addition, there are many pairs of words that sound very *similar* but are slightly different when pronounced carefully, as well as those that are similar enough in spelling or meaning that they are often confused for one another in speech and writing.

In this section, we'll look at various sets of words that are commonly confused in writing due to these factors, highlighting the specific part (or parts) of the words that give writers trouble. We'll also look at some other minor spelling errors that writers sometimes encounter.

Where possible, we'll try to offer some mnemonic devices and other quick tips to help remember which spelling is the correct one. We'll also include mini-quizzes for some of the more difficult sets to test your ability to use each word correctly.

a lot vs. *allot* vs. *alot*

We use the phrase *a lot* to indicate a large amount (of something), as in:
• "I have **a lot** of homework tonight."
• "She likes you **a lot**."

The word *allot*, on the other hand, is a verb meaning "to distribute, assign, or allocate." For example:
• "We were each **allotted** enough money to cover two meals and minor expenses for each day of the convention."
• "Our father chose to **allot** each sibling a portion of the land in his will."

Spelling Tricks and Tips

A very common mistake is to write *alot* instead of *a lot*—but *alot* is not a word. You can remember the proper spellings this way:
• "*A lot* is not a word—it's two!"
• If what you mean to write is ***allot***, remember that it means "to **allo**cate."

a while vs. *awhile*

A while and *awhile* have very similar pronunciations: /əˈwaɪl/ and /ə waɪl/, respectively. The pause between the two-word phrase is not very distinct, though, and, because the two terms have very similar meanings, they are often and easily confused.

The single word *awhile* is only ever an adverb meaning "for a short period of time"; it can only modify verbs, as in:
• "Why don't we stop **awhile**?"

The phrase *a while* is what's known as a noun phrase—a group of two or more words that together act as a noun in a sentence. *A while* means "a period of time" (not necessarily a short one), and, like other noun phrases of time (such as *one*

410

day, last year, etc.), it can be used adverbially as well. Because of this, it is therefore acceptable to use it in the same way as *awhile*. For example:

✔ "Why don't we stop **awhile**?"
✔ "Why don't we stop **a while**?"

However, there are some instances in which we can only use one or the other. For example, when we are using a preposition (typically the word *for*), then we have to use *a while*. This is because prepositions can only be followed by nouns or noun phrases when forming prepositional phrases. For instance:

✔ "They sat and chatted **for <u>a while</u>**."
✖ "They sat and chatted **for <u>awhile</u>**."

If we drop the preposition, then we can use either spelling, as we've seen already:

✔ "They sat and chatted **a while**."
✔ "They sat and chatted **awhile**."

There are also other instances in which *while* is a noun and *a while* must be spelled as two words. For example:

✔ "I have **a while** yet before class, if you want to go grab a coffee." (*A while* is a noun functioning as the object of the verb *have*.)
✖ "I have **awhile** yet before class, if you want to go grab a coffee."

✔ "Yes, we had a dog once, but that was **a while** ago." (*A while* is a noun functioning as the antecedent of the pronoun *that*.)
✖ "Yes, we had a dog once, but that was **awhile** ago."

Spelling Tricks and Tips

Because *a while* can correctly be used in all instances and *awhile* is only appropriate some of the time, simply use the two-word spelling if you are unsure of the usage—it will always be correct.

Quiz

(answers start on page 463)

1. Choose the sentence in which *awhile* can be used.

a) "I listened _____, but lost interest quickly."
b) "Let's rest for _____ before we head to the summit."
c) "I need to stop at the store, but I'll be home in _____."
d) "I hope you have _____, because there is a lot we need to talk about."
e) All of the above
f) None of the above

2. Choose the sentence in which *a while* can be used.

a) "The manager talked _____, but I don't think anyone was really listening."
b) "Come by whenever suits you; I'll be here _____."
c) "I had a girlfriend for _____ in college, but it never got very serious."
d) "You might have to wait _____ before the tests are available."
e) All of the above
f) None of the above

3. When can *awhile* **not** be used in a sentence?

a) When it follows a preposition in a prepositional phrase.
b) When it acts as the object of a verb.
c) When it follows a verb that it modifies.
d) A & B
e) A & C

accept vs. *except*

When properly and carefully pronounced, *accept* and *except* have slightly different pronunciations of their initial vowels: *accept* is pronounced /ækˈsɛpt/, while *except* is pronounced /ɪkˈsɛpt/.

In casual speech, though, the initial *a-* and *e-* get reduced to the unstressed speech sound schwa (/ə/), and both words are pronounced the same way: /əkˈsɛpt/. Because of this blending of pronunciations, the two words can sometimes be confused in writing.

Accept is a verb broadly meaning "to receive or take," "to give an affirmative or approving answer," or "to understand or regard as true, proper, correct, or normal." For example:
• "Please **accept** my apologies for not writing back sooner."
• "We're pleased to **accept** your invitation to dinner."
• "You shouldn't just **accept** that what someone tells you is the truth."

Except can also function as a verb, but it is much more common as a preposition or a conjunction (meaning "other than; excluding; apart from"). For example:
• "Everyone **except** Janet came to the movie." (preposition)
• "I would like a bit of everything **except** the broccoli, please." (preposition)
• "He had every reason for wanting to become a doctor, **except** that the tuition fees were so high." (conjunction)
• "Samantha never says a word in class, **except** when she's causing a disruption." (conjunction)

As a verb, *except* means "to leave out, exclude, or omit," as in:
• "He was **excepted** from the requirement due to his trouble walking."

However, this use as a verb is rather uncommon in everyday speech and writing. Most of the time, if you are describing the action of a verb, *accept* is almost certain to be the correct choice.

Quiz

(answers start on page 463)

1. Which of the following sentences is **incorrect**?

a) "He accepted that there were flaws in the report."
b) "Do you know which schools have excepted you yet?"
c) "I would have left already, except I haven't said goodbye to my granny yet."
d) "Janet's wife will accept the award on her behalf."

2. Choose the sentence in which *accept* is correct.

a) "I like anything on my pizza _____ olives."
b) "_____ for that one time in middle school, I've never cheated on a test."
c) "You have to _____ responsibility for your actions like an adult."
d) "Everyone _____ me is wrong!"

3. Choose the sentence in which *except* is correct.

a) "It was hard to _____, but I knew I'd been beaten."
b) "Just _____ that you have a problem!"
c) "Please _____ my sincerest thanks."
d) "I'd like to believe it, _____ that they've deceived me in the past."

ad vs. *add*

Ad is an informal shortening of the word *advertisement*, and it always functions as a noun. For example:

• "I saw a really funny **ad** on TV the other day."
• "All these **ads** on the website are a little annoying, but I guess they have to make money somehow."

(*Ad* can also function as a shortening of the word *advantage* when talking about tennis, but this is a much more specific usage.)

Add, on the other hand, is not a shortening of anything; it is a verb meaning "to combine, join, or unite," as in:

• "So, we simply **add** the two figures to find our result."
• "We are delighted to **add** you to our rapidly expanding team."
• "I'd like to **add** my thoughts on the matter, if I may."

Spelling Tricks and Tips

Just remember that when you *add* something, you must *add* two **D**s together.

adverse vs. *averse*

Adverse and *averse* are both adjectives that have similar—but distinct—pronunciations and meanings.

Adverse (/ædˈvɜrs/ or /ˈædvɜrs/) means "antagonistic, hostile, or inimical; unfavorable or harmful to one's interests, welfare, or wishes; contrary or in the opposite direction to." It relates to actions or forces that are external to oneself. For example:

• "While the new drug has some great potential benefits, it has too many **adverse** side effects for me to recommend it."
• "It is certainly an **adverse** situation, but I'll just keep trying my best."
• "The **adverse** current slowed our small boat considerably."

Averse (/əˈvɜrs/) has the similar meaning of "opposed to or disinclined; having a strong feeling of antipathy, repugnance, or distaste." Unlike *adverse*, it is used to describe personal feelings, tendencies, or thoughts, and it is usually followed by the preposition *to*, as in:

• "The company is notoriously **averse** to changing their centuries-old business model."
• "I've always been **averse** to the smell of onions, ever since I was a kid."

Spelling Tricks and Tips

As a quick mnemonic trick, just remember that *adverse* essentially means *bad* (both spelled with a *D*). And, if you are *averse* to something, you have an *aversion* to it (both spelled without a *D*).

Quiz
(answers start on page 463)

1. Choose the sentence in which *adverse* is the correct spelling.
a) "She always was rather _____ to having visitors."
b) "We may have to turn back if the conditions remain so _____."
c) "The group is not _____ to using physical force to achieve its goals."
d) "The encounter made me _____ to confrontation."

2. Choose the sentence in which *averse* is the correct spelling.
a) "Though dismayed by the _____ outcome, we're hopeful of a successful appeal."
b) "I found the environment too _____ to complete my research."
c) "The product was met with much _____ criticism when it was released."
d) "I'm not _____ to hearing suggestions."

advice vs. *advise*

Advice is a noun, meaning "an opinion, suggestion, or recommendation." *Advise* is the verb form, meaning "to give (someone) an opinion, suggestion, or recommendation." For example:
• "Allow me to give you some **advice**: travel as much as you can while you're still young."
• "My father **advised** me to travel as much as I can."

• "Can you give me some **advice** on which computer I should buy?"
• "Can you **advise** me on which computer I should buy?"

In addition to their difference in meaning, the two words are also pronounced slightly differently. *Advice* ends with an /s/ sound that rhymes with *nice*: /ædˈvaɪs/. *Advise*, meanwhile, ends with a /z/ sound that rhymes with *wise*: /ædˈvaɪz/.

Spelling Tricks and Tips

We can remember the spelling and pronunciation differences like this:
• It's **nice** to give **advice**, but only let a **wise** person **advise** you.

affect vs. *effect*

In everyday speech, *affect* and *effect* usually share the same pronunciation: /əˈfɛkt/ (although, when articulated carefully, *effect* is pronounced /ɪˈfɛkt/). They also have similarities in their most common meanings, which can cause many writers to confuse the two terms.

Affect is usually a verb meaning "to act upon or produce a change or effect in," as in:
• "Be aware that snowy conditions may **affect** your commute this morning."
• "I think all this dust is **affecting** my breathing."
• "I've never seen a film that **affected** me so deeply before."

Effect, on the other hand, is a **noun** meaning "a result produced by some cause or the action of an agent." For example:
• "The decision to create bike lanes had the unintended **effect** of slowing down traffic across the city."
• "Your writing really has a profound **effect** on me!"
• "That medication has some potent side **effects**."

Essentially, *effect* is the <u>result</u> of *affect*—that is, if you *affect* something, you produce an *effect*.

Other meanings of *affect* and *effect*

It's also important to note that both *affect* and *effect* have other meanings, though they are used less commonly.

Affect has a secondary meaning as a verb, which is "to simulate, imitate, make a pretence of, or put on a false appearance," as in:
• "He always **affects** a worldly and tolerant demeanor, but, in reality, he's a very narrow-minded individual."

Affect can also be a noun meaning "a feeling or emotion, especially as conveyed through facial expression or body language," as in:
• "I couldn't help but notice that he had a rather somber **affect** when I saw him in town earlier."

(Uniquely, when *affect* has this meaning as a noun, it is pronounced /ˈæfɛkt/.)

Finally, *effect* can also function as a <u>verb</u>, meaning "to cause, bring about, or accomplish." For example:
• "My efforts to **effect** change in the company's policies have so far been unsuccessful."

This secondary meaning of *effect* is perhaps what gives writers difficulty when trying to remember its spelling, as its meaning ("to cause or bring about") is similar to the meaning of *affect* ("to act upon or produce change"). Again, this use of *effect* refers specifically to producing a <u>result</u>—you *effect* some kind of outcome, such as *change, hope, a cure, a decision,* etc., that is stated immediately after the verb. With the verb *affect*, meanwhile, the result is often vague or implied. For example:

✔ "The bright lights **affected** my vision." (The lights acted upon the speaker's vision, with the specific outcome being implied, so *affect* is correct.)

✘ "The bright lights **effected** my vision." (*My vision* is not an outcome or result, so *effect* is incorrect.)

✔ "The group is trying to **effect** a repeal to the antiquated law." (*A repeal* is the result or outcome of *the group*'s action, so *effect* is the correct verb.)

✘ "The group is trying to **affect** a repeal to the antiquated law." (*The group* is probably not trying to act upon or influence *a repeal*, so *affect* is incorrect.)

Spelling Tricks and Tips

Just remember that *affect* refers to **acting** upon something or someone, while *effect* refers to the **end** result.

Quiz
(answers start on page 463)

1. Choose the sentence in which *affect* is the correct spelling.

a) "Let's hope that the medicine had the desired _____."
b) "The new legislation goes into _____ on the first of May."
c) "I hope this drought won't _____ our crops."
d) "The new CEO vowed to _____ an overhaul of the company's public image."

2. Choose the sentence in which *effect* is the correct spelling.

a) "Don't let your personal problems _____ your work."
b) "We can't _____ real change without gaining the support of the people."
c) "She chose to _____ a British accent in an attempt to blend in."
d) "Failing this exam will _____ your final grade in the class."

3. Which spelling means "to cause, bring about, or accomplish"?

a) affect
b) effect

aisle vs. *isle*

The homophones *aisle* ("a passageway that divides rows of seats") and *isle* ("an island, especially a small one") are both pronounced /aɪl/; the **S** is silent in both.

The confusion between these two terms actually goes back to their Middle English origins, *ele* (*aisle*) and *ile* (*isle*), which have been confused for one another since the 15th century. *Ile*, taken from Old French, was originally spelled the same as it is in modern English—*isle*. When the silent **S** was reintroduced to *isle* in the late 16th century, it was erroneously applied to the term *ele* as well, which acquired the initial *a-* shortly thereafter.

Spelling Tricks and Tips

As a quick way to remember the correct spelling, keep in mind that because *isle* refers to small islands, it has fewer letters and is thus the **smaller** of the two words.

all ready vs. already

The phrase *all ready* functions as an adjective meaning "completely equipped, prepared, or ready." For example:
• "Are we **all ready** for the presentation to begin?"
• "OK, I think I'm **all ready** for my trip to Europe!"

Unlike the term *alright* (an informal contraction of the phrase *all right*), *already* is <u>not</u> a contraction of *all ready*. Instead, it is a separate word that functions as an adverb, meaning "at or prior to a specified time" or "sooner or faster than expected," as in:
• "I can't believe that it's April **already**!"
• "She had **already** mowed the lawn by the time I got home."

Spelling Tricks and Tips

There are a couple of quick mnemonic tricks we can use to remember the difference between the two words:
• *All* essentially means "everything," so if you are *all ready*, then **everything** is ready.
• *Already* means "sooner or faster than expected," and it is **faster** to write *already* than *all ready*.

all right vs. *alright*

Alright is a common contraction of the phrase *all right*, which can function as an adjective meaning "safe, sound, or well; healthy in mind or body; or correct, proper, or acceptable." It can also be used as an adverb meaning "yes; satisfactorily; or certainly." For example:
• "That car nearly hit us! Are you and your sister **all right**?"
• "I've haven't gotten as much sleep as I should, but I've been **all right** otherwise."
• "We'll have to wait a little longer, but that's **all right**."

• "**All right**, we'll agree to the terms of the settlement."
• "You did **all right**, kid. Nice job."
• "Wow, this place is nice, **all right**."

Although *alright* is very common in casual writing, it is still considered a nonstandard and informal term. If in doubt (and especially in formal or professional writing), use *all right*, as it is always the preferred spelling.

all together vs. *altogether*

Like *all ready* and *already*, *all together* and *altogether* have separate meanings despite their similarity in appearance and pronunciation.

The two-word phrase *all together* has the general meaning of "at the same time or in the same place as a group." For example:
• "Now that we're **all together**, I'd like to make an announcement."
• "It's so nice hearing the group singing **all together** again after so many years."

Altogether, on the other hand, means "entirely or completely; all included; on the whole," as in:
• "The meal was very good, but it was **altogether** too expensive."
• "**Altogether**, we've seen a 20 percent rise in profits this year."

Spelling Tricks and Tips

As a quick test to see which spelling is correct, try moving *all* to a different part of the sentence. If it still makes sense, then *all together* is correct; if not, *altogether* is the right choice. For example:

• "He hid the cash **all together** in the floorboards beneath his bed."

✔ "He hid **all** the cash **together** in the floorboards beneath his bed." (The new sentence makes sense, so *all together* is correct.)

• "After failing the class, he decided to drop out of school **altogether**."

✘ "After failing the class, he decided to drop out of **all** school **together**." (The sentence no longer makes sense, so *altogether* is correct.)

allude vs. *elude*

In casual speech, the verbs *allude* and *elude* are both pronounced /əˈlud/, with their first vowels being reduced to the unstressed schwa sound. (When spoken carefully, though, *elude* is pronounced /ɪˈlud/.)

Allude means "to make an indirect, obscure, or oblique reference (to something or someone else)." For example:

• "The character's name clearly **alludes** to the Irish pirate Grace O'Malley."
• "Are you **alluding** to the incident that supposedly happened in the 1950s?"
• "One reporter **alluded** to the campaign scandal during the press briefing, but it was quickly dropped from the discussion."

Elude, on the other hand, means "to avoid or escape from," as in:

• "They **eluded** the police by hiding in the sewer system."
• "I'm sorry, but your name **eludes** me."
• "Victory **eluded** the team once again after a last-minute touchdown by the opposing side."

Spelling Tricks and Tips

An easy way to choose the correct spelling is to remember that *elude* means escape, so it is spelled with an **E**. (Just also remember to only use one **L**.)

allusion vs. *illusion*

In casual speech, *allusion* and *illusion* are both pronounced /əˈluʒən/, with their first vowels being reduced to the unstressed schwa sound. (When spoken carefully, though, *illusion* is pronounced /ɪˈluʒən/.)

Though they sound very similar, the nouns *allusion* and *illusion* have very different meanings. The more common word, *illusion*, means "a false, erroneous, deceitful, or misleading perception, belief, or impression," as in:

• "They were under the **illusion** that fans of the first film would automatically want to see the sequel."
• "Magicians are really just very good at creating **illusions** that trick the mind."
• "That mirage is an **illusion**—just ignore it."

An *allusion*, meanwhile, is "an indirect, obscure, or oblique reference to something or someone else." For example:

• "The character's name is a clear **allusion** to the Irish pirate Grace O'Malley."
• "There was an **allusion** to the campaign scandal during the press briefing, but it was quickly dropped from the discussion."

Spelling Tricks and Tips

One way to remember which spelling to use is to keep in mind that the noun *allusion* is formed from the verb *allude*—if someone *alludes* to someone or something, they are making an *allusion*. *Illusion*, on the other hand, does not have a related verb form. So, if you can rework the sentence with the word functioning as a verb instead of a noun, the correct spelling will be *allusion*. For example:

• "There was an **allusion** to the campaign scandal during the press briefing, but it was quickly dropped from the discussion."

✔ "One reporter **alluded** to the campaign scandal during the press briefing, but it was quickly dropped from the discussion." (The verb form works in the new sentence, so *allusion* is the correct spelling.)

• "Magicians are really just very good at creating **illusions** that trick the mind."

✘ "Magicians are really just very good at **illuding** the mind." (We cannot use a verb form in the new sentence, so *illusion* is the correct spelling.)

Quiz

(answers start on page 463)

1. Choose the sentence in which *allusion* is the correct spelling.

a) "Though no _____ was made to his recent misfortune, it was evident that everyone in the room knew what had happened."
b) "This is no _____; what you see before you is as real as I am."
c) "People who see bodies of water in the desert are usually experiencing an optical _____."
d) "Don't be under the _____ that you aren't in any trouble because of all this!"

2. Choose the sentence in which *illusion* is the correct spelling.

a) "I feel like the author tried to cram that _____ into the book to appear clever."
b) "She made an _____ to her uncle's successful media empire."
c) "He created a clever _____ that fooled the entire audience."
d) "The _____ to the 1950s film went over the heads of the students."

3. Which of these words has an associated verb form?

a) allusion
b) illusion

alter vs. *altar*

Although they have the same pronunciation (/ˈɔltər/), *alter* and *altar* have very different meanings.

Alter is a verb meaning "to change or become different in some way," as in:
• "We had to **alter** our plans once we found out our funding was cut."

Altar, though, is a noun referring to a raised pedestal, platform, or other structure typically used in religious rites or sacrifices, as in:
• "The priest placed the goblet upon the **altar** at the end of the ceremony."

Spelling Tricks and Tips

If you are describing an <u>action</u>, then you should spell the word *alter*, since it is a verb; if you are talking about an <u>object</u>, the word will be spelled *altar*.

amoral vs. *immoral*

Amoral and *immoral* are both formed by attaching prefixes to the adjective *moral*. The prefixes "a-" and "in-" (which changes to "im-" in front of words beginning with **M**) have very similar but distinct meanings in this usage: "a-" in this case means "without or not possessing," while "im-" means "not or non-."

If someone or something is **amoral**, it means they do not have a sense of morality whatsoever or are impartial to it, as in:
• "An insect is **amoral**; it only does what its instincts tell it to do."
• "Lawyers must in many ways be **amoral**, defending their client in a court of law regardless of personal beliefs or opinions."
• "A child is **amoral** before a certain age, simply unable to grasp the concept of right versus wrong."

An **immoral** person or thing, though, does that which goes against or subverts accepted or conventional moral principles. For example:
• "The company's decision to rescind employees' health benefits may not be illegal, but it is certainly **immoral** in my opinion."
• "The film was considered **immoral** in its home country due to some of its graphic depictions."
• "Your **immoral** habits have brought shame onto this family."

aural vs. *oral*

Aural means "relating to, characterized by, or perceived by the ear," and by extension describes that which is heard or consists of listening. *Oral*, on the other hand, means "relating to, characterized by, or perceived by the mouth"; by extension, it is used to describe that which is spoken or consists of speech.

Both words are most commonly pronounced /ˈɔrəl/, and they can be particularly tricky because they are often used in the same kind of way. Consider the following two examples:
• "There's going to be an **aural** exam on Wednesday."
• "There's going to be an **oral** exam on Wednesday."

Both sentences are completely correct, but mean different things. In the first, the exam is going to be based on **listening**, while the second sentence is describing an exam based on **speaking**.

Spelling Tricks and Tips

When we are deciding which spelling to use in our writing, we can remember that *aural* has the same general meaning as *audio*, while the **O** in *oral* looks like an open mouth.

In speech, though, it might be best to avoid *aural* where possible so as not to confuse the listener. For example, our previous example could be reworked as:
• "There's going to be a **listening** exam on Wednesday."
or
• "The exam on Wednesday **will be based on listening**."

Now the meaning is completely unambiguous, whether spoken or read.

bail vs. *bale*

The word *bail* has a variety of meanings. As a noun, it most often means "a security, usually money, paid to be released from imprisonment." As a verb, it can mean "to pay a security to release someone from prison," "to empty water from a boat," "to eject from an aircraft," or "to abandon something, such as a project or other enterprise." Informally, it can also mean "to help with or extricate from a difficult task or situation." For example:

• "You're just lucky we had enough money for your **bail**."
• "She posted **bail** last night."

• "I have to **bail** your brother out of jail."
• "The sailors began **bailing** out the dinghy."
• "We had to **bail** on the project after we found out our funding had been cut."
• "You can't always rely on me to **bail** you out of trouble."

The homophone *bale* has a much narrower definition. It can be a noun meaning "a large bundle, especially of raw materials, bound by ropes, cords, or wires," or a verb meaning "to wrap in or create a bale." For example:

• "I worked for a month **baling** hay at my friend's farm."

• "The warehouse was filled with giant **bales** of paper."

Spelling Tricks and Tips

Just remember that if you are going to *bail* out a boat, you would want to use something like a **pail** to scoop up water.

bait vs. *bate*

Bait refers to food or other lures used to trap or catch an animal (or, by extension, a temptation, enticement, or allurement). It can be used as a noun, referring to the lure itself, or as a verb, referring to the act of using a lure, temptation, or enticement. For example:

• "The worms haven't been working, so I'm going to try a different **bait**."
• "I tried to draw him into the argument by insulting him, but he didn't take the **bait**."

• "We **baited** the fly trap with honey."
• "They tried **baiting** me into staying with a pay raise, but my mind was made up."

Bate is an uncommon term that has largely been replaced by *abate*, meaning "to lessen, diminish, moderate, restrain, or take away from." However, *bate* is still preserved in modern English in the idiomatic phrase "with **bated** breath," which means "nervously, excitedly, or anxiously, as if holding one's breath." For example:

• "We waited *with bated breath* while they announced the results of the competition."

Because *bate* is so uncommon in all other usages, it is a frequent mistake to write "with **baited** breath." Just be sure to remember than one can only have "**bated**" breath," while we use *bait* in all other circumstances.

ball vs. *bawl*

A *ball* is any spherical object, especially as used in various sports (such as a base**ball**, soccer **ball**, basket**ball**, etc.). *Ball* can also be a verb meaning "to become or make into a ball." (It can also refer to formal social functions that feature dancing, though this is a more specific usage.)

Bawl, meanwhile, is usually used as a verb, meaning "to cry, sob, or shout loudly or vehemently," as in:
• "My brother started **bawling** when my parents grounded him."

As with *bait* and *bate*, the confusion for most writers occurs when using an idiomatic phrase—in this case, "**bawl** someone out," which means "to scold or reprimand someone very loudly and harshly." (It can also be reworked as "get **bawled** out," meaning "to receive a harsh or severe reprimand or rebuke.") For example:
• "The boss just ***bawled*** *Mike out* for how he handled the account."
• "I *got* ***bawled*** *out* by my teacher for falling asleep in class."

Because *ball* is much more common than *bawl* in everyday speech and writing—and because *bawl* is usually associated with crying, rather than shouting—it is a common mistake to write "**ball** someone out" or "get **balled** out." However, it's important to remember that, generally speaking, *ball* will only be used in reference to a spherical object or a game played with one. If you are talking about loud crying, sobbing, or yelling, *bawl* is the correct spelling.

bear vs. *bare*

As an adjective, *bare* means "without covering or clothing; lacking content, furnishings, or equipment; or unadorned or unembellished." As a verb, *bare* means "to uncover, expose, or reveal," or, more simply, "to make bare." For example:
• "In the early 20th century, women were not allowed to have **bare** legs when swimming in public."
• "The animal **bared** its teeth to appear threatening."

The homophone *bear* has a variety of different meanings as a verb, most usually "to carry, hold, or cause to move; to hold up, support, endure, or have tolerance for; to produce, yield, or give birth to; or to warrant, be worthy of, or be capable of," as in:
• "We all have our own burdens to **bear**."
• "It's important to know which kinds of plants **bear** edible fruit in the wild."
• "I don't know that this **bears** any further scrutiny."
(As a noun, of course, *bear* refers to the large omnivorous mammals with furry coats.)

The confusion for some writers comes when using certain idiomatic phrases and phrasal verbs that use the verb *bear*, such as:
• *grin and bear it* ("to endure or accept something unpleasant or difficult with good humor")
• *bear down (on someone or something)* ("to physically press or weigh down on someone or something; to try to accomplish something with all one's effort or energy; to advance upon or move toward something in a threatening or overbearing manner")
• *bear a resemblance to* ("to slightly resemble someone or something")
• *bear in mind* ("to keep a piece of information in one's mind when doing something or making a decision")

Perhaps the most commonly confused of these phrases is "bear arms," which means "to carry weapons." To "**bare** arms" is not correct, unless you are talking about arms that no longer have anything covering them.

birth vs. *berth*

The words *birth* and *berth* are both pronounced the same way: /bɜrθ/.

The more common term, *birth*, is primarily a noun referring to the act or process of being born or, by extension, ancestry, lineage, or origin. For example:
• "My son's **birth** is still the happiest moment of my life."
• "She's been a really happy, placid child since **birth**."
• "My grandfather was of Turkish **birth**."

Berth, meanwhile, has a number of different meanings. It is also primarily a noun, but it means "sufficient space for a vessel or vehicle to maneuver, dock, anchor, or park"; "a built-in bed or bunk in a vessel or train"; "accommodations, as at a hotel"; or "a job or employment, especially on a ship." For example:

• "Make sure you keep a wide **berth** of other boats around you."
• "Seamen are not allowed any personal items in, on, or around their **berths** during leave."
• "We eventually found a **berth** at an inn at the edge of town."
• "He secured a **berth** working as a chef aboard the cruise liner."

Berth is also used in the idiomatic phrase "give someone or something a wide berth," meaning to stay away from or avoid someone or something, as in:

• "I recommend you *give the boss a wide* **berth** today—I think he's in a foul mood."

Spelling Tricks and Tips

Because *berth* is much less common in everyday speech and writing, it can be easy to use *birth* in its place by mistake. If you're trying to determine which spelling is correct, just remember that one of the meanings of *berth* is "a bed," so it is spelled with an **E**.

break vs. *brake*

The word *break* has a huge variety of meanings, but its most common usage is as a verb meaning "to divide or cause to separate (something) into pieces, especially suddenly or violently" or "to cause to no longer function correctly or at all." For example:

• "Please be careful not to **break** that mirror!"
• "The cell phone company said they would replace my phone if I **break** it."

Another common use of the word *break* is as a noun meaning "a pause or interval from some activity, especially work," as in:

• "I'm going for a coffee **break** if anyone wants to come with me."

The word *brake* is pronounced the same way (/breɪk/), but it has a much narrower definition in everyday speech and writing. As a noun, it means "something that slows or stops movement or action," and it can function as a verb to mean "to cause to slow or stop," as in:

• "Use the **brakes**! You're going too fast!"
• "Be sure you have enough time to **brake** before you come to the intersection."
• "I think we need to put the **brakes** on this project for a little while."

If you are talking about something being separated into pieces, interrupted, or not working any more, then use the spelling *break*; if you are talking about slowing something down, then *brake* is the correct spelling.

breath vs. *breadth*

These two words sometimes cause confusion because their spelling and pronunciation are very similar.

Breath, by far the more common of the two, is pronounced /brɛθ/. It most simply refers to the act or an instance of breathing in air, as in:

• "I have to hold my **breath** every time we drive by the landfill."
• "Just take a deep **breath** and tell me what happened."

Breadth has a very similar pronunciation: /brɛdθ/. The /d/ sound (sometimes sharpened to a /t/ sound, depending on dialect) is often very subtly pronounced, with it blending into the /θ/ sound produced by **TH**. Because of this somewhat ambiguous pronunciation distinction, some writers mistakenly use *breath* when they mean to write *breadth*, which means "the linear measurement from side to side," or, by extension, "wideness of range, scope, tolerance, viewpoints, etc." For example:
- "The **breadth** and ornate décor of the cathedral was stunning."
- "For me, the greatest benefit of going to college is the **breadth** of new ideas and perspectives you can encounter."

Spelling Tricks and Tips

A quick way to remember the correct spelling is to keep in mind that, when used literally, *breadth* is roughly synonymous with *width*. If what you're writing does not have to do with the wideness of something, *breath* will be the correct spelling.

breath vs. *breathe*

The best known function of silent E is to mark a change in the sound of a vowel from "short" to "long," as in the difference between *cap* (/kæp/) and *cape* (/keɪp/).

However, it can also indicate changes in the pronunciation of certain consonant sounds. In the case of *breath* and *breathe*, the pronunciation changes from /brɛθ/ (rhyming with *death*) to /brið/ (rhyming with *seethe*). In addition to the pronunciation of the vowel digraph **EA** changing from /ɛ/ to /i/, the consonant digraph **TH** changes in pronunciation from /θ/ (as in *theme*) to /ð/ (as in *these*).

Finally, the silent E at the end of *breathe* indicates that the word shifts in meaning from a noun to a verb. A **breath** (noun) is an inhalation of air into the lungs; to **breathe** (verb) refers to the <u>action</u> of inhaling air into the lungs. For instance:
- "I stopped playing the saxophone for a minute to take a **breath**."
- "I have to hold my **breath** every time I drive past the landfill."

- "I started feeling very anxious and found it difficult to **breathe**."
- "Throughout the movie, I just couldn't believe that the characters could somehow **breathe** on the alien planet."

Several other pairs of words follow this pattern in which silent E indicates a shift in meaning from a noun to a verb related to that noun, as in *bath* vs. *bathe*, *cloth* vs. *clothe*, *teeth* vs. *teethe*, and *wreath* vs. *wreathe*.

canvas vs. *canvass*

A *canvas* is most often a tough, heavy cloth made from cotton, hemp, or linen, used especially to create sails, tents, or a surface on which to paint. In the case of paintings, *canvas* is the word for the surface itself, not just the materials from which it is made. (By extension, it can also refer figuratively to a background against which an event unfolds, as in, "The French Revolution began against a dark **canvas** of poverty and oppression.")

The similar word, *canvass*, has very different meanings. It is most often used as a verb meaning "to solicit votes, orders, advertising, or opinions (from people)" or "to investigate, examine, discuss, or scrutinize (something) closely or thoroughly." For example:
- "We've created a thinktank to **canvass** the issue of homelessness in the state."
- "I've been **canvassing** the city for the past three weeks to get people to vote 'Yes' in the upcoming referendum."
- "We plan to **canvass** residents about their opinion on the recent tax proposals."

Because *canvass* has such specific uses, and because it is very often used in the conjugated forms *canvassed* or *canvassing*, the common mistake many writers make is to use *canvas* instead when the verb is in its base form. Just be aware that the word must end "-ss" if you are using it as a verb; if you are describing a physical object, it is spelled with just one "-s."

censor vs. *sensor* vs. *censure*

The word *censor* was originally a noun referring to a magistrate who oversaw and upheld moral standards. In modern times, it means "a person authorized to examine various media, such as books, plays, and films, and suppress or expurgate vulgar, obscene, or otherwise objectionable content." Early in the 19th century, this use was extended to a verb meaning "to suppress or remove objectionable material." Here are some examples:

• "The experimental film never left the country due to the strict oversight of the state's **censor**."
• "The book, heavily **censored** upon its initial release, was republished in its entirety this year."
• "It came to light that upper management had been **censoring** employees' reports."

The homophone **sensor**, however, is only a noun, derived from the word *sense*. It uses the suffix of agency "-or" to mean "a device that senses and responds to signals or other physical stimuli," as in:

• "Most phones now have **sensors** that determine how bright the screen should be."

Spelling Tricks and Tips

We can remember the difference between these two spellings more easily by keeping in mind that *sensor* comes from *sense*. If what we're talking about doesn't have anything to do with *sensing*, then the correct spelling will likely be *censor*.

censure

There is also a third term with a similar spelling and pronunciation: *censure*. Like *censor*, this word can be a noun (meaning "a severe rebuke or an expression of strong disapproval") or a verb (meaning "to express such a rebuke or disapproval"), as in:

• "Following a review of the case, the committee concluded that no **censure** was necessary."
• "After being **censured** by the advisory board, Professor Keating considered an early retirement."

However, *censure* has a slightly different pronunciation than *censor* or *sensor*: /ˈsɛnʃər/ (SEN-sher). *Censor* and *sensor*, on the other hand, are both pronounced /ˈsɛnsər/ (SEN-ser).

Quiz
(answers start on page 463)

1. Choose the sentence in which *censor* is the correct spelling.
a) "The aircraft's _____ detected a breach in the hull."
b) "Despite numerous countries' attempts to _____ the book, it still became a huge worldwide success."
c) "The committee voted to _____ one of its members for his comments."
d) "We've installed a new _____ that can tell when your phone is in your pocket."

2. Choose the sentence in which *sensor* is the correct spelling.
a) "She received no _____ or punishment for her alleged involvement in the scandal."
b) "Many have accused the social media site of trying to _____ users who post political content."
c) "Before his time as a _____ for the state, he worked as a principal at a private high school."
d) "Electromagnetic radiation disrupted the _____ on the spacecraft."

3. Choose the sentence in which *censure* is the correct spelling.
a) "The board decided to _____ the manager, but did not recommend dismissal from the job."
b) "It is hypocritical to champion free speech and then try to _____ those who have a different opinion than you."
c) "The _____ that detects when the ink has been refilled isn't working properly."
d) "The _____ banned the book for its graphic content."

4. Which of these words is pronounced **differently** than the other two?
a) censor
b) sensor
c) censure

chord vs. *cord*

The consonant digraph CH can sometimes be difficult for writers because, while it is most commonly associated with the /tʃ/ sound (as in *church* or *chapter*), it can also form the "hard **C**" sound /k/ (as in *chemistry* or *archive*).

The word *chord* is one instance in which **CH** takes the /k/ sound (/kɔrd/). This can sometimes lead to confusion with the word *cord*, which is pronounced the same way.

Chord most commonly means "a combination of three or more musical notes played in combination to produce a single harmonic sound," as in:
• "I only learned how to play a few **chords** on guitar before I lost interest."

(*Chord* can also mean "a line that joins two points on a curve," but this is specific to mathematics and is not common in everyday speech and writing.)

Cord has a wider range of meaning, but it usually refers to a length of interwoven fibers—that is, a rope or a string. This extends to other things that have a shape similar to a rope, especially parts of anatomy, such as the *spinal **cord*** or *umbilical **cord***.

Spelling Tricks and Tips

As a quick trick to remembering the spelling of *chord*, keep in mind that it refers to multiple musical notes being played together to form a single sound; in the same way, we use the two consonants **C** and **H** together to form a single /k/ sound at the beginning of the word.

For any physical object, we must always use the spelling *cord*.

compliment vs. *complement*

These two words have the same pronunciation—/ˈkɒmpləmənt/—but they have very different meanings. The more common of the two, *compliment*, is usually a noun meaning "a remark, expression, or gesture of respect, praise, commendation, or admiration." It can also be used as a verb meaning "to make such a remark, expression, or gesture." For example:
• "One of my students gave me the nicest **compliment** today."
• "I would like to **compliment** you on your recent charity work!"

Complement, on the other hand, generally refers to something that completes, improves, or perfects something else. Like *compliment*, it can also function as a verb to describe the act of completing, improving, or perfecting something. For example:
• "Sweet flavors are often a great **complement** to spicy foods."
• "The new manager position will act as a **complement** to your existing role."
• "The company started by developing software, but that division now merely **complements** their lucrative hardware business."

(*Complement* also has a few other specific meanings that extend from this basic definition, such as "an angle related to another such that their sum is equal to 90°"; the quantity or amount that fills or completes something; and, in grammar, "a word or group of words necessary to complete the meaning of another part of a sentence.")

Spelling Tricks and Tips

Although *compliment* is the more common word, be careful not to use it in situations in which *complement* is the correct spelling. Remember, a *complement* **comple**tes something else, which is why it is spelled with an **E**.

Quiz

(answers start on page 463)

1. Choose the sentence in which *compliment* is the correct spelling.
a) "That suit really _____ your figure."
b) "I find that béarnaise sauce is the perfect _____ to high-quality steak."
c) "I appreciate your _____, but I really can't take credit."
d) "Now that the plane has its full _____ of passengers, we are ready to begin departure."

2. Choose the sentence in which *complement* is the correct spelling.
a) "Her strong communication skills really _____ her managerial talents."
b) "He seems a bit too quick to _____ his superiors' decisions, if you ask me."
c) "Jack is very talented but very humble, always trying to downplay any _____ he receives."
d) "I'd love to meet the chef so I can give him a _____ on this delicious meal."

cue vs. *queue*

A *cue* (pronounced /kju/) is either a signal or stimulus used to prompt or elicit a certain action, or a long, pointed stick used in the games of billiards and pool. *Cue* can also function as a verb based on the first definition, meaning "to give such a prompt or signal." For example:

• "He hit the ball with such force that the tip of his **cue** dug into the surface of the pool table."
• "I missed my **cue** and ended up walking onto the stage in the wrong part of the scene."
• "Will you please **cue** the lights so the audience knows we're about to begin?"

The homophone *queue* means "a line of people" or "to wait in a line of people," as in:

• "If you wish to speak to a member of the staff, please join the **queue**."
• "It feels like I've been **queueing** for hours!"

While *cue* has a very phonetic spelling (meaning its pronunciation is easy to deduce from its spelling, and vice versa), *queue* can be a bit more difficult due to the seemingly extraneous **UE** at the end of the word, which comes directly from its French origin.

Queue is also much more common in British English than it is in American English (whose speakers tend to just say "line" or "wait in line"), so many writers who have learned the American patterns of spelling and pronunciation incorrectly use the spelling *cue* instead. Unfortunately, there's no easy way to remember the correct spelling of *queue*; it just has to be committed to memory.

defuse vs. *diffuse*

The words *defuse* and *diffuse* are very often confused due to their similar pronunciations as well as a perceived overlap in meaning.

When pronounced carefully, the "de-" in *defuse* (/diˈfjuz/) receives a bit of extra stress, and the **E** takes the "long" pronunciation (/i/) found in words like *theme* or *discrete*. On the other hand, the **I** in *diffuse* (/dɪˈfjuz/) takes the standard "short **I**" sound found in words like *rip* or *dip*. In casual, everyday speech, though, the stress on the first syllable of both words is often reduced, resulting in the same pronunciation: /dəˈfjuz/.

The verb *defuse* is formed by combining the prefix "de-" (in this case, meaning "undo") with the noun *fuse* (a trigger used to detonate an explosive device) to mean "to remove, disable, or destroy a fuse from an explosive device," as in:
• "Officers were able to **defuse** the device before it was able to explode."

By extension, *defuse* can also be used figuratively to mean "to subdue, lessen, or remove tension, hostility, or danger." For instance:
• "The secretary of state has been in intense negotiations with the foreign ambassador in an attempt to **defuse** the crisis in the region."
• "He tried telling a joke to **defuse** argument, but it didn't go over very well."

Diffuse, on the other hand, is derived from the Latin *diffusus*. It is also primarily a verb, most often meaning "to spread, scatter, or pour out widely," as in:
• "The smoke from the burning paper **diffused** slowly throughout the room."
• "Rumors surrounding his source of income have **diffused** across the Internet."

By extension, *diffuse* can also mean "to weaken or make less intense due to scattering," as in:
• "The dirty window panes **diffused** the sunlight into a murky haze."
(Note that *diffuse* can also function as an adjective, usually meaning "widely spread, scattered, or dispersed," as in:
• "The room was filled with a soft, **diffuse** light."
• "The government's efforts have been too **diffuse** to be of any real effect."
In this usage, *diffuse* is pronounced with an /-s/ sound at the end, rather than /-z/: /dɪˈfjus/.)

It is the figurative application of *diffuse* that causes most confusion for writers, as it seems logical to use it in a way similar to the figurative use of *defuse*. For example, "**diffusing** tension" might seem correct, as it could be interpreted as meaning "making the tension less intense." Because this is so widespread, some sources even consider this as being correct.

However, most grammar and spelling resources do not accept this, arguing that the only reason *diffuse* can mean "to weaken" is that the thing being weakened is spread thinly across a wider area, which is not what happens when one lessens or weakens tension, danger, etc. When referring to making situations less tense, hostile, or dangerous, use *defuse* because it will always be correct.

Spelling Tricks and Tips

When trying to determine which spelling to use, remember that "de-" means "remove," and you'll know that *defuse* is the right word to *remove* a *fuse* from an explosive—or an explosive situation. **Diffuse** has a **diff**erent **use** altogether.

Quiz
(answers start on page 463)

1. Choose the sentence in which *defuse* is the correct spelling.
a) "Gossip tends to _____ through this town like ink through water."
b) "Negotiators have been trying to _____ the hostage crisis for nearly three hours."
c) "The crowd started to _____ as soon as law enforcement arrived."
d) "He was accused of trying to _____ anti-government sentiments across the region."

2. Choose the sentence in which *diffuse* is the correct spelling.
a) "We are closing the area until the bomb squad has been able to _____ the explosive device."
b) "A special ops team was sent in to _____ the rebels' plot."
c) "We're going to have a workshop to help employees _____ tensions in the workplace."
d) "The product was designed to slowly _____ fragrance in the room to help eliminate foul odors."

dependent vs. *dependant*

The suffixes "-ant" and "-ent" can cause writers a lot of confusion because they are pronounced the same and often have the same meanings (they are both used to form nouns of agency and adjectives that describe a state or quality).

Two words that typify this confusion are *dependent* and *dependant*. The word *dependent* is primarily an adjective meaning "relying or depending on someone or something for aid, support, direction, etc.," or "influenced, controlled, determined by, or contingent on something else," as in:

• "I've been **dependent** on financial aid to help pay for college tuition."
• "The company's profit will be **dependent** on whether this new device proves a popular success."

Dependant on the other hand, is only a noun meaning "one who relies or depends on someone else, especially for financial support," as in:

• "You are entitled to additional tax benefits if you have one or more **dependants** living with you at home."

This spelling is more common in British English, though; in American English, it is more common to use *dependent* for both the noun and adjective meanings. Just be aware that you can <u>only</u> use *dependent* when the word is functioning as an adjective.

independent vs. *independant*

The confusion between *dependent* and *dependant* leads to a similar mistake when trying to write *independent* ("not dependent on or determined by someone or something else"). Just keep in mind that the word *independent* is only ever an adjective, so, like the adjective-form of *dependent*, it is <u>always</u> spelled "-ent" (*independant* is not a word).

desert vs. *dessert*

This pair of words causes a lot of problems for writers because they have very similar spellings and pronunciations.

Desert has two primary meanings. As a noun, it is usually pronounced /ˈdɛzərt/ (with the stress on the first syllable) and means "a barren region devoid of vegetation, especially an arid region that has very little rainfall." As a verb, it is pronounced /dɪˈzɜrt/ (with the stress on the <u>second</u> syllable), and it means "to leave or abandon someone, something, or someplace" or "to forsake someone or something, especially in spite of a duty or responsibility." For example:

• "After spending a week camping in the **desert**, I gained a newfound appreciation for modern conveniences."
• "I can't believe he **deserted** the fledgling company to go work for some giant corporation."
• "The soldier was held on charges of **deserting** his post."

Dessert is pronounced the same way as the verb definition of *desert*: /dɪˈzɜrt/. It is only ever a noun, meaning "a sweet dish, typically served as the last course of a meal," as in:

• "Would you like ice cream or pudding for **dessert**?"

Spelling Tricks and Tips

Fortunately, there is a very common trick to determine which spelling to use:
• We always want <u>more</u> de**ss**ert, which is why it has <u>more</u> **S**'s than de*sert*.

"just deserts" vs. "just desserts"

While the two definitions of *desert* we already looked at are by far the most common, there is actually a third definition of the word. It is a noun (usually pluralized) meaning "something that is earned, deserved, or merited"; it has the same pronunciation as the verb form of the word, /dɪˈzɜrt/.

While not common in everyday speech and writing, this meaning of the word still survives in one phrase: *just deserts*, meaning "an outcome that one deserves, especially a punishment." For example:

• "The school bully got his **just deserts** when he was expelled for his behavior."

It is a very common mistake to write this phrase as *just desserts*, due to the similarity in the two words' spelling and their shared pronunciation, as well as because this meaning of *deserts* is very uncommon outside of this phrase. To remember this spelling, keep in mind that someone getting their *just **deserts*** is getting what they **deserve**—and they certainly don't deserve dessert!

discreet vs. *discrete* vs. *discretion*

The adjectives *discreet* and *discrete* are both pronounced the same way: /dɪˈskrit/.

Discreet is the more common of the two, meaning "unobtrusive; made, done, or situated so as to attract little or no notice" or "careful to avoid social awkwardness or discomfort, especially by not sharing delicate information." For example:
• "I would just ask that you be **discreet** regarding the ties between your father and this institution."
• "We are always **discreet** with our clients' personal information."
• "They chose a **discreet** location for their meeting."

The less common term, *discrete*, means "separate or distinct from another thing or things" or "consisting of unconnected, separate, and distinct parts," as in:
• "To help conceptualize the notion of time, we break it down into **discrete** units, such as seconds, minutes, and hours."
• "Speech is thought of as being **discrete**, a collection of unique individual sounds that form a system."

Adding to this confusion is the noun *discretion*, which looks like it should be derived from the adjective *discrete*, due to the single **E** before "-tion." *Discretion*, however, actually means "an act or instance of being *discreet*," as in:
• "Your **discretion** is appreciated while we investigate this issue."

(The noun form of *discrete*, on the other hand, is *discrete**ness**.*)

Spelling Tricks and Tips

Luckily, there is a helpful mnemonic we can use to help remember the appropriate meaning for the two different spellings:
• *Discrete* means "separate" or "distinct," so we must **separate** the two **E**s with a **T**.
• *Discreet* usually refers to keeping something "close to your chest," so the two **E**s are kept close together.

Quiz
(answers start on page 463)

1. Choose the sentence in which *discreet* is the correct spelling.

a) "He told her the results in a low, _____ voice."
b) "The phone's _____ components can be removed and replaced individually."
c) "The governor has established three _____ teams to investigate the issue."
d) "There are, of course, several _____ reasons for the company's failure."

2. Choose the sentence in which *discrete* is the correct spelling.

a) "He allegedly received illicit payments in _____ brown envelopes."
b) "Their staff is renowned for being exceptionally _____."
c) "He kept a _____ distance from the target."
d) "Our country as a whole is formed from _____ states, each with their own laws and cultural outlook."

3. Which of the following words can be made into the noun *discretion*?

a) discreet
b) discrete

disinterested vs. *uninterested*

In modern English, ***dis****interested* primarily means "impartial or free from bias," while ***un****interested* simply means "not interested or caring; indifferent." For example:

• "It is imperative to find jurors who are **disinterested** in the outcomes of the defendant or the plaintiff."
• "I've really become **uninterested** in video games in the last few years."

These two terms are often used interchangeably (with *disinterested* being more common) because of the similarity in meaning between the prefixes "dis-" and "un-", and because the specific usage of *interested* ("partial or biased") is less common than the more general meaning of "caring or having an interest."

Stricter grammarians decry using the two terms interchangeably, maintaining that they should only be used to express the separate meanings above (it is especially frowned upon to use *uninterested* to mean "impartial or unbiased"). In reality, the distinction has been eroded in recent years, and *disinterested* is very commonly used instead of *uninterested*. It's also worth mentioning that the original meanings of these words were actually the <u>opposite</u> until the 1700s, so there is historical precedence in using the two words in both ways.

However, especially in more formal writing, it is best to maintain the modern distinction in meaning between the two different terms, because it is always correct to do so.

dissociate vs. *disassociate*

These two terms are unique on this list because it is not a mistake to use one or the other—they are **synonyms**, so they have the exact same meaning: "to remove from or cause to break the association of." Some writers and guides prefer *dissociate*, possibly because it is shorter and more to the point, but it makes no difference to use *disassociate* instead; it just comes down to personal preference. For example:

✔ "He tried to **dissociate** himself from the company following the public scandal." (correct)
✔ "He tried to **disassociate** himself from the company following the public scandal." (also correct)

dissociate vs. *disociate*

One potential spelling error that may arise out of these two forms is to mistakenly spell *dissociate* with just one **S**—*disociate*. Because *disassociate* only has a single **S** initially, and because we pronounce the **SS** in *dissociate* as a single /s/ sound, it's easy to think the alternate spelling is only spelled with one **S**. Be careful not to fall into this trap, though, because it is always incorrect.

dual vs. *duel*

The adjective *dual* stems from the Latin word *duo* and shares its meaning, "two." For example:
• "This portable **dual**-speaker sound system is perfect for parties."
• "The position will have **dual** roles, both manager and content creator."

The meaning of the noun *duel*, "combat between two opponents," is also associated with *duo* (though it was actually derived from the Latin word *duellem*, meaning "war"), and it can also be used as a verb to describe the action of two people fighting. For example:
• "One of the classic tropes of old Westerns was the notion of being challenged to a **duel**."
• "The two politicians **dueled** during last night's debate."

Spelling Tricks and Tips

The two words share the same pronunciation, /ˈduəl/, which leads many writers to mix up their spellings. Just remember that *dual* is an **a**djective because it is spelled with an **A**, while *duel* is a noun that can function as a verb because it is spelled with an **E**.

elicit vs. *illicit*

The word *elicit* is only ever a verb meaning "to evoke, provoke, give rise to, or bring to light," as in:
• "The announcement **elicited** laughter from the audience."
• "I tried to **elicit** a confession from him, but he remained resolute in his silence."

Illicit, which is pronounced the same way as *elicit* (/ɪˈlɪsɪt/), is an adjective meaning "illegal, improper, or not permitted by moral or ethical customs." For example:
• "The major achievements from her time in office were marred by allegations of **illicit** deals with major businesses."
• "The **illicit** practice has steadily been gaining ground, with many hoping for legalization in the near future."

Spelling Tricks and Tips

Here are two quick mnemonic tips to remember the difference between these two terms:
• *Elicit* is a **v**erb, so it is spelled with an **E**.
• *Illicit* generally means **ill**egal, so it begins with *ill-*.

ensure vs. *insure*

It can be especially tricky to distinguish between the verbs *ensure* and *insure* due to their similarity in both pronunciation and meaning.

The two words have very similar pronunciations: /ɛnˈʃʊər/ and /ɪnˈʃʊər/, respectively. However, both tend to have the stress on their first vowel reduced in casual speech, resulting in the same pronunciation: /ənˈʃʊər/.

In addition to their pronunciations, the meanings of these two words also overlap. The most common definition of *ensure* is "to guarantee, secure, or make certain," as in:
• "The massive popularity of their new product has **ensured** the company's survival for the foreseeable future."
• "Our aim is to **ensure** that you have the most pleasant stay possible."

The most common definition of *insure* is "to protect or guarantee against damage, harm, loss, theft, etc.," or "to issue (someone) with an insurance policy." For example:
• "Legally, you must **insure** your car before you can drive it."
• "The insurance company refused to **insure** me again after the latest accident."
• "We recommend arriving early to **insure** against missing out on a spot in the theater."

In American English, though, *insure* is commonly used to mean the same thing as *ensure*, so it is generally accepted that the following sentences would be correct in American English writing:
✔ "The massive popularity of their new product has **insured** the company's survival for the foreseeable future."
✔ "Our aim is to **insure** that you have the most pleasant stay possible."

While you will probably be fine using *insure* in either instance if you are in the United States, it is always correct to use *ensure* to mean "make certain" and *insure* to mean "protect against harm or damage."

envelop vs. *envelope*

Envelop is a verb meaning "to cover, wrap up, fold over, or surround." For example:
• "A shroud of mist slowly **enveloped** the town."
• "The first thing I'm going to do when I get home is **envelop** my daughter in my arms."

Envelope, on the other hand, is a noun meaning "a wrapping or covering, especially that which covers and contains a letter," as in:
• "Please send the completed form in a plain white **envelope**."

Both words are ultimately derived from the French *envelopper*, though *envelope* comes from the French back-formation *enveloppe* and is much more recent in English.

The silent E at the end of *envelope* tells us that the previous **O** has a "long" vowel sound (/oʊ/), while the **O** of *envelop* has a reduced vowel sound known as a **schwa** (/ə/). However, there is also a difference in which **syllable** we emphasize. For *envelop*, the second syllable is emphasized (/ɛnˈvɛləp/), while we emphasize the <u>first</u> syllable for *envelope* (/ˈɛnvəˌloʊp/).

Finally, while the first syllable for both words is most often the same (/ɛn-/, rhyming with *when*), many speakers distinguish *envelope* further by pronouncing the first syllable more like the French original: /ˈɑnvəˌloʊp/ (rhyming with *fawn*). However, this is less common and up to personal preference.

environment vs. *enviroment*

The word *environment* originally comes from the verb *environ*, meaning "to surround, encircle, or envelop." The correct pronunciation of the word preserves the **N** in the middle of the word: (/ɛnˈvaɪrənmənt/). However, when we say *environment* aloud, it's common to glide over this /-n-/ sound, leading some to incorrectly write the word as *enviroment*. It's important that we don't neglect this N, though, at least in our writing.

exercise vs. *exorcise*

The words *exercise* and *exorcise* are very similar in pronunciation, but they have very different meanings. *Exercise*, pronounced /ˈɛksərˌsaɪz/, most often refers to activity that promotes bodily or mental health or personal development and improvement, either as noun or a verb. It also has a wide range of other meanings that stem from this core definition. For example:
• "I've started biking to work to get a little more **exercise**."
• "I usually end my class with a few **exercises** to let students apply what they've learned."

• "I need to **exercise** my legs a bit more."
• "This game will really **exercise** your brain!"

Exorcise, on the other hand, has a very narrow and specific definition: "to expel evil spirits or other malignant forces by religious ceremonies" or "to free a person or place from such evil elements." It can also be used figuratively. For example:
• "In the movie, they bring in a priest to **exorcise** a demon from the possessed girl."
• "These therapy sessions have really helped me **exorcise** some of my demons."

When spoken carefully, *exorcise* is pronounced /ˈɛksɔrˌsaɪz/. However, in quick, casual speech, the **O** in the middle of the word tends to have its stress reduced, resulting in a schwa sound that is identical to the pronunciation of *exercise*—/ˈɛksərˌsaɪz/. Because of this, the mistake is sometimes made to use *exercise* in place of *exorcise*, or vice versa.

Spelling Tricks and Tips

As a quick mnemonic trick, just remember that *exorcise* often relates to *demons*, both of which contain an **O**.

flaunt vs. flout

To *flaunt* means "to exhibit oneself or something in an ostentatious, shameless manner," as in:
• "She has been **flaunting** her success with a series of extravagant purchases."
• "I hate the way he **flaunts** through the office every morning in his expensive Italian suits."

The verb *flout*, meanwhile, means "to disregard or ignore, especially with disdain, derision, or scorn." For example:
• "Students caught **flouting** the school's regulations will be punished accordingly."
• "The up-and-coming politician has made a point of **flouting** the conventions of the established political parties."

Although they are not especially similar in pronunciation, *flaunt* is sometimes used incorrectly in instances in which *flout* is meant, perhaps because *flaunt* is more widely used and known by speakers and writers. In any case, we must be careful to only use *flaunt* when describing showing off, and *flout* when describing shirking or defying rules or laws.

Spelling Tricks and Tips

Here are a few ways to remember the difference between these two words:
• When someone *flaunts* something, they might be doing it as a way to t**aunt** other people (with their wealth, success, etc.).
• When you *flout* something, you are operating **out**side the rules.

flounder vs. founder

As a verb, *flounder* means "to struggle or move clumsily, awkwardly, or with difficulty," or, by extension, "to behave, act, or function in an awkward, confused, or directionless manner." For example:
• "I never learned to swim properly, so I usually just **flounder** in the shallow end whenever our family goes to the pool."
• "He **floundered** for a few years after college, with no real motivation or aim in life."
(*Flounder* can also function as a noun, referring to various types of flatfish.)

To *founder*, on the other hand, means "to sink" (when talking about a ship) or, more commonly, "to fail, fall apart, or break down." For example:
• "We began to **founder** after the hull struck an unseen reef beneath the water."
• "Our project **foundered** when our funding was cut by the head of the department."
• "Their relationship started to **founder** shortly after they moved to different states."
(*Founder* can also function as a noun, meaning "one who creates or establishes something.")

Because of its meaning "to struggle," *flounder* is often used incorrectly when *founder* is the correct verb, as in:
✘ "The company **floundered** soon after its latest product failed to attract customers."
✔ "The company **foundered** soon after its latest product failed to attract customers."

Likewise, we should not use *founder* when describing someone or something that is struggling or behaving awkwardly. We can illustrate this difference by reworking the two previous examples:
✔ "The company **floundered** *for several years* after its latest product failed to attract customers."
✘ "The company **foundered** *for several years* after its latest product failed to attract customers."

Note the italicized prepositional phrase *for several years*. The addition of this phrase changes the overall meaning of the sentence from one of finality (in which case *founder* would be the correct word) to one of progression (in which case *flounder* is correct).

This subtle difference in meaning is likely the reason many people struggle to choose the correct word. When you're trying to determine which is the correct spelling, remember that *flounder* describes a continuous or progressive action, while *founder* describes a finished state.

Quiz
(answers start on page 463)

1. Choose the sentence in which *flounder* is the correct word.
a) "Her career could _____ if it's discovered that she has avoided paying taxes for years."
b) "The crew was worried that the dock might _____ beneath their feet."
c) "If we don't secure funding soon, the project is sure to _____."
d) "I had a good grasp of the material at first, but I'm really starting to _____ in the class."

2. Choose the sentence in which *founder* is the correct word.
a) "It was pretty comical watching them _____ in the mud."
b) "Their relationship is likely to _____ if they don't seek some outside help."
c) "He began to _____ for a while after he lost his job."
d) "The nominee, who excels at prepared speeches, tends to _____ during debates."

gorilla vs. *guerrilla*

The words *gorilla* and *guerrilla* are both nouns with the same pronunciation—/gəˈrɪlə/—but they have very different meanings.

Gorilla refers to the genus of great apes indigenous to the forests of central Africa, the largest primates on Earth, divided into the species *Gorilla gorilla* (the Western gorilla) and *Gorilla beringei* (the Eastern gorilla). For example:
• "My favorite animals to see at the zoo as a kid were always the **gorillas**."

Guerrilla, on the other hand, refers to a member of an irregular army, usually motivated by political goals or ideologies, that relies on secretive, small-scale attacks meant to undermine and harass the enemy. In addition to referring to the members themselves, it can also function as an adjective to describe the tactics used by guerrilla soldiers. For example:
• "The government has been in negotiation with the leader of the **guerrillas** in an attempt to resolve the decades-long civil war."
• "The rebel group's **guerrilla** tactics have taken the dictatorship by surprise."

Spelling Tricks and Tips

One quick way of remembering the spelling difference is with this joke:
• Q: Where can an 800-pound **gorilla go**?
• A: Wherever it wants!

grisly vs. *grizzly* vs. *gristly*

The word *grisly* means "gruesome; causing horror, dread, or repugnance," as in:
• "A series of **grisly** murders have shocked the small town."
• "I can't believe she survived such a **grisly** car crash."

The adjective *grizzly* is derived from the noun *grizzle*, which means "hair that is gray or partly gray." One of its most common uses is in the name of the grizzly bear, so named because it has gray-tipped fur. For example:
• "After a month in the wilderness, he came back with a **grizzly** beard."
• "In these parts of the country, you need to watch out for **grizzly** bears and mountain lions."

The words *grisly* and *grizzly* are pronounced the same way: /ˈgrɪzli/. Because of this, it is very easy to confuse their spellings. Just remember that *grizzly* is based off the noun *grizzle*, and so it is spelled with two **Z**s rather than an **S**.

grisly vs. *gristly*

One last possible area of confusion comes from the word *gristly*, which is pronounced /ˈgrɪsli/. Like *grizzly,* it is based on a noun: *gristle* (tough, chewy cartilage, especially when present in meat). Because its pronunciation matches the "normal" speech sound associated with the letter **S** (and because the **T** is silent), it can be easy to mistakenly use the spelling *grisly*. Like *grizzly*, it's important to remember that *gristly* is derived from a noun, which is what determines its spelling.

hanger vs. *hangar*

The word *hanger* is formed by attaching the suffix of agency "-er" to the verb *hang*—it is a person or thing that performs the action of hanging or to which something is hung. For example:
• "Please put your coat on a **hanger** so it doesn't get wrinkled."
• "I've hired a professional painting **hanger** to find the perfect spot for my latest piece."

The noun *hangar*, though, is not formed using a suffix with a base verb; rather, it is derived directly from French and has a very specific meaning: "a shelter, workshop, or other structure in which aircraft are stored," as in:
• "There seems to be an issue with the engine, so we're bringing the plane back to the **hangar** for maintenance."

Because this word is used in such a specific context, it can be easy to mistakenly use the much more common *hanger* instead (especially as they have the same pronunciation, /ˈhæŋər/). When determining which spelling is correct, it's important to keep in mind that the "-er" denotes the agent of an action; if the noun we're writing is not associated with the action of *hanging*, then the correct spelling is probably going to be *hangar*.

hoard vs. *horde*

The homophones *hoard* and *horde* (both pronounced /hɔrd/) have related but different meanings.

Hoard, as a noun, means "a large supply or accumulated store gathered and carefully hidden or guarded for preservation or future use"; as a verb, it describes the action of accumulating such a hoard. For example:
• "It's rumored that the king kept a **hoard** of treasure beneath the dungeon of the castle."
• "I've been **hoarding** vintage toys since I was a teenager."

The noun *horde* similarly refers to a collection, but while *hoard* relates to collections of <u>things</u>, *horde* refers to large groups, crowds, or mobs of <u>people</u>. For example:
• "The movie star fled the restaurant when a **horde** of screaming fans descended upon her."
• "Many different nomadic **hordes** composed the tribe, descendants of which still travel the region to this day."

Spelling Tricks and Tips

If you are trying to remember which spelling is correct, keep this in mind:
• If such a collection can be kept beneath the floor**board**s, you are describing a *hoard*.

idiosyncrasy vs. idiosyncracy

The ending "-acy" is a suffix that indicates nouns of quality, state, or office, usually attaching to existing nouns or adjectives that end in "-ate," as in *accuracy* (from the adjective *accurate*), *candidacy* (from the noun *candidate*), *literacy* (from the adjective *literate*), or *piracy* (from the noun *pirate*).

This common spelling pattern very often leads to the misspelling *idiosyncracy*; however, the correct spelling is *idiosyncrasy*. Unfortunately, there is no easy way to remember this; it is just an unusual spelling that we have to memorize.

illusion vs. delusion

An *illusion* is an erroneous perception, belief, construal, or concept. It can refer to a trick of the senses, such as a sound or image that is not what it seems to be, or to a concept or idea that is wrongly presented or perceived. For example:
• "We thought there was a lake on the horizon of the desert, but it was merely an optical **illusion**."
• "The photographs give the **illusion** that the house is much bigger than it actually is."
• "Many people feel that our sense of freedom is really just an **illusion**."

The word *delusion* not only sounds similar to *illusion*, but has a similar meaning as well. It is also a noun, and it means "a mistaken, misleading, or false opinion, idea, or belief." Unlike *illusion*, *delusion* generally carries a negative connotation, suggesting something "abnormal" with a person's way of thinking. It most often refers to misperceptions that are deceptive, illogical, contrary to factual evidence, or (in psychiatry) the result of mental illness. For example:
• "I guess I was under the **delusion** that Geoffrey would stand by me no matter what happened."
• "They still adhere to the **delusion** that they have an inherent right to dictate the moral standards for the rest of society."
• "She has this unshakeable **delusion** of persecution by those around her."
• "He has been describing paranoid **delusions** consistent with symptoms of schizophrenia."

In some cases, either word will work when describing false or erroneous beliefs or ideas, as in:

✔ "Many people feel that our sense of freedom is really just an **illusion**."
✔ "Many people feel that our sense of freedom is really just a **delusion**."

✔ "They were under the **illusion** that the product's success was guaranteed."
✔ "They were under the **delusion** that the product's success was guaranteed."

However, using *delusion* instead of *illusion* in a sentence—even when there is no functional difference in meaning between the two—still carries an implied negativity; if you are trying to convey a more benign or innocent misperception, *illusion* is the better choice.

Spelling Tricks and Tips

Here's a way of remembering the difference between the two words:
• An *illusion* is usually an **i**nnocent trick of the **i**magination, so it begins with an **I**.
• A *delusion* is more often a **d**eceptive or **d**isturbed misbelief, so it begins with a **D**.

Quiz
(answers start on page 463)

1. Choose the sentence in which *illusion* is the correct spelling.

a) "Animation merely creates the _____ of images that move."
b) "You're laboring under the _____ that our society can operate without taxes."
c) "He's constructed an elaborate paranoid _____ existing entirely in his mind."
d) "The old man still has the _____ that he is relevant in the company."

2. Choose the sentence in which *delusion* is the correct spelling.
a) "The magician created the _____ that his assistant had been cut in half."
b) "The shadows on the street gave the _____ of someone following us."
c) "The successful persona he presents to the world is just a convincing _____."
d) "His _____ is so strong that even concrete evidence will not convince him."

3. Choose the sentence in which **either** *illusion* or *delusion* can be correct.
a) "I've been trying to figure out how this optical _____ works."
b) "Jeremy is under the _____ that he's a great writer, but he's only written a few poems."
c) "In his _____, he began firing people whom he thought were trying to undermine his authority."
d) "The mirrors create the _____ of a more spacious room."

incidence vs. *incidents* vs. *instances*

The word *incidence* is what's known as an uncountable noun, which means it cannot be divided or counted as individual elements or separate parts. (Subsequently, this means that uncountable nouns are usually not made into plurals, so we would normally not write *incidences*.) Most commonly, *incidence* means "the rate, degree, or extent of occurrence or effect," as in:
• "There has been a higher **incidence** of car thefts in the last few months than in the previous five years."

Where things get confusing is with the words *incident* and *instance*, both of which can mean "a particular occurrence." More specifically, writers have trouble with their plural forms: *incidents*, which has the exact same pronunciation as the singular *incidence* (/ˈɪnsɪdəns/), and *instances* (/ˈɪnstənsəz/), the ending of which sounds the same as the uncommon plural *incidences*. Because of these shared pronunciations, as well as the relative proximity in meaning, it's a common mistake to use the plural *incidences* in cases in which *incidents* or *instances* would be the correct term. For example:

✔ "There have been several such **incidents** throughout the late 20th century."*
✔ "There have been several such **instances** throughout the late 20th century."*
✘ "There have been several such **incidences** throughout the late 20th century."

Another possible mistake is to use *incidents* when *incidence* is the correct term, as in:

✔ "There has been a higher **incidence** of car thefts in the last few months than in the previous five years."
✘ "There has been a higher **incidents** of car thefts in the last few months than in the previous five years."

incident vs. *instance*

Be careful with these two words as well, because they are not always synonymous. While they both can mean "a certain case or occurrence," *incident* has another meaning of "a disruptive or violent occurrence that interrupts normal proceedings"; *instance* cannot be used this way. For example:

✔ "We had an **incident** in the workplace that shut down business for a week."
✘ "We had an **instance** in the workplace that shut down business for a week."

✔ "The international **incident** very nearly turned into a declaration of war."
✘ "The international **instance** very nearly turned into a declaration of war."

Instance, meanwhile, can be used to mean "an example cited to demonstrate or prove something," which is not how *incident* is used. For example:

✔ "There are several **instances** of gender-role subversion throughout Shakespeare's comedies."
✘ "There are several **incidents** of gender-role subversion throughout Shakespeare's comedies."

✔ "Density is not tied to weight; for **instance**, a heavy lump of iron will float on a pool of mercury because the latter is more dense than the former."
✘ "Density is not tied to weight; for **incident**, a heavy lump of iron will float on a pool of mercury because the latter is more dense than the former."

Spelling Tricks and Tips

One way to remember which spelling is correct is to look at the other words used in the sentence. While it is possible to pluralize *incidence* as *incidences*, this is not common and, as a result, we almost always find *incidence* accompanied by singular verbs (such as *has* in the first example). If we are using a verb that agrees with third-person subjects (such as *have* or *are*), then *incidents* or *instances* are much more likely to be correct.

Quiz
(answers start on page 463)

1. Choose the sentence in which *incidence* is the correct spelling.

a) "We had one _____ this year that required third-party mediation."
b) "The _____ of online fraud has skyrocketed in the last decade."
c) "This is a clear _____ of misappropriating funds."
d) "There was an _____ during the seminar that led to one person being removed from the audience."

2. Choose the sentence in which **only** *incident* is the correct spelling.

a) "There are a number issues. For _____, we still don't have a reliable manufacturer on board."
b) "Our efforts have led to a reduced _____ of crime in the city."
c) "We've noticed a higher _____ of infection in areas close to the river."
d) "The _____ led to his dismissal from the job."

3. Choose the sentence in which **only** *instance* is the correct spelling.

a) "We always strive to resolve a work-related _____ quickly and fairly."
b) "Since she took over, the _____ of work-related accidents has dropped significantly."
c) "This is just one _____ of a widespread problem."
d) "The experiment concluded without _____."

4. Choose the sentence in which **either** *incident* or *instance* is correct.

a) "One such _____ occurred just last week."
b) "The _____ on the plane has caused an uproar among passenger rights activists."
c) "Thanks to greater awareness about potential health issues, the _____ of deaths due to smoking continues to decline."
d) "This passage is an _____ of the author breaking the fourth wall."

it's vs. *its*

One of the most common spelling mistakes in all of English is to use an apostrophe with the word *its* when we want to indicate possession, or to <u>omit</u> the apostrophe when writing a contraction of *it is* or *it has*.

We usually express possession in writing by adding **'s** to the end of a noun, as in *Mary's, John's, the council's, the dog's*, etc. (As a matter of fact, this possessive **'s** is technically a contraction as well, stemming from the Old English suffix "-es"; however, this "-es" ending fell out of use, and we generally think of the possessive **'s** as a distinct syntactic and grammatical construct of its own.)

Curiously, the possessive form for the personal pronoun *it* does <u>not</u> have an apostrophe, just an **S**—*its*. However, the possessive form <u>was</u> originally spelled *it's*, <u>with</u> the apostrophe. This was dropped around the 1800s, most likely due to the established prevalence of the contraction of *it is*.

In any case, we can only use **'s** with *it* when **it's** is a contraction of *it is* or *it has*. If we write *its*, we are indicating gender-neutral possession for an object, animal, group, etc.

Let's look at a few examples just to see the difference more clearly:

✔ "I'm really glad **it's** (*it is*) starting to get warmer; I hate the wintertime!"

✘ "I'm really glad **its** starting to get warmer; I hate the wintertime!"

✔ "**It's** (*it has*) been a long time since I last saw you."

✘ "**Its** been a long time since I last saw you."

✔ "The corporation recently revised **its** *hiring policy* (possession of *hiring policy*)."

✘ "The corporation recently revised **it's** hiring policy."

lead vs. *led*

The past tense and past participle of the verb *lead* (pronounced /lid/) is *led* (pronounced /lɛd/). While this isn't too complicated in itself, the word *lead* can also be a noun that refers to a toxic, bluish-white metallic element that was formerly used to make paint and pipes. This noun is <u>also</u> pronounced /lɛd/, which often leads to the two spellings being used incorrectly in place of one another. For example:

✔ "The discovery has **led** to new innovations in the field."

✘ "The discovery has **lead** to new innovations in the field."

✔ "The **lead** in the old pipes began leaching into the town's drinking water."

✘ "The **led** in the old pipes began leaching into the town's drinking water."

Spelling Tricks and Tips

The best way to remember the correct spelling is to keep in mind that, if you're talking about the metallic element, you should dr**ead** its toxicity, so it is spelled *lead*. *Led*, meanwhile, is always a verb, so it is spelled with a single **E**.

lead vs. *lede*

One of the meanings of the word *lead* is "the initial part or introductory sentence of a news story." There is also another spelling of the term that is used to indicate this specific meaning: *lede* (also pronounced /lid/).

This used to be a more common variant spelling, but in modern English it has been relegated to journalism jargon, and the journalism-based idiom *bury the lede*, which means to open a news article (or simply an anecdote) with secondary or superfluous information, thus "burying" the central premise (the lead/lede) in a later part. Even in this usage, though, *lead* has become more common in modern English. However, it's worth knowing that *lede* <u>can</u> be used instead in specific situations and is not incorrect. (Just don't use *lede* for any other meanings.)

leech vs. *leach*

The word *leech* is relatively common in English. Most literally, it is a noun referring to an aquatic bloodsucking worm or a verb referring to the practice of draining the blood with a leech. It is also used figuratively as a noun to refer to someone who preys or depends on another person in the manner of a leech or other parasite, or as a verb to describe the actions of such a person. For example:

• "We were horrified to discover **leeches** all over our body coming out of the swamp."
• "The doctor **leeched** the snakebite in an attempt to draw out the venom from the boy."

• "When will you realize that your brother is just a **leech**? He's been living with us for years now and has barely contributed more than buying groceries once in a while."
• "Mary, you've been **leeching** off our money and goodwill for far too long now."

The less common *leach* (pronounced the same way as *leech*: /litʃ/) is most often a verb meaning "to dissolve or otherwise remove from a substance through the action of a percolating liquid," as in:
• "The lead in the old pipes began **leaching** into the town's drinking water."
• "The tainted water seeped into the soil, **leaching** it of minerals and nutrients needed to sustain plant life."

Spelling Tricks and Tips

Because *leach* is encountered much less often in everyday speech and writing, it's a common mistake to use *leech* in its place (especially because the notion of a substance being eroded or dissolved from something sounds kind of like the figurative meaning of *leech*.)

It can help to associate *leach* with *bleach*, which refers to removing the color from something.

lessen vs. *lesson*

Lessen and *lesson* are both pronounced /ˈlɛsən/.

The verb *lessen* is formed by attaching the suffix "-en" (which is most often associated with verbs) to the adjective/adverb *less*—it literally means "to make or become less." For example:
• "The new policy is meant to **lessen** the burden on low-income families."
• "The humor in the film doesn't **lessen** its emotional poignancy."

The noun *lesson* is not formed from a suffix; it comes from the Old French *leçon*, and means "something to be taught or learned." For example:
• "Tomorrow's **lesson** will be focused on Shakespeare's earliest plays."
• "Son, you need a **lesson** in manners."

Spelling Tricks and Tips

To remember the correct spelling, use the mnemonic hidden in that last example: One teaches a les**son** to one's **son**.

let's vs. *lets*

There are a few contractions that have become the standard form in modern English—that is, the uncontracted form is no longer used or sounds rather old fashioned in everyday speech and writing.

One of these is the contraction *let's*, which is a contraction of the words *let us*. This contracted form is only used when expressing a suggestion, as in, "**Let's** go to the beach." It sounds awkward and overly formal to say "**Let us** go to the beach."

However, because *let's* is solely associated with this meaning, there are other instances in which *let us* would be the only correct choice. This occurs when *let* means "to allow or give permission" or "to cause or make." For example:
✔ "I hope mom will **let us** go to the movies." (correct)
✘ "I hope mom will **let's** go to the movies." (incorrect)

✔ "Please **let us** know the results." (correct)
✘ "Please **let's** know the results." (incorrect)

Finally, we have to be careful not to confuse the contraction *let's* with **lets**, which is the conjugation of the verb *let* for third-person singular subjects.

One thing to remember is that *let's* is only used in imperative sentences, the sentence structure used to issue commands or, in this case, suggestions. Imperative sentences do not have a subject (the person or thing performing the action of a verb); instead, they simply use the bare infinitive of a verb on its own, as it is being used to command or instruct another person. *Lets*, on the other hand, can only be used in "normal" (non-imperative) sentences that *do* have subjects because it is dependent on the grammatical class of the subject used in the clause.

For instance:
✔ "**Let's** go get something to eat!" (correct)
✘ "**Lets** go get something to eat!" (incorrect)

✔ "This new technology **lets** people talk to each other from across the globe." (correct)
✘ "This new technology **let's** people talk to each other from across the globe." (incorrect)

Quiz

(answers start on page 463)

1. Choose the sentence in which *let's* is the correct spelling.

a) "Hey, _____ have pizza for dinner tonight."
b) "Do you think Tom will _____ take his car to the concert?"
c) "This TV _____ you watch shows in 3D!"
d) "_____ know as soon as your train has arrived."

2. Choose the sentence in which *lets* is the correct spelling.

a) "Welcome to the class, everyone; _____ begin."
b) "Please _____ stay up a little bit later, dad!"
c) "Janet's dad _____ her stay up past 10 PM, even on school nights!"
d) "_____ try adjusting the receiver and see if it resolves the issue."

3. Choose the sentence in which *let us* is the correct choice.

a) "I know it didn't work the last time, but _____ try restarting the computer again."
b) "When will the doctors _____ go in to see him?"
c) "Why should we spend money on movers? _____ just rent a truck and do the move ourselves."
d) "I hope the doctor _____ me go home soon."

lie vs. *lay*

This is an especially persistent spelling and grammar issue that causes no shortage of problems for learners and native speakers of English alike.

In the present tense, the word *lie* is an **intransitive verb**, meaning it does not require a grammatical object to receive its action. We use this spelling when we want to discuss reclining or resting flat on something, such as a bed, and it is often used with the adverb *down*. For example:

• "I think you should **lie** down for a while."
• "I miss being a teenager, when I could just **lie** in bed all morning on the weekend."

Lay, meanwhile, is a **transitive verb**, meaning it <u>does</u> require an object to receive the action. So, if we're talking about putting **something** (or someone) down flat on a surface, then we must use *lay* in the present tense, as in:

• "Please **lay** *the book* down carefully on the desk." (*The book* is a direct object being put down, so we use *lay*.)
• "Many people **lay** *flowers* on the monument on the anniversary of the uprising." (*Flowers* is a direct object being put down, so we use *lay*.)

Where things get *really* confusing, though, is when we start using these terms in the past tense, because the simple past tense of the word *lie* is *lay* (with the past participle *lain*), while the simple past tense of the word *lay* is *laid* (which is also its past participle). For example:

• "I **lay** under the tree for a while before heading home." (past tense of *lie*)
• "She **laid** the book down where she had found it." (past tense of *lay*)
• "We've **lain** here for too long already!" (past participle of *lie*)
• "I had already **laid** the card on the table when she walked into the room." (past participle of *lay*)

(It's also worth noting that *lie* has another meaning, "to intentionally communicate a nontruth or falsehood," which has the past tense and past participle form of *lied*.)

Unfortunately, there is no easy way to remember which word is correct in which context; we just have to commit them to memory.

Quiz
(answers start on page 463)

1. Choose the sentence in which *lie* is the correct spelling.

a) "Here, ___ your head on this cushion for a moment."
b) "Why don't you ___ on the sofa while I fix dinner?"
c) "Please ___ your finished exams on my desk as you leave."
d) "I'll just ___ this here, if you want to read it later."
e) A & B
f) B & D

2. Choose the sentence in which *lay* is the correct spelling.

a) "My father always just ___ around the house while my mother cleaned and cooked."
b) "Don't just throw your clothes into the wardrobe; fold them and ___ them neatly in their shelves."
c) "I can't wait to just ___ on the beach and soak up the sun."
d) "The future of this industry will ___ in smarter, more convenient technology."
e) A & B
f) B & D

3. What is the simple past tense of the word *lie* when it means "to relax or recline"?

a) lied
b) lay
c) laid
d) lain

4. What is the simple past tense of the word *lay*?

a) lied
b) lay
c) laid
d) lain

loath vs. *loathe*

This is a situation in which silent E helps determine not only pronunciation, but meaning as well. The word *loath* (which is an adjective meaning "unwilling or reluctant") is primarily pronounced /loʊθ/ (rhyming with *both*), while *loathe* (a verb meaning "to detest, hate, or feel disgust for") is pronounced /loʊð/ (rhyming with *clothe*).

(It's worth mentioning that *loth* is an acceptable variant spelling of *loath*, and it helps eliminate a lot of this confusion; however, it is less common, and some may consider it to be incorrect.)

However, to add extra confusion, some speakers pronounce *loath* the same way as *loathe*, choosing to use the "softer" /ð/ for both words; this is an accepted variant pronunciation that is present in most dictionary entries for the word. It's therefore important to look more closely at the words' meaning and function, rather than their pronunciation alone.

For example:

Examples of *loath*	Examples of *loathe*
"He was **loath** to leave the party so soon, be he had to work the next morning." "I'm **loath** to admit you are correct, but it is undeniable now." "She was always **loath** to accept the help of others."	"I don't **loathe** anyone, but that doesn't mean I enjoy everyone's company." "He **loathed** having to come in on a Sunday to work." "I really **loathe** the way they look at me now."

Loath is almost always followed by a phrase beginning with an infinitive (an uninflected verb preceded by *to*) that completes its meaning—this is known as an adjective complement. While *loathe* can also be followed by an infinitive phrase (functioning as a direct object), it doesn't have to; anything functioning as a noun can be its object.

Spelling Tricks and Tips

As a quick mnemonic trick, just remember that *loathe* functions as a verb, so it is spelled with an **E** at the end.

Quiz
(answers start on page 463)

1. Choose the sentence in which *loath* is the correct spelling.
a) "I'm just worried that she'll _____ me if this goes wrong."
b) "You know that I _____ to have my personal business known publicly."
c) "She seems _____ to give up her maiden name after getting married."
d) "I normally _____ this sort of thing, but I'm actually having a great time!"

2. Choose the sentence in which *loathe* is the correct spelling.
a) "Her father was _____ to help us out with the loan."
b) "I'm rather _____ to leave you so soon after the operation."
c) "Don't mind him; he's always been _____ to spend money where he can avoid it."
d) "I feel as though you _____ having me around for some reason."

3. Which word is almost always followed by an infinitive?
a) loath
b) loathe

4. *Loth* is an alternative spelling of which word?
a) loath
b) loathe

lose vs. *loose*

The similarity in spelling between these two words causes many writers to use them interchangeably, even though they have very different meanings and subtly different pronunciations.

Lose (pronounced /luz/, rhyming with *snooze*) is a verb with a wide variety of definitions. Most commonly, it means "to mislay," "to fail to win or use," or "to rid oneself of," as in:
- "I always **lose** my passport when I travel abroad."
- "There's no way we can **lose** this competition!"
- "He's been trying to **lose** weight for a few years."

Loose (pronounced /lus/, rhyming with *moose*) is most often an adjective meaning "not fastened, restrained, taut, or rigid." For example:
- "I think the bolts on the undercarriage have come **loose**."
- "There may be a **loose** wire causing the issue."
- "I love these boots, but they feel a little **loose**."

While the difference between spelling the word with one **O** or two is an easy one to mix up (and most readers will be able to understand what you mean based on context), it's important to use these words correctly, as failing to do so can greatly undermine your readers' confidence in your writing.

Spelling Tricks and Tips

Remember that when you *lose* something, you "lose" the second **O**.

main vs. *mane*

The words *main* and *mane* are both pronounced the same way (/meɪn/), but they have very different meanings.

The more common of the two, *main*, has a wide range of definitions, but it's most often used to mean "chief, principal, or most important," as in:
- "The **main** reason the product failed was a lack of consistent advertising."
- "She will be your **main** contact moving forward."

The word *mane* is a noun, and it has a much more specific meaning: "the long hair on the head and sides of the neck on certain mammals, such as horses, giraffes, or male lions." By extension, it can be used to describe long, thick hair on a person's head. For example:
- "He ran his fingers through the horse's **mane** as they trotted through the countryside."
- "The actor's fans were shocked when he cut off his trademark **mane** for a movie role."

metal vs. *mettle* vs. *medal*

metal vs. *mettle*

The word *mettle* means "the ability, determination, or resolve needed to meet a challenge or persevere under pressure." The term has now fallen into disuse in everyday speech and writing, generally being reserved for slightly formal phrases like *prove/show one's mettle* (meaning "to prove or demonstrate one's ability, determination, and resolve"). For example:
- "If you want to continue running this company, you'll have to **prove your mettle** to our investors."
- "I think he's definitely **shown his mettle** with his performance in that game."

Because it is so uncommon in modern speech and writing, it is easy to simply use the much more familiar *metal* instead, as both words are pronounced /ˈmɛtəl/. However, we must be careful not to do this, as the two words have discrete meanings and uses in modern English.

(It's worth mentioning, though, that these two words were actually interchangeable for most of their existence, with *mettle* being a variant spelling of *metal*. It was only in the 18th century when *mettle* diverged completely and took on its new, specific meaning.)

metal vs. *medal*

Another pair that sometimes causes problems for writers is *metal* and *medal*. A *metal* is a chemical element typically in solid form, such as tin, copper, or iron, or an alloy made from a combination of these elements, while a *medal* is a flat piece of metal formed into a certain shape and bearing a specific image or inscription, typically given as an award for some achievement.

Although they are pronounced differently when articulated carefully—*metal* is pronounced /ˈmɛtəl/, and *medal* is pronounced /ˈmɛdəl/—the /t/ sound in *metal* is commonly softened in casual speech, so that it sounds closer to a /d/ sound.

Perhaps what adds to the confusion is that a *medal* is typically made from some sort of *metal*. However, there are a few mnemonic tricks we can use to help distinguish them.

Spelling Tricks and Tips

To remember that *metal* is spelled with a **T**, just pronounce its adjective form, *metallic*, in which the **T** is always enunciated very crisply, and never sounds like a **D**. To remember that *medal* is spelled with a **D**, keep in mind that it is usually given as an *award*.

miner vs. *minor*

The suffixes "-er" and "-or" can cause a lot of confusion for writers because they sound the same (/-ər/) and behave the same way, usually denoting noun that performs an action.

This is the case when we write *miner*, someone who *mines* ore or other materials from the Earth, as in:
- "The **miners** are on strike until their pay reflects the danger of their work."
- "This town was inhabited almost entirely by coal **miners** and their families."

Minor, however, is taken directly from *Latin* as a gendered form of *minus*. It is usually an adjective meaning "lesser, smaller, or inferior," or a noun meaning "a person who is below the age of majority." For example:
- "The driving test is so strict here that you can fail for the most **minor** mistakes."
- "After a **minor** setback, the crew was quickly back on schedule."
- "We've had a problem with **minors** sneaking into the club with fake IDs."

When trying to determine which spelling is correct, just remember that ***miner*** <u>contains</u> the word *mine*, the action from which it is derived. If the word you're writing does not have to do with mining, then *minor* is the correct choice.

misspell vs. *mispell*

The word *misspell* is made up of the base word *spell* and the prefix "mis-" (meaning "badly or wrongly"). In careful diction, we pronounce each **S** separately: /mɪsˈspɛl/.

However, in more casual, informal speech, we tend to blend these two **S** sounds into one, sounding more like /mɪˈspɛl/. Because common pronunciation reduces the **S**s down to a single sound, this tends to be reflected in writing with the misspelling *mispell*. Just remember that *misspell* contains both *mis-* and *spell*, so we need both **S**s to write it correctly.

moose vs. *mousse*

The words *moose* and *mousse*, though having very different origins, spellings, and meanings, are both pronounced the same way: /mus/ (rhyming with *goose*).

Moose is a noun referring to a large, long-headed North American deer, typified by the enormous palmate antlers of the male. (Interestingly, *moose* is one of the few countable nouns whose plural form is the same as its singular—we would say "one moose" and "two moose.") For example:

• "Many people don't realize just how dangerous **moose** can be if you encounter them in the wild."
• "We were shocked to discover a **moose** that had wandered into our back yard."

Mousse, on the other hand, is taken directly from French, and, in English, typically refers to a chilled dessert consisting of whipped egg whites or cream flavored with chocolate, coffee, caramel, or other ingredients. For example:

• "I'd love to try the **mousse**, but I'm so full from dinner that I don't think I could handle something so rich."

muscle vs. *mussel*

The word *muscle* is taken from French and retains its non-phonetic pronunciation: ˈmʌsəl/ (with a silent C). While it has various meanings, it most often refers to the flesh and tissue in a body that contracts to create movement, as in:

• "Most people don't realize that the tongue is one of the strongest **muscles** in the human body."
• "I think I pulled a **muscle** in my back trying to lift that crate up the stairs."

The word *mussel* is a noun referring to a bivalve mollusk, typically those that are edible. For example:

• "This region is renowned for its delicious **mussels**, which they serve in a simple white wine sauce."

Mussel is also pronounced ˈmʌsəl/, and, because it has a much more phonetic spelling than *muscle*, this may lead to some confusion.

Spelling Tricks and Tips

If you're trying to remember which spelling is correct, keep in mind the related adjective *muscular*, in which the letter **C** is pronounced (/ˈmʌ**k**jələr/); if the noun you're writing has to do with mus**c**ular structures, then the spelling will be *mus**c**le*. Another trick is to remember that a *mu**ss**el* is a type of **s**hellfi**sh**, so it will be spelled with two **S**s.

oar vs. *ore*

Oar and *ore* are both pronounced /ɔr/.

Oar is usually a noun referring to a long, thin shaft of wood with a flat blade at the end, used to row or steer boats through the water. It can also function as a verb to describe the action of propelling a boat with an oar. For example:

• "Grab an **oar** and help us row, or it will take us forever to get to shore."
• "It took over an hour to **oar** from one side of the canal to the other."

Unlike *oar*, *ore* can only function as a noun, meaning "a mineral or aggregate of minerals found in nature from which valuable constituents can be extracted." For example:

• "The trucks haul the **ore** to the processing plant, where iron deposits are extracted and refined."

Spelling Tricks and Tips

If you're trying to remember which spelling is correct, it's useful to keep in mind that we use an ***oar*** to row a ***boat***, and both contain the vowel digraph **OA**.

pair vs. *pare* vs. *pear*

These three words are all pronounced the same way: /pɛər/.

The most commonly used term, *pair*, is typically a noun meaning "two of the same or similar people or things," though it can also function as a verb meaning "to form, belong to, or separate into a pair," or "to complement or complete." For example:

• "You two are just a **pair** of knuckleheads."
• "I need to buy a new **pair** of pants."
• "I want you all to **pair** off and discuss the themes of the chapter."
• "Chocolate **pairs** well with salty and spicy flavors."

The word *pare* is used in a much narrower way. It is only ever a verb meaning "to remove the outer covering, skin, edge, or part (of something)" or, by extension, "to reduce or trim in quantity or size." For example:

• "You need to **pare** your nails; they've become too long and sharp."
• "She **pared** the apple with her pocket knife."
• "We're going to need to **pare** down our expenses if we want to survive next year."

Finally, the word *pear* simply refers to a sweet, juicy fruit with a globular base that tapers toward the stem, as in:

• "I generally don't like **pears** unless they are perfectly ripe."

Spelling Tricks and Tips

Pare is much less commonly used in everyday speech and writing, which can lead some writers to mistakenly use the spelling *pair* in its place. If you need a trick to remember the correct spelling, keep in mind that when you *pare* something, you *prepare* it in some way. If you are describing two of something, remember that *pair* has a pair of vowels in the middle of the word—**A** and **I**. You can distinguish this from *pear*, because you **eat** pears, so it is spelled with the digraph **EA**.

pedal vs. *peddle* vs. *petal*

The words *pedal* and *peddle* are both pronounced the same way: /ˈpɛdəl/.

The more common of the two is **pedal**. It is primarily a noun meaning "a lever worked by the foot," originally referring to those on a pipe organ or piano, but now more commonly referring to those on bicycles. By extension, *pedal* can also function as a verb meaning "to operate or use the pedals (of something)." For example:

• "For me, the trickiest part of playing the piano has been using the **pedals** correctly."
• "My new bike has clip-in **pedals** and requires special shoes to ride."
• "You'll need to **pedal** faster than that if you want to keep up with me!"

Peddle can only ever be used as a verb, most often meaning "to travel around selling (something)," as in:

• "Many different vendors **peddle** overpriced souvenirs outside the tourist site."
• "Our town prohibits people from soliciting or **peddling** their wares in residential areas."

Spelling Tricks and Tips

One way of remembering the difference between these two spellings is to associate the word *peddle* with the similarly spelled verb *meddle* (meaning "to intrude into or interfere with other people's business or affairs"). When you try to *peddle* goods to someone, you are *meddling* with their decision to buy something. Olympic cyclists, on the other hand, *pedal* to win a *medal*.

pedal vs. *petal*

One other word that causes confusion for some writers is *petal*, which is a noun meaning "one of the brightly colored parts of a flower that surround the reproductive organ." For example:

• "He ran his fingers tenderly across the **petals** of the roses."

It has a very similar spelling as *pedal*, as well as a very similar pronunciation: /ˈpɛtəl/. In casual speech, the /t/ sound is commonly softened and pronounced quickly, sounding identical to a /d/ sound; this leads to the pronunciation of *petal* being the same as *pedal*, /ˈpɛdəl/, which adds to the confusion between the two spellings.

Just remember to pronounce *pedal* and *petal* carefully, and let that guide which spelling is correct to use.

pole vs. *poll*

The words *pole* and *poll* are both pronounced /poʊl/.

Pole is most commonly used to refer to a long, slender, rounded shaft, typically made of wood or metal. By extension, *pole* can function as a verb meaning "to propel, strike, or push with a pole" or "to stir, strike, or poke with a pole." For example:

• "As kids, we used to fish in the stream behind our house by tying string to wooden **poles** we found in our dad's workshop."
• "We watched them **pole** the small boats along the canal."

(*Pole* can also mean "either extremity of an axis that passes through a sphere," most commonly referring to the northernmost and southernmost points of the Earth. When capitalized, *Pole* also refers to a person of Polish origin.)

The word *poll* can similarly function as a noun or a verb describing an action based on the noun. As a noun, it most often means "a sample or collection of the opinions of a group of people regarding a specific question or topic" or "the act of voting or the recording and counting of such votes." As a verb, it means "to collect opinions from a group of people" or "to receive or record the votes of an election." For example:

• "Our latest **poll** shows that most people care more about a politician's personal life than his or her political strategy."
• "She won by a landslide in the **polls**."

• "We've been **polling** consumers about their spending habits in the mall."
• "The candidate, who always **polled** well in previous elections, suffered a disastrous defeat."

Spelling Tricks and Tips

A quick tip to remember the difference is that *poll* has to do with <u>multiple</u> people, so it will be spelled with multiple **L**s; a *pole* refers to a single point, and only has one **L** in it.

pore vs. *pour* vs. *poor*

The verb *pour* is very common, generally meaning "to cause liquid or granular solids to stream or flow out of or into a container" or "to stream, flow, or pass through profusely or continuously," as in:

• "He **poured** the substance from the vial."
• "Shall I **pour** you a cup of tea?"
• "Water continued to **pour** out of the broken pipe."
• "Protestors **poured** out onto the streets to voice their anger over the verdict."

Pore is most often used as a noun referring to a tiny opening on a surface, such as skin or rock. This meaning is completely lost when *pore* functions as a verb, in which case it usually means "to examine, study, or read with intense, careful

attention." For example:
• "She spent hours **poring** over the text, searching for a clue that might help solve the case."
• "I had to **pore** over the contract to find who is liable in such a situation."

Unlike the other two terms, *poor* is only used as an adjective. It most commonly means "lacking financial means to live well or comfortably," but it can also mean "inferior or inadequate," or "pitiable, unfortunate, or unlucky." For example:
• "We were too **poor** to afford a television when I was a kid."
• "Though well written, the play suffers from **poor** performances."
• "The **poor** guy has had a lot of bad luck this year."

Spelling Tricks and Tips

Because the usage of *pore* as a verb is relatively uncommon, many writers mistakenly use the homophone *pour* instead, especially because it seems to make a certain amount of logical sense—i.e., that you are *pouring* your attention onto something.

Just remember that you might start sweating from your **pores** if you spend a lot of energy *poring* over something, while you *pour* liquid **out** of something. The word *poor*, meanwhile, looks like it has two zeroes in the middle, indicating an absence of wealth, adequacy, or luck.

premier vs. *premiere*

Although *premier* and *premiere* are only separated in spelling by a silent E, they are very different in meaning.

Premier, without the final **E**, is primarily an adjective meaning "first, foremost, or principal in status or importance." It can also function as a noun, in which case it refers to the head of a government body (usually denoting a prime minister), especially in France or Canada. For example:
• "She is widely considered the **premier** violinist in Europe."
• "The **premier** responded to criticism of the government's response."

When we add the silent **E** to form *premiere*, the pronunciation remains the same: /prɪˈmɪər/. (Although in some dialects, especially British English, it <u>does</u> change slightly, with stress being placed on the first syllable: /ˈprɛmɪˌɛər/.) Primarily, *premiere* is a noun meaning "the first public performance or showing, as of a play, film, opera, etc." By extension, the word can also function as a verb meaning "to give or present the first public performance of a play, film, opera, etc." For example:
• "Several movie stars appeared at the film's **premiere**."
• "They chose to first **premiere** the play in a small theater before eventually moving to Broadway."

Unfortunately, there's no easy way to remember the difference; we just have to commit the correct meaning of each spelling to memory.

prescribe vs. *proscribe*

The terms *prescribe* and *proscribe* are often confused due to their similarities in spelling, pronunciation, and usage.

When enunciated carefully, *prescribe* is pronounced /prɪˈskraɪb/, while *proscribe* is pronounced /proʊˈskraɪb/. However, in casual speech, both words tend to have their first vowels reduced to a schwa sound (/ə/), resulting in the same pronunciation: /prəˈskraɪb/.

There is also a bit of an overlap in how these terms are used in a sentence, though their meanings are quite different. *Prescribe* means "to establish or lay down as a rule, law, directive, or order," or (most common in modern English) "to order a medicine or treatment or the use thereof." *Proscribe*, on the other hand, means "to condemn, denounce, prohibit, forbid, or outlaw," or "to banish or exile." For example:

• "The government **prescribes** the conditions by which states may form and enforce their own laws."
• "The doctor **prescribed** an experimental treatment to help combat the rare disease."

• "Behavior and lifestyles once **proscribed** by more puritanical societies are now accepted as the norm across the country."
• "The government **proscribed** the controversial group following their plan to demonstrate."

In conjunction with the relative ubiquity of the medical meaning of *prescribe*, part of the problem might be due to the prefixes used to create *proscribe*. Because "pro-" is often associated with the meaning "in favor of" (as in *pro-American, pro-peace, pro-business,* etc.), the fact that it appears in a verb that means "condemn or forbid" can sometimes trip writers up.

Even more commonly confused than these two verbs, though, are their adjectival forms: *prescriptive* and *proscriptive*.

prescriptive vs. *proscriptive*

While *prescribe* is a fairly common verb due to its use in medicine, the adjective *prescriptive* loses this association and in turn is much less common in everyday speech and writing.

Prescriptive means "of or related to the making of rules, laws, or directions." In discussions about linguistics, it describes the establishment of rules or norms for how a language should or should not be used (compared to how a language is actually used in common, everyday speech or writing).

This usage is where the term often gets confused with the adjective *proscriptive*, which describes a person or group that prohibits or condemns something. Because *prescriptive* grammarians advise on what should or shouldn't be used in language, they could also be considered **proscriptive** because they condemn certain things.

The difference can be very subtle, but it can change the structure of sentences in which the words appear. For example, consider the following two sentences:
• "**Prescriptive** linguists still maintain that *whom* <u>should be used</u> instead of *who* as an object of a verb or preposition."
• "**Proscriptive** linguists still maintain that *who* <u>cannot be used</u> instead of *whom* as an object of a verb or preposition."

Both sentences essentially mean the same thing, but their focus changes slightly depending on which adjective we choose to use. The sentence that uses *prescriptive* focuses on what is <u>recommended</u> or <u>established as a rule</u>, while the sentence that uses *proscriptive* focuses on what is <u>not allowed</u>.

Spelling Tricks and Tips

It may help to remember that **pro**scribe and **pro**scriptive deal with **pro**hibiting something. If you are talking about **pre**senting rules or laws, then **pre**scribe or **pre**scriptive are the correct terms.

Quiz
(answers start on page 463)

1. Choose the sentence in which *prescribe* is the correct word.

a) "I'm going to _____ you a round of antibiotics to fight the infection."
b) "The new law will _____ the use of cell phones while driving."
c) "The church plans to _____ the group for their views."
d) "Many grammar authorities _____ using the informal spelling *alright*."

2. Choose the sentence in which *proscribe* is the correct word.

a) "The terms of our agreement _____ how payment will be delivered."
b) "He needed to _____ strong pain medication following his patient's surgery."
c) "The company executives _____ our policies, not individual store managers."
d) "Jewish dietary laws _____ eating pork."

3. Choose the sentence in which *prescriptive* is the most correct word.
a) "The dress code here is pretty relaxed compared to the more _____ company I used to work for."
b) "Our father was always very _____ about our manners and etiquette at home."
c) "The requirements are so _____ that many artists don't even bother submitting their work."
d) "I find it better to let students express their learning in different ways, rather than being overly _____."

4. Choose the sentence in which *proscriptive* is the most correct word.
a) "The city has established several _____ laws in recent years, aimed at eliminating activities and behavior it deems undesirable."
b) "Tax forms are notoriously _____ regarding how they must be filled out."
c) "_____ English teachers focus too much on how the language is meant to be used, rather than how it is used in everyday speech and writing."
d) "I feel like the government is getting too _____. They need to just let people make their own choices and stop telling them what to do!"

principal vs. *principle*

This pair of words often causes trouble for English learners and native speakers alike, since they're both pronounced /ˈprɪnsɪpəl/.

Principal is both a noun and an adjective. As a noun, it most generally means "a person who holds a position of primary importance in or leads some event, action, or organization," most commonly referring to the head of an elementary, middle, or high school. As an adjective, *principal* means "chief, foremost, or primary; first in importance, value, rank, etc." For example:
• "The **principal** made an announcement to the school about the recent policy changes."
• "The **principal** actor in the play quit a week before the premiere."
• "Our **principal** interest is in maintaining steady growth over the first four quarters of the company's existence."

Principle can only function as a noun, generally meaning "an established, accepted, or fundamental rule, law, axiom, or doctrine," or "a personal set of moral standards, rules, or beliefs." For example:
• "It's not about the money; it's about the **principle** of sticking by your friends, no matter what!"
• "Can you explain the **principle** of the conservation of energy?"
• "A savvy businesswoman, she never deviates from her **principles** when striking a deal."

Spelling Tricks and Tips

Fortunately, there are a couple mnemonic tricks we can use to remember which spelling is correct:
• If what you're writing is an **adjective**, then the word will always be *principal*.
• If you're referring to a person, use *principal*, because a person can be your **pal**.
• A *principle* is a concept that can be taught to someone's disc**iple**.

rack vs. *wrack*

The word *wrack* (pronounced /ræk/, with a silent **W**) is related to the word *wreck*, meaning "a wreckage" or, as a verb, "to destroy or ruin." *Wrack* is now largely archaic, though, only appearing in the set phrase *wrack and ruin* (meaning "total collapse, destruction, or ruination"). For example:
• "It greatly pains me that my grandfather's estate has been left to go to **wrack and ruin**."
• "The terrible handling of the scandal has brought the company nothing but **wrack and ruin**."

Because of this specialized usage, there are a few other phrases in which *wrack* is often used, especially *wrack one's brains* (meaning "to exert a lot of mental effort to remember something") or *nerve-wracking* (meaning "causing anxiety; very stressful on the nerves"). It also appears in sentences like, "Pain **wracked** her body," though this is a bit less common.

However, in these phrases, the word *rack* is actually considered the more correct spelling to use. While *rack* most often refers to a structural framework that holds or contains something, it has a less common meaning of "to torture or cause great suffering to," a reference to a medieval torture device known as *the rack*.

Because *wrack* is associated with destruction or ruination, *wrack one's brains* and *nerve-wracking* seem logical because of the figurative sense of destroying one's brain or nerves, but, because the phrases are more about mental stress or suffering, *rack one's brain* and *nerve-racking* are the most correct.

All of that having been said, *wrack* is a widely accepted variant in these phrases, and (linguistic purists aside) few would judge this spelling as incorrect. If you want to be sure that your writing is absolutely accurate, though, *rack* is technically the better choice.

rein vs. *reign*

Rein and *reign* (both pronounced /reɪn/) can each function as a noun and a verb based on that noun's meaning.

Rein most literally means "either of two long straps attached to a bridle used to control a horse or other animal by its rider"; figuratively, it refers to any means of controlling, directing, or restraining. By extension, it functions as a verb to mean "to check, restrain, or control" (either literally or figuratively). For example:
• "He clutched the **reins** tightly as the carriage went across the narrow bridge."
• "The candidate vowed to loosen the **reins** of the government if he were to take office."

• "You need to **rein** in your mule if you want to keep control going down this ravine."
• "They brought in a financial advisor to try and **rein** in the firm's expenses."

Reign, one of the few words featuring a silent G, is primarily a noun meaning "the sovereign or royal rule of a monarch" or "the period during which a monarch holds power"; more figuratively, it can refer to any dominating power or influence. As a verb, it means "to possess and exercise sovereign power and rule" or "to have predominant or prevailing control or influence." For example:
• "The **reign** of Queen Elizabeth II is the longest in British history."
• "Following the coup, the military junta's **reign** of brutality came to an end."

• "The king **reigned** with an iron fist until he was dethroned in the early 11th century."
• "They strove to create a country where peace and virtue **reigned**."

Spelling Tricks and Tips

Because of its silent **G** and the overlap in meaning of "control," writers sometimes mistakenly use *rein* where *reign* would be correct. One way to remember the difference is to understand *reign*'s origin. The term is etymologically related to the word *regal*, meaning "of, relating to, belonging to, or befitting a monarch." So, if you're describing the control or authority that might be considered *regal*, the appropriate word to use is *reign*

rest vs. *wrest*

The homophones *rest* and *wrest* can sometimes give writers difficulty because of the silent W in the latter word. However, the two have very different meanings.

Rest has a wide range of definitions, but it primarily means "a period or state of motionlessness, inactivity, relaxation, or sleep," or, as a verb, "to be in or cause to be in a state or motionlessness, inactivity, relaxation, or sleep." For example:

• "We stopped for a **rest** on the banks of the river."
• "The computer is getting a little overheated; I think you should give it a **rest** for a while."

• "As a premium member, you'll be able to **rest** in our VIP lounge after the show."
• "The car **rested** to a stop on the top of the hill."

Wrest, on the other hand, is almost always used as a verb meaning "to take or remove with a forceful pulling or twisting motion" or "to obtain, take possession of, or usurp through forceful means or with persistent effort." For example:

• "He **wrested** the bicycle out of the tiny shed, nearly breaking it in the process."
• "The revolution led to the populace **wresting** power from the monarchy."
• "After hours of grilling the CEO, the panel finally managed to **wrest** an admission of guilt from him."

Spelling Tricks and Tips

A quick tip to remember the difference between these two words is that *wrest* is related in meaning and origin to *wrestle*, which also has to do with gaining control by force.

retch vs. *wretch*

Retch and *wretch* are both pronounced /rɛtʃ/; the **W** in *wretch* is silent. Other than the pronunciation, though, these two terms are entirely dissimilar.

Retch is a verb meaning "to vomit or try to vomit," as in:
• "The smell of the chemicals nearly made me **retch**."

Wretch, meanwhile, is a noun meaning "a person considered despicable, base, or morally repugnant," or "a pitiably or deplorably unhappy or unfortunate person." For example:
• "It makes me sick to know that such a boorish **wretch** is now running the company."
• "The poor **wretch** couldn't even afford a cup of coffee."

Spelling Tricks and Tips

To remember the difference in spelling between the two words, remember that a *wretch* is someone who you think does things that are *wrong*.

retched vs. *wretched*

The words *retch* and *wretch* also lead to two similar words, *retched* and *wretched*. *Retched* is simply the past tense of *retch*, while *wretched* is an adjective form of *wretch* (generally meaning "in a dismal state or characterized by woe or misfortune" or "despicable, contemptible, or base"). For example:
• "I **retched** after inhaling the fumes of the chemicals."
• "We lived in a **wretched** little apartment in Brooklyn for a few years."

In addition to the difference in meanings established by their base words, these terms are also pronounced slightly differently. *Retched* is pronounced /rɛtʃt/, with the final **E** being silent and **D** being pronounced /t/; *wretched* is pronounced /ˈrɛtʃɪd/, more phonetically representing the suffix "-ed."

ring vs. wring

The word *ring* is an extremely common word with a broad range of meanings. Very generally, *ring* has two primary meanings as a noun and (by extension) as a verb. As a noun, it most commonly means "a circular shape, object, line, or arrangement" (often referring to a circular band worn on a finger), or "the act of ringing something or the sound made by ringing" (usually referring to a bell). As a verb, it refers to the action of encircling or forming into a circle, or to the action of producing a sonorous or resonant sound. For example:

• "I always wear by grandfather's **ring** to remind myself of him."
• "We knew that the **ring** of the church bells in the evening meant it was time to come home for dinner."

• "Attendees **ringed** the monument with flowers."
• "Please **ring** the bell if you need any assistance."

The word *wring* is pronounced the same as *ring* (/rɪŋ/; the **W** is silent), but it has a much narrower definition. It is almost always used as a verb to mean "to twist, wrench, compress, or squeeze." It can refer to the literal action of twisting or squeezing a physical object, or it can be used figuratively to refer to applying force or pressure to a person to obtain or extract something. For example:

• "I had to **wring** out my shirt after the heavy rainfall."
• "We were finally able to **wring** an admission of guilt out of the suspect."

Spelling Tricks and Tips

Because *wring* has to do with applying force, it can help to associate it with the word *wrestle*, which also has a silent **W** before **R**. If what you're writing does not have to do with a forceful action, then *ring* is the correct spelling to use.

should've, would've, could've vs. should of, would of, could of

When words are formed into contractions, they sometimes create unique speech sounds that are not simply shortened versions of the full word's pronunciation. Because modern speech relies so heavily on contractions, this can occasionally lead to confusion as to what their proper spelling should be.

By far the most common of these is when *have* is contracted as *'ve* and attached to a word ending in a consonant, most commonly *should, would,* and *could*. This results in **'ve** being pronounced /əv/ (what's known as a syllabic consonant), which sounds the same as *of* when it is unstressed in speech. Because of this, it is a common mistake to think that *should've, would've,* and *could've* are instead spelled *should of, would of,* and *could of*. For example:

✔ "I **should've** known this wouldn't be easy."
✖ "I **should of** known this wouldn't be easy."

✔ "Who **would've** guessed that the answer could be so simple?"
✖ "Who **would of** guessed that the answer could be so simple?"

✔ "We **could've** won if you hadn't dropped the ball!"
✖ "We **could of** won if you hadn't dropped the ball!"

It's important to be aware that *should of, would of,* and *could of* are not correct in English, whether informal, colloquial, or otherwise; they literally do not mean anything. Be careful to always spell the shortened forms as the contractions *should've, would've,* and *could've*, and, if you are spelling them out in their entirety, *should have, would have,* and *could have*. These are the only correct spellings.

Finally, note that this also applies to the contractions *might've* and *must've*; the **'ve** in these is also pronounced like *of*, but *might of* and *must of* are always incorrect.

stationary vs. *stationery*

Stationary is an adjective meaning "not moving or incapable of being moved" or, by extension, "unchanging." For example:
• "The car remained **stationary** at the traffic light, despite the honking from the cars behind it."
• "Despite the company's overall evolution over the years, many of its policies have been obstinately **stationary**."

Stationery, on the other hand, is a noun meaning "writing paper or other materials used for writing, such as envelopes, pens, ink, etc.," as in:
• "The **stationery** with the company's logo on it finally arrived."
• "I had a personalized **stationery** case in high school that I absolutely loved."

Spelling Tricks and Tips

These two words give writers a lot of trouble, as they are very close in spelling and identical in pronunciation (/ˈsteɪʃənɛri/). Fortunately, there is a quick and easy trick to remembering the correct spelling. *Stationery* is usually referring to some form of *paper*, and is spelled with the letters **ER**; if we are not talking about paper, it will be spelled with the letters **AR** instead.

steak vs. *stake*

Stake and *steak* are both pronounced the same way: /steɪk/.

The word *stake* has a few different meanings. Most commonly, it is a noun referring to a pointed shaft made of metal or wood used to mark something or secure something to the ground; by extension, it can also function as a verb to describe the action of marking or securing something with a pointed shaft. For example:
• "Make sure you hammer down those **stakes** really firmly; we don't want the tent blowing away in the wind."
• "We finally finished **staking** out a patch of grass in the backyard where the dogs can run around."

Stake also has another common meaning: "money, property, or other valuables risked by a player in a bet or gambling game," or, by extension, "a financial interest or personal involvement in something." It can also function as a verb to describe the act of risking money or other valuables for a gamble. For instance:
• "I like poker, but I never play when there are real **stakes** involved."
• "She has a major **stake** in the company."

• "I can't believe he would **stake** his car for such a silly bet."
• "We've **staked** our company's future on the success of this product."

The homophone *steak* has a much narrower definition: it can only function as a noun, meaning "a thick slice of meat from an animal or large fish, usually beef," as in:
• "We went to that new restaurant last night, and I had the most delicious **steak** there."
• "Tuna **steak** is really tasty, but it can be pretty pricey."

Spelling Tricks and Tips

If you're trying to remember which spelling is correct, remember that a *steak* is a piece of *meat*, so it will be spelled with the digraph **EA**. If you are not talking about meat, the spelling should be *stake*.

sympathy vs. empathy

While the spelling, pronunciation, and meaning of *sympathy* and *empathy* are all different, they are each similar enough that the two words are very often confused in both speech and writing.

The older of the two, *sympathy*, originally meant "a relationship, harmony, or affinity between certain things or people." In modern English, *sympathy* more commonly means "a feeling of pity, sorrow, or regret in reaction to another person's distress or misfortune," or "support for or agreement with an opinion, position, cause, etc." For example:
• "I'm so sorry for your loss; you have my deepest **sympathies**."
• "It came to light that he had been in **sympathy** with the rebel cause."

Empathy is a newer term, originally referring to the act of projecting one's feelings, attitudes, or emotions onto an object, especially a piece of art. In modern English, it is more often used to describe the ability to understand and identify with the perspective, motivations, emotions, or experiences of another person. For example:
• "She has a great deal of **empathy** for the other children in class, and is always able to understand why they're upset."

The difference can seem a bit subtle, but it's important to know when each word is appropriate to use. When you have **sympathy** for someone, you are expressing your own regret or condolences for someone else's misfortune. When you have **empathy** for someone, you are able to understand at a fundamental level the emotions he or she is experiencing or the perspective he or she holds.

Finally, both *sympathy* and *empathy* can be made into verbs using the suffix "-ize," typically followed by the preposition *with*. These verbs are frequently confused as well, but their difference in meaning remains the same as their noun base words. Let's look at a couple of examples to see this difference more clearly:
• "I really do **sympathize** with your troubles, but I cannot grant any further extensions on the loan."
• "The president was criticized for seeming to **sympathize** with the rebel cause."

• "Having spent years as a fast food worker, I can **empathize** with anyone who works long hours for too little pay."
• "Even though the main character is very flawed and often unlikable, the reader is able to **empathize** with him after seeing the story unfold from his point of view."

There's no easy way to remember which word is correct in a given sentence, but here's a mnemonic trick to help keep the two words separate in your mind:
• When you have **s**ympathy for someone, you feel **s**orry for them.
• When you have **e**mpathy for someone, you can understand what it feels like to **e**xperience their **e**motions.

Quiz
(answers start on page 463)

1. Choose the sentence in which *sympathy* is the best choice.
a) "You have to have _____ for your students if you want to understand why they may be struggling."
b) "We've recently begun a program to help foster _____ in managers for their employees."
c) "He expected some amount of _____ for his difficulties, but only received a harsh rebuke."
d) "He speaks as though he has _____ for everyone in the world, but he never really seems to consider others' feelings."

2. Choose the sentence in which *empathy* is the best choice.
a) "He expressed _____ for the woman's loss."
b) "An important part of growing up is learning _____ for other people."
c) "One of the executives expressed his _____ for the workers' strike."
d) "You have my _____, but I still need the report finished by the end of the week."

then vs. *than*

When spoken with stress on their vowels, the words *then* and *than* are pronounced slightly differently—/ðɛn/ (rhyming with *when*) and /ðæn/ (rhyming with *ban*), respectively. However, we often say *than* without stress, leading to the pronunciation /ðən/, which sounds nearly identical to *then*. This closeness in pronunciation leads to *then* and *than* being regularly confused in written English, but they have very distinct functions grammatically.

Though it has multiple functions and meanings, *then* is most commonly used as an adverb meaning "at that time; next or immediately afterward." For example:
• "I'll be ready around 8 PM, if you want to come over **then**."
• "I miss being a kid; things were simpler **then**."
• "I'm just going to have lunch and **then** I'll start working on the report."

Than is a conjunction, rather than an adverb, most often used to compare or contrast two things, such as qualities, abilities, actions, opinions, etc. For instance:
• "My brother has always been faster **than** I am."
• "Her English is much better **than** it used to be."
• "I would rather make less money **than** spend every second of my life working."

Spelling Tricks and Tips

You can remember the difference between the two words by keeping in mind that when you use *then*, you are usually talking about what happens *next*, which is also spelled with an **E**.

therefore vs. *therefor*

The word *therefore* is sometimes mistakenly spelled *therefor* because of the silent E that appears at the end, but the two are unique words with different meanings.

Therefore is what most writers mean to use in modern English. It is an adverb and conjunction meaning "thus; hence; consequently; as a result." For example:
• "It is raining too heavily to cross the bridge safely; we must **therefore** find an alternative route."
• "Literature, **therefore**, is a means of empathizing with those for whom we would have no natural affinity in real life."

Therefor, without the silent **E**, is generally considered archaic in modern English. It is also an adverb, but it means "for or in exchange for this, that, or it." For example:
• "I've enclosed a list of required goods and the payment **therefor**."

Aside from certain legal contexts, you're most likely never going to use *therefor*; **therefore**, just remember that you probably need a silent **E** at the end.

they're vs. *there* vs. *their*

The contraction *they're* (*they are*) is very commonly confused with the words *there* (an adverb indicating location or direction) and *their* (a possessive determiner).

The main issue is that all three have the same pronunciation—/ðɛər/. If we are using the plural personal pronoun *they* and the verb *are*, then we have to use the contraction *they're*; if we are indicating direction or location, we use the adverb/pronoun *there*; and if we're saying that something belongs to a group of people, we use the possessive determiner *their*.

For example:
• "I think **they're** (*they are*) going to be here soon."
• "We parked the car over **there** (direction/location) on the hill."
• "I don't believe in giving students standardized tests, because **their** (possession) scores don't necessarily reflect **their** ability to learn."

Spelling Tricks and Tips

Here's a way of remembering the three different spellings:
• *They're* has an apostrophe in the middle because it comes from the words *they* and *are*.
• *There* contains the word **here**, another adverb/pronoun of direction and location.
• *Their* contains the word **heir**, which is a person who <u>possesses</u> something they have inherited.

to vs. *too* vs. *two*

These three words give writers a lot of trouble because they all have the exact same pronunciation: /tu/. However, each has a very specific meaning and usage, so it's important to understand the distinction between them.

To is most often a preposition; it has a broad range of meanings and uses, but it usually means "in a direction towards" or "reaching." For example:
• "We're going **to** Florida for our vacation."
• "The oil spill spread all the way back **to** the shore."

Too is an adverb most often meaning "in addition; also; as well; furthermore." It is also used as an intensifier, meaning "excessively or more than is useful, usual, fitting, or desirable," or "very; extremely." For example:
• "I think we should invite Dan, **too**; he'd really enjoy it."
• "The pizza was a bit **too** hot to eat right away."
• "He'd be only **too** happy to help you out."

Two is primarily a noun meaning "the cardinal number that is the sum of one plus one," "a set of this many people or things," or "something representing or represented by two units." *Two* is also commonly used as a determiner (a type of word similar to an adjective that introduces and provides information about a noun), meaning "amounting to two." For example:
• "I only needed one, but I bought **two** because they were on sale."
• "I just needed to get another **two** and I would have had a full house."
• "We only have **two** hours to get this done."

Spelling Tricks and Tips

There are few mnemonic tricks we can use to help determine which spelling is correct:
• *To* is most similar in meaning to the word *toward*; we simply cut off the -*ward* and we're left with *to*.
• *Too* most often means "in addition to," so we have a second **O** *in addition to* the first one.
• *Two* is spelled with a **W** (said aloud as "double U"), and the word *double* means "two."

More functionally, remember that *to* will almost always be followed by a noun (to form a prepositional phrase); *too* will always be describing a verb, adjective, or other adverb; and *two* will always describe or function as a noun.

tortuous vs. *torturous*

The word *tortuous* means "repeatedly bending, twisting, or winding; indirect, circuitous, or roundabout; or intricate or complex." For example:
• "Jim got sick after driving through those **tortuous** mountain roads."
• "Many students had trouble with the novel's **tortuous** plot."
• "The lawyer's **tortuous** legal arguments failed to convince the jury."

Torturous, on the other hand, means "of or related to torture; full of pain or suffering," as in:
• "Her **torturous** experiences with the company prompted her to go out on her own."
• "The dictator has been accused of establishing an oppressive regime through **torturous** methods."

Perhaps because of a more figurative application of the word *torture*, *torturous* can also be used to describe something that is strained, twisting, or overly complex (since this complexity or circuitousness could be thought of as painful to experience). Some language authorities dispute this shared meaning, though, so it is safer overall (especially in more formal writing) to reserve *torturous* for when you mean "of, causing, or relating to torture," and *tortuous* for when you mean "twisting, complex, devious, or circuitous."

weather vs. *whether*

In everyday speech, *weather* and *whether* are usually pronounced the same way: /ˈwɛðər/. (Some dialects *do* pronounce the **H** very subtly, though it comes <u>before</u> the /w/ sound—/ˈhwɛðər/. However, this isn't very common, especially in American English.)

Weather primarily functions as a noun or a verb. As a noun, it generally means "the atmospheric conditions at a given place and time, with respect to temperature, moisture, humidity, wind speed, etc." As a verb, it means "to affect or be affected by the actions of the weather" or "to survive, withstand, or endure some hardship, such as a crisis, storm, or other trouble." For example:
• "I think the **weather** is supposed to be nice this weekend."
• "The worst part of living in this country is the terrible **weather** all year."

• "The old car has **weathered** quite a bit over the years, its tires flat and its paint faded."
• "I just hope our rickety old house will be able to **weather** the storm."
• "The company managed to **weather** the financial crisis and is now dominating the market."

Whether, meanwhile, is a conjunction, most commonly used to introduce one or more alternatives, especially in an indirect question. For example:
• "I'll support your decision, **whether** you decide to stay in the job or not."
• "**Whether** by skill or pure dumb luck, he managed to make it into the finals of the tournament."
• "We weren't sure **whether** you would get here today or tomorrow."

Just remember that if you are describing something with physical properties or you are describing an action that someone or something performs, then the correct spelling is *weather*. If you are using a grammatical function word that joins parts of a sentence together, *whether* is correct.

wet vs. *whet*

Wet has the general meaning of "full of or covered with moisture" or "to cover or fill with moisture." *Whet*, on the other hand, has the very specific meaning "to sharpen or hone" or "to stimulate, enhance, or make more keen." For example:

• "My clothes were **wet** with perspiration."
• "He **wet** the cloth with cold water and applied it to the child's forehead."

• "She **whet** the edge of the blade against the stone."
• "Here are a few hors d'oeuvres to help **whet** your appetite."

Spelling Tricks and Tips

To remember the difference in spelling, keep in mind that *whet* means *sharpen*, and both have **H** as their second letter.

who vs. *whom*

This pair of interrogative pronouns is notoriously difficult for learners and native speakers alike.

Traditionally, *who* is only used when functioning as the subject of a verb's action, while *whom* is used when it functions as the object of a verb or preposition. For example:

• "It doesn't matter **who** completes the task, so long as it is finished in time!" (*Who* is the subject of the verb *complete*.)
• "**Who** could have done such a thing?" (*Who* is the subject of the verb *done*.)

• "Tell me, **whom** do you love most in the world?" (*Whom* is the object of the verb *love*.)
• "This is Mr. Carter, **whom** I worked for during college." (*Whom* is the object of the preposition *for*.)

This distinction carries over to the related pronouns *whoever* and *whomever*, as well:

• "**Whoever** can finish the proposal in time will get the contract." (*Whoever* is the subject of the verb *finish*.)
• "You may dance with **whomever** you like; it doesn't matter to me." (*Whomever* is the object of the preposition *with*.)

While it can be trickier to determine whether *who/whoever* or *whom/whomever* is functioning as the subject or object of a verb, it's much simpler when dealing with prepositions. Prepositions can only ever be associated with a grammatical objects to form a prepositional phrase, so they should only ever take *whom* or *whomever*.

In modern English, however, *who* (and, by extension, *whoever*) is used almost exclusively, even as the object of a preposition (especially when the two appear in different parts of a clause). *Whom* (and *whomever*) now tends to be reserved for more formal English, and it can even sound stuffy or old fashioned in conversational English. Still, it's important to know the difference between the two, and we should strive to use them correctly, especially in formal, professional, or academic speech and writing.

Quiz
(answers start on page 463)

1. Choose the sentence in which *who* is **traditionally** the correct word.
a) "I'm still not sure _____ this package is for."
b) "We're going to the airport to pick up Amy's brother, _____ she hasn't seen in five years."
c) "They're looking for someone _____ can speak fluent Spanish."
d) "_____ should we ask to be the master of ceremonies?"

2. Choose the sentence in which *whom* is **traditionally** the correct word.
a) "_____ could be calling us at this hour?"
b) "This is Andy, _____ is going to be Jeff's best man at the wedding."
c) "We need a writer _____ can deliver polished articles under strict deadlines."
d) "I wonder _____ they chose to be the new manager."

who's vs. *whose*

Because *who's* and *whose* have a similar appearance and are both pronounced /huz/, they can sometimes be confused for one another in writing. Another part of the problem is that we normally use "-'s" to form possession for nouns (as in *Amy's, the government's, parent's*, etc.), so single-word determiners that indicate possession can be tricky to remember—this is the same issue many writers encounter with *it's* and *its*.

Who's is a contraction of the pronoun *who* and the verbs *is* or *has*, and it is used when you are asking about or describing a person's actions or characteristics. For example:
• "Find out **who's** (*who is*) controlling the cameras."
• "I decided to ask Arnold, **who's** (*who is*) much better with computers than me."

• "**Who's** (*who has*) figured out the answer to the first problem?"
• "Does anyone know **who's** (*who has*) been eating my cookies?"

The possessive determiner *whose* is used when you are asking about or describing a person or thing's possession of something. For example:
• "Does anyone know **whose** car (possession of *car*) this is?"
• "The company, **whose** profits (possession of *profits*) have fallen since 2014, announced bankruptcy earlier today."

Spelling Tricks and Tips

Unfortunately, there isn't a simple trick to remember the difference; instead, we have to look at the rest of the sentence to help us determine which spelling is correct.

Who's, which is formed from the linking verb *is* or the auxiliary verb *has*, will be the correct choice if it is followed by an adjective that describes the subject or another verb that describes the subject's actions.

Since *whose* is a determiner, which functions like an adjective, it will usually be followed by the noun that it is describing.

yolk vs. *yoke*

Yolk and *yoke* share the same pronunciation: /joʊk/ (rhyming with *poke* or *stroke*).

The more common of the two, *yolk*, refers to the typically yellow, protein-rich portion of an egg, as in:
• "As a kid, I never liked to eat eggs with runny **yolks**."

Used literally, *yoke* refers to a wooden frame fitted around the neck or shoulders of a draft animal, or, as a verb, to the action of attaching a yoke or other harness to an animal. However, *yoke* is more often used figuratively to refer to some burden, oppression, or subjugation. For example:
• "The **yoke** smashed apart, and the ox broke free from the plow."
• "The country's economy has crumbled under the **yoke** of the dictatorship."
• "The loan helped us get our business started, but the debt has now become a **yoke** around our necks."

Because *yolk* is so much more common in everyday speech and writing, it is sometimes mistakenly used in places in which *yoke* is the correct spelling. Likewise, it can be tempting to use the spelling *yoke* when referring to the part of an egg because it has a much more phonetic spelling than *yolk* and its silent L. Nevertheless, it's important to know that these two spellings and their respective meanings are distinct and cannot be used interchangeably.

you're vs. *your*

One very common mistake many writers make is to use the word *your* when they mean to write *you're*.

You're is a contraction of *you* and the linking and auxiliary verb *are*; it is used when describing a person's actions or characteristics. For example:

• "She said **you're** (*you are*) leaving in the morning."
• "I don't know why **you're** (*you are*) so upset!"
• "**You're** (*you are*) a good student, so I'm sure you won't have any problem with this assignment."

Your is a possessive determiner (also called a **possessive adjective**), so it is used when describing a person's possession of something. Because it is a determiner, it is almost always followed immediately by the noun it is describing. For example:

• "I'm not sure *your point* (possession of *point*) is relevant."
• "We're going to remodel *your old room* (possession of *old room*), so put aside anything you don't want thrown away."

This difference (and the resulting confusion) between *you're* and *your* is the same as between many other homophonic pairs of contractions and possessive determiners, such as *it's* and *its*, *they're* and *their*, and *who's* and *whose*. Just remember that if you are describing a pronoun or any sort of action it performs, then you must use the spelling that features an apostrophe, as it is incorporating the verbs *is, has,* or *are*. If you are using a pronoun to describe possession of another noun, the spelling <u>without</u> an apostrophe is correct.

Quiz answers

Page. Article: Question-Answer

21. The Alphabet: 1-a, 2-b, 3-c, 4-b
31. Vowels: 1-d, 2-b, 3-d, 4-a, 5-c
59. Consonant Digraphs: 1-c, 2-a, 3-b, 4-d, 5-a, 6-c, 7-d
68. Trigraphs: 1-c, 2-b, 3-b, 4-a, 5-d, 6-b
71. Tetragraphs: 1-c, 2-b, 3-a, 4-d, 5-d
74. Other Letters, Marks, and Symbols: 1-c, 2-a, 3-d, 4-b
78. Diacritics: 1-b, 2-b, 3-a, 4-d
82. Ligatures: 1-f, 2-d, 3-c, 4-a
97. Spelling Conventions: 1-a, 2-b, 3-d, 4-b, 5-b, 6-c, 7-a, 8-d
111. Affixes: 1-a, 2-c, 3-b, 4-f, 5-d
122. Prefixes: 1-a, 2-b, 3-b, 4-e, 5-c, 6-b
137. Suffixes: 1-c, 2-b, 3-d, 4-a, 5-b, 6-d, 7-c
147. Commonly Confused Suffixes: -able vs. -ible: 1-a, 2-c, 3-b, 4-d, 5-b
154. Commonly Confused Suffixes: -ant vs. -ent: 1-b, 2-a, 3-d, 4-d, 5-c, 6-b
172. Commonly Confused Suffixes: -er, -or, and -ar: 1-b, 2-a, 3-d, 4-c, 5-a, 6-b
181. Commonly Confused Suffixes: -ic vs. -ical: 1-a, 2-c, 3-a, 4-b
192. Commonly Confused Suffixes: -tion vs. -sion: 1-d, 2-b, 3-a, 4-b, 5-a
198. Spelling Conventions with Suffixes: 1-b, 2-a, 3-d, 4-b, 5-c, 6-a
202. Changing Y to I with Suffixes: 1-c, 2-a, 3-d, 4-b, 5-b
208. Adding Suffixes after Silent E: 1-b, 2-c, 3-a, 4-c, 5-d
216. Doubling Consonants with Vowel Suffixes: 1-b, 2-d, 3-c, 4-b, 5-b
227. Inflection in Spelling: 1-d, 2-g, 3-b, 4-a, 5-e
231. Forming Plurals: 1-b, 2-d, 3-a, 4-b, 5-c
242. Forming Contractions: 1-b, 2-a, 3-b, 4-d, 5-c
244. Enclitics: 1-b, 2-b, 3-d, 4-a, 5-d
250. The Three-Letter Rule: 1-a, 2-c, 3-d, 4-b, 5-c, 6-a
254. I Before E, Except After C: 1-b, 2-f, 3-b, 4-a, 5-b
261. Rules for Capitalization: 1-c, 2-a, 3-d, 4-e, 5-c
265. Foreign Loanwords and Loan Translations: 1-a, 2-b
283. American English vs. British English Spelling: 1-b, 2-d, 3-a, 4-d, 5-b, 6-a
300. Pronunciation Conventions: 1-b, 2-d, 3-b, 4-c, 5-b, 6-b, 7-b, 8-a
305. Tricky Vowel Sounds (Monophthongs, Diphthongs, and Triphthongs): 1-c, 2-b, 3-d, 4-a
309. Diphthongs: 1-b, 2-d, 3-a, 4-f, 5-b
311. Triphthongs: 1-c, 2-b, 3-b, 4-a
319. Tricky Consonant Sounds: 1-b, 2-a, 3-b, 4-c, 5-b, 6-d
325. Forming the /k/ Sound: 1-c, 2-b, 3-c, 4-e, 5-a, 6-g
331. Forming the /z/ Sound: 1-c, 2-d, 3-b, 4-b
334. Forming the /ʒ/ (ZH) Sound: 1-c, 2-d, 3-c, 4-a
347. Pronouncing the Letter S: 1-c, 2-d, 3-a, 4-c, 5-d, 6-b
366. Silent Letters: 1-b, 2-c, 3-a, 4-c, 5-d, 6-a
373. Silent E: 1-c, 2-a, 3-b, 4-c, 5-b
386. Syllables: 1-b, 2-e, 3-b, 4-c, 5-a, 6-d, 7-c
406. Word Stress: 1-b, 2-a, 3-d, 4-b, 5-c, 6-a, 7-d
409. Sentence Stress: 1-a, 2-d, 3-c, 4-b
411. a while vs. awhile: 1-a, 2-e, 3-d
412. accept vs. except: 1-b, 2-c, 3-d
413. adverse vs. averse: 1-b, 2-d
415. affect vs. effect: 1-c, 2-b, 3-b

418. allusion vs. illusion: 1-a, 2-c, 3-a
424. censor vs. sensor vs. censure: 1-b, 2-d, 3-a, 4-c
426. compliment vs. complement: 1-c, 2-a
427. defuse vs. diffuse: 1-b, 2-d
429. discreet vs. discrete vs. discretion: 1-a, 2-d, 3-a
434. flounder vs. founder: 1-d, 2-b
436. illusion vs. delusion: 1-a, 2-d, 3-b
438. incidence vs. incidents vs. instances: 1-b, 2-d, 3-c, 4-a
441. let's vs. lets: 1-a, 2-c, 3-b
442. lie vs. lay: 1-b, 2-e, 3-b, 4-c
443. loath vs. loathe: 1-c, 2-d, 3-a, 4-a
450. prescribe vs. proscribe: 1-a, 2-d, 3-b, 4-a
456. sympathy vs. empathy: 1-c, 2-b
460. who vs. whom: 1-c, 2-d

Index

THE FARLEX
GRAMMAR BOOK

Dear Reader,

We hope you have reached the end of *Complete English Spelling and Pronunciation Rules* with a better understanding and a greater confidence in spelling and speaking. We think you'll find that it will continue to be a valuable reference.

If this book has helped you, we would like to ask you to consider supporting Farlex as an independent publisher by telling others about it in an Amazon review.

Your feedback helps us make all our books better! Thank you for choosing Farlex as your guide to the English language.

Sincerely,

The Farlex Team

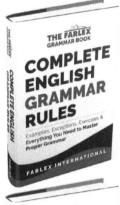

Complete English Grammar Rules

All the rules of English grammar, all in one book, explained in simple terms.

• 500+ pages of proper grammar instruction—2X more information than the leading grammar book!

• Hundreds of quizzes, thousands of example sentences, and more.

Complete English Punctuation Rules

The only punctuation guide with simple, easy-to-remember rules for how to use—and not use—every punctuation mark.

• Side-by-side examples of both correct and incorrect punctuation.

• Quizzes after every topic to help you retain what you learn.

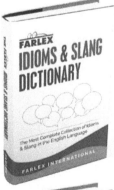

The Farlex Idioms & Slang Dictionary

The most complete collection of idioms and slang in the English language.

• 17,000+ entries covering idioms, slang, phrasal verbs, and more.

• Example sentences for every definition showing how the term is used in real life by native speakers.

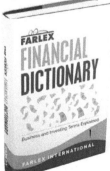

The Farlex Financial Dictionary

Define your success with the essential financial and business dictionary.

• 19,000+ entries covering both basic and advanced concepts—nearly 4X more than the leading financial dictionary!

• Cut through the jargon with clear, in-depth definitions backed by industry expertise.

Printed in the USA
CPSIA information can be obtained
at www.ICGtesting.com
LVHW082021200324
775025LV00007B/998

9 781978 0458